1969

HISTORY
OF THE
AMERICAN
THEATRE

BENJAMIN BLOM New York/London 1968

HISTORY

OF THE

AMERICAN

THEATRE

New Foundations.

George O. Seilhamer

First Published 1888-91
Reissued 1968
by Benjamin Blom, Inc. Bronx, New York 10452
and 56 Doughty Street London, W.C. 1

Library of Congress Catalog Card Number 68-58198

Printed in the United States of America

TO

ALBERT M. PALMER

THIS VOLUME OF

NEW FOUNDATIONS

IS INSCRIBED BY

THE AUTHOR,

IN TESTIMONY OF HIS TASTE AND SKILL AS A MANAGER,

AND

HIS EARNEST INTEREST IN THE HISTORY OF THE
AMERICAN THEATRE.

CONTENTS.

(v)

CHAPTER VI.

HALLAM AND HODGKINSON, 1794-5.

CHAPTER VII.

WIGNELL'S FIRST COMPANY.

CHAPTER VIII.

THE PHILADELPHIA COMPANY, 1793-4.

CHAPTER IX.

THE PHILADELPHIA COMPANY, 1794-5.

CHAPTER X.

THE PHILADELPHIA COMPANY, 1795-6.

CHAPTER XI.

THE BOSTON THEATRE, 1794-5.

CHAPTER XVIII.

The Boston Haymarket, 1796-7.

CHAPTER XIX.

A Rhode Island Interlude.

CHAPTER XX.

Hallam, Hodgkinson and Dunlap.

1792-1797

A History of the American Theatre:

NEW FOUNDATIONS.

CHAPTER I.

AMERICAN STROLLERS.

ENGLISH ACTORS LOOK TO THE WEST—THE KENNAS—VAUGHAN'S MIS-
HAP—"WALKING STEWART"—MRS. GARDNER—AN AMERICAN
WANDERING PATENTEE—SIGNOR TRISOBIO—McGRATH AND GOD-
WIN—VIRGINIA STROLLING—MR. AND MRS. SOLOMON.

DURING the first forty years of the American theatre there was
little change in the composition of the company that supplied
theatrical entertainments to the few towns that could support a theatre
at intervals; but even before 1792, when the Old American Company
was reorganized, English strollers began to make their way to the
United States. What the crown had lost Thespian royalty determined
to reconquer. As early as 1783 one of the London newspapers said
that as a taste for theatricals was beginning to prevail in America,
English actors may yet have one chance more—perhaps two or three
on that continent—if they differ with the managers of the British

theatres.   Three thousand miles, it was said, is a great journey; but that is nothing to a willing mind, spurred on by the goad of expectation.   English notions of American theatrical possibilities at that time were misty, as is apparent from a paragraph printed in the *Morning Post*, in February, 1783, in which it was said that Mr. Hallam, brother to Mrs. Mattocks, had lately had a letter from the American Congress inviting him to the direction of three theatres—namely, New York, Boston and Philadelphia.   "A gentleman is now in town," the *Post* said, "raising some theatrical troops for Mr. Hallam at handsome salaries;" and that journal added, "the war being now over, Congress has given him a genteel invitation to recompense him for his honorary banishment."   Notwithstanding this theatrical lie, that would have done no discredit to the "press agent" of a century later, Mr. Hallam seems to have met with little success in procuring recruits; and when English actors and actresses began to arrive on this side of the Atlantic, he was slow to accept them.   In spite of Hallam's disinclination to allow an invasion of the Old American Company's monopoly, the forecast of the London paragrapher proved well founded, and before the close of the century many of the London favorites of the decade succeeding the Revolution found their way to the United States.

In the first decade after the Revolution the earliest of the theatrical adventurers who found their way to America was the Kenna family. Mr. and Mrs. Kenna were actors of experience, and it may be assumed they were the Mr. and Mrs. Kenna to whose company Mrs. Entwistle, the mother of Harriet Mellon, was attached for a number of years, 1777 to 1783.   In America, as in England, Wales and Ireland, the Kennas were itinerants.   Mrs. Kenna especially seems to have been a woman of many resources, both as an actress and a manager.   She was equally ready to play all the leading roles in a drama, male and female, herself, or to teach them to unpromising candidates for public favor. Her labors, it must be confessed, were not always crowned with a success that honored them. The difficulties she had to contend with are illustrated by a misfortune that befell Mr. Vaughan one night at the theatre in the Northern Liberties, Philadelphia. A ludicrous actor named Purcell had advertised "Othello" for his benefit, the beneficiary appearing as the *Moor*. Vaughan had agreed to recite the famous epilogue, "Bucks Have at Ye All," between the play and the farce. Purcell's acting, unfortunately, resulted in an unceasing roar of laughter. This paved the way for Vaughan's downfall, for his habits were convivial, and during the play he devoted himself with great ardor to the flowing bowl at the "Noah's Ark" in the neighborhood of the theatre. When he came on the stage his condition was apparent to the audience, and there was a hiss. Undaunted by this mark of disapprobation, Vaughan began :

Ye social friends of claret and of wit,

when the hiss was repeated. Vaughan looked among the audience with indignation as if trying to discover the offenders, stamped on the floor, clenched his fist, and cried out in a loud voice, "Damn you, ye blackguards, I wish I had you here—I'd soon settle you." For once in his life poor Vaughan could say that the house rose at him, and the indignant elocutionist was pelted off the stage. Purcell, however, was equal to the occasion. He came forward with an apology. He hoped, he said, the ladies and gentlemen would not go for to say he was at all to blame—it was all Dr. Vaughan's fault—for though he had promised to keep sober till the play was over, he got as drunk as David's sow before it began. This unique harangue, as meritorious in its way as Purcell's performance of *Othello*, had the desired effect, and it was agreed that Vaughan should be allowed to recite the epilogue without hissing.   The promise was kept; but when the epilogue was finished, the drunken actor was pelted off again with the fury of a cloud-burst.   When it is remembered that Vaughan was for a number of years the principal member of the Kenna company outside of the Kenna family, some of the difficulties that beset this earliest band of American strollers will be appreciated.

Perhaps the most remarkable of the first appearances under the auspices of the Kennas was that of John Stewart, better known on both sides of the Atlantic as " Walking Stewart."   Stewart was the son of a linen-draper in Bond Street, who placed him at the Charter House for a classical education, and in due time secured him a writership in the service of the East India Company.   His representations of the abuses of the service receiving no attention, he conceived himself at liberty to quit the company's employ and seek employment among the native powers in India.   This resolution he carried into effect, and served both under Hyder Ally and the Nabob of Arcot.   The Nabob being in arrears for salary and seeing no hope of payment, Stewart resolved to return to Europe.   After his reappearance in England he wore for a time the Armenian habit.   He remained there only a short time, making his way to America, where he delivered eccentric lectures upon an eccentric philosophy of which he was the apostle.   When Stewart returned to England, from India, he had £3,000 besides his claim against the Nabob of Arcot.   This he deposited in the French Funds before his departure for America, in consequence of which he was reduced to so low a state in this country that he asked a very rich man whom he had known in India to allow him to sit by his kitchen fire, and to grant him a johnny-cake daily for food, both of which requests were refused. Stewart made two visits to the United States, the second being undertaken in the belief that the growth of French Revolutionary principles would destroy all regular government and give ascendency to the mob; Stewart believing, according to John Taylor, that America was the only secure asylum for the friends of order and rational freedom. It was during this second visit that he made his *debut* at the theatre in the Northern Liberties as *Altamont* in the " Fair Penitent" and *Captain Fitzroy* in the " Poor Soldier" on the 14th of November, 1792. Stewart again returned to England, however, and was contemplating an appearance as *Macheath* in the " Beggar's Opera " at the Haymarket Theatre, but luckily the fortunate adjustment of his affairs with the late Nabob, by which he came into possession of £16,000, frustrated this design. Although Stewart was a great traveler, he was not an observer of the manners and customs of the people, his " Travels to Discover the Sources of Moral Motion " being wholly devoted to the principles of justice and morality in the countries that he visited.

Soon after the advent of the Kenna family came a solitary adventurer, Mrs. Gardner, to try her fortunes in America. She never obtained recognition here; but in her day she was a distinguished actress. When Foote was the manager of the little theatre in the Haymarket she played the heroines in most of his productions. Subsequently she went to Jamaica, where she lived for a number of years, and managed to save a small fortune. In 1782 she returned to England, carrying with her in rums, sugars, etc., the provision she had made for her declining years. Unfortunately her little all was lost at sea. There was no resource left to her but to return to the stage. Her re-entry was made at the Haymarket for Mr. Wilson's benefit, on the 13th of August, 1782, as *Mrs. Cadwallader* in the "Author," a character in which she had been without a rival. Three days later she appeared in the farce of the "Female Dramatist" for the benefit of Mr. Jewel, the treasurer, but she did not succeed in obtaining a London engagement. It must have been previous to this that the incident related by John Bernard in his "Retrospections of the Stage" occurred in Dublin, if it occurred at all. She was, it appears, a member of a company that had been playing at Cork and Belfast under two moneyless managers, and undertook to play at Dublin in opposition to Crawford and Daly. The season ended abruptly; and Mrs. Gardner, unable to pay her debts, determined, as she could not satisfy her creditors, to elude them. In this she was assisted by some of her Dublin friends. Her illness and death were announced in the newspapers, to the dismay of numerous tradesmen, and preparations for a funeral were made with many demonstrations of sorrow. In the meantime a lady who very much resembled her took passage on a Holyhead packet, and two days afterward was drinking to Mrs. Gardner's repose in lodgings near the Strand. Mrs. Gardner, however, again returned to Dublin, where she gave the entertainment that she subsequently presented at Charleston and in New York.

The most remarkable itinerant of this period, however, was Christopher Charles McGrath. McGrath was the typical stroller of his epoch. He was a poet and singer as well as an actor; something of a dramatist as well as a manager. Godwin, under whom he had made his *debut* at Charleston in 1786, maliciously described him in a Baltimore paper as a spoiled priest, turned itinerant player—"capable of doing up a smart piece either in prose or verse." In 1796 McGrath advertised proposals for publishing his "Miscellaneous Poems,

Theatrical Pieces," etc. The work was to be in one volume, printed by Thornton at Dumfries, Va. The price was one dollar. "Any description or comment on the above design," the poet and comedian said, "would to many frequenters of the Virginia and Maryland theatres be altogether superfluous. The author has professionally brought forward several of his pieces in both States, and to the approbation with which they were occasionally honored he must now appeal for the hazard of a publication." Whether the publication was actually made I have been unable to ascertain. I have, however, met with some of his pieces in the newspapers. The *Oracle of Dauphin* printed one of his songs, addressed to Washington and Adams, and sung to the tune of " Nancy Dawson," which contained the following stanza:

> May his successors ever be
> What in immortal George we see,
> The guardians of our liberty,
> Protectors of their country.

This at least shows his patriotism. For the Fourth of July, 1798, McGrath wrote an "Address to the Young Men of America," in which he sang:

> With jealous eye has Europe long beheld
> This blooming paradise from war withheld;
> Its trade extending thro' the peopled world,
> The eagle tow'ring and the sails unfurled.
> Abounding harvests smiling o'er the soil
> To pay luxuriantly the farmer's toil;
> In laws and constitution standing high,
> Cemented all by unanimity.

Mr. McGrath, it is clear enough, was not a great poet. He seems, however, to have been an energetic manager in his way. In 1791, assisted by Mrs. McGrath and such local talent as he could procure, he gave performances at Hagerstown, Md., his repertoire comprising Dodsley's "Miller of Mansfield," Foote's "Devil Upon Two Sticks,"

Fielding's "Miser," Young's "Revenge," Vanbrugh's "Like Master Like Man" and Tyler's "Contrast." From this it may be inferred that he was the first American "pirate" of American copyright plays. On the 19th of November, 1792, McGrath's company of comedians gave a performance at York, Pa. Mr. McGrath in a card in the *Herald* thanked the "respectable citizens of York for their patronage, hospitality and support," and promised to repeat his visit. In September "An Eye-Witness in the Gallery" wrote to the newspapers from Lancaster that a part of the Old American Company had played there two months past. An honest countryman who had never seen a play was so wrought upon by the distress manifested by Miss Smith as *Jane Shore*, that he left his seat to go out and buy her some cakes that she might not die of hunger. This Miss Smith appeared in Boston in the Autumn under Mr. Harper's management, and afterward became Mrs. Harper. She was never with the Old American Company, but was probably McGrath's leading lady. In September, 1793, McGrath was at Baltimore with a company that he called the Maryland Company, giving performances at the New Theatre. On the 16th, which was the last night but one of the engagement, when he presented Henry's "School for Soldiers" and the "Miller of Mansfield" for Mrs. Kelly's benefit, he recited the "Epilogue in the character of Nobody with a hint to Somebody" between the play and the farce. On the 20th, McGrath advertised a second benefit, postponed to the 23d on account of the illness of one of the performers, when he presented the "Carmelite," an interlude from the "Good-Natured Man," and the farce of "Three Weeks After Marriage." In June, 1796, McGrath was at Norfolk, where he gave a concert at the borough tavern on the 29th, "the theatre being under repair." With

Mrs. Graupner, McGrath had assisted Signor Trisobio in trios and duets at a concert at the new theatre on the 16th. Trisobio advertised himself in the Norfolk *Herald* as from Italy. He claimed to have been three years in the service of the Queen of Portugal in the royal chapel, and to have sung in the concerts of ancient music in London before the royal family. In December, 1798, McGrath was at Harrisburg, where he produced the "Provoked Husband" and "Lovers' Quarrels" on the 13th, and later "Douglas," "Love and Latin" and the "Citizen," the "characters by young gentlemen of the town for their amusement." Between the play and the farce on the first night Mrs. McGrath recited the epilogue, "Belles Have at Ye All;" and the entertainment closed with "The Jockey Club; or, Jockeys of All Trades," described as "Mr. McGrath's dramatic whim." Preceding the play on the last night, McGrath delivered a patriotic address to the Sons of America in the character of an American tar. Mr. McGrath died at Reading, Pa., on the 23d of February, 1799.

In the earlier part of this epoch McGrath had a rival in the person of Mr. Godwin, under whose auspices he had originally appeared at Charleston. Godwin apparently had agreed to appear at Baltimore during the McGrath engagement there in 1793, but he left the city abruptly and went to Annapolis, where he announced in the *Maryland Gazette* of the 19th of September that he proposed and had long wished to settle in that city with his family. Godwin's abrupt departure called out a caustic communication from McGrath, printed in the Baltimore *Evening Post* on the 16th. To this "rhapsody of invectives against Mr. Godwin," one of Godwin's friends, "Toby Tickle," replied on the 18th, claiming that Godwin's theatrical abilities and character in private life were fully equal, and he believed superior, to his assailant's. "I have known Mr. Godwin near ten years," his champion wrote, "and always found him to be much of the gentleman ; and I can further say that in the line of his profession—the tragic walk— he has not his equal in America." A train of unforeseen embarrassments, it was claimed, occasioned Godwin's retirement to Annapolis, where he was waiting in expectation of being able to accumulate a sufficiency to pay off every demand that might be brought against him in Baltimore or elsewhere. To this McGrath replied with vigor, avowing full responsibility for the attack on Godwin, saying that Godwin's departure from Baltimore on the very day advertised for his performances was an imposition on the public, an escape from justice and a direct stab at Mrs. McGrath's benefit. McGrath added that on a previous occasion it was by a mortgage on his own property that Godwin's release was secured when he was locked up in jail. More than this, McGrath's bitterness toward Godwin was exhibited on the occasion of his second benefit in Baltimore, at this time by his choice of the interlude from the "Good-Natured Man"—a creditor in the hands of a bailiff. This gave great offense to Godwin's friends, but in a card McGrath declared that it was given *verbatim* from the book—not a line was foisted in. Godwin, however, was not always as loyal to his author as McGrath seems to have been on this occasion, for on the night that McGrath intended to present the interlude from the "Good-Natured Man" at Baltimore—September 20th, 1793—he was advertised to appear at Annapolis in the "Beaux' Stratagem" and "Lethe," his version of Farquhar's comedy being "a new edition, corrected and rendered pleasing to the most refined taste." I find no mention of Godwin after this last desperate effort until 1796, when he appeared at the City Theatre in Charleston as *Lovegold* in the "Miser," on the 28th of June, his first appearance there, the bills said, in ten years, when he delivered an address relative to his performing in that city several years past, with a humorous description of certain cities he had visited. One fancies he can catch a glimpse of this address in a prologue recited by John Bignall, at Richmond, in 1792:

> In Baltimore I found congenial spirits,
> Oh, could I worthily proclaim their merits;
> They frolic'd, danc'd and sung, and boldly roar'd,
> And "keep it up" was the perpetual word.
> But Philadelphia every praise demands—
> She boasts determined hearts, and heads, and hands—
> Hearts which will pay for claret and champagne,
> Heads which the former night's debauch disdain,
> And hands, untrembling, which the glass sustain.

And what better could Godwin have offered to Charleston than the sentiment of Bignall's lines of universal application:

> Thou city, foremost in the Union found;
> For beauty, wit and gallantry renowned;
> Thy patient sons the wreath of merit claim,
> And genius consecrates each hero's fame.

The Virginia towns at this period, although Bignall thought

> Too many Madisons in them are found,
> Instead of fun, who study now the nation,
> And talk of politics and reformation,

seem to have been overrun with strolling players. Among these Alexandria was prominent. A certain, or rather an uncertain, Mr. Fitzgerald was there in November, 1793, giving performances in Fullmore's Long Room. Before the play on the opening night Mr. Fitzgerald delivered "A Moral Defence of the Stage," and after the farce, "A Dissertation on Lying." On the second night, it will be

LIST OF PERFORMANCES—*Alexandria.*

1793.

Nov.		
7—Douglas	. . . .	Home
	Lying Valet	. . . . . Garrick
9—Contrast	. . . .	Tyler
	Miller of Mansfield	. . Dodsley
15—Roman Father	. . . .	Whitehead
	Poor Soldier	. . . . . O'Keefe

observed, Royall Tyler's comedy, the "Contrast," was played, apparently in defiance of stage morality. No names of performers are given,
but three years later, in 1796, at
Dumfries, Mrs. Moore and Mr.
and Mrs. Marriott were fellow-
players with Mr. Fitzgerald. Mrs.
Moore may have been the actress
who was with Allen at Albany in
1785. Mr. and Mrs. Marriott had
made their American *debut* with the Old American Company at Philadelphia in 1794. The full title of Mrs. Marriott's play was the "Death
of Major André; or, The Land we Live In." When it was announced for performance on the 16th of April, 1796, it was described
as performed but once in America. Mrs. Marriott died soon afterward.

LIST OF PERFORMANCES—*Dumfries.*

1796.
April 6—Venice Preserved . . . . . Otway
        Divorce . . . . Jackman
        (Mrs. Moore and Mr. Fitzgerald's
        Benefit.)
       16—Death of Major André
                          Mrs. Marriott
        Divorce
        (Mr. and Mrs. Marriott's Benefit).

Baltimore, as has already been indicated, was a favorite resort
of strolling players, and it was besides very strong in local amateurs.
On the 11th of
November, 1793,
Mr. and Mrs. Sol-
omon, aided by
Mr. Redfield, who was with them in the
first Boston attempt, and by a Mrs. Owens, played the "Romp" and
"Thomas and Sally" for the benefit of Mrs. Solomon. Afterward
Mrs. Solomon and her daughter, Miss Solomon, played regular en-
gagements with the Philadelphia, New York and other companies and
were recognized as legitimate members of the profession.

ROMP.

Barnacle . . . . . . Mr. Redfield
Old Cockney . . . . A Gentleman
Watty Cockney . . Mr. Solomon
Penelope . . . . . Mrs. Owens
Priscilla Tamboy . Mrs. Solomon

THOMAS AND SALLY.

Squire . . Mr. Solomon
Thomas . A Gentleman
Dorcas . . Mrs. Owens
Sally . . Mrs. Solomon

CHAPTER II.

_____

THE BEGINNING AT BOSTON.

HALLAM AND HENRY'S PETITION—PLAYS AT PORTSMOUTH AND SALEM—
REPEAL MEETINGS IN FANUEIL HALL—LEGISLATIVE ACTION—NEW
EXHIBITION ROOM—POWELL—THE LAW DEFIED—PLACIDE'S PAN-
TOMIMES—FIRST BOSTON CAMPAIGN—HARPER'S ARREST.

WHEN the Vauxhall was opened in Boston in 1785, the fear
was expressed that an attempt to establish a theatre would
follow. Mr. Hallam, as we have seen, had already looked with longing
eyes upon that city as an addition to his theatrical territory, but it was
not until 1790 that Hallam and Henry made a formal movement in
that direction. On the 5th of June, their petition asking to be allowed
to open a theatre was presented to the Massachusetts House of Representatives. The application of the petitioners was premature, and their
prayer was promptly denied. Boston had once more escaped invasion
by the profane players, and it was fondly hoped by the good people of
that good town that this denial would be a final rescue from the
impending evil. The players, however, were determined to obtain a
foothold in New England, and in midsummer, 1792, a company of
comedians appeared at Portsmouth, N. H., where the "Absent Man"
and "Lethe" were given on the 8th of August before a large audience.
It was said that the Governor of the State, who was at Portsmouth
at the time, was only prevented by illness from attending the per-

formance, but his wife gave it the sanction of her presence. A prologue was written for the occasion by Mitchell Sewall, Esq., and spoken by Mr. Watts. The theatre had previously been used as a warehouse, and the Prologue contained an apt description of its transformation into a playhouse, which fortunately has been preserved. Mr. Watts, who seems to have been the leading spirit in the enterprise, had been a provincial actor in England, and at a later period he became a member of West's company in the South. Watts is described by Dunlap as "a vulgar fellow with a wry neck." From Portsmouth the company went to Salem, where the "Beaux' Stratagem" and "Miss in her Teens" were given on the 11th, with Watts as *Archer* and *Captain Flash.* The "Miser" and "Thomas and Sally" followed. No restraint was attempted at Salem, and even the families of several of the clergy went to see the wicked players. From Salem, Watts carried his forces to Dorchester, and a few weeks later to Boston.

While the surrounding towns were enjoying such entertainments as the itinerant players could afford, Boston felt particularly aggrieved at being deprived of theatrical amusements. This feeling seems to have had its inception in the denial of the petition of Hallam and

EXTRACT FROM MR. SEWALL'S PROLOGUE.

———

The other manager, the courteous CIVIL,
Say, is he a magician, or the D—l?
Methinks I see him with his magic wand,
Like some old necromancer circl'd stand.
He strikes the *warehouse*, and the fabric, lo!
Turns to a theatre beneath the blow.
Where hogsheads, bales, were once conspicuous seen
Here frowns a monarch, and there stalks a queen;
That woods, that mountain and that beauteous valley,
Were where the worthy owner once kept tally;
Where porter-men, with muddy boots, once flock'd,
Great Chrononhotonthologos has stalked;
And where yon beauteous forms attract you, love,
Dry-goods, tier over tier, were piled above.
Then oh! this Conjurer favor with your nod;
If you refuse, that self-same potent rod,
Which from a warehouse reared this magic scene,
Shall turn all to a paltry store again.

Henry, and it grew so rapidly that in the autumn of 1791 two meetings were held in Fanueil Hall in favor of the repeal of the prohibitory act of 1750. At the first of these meetings, which was held on the 26th of October, the venerable Samuel Adams rose to speak against the theatre, but the meeting refused to hear him. Thereupon a frantic correspondent rushed into print in the *Argus*, hysterically asking, "Shall Europe hear, shall our Southern brethren be told that Samuel Adams rose to speak in the midst of his fellow-citizens and was silenced!—That while others who were born in season to enjoy the blessings which he earned were applauded, Samuel Adams could not be heard! Long may we remember that he rose to speak against the theatre in Boston and could not be heard. Was he in fault that he wished to speak the sentiments of his heart and to deliver the language of enlightened religion and truth? Do you blame him that he wished at death to leave his country virtuous as well as free?" This was transmuted into verse by one of the Hartford wits in No. 5 of the *Echo*, as follows:

> Shall Europe hear, shall Gallia's king be told,
> That Prince so spirited, so wise and bold,
> Whose duteous subjects, anxious to improve
> On common forms of loyalty and love,
> Took from their sovereign's hands the reins of state,
> For fear his royal nerves could not support the weight;
> And shall our worthy brethren of the South
> Be told Sam Adams could not ope his mouth?—
> That mouth whence streams of elocution flow'd,
> Like tail of saw-mill, rapid, rough and loud—
> Sweet as honey-dews that Maia pours
> O'er her green forests and her tufts of flow'rs—
> That potent mouth, whence issued words of force
> To stun an ox, or terrify a horse—
> Be told that while those brats whose feeble sight
> But just had op'd on freedom's dawning light,
> Born in the nick of time that bliss to know
> Which to his great and mighty toils we owe,

Received applause from sages, fools and boys,
The mighty Samuel could not make a noise.

*   *   *   *   *   *

Long may our souls the fond remembrance prove,
How, with a bosom crowded full of love,
To blast a wicked stage his voice he rear'd,
And yet that thundering voice could not be heard.

*   *   *   *   *   *

Was he to blame when, struck by mighty death,
He wish'd, by puffing his expiring breath,
To raze the pillars of a vicious stage,
And scatter virtue in his holy rage?

At the first Faneuil Hall meeting a committee was appointed to prepare instructions to the representatives of the town in the Legislature in the matter of repeal. This committee reported at the adjourned meeting on the 9th of November, and, in obedience to the instructions then reported and adopted, Mr. Tudor brought the question before the House on the 17th of January, 1792. The legislative proceedings were printed at considerable length in the *Massachusetts Magazine*,[1] from

---

[1] THE LEGISLATIVE PROCEEDINGS. (From the *Massachusetts Magazine*.) Jan. 17.—Mr. Tudor called the attention of the House to the subject of the repeal of the law prohibiting theatrical exhibitions. After stating the reasons which induced him thus early to rise, he read the law above mentioned, and moved that a committee be appointed to consider the expediency of bringing in a bill for the repeal of it. No person rising on the subject, the question was called for and put, when the members were, for the committee 37, against it 69.

On the speaker's declaring the vote in the negative, Mr. Gardiner rose, and moved for a reconsideration. Some attention, he said, was due to so respectable a town as Boston, three quarters of the citizens of which had in two public town meetings voted for the repeal. If on an individual's presenting a petition, or

complaining of a grievance, he was sure to have his case committed, he could not, he said, see the justice of refusing to take into consideration the request of so large a part of the community. He thought gentlemen had mistaken the motion and therefore wished the vote might be reconsidered.

Mr. Wedgery also thought the motion had been misunderstood. He had no idea of refusing to consider the request of so respectable a town as Boston, or even the poorest in the commonwealth. The committee, he said, was not chosen to bring in a bill to repeal the law—this was quite another thing—but merely to consider of the expediency or inexpediency of so doing. Surely, said he, the House can not refuse to do this. He, therefore, seconded Mr. Gardiner's motion.

Mr. Breck mentioned that the Legislature last year had sustained the petition of Mr.

which it appears that the House at first showed scant courtesy to the town of Boston. Although this summary action was reconsidered and a committee allowed, the committee reported the repeal of the prohibitory act inexpedient, and the House sustained the report.

It was clear that if Boston was to have a theatre it must be in evasion or defiance of the law. This was resolved upon by a few men

Henry, of the American Company of Comedians, on the same subject; he could not therefore see the propriety or consistency of refusing to commit the present subject.

Dr. Jarvis called on those who voted against the commitment to come forward with their reasons therefor. Perhaps, said he, they may be so forcible as to convince me that it is wrong to commit the subject. If they could demonstrate that the object of the institution was detrimental either to liberty, morality, religion, or the rights of society, he would readily vote with the majority. But until they did he should still vote as he' had done. Mr. Washburn and several other members mentioning that the motion had been misunderstood, the question of reconsideration was taken and passed in the affirmative. For it 71, against it 33.

The subject was then committed to Messrs. Gardiner, Greenleaf, Hitchborn, Bowers, Flagg, Washburn and Kingsley for to consider and report on.

———

Jan. 20.—Mr. Gardiner, chairman of the committee to whom was referred the instructions of the town of Boston to their representatives to procure a repeal of the law prohibiting theatrical exhibitions, as well as the remonstrance of a number of inhabitants against such repeal, as also the order of the House to consider the expediency of such repeal, reported verbally that it was inexpedient to repeal the said law. He observed that the committee consisted of seven members; that two were decidedly against the repeal, and that two others who voted against the report and repeal of that law as at present advised acknowledged in committee that they were not perfect masters of the subject, not being well acquainted with the whole nature and tendency of stage plays. That himself was decidedly in favor of the repeal of the law, which he considered as an undue restriction of the unalienable rights of the free citizens of this state; and that two others of the committee were for a repeal also.

Dr. Jarvis then moved that the house take up the subject matter of the report of that committee at 3 o'clock on the next Tuesday afternoon, which was accordingly ordered.

———

Jan. 26.—The House proceeded to take into consideration the report of the committee on the law for preventing stage plays and other theatrical entertainments, which was, that it was not expedient to repeal that law. The report was opposed in a sensible and judicious speech by Mr. Tudor; Mr. Gardiner delivered a learned and elaborate essay to prove the stage consistent with the principles of Christianity and good morals; and Dr. Jarvis displayed the blaze of eloquence in a speech pure, forcibly and refinedly ingenious. Yet all this, enforced by observations from other gentlemen, and not opposed by any other speaker, did not produce conviction on the House. On the question, Will you accept the report of your committee?—it passed in the affirmative, 99 to 44.

bolder than the rest.   An association was accordingly formed with this end in view, and a committee, consisting of Joseph Russell, Dr. Charles Jarvis, Gen. Henry Jackson, Joseph Barrell and Joseph Russell, Jr., was appointed to erect a building that should be a theatre in everything except in name.   Ground was purchased in Broad-alley near Hawley Street, and the building when erected was called the New Exhibition Room.   This was the first theatre in Boston.   It had a pit, a row of boxes forming three sides of a square, and a gallery, the theatre accommodating about five hundred persons.   The structure was a temporary one, but it served its purpose before it gave way to the more pretentious theatre in Federal Street two years later.

While the New Exhibition Room was building, Charles Stuart Powell, from the Theatre Royal, Covent Garden, arrived in Boston. Powell has generally been credited with being the father of the Boston stage and an actor of ability. The former he certainly was not, and if he was the latter his merit had been strangely overlooked on the London stage. His name first occurs in the Covent Garden bills, October 9th, 1789, as *Bagatelle* in the "Poor Soldier." This was his best part; but on the 17th of September, 1790, it was given to Mr. Marshall, although Powell was still with the company. Powell was three years at Covent Garden; but his last season, 1791–2, showed

MR. POWELL'S ENGLISH PARTS.

1789
Oct.   9—Poor Soldier . . . . . Bagatelle
Nov.   7—Miser . . . . Tailor
            9—Romeo and Juliet . . . . Peter
            13—Citizen . . . . Quilldrive
            14—Lady of the Manor . . . Vulture
            20—As You Like it . . . . William
            Bon Ton . . . . Mignon
            27—Clandestine Marriage . . Canton
Dec.   10—Hob in the Well . . . Old Hob
            11—Way to Keep Him . . Sideboard
1790
Feb.   23—Intriguing Chambermaid.Oldcastle
Mar.   13—Catharine and Petruchio
                                    Music Master
April 20—School for Wives . . . . Chastly
Sept. 15—Belle's Stratagem . French Valet
Dec.   20—Picture of Paris . . . Lemonadier
1791
Feb.   2—Upholsterer . . . . . . Feeble
Dec.   21—Bluebeard . . . . . . Doctor

him only where he began, as *Oldcastle* in the "Intriguing Chamber-maid," *Peter* in "Romeo and Juliet," and the *Tailor* in the "Miser," with two new parts—a small role in the "Day in Turkey," and as the *Doctor* in "Bluebeard." After the run of the pantomime, 1791–2, his name disappears altogether; and it was then, no doubt, that seeing no prospect of advancement at Covent Garden he determined to come to America. He seems to have landed at Boston, where he advertised two entertainments to be given at Concert Hall on the 15th and 17th of August, 1792. These entertainments were called "The Evening Brush for Rubbing off the Rust of Care." The programme for the first evening comprised such themes as modern spouters, stage candidates, tragedy tailors, wooden actors, butchers in heroics, and buffoons in blank verse; with original songs, "The Tragi-comedy of Human Life," the "Roman Veteran," and the "Golden Days of Good Queen Bess," ending with a whimsical "Transformation, or Humorous Dwarf Dance." That for the second evening was announced to comprise Dr. Dodd's moral and satirical lecture on "Human Hearts;" a song, "Poor Jack;" a duet, Mr. Pick giving "a song of his own composing on the harmoniac accompanied with the violin," a Dissertation on Noses, and finally a hornpipe by Mr. Powell. The latter entertainment, however, was postponed to accommodate Mr. Placide, who was to open the New Exhibition Room, Broad-alley, on that evening. Mr. Powell subsequently advertised his entertainment at Concert Hall for the 20th and 24th of August, and again for the 13th of September. On the last occasion Mr. Powell, who was suffering from a violent cold, gave "The Evening Brush," Mr. Murray "Twins of Latona," and Mr. Watts the "Drunken Sailor." The *Columbian Centinel* devoted nearly a column to an account of this entertainment.

Nov. 2—West Indian . . . . Cumberland
  Poor Soldier.
  (Mrs. Gray's Benefit.)
  7—She Stoops to Conquer
  Bird Catcher.
  Ghost . . . . . Mrs. Centlivre
  9—Catharine and Petruchio Shakspere
  Miller of Mansfield . . Dodsley
  Harlequin Balloonist.
  12—School for Scandal . . Sheridan
  Padlock . . . . . Bickerstaff
  (Mrs. Morris' Benefit.)
  14— Rivals . . . . Sheridan
  Love a la Mode . . . . Macklin
  Old Schoolmaster Grown Young.
  16—Catharine and Petruchio.
  High Life Below Stairs . Townley
  Padlock.
  (Mr. Robinson's Benefit.)
  19— George Barnwell.
  Inkle and Yarico . . Colman, Jr.
  (Mad. Placide's Benefit.)
  21—Douglas.
  Miss in her Teens.
  23—Love in a Village . . Bickerstaff
  Woodcutters.
  Citizen . . . . Murphy
  (Mr. Watts' Benefit.)
  26—Rivals.
  Lying Valet.
  Bear Hunters.
  28—Clandestine Marriage
      Garrick and Colman
  Devil to Pay . . . . . . Coffey
  (Mr. Solomon's Benefit.)
  30—Hamlet . . . . . . Shakspere
  Love a la Mode.
Dec. 3—Richard III . . . . . Shakspere
  Romp . . . . . . Bickerstaff
  (Mr. Adams' Benefit.)
  5—School for Scandal.
  True-Born Irishman.
  (Mr. Kenny's Benefit.)

Solomons remained throughout the season. Adams was with Harper at Providence and Newport the next year. Mr. Reinagle from Philadelphia was the leader of the orchestra. Mr. Roberts, whom Dunlap describes as "deformed and almost an idiot," appeared in the play on the 24th of October; and the same night Mr. O'Reilly, who had been with the Kennas at the Northern Liberties, Philadelphia, was in both the play and the farce. Mr. Kenna appeared in the "School for Scandal" for Mrs. Morris' benefit on the 12th of November; and Mr. Kenny, who had also been with the Kennas, played for Madame Placide's benefit on the 19th. A dwarf, three feet high, on the hornpipe, was Mr. Solomon's special benefit attraction. Mr. Powell played *Hamlet* on the 30th of November, with Mrs. Morris as *Ophelia*, and *Richard III* on the 3d of Decem-

ber, with Miss Smith as *Lady Anne.* The Shaksperean productions naturally excited the commendation of the Boston press; but in view of Mr. Powell's professional standing at Covent Garden, there was something almost grotesque in the *Centinel's* praise of his *Hamlet* as equal to everything the poet of nature designed by the character. Of Mrs. Morris as *Ophelia*, it was said she interested and affected every heart, and the tears which glistened on the cheeks of almost every one present, though a silent were yet an honorable tribute to her merit. Mr. Harper was described as a fine performer who richly merited his popularity; and it was said of Morris, "Few of the sons of Thalia exceed him." As *Richard III*, Mr. Powell's powers had ample scope, and were discovered to be very great. Miss Smith's *Lady Anne* gained her much applause, but she was simply set down as a promising actress. The farce of the "Romp," however, only seemed to the critic to be flat, stale and unprofitable. Mr. Kenny was described as a modest young man and promising performer. It was while Kenny's benefit was in progress that the season came to an abrupt end by the interference of the authorities under the law of 1750. Governor Hancock[1] seems to have taken the lead in rebuking the tolerant spirit that had been manifested toward the players, and in

GOVERNOR HANCOCK'S SPEECH.[1]

(As versified in *The Echo*, No. IX.)

But, Gentlemen, a thing unmention'd yet,
Enough to throw you in a dog-day sweat;
A thing, perchance, which you, as well as I,
Have seen sometimes, with many an aching
  eye;
Since, above measure bold, it scorns disguise,
And proudly stares us in the face and eyes;
A thing most vile, most dreadful in its kind,
Hangs, like a mill-stone, heavy on my mind.
By conscience urged, in duty's cause made
  bold,
To you this wicked thing I shall unfold,

Since plain enough to *me* is its intent,
An open insult on *my* government.
Long since, while Britain, with maternal hand,
Cheer'd the lov'd offspring of Columbia's
  land ;
Ere proud oppression bade that offspring brave
Assert their rights, and scorn the name of
  slave ;
Ere o'er the world had flown my mob-rais'd
  fame,
And George and Britain trembled at my name;
This State, then Province, pass'd with wise
  intent
An Act, Stage-Plays and such things to pre-
  vent.

urging their "condign punishment" for "an open insult upon the laws and government of the commonwealth." When the Legislature met at Concord on the 8th of November, he called the attention of the two Houses to the Act of 1750 as a law of the State, declaring that the principles upon which it was prèdicated had been recognized by and derived support from the consideration of several legislatures, and therefore ought to claim the respect and obedience of all persons who live or happen to be within the commonwealth. " Yet," he said, "a number of aliens and foreigners have lately entered the State, and in the metropolis of the government, under advertisements insulting to the habits and education of the citizens, have been pleased to invite them to, and to exhibit before such as attended Stage-Plays, Interludes

You'll find it, Sirs, among the laws sky-blue,
Made near that time on brooms when witches flew,
That blessed time when law kept wide awake,
Proscribed the faithless and made Quakers quake;
And thus, in terms sublime I state the fact,
Runs the Preamble of this precious Act.
Both for preventing, and avoiding, all
Those various evils which would sure befall
Our sober people, and their sober ways,
From Interludes and vile Theatric Plays;
To wit, all fiddling, fighting, gaming, raking,
Swearing profane, high broils and Sabbath breaking;
This Act, so full of wisdom and so good,
Has now become a law well understood;
Since it has often been confirmed, you see,
By many a Legislature great as we.
Yet, notwithstanding this, some chaps uncivil,
Grand emissaries of our foe the Devil,
Aliens and foreigners and actors funny,
Who less esteem our morals than our money,
Even in our holy Capital of late,
Have dar'd insult the majesty of state,

And to exhibit publicly, propose,
Stage-Plays and Interludes and Heathen shows;
Which, in the garb of Moral Lectures drest,
Of our good sober habits make a jest:
Yet so obnoxious to the people's notions,
So strange, so foreign to their constitutions,
That well I am convinced they never go,
From motives of amusement to the show;
But like good honest folks, with mere intent
To keep these actors under some restraint.

   *   *   *   *   *   *

Whether the magistrates all this have known
I do not know; but this I know, that none
Have taken care, whatever their intent,
These fellows' pranks and postures to prevent;
Ne'er have laid hold of them with law's strong hand,
And fairly brought the scoundrels to a stand,
Nor to the whipping post the rogues have tied,
Where oft cash-pay is chang'd to pay in hide.
With joy extreme, O Gentlemen, in you
The firm upholders of the law I view,
On you devolves the task—I grant it great—
To keep unstain'd the chasteness of our State.

and Theatrical Entertainments, under the style and appellation of
' Moral Lectures.' This fact is so notorious that it is in vain to attempt a concealment of its coming to our knowledge. Whether the
judicial departments, whose business it is, have attended to this subject
I am unable to determine; but this I am convinced of, that no measures
have been taken to punish a most open breach of the laws, and a most
contemptuous insult upon the powers of the government. You, gentlemen, are the guardians of the commonwealth's dignity and honor;
and our fellow-citizens rely upon your vigilance and wisdom for the
support of the sovereignty and importance of the government." That
the subsequent proceedings under which the performance of the 5th
of December was stopped were ascribed to Hancock is apparent from
these lines in the New Year's Verses of the *American Mercury:*

> Now, Hancock, fir'd with patriot rage,
> Proscribes these morals of the stage,
> Claps Harper under civil durance,
> For having dared, with vile assurance,
> By Interludes and Plays profane
> Pollute the glories of his reign.

The legal proceedings against the players were begun at the
instance of the Attorney-General, who made an application to Justices
Greenleaf and Barrett of the Supreme Court of Massachusetts for a
warrant for the arrest of Mr. Harper for violation of the law against
theatrical entertainments. The warrant was served on the evening of
the 5th of December, at the end of the second act of the " School for
Scandal," the sheriff threatening that if the performance was not
stopped he would arrest the whole company. A tumult followed.
Cries of " Go on, go on," were heard from the pit, and some of the
audience even leaped upon the stage, and, tearing down the arms of

the State, trampled it under foot. Judge Tudor made a short address, asking the audience to withdraw. Those who were present then retired, refusing to accept the admission money. Bonds were furnished for Mr. Harper's appearance before the court in Fanueil Hall on the following day, when the manager was defended by Mr. Otis and Mr. Tudor. Mr. Otis objected to the warrant as contrary to the Declaration of Rights, the application not being supported by an oath. In this view he was supported by Mr. Tudor, the Attorney-General arguing in favor of the legality of the proceedings. Justice Barrett, however, sustained the objection, and Mr. Harper was released.

Subsequently Mr. Placide announced that the performance advertised for the 8th of December was postponed at the request of the Selectmen of Boston, and Mr. Harper printed a card of thanks. Mr. Kenny, the beneficiary of the evening, also publicly thanked the audience for refusing to accept the return money. Thus ended the first theatrical campaign in Boston.

CHAPTER III.

HENRY'S RECRUITS.

HENRY IN ENGLAND—ACCOUNT OF JOHN HODGKINSON—MRS. HODGKIN-
SON—MISS BRETT—MRS. WRIGHTEN'S CAREER—KING AND WEST
—LUKE ROBBINS—PERSONAL DESCRIPTIONS OF HENRY'S RECRUITS.

WHEN Henry finally departed on his mission to England to obtain recruits for the Old American Company, he pursued it with great energy, so that in six months from the time he sailed from New York the actors and actresses engaged by him had arrived at that port. The only glimpse we have of Henry's manners and methods in England is that obtained from a pamphlet, published by Hodgkinson a few years later, detailing his grievances with the American managers. That Henry should have appeared at his best during his stay at Bath, where most of his recruits were obtained, and that he should have been a little more glowing in his accounts of the American cities and the American theatre than the facts warranted, was only natural. By these allusions Hodgkinson meant to convey the impression that he was deceived by Henry's genial manner and glowing representations; but, as he had been in treaty with the American managers before Henry sailed for England, and as Henry's recruits, with a single exception, were engaged at his instigation, his insinuations leave a more agreeable impression of Henry than he intended.

Hodgkinson's engagement for the Old American Company, if

he really was the great actor he has always been represented as being, seems, at the first glance, an anomalous one.   According to John Bernard in his "Retrospections," John Hodgkinson was "the provincial Garrick."   As Bernard had long been resident in America before his book was published, it was possible this high estimate of Hodgkinson's English standing was derived from his subsequent American pre-eminence; but I find it fully indorsed in a paragraph in the London *Gazetteer* in 1790, announcing his engagement for the Bath and Bristol theatres.   The writer declared that in such characters as the *Lyar*, *Deaf Lover* and *Young Quaker*, Mr. Hodgkinson had already given such powerful proofs of his talents that it was but justice to say such merit would prove an acquisition to any theatre in Europe.   It will be found in tracing the history of Mr. Hodgkinson's English career that, brilliant as his professional prospects were, his motives for seeking an American engagement were adequate to such a man at the time it was made with Hallam and Henry in 1792.

John Hodgkinson was the son of a small farmer—his family name was Meadowcroft—who afterward kept a public house at Manchester, where John was potboy.   The father dying, John's mother married again, and John was bound as an apprentice.   John as a boy sang in the choir of one of the Manchester churches, and at the same time he became an expert, self-taught performer on the violin.   He was also the leading spirit in a band of amateur Thespians who met for rehearsal, and gave their performances in a cellar in an obscure alley, with the strictest secrecy.   One day the little company was engaged in rehearsing the "Padlock."   John, as the best singer, was *Leander*, much against his will, as his favorite character was *Mungo*. Suddenly a noise was heard in the passage leading to the cellar:

Master Mungo stopped in the middle of a song. "What can it be?" the boys asked each other. "It's only one of the hogs in the alley," John answered. A moment later the door was burst open, and John's master entered. "Oh, my prophetic soul! did I not tell you it was a hog?" the lad exclaimed. Enraged at what he saw and heard, the man struck the boy with his fist, and smashed John's violin into pieces on his head. This ended John's apprenticeship, for he ran away from his master and from Manchester.

Already young Meadowcroft had begun to think of the theatre as a vocation. A few months previous to the incident that thus sent him out into the world to seek his fortune he was spending Sunday at the public house of his stepfather, where he busied himself making a bridge for a fiddle, at the same time singing *Linco's* laughing song in "Cymon." For this he was severely reprimanded by his foster-father, but two gentlemen stopping at the house interfered, one of them saying, "I'll be hanged if he doesn't sing it better than Wilder." Wilder was a Dublin actor, and the original *Linco* on the Dublin stage. The speaker was Mr. Dawson, a player, who was an assistant to Wilder's manager, and the stepfather of the celebrated William Lewis. Dawson's companion was a Dublin merchant named Comerford, who gave the boy a crown piece. John gave the money to his mother to keep for him, and it was the capital upon which he embarked upon the world. It was meagre, but it proved enough.

After running away from Manchester, young Meadowcroft changed his name to Hodgkinson, and made his way to Bristol. "I had no fear," Carpenter, his biographer in the *Mirror of Taste*, represents Hodgkinson as saying, "because I had health and strength to do several things to earn my bread (I could sing if I could do nothing else), and never once lost sight of the persuasion that I should one time or other be something better than a potboy or a mechanic. Nor did I meet anything in my journey to discourage me. Some suspected me of being a runaway, 'tis true, and looked severely at me; but I minded them not; and one man, a wagoner, who carried me a whole night in his wagon, owned that he had taken me in gratuitously for the purpose of having me delivered up, but that I fairly sang and talked him into a regard for me during the night. Few charged me anything for what I ate, and I brought more than half my crown into Bristol with me." Hodgkinson had scarcely arrived at his destination when he was recognized by a rustic, who said, "I'll tell thee what, thee art Jacky Meadowcroft; I know thee as well as I do that horse that stonds there before my eyes; so don't go vor to tell loies about it." The bumpkin had been a stable-boy at Manchester. After some persuasion he promised Hodgkinson not to betray him, and describing the vocal abilities of the Bristol company confirmed John's desire to go on the stage by telling him he was a better singer than any of them. The stable-boy proved a capable critic.

The company was at Bath at the time, but soon returned, when the lad made his application to Keasebury, the manager. "You wish to be an actor, you young rascal," Keasebury answered, laughing. "Pray, sir, what character have you thought of enacting?" The jibing manner in which this was said disconcerted the lad, but he managed to reply, "I can snuff candles if I can do nothing else; but I can do more: I can play the fiddle and sing a good song."—"A good song, I dare say, d—d badly sung," was the manager's discouraging response; "however, come this way, and let's hear what further you have to say for yourself." The boy soon found himself upon the stage of the

Bristol theatre where the company was rehearsing. While watching the actors go through their business, Hodgkinson of course thought he could do much of it better himself if he was bigger and had a beard. After the rehearsal the boy was heard. He first sang the beautiful finale to the first act of the "Padlock," accompanying himself on the violin, and followed this with one of *Lionel's* songs, "Oh, dry those tears," accompanied by the band. "My boy, you'll never be a candle-snuffer" was Keasebury's comment on these performances. The result of the trial was that Hodgkinson entered upon his theatrical apprentice-ship in the theatres at Bristol and Bath. Carpenter, his biographer, believes that this was in 1781, when he was in his fifteenth year.

How long Hodgkinson remained in Mr. Keasebury's employ at this time is uncertain, but it was a subject upon which the actor was always inclined to be reticent. The accounts of his subsequent wan-derings, previous to 1790, when he returned to Bath and Bristol to end his English career in the thea-tres in which it began, are equally meagre. Hodgkinson's position with Keasebury was necessarily an humble one, he being a mere boy without a chance of obtaining any of the parts that were afterward given to young Roscii. He helped to make up the crowd in the spec-tacles; his singing rendered him useful in the choruses; he occa-

MR. HODGKINSON'S PARTS—*Bath and Bristol.*

1790.
Oct. 4 (Br.)—Lyar . . . Young Wilding
      30 (B.)—Know Your Own Mind
                              Dashwood
Nov. 4   —Othello . . . . . Othello
     11   —Battle of Hexham . Montague
              Deaf Lover . . . Meadows
     20   —Country Girl . . . Harcourt
              Gentle Shepherd . . Bauldy
     22 (Br.)—Recruiting Officer
                          Capt. Plume
Dec. 4 (B.)—Suspicious Husband
                              Frankly
              Highland Reel . Sergt. Jack
      6 (Br.)—Cymbeline . . . Arviragus
      23 (B.)—Julia de Roubigne
                              Montauban
              No Song No Supper . Robin
1791.
Jan. 20 (B.)—Tancred and Sigismunda
                              Osmond

Jan. 24 (Br.)—German Hotel . . Dorville
Feb.   1 (B.) —Inconstant . Young Mirabel
       8   —Young Quaker
                     Young Sadboy
            Flitch of Bacon
                     Maj. Benbow
      14 (Br.)—Isabella. . . . . . Villeroy
      26 (B.)—All in the Wrong
                     Sir John Restless
Mar. 14 (Br.)—St. Patrick's Day . Lieutenant
      21   —As You Like It . . Jacques
      29 (B.)—Clandestine Marriage
                     Sir John Melville
April 4 (Br.)—Bold Stroke for a Husband
                     Don Carlos
      11   —Merchant of Venice . Antonio
            Ways and Means . Random
May   2   —School for Arrogance
                     McDermot
       7 (B.)—Modern Antiques . . Frank
      12   —Heiress . . . . . Clifford
      17   —Love in a Camp . . Darby
      19   —Such Things Are . Twineall
      26   —Busybody . . . . Marplot
      28   —Deuce is in Him
                     Col. Tamper
      30 (Br.)—Padlock . . . . . Mungo
June 13   —Hamlet . . . . . Horatio
      27   —Orphan . . . . . Polidore
      29   —Gamester . . . . Lewson
            Catharine and Petruchio
                     Petruchio
July 11   —Cheats of Scapin . . Scapin
      13   —Mahomet . . . . Mahomet
Oct.   3   —Wonder . . . Col. Briton
       5   —Inkle and Yarico . . Inkle
            Scheming Lieutenant
                     Lieut. O'Connor
      10   —Grecian Daughter
                     Dionysius
      21   —Brystone . . . Neptune
      24   —Conscious Lovers . Myrtle
      26   —Farmer . Farmer Blackberry
Nov. 10 (B.)—Richard III . . . Richard
      24   —Quaker . . . . . Steady

sionally "went on" with a letter or message. In the dirge in "Romeo and Juliet" his singing attracted the notice of a person of consequence, who asked the manager which of the ladies it was whose voice so far exceeded the others in sweetness and power. The first applause he ever received on his own account was after the delivery of a letter to one of the comedians, who received it so ruefully that Hodgkinson, as he was about to retire, could not help turning round and looking back, when he burst into a fit of laughter which he endeavored to suppress by putting his hand to his mouth. The audience, thinking it was purposely done in character, was astonished at the natural way in which the boy acted it, and gave him loud marks of approbation. "I dare say I looked devilish odd at the time," said Hodgkinson afterward, relating the incident to a party of friends in Philadelphia. "Ay, ay," gravely responded a young Irishman who was present, "no doubt it was your game eye they laughed at." One of Hodgkinson's eyes was smaller than the other, which sometimes gave him a very whimsical look. As he was exceedingly proud of his personal appearance, this indiscreet remark gave him great annoyance. The list of Hodgkinson's parts after his return to the Bristol and Bath theatres in 1790, printed herewith, which I obtained from the file of bills in the possession of

Nov. 28	(Br.)—Wild Oats . . .	John Dory
Dec. 22	(B.)—Rivals . . .	Capt. Absolute
1792.		
Jan. 2	(B.)—Macbeth	Hecate
12	—Dramatist	Floriville
17	—Notoriety	Clairville
31	—Love in a Village .	Hawthorn
Feb. 9	—Douglas	Glenalvon
16	—Romeo and Juliet .	Romeo
Mar. 24	—Flitch of Bacon . Capt.Wilson	
26	(Br.)—Which is the Man? Belville	
	Family Party	Pinch
31	—More Ways Than One . Bellair	
April 9	—Cymbeline	Pisanio
10	(B.)—Mayor of Garratt	
		Maj. Sturgeon
19	—Fair Penitent . . .	Horatio
May 1	—I'll Tell You What	
		Maj. Cypres
22	—Duplicity . Sir Harry Portland	
26	—Prisoner at Large	
		Jack Connor

Mr. James H. Brown, of Malden, Mass., the only full collection I know of, shows, however, that he was not an accidental comedian.

Where Hodgkinson betook himself after leaving Keasebury, is unknown. It is inferred that he was for a time with a company managed by an itinerant named Miller; but the first certain knowledge we have of him is after his engagement by the eccentric James Whiteley, whose circuit comprised the Worcester, Wolverhampton, Derby, Nottingham, Retford and Stamford theatres. The young comedian was introduced to Whiteley by a gentleman named Mills, who had previously warned Hodgkinson not to take offense at anything the manager might say. "So this is the chap," said Whiteley, addressing Mills, "about whom you gave me such a platter of stirabout with Ballyhack butter in it yesterday." Instead of being vexed at this extraordinary greeting, Hodgkinson found it difficult to suppress a smile of merriment, whereupon Whiteley turned to his friend and said, "The black-guard has some fun in him I see, but he looks as if a dinner would not come amiss to him—he's as slim as a greyhound." Then casting a glance at Hodgkinson's clothes, which were new and neat, he added, "Why boy, your belly ought to swear its life against your back, for you are killing the one to cover the other." "You are mistaken," said Mills; "there is not a man in your company eats better than John." "Where does he get it?" demanded Whiteley; "he can't have above half a guinea a week for his salary, and the clothes now on his back must have cost at least twenty half-guineas—half a year's pay!" Hodgkinson laughed heartily, and, forgetting himself, he sat down un-bidden in a large armchair that stood behind him. "What's this his name is?" Whiteley asked. "Hodgkinson," Mills answered. "I thought there must be an O or a Mac to it by the aisy affability with which he helped himself to the great chair. Old Maclaughlin, that blackguard Jew that calls himself Macklin, could not surpass it for modesty." Hodgkinson rose. "Och, to the d—l with your manners, honey," exclaimed Whiteley, pressing the actor back into the chair; "stay there since you are in it, and be d—d to you." Mills and Hodgkinson remained to dinner. Before dinner was announced the torrent continued, but not a word of the stage could Whiteley be in-duced to speak. At dinner the ribald, often witty and always coarse, turned into the generous and genial host. When his guests were about to depart, Whiteley turned to Hodgkinson and said, "Look you, my lad, when the waiter of a tavern or the potboy of a porter-house brings me a pot of beer, I always blow off the froth, and bring it to the light, so that I may look down through it, lest it be muddy or foul—in a word, I want to know what I am about to swallow. While

I was blackguarding you, and you staring and laughing at me, I was looking down through your contents, from your frothy powdered head to the very bottom. If your friend and you will call here to-morrow morning, I shall try to bring my tongue down to some serious conversation with you." The result was an engagement that was continued over a considerable period, of which Hodgkinson always spoke with gratitude, a quality he often lacked.

Hodgkinson's next engagement was on the northern circuit, comprising Newcastle, Sheffield, Lancaster, Preston, Warrington and Chester, then under the control of Whitlock and Munden. Charles Whitlock married Eliza Kemble, a sister of Mrs. Siddons, with whom he subsequently came to America. Joseph Munden was afterward the distinguished London comedian. "John had as much work in him as any two players I ever knew," Whitlock said many years later. "I have known him after performing in both play and after-piece at Newcastle, in Northumberland, to set off in a postchaise, travel all night, rehearse the next day, and perform at night in play and farce at Preston in Lancashire." At this time Hodgkinson was especially esteemed for his musical talents, so much so indeed that a capable actor and singer was deprived of *Lubin* in the "Quaker," that he might make his *debut* in the part at Preston. As sometimes happens under such circumstances, Hodgkinson's success on that occasion was not great. In spite of occasional failure, his fame more than kept pace with his years, and he was soon looked upon as the most promising young actor of the time. "Co-ordinate with the rise of his fame and fortune," says Carpenter in the *Mirror of Taste*, "was the growth of the evils which were fated to endanger the one and make shipwreck of the other; his professional success and his gallantries, running parallel with each other like the two wheels of a gig, left their mark on every road he travelled." The first affair of this kind of which there is any record occurred at Chester, where Miss Chapman, an American girl long resident in England, who had run away from her husband, placed herself under his protection. This attachment, if any existed, must have been of brief duration, for as early as October 22, 1788, Miss Chapman made her *debut* at Covent Garden as *Yarico* in " Inkle and Yarico," and previous to that time she had been the heroine at Brighton both in sentimental and lively comedy. She was an elegant young woman, with expressive features and a figure equal to that of Miss Farren, according to the prints of the time. The improbability of the story is enhanced by the fact that the relation must have ended soon after Hodgkinson attained his majority. When Hodgkinson left the Newcastle Company in 1789 he carried with him the so-called wife of Munden, going to Exeter. On the occasion of his *debut* at Bristol, October 4, 1790, he was announced in the bills as "from the Theatre Royal, Exeter," which brings his record down to his last engagement in England, just before his departure for America.

Carpenter gives a glowing account of Hodgkinson's life at Bath, which, unfortunately, must be set down as pure fiction. It was derived from Hodgkinson himself. Like most inventions of the kind, his stories have not even the merit of originality. Coming among the simple republicans of the United States, the Bath favorite, like many of his successors in America, was always ready to boast

MRS. HODGKINSON'S PARTS—*B. and B.*

1790.
Oct. 29 (Br.)—Castle of Andalusia . Catalina
Nov. 13 (B.)—Cross Purposes . Housemaid
      22 (Br.)—Recruiting Officer . . Lucy
      27 (B.)—Provoked Husband . Myrtilla
      30   —He Would be a Soldier
                                   Nancy
Dec. 23   —No Song No Supper
                              Grandmother

of his associations with the great. With a vulgar and illiterate woman bearing his name on the Bath stage, and playing parts so insignificant that they could bring no credit either to her or to him, as her list shows, a woman who had played similar roles at Newcastle as Mrs. Munden, and had borne the Newcastle manager four children whom she deserted, Hodgkinson asserts for himself a high social and professional standing in the most fashionable city in England. He was, he said, a member of the Noblemen's Catch Club at Bath. Out of gratitude for his championship of her play, se-

1791.
Feb.   8 (B.)—Young Quaker
                        Mrs. Millefleur
       14 (Br.)—Isabella . . . . . . Nurse
       24 (B.)—Funeral . . . . Tattleaid
Mar. 10   —Jealous Wife . . . . Toilet
April 4 (Br.)—Bold Stroke for a Husband
                        Inis
       12 (B.)—Fontainebleau . Mrs. Casey
       14   —Richard III
                        Duchess of York.
May   7   —Modern Antiques . . Betty
June 9   —Way to Keep Him
                        Mignonette
July 29 (Br.)—⎰ Beggar's ⎱ Lady
Oct. 29 (B.)—⎱ Opera. ⎰ Diana Trapes
      31 (Br.)—Haunted Tower . . Maud
1792.
Jan.   5 (B.)—Macbeth . Speaking Witch
Mar. 26 (Br.)—Which is the Man?
                        Mrs. Johnson
      31 (B.)—Devil to Pay . . . Lettice
April 11   —Battle of Hexham . Villager
      30 (Br.)—Road to Ruin . Mrs. Ledger
May   26 (B.)—Prisoner at Large . Landlady
      29   —Measure for Measure
                        Francisca
July   5 (Br.)—He Would be a Soldier
                        Nancy

curing its production and playing the hero with great effect, he was, he averred, the annual pensioner of a single lady of high rank to the amount of £200, besides which his patroness secured him many supporters, including the Prince of Wales and other members of the royal family. He was, he boldly claimed, the *protege* of Mrs. Siddons, who offered to play *Lady Randolph* to his *Douglas*, and *Catharine* to his *Petruchio*, when he should make his first appearance in London. He was not only promised the favor of the Prince of Wales when he went to Brighton to play an engagement in the Summer of 1791, but his Royal Highness applauded him on his opening night, notwithstanding the friends of the Duke of York had arranged that he should be hissed from the stage. According to Hodgkinson, as the story is related at great length by Carpenter, the actor, who had been promised the favor at the Brighton Theatre of his Royal Highness the Prince of Wales, was one day walking along the Stein when he found a young man named Fox, a member of the company, beset by a party, headed by Lord Barrymore, which also included the Duke of York. Hodgkinson chivalrously rushed to the defense of the young comedian thus beset, crying, as it happened, to his Royal Highness the Duke, "D—n you, you cowardly rascal, and all your d——d breed." Just then the Prince of Wales came up, and separated the combatants. When Hodgkinson learned that he had thus unwittingly insulted the whole royal family, he determined to leave Brighton before he could be visited with the resentment of the Prince and all his friends; but the manager refused to listen to the actor's appeal, and threatened to have him arrested if he persisted in his design. The result was that when Hodgkinson opened at Brighton the magnanimous Prince stood up in his box, and loudly applauded at the very moment his brother's friends were expecting him to give the signal for hissing the actor.

Hodgkinson was accustomed to speak of the sacrifices he had made in coming to America. Had his stories been true, these would have been too great to counterbalance the motives that actually induced him to cross the Atlantic. This, however, was not a purpose hastily formed. He sought the American engagement before the engagement sought him. This is clearly shown by his letter to Hallam and Henry, which also betrays the motive of the application. He desired to quit England as a means of repudiating the woman who bore his name at Bath, so that another woman might bear it in America.

That Hodgkinson might have obtained an engagement in London at this time need not be doubted: his merit and reputation warranted it. Beyond this, his alleged sacrifices are incredible. His pension, in itself greater than his American salary, was a myth. The only new play in which he performed the hero at Bath was "Julia de Robigne," by Catharine Metcalfe. The Siddons story falls by the weight of its own inherent absurdity. His chivalrous defense of Fox at Brighton was only a fictitious adaptation of a fracas that actually occurred there in the Summer of 1791. It happened in Castle Square, not on the Stein. Lord Barrymore was concerned in it, and so was his brother,

HODGKINSON'S LETTER.

To Messrs. Hallam and Henry, Managers of the Theatre, New York.

GENTLEMEN,

An ardent desire to visit America has forced me to an inquiry how your theatres are situated. Have you a *first line* vacant? or would you be glad to make one for a principal character in this kingdom? I have in all the first theatres out of the capital, maintained one, as I do now in Bath. Among my range of characters here, are Young Mirabel, Young Quaker, Dashwood, Sir John Restless, The Liar, Othello, Iachimo, Belville (*Wives*), Clifford (*Heiress*), Mahomet, Scapin, Captain Plume, Jaques, Deaf Lover, Myrtle, Villeroy, Petruchio, Marplot, Don Carlos (*B. S. Husband*), Zanga, Richmond, Don John (*Chances*), Dyonisius, etc.

Now as it may seem singular that a man in possession of so great a line, and in a first theatre, who has refused, and has now offers of a considerable nature from London, should wish to emigrate, give me leave to say that no pecuniary extravagance has caused the idea, nor could that, without great imprudence,

be the case, my receipts being near four hundred pounds a year from the theatre.

I know many who, were they once convinced of the firm establishment of your country would be glad to visit it; and I can treat for you with as capital a singer as any this country has, Mrs. Billington excepted. My wish is, you would be candid with regard to every information relative to your towns, etc. What salary you can give *two* such people as I have mentioned; and should this meet your approbation do not disappoint in anything, for my part or those mentioned, should any take place, you shall be at liberty to relinquish in an instant. Our vacancy here takes place the beginning of August. Some time between that and September my wish would be to set sail.

I should thank you to attend to these points. I am sure you'll pardon my being particular in them all, and in requesting an answer by the first return. Rest assured that on my part, or the person I treat for, no failure shall take place.

I am, gentlemen,
Your servant,
JOHN HODGKINSON.

Bath, December 28, 1791.

Mr. Barry, attended by a bruiser. They were joined by the *ci-devant* French Duke de la Paine, presumably the Duke of York. When the Duke asked who the victim of their wrath was, Young Barry answered: "A d——d scoundrel who has been insulting my brother." It was this phrase that was turned into the Hodgkinsonian insult to royalty. There was no Fox concerned in the affair—Fox was the manager of the theatre. There was no Hodgkinson to defend Lord Barrymore's victim, who was so badly beaten that he took to his bed. The Prince of Wales caught a glimpse of the fracas from his room, where he was dressing, but instead of the dramatic scene in the theatre he simply advised the Duke to quit Brighton. Besides, there was nothing chivalrous in Hodgkinson's nature. This is illustrated by the fact that when he was about "embarking for America with an actress of the name of Brett" he wrote to Munden, whom he always spoke of in this country as one who had foully wronged him and sought to destroy him in his youth, asking him to care for the deserted woman's children, one of whom had been born at Bath or Exeter after the elopement.

Miss Brett, whom Hodgkinson described as second only to Mrs. Billington as a singer, and who was known in America as Mrs. Hodgkinson, was a daughter of Brett, the celebrated singer of Covent Garden and the Haymarket theatres. Mr. Brett made his first appearance at Covent Garden in 1782 after singing in the Summer at the Haymarket. For some years he had been known as the Orpheus of Bath, and at this time he was

MISS BRETT'S PARTS—*B. and B.*

1789.
Sept. 23 (Br.)—Padlock . . . . . Leonora
Oct.   2   —Waterman . . Wilhelmina
       7   —School for Scandal . Maria
             Farmer . . Molly Maybush
      17 (B.)—Rosina . . . . . . Rosina
      19 (Br.)—As You Like It . . Audrey
Oct. 24 (B.)—Love in a Village . Lucinda
Nov. 14   —Agreeable Surprise . Cowslip
      28   —Inkle and Yarico . Narcissa
      30 (Br.)—Poor Soldier . . Kathleen

said to be the best singer that had been heard in England for twenty years. Mr. Brett had been at the Haymarket in 1778, and he now made his reappearance, after an absence of four years, as *Captain Greville* in the "Flitch of Bacon." On the 19th of August he appeared as the *Genius of Ireland* in a successful pantomime called "Harlequin Teague," his son Master Brett making his *debut* as the *Giant of the Causeway*. This lad was a prodigy, his voice being said to have a greater compass and finer tone than were ever before displayed by a youth of his age in the United Kingdom. Master Brett unfortunately died on the 30th of October, 1782. At this time the future Mrs. Hodgkinson was too young for the stage; but two years later, August 2d, 1784,

1790.
Sept. 29 (Br.)—West Indian . Miss Dudley
Oct. 16 (B.)—Highland Reel . . . Jenny
20 (Br.)—Love in a Village . Rosetta
29 —Castle of Andalusia . Lorenza
30 (B.)—Know Your Own Mind
Miss Neville
Nov. 20 —Gentle Shepherd . . Peggy
Dec. 11 —Flitch of Bacon . . . Eliza

1791.
Jan. 4 (B.)—No Song No Supper . Louisa
29 —Lionel and Clarissa . Diana
Feb. 10 —Brystone . . . . . Nymph
24 —Funeral . . Lady Charlotte
26 —Poor Vulcan . . . . Venus
Mar. 10 —Sultan . . . . . . Ismena
14 (Br.)—Fontainebleau . . . . Rosa
24 (B.)—Milesian . . . . . Isabella
29 —Deserter . . . . . Louisa
April 11 (Br.)—Merchant of Venice . Jessica
Ways and Means . . Kitty
May 12 (B.)—Heiress . . . . Miss Alton
July 11 (Br.)—Cheats of Scapin . . Lucia
Oct. 29 (B.)—Beggar's Opera . . . Polly
31 (Br.)—Haunted Tower . . Adda
Nov. 12 (B.)—Spoiled Child . Miss Pickle
24 —Quaker . . . . . . Gillian
Dec. 17 —Cymon . . . . . . Sylvia

1792.
Jan. 3 (B.)—No Song No Supper
Dorothy
5 —Macbeth . . Singing Witch
Feb. 1 (Br.)—Spoiled Child . . . Susan
2 (B.)—Rival Candidates . Narcissa
18 —Double Disguise . . Emily

when Holcroft's "Noble Peasant" was first produced at the Haymarket, she played the *Dwarf*, Miss George, afterward Mrs. Oldmixon, being the *Adela*. Dunlap, who saw her at the Haymarket during the run of the opera, speaks of her as a page, but the bills show that she really appeared in the character of a dwarf. Miss Brett failed to make anything like the impression created by her brother two years before; and, except that she sang in a duet with her father in the Summer of 1785, her name does not again occur in the bills of the Haymarket until the 19th of June, 1786, when she created the part of *Maria* in "Hunt the Slipper." A few weeks later she was one of the *Bacchants* in "Comus." Miss Brett subsequently sang in Dublin, and when she made her first appearance on the Bristol stage, September 23, 1789, she was underlined from the Theatre Royal, Dublin. That she had achieved some distinction as a singer is apparent from the part accorded her for her *debut* at Bristol, and her subsequent roles show her professional standing when she was engaged by Henry for America. When this engagement was made it was signed only by Hodgkinson, Miss Brett being named as Mrs. Hodgkinson, although the other Mrs. Hodgkinson was acting at Bath at the time as Hodgkinson's acknowledged wife. Mrs. and Miss Brett, the mother and sister of Hodgkinson's intended wife, were also included in the agreement. Mrs. Brett shrank from the long voyage to a strange country, but the younger Miss Brett accompanied her sister. This Miss Brett had inherited little of the genius of the family. Another Miss Brett, who remained behind, is mentioned in a paragraph in a London paper, saying she was the *Lucy* in the "Beggar's Opera" in Dublin, early in November, 1791.

Owing to the failure of Mrs. Brett to make the voyage to America on the ship "Bristol" from London to New York with her two daughters and prospective son-in-law, Mr. Henry succeeded in filling her place by an engagement that was the most important yet made for the United States.

MRS. WRIGHTEN'S PARTS—*Drury Lane.*

1770.
Feb. 8—Lionel and Clarissa . . . Diana
1771.
May 8—Ephesian Matron . . . Matron
Sept. 21—Beggar's Opera . . . . . Polly

This was that of the celebrated Mrs. Wrighten, of Drury Lane, known on the American stage as Mrs. Pownall, who came out with Henry on the "Betsy," arriving a month after the others. Her story is one of unusual interest. When James Wrighten, afterward for many years prompter at Drury Lane, was a strolling player, he met Miss Marshall, a vivacious country girl, whom he married and trained for the stage. She was still very young when, as Mrs. Wrighten, she made her *debut* at Drury Lane, February 8th, 1770, in the character of *Diana* in "Lionel and Clarissa." At this time Garrick's company was weak in singing chambermaids; and as Mrs. Wrighten was not only a singer but an excellent actress, she soon made her mark. This is shown by the fact that early in the season of 1771–2 she was given the part of *Polly* in the "Beggar's Opera," Miss Pope, who was not a good singer, being the *Lucy*. Later

1773.
Feb. 1—Wedding Ring . . . . . Lisetta
Mar. 27—Frenchified Lady . . . Doralice
Nov. 2—Deserter . . . . Jenny
Dec. 27—Christmas Tale . . . . Robinette
1774.
April 15—Ladies' Frolick . . . . . Rachel
May 9—Gentle Shepherd . . . . Peggy
Oct. 21—Election . . . . Sally
Dec. 9—Cobbler . . . . Alice
1775.
Feb. 1—Rival Candidates . . . . Jenny
May 13—Tom Thumb . . . . . . Queen
Sept. 23—Theatrical Candidates . Comedy
Oct. 28—May Day . . . . Dolly
Nov. 9—Old City Manners . . . Gertrude
      24—Love in a Village . . . Margery
Dec. 12—Peep into the Seraglio . . Imena
1776.
Jan. 26—Author . . . . . Mrs. Cadwallader
Feb. 1—Blackamoor Washed White
                              Lady Oddfish
      15—Runaway . . . . Susan
Mar. 23—Valentine's Day . . . . Pinner
April 15—Love's Metamorphosis . Feather
May 16—Wonder . . . . Flora
Sept. 21—New Brooms . . . Mrs. Quaver
Nov. 21—Hotel . . . . Tabby
1777.
Jan. 16—Rivals . . . . Lucy
Oct. 7—Quaker . . . . Floretta
      9—Old Batchelor . . . . . . Lucy
Nov. 8—Beggar's Opera . . . . . Lucy
Dec. 22—Comus . . . . . First Bacchant
1778.
Jan. 17—Cymon . . . . Fatima
Mar. 16—Belphegor . . . . . Dame Din
      30—Second Thought is Best . Agnes
April 29—Waterman . . . . Mrs. Bundle
      30—Lucky Escape . . . . . Letitia
May 23—Devil to Pay . . . . . . Nell
Sept. 15—Camp . . . . Nell
1779.
Mar. 25—Peep Behind the Curtain . Rhodope
April 10—Who's the Dupe ? . . . Charlotte
Nov. 19—Lionel and Clarissa . . . Jenny

1780.
Mar. 14—Artifice . . . . . . Margaritta
Oct. 5—As You Like It . . . . Audrey
Dec. 27—Lord of the Manor . . . Peggy
1781.
Feb. 20—Catharine and Petruchio .Catharine
Mar. 6—Maid of the Mill . . . . Fanny
8—Chapter of Accidents . . Bridget
April 24—Way to Keep Him . . . Muslin
Nov. 12—Divorce . . . . Biddy
Dec. 13—Carnival of Venice . . Francisca
1782.
May 18—Fair American . . . . . Rachel
Dec. —Best Bidder.
1783.
April 7—Double Gallant . . . . Wishwell
Oct. 7—Comus . . . . . . Euphrosyne
Nov. 4—Thomas and Sally . . . Dorcas
Dec. 5—Metamorphosis . . . . . Mary
1784.
Mar. 8—Double Disguise . . . . Rose
April 12—Way of the World . . . Foible
Nov. 4—Spanish Rivals . . . . . Lucett
1785.
April 1—Clandestine Marriage
Chambermaid
Intriguing Chambermaid . Lettice
Dec. 8—Strangers at Home . . . . Alice
26—Hurly-Burly . . . . . Nannette
1786.
April 24—Daphne and Amintor . Mendora
May 17—Provoked Wife . . Mademoiselle
Sept. 21—Country Girl . . . . . Lucy
Nov. 25—School for Greybeards . . Rachel

Mrs. Wrighten, herself, was *Lucy*, yielding *Polly* to Mrs. Baddeley. But even as *Lucy* one of the London critics said of her in 1784 that she could not be equalled on the stage. The parts here given are either original creations or first appearances in familiar roles. — Among the latter it will be noted that she did not play *Audrey* in "As You Like It" until 1780, when she had been more than ten years in the theatre, and her first appearance as *Catharine* in "Catharine and Petruchio" was not until 1781. She played *Audrey* when Mrs. Siddons failed as *Rosalind* and *Catharine* among others to John Philip Kemble's *Petruchio*. Her last appearance in London in the latter part was to the *Petruchio*

of Palmer. During the Summer she was accustomed to sing at Vauxhall, where she was a great favorite for many years, sharing the honors with Darley, afterward a popular member of the Philadelphia Company. In the Summer of 1783, however, she was at the Haymarket, where she created the part of *Belinda* in the "Lawyer" to the *Charles Powys* of Williamson, subsequently the noted Boston and Charleston manager. In May, 1784, she was so dangerously ill that her life was despaired of. In 1785 she returned to Vauxhall, and sang there for the last time in 1786. As a singer, she was surpassed only by Mrs. Billington and Miss George, better known as Mrs. Oldmixon, and her comic powers were remarkable. One of the wits of the time suggested that she should be painted as the Goddess of Mirth, attended by St. Cecilia; and Anthony Pasquin celebrated her in his "Children of Thespis" as

> The prop of burlettas and mistress of mirth,
> Of female comedians an excellent sample—
> Of Abagail singers the first great example.

According to the "Thespian Dictionary," Mrs. Wrighten basely eloped from her husband, and deserted her daughters, in consequence of which poor Wrighten died of a broken heart. As the elopement occurred during the holiday season of 1786–7, and James Wrighten lived until 1793, his wrongs were more than seven years in culminating fatally. That she should quit Drury Lane in the middle of the season was a surprise; but from their frequent skirmishing it was expected that she would separate from her husband, one of the London papers saying that she had lived for some time O. P. instead of P. S. After her disappearance she was not again seen in London until the following April. There were rumors that she had eloped with an earl, but on the other hand it was positively asserted: "Mrs. Wrighten did not soar in her late flight—the coronet she despised, and looked for more substantial bliss in the snug retreat of a dealer in strong spirits." Mrs. Wrighten's flight was the subject of many rhymed effusions, one of the newspaper poets even celebrating her supposed return. He sang of her assumed abode as heaven; and it was intended, according to the poet, to send the aeronaut whose balloon was destroyed by the mob at the vitriol works in Tooley Street on the 1st of August, 1787, to offer her a passage back to earth.   Indeed, the poet imagined the balloonist's mission accomplished, and sang of his achievement:

> The moment he pronounced her name,
> Out skipping came the laughing dame,
> Right glad to leave the blest abodes,
> For mortals she prefers to gods;
> Besides, her life was irksome there,
> And scanty was her bill of fare;
> Would change her nectar if they'd let her;
> She lik'd a pot of porter better.

Rumors of Mrs. Wrighten's return to Drury Lane often found expression in the newspapers, but she seems to have lived in retirement in France until Mr. Henry found her there and engaged her for America.   The acquisition was a great one, but it was never utilized, because the Hodgkinsons barred the way.   Her American history, however, was worthy of her great career.

Dunlap speaks of King as next in importance to Hodgkinson among Henry's recruits, but adds that he could do nothing except as instructed by Hodgkinson.   His position at Bath and Bristol was a very humble one, as his list of parts shows; equally humble was that of West.   Their parts, however, assume a significance far beyond their importance in showing that, through the influence of Hodgkinson, Henry was induced to engage feebler actors in England

MR. KING'S PARTS—*B. and B.*

1791.
Sept. 28 (B.)—Farm House . Shacklefigure
    29   —Child of Nature . Evander
    30   —Inkle and Yarico
                                Second Planter
Oct.   1   —Isabella . . . . . . Pedro
    10 (Br.)—Grecian Daughter
                                Greek Soldier
    12   —Rosina . . . . . . Rustic
    19   —Know Your Own Mind
                                Charles
           No Song No Supper
                                William
    21   —Brystone . . . Scaramouch

than he had left in the same walk at home. They came simply as the satellites of the man whose aim in coming to America was to drive Henry from his managerial throne. Beyond their professional history during the two years preceding their American engagement I have been able to find nothing concerning either King or West. Another West, whom Dunlap speaks of as West, Jr., was with the company, as was also a very tall young man, Luke Robbins, who painted some of the scenery, sang in the chorus, and occasionally played small parts. These comprised the recruits with whom the Old American Company began the season of 1792–3.

In Jefferson's Company at Plymouth was Mr. Prigmore, according to John Bernard "a gentleman of some vanity and little merit, whose opinion of himself was in an inverse proportion to that of the public." Bernard found him there in 1787, when he joined

Oct.	29	(B.)—Farmer	. . . .	Flummery
	31	(Br.)—Haunted Tower	. .	Hubert
Nov.	2	—Humorist	. . . . .	Blunt
	5	(B.)—Fontainebleau	. . .	Gagg
	10	—Richard III	. . .	Ratcliff
	17	—Venice Preserved	.	Officer
	21	(Br.)—Deaf Lover	. . . .	Groom
	22	(B.)—Ways and Means		
				Old Random
Dec.	1	—Heiress	. . . . .	Servant
		Virgin Unmasked	.	Thomas
	3	—Drummer	. . .	Coachman
	8	—Midnight Hour	. .	Mathias
	22	—Rivals	. . . . .	Coachman
1792.				
Jan.	5	(B.)—Macbeth	. .	Singing Witch
	14	—Catharine and Petruchio		
				Music Master
Feb.	4	—Country Girl	. . .	Servant
	7	—Wild Oats	. . . . .	Trap
	9	—Douglas	. .	Second Officer
Mar.	3	—Robin Hood	. . .	Bowman
	8	—Provoked Husband	.	James
	10	—Clandestine Marriage		
				Traverse
		Devil Upon Two Sticks		
				Dr. Sligo
	19	—Fair Penitent	. . .	Servant
	24	—Flitch of Bacon	. . .	Putty
	26	(Br.)—Which is the Man?		Servant
April	9	—Cymbeline	. . . .	Philario
	10	(B.)—Inkle and Yarico	. .	Mate
		Mayor of Garratt	.	Heeltap
	11	—Battle of Hexham	.	Somerset
	30	(Br.)—Road to Ruin	. . .	Marker
May	19	(B.)—Follies of a Day		
				Pedro Bounce
	21	(Br.)—Citizen	. . . .	Quilldrive
	24	(B.)—Robinson Crusoe	. .	Pierrot
	26	—Prisoner at Large		
				Father Frank
	29	—Measure for Measure		
				Darnadine
	31	—Much Ado About Nothing		
				Borachio
		Devil to Pay	. . . .	Butler

June 2　—She Wou'd and She Wou'd
　　　　　Not . . . . . Alguazil
　　　　Agreeable Surprise . . John
　　7　—Roman Father . Volscinius
　　　　Modern Antiques . Thomas
　　9　—Highland Reel . . Croudy

accompanied Bernard to Guernsey, and he was still with Bernard and back at Plymouth in 1792 when Henry engaged him for the Old American Company. Prigmore was not free to make an engagement at the time, and so instead of sailing with the rest of Henry's recruits from London he concealed himself among the bales and boxes on an American brig, then at Plymouth, where he was found the next day by the captain. His unexpected desertion caused some inconvenience in the theatre where he was cast for a small part in "He Would be a Soldier." In consequence, young John Emery who was in the orchestra was substituted to read the part, but he mastered the lines before his scene was reached and played with such effect that Dr. Gaskin, a friend of Bernard's, went behind to ask the name of the new actor in the last act. "Young Emery,

hands with Jefferson in the management of the Plymouth Theatre. Afterward Prigmore, who called himself "a low comedian,"

Mr. West's Parts—*B. and B.*

1791.
April 30 (B.)—Waterman . . . Tom Tug
May　5　—Battle of Hexham . . Fool
　　24　—Robin Hood . . . . Edwin
　　26　—Busybody . . . . Charles
June 13 (Br.)—Hamlet . . . . Rosencranz
　　22　—Duenna . . . Don Antonio
　　29　—Catharine and Petruchio
　　　　　　　　　　　Hortensio
July　8　—Such Things Are
　　　　　　　　First Keeper
　　11　—Cheats of Scapin . Octavian
　　13　—Mahomet . . . . . Pharon
　　18　—Roman Father . . Valerius
　　27　—Cymbeline . . . Arviragus
Sept. 28 (B.)—Percy . . . . . Sir Hubert
　　30　—St. Patrick's Day . Sergeant
Oct.　1　—Isabella . . . . . Belford
　　3 (Br.)—Poor Soldier . Capt. Fitzroy
　　5　—Inkle and Yarico . Campley
　　7　—Scheming Lieutenant
　　　　　　　　　Trounce
　　8 (B.)—Farmer . . . . . . Rundy
　　　　Merchant of Venice . Solanio
10 (Br.)—Grecian Daughter . . Arcas
　　12　—Rosina . . . Capt. Belville
　　14　—Way to Keep Him . William
　　　　Two Strings to Your Bow
　　　　　　　　　　Octavio
　　17　—Farm House . . Heartwell
　　19　—Know Your Own Mind
　　　　　　　　　Sir Harry
　　　No Song No Supper
　　　　　　　　Frederick

the musician," was Bernard's an-swer. "You mean young Emery, the comedian," the Doctor replied. When informed by the captain of the brig of Prigmore's intended departure, Bernard, accepting his loss, assented to it, and thus America obtained a buffoon, and England gained a great comedian.

Dunlap is almost the only source of information we have in regard to the personal qualities and appearance of these acquisitions to the American stage. Hodg-kinson he describes as six feet ten inches in height, but too fleshy to appear tall — well formed in the neck, chest, shoulders and arms, but clumsy in his lower extremi-ties, his ankles being thick and his knees inclining inward. His face was round, his nose broad, and his eyes, which were of unequal sizes, gray, with large pupils and dark eyelashes. His complexion was almost colorless, and his hair dark-brown. His manners were agree-able and his habits convivial, so

Oct.	21	—George Barnwell . . Blunt
		Brystone . . . . Macarino
	26	—Beggar's Opera . . . Mat
	31	—Haunted Tower . . Charles
Nov.	5 (B.)	—Fontainebleau . . . Henry
		Romp . . . . Capt. Sightly
	7 (Br.)	—Highland Reel . Capt. Dash
	10 (B.)	—Richard III . . . Catesby
	12	—School for Scandal . . Trip
	15	—Deaf Lover . . . Canteen
	17	—Venice Preserved . Spinosa
Dec.	1	—Heiress . . . . . Prompt
		Virgin Unmasked . Quaver
	3	—Suspicious Husband . Buckle
	5 (Br.)	—Wild Oats . . . . Twitch
		Drummer . . . . Fantome
	10	—Provoked Husband . Basset
	13	—Cross Purposes . . . Robin
	17	—Much Ado About Nothing
		Conrade
	22 (B.)	—Rivals . . . . . . David

1792.

Jan.	2 (Br.)	—Macbeth . . . . . Rosse
	12 (B.)	—Dramatist . . . . . Peter
		Lyar . . . Sir James Elliot
	17	—Notoriety . . . . Saunter
	28	—Chapter of Accidents . Vane
	31	—Love in a Village . Eustace
Feb.	4	—Country Girl . . . Belville
	9	—Douglas . . . . . Officer
	18	—West Indian . . . Stukely
		Double Disguise . . . Sam
	25	—Battle of Hexham . Egbert
Mar.	6	—Romeo and Juliet . . Tibalt
	10	—Devil Upon Two Sticks
		Invoice
	15	—Belle's Stratagem . . Villars
	24	—Bold Stroke for a Husband
		Garcia
	26 (Br.)	—Family Party . Capt. Rampart
	29 (B.)	—I'll Tell You What
		Sir Harry
	31	—More Ways Than One
		Lawyer's Clerk
		Devil to Pay . . . . Butler

April   9 (Br.)—Cymbeline . . . First Lord
       12 (B.)—Robin Hood . . . Scarlet
       30 (Br.)—Road to Ruin   . . Officer
May   14   —Maid of the Mill . . Mervin
       21   —Citizen . . Young Wilding
       26 (B.)—Way to Keep Him . William
             Prisoner at Large . . Trap
       29   —Measure for Measure
                            Abhorson
             Bold Stroke for a Wife
                            Sir Philip
June   2   —She Wou'd and She Wou'd
             Not . . . . Soto
             Agreeable Surprise . Eugene
       18 (Br.)—Village Lawyer . Young Snarl

that he soon became the delight of the town, the companion of the wits and the soul of the musical societies. The early friends that he made in America may have fallen away from him, as Dunlap asserts, but it is more likely this was due to his irascible temper and want of principle rather than the coarseness of his nature and an ignorance that "beyond theatrical limits was profound." As a proof of his want of knowledge, Dunlap declares he did not know the name of the author of "High Life Below Stairs" at the time he was playing the principal character in the piece; but, on the other hand, Carpenter says that he had ready at his call all the criticisms and commentaries on the dramatic poets, and concerning disputed points in Shakspere he could instantly repeat the opinions of every great annotator. His reading, it was said, was extensive, and he was ambitious not only to act well but to write well. It is unnecessary, however, to anticipate an estimate of his abilities, as this can best be done in the light of his achievements. Mrs. Hodgkinson was petite and girlish in figure, with a nose that was too prominent for her stature. Her face was oval, and she was very fair, with blue eyes and hair that approached the flaxen. Apart from her merits as an actress and singer, she was, in the words of Dunlap, "an amiable woman and a good wife." Unlike her sister, Miss Brett scarcely attained to the comely, and she possessed little of her sister's talent. Better than any description of Mrs. Pownall, as Mrs. Wrighten was now called, is the engraved portrait by Dighton, which may still be occasionally met with. The accounts of the minor players among the men are meagre. There is no description of Prigmore beyond the fact that he was a very vain and ludicrous person. King was tall and manly in figure, with a fine face, but he was dissipated and negligent of duty. West was something of a dandy, Dunlap calling him the "leather-breeches beau" because he was arrested for debt by a New York breeches-maker, having obtained six pairs of leather breeches which he was unable to pay for. "Six pairs of leather breeches!" exclaimed the old printer, Hugh Gaine, who went his bail; "how many legs has the fellow got?" West usually appeared in the street in boots and leather breeches, always new, and with three gold-laced buttonholes on each side of the high, upright collar of his scarlet coat. Robbins, who was the least important member of the company, in addition to the gold-laced collar, wore three gold hatbands. Even Hodgkinson assumed the air that was known as theatrical a hundred years ago, as it is still. He wore breeches and buckled shoes instead of trousers and boots, and retained the powdered curls on each side of his head, and the cue behind, long after short, cropped hair had come into fashion.

Having thus introduced Henry's recruits to the reader, it only remains to follow them at their work in the following chapters.

CHAPTER IV.

―――

HALLAM AND HENRY, 1792–3.

THE SEASON IN PHILADELPHIA—HODGKINSON'S FIRST APPEARANCE—
THE OTHER DEBUTS—CONTEMPORARY OPINIONS OF THE ACTORS
—CASTS AND PARTS—MR. CHAMBERS—NEW YORK SEASON, 1793
—YOUNG HALLAM'S DEBUT—RETURN TO PHILADELPHIA.

THE first engagement of the Old American Company as reorganized by Mr. Henry was played at the Southwark Theatre, Philadelphia. The season began on the 26th of September, 1792, with the comedy of the "Wonder" and the musical farce, the "Padlock," as the opening pieces. Strong as the new company was, the management felt that the new theatre in Chestnut Street would soon become a dangerous competitor, and so the aid of the newspapers was invoked to convince the public that the old theatre was not so inaccessible as some people imagined. "Access to the Old American Theatre in Southwark," said Dunlap's *Advertiser* on the morning when the old house was announced to be reopened with the new company, "is becoming every day more and more easy. From the progress of pavements in that part of the town, riding and walking to it will soon in no season be disagreeable or difficult." This paragraph caused a smile in Philadelphia, and it was even copied into the newspapers of other cities as a species of unconscious humor. For more than a quarter of a century the Southwark Theatre had been the only place of amusement in Philadelphia. During that whole period it had suffered in patronage because of its inaccessibility. It was now about to enter the epoch of its decline, leading to its virtual and finally its complete abandonment as the home of the Old American Company.

The season of 1792-3 lasted from the 26th of September to the 12th of January following. For many weeks nothing that was new to Philadelphia playgoers was attempted. The repertoire consisted of the best of the pieces that had met with favor in the past. These, no doubt, served as an excellent vehicle for the introduction of the recruits engaged by Mr. Henry in England, most of whom made their American *debut* on the opening night, including Mr. and Mrs. Hodgkinson. Mr. Henry upon his return did not arrive in New York until the 1st of October, but he reached Philadelphia in time to play *Sir Peter* in the "School for Scandal" on the 8th. The first new production of the season was the afterpiece, the "Romp," first played on the 22d. President Washington attended the theatre November 14, when the "Maid of

LIST OF PERFORMANCES—*Philadelphia.*

1792.

Sept. 26—Wonder . . . . . Mrs. Centlivre
Padlock . . . . . . Bickerstaff
28—West Indian . . . . Cumberland
Padlock.
Oct. 1—Clandestine Marriage
Garrick and Colman
Flitch of Bacon . . . . . Bate
3—She Stoops to Conquer . Goldsmith
Deserter . . . . Dibdin
5—Beaux' Stratagem . . . Farquhar
Flitch of Bacon.
8—School for Scandal . . . Sheridan
Deserter.
10—Love in a Village . . Bickerstaff
Catharine and Petruchio
Shakspere
12—Jane Shore . . . . . . Rowe
Lying Valet . . . . . . Garrick
15—Maid of the Mill . . Bickerstaff
Love a la Mode . . . . Macklin
17—Maid of the Mill.
Mayor of Garratt . . . . Foote
19—Richard III . . . . . Shakspere
Devil to Pay . . . . . . Coffey
22—Busybody . . . . Mrs. Centlivre
Romp . . . . . . Bickerstaff
24—Miser . . . . Fielding
Rosina . . . . . . Mrs. Brooke
26—Clandestine Marriage.
Romp.
29—Othello . . . . Shakspere
Romp.
31—Dramatist . . . . . . Reynolds

Oct. 31—Devil to Pay.
Nov. 2—Dramatist.
      Rosina.
      5—Henry IV . . . . . Shakspere
      Padlock.
      7—Dramatist.
      Romp.
      9—Love in a Village.
      Lying Valet.
      14—Maid of the Mill.
      Romp.
      16—Miser.
      Farmer . . . . O'Keefe
      17—Dramatist.
      Romp.
      19—Othello.
      Farmer.
      23—Busybody.
      Midas . . . . O'Hara
      24—Douglas . . . . Home
      Rosina.
      26—School for Scandal.
      Flitch of Bacon.
      28—Mysterious Husband . Cumberland
      Prisoner at Large . . . O'Keefe
      30—More Ways Than One
                        Mrs. Cowley
      No Song No Supper . . Hoare
Dec. 3—All in the Wrong . . . Murphy
      Poor Soldier . . . . . O'Keefe
      5—Romeo and Juliet . . Shakspere
      No Song No Supper.
      7—More Ways Than One.
      No Song No Supper.
      10—Road to Ruin . . . . Holcroft
      Romp.
      12—Road to Ruin.
      Romp.
      14—Fair Penitent . . . . . Rowe
      Agreeable Surprise . . O'Keefe
      17—Road to Ruin.
      No Song No Supper.
      19—Dramatist.
      Don Juan.
      20—Dramatist.
      Don Juan.

the Mill" and the "Romp" comprised the bill. The first production of O'Keefe's "Farmer" by the Old American Company occurred on the 16th of November. It was first played in this country by Bignall and West's Virginia Company at Richmond in 1790. Prince Hoare's musical drama, "No Song No Supper," had its first production in America on the 30th, and Holcroft's "Road to Ruin" received its initial performance on the 10th of December. The pantomime ballet, "Don Juan," first given on the 19th, was announced "by permission of John Palmer, manager of the late Royalty Theatre." Two new plays were played for the first time in this country at the benefits, Mrs. Hodgkinson and her sister, Miss Brett, giving Mrs. Inchbald's "Child of Nature," and Messrs. West and Prigmore the younger Colman's "Ways and Means." Only joint benefits were given this season, and these were con-

fined to the new members of the
company. There were only three
postponements of the performances
on account of indisposition during the engagement, those of November 12th and December 17th,
owing to the illness of Mr. Henry,
and that of November 21st because of the illness of Miss Tuke.
The most successful of the new
pieces was the " Romp," which
had eight performances. The
other farces were less fortunate,
" No Song No Supper " having
only five performances, " Don
Juan " four, and the " Farmer "
two. The " Road to Ruin," which
continued to be a stock piece until
stock companies almost ceased to

Dec. 22—All in the Wrong.
  Don Juan.
  26—Earl of Essex . . . . . . Jones
  Don Juan.
  28—He Would be a Soldier . . Pilon
  Agreeable Surprise.
  29—Fashionable Lover . Cumberland
  Don Juan.
  (Entertainment of the Wabash
  Indian Chiefs.)
  31—He Would be a Soldier.
  No Song No Supper.
1793.
Jan. 2—Hamlet . . . . Shakspere
  Agreeable Surprise.
  (Hodgkinson and King's Benefit.)
  4—Venice Preserved . . . . Otway
  Farmer.
  (Mrs. Pownall and Mr. Chambers'
  Benefit.)
  7—Child of Nature . . . . Inchbald
  Cymon and Sylvia.   Garrick
  (Mrs. Hodgkinson and Miss Brett's
  Benefit.)
  9—Ways and Means . . Colman, Jr
  Romp.
  (West and Prigmore's Benefit.)
  11—Fair Penitent.
  Rosina.
  12—More Ways Than One.
  Prisoner at Large.

exist, was played only three times. At that time, however, eight, or
even five, performances were a measure of great success.

Few casts of this interesting season have come down to us.
Fortunately, among these few are those of the opening night, when
Mr. Hodgkinson made his *debut* as *Don Felix* in the " Wonder," and
Mrs. Hodgkinson as *Leonora* in the "Padlock." It has always been
asserted that Hodgkinson made his first appearance in America as
Belcour in the "West Indian," a mistake that was first made in the
biography published in the *Mirror of Taste*. It would have been sur-

prising if Mr. Hodgkinson had recited an address,[1] written by himself, on the opening night, and yet have refrained from taking advantage of an occasion so favorable for his *debut;* but that he did so is supported both by tradition and personal recollection. Indeed, Charles Durang, in his " History of the Philadelphia Stage," goes so far as to say that Hodgkinson, as *Belcour,* on meeting *Stockwell* in his opening scene on his opening night, had completely forgotten the first line of his

WONDER.

Don Felix . . Mr. Hodgkinson
(His first appearance in America)
Colonel Briton . . . Mr. King
(His first appearance in America)
Don Pedro . . . . Mr. Ashton
Don Lopez . . . . Mr. Ryan
Gibby . . . . Mr. Bisset
Alguazile . . . Mr. Hammond
English Soldier . Mr. Robinson
Vasquez . . . . . Mr. Durang
Lissardo . . . . Mr. Prigmore
(His first appearance in America)
Isabella . . . . . Miss Tuke
Flora . . . . . . Mrs. Rankin
Ines . . . . . Mrs. Hamilton
Violante . . . . Mrs. Henry

PADLOCK.

Mungo . . . . . Mr. Hallam
Don Diego . . . . Mr. Woolls
Leander . . . . . . Mr. West
(His first appearance in America)
Ursula . . . . Mrs. Hamilton
Leonora . . Mrs. Hodgkinson
(Her first appearance in America)

---

[1] MR. HODGKINSON'S ADDRESS.

Across the vast Atlantic we have steered
To view that liberty so much revered;
To view the genuine sons of freedom's cause,
The favor'd land govern'd by reason's laws—
The empire whose bright fame the muse shall sing, [king.
Where virtue reigns, where every man's a
And, thank my stars, upon this wish'd for spot
I'm landed safe, whate'er's my future lot;
But, ah! that rests with you; yours the kind task
To grant the welcome I scarce dare to ask.
Yet balmy hope assures me there's no danger
In craving your protection for a stranger,
Who, if his poor exertions you approve,
Will ever study to deserve your love; [care,
Who's brought among you, trusted to your
A wife and sister—all he has that's dear.
Consign'd to you, refuse them if you can—
You can't, you sacred hold the Rights of Man.

From you they sprang, 'twas yours to give them birth [earth.
And deal the heav'n-born blessing round the
Those rights proclaim; your first, your darling care,
Is to exert protection for the fair. [favor,
We've others, too, who, anxious for your
Will ever use their ardent, firm endeavor;
Who to this shore most cheerfully are come
Trusting they'll meet a kind and welcome home; [from you
Trusting that while deserv'd, they'll meet
The kind reward to modest merit due.
(*Bell rings.*)
There goes the knell that summons to my fate,
And now your judgment tremblingly I wait;
One poor request, my trial ere I meet,
I beg to lay before my jury's feet:
If to my condemnation you incline,
Do it with mercy—to submit be mine.
But if not guilty prov'd, support my cause,
And my acquittal crown with your applause.

part in the excitement of a first appearance in a new land. The incident is reported on the authority of John North, the caretaker of the old Southwark Theatre. " The night Hodgkinson made his first appearance in this theatre," North is quoted as saying, " he entered on the P. S. side as *Belcour* in the ' West Indian.' He went down to the footlamps and made a very low bow, and after the applause he went to the prompt side, and said to the prompter (who was old Bignall), loud enough for the audience to hear him, ' Mr. Prompter, give me the word,' which was *Mr. Stockwell.* A general surprise seized upon all. It was wondered whether this action should be attributed to freak, or really a want of the word. After he got the word, he went on glibly and smoothly with the dialogue of the scene. Why it so happened Hodgkinson said afterward he could not tell; such a thing never occurred to him again. He said a strange sensation came over him. He had forgotten the character he was to personate — he had forgotten the play." If anything of this

WEST INDIAN.

Belcour . . . Mr. Hodgkinson
Varland . . . . Mr. Prigmore
Major O'Flaherty . . Mr. King
Charlotte Rusport . Mrs. Henry

SHE STOOPS TO CONQUER.

Hardcastle . . . Mr. Prigmore
Young Marlow. Mr. Hodgkinson
Tony Lumpkin . . Mr. Hallam
Miss Hardcastle . Mrs. Henry

kind happened on the night of Hodgkinson's *debut*, it is evident that somebody else forgot the character he was to personate and the play in which he appeared. Hodgkinson was not only announced to make his first appearance as *Don Felix* on the opening night, but his address shows he was ready for the summons to his fate. Besides, there are at least two contemporary criticisms of his acting in the part on that occasion. The *Federal Gazette* said that in the character of *Don Felix* he portrayed in a manner the most striking all the various excesses of love and jealousy, while a Philadelphia correspondent, writing to the

Columbian Centinel, declared that he supported the part with great strength and propriety. From his energetic performance of the more pathetic scenes, this writer was induced to think well of his abilities. It is certain that *Belcour* was Hodgkinson's second part, and on the fourth night of the season he played *Young Marlow* in " She Stoops to Conquer," but the newspapers failed to comment on his parts in these comedies, of which only partial casts have been preserved. The allusion to old Bignall as the prompter of the Old American Company at this time was another curious mistake, as Bignall never played in Philadelphia, but was still the manager of the Virginia Company.

Mrs. Hodgkinson made her *debut* on the opening night as *Leonora* in the " Padlock," and appeared as *Rosetta* in " Love in a Village " two weeks later, with Mrs. Pownall as *Madge,* and Mr. Hodgkinson as *Young Meadows.* The *Federal Gazette* said Mrs. Hodgkinson acted *Leonora* inimitably —" All ears were charmed with her voice and all eyes delighted with her manner." The writer in the *Centinel* also acknowledged her charm, and

ROMP.

———

Watty Cockney ·	Mr. Prigmore
Barnacle	Mr. King
Old Cockney . . .	Mr. Ashton
Captain Sightly . . .	Mr. West
Priscilla Tomboy	
	Mrs. Hodgkinson
Penelope	Miss Brett
Miss La Blond . .	Mrs. Rankin

ROSINA.

———

Belville . . .	Mr. Chambers
Captain Belville . .	Mr. West
William	Mr. Prigmore
Irishman	Mr. King
Rosina . . .	Mrs. Hodgkinson
Phoebe	Mrs. Pownall
Old Woman . .	Mrs. Hamilton

added: " In her Mrs. Henry at last finds a rival worthy of her vocal abilities." As *Priscilla Tomboy* the *Federal Gazette* said Mrs. Hodgkinson caused the greatest laughter, and acted inimitably; but some exception was taken to her manner of speaking as *Rosina* as too quick and lively. It was conceded, however, that she sang delightfully. Apparently, there was some arrangement for the distribution of parts between Mrs. Hodgkinson, Mrs. Henry and Miss Tuke—the last-named soon to become Mrs. Hallam—Mrs. Hodgkinson being accorded the leading singing roles, such as *Molly Maybush* in the "Farmer," and *Margaretta* in "No Song No Supper," besides those already named, while Mrs. Henry and

FARMER.

Farmer Blackberry	Mr. King
Valentine	Mr. West
Fairly	Mr. Heard
Colonel Dorimont	Mr. Ashton
Jemmy Jumps	Mr. Chambers
Flummery	Mr. Ryan
Rundy	Mr. Martin
Stubble	Mr. Woolls
Louisa	Mrs. Kenna
Molly	Mrs. Hodgkinson
Betty Blackberry	Mrs. Pownall
Landlady	Mrs. Rankin

NO SONG NO SUPPER.

Robin	Mr. Hodgkinson
Endless	Mr. Martin
Crop	Mr. Prigmore
Frederick	Mr. West
Thomas	Mr. Ryan
William	Mr. Robbins
Margaretta	Mrs. Hodgkinson
Dorothy	Mrs. Pownall
Nelly	Mrs. Rankin
Louisa	Miss Brett

Miss Tuke divided the tragedy and comedy lead. Mrs. Henry, as we have seen, was *Violante* in the "Wonder" on the opening night, and *Charlotte Rusport* in the "West Indian," and *Miss Hardcastle* in "She Stoops to Conquer" in quick succession. Miss Tuke is first noticed in the "Lying Valet," when Garrick's farce was given with "Love in a Village" on the 9th of November. It is probable she

LYING VALET.

Sharp	Mr. Hallam
Guttle	Mr. Ashton
Beau Trippet	Mr. Hammond
Kitty Pry	Miss Tuke

LOVE IN A VILLAGE.

Young Meadows	Mr. Chambers
Woodcock	Mr. Ashton
Sir William	Mr. Hammond
Hodge	Mr. Hallam
Madge	Mrs. Pownall
Rosetta	Mrs. Hodgkinson

played *Kitty* when the "Lying Valet" was first presented this season a month earlier. The opera had been produced earlier in the season with Hodgkinson as *Young Meadows.* A correspondent wrote to the *Federal Gazette* concerning this performance, that as Hodgkinson and Prigmore, who had been the life of the theatre, were not in the bill, his curiosity led him to the playhouse, but he found the characters supported beyond his expectations.

Mr. Prigmore made his *debut* on the opening night as *Lissardo* in the "Wonder," subsequently appearing as *Varland* in the "West

MAID OF THE MILL.	Indian," and	DRAMATIST.
Aimworth . . Mr. Hodgkinson	*Watty Cockney*	Vapid . . . . Mr. Hodgkinson
Sir Harry Sycamore		Lord Scratch . . Mr. Prigmore
Mr. Prigmore	in the "Romp;"	Ennui . . . . . . Mr. King
Mervyn . . . . . . Mr. West	*Mr. Hardcastle*	Floriville . . . . Mr. Hallam
Fairfield . . . Mr. Ashton		Willoughby . . Mr. Hammond
Giles . . . . . . Mr. Woolls	in "She Stoops	Neville . . . . . Mr. Martin
Ralph . . . . . . Mr. Hallam	to Conquer," *Sir*	Peter . . . . Mr. Ryan
Lady Sycamore . Mrs. Hamilton		Marianne . . . . . Miss Tuke
Fanny . . . . . Mrs. Kenna	*Harry Sycamore*	Lady Waitfort . Mrs. Hamilton
Theodosia . . . . Miss Tuke		Louisa . . . . . . Miss Brett
Patty . . . . . . Mrs. Pownall	in the "Maid of	Letty . . . . . . Mrs. Rankin

the Mill," *Jobson* in the "Devil to Pay," *Crop* in "No Song No Supper," and *Lord Scratch* in the "Dramatist." At the outset, Prigmore was received with more favor than he deserved. He succeeded in making a good impression as *Lissardo ;* and when he played *Jobson* to Mrs. Pownall's *Nell,* one of the Philadelphia critics said of him that in low comedy he had few equals, while he reminded the correspondent of the Boston *Centinel* of Wignell, whose absence in consequence was to be the less regretted. On the night when President Washington[1] attended the theatre to witness the performance of the "Maid of the Mill" and the "Romp," another Philadelphia critic described his

---

[1] WASHINGTON AT THE PLAYHOUSE. — (From the *Federal Gazette,* Nov. 17th, 1792.) When Mr. Hodgkinson as *Lord Aimworth* exhibited nobleness of mind in his generosity to the humble miller and his daughter, *Patty;* when he found her blessed with all the qualities that captivate and endear life, and knew that she was capable of adorning a higher sphere; when he had interviews with her upon the subject on which was painted the amiableness of an honorable passion; and after his connection, when he bestowed his benefactions on the relatives, etc., of the old miller, the great and good Washington manifested his approbation of this interesting part of the opera by the tribute of a tear. Nor was his approbation withheld in the afterpiece when Mrs. Hodgkinson as *Priscilla Tomboy,* and Mr. Prigmore as *Young Cockney,* played truly up to nature. The humorous scenes unfolded in this piece, being acted to the life, received the approving smiles of our President, whose plaudits they have studiously endeavored and, we hope, will endeavor to merit.

Young Cockney as " truly up to nature." It must be said, however, that the critics were not so lavish in praise of the other new members of the company, with the exception of Mrs. Pownall. This distinguished actress arrived in America on the same vessel with Mr. Henry, on the 1st of October. It is probable she made her American *debut* as *Catharine* in " Catharine and Petruchio" on the 10th, and in a musical part as *Patty* in the " Maid of the Mill" on the 15th. One critic, speaking of Mrs. Hodgkinson as *Molly Maybush* and Mrs. Pownall as *Betty Blackberry* in the " Farmer," said that the difference in the abilities of these ladies was that the former charmed in lively characters, and the latter in all characters. On the other hand, Mr. West as *Captain Belville* in " Rosina" was described as "just yet as truly unamiable," and Mr. King as *Colonel Briton* in the " Wonder" played the part only with " appropriate firmness." Miss Brett, who is first noticed as *Louisa* in the " Dramatist," was kindly treated; but it was said, " She speaks rather too low and quick, and, inclining a little, looks too much toward the floor of the stage."

Mr. Hodgkinson probably made his *debut* in a Shaksperean character as *Petruchio* to Mrs. Pownall's *Catharine ;* but he appeared later in the season as *Richard*, *Othello* and *Hamlet*. Besides these the only tragedy role he is known to have played at this time was the *Earl of Essex*.

OTHELLO.

Othello	Mr. Hodgkinson
Iago	Mr. Hallam
Cassio	Mr. King
Desdemona	Miss Tuke

EARL OF ESSEX.

Essex	Mr. Hodgkinson
Lord Burleigh	Mr. King
Sir Walter Raleigh	Mr. Ashton
Lieutenant	Mr. Woolls
Southampton	Mr. Martin
Queen Elizabeth	Mrs. Kenna
Countess of Nottingham	Mrs. Hamilton
Countess of Rutland	Mrs. Henry

" Though we do not pretend to say that Mr. Hodgkinson equals a Kemble," the *Federal Gazette* said, speaking of his *Richard III,*

" yet he certainly did great justice to the part. His action was violent, as the character requires, and at the same time not unstrained. If we must censure him, it is for his manner of speaking—he lets his voice fall too suddenly, speaking, to borrow a term from music, in octaves; he, however, excels any that ever appeared here in the character of *Richard*." When he appeared as *Othello* ten days later, the same authority spoke of him as " the American Kemble," adding, " His address to the Senate was spoken with judgment; the whole of his acting, where *Iago* so artfully excites his jealousy, was very natural; the heaving of his breast, the expression of his countenance and the rage which *Iago* causes when he determines to kill *Desdemona*, was a masterly piece of acting." Mr. Hallam as *Iago* " performed to admiration;" Mr. King as *Cassio* " performed well in the drunken scene;" and Miss Tuke as *Desdemona* " pleased the audience—there is a natural diffidence truly engaging in this graceful young actress." There was no criticism of Mr. Hodgkinson's *Hamlet* or of his *Earl of Essex* in Jones' tragedy.

In the familiar pieces this season Hallam and Henry frequently gave up the roles in their possession to Hodgkinson, and even to West. Mr. Henry indeed seldom appeared, while the only part that Mr. Hallam kept to himself at the beginning of the season, as of the first importance, was *Marplot* in the " Busybody." In the " Beaux' Stratagem " he played the low comedy, *Scrub*, and was secondary to Hodgkinson

BEAUX' STRATAGEM.

Archer . Mr. Hodgkinson
Aimwell . . . Mr. West
Scrub . . . Mr. Hallam
Mrs. Sullen . Mrs. Henry
Dorinda . . Mrs. Kenna
Cherry . . Mrs. Pownall

ALL IN THE WRONG.

Sir John Restless . Mr. Hodgkinson
Beverly . . . . . . Mr. Hallam
Sir William Belmont . Mr. Prigmore
Young Belmont . . . Mr. Martin
Lady Restless . . . Mrs. Pownall
Belinda . . . . Miss Tuke
Clarissa . . . . Miss Brett
Tattle . . . . . . Mrs. Hamilton

in "All in the Wrong." In Pilon's play, " He Would be a Soldier,"
on the 28th of December, both the managers appeared, as well as Miss
Tuke and Mrs. Henry; Mr. Hodgkinson and Miss Brett being the

only new members of the company in the cast. The others, however, with the exception of Mrs. Pownall, were seen in the "Agreeable Surprise," which was the afterpiece of the

HE WOULD BE A SOLDIER.

Colonel Talbot . .	Mr. Henry
Capt. Crevalt .	Mr. Hodgkinson
Caleb	Mr. Hallam
Mandeville	Mr. Martin
Sir Oliver Oldstock .	Mr. Ashton
Johnson	Mr. Hammond
Wilkins	Mr. Woolls
Amber	Mr. Ryan
Harriet	Miss Tuke
Lady Oldstock . .	Mrs. Rankin
Mrs. Wilkins .	Mrs. Hamilton
Betty	Mrs. Kenna
Nancy	Miss Brett
Charlotte	Mrs. Henry

AGREEABLE SURPRISE.

Lingo . .	Mr. Hodgkinson
Eugene	Mr. West
Compton . .	Mr. Chambers
Sir Felix Friendly .	Mr. King
Chicane . . .	Mr. Ashton
Cuddon	Mr. Ryan
John	Mr. Martin
Harry . . .	Mr. Hammond
Laura	Mrs. Kenna
Mrs. Cheshire .	Mrs. Rankin
Fringe . . .	Mrs. Hamilton
Cowslip .	Mrs. Hodgkinson

evening. Only three new comedies were produced this season—
Holcroft's " Road to Ruin," on the 10th of December; Mrs. Inchbald's " Child of Nature," for the
benefit of Mrs. Hodgkinson and
Miss Brett; and the younger Colman's "Ways and Means," for the
benefit of West and Prigmore.
Only one of these continued to
hold the stage, the " Road to
Ruin " being in the list of " old
comedy" favorites until within a

ROAD TO RUIN.

Goldfinch	Mr. Hallam
Mr. Dornton	Mr. Henry
Harry Dornton	Mr. Hodgkinson
Milford	Mr. Martin
Silky	Mr. Prigmore
Sulky	Mr. King
Smith	Mr. Ashton
Jacob	Mr. Ryan
Widow Warren	Mrs. Pownall
Sophia	Miss Tuke
Jenny	Mrs. Hamilton
Mrs. Ledger	Mrs. Kenna

few years. It was the best of Holcroft's pieces, and had been printed in
London only a few months before its first production in America. Its
success at Covent Garden was largely due to Munden's admirable
acting as *Old Dornton*. That Mr. Henry equalled the original would

be a violent assumption. Mrs. Inchbald's "Child of Nature" was based on the "Zelie" of Madame de Genlis. This piece was also a Covent Garden success. Young Colman's "Ways and Means" was from the Haymarket. The casts of both pieces were made up almost wholly of the new members of the company, the production of the latter being due apparently to Prigmore's desire to play *Sir David Dunder.*

CHILD OF NATURE.

Duke Mercia . . . Mr. Prigmore
Marquis Almanza . . . Mr. King
Count Valentia . Mr. Hodgkinson
Granada . . . . . . Mr. Martin
Seville . . . . Mr. Ryan
Marchioness Merida . Mrs. Pownall
Amanthis . . . Mrs. Hodgkinson

WAYS AND MEANS.

Sir David Dunder. Mr. Prigmore
Random . . . Mr. Hodgkinson
Scruple . . . . . . Mr. West
Tiptoe . . . . . . Mr. King
Paul Peery . . . . Mr. Ashton
Lady Dunder . . Mrs. Rankin
Harriet . . . . . . Miss Brett
Kitty . . . . Mrs. Hodgkinson

Mr. Prigmore was certainly accorded extraordinary opportunities. He created new low comedy roles in which Mr. Wignell had not been seen; and in the hope that he would outrival Wignell, he was accorded the parts in which that favorite comedian was famous.

DON JUAN.

Don Juan . Mr. Hodgkinson
Don Guzman . Mr. Hallam
Don Ferdinand, Mr. Chambers
Scaramouch . Mr. Prigmore
Confidante . Mrs. Hamilton
Donna Anna . Mrs. Henry

POOR SOLDIER.

Patrick . . Mr. Hodgkinson
Captain Fitzroy . Mr. West
Father Luke . . Mr. King
Darby . . . Mr. Prigmore
Norah . . . Mrs. Pownall
Kathleen . Mrs. Hodgkinson

He was the original *Scaramouch* in this country in the great Royalty Theatre success, "Don Juan." He succeeded Wignell as *Darby* in the "Poor Soldier." The attempt was vain, however, for when Wignell reappeared, Prigmore disappeared.

In the Philadelphia cast of "Don Juan" Mr. Chambers was the *Don Ferdinand;* but when the ballet was given in New York, he was succeeded by Mr. West. Chambers played a number of parts during the Southwark season, as the casts show; but it does not appear that he went with the company to New York. Indeed, it may be doubted whether, at any time, he was a regular member of the company. Mr. Chambers had appeared at the summer theatres in London, being at the Royalty in 1787 and 1788, and at the Haymarket in 1789. At the Royalty he was *Clink* in " Poll of Plympton," and the *Wizard* in " Harlequin Mungo." At the Haymarket he was among the vocalists in the " Battle of Hexham," and played *Castinicio* in the " Enraged Musician," his only serious part being *Guildenstern* in " Hamlet." It is probable Chambers came to America without an engagement, as his name is not among the list of Henry's recruits who took passage on the ship " Bristol."

From Philadelphia the company journeyed to New York, where the old theatre in John Street was reopened on the 28th of January, 1793. The intention was to begin the season with the "Wonder" and " Prisoner at Large;" but the bill was changed " at the request of many friends." On the opening night Mr. Prigmore, who was cast for *Lord Scratch* in the comedy, refused to appear; and with the consent of the audience Mr. Henry read the part. Why Prigmore refused the part is not very clear, as he had previously played it in Philadelphia; but in an insolent card that he succeeded in having printed in one of the news-

List of Performances—*New York.*

1793.

Jan. 28—Dramatist . . . . Reynolds
Padlock . . . . Bickerstaff
30—Maid of the Mill . . . Bickerstaff
Love a la Mode . . . . Macklin
Feb. 1—Richard III . . . . . Shakspere
Flitch of Bacon . . . . . . Bate
4—Love in a Village . . Bickerstaff
Catharine and Petruchio. Shakspere
6—Othello . . . . Shakspere
Romp . . . . Bickerstaff
8—Road to Ruin . . . . . Holcroft
Flitch of Bacon.
11—All in the Wrong . . . Murphy
Rosina . . . . . . Mrs. Brooke
12—Road to Ruin.
Romp.
15—Miser . . . . Fielding
No Song No Supper . . . Hoare
18—Dramatist.
Farmer . . . . O'Keefe
20—Maid of the Mill.
Mayor of Garratt . . . . . Foote

Feb. 22—Child of Nature . Mrs. Inchbald
No Song No Supper.
25—Wonder . . . . . Mrs. Centlivre
Agreeable Surprise . . . O'Keefe
27—West Indian . . . . Cumberland
No Song No Supper.
Mar. 1—She Stoops to Conquer . Goldsmith
Poor Soldier . . . . . O'Keefe
4—Child of Nature.
Agreeable Surprise.
6—Love in a Village.
Ways and Means . . Colman, Jr.
Beaux' Stratagem . . . Farquhar
Romp.
11—Earl of Essex . . . . . . Jones
Devil to Pay . . . . . . Coffey
13—More Ways than One . Mrs. Cowley
Don Juan.
15—School for Scandal . . Sheridan
Don Juan.
18—Wild Oats . . . . . . O'Keefe
Devil to Pay.
20—Dramatist.
Romp.
22—Wild Oats.
Padlock.
23—He Would be a Soldier . . Pilon
Agreeable Surprise.
26—Fashionable Lover . Cumberland
No Song No Supper.
(Benefit of Widows and Orphans.)
April 1—Romeo and Juliet . . Shakspere
Lying Valet . . . . . . Garrick
3—Wild Oats.
Cymon and Sylvia . . . Garrick
5—More Ways than One.
Prisoner at Large . . . O'Keefe
8—Clandestine Marriage
Garrick and Colman
King of the Genii.
10—George Barnwell . . . . . Lillo
Deserter . . . . Dibdin
12—Dramatist.
Lying Valet.
15—West Indian.
St. Patrick's Day . . . Sheridan

papers he accused the managers of treating him unfairly. His conduct, no doubt, had the support of Hodgkinson, and had no higher purpose than to distract the management and the company. In imputing so grave a charge to Hodgkinson it is scarcely possible to do him injustice. From the outset he was not only the despot of the company, but its marplot. He allowed no opportunity to escape him, by which he could create discord or harass Henry. He would tolerate no rival either for himself or Mrs. Hodgkinson. The repertoire was always moulded so as to meet his aims. The substitution of the "Dramatist" for the "Wonder" on the opening night had for its object the prevention of Mrs. Henry's appearance as *Violante*. It was a piece, too, in which Hodgkinson as *Vapid* could be seen in one of his most effective roles. In the "Maid of the Mill" which followed he was able to show his versatility

as *Aimworth*, while Mrs. Hodgkinson was brought forward in her
favorite part of *Patty*. Then, on
the third night, he crowned his
previous triumphs by appearing as
Richard III, and a few days later
as *Othello* at the same time that
Miss Tuke, who had just become
Mrs. Hallam, was successively the
Lady Anne and *Desdemona*, as
she had previously been *Marianne*
in the "Dramatist" to the exclu-
sion of Mrs. Henry. By the.same
arrangement Mrs. Pownall, who
was a greater actress and better
singer than Mrs. Hodgkinson,
was relegated to secondary roles.
Hodgkinson not only had his own
way in everything, but his favor
was the only road to success.
Such a man could not fail to find
in Prigmore a convenient tool,
only too willing to insult the managers and offend their patrons.
Not content with refusing to appear
in the "Dramatist" on the opening night, this ignorant and insolent man, who was in fact a

April 17—King Henry IV . . . Shakspere
Agreeable Surprise.
(Mr. Woolls' benefit.)
19—Suspicious Husband . . Hoadley
Cymon and Sylvia.
(Mr. Hodgkinson's benefit.)
22—Notoriety . . . . . . Reynolds
Romp.
(Mrs. Hodgkinson's benefit.)
24—Hamlet . . . . Shakspere
Deserter.
(Mr. Heard's benefit.)
May 3—Rivals . . . . Sheridan
Cymon and Sylvia.
(Mr. Ryan's benefit.)
6—Recess.
Robinson Crusoe . . . Sheridan
(Mrs. Hamilton's benefit.)
8—Alexander the Great . . . . Lee
Rival Candidates . . . . . Bate
(Mrs. Henry's benefit.)
10—Provoked Husband . . Vanbrugh
Ways and Means.
(Mrs. Kenna's benefit.)
13—Such Things Are . Mrs. Inchbald
Padlock.
(Mr. King's benefit.)
15—Notoriety.
Rosina.
(Mrs. Rankin's benefit.)
17—Such Things Are.
Look Before You Leap . Robson
Harlequin Fisherman.
(Mr. Martin's benefit.)
20—Wedding . . . . Dunlap
Agreeable Surprise.
(Miss Brett's benefit.)
22—Chapter of Accidents . . Miss Lee
Waterman . . . . Dibdin
(Mrs. Pownall's benefit.)
24—Tempest . . . . Dryden
No Song No Supper.
(Mrs. Hallam's benefit.)
27—Conscious Lovers . . . . Steele
Critic . . . . Sheridan
(Mr. Hammond's benefit.)

May 29—Jealous Wife . . . . . . Colman
Comus . . . . Milton
(Mr. Ashton's benefit.)
31—Animal Magnetism . Mrs. Inchbald
Hunt the Slipper . . . . Knapp
Death of Captain Cook.
(Mr. Prigmore's benefit.)
June 3—Chapter of Accidents.
Midas . . . . O'Hara
(Mr. West's benefit.)
5—Merchant of Venice . . Shakspere
Irishman in London . . Macready
(Mr. Henry's benefit.)
7—Fashionable Lover.
Harlequin Shipwrecked.
(Durang's and Bisset's benefit.)
20—Jealous Wife.
Prisoner at Large.
(Robbins' and West, Jr.'s, benefit.)
July 12—Jane Shore . . . . Rowe
No Song No Supper.
(Mrs. Kenna's benefit.)
14—Road to Ruin.
Rosina.

buffoon, not a comedian, seized the occasion of the second production of the comedy on the 18th of February, when he played *Jemmy Jumps* in the afterpiece, to introduce politics into the opera. This gave great offense to the Federalists, who objected to Prigmore's rabid Democracy. In view of his "awkward and offensive introduction of politics" into the "Farmer," a correspondent wrote to the New York *Daily Gazette* to say that there was no more power in the wisest forms of government to make men politically and equally free than there was in Governors Hallam and Henry to make Prigmore play like Wignell. "But though they cannot make a tolerable performer of him," the writer added, "it is to be hoped, since they pay him wages, they have at least the power of checking his impertinence." Unfortunately the managers possessed no such powers, as it was the astute Hodgkinson who was behind the insolent Prigmore.

The first piece of the season, new to New York audiences, was the afterpiece, the "Romp," which was followed in rapid succession by Holcroft's comedy, the "Road to Ruin," Prince Hoare's "No Song No Supper," O'Keefe's "Farmer," Mrs. Inchbald's comedy, the "Child of Nature," the younger Colman's "Ways and Means," and the pantomimic ballet, "Don Juan." All these had been previously presented

in Philadelphia, the only noteworthy change in the cast being the substitution of Prigmore for Chambers as *Jemmy Jumps* in the "Farmer."
In the familiar pieces there were also a few changes, Hodgkinson succeeding Chambers as *Belville* in "Rosina" and as *Young Meadows* in
"Love in a Village," and West as *Don Ferdinand* in "Don Juan."
When the "West Indian" was presented, on the 15th of April, Mr.
Hallam played *Stockwell* for the first time, and his son by his first
wife, Mirvan Hallam, made his first appearance on the New York
stage as *Belcour*. The younger Hallam appeared a number of times
during the season in unimportant roles, including *Carlos* in "Recess,"
with Mr. Hallam as *Muscato* and Mrs. Hamilton as *Aurora* for the
actress' benefit. He was possessed of little talent, and never succeeded.

The first of the pieces to have its initial American production
this season was O'Keefe's "Wild Oats," which proved one of the most
successful comedies of the epoch.
It was a piece in which the broad
laugh and the tear of sensibility,
to use the language of the period,
alternately followed each other,
and the comedy at once became
popular with American audiences.
The late William B. Wood, for
many years manager of the Philadelphia theatre, saw this pro-

WILD OATS.
___

Rover	Mr. Hodgkinson
Sir George Thunder	Mr. Prigmore
Harry Thunder	Mr. West
Banks	Mr. Heard
John Dory	Mr. King
Ephraim Smooth	Mr. Henry
Jim	Mr. Hallam
Farmer Gammon	Mr. Hammond
Lamp	Mr. Durang
Trap	Mr. Ashton
Lady Amaranth	Mrs. Henry
Amelia	Mrs. Kenna
Jane	Mrs. Pownall

duction with its original cast when he was a boy, just entering upon
his teens. Mrs. Henry's acting as *Lady Amaranth*, he says in his
"Personal Recollections of the Stage," and Mr. Henry's as *John Dory*,
were both fresh in his memory after sixty years. "They must have

been excellent," he adds, "for I have no remembrance of *Rover*, the principal character, though acted by Mr. Hodgkinson." It is probable that Mr. Wood's deductions are more trustworthy than his facts. Not only did Mr. Henry not play *John Dory*, as the cast shows, but there is a portrait of him as *Ephraim Smooth*, of which, unfortunately, only two copies are known to exist.

With the beginning of the benefits the production of novelties began in earnest, a number of beneficiaries choosing recent London pieces as special attractions. Mrs. Hodgkinson offered Reynolds' new comedy, "Notoriety," notwithstanding it had failed to achieve anything like the success of the "Dramatist" at Covent Garden, and Mr. King followed with Mrs. Inchbald's play, "Such Things Are," in which Mr. Hallam played *Haswell*, a part that was intended as a portrait of Howard, the philanthropist. To the latter Mr. Martin added a one-act comedy, "Look Before You Leap," in which a mother, still young and handsome, becomes the successful rival of her daughter, and the pantomime, "Harlequin Fisherman."

NOTORIETY.

Nominal . .	Mr. Hodgkinson
Lord Jargin . .	Mr. Hammond
Sir Andrew Acid .	Mr. Heard
Colonel Hubbub .	Mr. Prigmore
Clairville	Mr. Hallam
Blunder O'Whack .	Mr. King
Saunter	Mr. West
James . . .	Mr. West, Jr
Lady Acid . .	Mrs. Hamilton
Honoria	Mrs. Hallam
Sophia Strangeway .	Mrs. Henry

SUCH THINGS ARE.

Twineall . .	Mr. Hodgkinson
Sultan	Mr. Hallam
Sir Luke Tremor .	Mr. Prigmore
Haswell	Mr. Hallam
Lord Flint . .	Mr. Hammond
Meanright	Mr. West
Elvirus	Mr. Martin
Zedan	Mr. King
Lady Tremor . .	Mrs. Kenna
Aurelia	Mrs. Hallam
Arabella	Mrs. Henry

LOOK BEFORE YOU LEAP.

Lucas . .	Mr. Hodgkinson
Duval	Mr. Martin
Corporal . .	Mr. Hammond
Lawyer . . .	Mr. Ryan
Lucette . . .	Mrs. Hallam
Margaret . . .	Mrs. Kenna

HARLEQUIN FISHERMAN.

Harlequin . . .	Mr. Martin
Pantaloon . . .	Mr. Heard
Clown	Mr. Ryan
Lover . . .	Mr. Hammond
Magician . . .	Mr. Robbins
Columbine . . .	Miss Brett
Sylph	Mrs. Kenna

Among those who were first to bow before Hodgkinson, as the rising sun of the American theatrical firmament, was William Dunlap. The aspiring young dramatist had a comedy ready for production when the company returned to New York, but Mr. Henry wisely declined to produce it. When it was produced it was through the favor of Hodgkinson, who brought it out for Miss Brett's benefit on

WEDDING.

Commodore Welldon . . . . . Mr. Hallam
Quibble . . . . Mr. Hodgkinson
McSkinflint . . . . Mr. Prigmore
Lovejoy . . . . Mr. Martin
O'Banter . . . . Mr. King
Crackjaw . . . . Mr. West
Toupee . . . . Mr. Ryan
Mrs. Sugarcane . . . . Mrs. Rankin
Dinah . . . . Mrs. Hamilton
Julia . . . . Mrs. Hallam

the 20th of May, not in the hottest weather, early in June, as Dunlap says. It was originally intended that Henry should play *Commodore Welldon,* but he refused—"very properly under the circumstances," the author declares in his character of historian—whereupon Hallam accepted the part in opposition to his partner. According to Dunlap, the piece, which he calls the " Miser's Wedding," though it was advertised as the " Wedding," was played without study or rehearsal and, of course, murdered. The author admitted, however, that it deserved death, and it was never repeated.

The remaining new pieces of the season, presented at benefits, were Dibdin's ballad opera, the " Waterman," produced by Mrs. Pownall; Mrs. Inchbald's farce in three acts, "Animal Magnetism;" the Rev. Henry Knapp's

WATERMAN.

Tom Tug . . Mr. Hodgkinson
Bundle . . . . . Mr. Ashton
Robin . . . . . Mr. Prigmore
Mrs. Bundle . . Mrs. Pownall
Wilhelmine . Mrs. Hodgkinson

ANIMAL MAGNETISM.

Marquis Delancy . Mr. West
Dr.Mundungus,Mr.Prigmore
Lafleur . . Mr. Hodgkinson
Jeffrey . . . . Mr. Martin
Constance . . Mrs. Hallam
Lisette . . . Mrs. Pownall

musical farce, " Hunt the Slipper," and the serious pantomime, " Death of Captain Cook," brought out together by Mr. Prigmore; and the "Irishman in London," included in his benefit bill by Mr. Henry for the purpose of showing himself in a new Irish part. To these may be added the cast of "St. Patrick's Day," produced a night or two before the benefits began. All these pieces, which were Covent Garden or Haymarket successes, became very popular, and some of them held the stage until within a comparatively recent period. The most successful of these productions was the "Waterman," in which Hodgkinson as *Tom Tug* had a fine opportunity to emphasize the versatility of talent he had shown throughout the season. In "Hunt the Slipper" Miss Brett was announced as Mrs. King. Two days before, when she played the *Lady* in "Comus" for Mr. Ashton's benefit, she was still Miss Brett. According to Dunlap, Miss Brett was a feeble actress who owed whatever supremacy she obtained to the influence of Hodgkinson. As the virtual dictator of the company, this accomplished actor, but unscrupulous man, made everything bend to his own interest.

A few casts of familiar pieces that had not been played by the reorganized company in Philadelphia during the engagement there

HUNT THE SLIPPER.

Billy Bustle . .	Mr. Prigmore
Winterbottom . . .	Mr. Ashton
Captain Clement . .	Mr. West
Glib	Mr. Martin
Miss Winterbottom .	Mrs. Rankin
Harriet	Mrs. King
Maid	Mrs. Kenna

DEATH OF CAPTAIN COOK.

Captain Cook .	Mr. Hodgkinson
Lieutenant . . .	Mr. Prigmore
Terreoboo	Mr. Robbins
Oroondo	Mr. Martin
Perea	Mr. West
Kosh	Mr. King
High Priest	Mr. Heard
Emai	Mrs. Kenna

IRISHMAN IN LONDON.

Murtoch Delany . .	Mr. Henry
Mr. Cullooney . . .	Mr. King
Captain Seymour . .	Mr. West
Edward	Mr. Martin
Frost	Mr. Heard
Cymon	Mr. Hallam
Caroline	Mrs. Hallam
Louisa	Mrs. Kenna
Cubba	Mrs. Hamilton

ST. PATRICK'S DAY.

Lieut. O'Conner,	Mr. Hodgkinson
Dr. Rosy	Mr. Martin
Justice Credulous .	Mr. Prigmore
Sergeant Trounce . .	Mr. West
Lauretta	Mrs. Hallam
Mrs. Bridget . .	Mrs. Hamilton

have been preserved. These are given herewith to make the record as complete as possible. It must be said, however, that it is to the long list of benefits this season rather than to the casts that we owe our knowledge of the *personnel* of the company. The casts on the other hand show Hodgkinson's aggressiveness in the distribution of parts, the American element in the company being ruthlessly pushed aside in favor of the English contingent. Poor old Woolls, after a service of more than thirty years on the American stage, was seldom heard, even in the parts that had long been in his possession. Heard, Ashton, Hammond, Bisset, Mrs. Kenna, Mrs. Rankin and Mrs. Hamilton received little consideration. Bisset asserted his right to play his favorite Scotchman, *Colin McLeod*, in the "Fashionable Lover" for his benefit, but the others were generally content with subordinate roles, even on their benefit nights. Even Martin, who made some

NEW CASTS OF FAMILIAR PIECES.

ALEXANDER THE GREAT.

Alexander . . . Mr. Hodgkinson
Clytus . . . . Mr. King
Lysimachus . . . . Mr. Hallam
Statira . . . . Mrs. Henry
Roxana . . . . . . Mrs. Kenna
Parisates . . . . . Mrs. Hallam

CHAPTER OF ACCIDENTS.

Woodville . . . Mr. Hodgkinson
Governor Harcourt . Mr. Prigmore
Captain Harcourt . . Mr. Martin
Lord Glenmore . . . . Mr. King
Grey . . . . Mr. Heard
Vane . . . . Mr. West
Jacob Gawky . . . Mr. Hallam
Miss Mortimer . . Mrs. Hallam
Celia . . . . Mrs. Henry
Bridget . . . . Mrs. Pownall
Mrs. Warner . . Mrs. Hamilton

COMUS.

Comus . . . . . Mr. Hodgkinson
Elder Brother . . . . Mr. Martin

Younger Brother . Mr. Hammond
Lady . . . . Miss Brett
Sabrina . . . . . . Mrs. Rankin
Euphrosyne . . Mrs. Hodgkinson

JEALOUS WIFE.

Mr. Oakley . . Mr. Hodgkinson
Major Oakley . . . Mr. Ashton
Charles . . . . . . Mr. West
Russet . . . . . . Mr. Prigmore
Lord Trinket . . Mr. Hammond
Sir Harry Beagle . . Mr. Martin
Captain O'Cutter . . . Mr. King
Paris . . . . Mr. Durang
Mrs. Oakley . . . Mrs. Pownall
Lady Freelove . . . Mrs. Kenna
Harriet . . . . . . Mrs. Hallam
Toilet . . . . . Mrs. Hamilton

KING OF THE GENII.

King . . . . Mr. Woolls
Harlequin . . . . . Mr. Martin
Pantaloon . . . . . . Mr. Ryan
Clown . . . . . . Mr. Prigmore
Columbine . . . . . Mrs. Kenna

MERCHANT OF VENICE.

Shylock . . . . . . Mr. Henry
Gratiano . . . Mr. Hodgkinson
Bassanio . . . . . . Mr. Martin
Antonio . . . . . . Mr. Hallam
Launcelot . . . . . Mr. Prigmore
Portia . . . . Mrs. Henry
Nerissa . . . . . . Mrs. Kenna
Jessica . . . . . . Mrs. Hallam

MIDAS.

Midas . . . . . . Mr. Prigmore
Apollo . . . . Mr. West
Pan . . . . Mr. King
Mysis . . . . Mrs. Rankin
Nysa . . . . . Mrs. Hodgkinson
Daphne . . . . . Mrs. Pownall

RIVAL CANDIDATES.

General Worry . . . Mr. Henry
Sir Harry Muff . . . Mr. Martin
Spy . . . . Mr. Prigmore
Narcissa . . . Mrs. Hodgkinson
Jenny . . . . Mrs. Rankin

progress, fared little better than the others.   A like fate befell such of
Henry's recruits as were likely to prove dangerous either to Mr. or
Mrs. Hodgkinson.   Mrs. Pownall was the first victim of Hodgkinson's
displeasure, as the rival of Mrs. Hodgkinson.   Mr. Chambers, too, he
pushed aside, as a possible rival of his own in singing parts.   This
occurred in Philadelphia before the company went to New York.
Chambers and Mrs. Pownall had been announced to sing at Oeller's
tavern, on the 19th of January.   Hodgkinson intervened with a concert for the benefit of Mrs. Hodgkinson, which he advertised for the
same night.   In consequence of the strenuous opposition which this
action provoked, he was compelled to postpone Mrs. Hodgkinson's
concert until the 21st.   He did this, he said, because he was not in
immediate necessity, and would rather let those who were be served
before him.   In his card in the newspapers he assumed an air of in-
jured innocence; but as a further expression of his malice he recited
Foote's prologue on the impossibility of pleasing everybody, on the
night of his wife's concert.   This incident marked the beginning of a
long series of intrigues, which finally culminated in Henry's surrender
of his supremacy with a public that he had served so long.

After the close of the New York season the company returned
to the Southwark Theatre to reap a second harvest in Philadelphia
before the arrival of Wignell's forces at the New Theatre in
Chestnut Street.   Before the season opened, which was on the first
day of July, Hallam and Henry advertised a ventilator on a new
system, as in preparation for the

LIST OF PERFORMANCES—*Philadelphia.*

1793.
———

July   1—Road to Ruin . . . . . Holcroft
       Love a la Mode . . . . Macklin
       3—Maid of the Mill . . . Bickerstaff
       Irishman in London . . Macready
       5—Such Things Are . Mrs. Inchbald
       Devil to Pay . . . . . . Coffey
       8—George Barnwell . . . . . Lillo
       Irishman in London.

hot weather. Later they announced that their new steam ventilator was completed. Devices
for cooling the Southwark Theatre
in Summer had been adopted even
before the Revolution, and like
attempts, all inadequate in result,
continue to be made after the lapse
of more than a century. French
feeling ran very high in Philadelphia at this time. Two benefits
were given during the season for
the refugees from San Domingo,
and the performance of the 9th of
August was bespoke by the Patriotic Society, at whose instance
the Marseillaise Hymn was sung.
The only pieces new to Philadelphia that were given at this time
were those that had previously
been produced in New York. This
is explained by the fact that the
season was brought to an abrupt
close by the yellow fever epidemic
of that year, just as the benefits
were beginning. Mrs. Pownall's
was the only one that actually occurred, and she had nothing new to offer.

July 10—Notoriety . . . . . . Reynolds
Prisoner at Large . . . O'Keefe
12—Notoriety.
Prisoner at Large.
15—Chapter of Accidents . . Miss Lee
Lying Valet . . . . . . Garrick
18—Notoriety.
No Song No Supper . . . Hoare
20—Wild Oats . . . . . . O'Keefe
Padlock . . . . . . Bickerstaff
23—Wild Oats.
Romp . . . . Bickerstaff
25—Animal Magnetism . Mrs. Inchbald
Rosina . . . . . . Mrs. Brooke
27—Lionel and Clarissa . . Bickerstaff
Register Office . . . . . . Reed
29—Clandestine Marriage . . Garrick
Romp.
(Benefit distressed French emigrants.)
31—School for Scandal . . . Sheridan
Deserter . . . . Dibdin
Aug. 2—Richard III . . . . . Shakspere
Rival Candidates . . . . . Bate
5—Lionel and Clarissa.
Register Office.
7—Wild Oats.
St. Patrick's Day . . . Sheridan
9—More Ways than One . Mrs. Cowley
Agreeable Surprise . . . O'Keefe
(Benefit distressed emigrants from
Hispaniola.)
10—Cato . . . . Addison
Irishman in London.
12—Lionel and Clarissa.
Critic . . . . Sheridan
14—Tempest . . . . Dryden
Catharine and Petruchio, Shakspere
16—Dramatist . . . . . Reynolds
Farmer . . . . O'Keefe
19—Child of Nature . . Mrs. Inchbald
Ways and Means . . Colman, Jr
23—Wild Oats.
No Song No Supper.
(Mrs. Pownall's benefit.)

Mr. Hodgkinson's benefit

was to have taken place on the 26th of August, for which he had announced the first production in this country of Mrs. Inchbald's " I'll Tell You What." It was postponed, however, on account of the indisposition of Hodgkinson, King and Mrs. Hallam. In consequence of the rapid spread of the plague it was abandoned altogether, the house remaining closed. The failure of the benefits, in consequence of the epidemic, led to another quarrel between Hodgkinson and Henry, in which Hallam sided with Hodgkinson. To the charge of failure to fulfil the engagement made with Hodgkinson and his wife in regard to benefits, the actor further alleged neglect and inhumanity, while he was ill and fleeing from the yellow fever. The affair was afterward submitted to arbitration, the arbitrators deciding that Henry had not been guilty of any inhumanity toward Hodgkinson, but giving the latter four hundred dollars, the estimated profits of two benefits. Henry submitted without making any defense, amazed at the audacity of his accuser and the duplicity of his partner. The charge of inhumanity was probably based on Mrs. Hodgkinson's condition, as her first child, a daughter, was born on the 16th of June, 1793, just before the company left for Philadelphia.

CHAPTER V.

MR. HENRY'S LAST SEASON, 1793-4.

HODGKINSON'S OPPOSITION TO HENRY—MRS. MELMOTH—MISS CHEER, NOW MRS. LONG—MR. RICHARDS AND MRS. WILSON—MRS. POWNALL'S "NEEDS MUST"—"TAMMANY"—DUNLAP'S "FATAL DECEPTION"—PIECES PRODUCED—DEATH OF MR. AND MRS. HENRY.

THE New York season of 1793-4 was the last of Mr. Henry's connection with the Old American Company. It was throughout a season of discord. Hodgkinson, intent from the outset upon driving Henry and his wife from the company, had so far succeeded to his satisfaction. In this intrigue he was abetted by Hallam, who almost openly contributed to his partner's downfall. Henry had been compelled to yield up part after part to Hodgkinson; and even when he was in possession of roles that Hodgkinson had no wish to play, the actor found means for preventing the manager from producing the pieces. Hodgkinson's opposition to Henry was not so much due to professional jealousy as to a desire to obtain Henry's share in the property. His hostility to Mrs. Henry, on the other hand, was conceived in mere wantonness—it had no purpose except that it may have seemed necessary to Hodgkinson that in order to crush the husband he must also crush the wife—that, to overcome the manager, it was needful to overthrow the actress. Mrs. Henry's roles at that time were confined to the heroines of tragedy. To deprive her of these, Hodg-

(77)

kinson insisted that Mrs. Melmoth, who had recently arrived in the country, should be brought forward in parts akin to Mrs. Henry's— a plan in which he succeeded through Hallam's connivance.

The season, which began on the 11th of November, 1793, with a performance in aid of the Philadelphia sufferers, was a long one, lasting until the 28th of July, 1794. The theatre had not been open a fortnight, when Mrs. Melmoth made her first appearance in America as *Euphrasia* in the " Grecian Daughter." Mrs. Melmoth came to the United States without an engagement, arriving in New York in February, 1793. It was announced at the time that her views were not theatrical—that her intention was to give a course of readings. She actually attempted this plan, giving a reading at the City Assembly Room, New York, on the 9th of April; but finding dramatic readings unappreciated, her thoughts again turned to the stage, for which her abilities and experience fitted her. Mrs. Melmoth was the daughter of a respectable farmer in Surrey, England. While at boarding-school

LIST OF PERFORMANCES.

1793.
Nov. 11—Clandestine Marriage
　　　　　　　　Garrick and Colman
　　　Padlock . . . 　　　　Bickerstaff
　　(Benefit of the Philadelphia sufferers.)
　　13—Dramatist . . . . . . Reynolds
　　　　Romp . . . . Bickerstaff
　　15—She Stoops to Conquer . Goldsmith
　　　　Deserter . . . . Dibdin
　　18—Wonder . . . . . Mrs. Centlivre
　　　　Ways and Means . . Colman, Jr
　　20—Grecian Daughter . . . Murphy
　　　　Romp.
　　22—More Ways than One . Mrs. Cowley
　　　　Ways and Means.
　　25—Grecian Daughter.
　　　　Lying Valet . . . . . . Garrick
　　27—Provoked Husband . . Vanbrugh
　　　　Romp.
　　29—Notoriety . . . . . . Reynolds
　　　　Agreeable Surprise . . . O'Keefe
Dec. 2—Jealous Wife . . . . . Colman
　　　　Agreeable Surprise.
　　4—Venice Preserved . . . . Otway
　　　　Love a la Mode . . . . Macklin
　　6—All in the Wrong . . . Murphy
　　　　Deserter.
　　9—Venice Preserved.
　　　　Miss in Her Teens . . . Garrick
　　11—Notoriety.
　　　　Don Juan.
　　13—Percy . . . . . . Hannah More
　　　　Padlock.
　　16—Child of Nature . . Mrs. Inchbald
　　　　Don Juan.
　　18—I'll Tell You What . Mrs. Inchbald

she was induced to elope with a young man of literary and theatrical aspirations, named Pratt, at one time well known as Courtney Melmoth. During the season of 1772–3, Melmoth made his first appearance on the stage at Smock Alley in Dublin as *Antony* in "All for Love." Mrs. Melmoth also made her *debut* there as *Monimia* in the "Orphan." She was at that time possessed of a beautiful figure and a very sweet voice. The Melmoths were at Covent Garden during the season of 1774 and 1775. Mrs. Melmoth obtained an introduction there through Younger, for whose benefit she played *Mandane* in "Cyrus," April 11th, 1774. Her formal *debut* at Covent Garden was made October 4th, 1774, as *Roxana* in "Alexander the Great." Among her parts at this time were *Bellario* in "Philaster," *Queen Elizabeth* in "Richard III," the *Queen* in "Henry II," and *Hermione* in "A Winter's Tale." In January, 1775, Mel-

Dec. 18—Agreeable Surprise.
20—Percy.
St. Patrick's Day . . . Sheridan
23—I'll Tell You What.
Needs Must . . . **Mrs.** Pownall
26—Such Things Are . Mrs. Inchbald
Needs Must.
28—Barbarossa . . . . . . Browne
30—Dramatist.
Don Juan.

1794.
Jan. 1—Grecian Daughter.
Flitch of Bacon . . . . . . Bate
3—Barbarossa.
Romp.
6—Belle's Stratagem . Mrs. Cowley
Cymon and Sylvia . . . Garrick
8—Belle's Stratagem.
Ways and Means.
10—Such Things Are.
Romp.
13—Tempest . . . . Dryden
Guardian . . . . Garrick
15—Douglas . . . . Home
Irishman in London . Macready
20—Belle's Stratagem.
Highland Reel . . . . O'Keefe
22—School for Scandal . . Sheridan
Flitch of Bacon.
24—Fair Penitent . . . . . . Rowe
Highland Reel.
27—West Indian . . . . Cumberland
Who's the Dupe? . Mrs. Cowley
29—Henry IV . . . . . . Shakspere
True-Born Irishman . . Macklin
Feb. 1—Carmelite . . . . . Cumberland
Highland Reel.
3—Love in a Village . . Bickerstaff
Ways and Means.
5—Wild Oats . . . . . . O'Keefe
Padlock.
8—Mourning Bride . . . Congreve
Irishman in London.
10—Carmelite.
All the World's **a** Stage . Jackman

Feb. 12—Fair Penitent.
    No Song No Supper . . . Hoare
    14—Road to Ruin . . . . . Holcroft
    Rival Candidates . . . . . Bate
    17—Macbeth . . . . . . Shakspere
    High Life Below Stairs . Townley
    19—Chapter of Accidents . Miss Lee
    True-Born Irishman.
    21—Lionel and Clarissa . . Bickerstaff
    Irishman in London.
    24—Cato . . . . Addison
    Rosina . . . . . . Mrs. Brooke
    26—Lionel and Clarissa.
    Catharine and Petruchio.Shakspere
    28—Cato.
    Highland Reel.
Mar. 3—Tammany . . . . . Mrs. Hatton
    Register Office . . . . . . Reed
    6—Tammany.
    High Life Below Stairs.
    8—Tammany.
    (Mrs. Hatton's benefit.)
    10—Barbarossa.
    No Song No Supper.
    12—Grecian Daughter.
    Irish Widow . . . . . Garrick
    14—Julius Cæsar . . . . . Shakspere
    No Song No Supper.
    18—Tamerlane . . . . Rowe
    Highland Reel.
    20—Battle of Hexham . . Colman, Jr
    Rosina.
    22—Gamester . . . . Moore
    Prisoner at Large . . . O'Keefe
    24—Battle of Hexham.
    Irish Widow.
    26—Beggar's Opera . . . . . . Gay
    Irishman in London.
    28—He Would be a Soldier . . Pilon
    Highland Reel.
    31—Beggar's Opera.
    Cross Purposes . . . . . O'Brien
April 2—Percy.
    Don Juan.
    4—Carmelite.
    No Song No Supper.

moth attempted *Hamlet*, Mrs. Melmoth appearing as *Queen Gertrude*. She was engaged at Drury Lane for the season of 1776–7, making her first appearance at that house November 25th, 1776, as *Lady Macbeth*. Mrs. Melmoth, notwithstanding she had opportunities at the two great houses, failed to make a marked impression in London; but afterward, at the theatres of Edinburgh and Dublin, she took high rank. She now played comedy as well as tragedy, and even appeared in comic opera, her first appearance at the English Opera House, Capel Street, Dublin, being made December 19th, 1783, in Houlton's "Gibraltar," which was brought out at that house. For her benefit, March 24th, 1784, Mrs. Melmoth played *Lady Mary Woodley* in Mrs. Griffith's comedy, "The Times." Long before Mrs. Melmoth's arrival in America her girlish figure had been supplanted by the immense proportions of an

English matron, in consequence of which her *debut* in New York, November 20th, 1793, as *Euphrasia* in the "Grecian Daughter," came near meeting with disaster. In the scene where she asked *Dionysius* to strike her instead of her feeble father, "Strike here, here's blood enough," the realism of the situation provoked a laugh. Although she often played *Euphrasia* afterward, she never repeated "here's blood enough." Her sense of the incongruous, however, did not prevent her from playing the rolicking *Roxalana* in the "Sultan" for her benefit, when she was again laughed at. Mrs. Melmoth's accession was marked by the revival of the sombre tragedies of Congreve, Rowe and Addison, which had already fallen into desuetude. Early in the season another event occurred that has at least a reminiscent interest—the appearance of Mrs. Long as *Mrs. Oakly* in the "Jealous Wife," on the 2d of December. This lady was Miss

April 7—Othello . . . . Shakspere
Devil to Pay . . . . . . Coffey
9—World in a Village . . . O'Keefe
Rosina.
11—Tammany.
Agreeable Surprise.
12—World in a Village.
Highland Reel.
21—Surrender of Calais . . Colman, Jr
Inkle and Yarico . . Colman, Jr
(Mrs. Henry's benefit.)
24—Fatal Deception . . . . Dunlap
Shelty's Travels . . . . Dunlap
Farmer . . . . O'Keefe
(Mr. Hodgkinson's benefit.)
26—Every One has His Fault
Mrs. Inchbald.
No Song No Supper.
(Mr. Ashton's benefit.)
28—Liberty Restored.
Wedding Ring . . . . . Dibdin
(Mrs. Pownall's benefit.)
30—Robin Hood . . . . . MacNally
Lyar . . . . Foote
(Mrs. Hodgkinson's benefit.)
May 3—Isabella . . . . Southerne
Sultan . . . . Bickerstaff
(Mrs. Melmoth's benefit.)
5—How to Grow Rich . . Reynolds
Shelah's Voyage to America.
Highland Reel.
(Mrs. Hallam's benefit.)
7—Jane Shore . . . . Rowe
Guardians Outwitted, Mrs. Centlivre
(Mr. Henry's benefit.)
9—Fatal Deception.
Robinson Crusoe . . . Sheridan
(Mr. Richards' benefit.)
12—Young Quaker . . . . O'Keefe
Robinson Crusoe.
(Mr. King's benefit.)
14—Surrender of Calais.
Prisoner at Large.
(Mr. Richards' benefit.)

May 16—Young Quaker.
　　　Three Weeks After Marriage
　　　　　　　　　　　　Murphy
　　　(Mrs. Hamilton's benefit.)
　19—Bold Stroke for a Husband
　　　　　　　　　　Mrs. Cowley
　　　Hob in the Well . . . . Cibber
　　　Trick Upon Trick . . . Yarrow
　　　(Mr. Martin's benefit.)
　21—Such Things Are.
　　　Three Weeks After Marriage.
　　　(Mrs. Wilson's benefit.)
　23—Beggar's Opera.
　　　Midnight Hour . . Mrs. Inchbald
　　　(Mr. King's benefit.)
　26—School for Wives . . . . Kelly
　　　Midnight Hour.
　　　(Mrs. Miller's benefit.)
　28—Gamester.
　　　Shelah's Voyage.
　　　Animal Magnetism . Mrs. Inchbald
　　　(Mrs. Long's benefit.)
　30—Belle's Stratagem.
　　　True-Born Irishman.
　　　(Mrs. Kenna's benefit.)
June 2—New Peerage . . . . . Miss Lee
　　　Poor Soldier . . . . . O'Keefe
　　　(Mr. Hallam's benefit.)
　5—Patriot.
　　　Bold Stroke for a Wife
　　　　　　　　　Mrs. Centlivre
　　　Nootka Sound.
　　　(Mr. Prigmore's benefit.)
　7—Rivals . . . . Sheridan
　　　Devil to Pay.
　　　(Mr. Heard's benefit.)
　9—Young Quaker.
　　　Midnight Hour.
　　　Trick Upon Trick.
　　　(Mr. Ryan's benefit.)
　11—Patriot.
　　　Love in a Camp . . . . O'Keefe
　　　Tammany's Frolics.
　　　(Miller, Bergman, Durang and Mrs.
　　　　　Wilson's benefit.)
　13—Bold Stroke for a Husband.
　　　Romp.
　　　(Robbins, West and Faulkner's benefit.)

Cheer, of the Colonial stage. She had not played in New York for twenty years, but had occasionally appeared with Hallam's forces in Jamaica in 1781. During the season she appeared as *Almeria* in the "Mourning Bride," *Sancha* in "A Bold Stroke for a Husband," and *Mrs. Grub* in "Cross Purposes." "Mrs. Long," Dunlap says, "was received in silence by the audience, and never heard of more." There were others, however, who manifested a more chivalrous feeling toward the old-time favorite, one of these writing to the *Daily Advertiser* in anticipation of her benefit: "Who does not remember Miss Cheer? Now descended into the vale of years, it is supposed this lady will retire after this season—let us pay a tribute to her former powers, and render her retiring cheerful."

Besides Mrs. Melmoth, the debutants of the season were Mr. Richards, whose first appearance was made December 28th, 1793, as *Barbarossa*, and Mrs. Wilson, who appeared as *Mrs. Brady* in the "Irish Widow," March 12th, 1794. Richards was an assumed name for Sir Richard Crosby, an Irish Baronet. Richards was a pudding-faced giant, who realized Foote's description of a nobleman of his day—"He looks like a greyhound that has got the dropsy."

June 20—Heiress . . . . Burgoyne
 Death of Harlequin.
 No Song No Supper.
 (Woolls and Richards' benefit.)
23—Every One has His Fault.
 Wapping Landlady.
 Spoiled Child . . . . Bickerstaff
 (Mr. Ashton's benefit.)
25—Dramatist.
 Padlock.
 (Heard and Hammond's benefit.)
28—Barbarossa.
 Agreeable Surprise.
 (Benefit for Algerine Captives.)

Among his previous achievements, Sir Richard had built a balloon and gone up in it, to come down in the Irish Channel at the peril of his life. Having dissipated a fortune, there was one distinction left to him—to become the first baronet to appear on the American stage. Who Mrs. Wilson was it is impossible to say. The name had been a common one on the English stage a few years before. One Mrs. Wilson was a daughter of Lee Lewes, and the wife of Mr. Wilson, of the Haymarket, who left her a widow. Mrs. J. Wilson, who had played at Birmingham, Brighthelmstone and Portsmouth with success, was announced for a London *debut* in 1783. Our Mrs. Wilson, whoever she was, is less interesting to American readers than the Mrs. Wilson, of Covent Garden, celebrated in the prints of the time as "Sally the Small," the "yellowhammer" and the "goldfinch." She married Weston, but eloped with Wilson, and was, perhaps, the most notorious actress of her time. She was a daughter of the Mr. and Mrs. Adcock, who came to America with the original Hallam company in 1752, and her age at the time of her death in 1787—thirty-four years—shows that she was born in this country.

Mrs. Pownall was unable to appear during the first few weeks of the season, having broken her leg, and when she again came before the public she was still on crutches. A musical trifle, called "Needs Must, or the Ballad Singers," served as a vehicle for her reappearance. For this piece Mrs. Hatton, a sister of Mrs. Siddons, furnished the plot, which was slight and wrote one of the songs; the whole of the dialogue was the work of Mrs. Pownall. The only example of the songs in "Needs Must" that has come down to us is the following:

NEEDS MUST.

Hardwell	Mr. Prigmore
Anthony	Mr. Martin
Rushbrook	Mr. Bergman
Delia	Mrs. Hallam
Marian	Mrs. Pownall

> To her enraptured fancy flies
>   Whose image fills the heart;
> Swells on the beam of her dear eyes,
>   Whose smiles ecstatic joy impart.
>
> And now while gentle dews descend,
>   And misty evening veils the sky,
> Oh, love, thy vot'ry's suit befriend
>   And whisper, Delia, Henry's nigh.

One of the newspapers, in contradicting the report that Mrs. Hatton had written "Needs Must," spoke of her as the lady from whose pen was soon to be expected a new opera—"Tammany, or the Indian Chief." This lady was Mrs. Anne Julia Hatton, a sister of Mrs. Siddons, who aspired to be a poet and playwright. In 1783, when she was Mrs. Curtis, she published a volume of "Poems on Miscellaneous Subjects," of which one of the reviews said, "The public is frequently addressed in

TAMMANY.

Tammany	Mr. Hodgkinson
Columbus	Mr. Hallam
Perez	Mr. King
Ferdinand	Mr. Martin
Wegan	Mr. Prigmore
Indian Dancers	{ Mr. Durang { Mr. Miller
Manana	Mrs. Hodgkinson
Zulla	Mrs. Hamilton

worse poetry." In 1793, after she had become Mrs. Hatton, she attempted the stage, appearing at the Haymarket in June of that year as *Kitty* in "Seeing is Believing," and *Nancy* in a piece called the "Pad." She arrived in New York in the Winter of 1793-4, and at once became the bard of the American Democracy. When the Democratic Society of New York celebrated the recapture of Toulon, she furnished the ode for the occasion for which she was voted the thanks of the Society. She also succeeded in interesting the Tammany Society in her opera, the wish of this powerful organization for its production being equal to a command. Elaborate preparations were made for bringing it out. The prologue, which was spoken by Mr. Hodgkinson, was written by Richard Bingham Davis, a young New York poet, then only in his 23d year. It was included in a volume of "Poems,' collected and published after his death, which occurred of yellow fever in 1799. The music was by James Hewitt, who had been the leader of the orchestra for many years. This was the first important attempt at the

EXTRACT FROM DAVIS' PROLOGUE.

———

Secure the Indian roved his native soil,
Secure enjoy'd the produce of his toil,
Nor knew, nor feared a haughty master's pow'r
To force his labors, or his gains devour.
And when the slaves of Europe here unfurl'd
The bloody standard of their servile world,
When heaven, to curse them more, first deign'd to bless
Their base attempts with undeserved success,
He knew the sweets of liberty to prize,
And, lost on earth, he sought her in the skies;
Scorn'd life divested of its noblest good,
And seal'd the cause of freedom with his blood.

For you, this night, we bid those scenes return—
Scenes that must make each patriot bosom burn;
While the brave deeds of former times renew'd,
Exhibit what yourselves but late have view'd.
When Tammany his country's champion glows,
"Thus," says the patriot, "Washington arose;"
And when his hand illumes the fatal pyre,
"Thus glory saw Montgomery expire."
In each heroic act we fondly trace
Those features which Columbia's worthies grace;
In every eye with exaltation see
Columbia's sons determined to be free.
And oh! may this exalted spirit glow,
Long as the rolling tide of time shall flow.

composition of operatic music in America; but, like most pioneer com-
posers, Mr. Hewitt met with faint recognition, so far as his original work
was concerned, and he even suffered the mortification of being hissed
by an angry audience on the first night of "Tammany" for not being
ready with a popular air when it was called for. The scenery was all
new, being specially painted by Charles Ciceri for the production.
Ciceri was not without experience as a scene-painter. He had found
employment on the paint-frames in some of the leading theatres of
Paris and London, and he was engaged by Milbourne to assist in
painting the stock scenes for the New Theatre in Philadelphia. The
yellow fever of 1793 drove him to New York, where he soon found
occupation in repairing and replacing the well-worn scenery in the
theatre in John Street. Dunlap said of the scenes for "Tammany"
that "they were gaudy and unnatural, but had a brilliancy of coloring,
reds and yellows being abundant." Although Dunlap speaks of the
opera itself as "a melange of bombast" and as "seasoned high with
spices hot from Paris, and swelling with rhodomontade for the sonor-
ous voice of Hodgkinson," it does not follow that, as a literary performance, it was worse than similar performances of his own. The
fact is that the political character of the work—its pronounced republicanism—was peculiarly offensive to Dunlap and to the Federalists
generally. This is what the historian meant by "spices hot from
Paris." While Republicans were called upon to support the effort on
the one hand, there were rumors that a party had been got up to hiss
it on the other. While it was admitted that the opera was "received
with unbounded applause," it was said with a sneer that the audience
was made up of "the poorer class of mechanics and clerks." Whatever may have been the merits of the piece, *Tammany* received much

applause for his independent and noble spirit, and *Columbus* was also applauded. The only hint of the plot is contained in one of the criticisms, in which it is said that the Spaniards got the better of the brave *Tammany*, and burnt him up in his cabin with poor *Manana*. The opera was given in Philadelphia in the following Autumn, and a few years later Hodgkinson revived it in Boston.

After the production of his first comedy, "The Father," Dunlap's activity as a dramatist was very great. As early as 1790 he wrote a tragedy, which was not produced until 1794, when Hodgkinson was induced to bring it out for his benefit. It was originally called "Lord Leicester," but was produced as "The Fatal Deception, or The Progress of Guilt." It was afterward published with the simple title of "Leicester." The author, who was always fond of

FATAL DECEPTION.

Lord Leicester	Mr. Hallam
Henry Cecil	Mr. Hodgkinson
Dudley Cecil	Mr. King
Eldred	Mr. Richards
Howard	Mr. Martin
Elwina	Mrs. Hodgkinson
Matilda	Mrs. Melmoth

his offspring, though he sometimes speaks of his pieces deserving the early death that overtook them, describes this so-called tragedy as a poem. It certainly was poetic in form, but it was not poetry; nor was it tragedy. It was prose with a capital letter at the beginning of each line, and, what is now unendurable, turgid melodrama without action. In length its speeches were Shakspearean, but only in length. Although historical characters were introduced, it had no historical basis. The supposed wife of Leicester presents her lover to her husband as her brother—the guilty wife and her paramour exchange all the servants of the great castle of Kenilworth for strangers in the earl's absence. They attempt Leicester's murder in a way that is at once commonplace and cowardly. These two characters, Dunlap says, were played by Hodgkinson and Mrs. Melmoth with great effect. He also says that Mrs. Hodgkinson as *Elwina*—the fainting and distressed heroine of melodrama—"first played an important part in this branch of the drama, and evinced great powers." Whatever success these players had, must have been entirely due to their declamation. Dunlap says the success of this play confirmed his attachment to the drama—it was in fact a failure. It was repeated for Richards' benefit, which also failed, and again tried in Philadelphia during the Autumn season of 1794, after which it was never revived. As an afterpiece to the tragedy, when Hodgkinson first produced it, Dunlap contributed an interlude called " Shelty's Travels," in which Hodgkinson's success as *Shelty* was as celebrated as Wignell's *Darby* had been in " Darby's Return."

The new English pieces produced in New York for the first time during the regular season were Mrs. Inchbald's " I'll Tell You What," previously announced for Mr. Hodgkinson's benefit in Philadelphia, but not given because of the yellow

I'LL TELL YOU WHAT.	HIGHLAND REEL.
Col. Downright . . . Mr. Hallam	Shelty . . . . . Mr. Hodgkinson
Anthony Euston . Mr. Hodgkinson	McGilpin . . . . . Mr. Prigmore
Mr. Euston . . . . Mr. Prigmore	Sergeant Jack . . . . . Mr. King
Sir George Euston . . Mr. Ashton	Charley . . . . Mr. Martin
Charles Euston . . . . Mr. Martin	Sandy . . . . . . Mr. Bergman
Major Cyprus . . . . . Mr. King	Captain Dash . . . Mr. Hammond
Sir Harry Harmless . Mr. Hammond	Raasay . . . . Mr. Kenna
Lady Euston . . . . Mrs. Hallam	Coll . . . . Mr. Ashton
Lady Harriet Cyprus . Mrs. Kenna	Moggy McGilpin . Mrs. Hodgkinson
Young Lady . . Mrs. Hodgkinson	Jenny . . . . Mrs. Hallam
Bloom . . . . Mrs. Miller	

fever; O'Keefe's " Highland Reel," which proved exceedingly popular, and was included in the repertoires of all the new American companies; Cumberland's "Carmelite," in which Hodgkinson played *St. Valori*, and Mrs. Melmoth *Matilda*, a part in which her great abilities were unequalled; the younger Colman's "Battle of Hexham," of which I have not been able to find the original cast; and O'Keefe's "World in a Village," the least popular of all that prolific writer's pieces. Mrs. Inchbald's comedy had

CARMELITE.

St. Valori . Mr. Hodgkinson
Hildebrand . . Mr. Richards
De Courcy . . . Mr. King
Montgomeri . . Mr. Martin
Gyfford . . . . Mr. Ashton
Fitz Allan . . . Mr. Kenna
Matilda . . Mrs. Melmoth

WORLD IN A VILLAGE.

Dr. Grigsby . . . Mr. Hodgkinson
Jollyboy . . . . . . Mr. Hallam
Alebut . . . . . . Mr. Prigmore
Charles Willows . . . . Mr. King
William Bellevue. . . Mr. Martin
Capt. Mullenahack . Mr. Richards
Sir Henry Check . . . Mr. Ashton
Capt. Vansheisen . . . Mr. Ryan
Jack . . . . Mr. Bergman
Hedgeworth . . . Mr. Hammond
Briers . . . . . . Mr. Woolls
Willows . . . . Mr. Heard
Louisa . . . . . . Mrs. Henry
Maria . . . . Mrs. Hallam
Mrs. Alebut . . . . Mrs. Pownall
Mrs. Bellevue. . . . Mrs. Kenna

been first acted at the Haymarket in 1785, and was well received, but in this country it was soon jostled aside by more popular productions. The first cast of the "Highland Reel" is especially worthy of remembrance because of the character portrait of Martin as *Charley*, published in 1794, of which only one copy is known to exist. This one I picked out of the "five-cent box," at a second-hand bookstore in New York in 1880. The cast of the "World in a Village" is only noteworthy in showing the subordinate strength of the company. Mr. Bergman, who played the little part of *Jack*, was a musician and a member of the orchestra.

When the benefits began, new plays followed each other in rapid succession. Another of the younger Colman's pieces, the "Surrender of Calais," was brought out on Mrs. Henry's night, and Mrs. Inchbald's best comedy, "Every One has His Fault," was played for Mr. Ashton. In Colman's play, notwithstanding it was produced for Mrs. Henry's benefit, Mr. and Mrs. Hodgkinson had the best parts. A solecism in the cast was Hammond as *King Edward*, Williamson's part, when the play was first produced at the Haymarket in 1791. The plot of this piece was borrowed from a novel called "The Siege of Calais," published in 1751. In Mrs. Inchbald's comedy the characters of *Lord Norland* and *Harmony* were drawn from her novel, "A Simple Story." The solecism in this cast was Mr. Ashton as *Harmony.*

SURRENDER OF CALAIS.	
Eustache de St. Pierre	. Mr. Henry
La Gloire	. Mr. Hodgkinson
Ribbemont	. Mr. Martin
John de Vienne . . .	Mr. Richards
O'Carroll	. Mr. King
Edward III	Mr. Hammond
John D'Arie	Mr. Ashton
Sir Walter Mauny . .	Mr. Woolls
Sergeant	. Mr. Prigmore
Carpenter	Mr. Hallam
Old Man	. Mr. Heard
Queen Phillipa . . .	Mrs. Hallam
Julia	. Mrs. Henry
Madelon	. Mrs. Hodgkinson

EVERY ONE HAS HIS FAULT.	
Lord Norland . .	Mr. Richards
Sir Robert Ramble .	Mr. Martin
Captain Irwin .	Mr. Hodgkinson
Placid	. Mr. Hallam
Solus	. Mr. Prigmore
Harmony	. Mr. Ashton
Hammond	. Mr. Durang
Edward . .	A young gentleman
Lady Elinor . . .	Mrs. Melmoth
Mrs. Placid . . .	Mrs. Pownall
Miss Wooburn . .	Mrs. Hallam
Miss Spinster . .	Mrs. Hamilton

Its production in New York had been anticipated by Mr. Wignell's company with a cast in every way superior. Mrs. Pownall chose for her benefit bill a piece called "Liberty Restored" and Dibdin's "Wedding Ring." Her selection of the "Wedding Ring" is easy enough to understand, as her early fame

LIBERTY RESTORED.	
A la Grecque .	Mr. Hodgkinson
Ibrahim	. Mr. King
Mustapha . . .	. Mr. Martin
Azim	. Mr. Prigmore
Selim	. Mr. Bergman
Orloff	. Mr. Hallam
Muley	. Mr. Ashton
Ismael	Mr. Hammond
Old Man	. Mr. Heard
Son	. Mr. West
Alexina	Mrs. Melmoth
Lauretta	Mrs. Hamilton
Fatima	. Mrs. Wilson
Paulina	Mrs. Pownall

WEDDING RING.	
Zerbino	. Mr. Prigmore
Pandolfo	Mr. Richards
Henrico	. Mr. King
Lisetta	Mrs. Pownall
Margaretta . .	Mrs. Hodgkinson

was associated with the part of *Lisetta* of which she was the original when the opera was first produced at Drury Lane in 1773. The choice of the play, it must be confessed, is a puzzle. In the fact that Mr. Prigmore a few weeks later produced a piece called the "Patriot, or Liberty Asserted," may be found a possible explanation of the phenomenon. In consequence of the French Revolution and the establishment of the

Swiss Confederation there was a great deal of cant about liberty with which the stage naturally sympathized. That there was either a public or a political demand for the production of such pieces is made clear by the fact that in March of this year, 1794,

PATRIOT.		NOOTKA SOUND.	
William Tell .	Mr. Hodgkinson	Captain Douglas .	Mr. Prigmore
Melchdale . . .	Mr. Prigmore	Sam Stern	Mr. Robbins
Edwald	Mr. King	Tom Grog	Mr. Woolls
Grisler	Mr. Richards	Lieutenant . . .	Mr. Bergman
Werner	Mr. Hallam	Don Guzman	Mr. King
Lieutenant	Mr. Martin	Don Frederick . .	Mr. Martin
Provost	Mr. Ashton	Alknomook	Mr. West
Bowman	Mr. West	Wampumpoo . . .	Mrs. Miller
Serena	Mrs. Wilson		
Lucella	Mrs. Kenna		
Marina	Mrs. Melmoth		

a number of correspondents wrote to the *Daily Advertiser* in Philadelphia demanding that the managers of the New Theatre should produce an opera called " Helvetic Liberty, or the Lass of the Lakes," founded on the story of William Tell. While Wignell resisted these appeals, it is not surprising that Prigmore, who always manifested a disposition to foist political allusions into his lines, should adopt the theme as a good one for a benefit play. Mrs. Pownall also may have found a reason for her production in the same feverish condition of public feeling. Prigmore's

ROBIN HOOD.		HOW TO GROW RICH.	
Robin Hood	Mr. King	Pave	Mr. Hodgkinson
Little John . . .	Mr. Prigmore	Hippy	Mr. Hallam
Baron Fitzherbert .	Mr. Richards	Latitat	Mr. Martin
Edwin	Mr. Bergman	Warford	Mr. King
Ruttekin . . .	Mr. Hodgkinson	Sir Thomas Roundhead .	Mr. Richards
Will Scarlet	Mr. Martin	Sir Charles Dazzle	Mr. Ashton
Allan-a-Dale . . .	Mr. Ashton	Plainly	Mr. Hammond
Clorinda . .	Mrs. Hodgkinson	Smalltrade	Mr. Prigmore
Angelina	Mrs. Pownall	Lady Henrietta	Mrs. Hallam
Stella	Mrs. Hallam	Rosa	Mrs. Hodgkinson
Annette	Mrs. Wilson	Miss Dazzle	Mrs. Wilson
		Betty	Mrs. Hamilton

afterpiece, " Nootka Sound " was a pantomimic trifle whose only merit was in the fact that it was new. There was a more genuine dramatic purpose in the other new pieces presented at benefits during the season, Mrs. Hodgkinson giving Mr. MacNally's "Robin Hood," Mr. Hallam Reynold's new comedy, "How to Grow Rich," and Mr. King O'Keefe's "Young Quaker" at a first attempt, and Mrs. Inchbald's "Midnight Hour" for his second benefit. Besides these, a ballet, that was original at least in name, the "Huntress, or Tammany's Frolics," was produced by Miller, Bergman, Durang and Mrs. Wilson. In this skit Mr. Ashton was *Tammany*, and Mrs. Wilson the *Huntress*. The interest in "Robin Hood" was to a great extent owing to the music by Shields, which was excellent.

In this opera Goldsmith's *Edwin* and *Angelina* were introduced among the legendary heroes and heroines of Sherwood Forest. Its performance in Philadelphia antedated that in New York. Reynolds' comedy, "How to Grow Rich," had some merit, but failed to obtain the popularity of the "Dramatist." Its performance in New York was not anticipated by the Philadelphia company.

YOUNG QUAKER.

———

Young Sadboy	Mr. Hodgkinson
Old Sadboy	Mr. Richards
Chronicle	Mr. Prigmore
Captain Ambush	Mr. Martin
Spatterdash	Mr. King
Clod	Mr. Hallam
Shadrach	Mr. Hammond
Malachi	Mr. Woolls
Lounge	Mr. West
Twig	Mr. Durang
Lady Rounceval	Mrs. Miller
Dinah Primrose	Mrs. Hallam
Araminta	Mrs. Hodgkinson
Pink	Mrs. Pownall
Judith	Mrs. Hamilton
Mrs. Millefluer	Mrs. Kenna

MIDNIGHT HOUR.

———

Marquis	Mr. Hodgkinson
General	Mr. Richards
Nicholas	Mr. Prigmore
Sebastian	Mr. Martin
Matthias	Mr. Hammond
Ambrose	Mr. West
Julia	Mrs. Wilson
Flora	Mrs. Pownall
Cicely	Mrs. Hamilton

Although the "Young Quaker" was originally acted as early as 1783, and was one of O'Keefe's most amusing works, this first production in America was delayed, no doubt, to avoid offense to the Quaker element. Mrs. Inchbald's "Midnight Hour" was "considerably altered from the French," but it proved an interesting play, as so many English pieces from the same source have done ever since.

The new casts of the familiar pieces form the basis of an interesting study of the condition of the Old American Company under the domination of Hodgkinson. In these casts the absence of Mr. and Mrs. Henry, the subordination of Mrs. Pownall to Mrs. Hodgkinson, and the prominence of Mrs. Melmoth are especially noteworthy. In

NEW CASTS OF FAMILIAR PIECES.

BEGGAR'S OPERA.

Macheath . . . Mr. Hodgkinson
Peachum . . . . . Mr. Prigmore
Lockit . . . . Mr. Ashton
Filch . . . . Mr. Martin
Mat o' the Mint . . Mr. King
Polly . . . . . Mrs. Hodgkinson
Lucy . . . . . . Mrs. Pownall
Mrs. Peachum . . . Mrs. Miller
Mrs. Coaxer . . . Mrs. Hamilton
Mrs. Slammekin . . Mrs. Wilson

BELLE'S STRATAGEM.

Doricourt . . . Mr. Hodgkinson
Flutter . . . . . . Mr. Hallam
Sir George Touchwood . Mr. King
Hardy . . . . . . Mr. Prigmore
Letitia Hardy . Mrs. Hodgkinson
Widow Racket . . Mrs. Melmoth

BOLD STROKE FOR A HUSBAND.

Don Julio . . . Mr. Hodgkinson
Don Vincentio . . . Mr. Martin
Don Cæsar . . . . Mr. Prigmore
Don Carlos . . . . . Mr. King
Don Garcia . . . Mr. Hammond
Gasper . . . . . . Mr. Richards
Victoria . . . . . . Mrs. Wilson
Olivia . . . . . . Mrs. Hallam
Laura . . . . . Mrs. Kenna
Minette . . . . . Mrs. Pownall
Marcelia . . . . Mrs. Hamilton
Sancha . . . . . . Mrs. Long

CATHARINE AND PETRUCHIO.

Petruchio . . . Mr. Hodgkinson
Catharine . . . . . . Mrs. Long

CATO.

Cato . . . . Mr. Hallam
Portius . . . . . . Mr. Henry
Juba . . . . . . Mr. Hodgkinson
Sempronius . . . . Mr. Richards
Marcius . . . . . Mr. Martin

Syphax . . . . . . Mr. Ashton
Lucius . . . . . . Mr. Kenna
Decius . . . . . . Mr. Woolls
Marcia . . . . . Mrs. Melmoth
Lucia . . . . . . Mrs. Hallam

CROSS PURPOSES.

Chapeau . . . . . Mr. Hallam
Robin . . . . . . Mr. Martin
Grub . . . . . . Mr. Prigmore
Mrs. Grub . . . . . Mrs. Long

FAIR PENITENT.

Sciolto . . . . . Mr. Henry
Horatio . . . Mr. Hodgkinson
Lothario . . . . . Mr. Hallam
Altamont . . . . . Mr. Martin
Calista . . . . . Mrs. Melmoth
Lavinia . . . . . Mrs. Hallam

GAMESTER.

Beverly . . . Mr. Hodgkinson
Stukely . . . . Mr. King
Lewson . . . . . Mr. Hallam
Mrs. Beverly . . . Mrs. Melmoth

GUARDIANS OUTWITTED.

Colonel Feignwell . . Mr. Hallam
Periwinkle . . . . Mr. Prigmore
Obadiah Prim . . . . Mr. Henry
Freeman . . . . . . Mr. Martin
Sir Philip Modelove . Mr. Ashton
Tradelove . . . . . Mr. King
Simon Pure . . . . Mr. Woolls
Ann Lovely . . . Mrs. Henry
Mrs. Prim . . . . Mrs. Hamilton
Betty . . . . . . Mrs. Kenna

Obadiah Prim . . . Mr. Prigmore
Ann Lovely . . . Mrs. Hallam

HEIRESS.

Clifford . . . . Mr. Hodgkinson
Sir Clement Flint . Mr. Richards

Lord Gayville . . . . Mr. Martin
Alscrip . . . . . . Mr. Prigmore
Blandish . . . . . . Mr. Ashton
Rightly . . . . Mr. King
Prompt . . . . . . Mr. Woolls
Lady Emily . . . . Mrs. Hallam
Miss Alscrip . . . Mrs. Pownall
Miss Alten . . Mrs. Hodgkinson
Mrs. Blandish . . . . Mrs. Miller
Tiffany . . . . . . Mrs. Wilson

HOB IN THE WELL.

Hob . . . . Mr. Hallam
Dick . . . . Mr. Martin
Roger . . . . . . Mr. Prigmore
Flora . . . . . . Mrs. Kenna

INKLE AND YARICO.

Inkle . . . . Mr. King
Curry . . . . Mr. Henry
Trudge . . . . . . Mr. Hallam
Yarico . . . . . Mrs. Hallam

IRISH WIDOW.

Widow Brady . . . Mrs. Wilson

ISABELLA.

Biron . . . . . Mr. Hodgkinson
Count Baldwin . . Mr. Richards
Carlos . . . . Mr. King
Villeroy . . . . . . Mr. Hallam
Belford . . . . . Mr. Hammond
Sampson . . . . . Mr. Prigmore
Pedro . . . . Mr. West
Child . . . . . . Master Pownall
Isabella . . . . . Mrs. Melmoth
Nurse . . . . . . Mrs. Hamilton

JANE SHORE.

Hastings . . . . Mr. Hodgkinson
Gloster . . . . . . Mr. Hallam
Dumont . . . . . . Mr. Henry
Belmour . . . . . . Mr. Martin
Jane Shore . . . . Mrs. Henry
Alicia . . . . . Mrs. Melmoth

regard to Mrs. Pownall, Dunlap said had she been permitted by Hodgkinson to play *Margaretta* in " No Song No Supper," Mrs. Hodgkinson would not have played the part again.   This conclusion may be
doubted.   Mrs. Pownall could easily have asserted her rank had not
the public of Philadelphia and New York been alike indifferent to her

NEW CASTS OF FAMILIAR PIECES.

JEALOUS WIFE.

Mrs. Oakly . . . . . Mrs. Long

JULIUS CÆSAR.

Julius Cæsar . . . Mr. Richards
Marc Antony . . Mr. Hodgkinson
Brutus . . . . Mr. Hallam
Cassius . . . . Mr. Henry
Octavius . . . . . . Mr. Martin
Casca . . . . Mr. King
Trebonius . . . . . . Mr. Woolls
Pindarus . . . . Mr. Hammond
Decius Brutus . . . . Mr. Ashton
Metellus Cimba . . . Mr. Ryan
Lucius . . . . . . Mr. Bergman
Cinna . . . . Mr. Prigmore
Marcellus . . . . . . Mr. Bisset
Lucilius . . . . Mr. West
Artimedorus . . . . Mr. O'Reilly
Portia . . . . . . Mrs. Melmoth
Calphurnia . . . . Mrs. Hallam

LIONEL AND CLARISSA.

Lionel . . . . . Mr. Hodgkinson
Colonel Oldboy . . Mr. Prigmore
Sir John Flowerdale . . Mr. King
Harman . . . . . Mr. Hammond
Jessamy . . . . . . Mr. Martin
Jenkins . . . . Mr. Woolls
Clarissa . . . . . . Mrs. Pownall
Diana . . . . . Mrs. Hodgkinson
Lady Oldboy . . Mrs. Hamilton
Jenny . . . . Mrs. Hallam

LOVE IN A CAMP.

Captain Patrick . . . . Mr. King
Fehrbellin . . . . . Mr. Ashton
Rupert . . . . Mr. Woolls
Father Luke . . . . Mr. Richards
Darby . . . . . . Mr. Prigmore
Quiz . . . . Mr. Bergman
Adjutant . . . . . Mr. Hammond
Mabel Flourish . . . Mr. Martin
Flora . . . . Mrs. Wilson
Norah . . . . . Mrs. Pownall

LYAR.

Young Wilding . Mr. Hodgkinson

MACBETH.

Macbeth . . . . Mr. Hodgkinson
Macduff . . . . Mr. Hallam
Banquo . . . . . . Mr. Richards
Lady Macbeth . . Mrs. Melmoth

MOURNING BRIDE.

Osmyn . . . . . Mr. Hodgkinson
Manuel . . . . . . Mr. Richards
Heli . . . . Mr. King
Gonzales . . . . . . Mr. Kenna
Zara . . . . Mrs. Melmoth
Almeria . . . . . . Mrs. Long

NEW PEERAGE.

Vandercrab . . . . . Mr. Hallam
Charles . . . . Mr. Hodgkinson
Lady Charlotte . . Mrs. Melmoth
Miss Harley . . . . Mrs. Hallam

PERCY.

Percy . . . . . Mr. Hodgkinson
Earl Douglas . . . . Mr. Hallam
Lord Raby . . . . . . Mr. King
Sir Hubert . . . . Mr. Prigmore
Edric . . . . Mr. Martin
Harcourt . . . . . . Mr. Ashton
Elwina . . . . . Mrs. Melmoth
Birtha . . . . Mrs. Hallam

POOR SOLDIER.

Darby . . . . . . Mr. Hallam
Norah . . . . . . Mrs. Wilson
Kathleen . . . . . Mrs. Pownall

RICHARD III.

Richard . . . . Mr. Hodgkinson
Henry VI . . . . . . Mr. Henry
Richmond . . . . . Mr. Hallam
Buckingham . . . Mr. Prigmore

[Prince of Wales column]

Prince of Wales . . . Mr. Martin
Tressel . . . . Mr. King
Queen Elizabeth . Mrs. Melmoth
Lady Anne . . . . Mrs. Hallam

RIVALS.

Bob Acres . . Mr. Hodgkinson
Captain Absolute . . Mr. Hallam
Lydia Languish . . Mrs. Hallam
Julia . . . . . . Mrs. Melmoth

SUCH THINGS ARE.

Arabella . . . . . Mrs. Melmoth

SULTAN.

Solyman . . . . . Mr. Richards
Osmyn . . . . . . Mr. Prigmore
Elmira . . . . Mrs. Hallam
Ismena . . . . . . Mrs. Pownall
Roxalana . . . . Mrs. Melmoth

TAMERLANE.

Tamerlane . . . Mr. Hodgkinson
Bajazet . . . . . . Mr. Hallam
Moneses . . . . Mr. King
Axalla . . . . Mr. Martin
Arpasia . . . . . Mrs. Melmoth
Selima . . . . . . Mrs. Hallam

TRUE-BORN IRISHMAN.

O'Dogherty . . . . . Mr. King
Hamilton . . . Mr. Richards
Count Mushroom . . Mr. Martin
Major Gamble . . Mr. Prigmore
Mrs. Diggerty . . . Mrs. Henry
Lady Kinnegad . . Mrs. Kenna
Lady Bab Frightful . Mrs. Miller
Lady Farrel . . . Mrs. Hallam

VENICE PRESERVED.

Pierre . . . . Mr. Hallam
Jaffier . . . . . Mr. Hodgkinson
Priuli . . . . Mr. King
Belvidera . . . . Mrs. Melmoth

abilities. She sang *Polly* in the " Beggar's Opera " after Mrs. Hodgkinson had been heard in the part. She had many good parts in
which her singing and acting were displayed to great advantage.
Hodgkinson was able to keep her in the background, because then, as
now, youth and beauty were preferred to mere artistic merit. With
Mrs. Melmoth and Mrs. Henry the case was different. Through
Hodgkinson's manipulations of public sentiment and Hallam's quies-
cence, a call was created in Mrs. Melmoth's behalf; she appeared, and
her abilities at once enabled her to usurp the place that Henry had
held in reserve for his wife. It was peculiarly easy for Hodgkinson to
achieve his purpose of dethroning Henry. His popularity was at its
height. Even the press, blinded by his versatile talents and accomplishments, gave him assistance. A remarkable instance of this was
afforded by the *Daily Advertiser*, when Henry played his favorite part
of *Beverly* in the " Gamester," on the 22d of March, with Mrs. Henry
as *Mrs. Beverly*. The house was a thin one, and thereupon the public
was told that this was owing to the preoccupation of parts by incom-
petent persons, when others more capable were willing to play them.
Henry yielded ; and on the 28th of May following, Hodgkinson played
Beverly, and Mrs. Melmoth *Mrs. Beverly*. After this, Mr. and Mrs.
Henry appeared in only one new play, the former as *St. Pierre* and the
latter as *Julia* in the " Surrender of Calais " for Mrs. Henry's benefit.
Subsequently Mrs. Henry played the title-role in " Jane Shore," with
Henry as *Dumont*, and *Ann Lovely* in " Guardians Outwitted," an
alteration of Mrs. Centlivre's " Bold Stroke for a Wife," with Henry as
Obadiah Prim. In the latter they made their last appearances on the
stage, negotiations for the sale of Henry's interest in the theatre being
consummated a few days later. With the disappearance of the Henrys

this season was also the final retirement of Mrs. Long, formerly Miss Cheer, who no longer found favor with the new generation of playgoers.

Hodgkinson's popularity, great as it was, was often severely strained. An incident that happened early in the season of 1793–4 is a curious illustration of his manner of alienating his friends. One evening in December he was late in making his appearance, in consequence of which he was hissed by one or two persons in the audience. Putting on an air of authority, Hodgkinson demanded the cause of the dissatisfaction, and he then went on to tell how Mrs. Hodgkinson had been insulted on the way to the theatre, and how he had beaten the ruffian. The manner and language in which his story was conveyed gave offense to persons who were not disposed to find fault with his tardiness on a single occasion. In his speeches Hodgkinson seldom failed to give offense, and this he often aggravated by communications in the newspapers. An unfortunate affair of this kind happened when he came on the stage as *Captain Flash* in " Miss in Her Teens," on the 8th of March, 1794. He wore an English uniform, as he was bound to do, but some unreasoning French partisans among the " fierce democracie" of Tammany Hall hissed him, and ordered him to "take it off." Instead of appealing to long-established custom, and the propriety of an English officer wearing an English uniform in an English farce, he appeased the French party by saying he represented a coward and a bully,. which, of course, incensed the English partisans in the audience. Then, to make bad worse, he wrote to the *Daily Advertiser*, professing to give the exact words of his speech.[1] The statement

[1] HODGKINSON'S SPEECH.—*First Corrected Version.*—Sir : The character I am going to portray is a bully and a coward, and however you may choose to quarrel with a red coat, you would probably be a great deal more offended had I improperly disgraced the uniform of this or any other country by wearing it on the back of a poltroon.

in which this speech was contained, was signed "Verax;" but, as it failed to give satisfaction, Hodgkinson, on the 13th of March, 1794, printed a card[1] over his own name, in which he endeavored still further to soften his unfortunate phraseology. The result was that he made enemies in both factions, in a trivial matter that he could safely have left to his audience.

This man, at once so impulsive and so prone to juggle with the truth, was often the victim of his own disingenuousness; but John Henry, and even Mrs. Henry, suffered from it in a way that had it been foreseen the engagement of John Hodgkinson would not have been made. Poor Henry had long been subjected to the insidious arts and practices of Hallam. When the public demand for better per-formers was made in Philadelphia, in 1791, Henry was prevented by his partner from moving in the matter, the latter promising the mission

MR. AND MRS. HENRY'S PARTS.

Plays.	Mr. Henry.	Mrs. Henry.
Alexander the Great	. . . .	Statira
Chapter of Accidents	. . . .	Cecelia
Don Juan	. . . .	Donna Anna
Earl of Essex	. . . .	Countess of Rutland
Gamester	Beverly	. . . . Mrs. Beverly
Guardians Outwitted	Obadiah Prim	. . . . . Ann Lovely
Irishman in London	Delany	. . . .
Jane Shore	Dumont	. . . . Jane Shore
Julius Cæsar	Cassius	. . . .
Merchant of Venice	Shylock	. . . . Portia
Notoriety	. . . .	Sophia Strangeway
Rival Candidates	General Worry	. . . .
Road to Ruin	Old Dornton	. . . .
Surrender of Calais	St. Pierre	. . . . Julia
True-Born Irishman	O'Dogherty	. . . . Mrs. Diggerty
Wild Oats	Ephraim Smooth	. . Lady Amaranth
World in a Village	. . . .	Louisa

[1] HODGKINSON'S CARD.—The situation I was placed in on Saturday evening last, and the explanation I was compelled to enter into, having given an opportunity to some evil-minded person to grossly mistake my words, I beg, through the medium of your paper, to lay before that part of the public who have heard the fabrication the true meaning of what I said—"However angry you may be at the sight of a red-coat, you would probably be more displeased, had I appeared in the uniform of this or any other country, usually worn on the stage, for a character that is a disgrace to his cloth, by being a bully and a

to England to engage recruits to Wignell. Jealousy of Wignell afterward led Hallam to side with Henry. While Hallam escaped animadversion almost entirely, Henry, in consequence, became very unpopular in the Quaker City, where, as late as January, 1793, he felt obliged to deny the calumnies then current in regard to his unwillingness to strengthen the Old American Company under oath. To some extent, a like feeling against him was cherished in New York, but there the opposition in the main was within his own theatrical household. One by one, under various pretexts, he saw his favorite roles slipping out of his keeping. Hodgkinson now played *Othello*, and wrested *Beverly* from him, with a public insult in the newspapers impugning his capacity. Even *O'Flaherty*, in which he was long unrivalled, was given to Hodgkinson's prospective brother-in-law, King. For a brief period after the reorganization, Mrs. Henry enjoyed a better fortune. She had at last become what she had long aspired to be—the leading tragic actress on the American stage. While Henry retained *Shylock*, she was the *Portia;* when Henry played *Dumont* in " Jane Shore," she was the heroine; when Henry appeared as *Beverly* for the last time, she was *Mrs. Beverly*. A few parts that had formerly belonged to Mrs. Morris were accorded her, as the *Countess of Rutland* in the " Earl of Essex," and she now played *Statira* in " Alexander the Great," and *Ann Lovely* in "A Bold Stroke for a Wife" under its new name. With Mrs. Hodgkinson filling the first place in opera and the

poltroon." This was my meaning, and so plain, that I thought to misrepresent it was impossible; for I trust it will need no great argument to convince that if I, who have constantly worn a British uniform for a British officer, had upon this occasion altered it, I might have expected that just resentment which pointed insult deserves. However, upon this, as every other occasion, I trust to the candor of my fellow-citizens at large, and leave the being, capable of an endeavor at injury, to the disappointment and malice of his own heart.

JOHN HODGKINSON.

romps ; Miss Tuke, now Mrs. Hallam, in comedy, and Mrs. Melmoth in tragedy, there was no place in her husband's company for Mrs. Henry, who had been such a great favorite for many years, growing up from childhood on the American stage, as there was no place for Henry himself in the company he had twice reorganized.

At last, wearied by opposition, Henry offered, through his friend, Hugh Smith, to sell his interest in the property to Hodgkinson for $10,000. Hodgkinson was not only willing but anxious to buy; and Hallam assented, stipulating, however, that he should be the purchaser from Henry, and that Hodgkinson should repurchase from Hallam. To this Hodgkinson agreed, but he afterward claimed that Hallam had bought one-half the property from Henry, but reconveyed only two shares, one-third, out of six. The property at this time was burdened by an annuity to Stephen Woolls, of which a full half was saddled upon Hodgkinson.

John Henry's death followed quickly upon his retirement. The worry and anxiety that had induced him to sell his interest in the Old American Company undermined his health, and he died of a rapid consumption on the 16th of October, 1794, in the forty-eighth year of his age, on a sloop on Long Island Sound. He was buried in the sand on Fisher's Island in the Sound, but his remains were disinterred the next day and taken for reburial to Bristol. Mrs. Henry never recovered from the shock of Mr. Henry's death, and died at her home, in the rear of the Southwark Theatre, on the 28th of April, 1795, a raving maniac.

CHAPTER VI.

―――

HALLAM AND HODGKINSON, 1794-5.

UNDER NEW MANAGEMENT—LAST SEASON IN PHILADELPHIA—SOME NEW PLAYERS—MR. AND MRS. MARRIOTT—BENJAMIN CARR—"CHIMERA" —THE SEASON IN NEW YORK—DUNLAP'S SECOND TRAGEDY— ESTIMATES OF THE ACTING—RYAN'S DEATH.

THE Old American Company, under the management of Hallam and Hodgkinson, ventured to Philadelphia in the Autumn while the Chestnut Street Theatre Company was absent at Baltimore, reopening the old Southwark Theatre on the 22d of September, 1794, with a prelude called "Old and New Houses," in which the characters were taken by Hodgkinson, King, Martin, Ryan, Mrs. Miller, and others. The old house was now advertised as the Theatre in Cedar Street. The names of West, Heard, Bisset, Mr. and Mrs. Kenna and Mrs. Long, as well as those of Mr. and Mrs. Henry, were no longer in the bills. In their stead was a number of new candidates for public favor, none of whom, however, succeeded in making any deep impression. The prelude recited on the opening night was not printed, but it is easy to imagine its rhymed platitudes. As a matter of course, the Philadelphians were told that they had a place in their generous hearts for their earnest servants of the old theatre, who had just returned to them, as well as for the excellent performers of the new house. According to Dunlap, however, such of the citizens as were friends of the drama gave their countenance to the splendid establishment of Wignell and Reinagle, and frowned on those whom they regarded as intruders. Whatever may be the value of this statement, it is certain that Hallam and Hodgkinson put their welcome to a full test and refused to retire from the field until the company at the new theatre was ready to begin the season of 1794-5.

This season was the last ever played by the Old American Company in Philadelphia. With Mr. and Mrs. Hallam's benefit on the 4th of December, this old temple of the drama closed its doors upon a past that covered more than twenty-eight years. For the future it was to stand untenanted, or be given over to itinerant mountebanks or strolling companies. In as marked contrast as was the new theatre with the old, was the repertory at both houses in 1794, with the lists of performances before and after the Revolution. Theatrical taste had undergone a complete change. Few of the works of the older dramatists were in the bills, and of these the tragedies that were retained at the Southwark were such as displayed the powers of Mrs. Melmoth in comparison with the abilities of

LIST OF PERFORMANCES.

1794.
Sept. 22—Old and New Houses.
    Grecian Daughter . . . Murphy
    Romp . . . . Bickerstaff
    24—Love in a Village . . Bickerstaff
    26—Young Quaker . . . . O'Keefe
    Midnight Hour . . Mrs. Inchbald
    29—Fair Penitent . . . . . . Rowe
    No Song No Supper . . . Hoare
Oct.   1—Young Quaker.
    Padlock . . . . . . Bickerstaff
    3—Percy . . . . Miss More
    Highland Reel . . . . O'Keefe
    6—I'll Tell You What . Mrs. Inchbald
    Quaker . . . . Dibdin
    8—Dramatist . . . . . . Reynolds
    Danaides . . Quenet and Pelisier
    10—Robin Hood . . . . . MacNally
    Danaides.
    13—Bold Stroke for a Husband
                   Mrs. Cowley
    Danaides.
    15—Macbeth . . . . . Shakspere
    Rival Candidates . . . . . Bate
    17—Beggar's Opera . . . . . . Gay
    Three Weeks after Marriage
                     Murphy
    18—Tammany . . . . . Mrs. Hatton
    Bold Stroke for a Wife
                 Mrs. Centlivre
    20—Beggar's Opera.
    Three Weeks after Marriage.

Oct. 22—World in a Village . . O'Keefe
High Life below Stairs . Townley
24—Barbarossa . . . . . . Browne
Two Philosophers.
No Song No Supper.
27—Wild Oats . . . . . . O'Keefe
Don Juan.
29—Fatal Deception . . . . Dunlap
Rosina . . . . . Mrs. Brooke
31—Carmelite . . . . . Cumberland
Bold Stroke for a Wife.

Nov. 1—West Indian . . . . Cumberland
Sophia of Brabant.
3—Such Things Are . Mrs. Inchbald
Intrigues of a Morning
Mrs. Parsons
(Ashton and Woolls' benefit.)
5—Young Quaker.
Highland Reel.
(King and Richards' benefit.)
7—Battle of Hexham . . Colman, Jr
Citizen . . . . Murphy
(Mr. Munto and Mrs. Solomon's
benefit.)
10—Tammany.
True-Born Irishman . . . Macklin
(Mrs. Miller, Mrs. Hamilton and
Mr. Ryan's benefit.)
12—Gamester . . . . . Moore
Wedding Ring . . . . . Dibdin
(Mrs. Melmoth and Mrs. Pownall's
benefit.)
14—Love's Frailties . . . . Holcroft
Busybody . . . . Mrs. Centlivre
(Mr. and Mrs. Hallam's benefit.)
17—Alexander the Great . . . . Lee
Chimera . . . . . Mrs. Marriott
(Mr. and Mrs. Marriott's benefit.)
19—Country Girl . . . . . Garrick
Birth of Harlequin.
(Mrs. King, Mr. Durang and Mr.
Berwick's benefit.)
21—Love's Frailties.
Bird Catcher.
Harlequin Pastry Cook.
(Mr. Ashton and Mad. Gardie's
benefit.)

Mrs. Whitlock. This distinguished actress made her first appearance in Philadelphia on the opening night as *Euphrasia* in the "Grecian Daughter," and a week later she played *Calista* in the "Fair Penitent." Among the pieces presented during the season that were new to Philadelphia, were Mrs. Hatton's "Tammany," and Dunlap's "Fatal Deception." The first of the pieces, never before produced, was a pantomime called the "Danaides" by M. Quenet, a dancer in the company—the music by M. Pelisier. It was very popular, and was followed by another pantomime, "Sophia of Brabant," in which Madame Gardie was the heroine. This work differed from anything that had ever before been seen on our stage. It was the first attempt at serious pantomime in this country, and Madame Gardie as *Sophia* gave theatre-goers a delight altogether new. Her figure, face and action were enchanting. "The appearance and manner of this lady," said a New York critic a few weeks later, "are prepossessing beyond any example on our stage." These pantomimes were the only new pieces produced during the regular season, the others being brought forward at the benefits. Ashton and Woolls were first in the field, offering Mrs. Parsons' "Intrigues of a Morning;" the Marriotts produced a piece by

Nov. 24—Suspicious Husband . . Hoadley
Children in the Wood . . . Morton
(Hallam, Jr., and Carr's benefit.)
26—Notoriety . . . . . . Reynolds
Hunt the Slipper . . . . Knapp
(Prigmore and Martin's benefit.)
28—Wild Oats.
Romp.
(Nelson and Mrs. Wilson's benefit.)
Dec. 2—Haunted Tower . . . . . Cobb
Lyar . . . . Foote
(Mr. and Mrs. Hodgkinson's benefit.)
4—Young Quaker.
Two Philosophers.
Children in the Wood.
(Mr. and Mrs. Hallam's benefit.)

Mrs. Marriott called " Chimera, or Effusions of Fancy ; " the Hallams brought out Holcroft's new comedy, " Love's Frailties ; " Mrs. King and Messrs. Durang and Berwick gave Garrick's " Country Girl," based on Wycherly's " Country Wife," its first American production ; the younger Hallam and Mr. Carr gave Thomas Morton's " Children in the Wood," with additional songs by Mr. Carr ; and the Hodgkinsons closed the list with Cobb's " Haunted Tower." Mr. and Mrs. Hodgkinson's benefit was advertised for the 1st of December, but it was postponed till the 2d because of the illness of the lady and Mr. Prigmore, Mr. King finally taking Prigmore's part of the *Baron of Oakland*. The additional songs by Mr. Carr to the " Children in the Wood " was not the only time during the season that liberties were taken with the author, for the " Battle of Hexham " was advertised " with alterations by Mr. Hodgkinson."

Only two casts were advertised in the newspapers this season— those of the " Young Quaker " and the " Midnight Hour." These, however, show a number of additions to the company. Mr. Munto appeared as *Lounge* and Miss Hatton as *Goliah* in the former, while Mr. Berwick made his first appearance as *Matthias* and Mrs. Marriott effected her American *début* as *Julia* in the latter. Mr. Marriott, who was announced as from the Edinburgh Theatre, appeared for the first time in this country as *Lothario* in the "Fair Penitent." Besides these there were other debutants, including Benjamin Carr, who probably made his first appearance as *Young Meadows* in " Love in a Village," with Munto as *Eustace*, and Mrs. Solomon as *Lucinda*, on the 24th of September. Mr. Nelson's first appearance was probably as *Lubin* in the " Quaker," on the 1st of October. These opinions are based on the facts that these were their opening parts in New York the following season. All the New York casts extant for the season of 1794–5, of pieces that were played in Philadelphia during the season of 1794, are appended as an illustration of the last work of the Old American Company at the Southwark Theatre. These casts may be accepted as substantially accurate for both cities, and their use in this place seems necessary to indicate the parts played by the new members of the company in Philadelphia. As " Love in a Village" was played on the second night of the Southwark season, it is fair to assume that the *Young Meadows, Eustace* and *Lucinda* were the same in both cities. Mr. Carr was a resident of Philadelphia, where he was in busi-

YOUNG QUAKER.

Young Sadboy . Mr. Hodgkinson
Chronicle . . . . . Mr. Prigmore
Clod . . . . . . Mr. Hallam
Captain Ambush . . Mr. Martin
Shadrach Boaz . Mr. Hammond
Old Sadboy . . . Mr. Richards
Malachi . . . . . Mr. Woolls
Lounge . . . . . . Mr. Munto
Twig . . . . . . Mr. Durang
Goliah . . . . . Miss Hatton
Spatterdash . . . . . Mr. King
Araminta . . Mrs. Hodgkinson
Pink . . . . . . Mrs. Pownall
Lady Rounceval . . Mrs. Miller
Mrs. Millefluer . Mrs. Hamilton
Judith . . . . . . Mrs. King
Dinah Primrose . Mrs. Hallam

MIDNIGHT HOUR.

Marquis . Mr. Hodgkinson
Sebastian . . . Mr. Martin
Nicholas . . . Mr. Prigmore
Matthias . . . Mr. Berwick
Ambrose . . . . Mr. Ryan
General . . . Mr. Richards
Julia . . . . Mrs. Marriott
Cicely . . . Mrs. Hamilton
Flora . . . . Mrs. Pownall

ness as a music publisher and dealer in music. He had a pleasing and comprehensive voice, and as *Young Meadows* he displayed good sense and modesty united to a perfect knowledge of his profession as a musician. Munto as *Eustace* was manly and pleasing. He was timid, however, and seems to have been without stage experience. Mrs. Solo-

NEW YORK CASTS OF PHILADELPHIA PRODUCTIONS.

ALEXANDER THE GREAT.

Alexander . . . Mr. Hodgkinson
Lysemachus . . . . Mr. Hallam
Clytus . . . . . . Mr. Marriott
Roxana . . . . . Mrs. Melmoth
Statira . . . . . . Mrs. Marriott
Parisatus . . . . . Miss Chaucer

BUSYBODY.

Marplot . . . . . . Mr. Hallam
Sir George Airy . Mr. Hallam, Jr
Sir Francis Gripe . Mr. Prigmore
Charles . . . . . . Mr. Martin
Miranda . . . . . Mrs. Hallam
Patch . . . . . . Mrs. Hamilton

CHILDREN IN THE WOOD.

Walter . . . . . Mr. Hodgkinson
Lord Alford . . . . . Mr. Carr
Sir Rowland . . . . Mr. Marriott
Apathy . . . . . . Mr. Nelson
Gabriel . . . . . . Mr. Martin
Oliver . . . . Mr. Lee
Children, . . . { Miss Harding
{ Miss Solomon
Lady Helen . . . Mrs. Solomon
Josephine . . . Mrs. Hodgkinson
Winifred . . . . Mrs. Hamilton

COUNTRY GIRL.

Moody . . . . Mr. Hodgkinson
Sparkish . . . . . . Mr. Martin
Harcourt . . . . . Mr. Marriott
Belville . . . . Mr. Hallam, Jr
Will . . . . Mr. Miller
Peggy . . . . Mrs. Hodgkinson
Alithea . . . . . . Mrs. Solomon
Lucy . . . . Mrs. Pownall

GAMESTER.

Beverly . . . . Mr. Hodgkinson
Lewson . . . . . . Mr. Marriott
Charlotte . . . . . Mrs. Marriott
Mrs. Beverly . . . Mrs. Melmoth

HAUNTED TOWER.

Lord William . Mr. Hodgkinson
Oatland . . . . . . Mr. King
Edward . . . . . Mr. Martin
Charles . . . . Mr. Carr
Hugo . . . . . . Mr. Richards
De Courcey . . Mr. Hallam, Jr
Robert . . . . . . Mr. Nelson
Lewis . . . . . . Mr. Berwick
Lady Elinor . . . . Mrs. Pownall
Adela . . . . . Mrs. Hodgkinson
Cicely . . . . . Mrs. Solomon
Maud . . . . . . Mrs. Hamilton

HIGHLAND REEL.

Sandy . . . . Mr. Carr

LOVE IN A VILLAGE.

Young Meadows . . . Mr. Carr
Hodge . . . . . . Mr. Hallam
Eustace . . . . . . Mr. Munto
Justice Woodcock . Mr. Prigmore
Sir William Meadows
Mr. Richards
Hawthorn . . . Mr. Hodgkinson
Madge . . . . . Mrs. Pownall
Lucinda . . . . Mrs. Solomon
Deborah . . . . Mrs. Hamilton
Rosetta . . . . Mrs. Hodgkinson

LOVE'S FRAILTIES.

Craig Campbell . . . Mr. Hallam
Muscadel . . . Mr. Hodgkinson
Sir Gregory Oldwit, Mr. Prigmore
Seymour . . . . Mr. Marriott
James . . . . . Mr. Martin
Lady Fancourt . . Mrs. Hallam
Lady Louisa . . . Mrs. Marriott
Paulina . . . . Mrs. Hodgkinson
Nanette . . . . . Mrs. Pownall
Mrs. Wilkins . . . . Mrs. Miller

MACBETH.

Macbeth . . . . Mr. Hodgkinson
Duncan . . . . . Mr. Richards
Macduff . . . . . . Mr. Hallam
Malcolm . . . . . Mr. Martin
Donalbain . . . . . . Mr. Miller
Lenox . . . . Mr. King
Siward . . . . . . Mr. Munto
Fleance . . . . . Miss Harding
Apparition . . . . Miss Solomon
First Assassin . . . . . Mr. Lee
Hecate . . . . Mr. Woolls
First Witch . . . Mrs. Hamilton
Second Witch . . . . Mr. Nelson
Third Witch . . . Mr. Berwick
Lady Macbeth . . Mrs. Melmoth

QUAKER.

Lubin . . . . Mr. Nelson
Steady . . . . Mr. King
Easy . . . . Mr. Ashton
Solomon . . . . Mr. Hodgkinson
Gillian . . . . Mrs. Hodgkinson
Floretta . . . . Mrs. Solomon
Cicely . . . . . . Mrs. Miller

SUCH THINGS ARE.

Sir Luke Tremor . Mr. Prigmore
Zedan . . . . Mr. King
Elvirus . . . . . . Mr. Martin
Lady Tremor . . . Mrs. Pownall
Arabella . . . . . Mrs. Marriott

THREE WEEKS AFTER MAR-RIAGE.

Sir Charles Racket
Mr. Hodgkinson
Drugget . . . . . Mr. Prigmore
Lovelace . . . . . Mr. Martin
Woodley . . . . . . Mr. King
Lady Racket . . . Mrs. Hallam
Mrs. Drugget . . . Mrs. Miller
Nancy . . . . . . Mrs. King
Dimitry . . . . . Mrs. Pownall

mon as *Lucinda* was considered an acquisition. She had been with Harper and Placide's company in Boston in 1792. As Miss Harding was *Fleance*, Miss Solomon the *Apparition* and Mr. Lee the *First Assassin* in " Macbeth," in New York, it is probable they had the same unimportant roles in Philadelphia. Miss Harding was a ward of the Hodgkinsons. That these girls were very young is apparent from a remark of a New York critic when they appeared in the "Children in the Wood" as the *Children*—parts they probably had previously played in Philadelphia. " In speaking, singing and action," he said, " they surpassed all we could have conceived of children of their age." Mr. Lee had previously been a supernumerary at the Chestnut Street Theatre. The younger Hallam was also with the company. As the first piece played in Philadelphia in which his name occurs in the New York casts was the " Country Girl," *Belville* must be accepted as his earliest known part—a role in which it was said he appeared to advantage. Madame Gardie, who had been with Wignell's company for a short time, also joined Hallam and Hodgkinson's forces during their Philadelphia engagement, making her first appearance in the title-role of " Sophia of Brabant." With the exception of Madame Gardie, none of these acquisitions made any decided impression.

Although Mrs. Marriott's " Chimera " was originally played in Philadelphia, it is the New York cast that is given herewith. The two were probably identical. When Mrs. Marriott first advertised her " Chimera," as this piece evidently was, she spoke of it as " an effort of juvenile fancy," and indulged in the twaddle that has shown such

CHIMERA.

———

Lord Aberford	Mr. Prigmore
Captain Rupert	Mr. Marriott
Frolic	Mr. Martin
Miss Martin	Mrs. Hamilton
Matilda	Mrs. Marriott
Dolly	Mrs. Miller

surprising vitality about Americans being supporters of genius, however lowly. She was apparently a young woman of little talent, but great literary ambition. After the play when Mr. Marriott made his *debut* as *Lothario*, on the 29th of September, he recited an ode on the French Revolution, written by his wife. Mrs. Marriott afterward wrote a piece called the " Death of Major André," which she played in the small Virginia towns in 1796. With a single exception, all the new English pieces, which like Mrs. Marriott's " Chimera," were first presented on benefit occasions this season, proved of decided merit and long continued to hold the stage. The exception was Mrs. Parsons' " Intrigues of a Morning," the choice of Ashton and Woolls. Why they chose it is not apparent. It had been acted at Covent Garden in 1792 for the benefit of Mrs. Mattocks, but had met with too little success to warrant expectations of better results here. Holcroft's " Love's Frailties " was also a Covent Garden production, where it succeeded in spite of some opposition excited by its democratic sentiments. These views, apart from its merits as a play, helped its popularity in the leading American cities, and for some years it was often played. Mrs. Pownall as *Nanette* was the feature of its first production in this country. The performance of Garrick's " Country Girl " at this time was due, no doubt, to Mrs. Jordan's popularity as *Peggy* in England. Hodgkinson made a great success as *Moody*, and Mrs. Hodgkinson as *Peggy* was admirable in the letter scene. The latest *Peggy* on our stage is Miss Ada Rehan. Thomas Morton's " Children in the Wood," the music by Dr. Arnold, found a welcome here almost equal to that accorded it at the Haymarket in 1793. Hodgkinson's *Walter* was scarcely inferior to Bannister's. Morton was brought forward on the American stage by Mr. Carr; but Mr.

Hodgkinson's introduction of another new English dramatist, Cobb, by the production of the " Haunted Tower," was even more happy. In the composition of this work, Mr. Cobb had the assistance of the celebrated Stephen Storace, the composer, their joint work being the first real attempt at English opera.   Instead of single airs and duets to relieve the dialogue, customary in English musical pieces, the story of the " Haunted Tower" was told in music, and the success of the opera was extraordinary.   It ran for sixty nights during its first season at Drury Lane in 1789.   Its popularity in this country was very great also, but, for obvious reasons, not equal to its English reception.

From Philadelphia the Old American Company made its way to New York for the Winter season of 1794–5, carrying with it the additions to the force that had been previously introduced to the public at the Southwark Theatre. These comprised for the opening night, the 15th of December, 1794, Carr as *Young Meadows*, Munto as *Eustace*, and Mrs. Solomon as *Lucinda* in " Love in a Village." The same evening Miss Chaucer, who seems to have been a more recent acquisition, made her first appearance as *Miss Godfrey* in the " Lyar." She was a young lady of pleasing figure, and her voice was described as low, but not without melody.   Before the

LIST OF PERFORMANCES.—*New York.*

1794.

Dec. 15—Love in a Village. . . Bickerstaff
       Lyar . . . . Foote
     17—Venice Preserved . . . . Otway
       Highland Reel . . . . O'Keefe
     19—Such Things Are . Mrs. Inchbald
       Sophia of Brabant.
     22—Country Girl . . . . . . Garrick
       True-Born Irishman . . Macklin
     24—Carmelite . . . . . Cumberland
       Quaker . . . . Dibdin
     26—School for Wives . . . . . Kelly
       Children in the Wood . . Morton
     29—Dramatist . . . . . . Reynolds
       Sophia of Brabant.
     31—Robin Hood . . . . MacNally
       Midnight Hour . . Mrs. Inchbald
1795.
Jan. 1—Alexander the Great . . . . Lee
       Harlequin Animation.
      2—Country Girl.
       Children in the Wood.
      5—Percy . . . . . . Miss More
       Quaker.

play Mr. Hodgkinson addressed the audience in his new capacity as manager, promising to suppress the insults that the gallery considered itself privileged to bestow on every other part of the house, especially upon the gentlemen who composed the orchestra. The gallery element at this period was exceedingly disorderly everywhere. In Boston, as we have seen, it was necessary for the orchestra to make a public appeal for more considerate treatment. In Philadelphia even the vigilance of Mr. Reinagle could not always prevent disturbances in the gallery or protect the audience and the orchestra from insult. All this was a part of the rudeness of the time—a condition that has entirely passed away in our places of amusement. On the second night of the season Mr. Marriott was brought forward as *Pierre* in " Venice Preserved," in which he failed, and was condemned in the newspapers. One of Marriott's

Jan. 7—Haunted Tower . . . . . Cobb
Midnight Hour.
9—Haunted Tower.
Midnight Hour.
10—I'll Tell You What . Mrs. Inchbald
Children in the Wood.
12—Haunted Tower.
Bold Stroke for a Wife
Mrs. Centlivre
14—Macbeth . . . . . . Shakspere
Romp . . . . Bickerstaff
16—Love's Frailties . . . . Holcroft
Sophia of Brabant.
19—Notoriety . . . . . . Reynolds
Children in the Wood.
21—Mahomet . . . . Miller
Agreeable Surprise . . . O'Keefe
23—Bold Stroke for a Husband
Mrs. Cowley
Danaides . . Quenet and Pelisier
26—Love's Frailties.
No Song No Supper . . . Hoare
28—Child of Nature . Mrs. Inchbald
Two Philosophers.
Children in the Wood.
31—Every One Has His Fault
Mrs. Inchbald
Harlequin Animation.
Feb. 2—Haunted Tower.
Sultan . . . . Bickerstaff
4—Young Quaker . . . . . O'Keefe
Highland Reel.
6—Belle's Stratagem . Mrs. Cowley
Don Juan.
9—Child of Nature.
Two Philosophers.
Children in the Wood.
11—Isabella . . . . Southerne
Prize . . . . Hoare
13—Every One Has His Fault.
Children in the Wood.
16—Fontainville Abbey . . . Dunlap
18—Wild Oats . . . . . . O'Keefe
Prize.
20—Child of Nature.
Intrigues of a Morning, Mrs. Parsons
Romp.

Feb. 23—Fontainville Abbey.
   Purse . . . . Cross
  25—Jew . . . . Cumberland
   Rival Candidates . . . . . Bate
  28—Romeo and Juliet . . Shakspere
   Padlock . . . . . . Bickerstaff
Mar. 2—Gamester . . . . Moore
   Purse.
  4—Jew.
   Purse.
  6—Battle of Hexham . . Colman, Jr
   Purse.
  9—Fontainville Abbey.
   Two Philosophers.
   Deaf Lover . . . . . . Pilon
  11—Grecian Daughter . . . Murphy
   Spoiled Child . . . Bickerstaff
  13—How to Grow Rich . . Reynolds
   Tammany . . . Mrs. Hatton
  16—Heigh-ho for a Husband, Waldron
   Highland Reel.
  18—Haunted Tower.
   Deaf Lover.
  20—Every One Has His Fault.
   Le Foret Noire.
  21—George Barnwell . . . . . Lillo
   Spoiled Child.
  23—Jew.
   Purse.
  25—School for Scandal . . . Sheridan
   Village Lawyer . . . Macready
  27—Lear . . . . Shakspere
   Three Weeks after Marriage
          Murphy
  30—Lear.
   Le Foret Noire.
April 6—Tempest . . . . Dryden
   Purse.
  7—Fair Penitent . . . . . . Rowe
   Poor Jack.
   Rosina . . . . . Mrs. Brooke
  10—World in a Village . . . O'Keefe
   Le Foret Noire.
  13—Fatal Deception . . . . Dunlap
   Le Foret Noire.
  15—Duenna . . . . Sheridan
   Busybody . . . . Mrs. Centlivre

critics said that a certain part of the audience applauded him; whether they were the same who laughed at the distresses of *Jaffier* and *Belvidera*, the critic was unable to say. Mrs. Marriott made her New York *debut* on the third night as *Arabella* in "Such Things Are." She was greatly frightened, probably in consequence of her husband's failure the previous evening. The same night Madame Gardie, who became a great favorite, captivated New York in the title-role of the pantomime, "Sophia of Brabant." There could be no greater contrast than the treatment of these ladies by the New York critics. When, later in the season, Mrs. Marriott presented her farce "Chimera" for her benefit, an unfeeling censor said that the farce was unequalled by anything except its own prologue, and the prologue unrivalled by anything except the farce. On the occasion of Madame Gardie's appearance in "Jeanne d'Arc" for her benefit, the same writer declared that, though often seen with delight, she was now heard for the first time, and heard with much pleasure. The other introductions followed in quick succession. The younger Hallam appeared as *Belville* in the "Country Girl" on the 22d of December; Mr. Nelson as *Lubin* in the "Quaker" on the 24th; and Mr. Lee as *Oliver*, and the Misses Harding and Solomon as the *Children* in the "Children in the Wood," on the 26th. The production of "Mahomet," on the 21st of January, 1795, served for the *debut* of another new actor in the title-role—Mr. Fawcett. According to a writer in the *New York Magazine*, Mr. Fawcett never before appeared on any stage; but this is contradicted by a tradition in the Fawcett family, Owen Fawcett, the comedian, having been told by his father that John Fawcett, his father's uncle, had previously played in English provincial theatres. At the time of his *debut*

April 17—Young Quaker.
    Children in the Wood.
  20—School for Greybeards, Mrs. Cowley
    Shelty's Travels . . . . Dunlap
    No Song No Supper.
    (Mr. Hodgkinson's benefit.)
  22—Highland Reel.
    Poor Jack.
    Children in the Wood.
    (Mr. Carr's benefit.)
  24—Know Your Own Mind . Murphy
    Purse.
    (Mrs. Hodgkinson's benefit.)
  27—Natural Son . . . . Cumberland
    Selima and Azor . . . . Collier
    (Mrs. Hallam's benefit.)
  29—Heigh-ho for a Husband.
    Double Disguise . . . Mrs. Hook
    (Mrs. Pownall's benefit.)
May 2—Zenobia . . . . Murphy
    Children in the Wood.
    (Mrs. Melmoth's benefit.)
   4—School for Greybeards.
    Jeanne d'Arc.
    (Madame Gardie's benefit.)
   7—Which is the Man ? . Mrs. Cowley
    Deserter . . . . Dibdin
    (Mr. Hallam's benefit.)
   9—Richard III . . . . . Shakspere
    Farm House . . . . . Kemble
    (Mrs. King's benefit.)
  11—Know Your Own Mind.
    Edgar and Emmeline, Hawksworth
    (Mr. Martin's benefit.)
  14—Robbers . . . . Schiller
    (Mr. Marriott's benefit.)
  16—Carmelite.
    Beggar's Opera.
    (Mr. Richards' benefit.)
  18—Which is the Man ?
    Edgar and Emmeline.
    (Mr. Woolls' benefit.)
  20—Chapter of Accidents . . Miss Lee
    Deserter.
    (Mrs. Hamilton's benefit.)

May 22—Earl of Essex . . . . . . Jones
Chimera . . . . . Mrs. Marriott
(Mrs. Marriott's benefit.)
25—Rage . . . . Reynolds
Agreeable Surprise.
(Mr. Hallam, Jr.'s, benefit.)
27—Zenobia.
Don Juan.
(Mr. Nelson's benefit.)
29—Rage.
Jack in Distress.
Modern Antiques . . . O'Keefe
(Mr. Faulkner's benefit.)
June 1—Critic . . . . Sheridan
Irishman in London . . Macready
Florizel and Perdita . . Shakspere
(Mr. Fawcett's benefit.)
3—Inconstant . . . . . . Farquhar
Authoress . . . . Reed
Children in the Wood.
(Mrs. Miller and Miss Harding's benefit.)
5—He Would be a Soldier . . Pilon
Gentle Shepherd . . . . Ramsay
(Mr. King's benefit.)
8—Road to Ruin . . . . . Holcroft
Demolition of the Bastile.
(Mr. Prigmore's benefit.)
10—Douglas . . . . Home
Prize.
(Benefit of eight performers.)
12—Inconstant.
Love a la Mode . . . . Macklin
(Lee and Berwick's benefit.)
15—Recruiting Officer . . . Farquhar
Lyar.
(Mr. Munto's benefit.)
18—English Merchant . . . Colman
Critic.
(Benefit of Humphrey and Ryan's family.)
20—Seduction . . . . . . Holcroft
Old Soldier.
As It Should Be . . . . Oulton
(Mr. Ashton's benefit.)
23—Try Again.
Tyranny Suppressed.
No Song No Supper.
(Mrs. Marriott's benefit.)

Fawcett was too young in appearance to be the father of *Zaphna* and *Palmira*, as played by Hodgkinson and Mrs. Melmoth; but, as a first appearance, his effort was pronounced very creditable to his talents, and it was said that in a younger part he would appear to greater advantage. He made his second appearance as *Saville* in the "Belle's Stratagem," but, unfortunately, did not know his lines. In person he was handsome; his action and walk were good, and his voice was full and harmonious, but his articulation was sometimes faulty. Mrs. Spencer made her *debut* as *Juliet* on the 28th of February, but made no impression. She afterward appeared as *Lady Henrietta* in "How to Grow Rich" and as *Maria* in "Heigh-ho for a Husband," and then disappeared. Finally, Mrs. Munto appeared as *Sylvia* in the "Recruiting Officer" for her husband's benefit, but the critics declined to praise her.

The repertory of the season

was a remarkable one, and in many ways, including, as it did, numerous revivals, the production of the new pieces previously presented by the company in Phila-

June 25—Young Quaker.
　　Demolition of the Bastile.
　　(Mr. and Mrs. King's benefit.)
　27—School for Soldiers . . . . Henry
　　Children in the Wood.
　　(Mr. Hallam's benefit.)

delphia, the initial performance in New York of a number of new comedies, operas and pantomimes, and the first production of another

FONTAINVILLE ABBEY.

La Motte . . . . Mr. Hodgkinson
Marquis . . . . Mr. King
Peter . . . . Mr. Prigmore
Madame La Motte . . . . . Mrs. Melmoth
Adeline . . . . Mrs. Hodgkinson

so-called tragedy from the pen of the prolific Dunlap—"Fontainville Abbey." Dunlap's play was based on Mrs. Radcliff's "Romance of the Forest," but it was announced

for production without any allusion to the name or nationality of the dramatist. In view of this suppression the *New York Magazine* asked whether the author believed that an avowal of his work would operate against it, and Dunlap afterward said not only that he thought so, but that such an avowal at that time would have been enough to condemn the piece. He adds that the writers of the day praised it in good set terms, and dismisses it with the remark that after a few repetitions his second tragedy was allowed to sleep with its predecessor. Dunlap, the historian, treated Dunlap, the playwright, very tenderly. As a matter of fact, the piece was repeated only twice, and most of the praise was bestowed on the actors. This praise in itself showed what would now be thought the faults of the play. Mrs. Hodgkinson, it was said, related the narrative of *Adeline's* story admirably, and for reading the scroll she was warmly commended. Besides it was said that Hodgkinson and Mrs. Melmoth were excellent just before and after the appearance of the *Marquis;* that Mr. Richards drew a burst of applause to the honest and simple *Peter*, and that Mr. King's acting in the last act was a treat. When the piece was played the second time, Mr. King was ill, and Mr. Fawcett read his part. The play did not go well, and was not again attempted except for the author's night.

Many of the pieces produced during the season that were new to New York had already been presented either in Philadelphia or Baltimore by Wignell and Reinagle's company. These comprised some pieces of which the casts have already been given—" Robin Hood," the " Country Girl" and the " Haunted Tower." The others included, besides those of which the casts are appended, Madame Gardie's opera " Jeanne d'Arc." As *Lucille* in " Le Foret Noire," Madame Gardie was pronounced wonderful, and Miss Harding as

FIRST NEW YORK PRODUCTIONS—CASTS.

FARM HOUSE.

Modely . . . . . Mr. Hallam, Jr
Heartwell . . . . . . Mr. Martin
Freehold . . . . . Mr. Marriott
Shacklefigure . . . . Mr. Woolls
Flora . . . . Mrs. King
Aura . . . . Mrs Marriott

JEW.

Sheva . . . . . Mr. Hodgkinson
Sir Stephen Bertram, Mr. Richards
Frederick Bertram . Mr. Fawcett
Charles Ratcliff . . . Mr. Martin
Jabal . . . . Mr. Hallam
Saunders . . . . . . Mr. Ashton
Eliza Ratcliff . . . Mrs. Hallam
Mrs. Ratcliff . . Mrs. Hamilton
Dorcas . . . . . . Mrs. Miller
Mrs. Goodison . . Miss Chaucer

LE FORET NOIRE.

La Terreur . . Mr. Hodgkinson
Geronte . . . . . Mr. Hallam
Lauridan . . . . . . Mr. King
Abbe . . . . Mr. Martin
Peasant . . . . . . Mr. Woolls
Adolphus . . . . . Miss Harding
Lucille . . . . . Madame Gardie
Confidante . . . Mrs. Hamilton

MODERN ANTIQUES.

Cockletop . . . . Mr. Prigmore
Frank . . . . Mr. Martin
Joey . . . . Mr. Hallam
Napkin . . . . . . Mr. Ashton
Hearty . . . . Mr. Munto
Mrs. Cockletop . Mrs. Hamilton
Belinda . . . . . Mrs. Marriott
Mrs. Camomile . . Mrs. Wilson
Nan . . . . Mrs. Miller
Flounce . . . . . . Mrs. King

NATURAL SON.

Sir Jeffrey Latimer, Mr. Richards
Blushenly . . . Mr. Hodgkinson
Maj. O'Flaherty . . . Mr. King
Jack Hastings . . . Mr. Hallam
Rueful . . . . . Mr. Marriott
Dumps . . . . . Mr. Prigmore
Lady Paragon . . . Mrs. Hallam
Phœbe Latimer . Mrs. Hamilton
Penelope . . . . . Miss Chaucer

POOR JACK.

Poor Jack . . . . . Mr. Durang
Ben Bobstay . . . . Mr. Munto
Landlady . . . . . . Mr. Lee
Orange Girl . . Madame Gardie

PRIZE.

Dr. Lenitive . . Mr. Hodgkinson
Heartwell . . . Mr. Hallam, Jr
Caddy . . . . Mr. Ashton
Label . . . . Mr. Martin
Juba . . . . Mr. Carr
Mrs. Caddy . . . . Mrs. Miller
Caroline . . . . . Mrs. Pownall

SPOILED CHILD.

Little Pickle . . . Miss Harding
Old Pickle . . . . Mr. Prigmore
Tag . . . . Mr. Martin
John . . . . Mr. Lee
Thomas . . . . . . Mr. Durang
Maria . . . . . . Miss Chaucer
Miss Pickle . . . Mrs. Hamilton
Susan . . . . . . Mrs. Wilson
Margery . . . . . . Mrs. Miller

TRIUMPH OF MIRTH.

Harlequin . . . . . . Mr. Martin
Clown . . . . . Mr. Hodgkinson
Pantaloon . . . . . Mr. Ashton
Lover . . . . . . Mr. Durang
Gladiator . . . . . . Mr. King
Mirth . . . . . . Mrs. Solomon
Pantalina . . . Mrs. Hamilton
Columbine . . . Madame Gardie

Adolphus was charming. Mr. Carr as *Juba* in the "Prize" was "better than ever before." The first production of the "Jew" was marked by a scandal that resulted in the temporary withdrawal of Mrs. Hallam. While playing *Eliza Ratcliff*, she exhibited many of the incoherencies of intoxication. Hallam attributed her conduct to opium. Her behavior shocked her friends and disgusted the audience. In view of all this, her appearance for a time became impossible. Her sequestration, however, was for only a brief period, as a month later she played *Cordelia* in "Lear," and probably repeated her unfortunate role in the "Jew." This was the beginning of her decline.

When Dunlap's "Fontainville Abbey" was played the second time, a little musical drama called the "Purse," by Mr. Cross, of Covent Garden Theatre, was added as an afterpiece. This was the

NEW PRODUCTIONS—ORIGINAL CASTS.

DEMOLITION OF THE BASTILE.

Mereau de St. Merry	Mr. Hodgkinson
La Braint	Mr. Hallam
Henry Dubois	Mr. King
De Lany	Mr. Fawcett
Leontine	Mr. Martin
Sophia	Mrs. Wilson
Matilda	Mrs. Pownall

HEIGH-HO FOR A HUSBAND.

Justice Rackrent .	Mr. Prigmore
Timothy	Mr. Hallam
Frank	Mr. Martin
Squire Edward .	Mr. Hallam, Jr
General Fairlove .	Mr Marriott
Maria	Mrs. Spencer
Charlotte · . . .	Mrs. Marriott
Dorothy	Mrs. Pownall
Mrs. Millclack . . .	Mrs. Miller

PURSE.

Will Steady . .	Mr. Hodgkinson
Baron	Mr. Richards
Edmund	Mr. Carr
Theodore	Mr. Fawcett
Page	Miss Harding
Sally	Mrs. Hodgkinson

RAGE.

Gingham . . .	Mr. Hodgkinson
Darnley	Mr. Hallam
Hon. Mr. Savage,	Mr. Hallam, Jr
Sir Paul Perpetual .	Mr. Prigmore
Sir George Gauntlet,	Mr. Marriott
Flush	Mr. Richards
Signor Cygnet . . .	Mr. Martin
Ready	Mr. Munto
Mrs. Darnley . .	Mrs. Melmoth
Hon. Mrs. Savage .	Mrs. Wilson
Clara Sedley . . .	Mrs. Marriott

SCHOOL FOR GREYBEARDS.

Don Henry . .	Mr. Hodgkinson
Don Alexis	Mr. Hallam
Don Gaspar . . .	Mr. Prigmore
Don Octavio . . .	Mr. Martin
Don Sebastian .	Mr. Hallam, Jr
Peter	Mr. Ashton
Antonia	Mrs. Hodgkinson
Seraphina	Mrs. Hallam
Rachel	Mrs. Pownall
Viola	Mrs. Marriott
Clara	Mrs. King
Carlotta	Mrs. Miller

TRY AGAIN.

Sidney	Mr. Martin
Du Cheone	Mr. Marriott
Antoine	Mr. Berwick
Picard	Mr. Munto
Le Fourbe	Mr. Prigmore
Lauretta	Mrs. Marriott
Rosalie	Mrs. Hallam
Marinette	Mrs. Miller

TYRANNY SUPPRESSED.

Captain Douglass .	Mr. Prigmore
Terizabes	Mr. Martin
Mrs. Douglass . .	Mrs. Marriott
Mellamor	Madame Gardie

ZENOBIA.

Rhadamistus . .	Mr. Hodgkinson
Pharasmanes	Mr. King
Teribazus	Mr. Fawcett
Megistus	Mr. Richards
Tigranes	Mr. Marriott
Zepiron	Mr. Ashton
Zenobia	Mrs. Melmoth
Zelmira	Mrs. Marriott
Ariadne	Mrs. Wilson
Irene	Miss Chaucer

first of the new English pieces to have its initial production in America this season. It was an interesting little piece, and long continued to hold the stage. This and Waldron's comedy, "Heigh-ho for a Husband," were the only productions of this character brought forward during the regular season. The comedy was a sort of counterpart of Farquhar's "Beaux' Stratagem." The two giddy girls, *Charlotte* and *Maria*, were the reverses of *Archer* and *Aimwell;* the landlady, *Mrs. Millclack*, was the female *Boniface;* her son, *Frank*, was the alternate for *Cherry*, and so on. That it was unequal to the original, goes without the saying; but the dialogue was sprightly, and the comedy entertaining. For his benefit Mr. Hodgkinson offered Mrs. Cowley's "School for Greybeards." This comedy was borrowed, to some extent, from Mrs. Behn's "Lucky Chance;" but it had none of the indecencies of the older play, although, like Mrs. Behn's comedy, Mrs. Cowley's was disapproved on its first production at Drury Lane by the goody-good with a nose at an inuendo. Mrs. Melmoth presented Murphy's tragedy, "Zenobia," in which Mrs. Dancer, afterward Mrs. Crawford, was the London heroine. Then came Mr. Marriott with an English translation of Schiller's "Robbers," to which the company was pronounced unequal. The cast was not preserved. Young Hallam had a new piece in his bill, the "Rage" by Reynolds. Mr. Reynolds' comedy had been produced at Covent Garden in 1794. It was played in London with success, but was pronounced by the New York critics unequal to the author's previous works. Mr. Prigmore, as a fresh proof of his political principles, produced an afterpiece called the "Demolition of the Bastile;" and for a second attempt, at a benefit, Mrs. Marriott presented an English anonymous farce called "Try Again," and a new pantomime, "Tyranny Suppressed." It is easy to understand that Mrs. Marriott chose her farce for its name. The others, whatever their origin, were mere theatrical contributions to the French partisanship of the period. Mr. Ashton's production, Holcroft's comedy, "Seduction," was a good piece in spite of its name.

A number of pieces was presented during the season of 1794-5, either for the first time since the reorganization of the Old American Company or with first casts, as shown by existing theatrical records. These are given on the next page in alphabetical order. The "Authoress," which leads the list, was merely a scene from the "Register Office." The "Benevolent Merchant" was the elder Colman's "English Merchant." Sheridan's two pieces, the "Critic" and the "Duenna," and Dibdin's "Deserter," were all familiar. The little musical piece "Edgar and Emmeline" had not been revived since the Revolution. Garrick's adaptation of the sheap-shearing scene from the "Winter's Tale," known as "Florizel and Perdita," was in the repertory of the American Company in Jamaica, but it was first played in the United States by the Kenna family. Tickell's version of Ramsay's "Gentle Shepherd" had been presented by Hallam and Henry in Philadelphia in 1791. Apparently, "George Barnwell" was revived to allow Martin to play the title-role, and to afford Mrs. Marriott an opportunity to satisfy her ambition as *Millwood*. Hodgkinson as *Young Mirabel* could not fail to make the revival of the "Inconstant" acceptable. Murphy's "Know Your Own Mind" had never been played except by the Virginia Comedians in 1790. Hallam's *Lear* was complimented by a New York critic as in his very best manner, but Miss Harding was pronounced not quite equal to *Ariel* in the "Tempest."" In the latter Mr. Marriott only read the part of *Prospero*, Mr. Hallam being ill. Notwithstanding it was a favorite stock piece in England, Mrs.

Cowley's "Which is the Man?" had only been played by the Kenna troupe at the theatre in the Northern Liberties, Philadelphia.

A LIST OF REVIVALS—CASTS.

AUTHORESS.

Gulwell . . . . . . Mr. Ashton
Mrs. Doggerell . . . Mrs. Miller
Melpomene . . . . Miss Harding

BENEVOLENT MERCHANT.

Freeport . . . . Mr. Hodgkinson
Lord Falbridge . . . Mr. Martin
Sir William Douglas
            Mr. Richards
Spatter . . . . . . Mr. Prigmore
Owen . . . . Mr. Woolls
Tripwell . . . . . . Mr. Munto
Lady Alton . . . Mrs. Melmoth
Amelia . . . . . Mrs. Hallam
Molly . . . . . . Mrs. Pownall
Mrs. Goodman . . Mrs. Hamilton

CRITIC.

Puff . . . . . Mr. Hodgkinson
Sir Fretful . . . . Mr. Prigmore
Dangle . . . . . . Mr. King
Leicester . . . . Mr. Richards
Raleigh . . . . . . Mr. Munto
Don Whiskerandos . Mr. Martin
Sneer . . . . . . Mr. Fawcett
Prompter . . . Mr. Humphreys
Governor . . . . . Mr. Woolls
Mrs. Dangle . . . Mrs. Hamilton
Tilburina . . . . . Mrs. Miller

DESERTER.

Skirmish . . . . . . Mr. Hallam
Henry . . . . Mr. Hodgkinson
Louisa . . . . Mrs. Hodgkinson
Jenny . . . . . . Mrs. Pownall

DUENNA.

Don Jerome . . . Mr. Richards
Ferdinand . . . Mr. Hodgkinson
Carlos . . . . . . Mr. Nelson
Antonio . . . . Mr. Carr
Father Paul . . . . . Mr. King
Isaac Mendoza . . Mr. Prigmore
Lopez . . . . Mr. Martin
Clara . . . . Mrs. Hodgkinson
Louisa . . . . . . Mrs. Pownall
Margaret . . . . . Mrs. Miller

EDGAR AND EMMELINE.

Edgar . . . . . Mr. Hodgkinson
Florimund . . . . . Mr. Martin
Elfina . . . . . . Miss Harding
Emmeline . . . . Mrs. Marriott

FLORIZEL AND PERDITA.

Florizel . . . . . . Mr. Fawcett
Polixenes . . . . . Mr. Richards
Antigonus . . . . . Mr. Marriott
Autolycus . . . M:. Hodgkinson
Camillo . . . . . . Mr. Munto
Clown . . . . . . Mr. Durang
Perdita . . . . . Mrs. Marriott
Mopsa . . . . . Mrs. Wilson
Dorcas . . . . . . Mrs. Miller
Shepherdess . . Madame Gardie

GENTLE SHEPHERD.

Patie . . . . Mr. Carr
Roger . . . . . . Mr. Martin
Bauldy . . . . Mr. Hodgkinson
Worthy . . . . . Mr. Richards
Glaud . . . . . Mr. Prigmore
Symon . . . . . . Mr. Nelson
Peggy . . . . . . Mrs. Pownall
Jenny . . . . . . Mrs. Wilson
Mause . . . . . . Mrs. Miller
Elspa . . . . . . Mrs. Hamilton

GEORGE BARNWELL.

George Barnwell . . Mr. Martin
Millwood . . . . . Mrs. Marriott

INCONSTANT.

Young Mirabel . Mr. Hodgkinson
Old Mirabel . . . Mr. Prigmore
Duretete . . . . . Mr. Hallam
Dugard . . . . . Mr. Fawcett
Petit . . . . Mr. Martin
Bravo . . . . . Mr. Ashton
Page . . . . . . Miss Harding
Bisarre . . . . Mrs. Melmoth
Oriana . . . . Mrs. Marriott
Lamorce . . . . . Mrs. Wilson

KNOW YOUR OWN MIND.

Dashwould . . Mr. Hodgkinson
Millamour . . . Mr. Hallam, Jr
Sir John Millamour . Mr. Richards
Bygrove . . . . . Mr. Prigmore
Captain Bygrove . . Mr. Fawcett
Malvil . . . . . . Mr. Marriott
Sir Harry Lovewit . Mr. Martin
Charles . . . . Mr. King
Robert . . . . . . Mr. Munto
Lady Bell . . Mrs. Hodgkinson
Lady Jane . . . . Mrs. Marriott
Miss Neville . . . Mrs. Hallam
Mrs. Bromley . . Mrs. Hamilton
Mad. Larouge . . Mrs. Pownall

LEAR.

Lear . . . . Mr. Hallam
Edgar . . . . . Mr. Hodgkinson
Edmund . . . . Mr. Hallam, Jr
Kent . . . . Mr. Prigmore
Gloster . . . . . Mr. Richards
Albany . . . . . Mr. Marriott
Cornwall . . . . . Mr. Fawcett
Burgundy . . . . . Mr. Ashton
Usher . . . . Mr. Martin
Peasant . . . . . . Mr. Woolls
Cordelia . . . . Mrs. Hallam
Regan . . . . . . Mrs. Marriott
Goneril . . . . Mrs. Hamilton
Aranthe . . . . Miss Chaucer

TEMPEST.

Prospero . . . . . Mr. Marriott
Ariel . . . . . . Miss Harding

WHICH IS THE MAN?

Beauchamp . . Mr. Hodgkinson
Lord Sparkle . . Mr. Hallam, Jr
Bobby Pendragon . Mr. Hallam
Fitzherbert . . . . Mr. Richards
Belville . . . . . . Mr. Martin
Tom . . . . Mr. Durang
Lady Bell Bloomer . Mrs. Hallam
Sophy Pendragon
            Mrs. Hodgkinson
Julia . . . . . . Mrs. Marriott
Kitty . . . . . . Mrs. Pownall
Clarinda . . . Mrs. Hamilton
Mrs. Johnson . . . . Mrs. Miller

Among the pieces revived during the season, of which the casts were previously given, there was a number in which there were changes worthy of mention. It is only necessary to indicate these. In giving them, an opportunity is afforded for reproducing some of the criticism of the season. Speaking of the " Belle's Stratagem," on the occasion of Mr. Fawcett's appearance as *Saville*, it was said of Mrs. Hodgkinson's *Letitia Hardy* that it was "equal to the wishes of her warmest admirers." In " Every One Has His Fault " Miss Harding's little *Edward* was pronounced "truly charming." Mrs. Marriott played *Miss Wooburn* only once, on account of the illness of Mrs. Hallam. In the " Highland Reel " Mr. Carr made a " great deal of the little part of *Sandy;*" Munto's *Captain Dash* " did him credit," and Mrs.

CONTRASTED CASTS—CHANGES.

PLAYS.	1794-5.	1792-4.	PLAYS.	1794-5.	1792-4.
Belle's Stratagem.			*Midnight Hour.*		
Saville	Mr. Fawcett		Marquis	Mr. Hallam, Jr.	Mr. Hodgkinson
			Nicholas	Mr. Hallam	Mr. Prigmore
Children in the Wood.			Julia	Mrs. Marriott	Mrs. Wilson
Lord Alford	Mr. King	Mr. Carr			
Lady Elinor	Mrs. Melmoth	Mrs. Solomon	*Richard III.*		
			Richmond	Mr. King	Mr. Hallam
Every One Has His Fault.			Prince	Miss Harding	Mr. Martin
Harmony	Mr. Richards	Mr. Ashton			
Edward	Miss Harding	Young Gentleman	*Rival Candidates.*		
Miss Wooburn	Mrs. Marriott	Mrs. Hallam	Gen. Worry	Mr. Richards	Mr. Henry
			Jenny	Mrs. Pownall	Mrs. Rankin
He Would be a Soldier.					
Capt. Crevalt	Mr. King	Mr. Hodgkinson	*Robin Hood.*		
Harriet	Mrs. King	Miss Tuke	Clorinda	Mrs. Pownall	Mrs. Hodgkinson
Highland Reel.			*Romeo and Juliet.*		
Sandy	Mr. Carr	Mr. Bergman	Mercutio	Mr. Hallam	
Capt. Dash	Mr. Munto	Mr. Hammond	Juliet	Mrs. Spencer	
How to Grow Rich.			*Romp.*		
Lady Henrietta	Mrs. Spencer	Mrs. Hallam	Watty	Mr. Martin	Mr. Prigmore
Irishman in London.			*School for Scandal.*		
Delany	Mr. Richards	Mr. Henry	Lady Teazle	Mrs. Hallam	
Isabella.			*Such Things Are.*		
Villeroy	Mr. Fawcett	Mr. Hallam	Sir Luke	Mr. Richards	Mr. Prigmore
Carlos	Mr. Hallam, Jr.	Mr. King	Lady Tremor	Mrs. Pownall	Mrs. Kenna
			Arabella	Mrs. Marriott	
Lyar.			*Venice Preserved.*		
Papillion	Mr. Martin		Pierre	Mr. Marriott	Mr. Hallam
Miss Godfrey	Miss Chaucer		Prinli	Mr. Richards	Mr. King

Hallam's *Jenny* was delightful, even without the songs. The scene where she dances round the *Captain*, one critic declared, was charming, and he hoped she would never withdraw her very pleasing figure and acting from it. In "Robin Hood" Mrs. Pownall was said to be entirely out of place as *Clorinda*—one of the instances in which she was adversely criticised. Martin played *Young Cockney* in the "Romp" once or twice, because of the illness of Prigmore, and Richards read the part of *Sir Luke* in "Such Things Are" for the same reason, taking the words from the prompter instead of the book. This was a practice to which one of the critics strenuously objected. What was called reading a part was of frequent occurrence; but these substitutes were not the only actors who were complained of as imperfect in the words. Fawcett, as we have seen, attempted *Saville* without knowing the lines; and when Dunlap's "Fontainville Abbey" was played the last time, Mrs. Hodgkinson was the only performer who had full possession of the words. The deductions from all this are obvious. It may be doubted whether Dunlap's play would have succeeded had it been well played. There was no tenderness toward American plays or playwrights. When Mrs. Hatton's opera was revived this season, it was asked, "Why is that wretched thing 'Tammany' again brought forward?" The revival of Mr. Henry's "School for Soldiers" also led a critic to remark that the author was a better actor than dramatist. This unfriendly spirit was not unjust in these particular cases, but it was disastrous in its consequences.

Early in the season Mr. Ryan, the prompter, died, as is shown by the fact that what would have been his benefit was divided between his children, and Mr. Humphrey, his successor. Mr. Ryan had been with the company since its return from Jamaica, serving as prompter and occasionally playing small roles until his death. During the period between the secession of Wignell and the accession of Henry's recruits, he was very active on the stage, as his list of parts at the close of that epoch shows. After the reorganization of the company he appeared less frequently, but he was still sometimes made useful in small parts. Ryan played with the Hartford contingent in 1794, as will be told hereafter. The vacancy caused by Ryan's death was not the only change either at its close or during the

MR. RYAN'S PARTS.

Plays.

Child of Nature	Seville
Dramatist	Peter
He Would be a Soldier	Amber
Julius Cæsar	Matellus Cimba
Midnight Hour	Ambrose
Road to Ruin	Jacob
Wedding	Toupee

Operas and Farces.

Agreeable Surprise	Cordon
Farmer	Flummery
Harlequin Fisherman	Clown
King of the Genii	Pantaloon
Look before You Leap	Lawyer
No Song No Supper	Thomas
World in a Village	Van Sluisen

season. Mrs. Solomon and her daughter, Miss Solomon, remained with the company only a short time. Mrs. Spencer and Miss Chaucer failed to establish a permanent connection with the New York theatre. Carr retired from the stage, and Fawcett and Nelson joined West's company in the South.

When the Old American Company was next seen in New York, it was reorganized and greatly strengthened.

CHAPTER VII.

WIGNELL'S FIRST COMPANY.

IMPORTANT ENGAGEMENTS—MISS GEORGE—MR. FENNELL—MR. CHALMERS —MR. AND MRS. WHITLOCK — MR. AND MRS. MARSHALL—MRS. WARRELL—MR. DARLEY—MISS BROADHURST—MR. BATES—MR. AND MRS. FRANCIS—THE ROWSONS—OTHER ENGAGEMENTS.

UNLIKE Mr. Henry, who showed great energy in engaging recruits in England, Mr. Wignell was singularly slow in selecting his company. As early as the 4th of January, 1792, the London *Gazetteer* announced that the manager of the Philadelphia Theatre, who was then in London, had contracted with the master of an American vessel to carry out his kings and queens with all their equipages, regalia and servants at so much per household. A year later it was said that Wignell and his dramatic corps had arrived in New York in December, and this was followed by the astounding statement that the theatre just finished in Philadelphia, which had been opened with the play of "Brutus," from the French of Voltaire, translated by Mr. Smith, of Marianne College, was capable of seating ten thousand persons. Finally, on the 22d of May, 1793, came a paragraph in which Mrs. Melmoth, the once intimate friend of Courtney Melmoth, Chalmers, the late *Harlequin* of Covent Garden, Miss George, Fennell and Miss Broadhurst were mentioned as having been engaged by Wignell for his new theatre. At that time Mrs. Melmoth was already in America, but without an engagement. The others, however, had really been engaged by Wignell, and, with still others almost equally important, they formed a company strong enough for either of the great London houses.

The most distinguished member of Mr. Wignell's company was Miss George, known to the American stage as Mrs. Oldmixon. She made her first appearance on any stage at the Haymarket Theatre as *Rosetta* in " Love in a Village," June 2d, 1783. Previous to her *debut* she had never seen a play and had received no theatrical education. She was the daughter of a clergyman at Oxford, and for some time previous to her appearance in London she had been a principal singer in the concerts there. For a long time the London papers spoke of her as " from the pipe-office, Oxford." In person, though rather small, she was neat, and her manner was vivacious, easy and agreeable. Her eyes were expressive, and her features large, but pleasing and excellently adapted to the stage. The compass of her voice was astonishing, and her melody had a sweetness, roundness and variety of tone

MISS GEORGE'S PARTS.

1783. *Haymarket.*
June 2—Love in a Village . . . . Rosetta
       28—Comus . . . . . . Euphrosyne
July 16—Artaxerxes . . . . . . Mandane
Aug. 12—Birthday . . . . Florina

1783. *Drury Lane.*
Sept. 22—Love in a Village . . . . Rosetta
Oct. 7—Comus . . . . . First Bacchante
       30—Lionel and Clarissa . . . Diana
Nov. 4—Thomas and Sally . . . . Sally
       18—Lord of the Manor . . . Annette
Dec. 5—Metamorphosis . . . . Charlotte

1784.
April 14—Cymon and Sylvia . . . . Sylvia
       28—Tom Thumb . . . Huncamunka

1784. *Haymarket.*
June 19—Two to One . . . . . . Tippet
July 24—Midas . . . . Nysa
Aug. 2—Noble Peasant . . . . . Adela
       3—Young Quaker . . . . Araminta
       10—What D'ye Call It . . . . Susan
       24—Deserter . . . . Jenny

1785. *Drury Lane.*
Jan. 10—Cymon . . . . Urganda
Feb. 8—Liberty Hall . . . . . . Aurelia
Mar. 28—Rosina . . . . Phœbe
April 6—Confederacy . . . . . . Corinna

1785.   *Haymarket.*

July 9—Turk and No Turk . . . . . Fib
      20—Gretna Green . . . Miss Plumb

1786.

July 19 —Provoked Husband . . . . Jenny
      20—Beggar's Opera . . . . . Lucy
Aug. 3—Romp . . . . Priscilla Tomboy
      12—Siege of Curzola . . . . Teresa
      29—Orpheus . . . . Rhodope

1787.

May 16—Harvest Home . . . . . Unah
July 16—Golden Pippin   . . . . Juno
Aug. 4—Inkle and Yarico . . . Wowski

1787.   *Royalty.*

Sept. 27—Thomas and Susan . . . . Susan
Dec. 3—Apollo Turned Stroller . . Apollo

1789.   *Haymarket.*

May 18—Enraged Musician . . Milk Girl
July 31—Portrait . . . . Isabella

that the *Morning Post* declared the morning after her *debut* were rarely to be met with even on the other side of the Haymarket—that is, the English Opera House. Her articulation was said to be equal to that of Mrs. Kennedy; her taste and execution were pronounced equal to any, and it was predicted that the public would stamp her as one of the first singers of the English stage. The same critic afterward said that as *Rosetta* she cast her eyes down, but as *Euphrosyne* in "Comus," her second part, she looked as if ready to cry, "Who's afraid?—it is a wonderful town this, and a theatre is not the worst academy a young lady can go to." This remark was curiously supplemented when she appeared as *Euphrosyne* the second time. While she was singing, a gentleman in the boxes, dressed like a clergyman, began to hiss, shout and otherwise disturb the audience, the effect of which was to cause Miss George to faint. It may be inferred that the disturber was her father, manifesting his opposition to her choice of a profession. It is not surprising that parental authority was of little avail, for her success was so great that before the close of her first season at the Haymarket she was hailed as the English Allegranti.

Before the close of her first season at the Haymarket Miss George secured an engagement at Drury Lane for three years at £10 per week, where she made her first appearance September 22, 1783, as *Rosetta.* Great improvement in her acting was noticed by the critics on this occasion, as the result of her brief experience at the Summer theatre, but her singing was subjected to severer criticism. The *Independent Gazetteer*, for instance, regretted that she was not under the immediate direction of Mr. Linley, as she had been taught apparently rather to astonish the ear than to please the heart—was a sublime warbler rather than a pleasing singer. It was imputed to her as a fault that she copied the Italian school in her singing and the French in her manners; but these qualities commended her to the musical public; and, beginning with the season of 1784, she was engaged for the oratorios that were then annually given at Drury Lane, and were very popular. During her first season as an oratorio singer Miss George was heard in " L'Allegro el Pensoroso," the " Messiah," "Samson," "Alexander's Feast," " Jepthah," " Judas Maccabæus" and "Acis and Galatea." In 1785 she was one of the vocalists engaged for the Handel commemoration at Drury Lane, and she was re-engaged for the oratorio season. These oratorio engagements were made year after year for a number of years, even after Miss George had ceased to appear at Drury Lane during the regular season. When Mrs. Siddons made her first appearance as *Lady Macbeth* at Drury Lane, in 1785, Miss George and Mrs. Wrighten were both among the vocalists. One of Miss George's greatest successes during the season of 1784–5 was her first song in Dibdin's " Liberty Hall," in which she was sprightly and original, and never failed of being received with repeated plaudits and a general recall. When she took her benefit this season, one of the papers said, "Little George beat Miss Phillips by half a neck."

Dunlap saw Miss George at the Haymarket in the Summer of

1785, and at Drury Lane early in 1786, and he speaks of her as so distinguished at that time that her portrait, in company of that of John Palmer, was exhibited at Somerset House by Russell, one of the best painters in pastel of the period. This opinion of her merit is corroborated by the *Independent Gazetteer*, which pronounced her the best singer then on the English stage. Her voice was flexible and sweet, and its compass greater than that of any singer before the public. One of the operas in which Dunlap heard her was the "Noble Peasant," and it was said by one of the newspapers that the manner in which she sang the airs allotted to her in that work could never be forgotten.

After the close of the Haymarket season of 1785 Miss George suffered from a long illness, so that her last season at Drury Lane offered few opportunities for the display of her peculiar talents. She was again at the Haymarket in the Summer of 1786, where, for her benefit, she appeared for the first time as *Priscilla Tomboy* in the "Romp," in which Mrs. Jordan was then so popular. In order to deprecate prejudice and comparison, Mr. Bannister, Jr., recited a poetical address written for the occasion, which was supposed to be made up of extracts from the newspapers. Miss George was always considerately treated by the

MISS GEORGE'S ADDRESS.

[Newſpapers lying on the table.

The Play quite over the Addreſs not written! What ſhall I do? Miſs George is fairly bitten.

Flat as a cit 'fore dinner—hipped by vapours, But can't I ſteal from all theſe morning papers?

The POST—" Miſs George this evening plays the Romp;

"'Tis hop'd no nibbling critic in ſtiff pomp

" Will ſneer at her eſſay and voice melodious;

" Remember, "All compariſons are odious." What have we here? "*The* PUBLIC ADVERTISER—

" Theatricals—*daſh*---AND—*daſh*—we *adviſe* her——

"*Daſh*—let Miſs George——*daſh*——*teipſe noſce*——

"*Daſh*—ſhe's not Jordan—*daſh*—nor Madam Pozzy "——

Daſh—*daſh*—*ſlapdaſh*—*The* CHRONICLE at laſt,

Fame's pleaſing *trump*, without one envious blaſt,

What's here? " Miſs George's great attempt to-night

London press; and this occasion, notwithstanding Mrs. Jordan's popularity, proved no exception. "With the warmest prejudices in favor of Mrs. Jordan," said the *Gazetteer*, "we must bear testimony to the spirit, the volatility, the gamesomeness of Miss George. She sang the songs with such taste and excellence as to excite a tumult of applause and, in all but one or two, a general encore. She has reason to be fully satisfied with her benefit, both from the accession of fame and of cash, for the house overflowed in every part."

"Cannot offend, but may give some delight;
"She's young and volatile—has fun and rig,
"Her *Tippet* and *Mifs Jenny* prove fhe's gig.
"Though wond'rous Jordan be Dame Nature's choice,
"Yet fprightly George has got a charming voice.
"Had no young candidate e'er try'd their art
"To play a great performer's choiceft part,
"*Jordan* and *Siddons* we had never gain'd,
"For *Clive* and *Cibber* would have always reign'd."
Let candour, then, not cynick fnarls prevail;
Let no one cock his glafs, and fay "fhe'll fail!
"She's *not the Jordan!*" that fhe *knows* indeed,
But none can be more anxious to fucceed
Than fhe, to make you merry—not to teize you,—
She'll do her beft—none can do more—to pleafe you.

One of Miss George's greatest successes at the Haymarket this season was her singing of Dr. Arnold's "*Je ne scai quoi*" in the "Siege of Curzola," originally written for the Prince of Wales' birthday in 1783. One of the penalties of her popularity at this time was a report in a newspaper that she was to marry a Mr. Martyr, which, of course, suggested "St. George, the Martyr," to the sapient paragrapher. In November and December, 1786, Miss George, being then disengaged, sang operatic arias at a series of readings by Mr. Lacy at Free-Mason's Hall. A few weeks later, in consequence of the secession of the laughter-loving Wrighten, it was suggested in the *Gazetteer* that, as one star had fallen, the managers could not do better than to secure the wandering but brilliant Georgina Sidus. Again, in February, 1787, Miss George sang at Mr. Lacy's readings, and she was also engaged for the Drury Lane oratorio. Her singing in the " Redemption " gained her " an encore from the pit even unto the gods." In the Summer of 1787 she was engaged as the principal singer at Ranelagh, and she was again at the Haymarket, where she greatly distinguished herself, both as singer and actress, as *Unah* in " Harvest Home " on the opening night. As *Juno* in the " Golden Pippin " and as *Wowski* in the younger Colman's new opera, " Inkle and Yarico," she was highly complimented.

When the new Royalty Theatre, projected by John Palmer, was opened for the season of 1787–8, Miss George was engaged, making her first appearance at the new house on the 27th of September as *Susan* in " Thomas and Susan." " We cannot too much commend Mr. Palmer in engaging this little syren," said the *Gazetteer,* " and we have no doubt she will be as great a favorite in the East as she was in the West." In Sir John Oldmixon's " Apollo Turned Stroller," she was as successful as usual, but, owing to the opposition of the patent houses, the Royalty was soon closed as a Winter theatre. Miss George again sang in the Drury Lane oratorio in 1788, and subsequently she played a brief engagement at Edinburgh, making her first appearance there March 14, 1788, as *Rosetta* in " Love in a Village." In her return journey for the season of 1788 at the Haymarket she was seized with a fever near Carlisle, in consequence of which her life was despaired of, and the fulfilment of her engagement rendered impossible. When she recovered she went to London, which she left in October, 1788, to play an engagement of twelve nights in Dublin. She was extremely well received in the Irish capital, but, taking offense at her treatment behind the scenes, she terminated her engagement early in December, and went to Edinburgh, but she reached London in time for the Haymarket season of 1789, appearing on the opening night as the *Milk Girl* in an afterpiece called the " Enraged Musician." This was her last engagement in London, and she seems to have lived in retirement until Mr. 'Wignell engaged her for Philadelphia.

Previous to her American engagement, Miss George married Sir John Oldmixon, a noted beau of that time. Little authentic information has been preserved in regard to Sir John. Bernard knew him at Bath in 1784, where he was distinguished for the refinement of his dress and manners and, in all points of good breeding, looked up to as an oracle. Indeed, Bernard professed to have chosen Sir John as the model of his *Lord Sparkle* in Mrs. Cowley's " Which is the Man ? " " Bernard, I saw your *Sparkle* last night," the comedian represents Sir John as saying ; " they say you imitate me, but your dress was incorrect ; you wear only twelve curls to a side—I never wear under sixteen." It may be inferred, however, that the objections were couched in stronger terms, as, according to the late William B. Wood, Bernard was the worst dresser on the stage. Sir John Oldmixon was the grandson of that John Oldmixon whom Pope included in the " Dunciad," being a son of Oldmixon's daughter, who had married a musician named Morella. Young Morella had his name changed to Oldmixon, after his grandfather, and, while serving under the Duke of Portland in Ireland, he was knighted by the viceroy. It is not unlikely that Sir John first met Miss George during her Royalty engagement in 1787. I have been unable to find the date of their marriage; but when she made her first appearance in America, in Philadelphia in 1794, Lady Oldmixon was announced in the bills simply as Mrs. Oldmixon.

Next in reputation after Mrs. Oldmixon, among Wignell's recruits, was Mr. Fennell. James Fennell was the son of an official in the pay department of the Royal Navy, who had been for some years a resident of New York about the middle of the century. James was born in London, December 11, 1766. He was educated at Eton and Trinity College, Cambridge, and was intended for the bar. His irregular habits and extravagance defeated this design, for, in the foolish expectation of revenging himself upon his father for refusing him money to pay a gambling debt, he resolved to go upon the stage, and immediately set off for Edinburgh to carry his purpose into execution. This was in June, 1787. Mr. Jackson, the manager of the Edinburgh Theatre, agreed to give him an appearance, as an amateur, in the character of *Othello*, which he played with such success that during the Summer he performed six times in Edinburgh and repeated his performances in Glasgow. Although he played under the assumed name of Cambray, his course so incensed his family that upon his return to London in the Autumn he found the doors of all his relations closed against him. Then came an engagement at Covent Garden.

Mr. Fennell's London *debut*, which was also in the name of Cambray, was effected with a considerable flourish of trumpets. The manager of Covent Garden, the newspapers said, had found a phenomenon, who had presented himself unrecommended to Mr. Harris, and, by reciting some passages from leading characters, had instantly won an essay—his engagement to be contingent upon his first attempt. Fennell accordingly appeared on the 12th of October,

MR. FENNELL'S C. G. PARTS.

1787.
Oct. 12—Othello . . . . Othello
22—Alexander the Great . Alexander
29—Venice Preserved . . . Jaffier
Nov. 16—Macbeth . . . . . . Macbeth
Lyar . . . . . Young Wilding
1789.
Nov. 2—Henry IV . . . . . . Hotspur
21—Lear . . . . Bastard
1790.
Oct. 27—Orphan . . . . Castalio
Dec. 10—Love Makes a Man . . . Duart
11—Author . . . . . . Young Cape
20—Douglas . . . . . Douglas

1787, as *Othello*, Mrs. Pope being the *Desdemona*. He was described, after his *debut*, as being a most elegant and striking figure—tall, finely proportioned and graceful. His voice, it was said, had great volume, and was not destitute of music, but his management of it was faulty; he seldom erred in the conception of the character, but in the delivery of the passion he stretched his voice beyond its powers. When he essayed *Alexander*, Miss Brunton, best known to the American stage as Mrs. Merry, played *Statira* for the first time. On this occasion, also, his great volume of voice, with its lack of variety and modulation, was noticed. "He possesses feeling, and strives to make others feel," said one of his critics, "but the want of natural tenderness of voice makes him degenerate into a whine which destroys the interest, and neither gratifies the ear nor reaches the heart." For his benefit Fennell played *Macbeth* to the *Lady Macbeth* of Mrs. Pope, and, like most young tragedians, he "gave various new readings." All the clubs of which he had been a member at Cambridge came to London to attend his benefit, which proved a very profitable one.

Before Mr. Fennell left Edinburgh, after his first attempts, he entered into articles with Mr. Jackson for the following season, should he continue on the stage. Mr. Harris offered to pay the penalty named in the articles—£200—and additional damages if Mr. Jackson would release him, but Jackson declined, and Fennell felt bound to fulfil his contract. He accordingly played in Edinburgh throughout the Winter season of 1787–8. After the close of the regular season Jackson engaged Mrs. Siddons for the week of the Leith races, and induced Fennell to agree to support her. In casting the play of "Venice Preserved," the manager gave *Jaffier* to Fennell and *Pierre* to Woods, another member of the company. Both these actors had played *Jaffier*, but Fennell had never played *Pierre*. The friends of Woods, however, insisted that he should be allowed to play *Jaffier*, and created a disturbance in the theatre because the change was not made. Mr. Jackson was forewarned of this disturbance by means of an anonymous letter, to which Fennell incautiously referred as " a scene of villainy." For this an apology was demanded, which the young tragedian refused to make. Fennell was finally withdrawn by the manager, but nothing short of an apology would appease his enemies, and he was consequently driven from the Edinburgh stage altogether. Singularly enough, the conspirators were composed of advocates and writers of the Scotch bar, against whom Fennell afterward brought an action. It was with difficulty that he obtained counsel, most of the attorneys who were not in the conspiracy refusing to accept a brief against their brethren. A year later, as the cause would not be likely to be disposed of under six years, Mr. Fennell withdrew the action. After the action was withdrawn, in the Summer of 1789, Fennell appeared twice on the Edinburgh stage, with the approbation of the audience, which ended his professional career in Scotland.

Having left Edinburgh, Fennell appeared for one night at Newcastle for the benefit of Mrs. Whitlock, and on the 26th of August, 1789, he played *Othello* at York, Miss Farren being the *Desdemona*. On the 16th of October he reappeared at Covent Garden, also as *Othello*, a role that one of the newspapers said was beyond his reach, adding that there were many parts in which he would be a useful actor. He seems to have acted on the hint, for he subsequently appeared as *Hotspur* in " Henry IV," and other roles less trying. To some of them he failed to take kindly, however; and, after playing the *Abbe Maury* for one night in the " Picture of Paris," he retired from the theatre, disgusted with the tomfooleries of the part and the play. Fennell, in his "Apology" for his life, confesses that at this time— 1790–91—he was very much in love with Miss Brunton, but she did not discover the fact until after she was the wife of her third husband, William Warren. He was soon consoled, however, and early in 1792 he was married, going to France on his wedding excursion. In Paris he and his bride met Mr. and Mrs. Merry (Miss Brunton), and they returned to London together. While in Paris, Merry proposed that they should sail for America, with a view of joining the theatrical forces in this country. Fennell declined, and Merry abandoned the project. A year later Fennell changed his mind, and, engaging with Wignell, he set sail in advance of the rest of the Philadelphia company.

For the lead in genteel comedy and for secondary roles in tragedy Mr. Wignell engaged Mr. Chalmers, whom he probably found at Dublin. Chalmers was an actor of experience and of some merit, though not of the first rank. He made his London *debut* at Covent Garden on the 8th of October, 1783, as *Tom* in the "Conscious Lovers." Mrs. Chal-

MR. CHALMERS' C. G. PARTS.

1783.
Oct. 8—Conscious Lovers . . . . . Tom
1784.
Mar. 16—Which is the Man ? . Lord Sparkle
May 4—Merry Wives of Windsor . Fenton
Sept. 17—As You Like It . . . . . Silvius
    20—Harlequin Rambler . Harlequin
    29—Henry IV . . . . Poins

mers, who was a sister of Mills, at that time at Covent Garden, had appeared a few nights before as *Rose* in the "Recruiting Officer." She was esteemed in Edinburgh, where she received the rudiments of her theatrical education, and much was expected from her in London, which, however, she failed to realize. Mrs. Chalmers died in Dublin in May, 1792. Mr. Chalmers remained at Covent Garden only one season, but with his wife he was engaged for Dublin for the season of

1784-5. It is unnecessary to trace his subsequent wanderings, except to say that for three years—1789-91—he was at Weymouth. In 1789 he performed *Marplot* in the " Busybody," *Young Wilding* in the " Lyar " and *Petruchio* in " Catharine and Petruchio," before the king and Queen Caroline. His last part at Weymouth in 1791 that I find noticed in the newspapers was *Doricourt* in the " Belle's Stratagem," which he played on the 10th of September, it was said, with approbation. At the time of his London *debut* one of the critics found Chalmers wanting in the sprightliness and flippancy necessary to the coxcomb and in that flow of words and spirit that makes the dialogue trip lightly from the tongue and the feet bound airily from the boards. Durang speaks of him as the reverse of this, saying he could never play a part without a jump or a turn in it; that he had taken Lewis as his model, but only caught the nimbleness of that actor's legs. Dunlap accords him talents and power as an actor in comedy, but says his consummate vanity and indifference to everything except selfish gratification ruined him.

Among Mr. Wignell's recruits none was more noteworthy than Mr. and Mrs. Whitlock. Charles Whitlock had long been a provincial actor and manager in England. He was best known, perhaps, as the associate of Munden in the management of the theatre at Newcastle. As an actor he was excellent in the heavy fathers, *Lord Norland* in " Every One Has His Fault" being esteemed his best part. Mrs. Whitlock was Eliza Kemble, the youngest sister of Mrs. Siddons. Like the other members of the

ELIZA KEMBLE'S D. L. PARTS.

1783.
Feb. 22—Merchant of Venice . . . Portia
Oct. 16—As You Like It . . . . Rosalind
Nov. 4—New Way to Pay Old Debts
Margaret
1784.
Jan. 23—Revenge . . . . Leonora
1785.
April 27—Earl of Essex
Countess of Rutland

Kemble family she had received her theatrical education in the provinces. When Sarah had gained her great triumph at Drury Lane, she brought out her sister Fanny as *Alicia* to her *Jane Shore;* and a few weeks later Betsy, who had been at York, followed as *Portia.* Some of Miss Betsy's tones, one of the newspapers said, resembled her sister's, but she was criticised for sinking her voice so that several words were lost in every sentence, and for making use of too many airs and attitudes. In the Summer of 1784 Eliza Kemble was at Lancaster, where she was married in June, 1785, to Mr. Whitlock, who was then one of the managers of the Chester Theatre. She was afterward the chief attraction of the Newcastle circuit. When the new theatre at Newcastle was opened, January 21st, 1788, Mrs. Whitlock appeared as *Mrs. Lovemore* in the "Way to Keep Him," the opening play. As a mark of the esteem in which the Whitlocks were held at Newcastle, it may be noted that at the close of their season there, in June, 1791, they were presented by a select party of gentlemen with a purse containing fifty guineas. Mrs. Whitlock was not again seen in London until June, 1792, when she appeared at the Haymarket on the 18th as *Queen Margaret* in the "Battle of Hexham," and on the 23d as *Julia* in the "Siege of Calais." Mr. and Mrs. Whitlock were engaged for the Edinburgh and Glasgow theatres, under Mrs. Esten's management, for the season of 1792–3. Among Mrs. Whitlock's parts at Edinburgh was *Elvira* in "Percy," a part that she was soon to play in America, under Mr. Wignell's management. The Whitlocks were exceedingly amiable and worthy people.

Mr. Wignell selected his company with a view to a strong operatic department, choosing singers who were at the same time actors and actresses. Mr. and Mrs. Marshall were excellent examples of his method. That Mr. Marshall was a good actor in fops and Frenchmen is proved by his list of parts at Covent Garden during a period of three years; only a fair singer, as well as a good actor, could have succeeded Wewitzer as *Bagatelle*, which Marshall did with entire acceptability on the occasion of his London *debut*. After that performance he was commended for his comic talents, and it was predicted that he would prove an attractive and useful performer. Marshall was still at Covent Garden at the beginning of the season of 1792–3; but early in January a newspaper paragraph said his situation at Bath was a pitiable one, adding, by way of explanation, that it was natural a son

Mr. Marshall's C. G. Parts.

1790.
Sept. 17—Poor Soldier . . . . . Bagatelle
Oct. 15—Fontainebleau . Col. Epaulette
Dec. 20—Picture of Paris . . . . . Poet
    27—Recruiting Officer . Capt. Brazen
1791.
Jan. 3—Henry IV . . . . Poins
    14—Little Hunchback, French Doctor
Feb. 4—School for Arrogance . . Picard
May 2—Alexander the Little . Lysimachus
    19—He Wou'd be a Soldier . Pierpont
June 1—Chances . . . . Don Frederick
Oct. 27—Provoked Husband . Count Basset
Nov. 1—Duenna . . . . . . Anthonio
    19—Midnight Hour . . Marquis
Dec. 21—Bluebeard . . . . . . Bounce
1792.
Mar. 26—Mermaid . . . . . . Raymond
May 18—Cymbeline . . . . . . Cloten
Sept. 28—Suspicious Husband, Jack Meggot

of the sock should become entangled in a dramatic Webb. This was the actress known on the American stage as Mrs. Marshall and afterward as Mrs. Wilmot. When the " Beggar's Opera " was produced at the Haymarket Theatre in 1786, Mrs. Brett, the mother of Mrs. Hodgkinson, was the *Lucy*, but she was succeeded at the second performance by Mrs. Webb, and Mrs. Webb in turn gave way to Miss George. Notwithstanding this failure, she became a very capable actress and singer. Her *Edward* in " Every One Has His Fault " was long celebrated as a matchless performance. Mrs. Marshall was *petite* in figure, with a round face, sparkling eyes, and an arch and sprightly expression of features.

The engagement of the Warrells was in line with Mr. Wignell's general policy. Mr. Warrell had few pretensions as an actor, but, with his young sons, Master Warrell and Master T. Warrell, was often useful in filling out a cast. Mrs. Warrell, on the other hand, was an important acquisition both as an actress and a singer. Before her first London appearance at the Royalty Theatre, July 15th, 1788, in the title-role of the little piece called "Poll of Plympton," Mrs. Warrell had been at Bath, where she was held in esteem for her vocal

MRS. WARRELL'S PARTS.

Royalty.

1788.
July 15—Poll of Plympton . . . . . Poll
Sept. 1—Honoria . . . . Honoria

Covent Garden.

1790.
Feb. 18—Fontainebleau . . . . . . Rosa
Mar. 18—Flitch of Bacon . . . . . Eliza
May 13—Lionel and Clarissa . . . Diana
Oct. 13—Robin Hood . . . . Angelina
Nov. 3—Wives Revenged . . Mrs. Tokay
1791.
May 24—Primrose Green.

powers. As she had pleased the fashionable circles at Bath, one of the newspapers said, previous to her *debut*, that there was little doubt of her captivating a London audience. She failed to make an immediate impression, however; and, although her engagement at one of the Winter theatres was talked of, it was not until the season of 1790–91 that she was retained in the vocal department at Covent Garden. There her position was a subordinate one, as her parts show, but she was useful as one of the singers in such pieces as the "Picture of Paris" and the "Woodman." Mrs. Warrell remained at Covent Garden only one season, going to Brighton for the Summer of 1791, where she appeared on the 17th of July as *Rosetta* in "Love in a Village." It is probable that Mr. Wignell found her at Edinburgh, where she was a member of Mrs. Esten's company during the season of 1792–3.

The engagement of Mr. Darley could only have been possible in an American company modelled after those of the two great London theatres. Mr. Darley was not a good actor, but in singing parts his faults were overlooked.   The first mention of him as an actor that I have been able to find was as *Charles the Wrestler* in "As You Like It" in 1784.   He was a large man—in fact, when he came to America he was a fat man—and he was probably chosen for *Charles* because he looked the athlete.   In person and features he was said to bear such a striking resemblance to Henry VIII that in 1786 he sat to an eminent artist for a portrait of the king.   For fully ten years Darley, as a singer, was a Covent Garden favorite. An incident related by Dunlap, who was present, well illustrates Darley's acceptability.   In the Winter of 1785–6 a farce was revived that had owed its success the previous season to a song sung by the celebrated Mrs. Kennedy. This song was omitted when the piece was revived, which was the occasion of an uproar.   Finally, however, the audience consented to hear Darley sing it, Mrs. Kennedy not being in the theatre, and it was received with great applause.

Mr. Darley's Parts.

1784.
Sept. 17—As You Like It . . . . Charles
       20—Harlequin Rambler . Friar Bungy
Nov. 6—Fontainebleau . . . . . Robin
1785.
Mar. 12—Robin Hood.
       Midas . . . . Jupiter
April 12—Nunnery . . . . Friar
Dec. 20—Omai . . . . Otoo
1786.
Oct. 16—Richard Cœur de Lion
                       Principal Knight
Nov. 17—Love in a Village . . Hawthorn
       22—Tom Thumb . . . . . . Ghost
       24—Castle of Andalusia . Sanguino
       30—Two Misers . . . . Ali
1787.
Jan. 15—Artaxerxes . . . . . Artabanes
May 21—Rose and Colin . . . . Gregory
Sept. 21—Cymon . . . . Demon
       26—Poor Vulcan . . . . . Sergeant
Oct. 1—Macbeth . . . . Hecate
       Love and War . . . . . Rifle
       31—Farmer . . . Farmer Blackberry
1788.
Jan. 25—Much Ado About Nothing
                           Balthazar
       28—Lady of the Manor
                      Farmer Sternhold
May 22—Marian . . . . Thomas
1789.
Feb. 24—Hide and Seek . . . . Brigadier
April 29—Beggar's Opera . Mat o' the Mint
May 2—Sultan . . . . Selim
Oct. 30—Positive Man . . . . . . Cable
1790.
Mar   2—Maid of the Mill . . . Fairfield
April 8—Inkle and Yarico . . . . Mate
1791.
Sept. 26—Crusade . . . . Daran
Nov. 1—Duenna . . . . . . Father Paul

So great and so lasting was Darley's popularity that at Vauxhall,
after the flight of Mrs. Wrighten, he
almost compensated the audiences
for her loss. During the season of
1790–91 Darley was out of the

Dec. 10—Woodman . . . . Fairlip
15—Jovial Crew . . . . . Hearty
21—Bluebeard . . . . . Bluebeard
1792.
Feb. 28—Orpheus and Euridice.
Sept. 28—Flitch of Bacon . . Capt. Wilson
Oct. 5—Highland Reel . Sergeant Jack
1793.
May 11—Sprigs of Laurel . . . . Corporal

Covent Garden Company, being engaged at Portsmouth. He was
soon back again, however, playing his most famous role, *Farmer
Blackberry* in the " Farmer," on the opening night of the next season.
Darley was often commended for his singing, but seldom for his acting.
As *Farmer Blackberry* he was excellent ; as *Daran* in the " Crusade " it
was conceded that he acted well ; and it was said he made *Fairlip* in the
" Woodman " as fine a character as any of his predecessors. When he
came to America, Darley brought with him his son, John Darley, the
younger, who was destined to become one of the most distinguished
actors on the American stage.

Early in December, 1790, a London paper announced that Miss
Broadhurst, the promising pupil of the ingenious Mr. Percy, would

Miss Broadhurst's Parts.

1791.
Jan. 15—Beggar's Opera . . . . . Polly
Feb. 10—Padlock . . . . Leonora
May 12—Rosina . . . . Rosina
June 3—Cottage Maid.
Sept. 23—Comus . . . . Pastoral Nymph
Oct. 20—Oscar and Malvina.
1792.
Feb. 28—Orpheus and Euridice.
April 17—Will o' the Wisp . . . . Zelma
Sept. 19—Duenna . . . . Clara
28—Flitch of Bacon . . . . . Eliza
Oct. 3—Fontainebleau . . . . . Celia
Sultan . . . . Ismene

soon make her theatrical *entree* in
a new comic opera to be called
the " Will o' the Wisp." Miss
Broadhurst was then only 16, but
she was not entirely unknown to
the musical public, as she had sung
some time previously at Free-Mason's Hall. The part for her *debut*
was afterward changed to *Polly* in
the " Beggar's Opera," in which she

Oct. 5—Highland Reel . . . . . Jenny   made her first appearance January
      17—Poor Soldier . . . . . . Norah
      18—Maid of the Oaks . . . . Maria   15th, 1791. Considering her age, it

was said her musical acquirements were truly wonderful. Her voice
was pleasing and flexible, and when she became more accustomed to
the stage it was predicted that she would prove a distinguished orna-
ment to the musical department of the theatre. She sang *Polly* five
times in succession before she was heard in her second part—*Leonora*
in the " Padlock." She had also the distinction, previously accorded
only to Miss George, of appearing in the Drury Lane oratorio during
her first season on the stage. For her benefit on the 3d of June she
produced a new piece, the " Cottage Maid," and sang an Italian aria
in the masquerade scene in the " Belle's Stratagem " and a new ballad
at the end of the first act. When Incledon made his first appearance
as *Macheath* at Covent Garden, she was again the *Polly*. Miss Broadhurst never developed much skill as an actress, and according to Dunlap she was deficient in personal beauty. Wignell engaged her solely
for her musical abilities. She came to this country accompanied by
her mother. There is a portrait of her, but it is seldom met with.

The low comedian engaged by Mr. Wignell was Bates, famili-
arly known as Billy Bates. His low comedy, it is said, was very coarse,
and his talents were not of a high order; but he was an actor of long
experience, and understood his business thoroughly. John Bernard found him at Bristol in 1783; and Ryley in the " Itinerant"
speaks of him as a member of the Manchester company a year or two
later. In 1786-7 he was at Drury Lane, where he seems to have remained in a subordinate position, although his name seldom appears
in the casts. His parts at Drury Lane, as his brief list shows, were
second low comedy. Bates was engaged at the Royalty Theatre in

the Summer of 1787 and again in 1788. At the Royalty he played *Harlequin* in the pantomime, "Hobson's Choice," on the opening night, July 3d, 1787, and in "Har-lequin Mungo" August 29th, 1788. Bates was the author of a piece called "Gil Blas," produced at the Royalty in 1788, in which he played the title-role, with Watts, who

MR. BATES' D. L. PARTS.

1787.
Mar. 13—Seduction . . . . Lapell
Oct. 6—Englishman in Paris . . Killean
1788.
May 15—Lear . . . . Burgundy
16—Constant Couple . . Tom Errand
21—Merry Wives of Windsor . Bardolph

was with Harper in Boston in 1792 as *Father Dominic*, and Chambers, who appeared in Philadelphia the same year with the Old American Company as a *Lay Brother* and *Fabricius*. Bernard tells a story of Bates at rehearsal, at Bristol, that seems to have been characteristic of the man. He had only a few lines, but he spoke them in a very ener-getic manner. "Do you mean to speak that way at night?" asked Holland, one of the managers. "Certainly," Bates answered; "I have a benefit to make as well as you, Mr. Holland." In Philadelphia he sometimes advertised his benefits in verse, one of his advertisements beginning as follows:

On Friday eve next, as the play-bill relates,
(To discount other bills) is a bill for Bill Bates,
To which he invites all the town, grave and gay,
To see wit and humor portrayed in a play.

Mrs. Bates was engaged with her husband, but she appeared only in unimportant parts.

What proved two of the most important engagements made by Mr. Wignell were those of Mr. and Mrs. Francis. William Francis had been the *Harlequin* at Manchester and Birmingham since 1787, and was noted for the skill with which he prepared pantomimic ballets for the stage and superintended their production. Mr. Wignell saw a specimen of his work in the " Enchanted Wood " at the Haymarket in 1792, and engaged him principally for similar services in Philadelphia. Francis was the second dancer of the name known to the American stage. The other, whose real name was Menzius, but who was here called Francis Mentges, was from Holland. He had danced with Douglass' company before the Revolution, but early in that struggle he entered the Revolutionary army as adjutant of Colonel Atlee's Musketry Battalion, to which position he was appointed March 22d, 1776. He was promoted to be first lieutenant on the 7th of August following. In October he was transferred to the Eleventh Pennsylvania Regiment, of which he was made major; and on the 9th of October, 1778, he succeeded Persifor Frazer as lieutenant-colonel of the Fifth Pennsylvania, where he rendered distinguished service. After the Revolution he was inspector of United States troops in the Northwest Territory. Heckwelder in his diary speaks of meeting Mentges near Cincinnati in 1792. This first Francis was, so far as I know, the only person connected with the colonial stage who took part with the colonies in the struggle for independence. I speak of him thus at length because unfortunately I confounded him in my first volume with his successor of the same name, the subject of the present sketch. Little is known of William Francis in the English provincial theatres except that he there won the esteem of Cooke and other actors who afterward met him in this country. Ryley speaks of him in the " Itinerant " in connection with the discovery of a Jacobite plot at Manchester to carry off the king, which turned out to be a memorandum of Francis' new pantomime. Mrs. Francis was with her husband in the Manchester and Birmingham companies, and there received the theatrical education that at once made her so acceptable here as an actress.

Among the most interesting, if not the more important engagements made by Mr. Wignell were those of the Rowsons. According to Mr. Nason, Mrs. Susanna Rowson's biographer, William Rowson was, at the time of their marriage in 1786, a hardware merchant and a trumpeter in the Royal Horse Guards. Mrs. Rowson was the only daughter of Lieutenant William Haswell, of the British navy. She was born at Portsmouth, Hampshire, Eng., in 1762. Lieutenant Haswell held a position in the revenue service at Boston, making his home at Nantasket. In 1767 he sent for his little daughter Susanna, who, in consequence, spent her early years at that place, where she witnessed some of the opening scenes of the Revolution. Lieutenant Haswell's loyalty to his king caused him to be kept in constant surveillance after the evacuation of Boston, and, to render him harmless, he was ordered to live at Hingham. In 1777 he was removed to Abington, and early in the next year he was sent with his family under a flag of truce to Halifax. Miss Haswell soon afterward returned with the family to England, where she obtained a situation as governess. Her first novel, " Victoria," was published soon after her marriage, under the patronage of the Duchess of Devonshire. Her other books, " The Inquisitor," " Mary," " Trip to Parnassus," " Charlotte Temple," " Mentoria " and " Rebecca," followed in rapid succession between 1788 and 1792. The husband becoming bankrupt in the latter year, the family, including Mr. and Mrs. Rowson and Miss Charlotte Rowson, Mr. Rowson's sister, resolved to go upon the stage, and in 1792–3 they were engaged at the Edinburgh Theatre, under Mrs. Esten's management. Mr. Wignell found them there, and engaged them for his Philadelphia Theatre, Mr. Rowson to be the prompter, and Mrs. and Miss Rowson for subordinate roles in opera and comedy.

The other members of Mr. Wignell's company engaged in England were not noteworthy at the time of their engagement. Mrs. Shaw, who was engaged for the "comedy old ladies," a large, corpulent woman, was unknown to fame; but her husband, who came out to join the orchestra under Mr. Reinagle, had been a musician at Drury Lane. Mr. and Mrs. Cleveland, who filled minor roles, the former "walking gentlemen" and the latter "smart chambermaids," were also devoid of previous reputation. Miss Willems, a very pretty girl, afterward Mrs. Green, had had no theatrical experience, and the same thing was true of Messrs. Moreton, Harwood, Green and Blissett, four young men who were destined to become distinguished actors. John Pollard Moreton, whose real name was Pollard, was the son of an English officer who had served in America, and it is said he was born in this country. Going to England with his father, he was well educated, and when still a very young man he went to India, where he held an important position in the Bank of Calcutta. An indiscretion, involving the loan of the bank's money, which, however, was repaid, sent him back to England in disgrace and despondent, where Mr. Wignell met him and engaged him for the American stage. John E. Harwood was a well-educated and accomplished young Englishman, ardent and impulsive, to whom the offer of a theatrical engagement in America could not fail to prove tempting. Harwood married Miss Bache, a granddaughter of Benjamin Franklin. William Green had been a friend of Moreton in India, whom he joined in seeking theatrical honors in the United States. Francis Blissett, the younger, was the son of Blissett, the Bath comedian; but he never acted in England. Mr. and Mrs. Morris, Mr. Finch, who had been a teacher of languages, and others, were engaged on this side of the Atlantic.

CHAPTER VIII.

THE PHILADELPHIA COMPANY, 1793-4.

DESCRIPTION OF THE NEW THEATRE—ARRIVAL OF THE COMPANY—
BRIEF SEASON AT ANNAPOLIS—OPENING OF THE NEW HOUSE—
"SLAVES IN ALGIERS"—"EMBARGO"—FRANCIS' PANTOMIMES—
OPENING PIECES—THE CASTS AND THE PLAYERS.

THE project of building a new theatre in Philadelphia originated in the differences between Wignell and the managers of the Old American Company in 1791. When it was once conceived it took shape rapidly. Public meetings were held at the old City Tavern, where the stock was subscribed for and the details of the management agreed upon. A. Reinagle, an eminent musician, and Thomas Wignell were made the managers, the former to have the direction of the musical department, and the latter of the stage. The managers were equal in authority in the business department. Mr. Reinagle was a brother of the great London animal painter and the father of Hugh Reinagle, afterward well known as an accomplished scene-painter. The elder Reinagle had long lived in Philadelphia, where he held the first rank as a musician and composer. He was a man of very impressive appearance, and was held in high esteem by all the best people in the Quaker City. Upon him devolved the actual work of superintending the erection of the theatre, Mr. Wignell being absent in England engaging the company, and the house was completed with so little delay that it was ready for the opening before the company was engaged for the theatre.

The site chosen for the New Theatre was in Chestnut Street, above Sixth, on the north side of the street. The plans for the theatre were supplied by Mr. Richards, Mr. Wignell's brother-in-law, who had furnished the designs for the remodelled Covent Garden Theatre, which was then the pride of the British metropolis. His model was shipped in two sections. Charles Durang speaks of seeing it in the property-room over the dome many years afterward. The interior of the new theatre was a perfect copy of the Theatre Royal at Bath. The façade, which was not finally finished until 1805, measured ninety feet in Chestnut Street, including two wings of fifteen feet each. The theatre stood back from the street with the projections of the wings or pavilions in front of the main building extending to the line of the street. These pavilions were connected by a colonnade of ten Corinthian columns, and decorated by emblematic figures in tablets. The centre building was ornamented by two spirited and well-executed figures of Tragedy and Comedy by Rush. In the centre of the building was a great Venetian window, the niches in which the figures were placed being on each side of this window. Over the niches in two circular tablets were emblematic insignia. The top of the centre building was crowned by a pediment. The wings above receded a little from the line of the main building, but below, as already indicated, projected twelve feet to the street. These projections were faced with marble, and a large window opened into each of the wings above. In each of the wings was a green-room, one being used for music rehearsals, dancing practice, etc., and that in the west wing as a green-room in the proper meaning of the term. The dressing-rooms, which were numerous, were also in the wings. The entrances to the theatre were through the projecting wings. The stairs of the galleries were under the colonnade. The left-hand door led to the pit. To the boxes the ascent was by a flight of marble stairs in front to a lobby which communicated by corridors with all the boxes. The fronts of the boxes were handsomely gilt and decorated to correspond with the ceiling and hung with corresponding drapery between the columns. Those in front of the stage were arranged in the form of an amphitheatre. The seats, including those of the pit and gallery, were well disposed. The extreme depth of the theatre was one hundred and thirty-four feet; that of the stage upward of seventy-one feet. Between the boxes the stage occupied a front of thirty-six feet. Over the stage, occupying a part of the entablature, was an emblematic representation of " America Encouraging the Drama," with the motto, " The eagle suffers little birds to sing." For this was afterward substituted the words, " For useful mirth or salutary woe." It was computed that the theatre would hold about two thousand people, of which number nine hundred could be accommodated in the boxes.

The corner-stone of the New Theatre was laid with Masonic ceremonies, Mr. Reinagle being a Master Mason; and Jared Ingersoll, an eminent Philadelphia lawyer, delivered an address. While the work was in progress, there were frequent references to it in the Philadelphia papers, a paragraph in the *Federal Gazette* in November, 1792, saying that the workmen on the New Theatre were employed sixteen hours out of the twenty-four, and that it was expected the house would be completed by the middle or end of December. It was not, however, until the 30th of January, 1793, that the subscribers were afforded an opportunity to see it, after which it remained closed until the 2d of

February, when it was opened to the public with a grand concert, the prices being one dollar to the boxes, seventy-five cents to the pit, and fifty cents to the gallery. Notwithstanding it was an inclement night, the house was crowded in every part. The boxes, one of the newspapers said, exhibited a blaze of beauty; the pit was a display of respectable judges, and the gallery was filled with orderly, well-disposed citizens, whose decency of behavior deserved the greatest applause. Oddly enough, there was no comment on the character of the entertainment, which must be judged by the programme as it was advertised. The concert was repeated on the 4th and again on the 7th of February, after which the doors of the theatre remained closed for more than a year, waiting for the players.

It was only natural that Mr. Wignell's delay in engaging a company should occasion a feeling of dissatisfaction among the subscribers; and on the 28th of January, only two days before the private view of the completed edifice, a meeting was held at the City Tavern to hear and consider his reasons for the course he was pursuing.

PROGRAMME OF THE CONCERT.

Act I.

New Overture . . . . Mr. Reinagle
Song—" On by the Spur of Valor "
　　　　　　　　Mr. Chambers
Concerto—Violin . . . . Mr. Boulay
Song—" Kiss me now or never ". Mrs. Morris
Quartette—Despetit avis
　　Messrs. Pettit, Boulay, Mallet and Reinagle
Song—" Poor Tom Bowling " . Mr. Harper
Symphonia . . . . Mr. Hozeluch
Glee—" Sigh no more, Ladies "
　　Messrs. Chambers, Harper and Reinagle

Act II.

Grand Overture . . . . Haydn
Italian Song . . . . Mr. Mallet
Sonata—Pianoforte . . . . . Mr. Guenin
Song—" My Poll and Partner Joe ", Mr. Harper
Sonata—Harp . . . . Mr. Saloman
Song—" A Smile from the Girl of my Heart "
　　　　　　　　Mr. Chambers
Symphonia Concertant
　　　　　Messrs. Pettit and Boulay

Act III.

Symphony . . . . Stametz
Song—" Blithe Colin " . . . . Mrs. Morris
Concerto—Violin . . . . Mr. Pettit
Song—" Cottage Boy " . . . Mr. Chambers
Glee—" How Merrily We Live "
　　Messrs. Chambers, Harper and Reinagle
　　Dancing by Master Duport in the character of *Harlequin* and in the dance, " Le Noble, or Henry IV."

These reasons were not made public; but whatever they were, they proved satisfactory, and resolutions were passed approving his action and expressing full confidence in his exertions. In the meantime, preparations were continued for the opening, which it was confidently expected would occur in the following September. Charles Milbourne, an able and experienced scene-painter from London, had long been at work upon the scenery and decorations. The latter being finished, additions continued to be made to the stock scenes that had already been painted. Besides, Wignell was presented with some fine drop-scenes by his brother-in-law, Richards, of Covent Garden. Mr. Richards also painted the act-drop, which was a very handsome piece of work. Early in April, 1793, the *Federal Gazette* announced that the furniture of Lord Barrymore's theatre, which had been purchased for the New Theatre, had arrived by the "George Barclay." It only remained for the "Barclay" to return to bring out the company, which it did, sailing from London on the 15th of July, and arriving in the Delaware a few weeks later.

The only account that we have of the arrival of the "George Barclay" with the company is that given by Mr. Fennell in his autobiography. Fennell had come out by another vessel, arriving in New York five weeks in advance of the others. The first tidings he had upon landing was that the yellow fever was raging in Philadelphia, but he continued his journey to the plague-stricken city, which he found almost deserted. Mr. Reinagle, however, had remained at his post; and Mr. Morris, the veteran comedian, was apparently living at his own house in the city, for it was there that Fennell encountered Mr. Wignell immediately upon his arrival. Wignell had left the "George Barclay" anchored in the Delaware off Gloucester, with the

company on board, fifty-six in all. Securing a supply of fresh vege-
tables and other provisions, the manager returned to the ship, accompanied by the tragedian. As soon as possible the members of the
company were landed, Harwood, Fennell says, on touching the shore
in the Jerseys, falling on his knees and kissing it in imitation of an
English king, who had played the same prank to acquire popularity.
The families were cared for by the farmers in the neighborhood, and
the single men found lodgings at a tavern at Sandtown. There they
remained for several weeks, and were then conducted to Annapolis,
where the theatrical campaign finally began.

It was scarcely to be expected that the Annapolis season would
prove profitable, but that city was the only place open to the company.
Philadelphia, owing to the plague, was certain to be unavailable until
midwinter. The only theatre in Baltimore belonged to Hallam
and Henry. Fortunately for Wig-nell, the terms on which the Old
American Company had held the playhouse at Annapolis had been
practically surrendered. In that house, accordingly, the company
opened on the 20th of December with the " Castle of Andalusia " for a brief holiday season. The subjoined list of performances is far from complete, but the only additional
play that I have seen mentioned was " Othello," in which Fennell
played the title-role. A country gentleman in the boxes who had
never seen the play before, according to the veracious tragedian, was

LIST OF PERFORMANCES—*Annapolis.*

1793.
Dec. 20—Castle of Andalusia . . O'Keefe
    26—Belle's Stratagem . . Mrs. Cowley
        Flitch of Bacon . . . . . . Bate
1794.
Jan. 3—Rivals . . . . Sheridan
        Poor Soldier . . . . . O'Keefe
    13—Every One Has His Fault
                    Mrs. Inchbald
        Agreeable Surprise . . . O'Keefe
    17—Road to Ruin . . . . . Holcroft
        Deserter . . . . Dibdin
        Caledonian Frolic . . . Francis
    24—Robin Hood . . . . . MacNally
        Village Lawyer . . . Macready

so impressed with the intelligence of the *Moor* that he was willing to pay $500 for the negro, but failed to make the purchase. The company was received with great hospitality by the Maryland gentry, but Annapolis had already ceased to be a theatrical town.

At last, after more than thirteen months' delay since its completion, the New Theatre in Philadelphia was opened to the public on the 17th of February, 1794. The house was crowded to its full capacity, the receipts being $850. The order of productions on the earlier nights of the season, it will be observed, was an alternation of opera, tragedy and comedy, with accompanying farces, ballets and pantomimes. The "Castle of Andalusia," on the opening night, served to introduce some of the leading singers—Darley, Mr. and Mrs. Marshall, Mrs. Warrell and Miss Broadhurst—with Mrs. Francis and Mrs. Rowson in the farce. In "Isabella," on the second night, Mr. Fennell and Mr. and Mrs. Whitlock were brought forward. The third night served for the introduction of Chalmers as *Vapid* in the "Dramatist." Mr. Francis, who had previously appeared as

LIST OF PERFORMANCES.

1794.

Feb.	17—Castle of Andalusia . .	O'Keefe
	Who's the Dupe? .	Mrs. Cowley
	19—Isabella	Southerne
	Rosina	Mrs. Brooke
	21—Dramatist	Reynolds
	Flitch of Bacon	Bate
	24—Venice Preserved	Otway
	Lying Valet	Garrick
	26—Love in a Village . .	Bickerstaff
	Caledonian Frolic . . .	Francis
	Guardian	Garrick
	28—Jealous Wife	Colman
	Scheming Clown . . .	Francis
	Lyar	Foote
Mar.	3—School for Scandal . .	Sheridan
	Poor Soldier	O'Keefe
	5—Carmelite	Cumberland
	Spoiled Child	Bickerstaff
	7—Every One Has His Fault	
		Mrs. Inchbald
	Village Lawyer . . .	Macready
	8—Every One Has His Fault.	
	Poor Soldier.	
	10—Robin Hood . . .	MacNally
	Who's the Dupe?	
	12—Douglas	Home
	Farmer	O'Keefe
	14—Robin Hood.	
	Lyar.	
	17—Isabella.	
	St. Patrick's Day . . .	Sheridan
	19—Castle of Andalusia.	
	Sailor's Landlady . . .	Francis

Mar. 19—Spoiled Child.
   21—School for Wives . . . . Kelly
      Deserter . . . . . . Dibdin
   22—Jealous Wife.
      Virgin Unmasked . . . Fielding
   24—Every One Has His Fault.
      Poor Soldier.
(For American captives in Algiers.)
   26—Fair Penitent . . . . . Rowe
      Catharine and Petruchio
                  Shakspere
   28—Dramatist.
      Farmer.
   29—Love in a Village.
      Village Lawyer.
   31—Grecian Daughter . . . Murphy
      Spoiled Child.
April 2—Grecian Daughter.
      Son-in-Law . . . . . . O'Keefe
    4—Highland Reel . . . . O'Keefe
      Lying Valet.
    5—Highland Reel.
      Catharine and Petruchio.
    7—Macbeth . . . . . . Shakspere
      Flitch of Bacon.
    9—Rivals . . . . Sheridan
      Agreeable Surprise . . O'Keefe
  11—Gamester . . . . . . Moore
      Guardian.
  12—Macbeth.
      Miss in Her Teens . . . Garrick
  14—Road to Ruin . . . . . Holcroft
      Agreeable Surprise.
  17—Highland Reel.
      Miss in Her Teens.
  21—Richard III . . . . . Shakspere
      Son-in-Law.
  23—School for Scandal.
      Peeping Tom of Coventry
                  O'Keefe
  25—Hamlet . . . . . . Shakspere
      Wrangling Lovers . . . . Lyon
  26—Rivals.
      Le Foret Noire.
  28—Hamlet.
      Le Foret Noire.

the *Officer* in "Venice Preserved," played *Hodge* in "Love in a Village" on the 26th of February. The same night he presented the first of his dances, a Scotch dance called the "Caledonian Frolic," in which he took part, together with Miss Willems and Mrs. De Marque. This dance had its first production at Annapolis in January. The first mention of Mrs. De Marque was an announcement in a Baltimore paper that Mr. and Mrs. De Marque, recently arrived from Europe, would give a concert in Mr. Storck's Long Room, November 25, 1793. Mrs. De Marque also appeared with Francis and the younger Darley in the second of Francis' dances, the "Scheming Clown." Mr. Reinagle furnished the music for the third in the series of pantomimical dances arranged by Francis, the "Sailor's Landlady," one of the songs of which, sung by Darley, was published. It was patriotic in character, and became very popular. A single stanza will show its character :—

For, under snug sail, we laugh at the gale,
 And, though landsmen look pale, never
  heed 'em ;
But toss off the glass to a favorite lass,
 To America, Commerce and Freedom.

In the fourth of Francis' dances, " Fruitless Precaution," M. Bellona, a French dancer and pantomimist, made his first appearance in America. In this piece, also, was Madame Gardie, whose American *debut* had been made on the 26th of April as *Lucille* in the French pantomime, " Le Foret Noire." Madame Gardie was announced " from the theatre at Paris." According to Dunlap, she was the nominal wife of M. Gardie, the son of a nobleman, receiver-general at La Rochelle for Louis XVI. One evening at the theatre, after the Revolution in France, the audience demanded the " Marsellaise," but she refused to sing it. Her withdrawal from the Parisian stage and a subsequent flight were the consequences. Accompanied by M. Gardie, the beautiful dancer

April 30—Highland Reel.
 Le Foret Noire.
May 2—Othello . . . . . . Shakspere
 Peeping Tom of Coventry.
 3—Dramatist.
 Le Foret Noire.
 5—Inkle and Yarico . . Colman, Jr
 Village Lawyer.
 7—Provoked Husband . . Vanbrugh
 Le Foret Noire.
 9—Inkle and Yarico.
 Wrangling Lovers.
 10—Othello.
 Peeping Tom of Coventry.
 12—Recruiting Officer . . Farquhar
 Le Foret Noire.
 14—Robin Hood.
 Who's the Dupe ?
 16—Maid of the Mill . . Bickerstaff
 Fruitless Precaution . . Francis
 Quality Binding . . . . . Rose
 19—Surrender of Calais . Colman, Jr
 Sultan . . . . . . Bickerstaff
 (Mr. Fennell's benefit.)
 21—West Indian . . . Cumberland
 Triumph of Mirth.
 (Mr. Chalmers' benefit.)
 23—Duenna . . . . Sheridan
 Robinson Crusoe . . . Sheridan
 (Mr. Bates' benefit.)
 26—She Wou'd and She Wou'd Not
  Cibber
 Prize . . . . Hoare
 (Mr. Morris' benefit.)
 28—Julia . . . . Jephson
 Bon Ton . . . . Garrick
 (Mr. Whitlock's benefit.)
 30—As You Like It . . . Shakspere
 Hartford Bridge . . . . Pearce
 (Mr. Marshall's benefit.)
June 2—Lionel and Clarissa . Bickerstaff
 Modern Antiques . . . O'Keefe
 (Mrs. Warrell's benefit.)
 4—Romeo and Juliet . . Shakspere
 Romp . . . . Bickerstaff
 (Mrs. Marshall's benefit.)

June   6—Every One Has His Fault.
   No Song No Supper.
   (Mr. Darley's benefit.)
  9—Battle of Hexham . . Colman, Jr
   True-Born Irishman . . Macklin
   (Mrs. Morris' benefit.)
  11—Mourning Bride . . . Congreve
   Three Weeks After Marriage
           Murphy
   (Mrs. Whitlock's benefit.)
  13—Merchant of Venice . Shakspere
   Embargo.
   (Mr. Finch's benefit.)
  16—Gustavus Vasa . . . . . Brooke
   Harlequin Shipwrecked.
  (Mr. and Mrs. Francis' benefit.)
  18—Woodman . . . . Bate Dudley
   Critic . . . . Sheridan
   (Miss. Broadhurst's benefit.)
  20—How to Grow Rich . . Reynolds
   Le Foret Noire.
   (Mr. Green's benefit.)
  23—Julia.
   Waterman . . . . . . Dibdin
   (Mrs. Shaw's benefit.)
  25—Wonder . . . . Mrs. Centlivre
   Comus . . . . Milton
  (Moreton and Harwood's benefit.)
  27—Macbeth.
   Jeanne d'Arc.
  (Mad. Gardie and Miss Willems' benefit.)
  30—Slaves in Algiers . Mrs. Rowson
   Citizen . . . . . . Murphy
  (Mr. and Mrs. Rowson's benefit.)
July 2—Widow of Malabar . Humphreys
   L'Americain.
   Selima and Azor . . . . Collier
  (Mr. and Mrs. Cleveland's benefit.)
  7—Spanish Barber . . . . Colman
   Scheming Milliners . . . Francis
   Prisoner at Large . . . O'Keefe
   (Mrs. Oldmixon's benefit.)
  9—Cymbeline . . . . . Shakspere
   Irish Lilt . . . . . . Francis
   Devil Upon Two Sticks . . Foote
  (Blissett and Mrs. De Marque's benefit.)
  11—Comus.

first went to Saint Francoise, and from San Domingo they came to Philadelphia. Madame Gardie does not appear to have created the impression in Philadelphia that she afterward made in New York, for she retired from Wignell and Reinagle's company at the close of the season, joining the Old American Company during Hallam and Hodgkinson's Southwark engagement in the Autumn. The repertory of the first season at the New Theatre was remarkably strong in operatic productions, or what was called opera. But even the tragedies were given with a musical completeness before unknown in this country, the great number of singers in the company affording the managers facilities for embellishing such plays as "Romeo and Juliet" and "Macbeth" with genuine artists in the vocal parts. In the choruses, at this time, were all the singers in the company not engaged in the casts. In these, too, the beginners, as Miss Oldfield this season, took their first lessons in facing an audience. Besides, Mr. Reinagle frequently composed new overtures and furnished additional airs for the musical productions. Among the pieces to which he added new songs were "Robin Hood," the " Highland Reel "—

Ways and Means . . Colman, Jr
Prize.
(Mr. Franklin's benefit.)
July 14—Tempest . . . . Dryden
Birth of Harlequin.
(Mr. Milbourne's benefit.)
16—Gamester.
Irish Lilt.
Sultan.
(Blissett, De Moulin, Mrs. De Marque and Madame Gardie's benefit.)
18—Every One Has His Fault.
Birth of Harlequin.
(For a Dramatic Fund.)

a song for Darley, words by Mrs. Rowson—and " Le Foret Noire," of which the overture and music were entirely new. Mr. Reinagle also furnished incidental music for many other productions. Among those who profited by the benefits were Mr. Milbourne, the scene-painter, and Mr. Franklin, the box-keeper.

Two American productions were presented during the season —a comedy by Mrs. Rowson, called " Slaves in Algiers," and an after-piece, the " Embargo, or Every One Has His Own Opinion," by a citizen of Philadelphia. Both pieces were the outcome of American feeling. Not fewer than fifteen American vessels had been captured, and one hundred and eighty

SLAVES IN ALGIERS.

Muley Moloch . . . Mr. Green
Frederick . . . . . Mr. Moreton
Henry . . . . . Mr. Cleveland
Constant . . . Mr. Whitlock
Sebastian . . . . . Mr. Bates
Ben Hassan . . . Mr. Francis
Mustapha . . . Mr. Darley, Jr
Sadi . . . . . Master Warrell
Selim . . . . . . Mr. Blissett
Zoriana . . . . Mrs. Warrell
Fetnah . . . . Mrs. Marshall
Rebecca . . . . Mrs. Whitlock
Selima . . . . Mrs. Cleveland
Olivia . . . . Mrs. Rowson

EMBARGO.

Mr. Neverfret . . . Mr. Bates
Captain Standby . Mr. Darley
Ben Standby . . . Mr. Green
Jack Mainstay . . Mr. Francis
Bob Overhaul . . Mr. Blissett
Patrick O'Flanagan . Mr. Finch
Mrs. Neverfret . . . Mrs. Shaw
Lucy . . . . . . Mrs. Warrell
Ruth Doublescore . Mrs. Bates

American officers and seamen made slaves by the Algerines before the close of 1793. This furnished Mrs. Rowson with her theme, but the result was only a turgid drama, equally faulty in dramatic construction and as a literary production. The style was wretched, the dramatic quality tawdry, and the sentiment strained and stilted. The play was published soon after its initial performance, and would probably have been forgotten in a few months had it not had the good fortune to fall under the lash of the celebrated William Cobbett. He jeered at Mrs. Rowson as a self-constituted poetess laureate of the Sovereign People of the United States, doubted the sincerity of her sudden conversion to republicanism, and ridiculed her disjointed lines and illogical speeches. The " Embargo," on the other hand, was not so intensely political, notwithstanding it was a satire on the political topic that was uppermost at the time. This skit can be judged only from the names of the characters, as it was not printed, and no mention of it was made in the newspapers. It was probably local in its satire, directing its shafts at both sides to the embargo dispute of 1794, as its subtitle indicates. Although this embargo was for only thirty days, it brought the country to the verge of war. Without either army or navy, the Democratic societies were hotly in favor of its continuance. It may be assumed, however, that *Mr. Neverfret* was inclined to support President Washington, who preferred diplomacy to war for the settlement of all questions affecting the depredations on American commerce in consequence of the British Orders in Council. The names of *Patrick O'Flanagan* and *Ruth Doublescore* suggest the meeting of the captains and mates of all the brigs, snows and schooners in the Delaware, at the Harp and Crown tavern of Barnabas McShane, who adopted a little ten days' embargo of their own. The soldier, *Captain Standby*, no doubt represented the military fervor for defense that was then blazing all over the country, and the two sailors, *Jack*

Mainstay and *Bob Overhaul*, the intrepid spirit that humbled the naval supremacy of Great Britain by removing the mainmast of a British merchantman at her dock. It is to be regretted that the piece is lost, as it would show the theatrical treatment of the first great warlike wave that swept over the new republic.

While the production of Mrs. Rowson's turgid drama and of the anonymous skit on the embargo was no sign of the development of American dramatic writing, the new dances and pantomimic ballets composed by William Francis for the New Theatre this season

SAILOR'S LANDLADY.

Jack . . . . Mr. Francis
Ned Halyard . . . . Mr. Darley, Jr
Landlady . . . . Mr. Rowson
Orange Girl . . . . Mrs. De Marque

were indications of progress in the art of providing for the public amusement. Of Mr. Francis' six dances his Scotch pastoral, the "Caledonian Frolic," has been mentioned as given at Annapolis. Three of the others—the "Scheming Clown," the "Sailor's Landlady" and " L'Amour Trouve les Moyens, or Fruitless Precaution "—have already been named as serving for the introduction of distinguished dancers. The cast of the " Sailor's Landlady," the only pantomime in which the characters were named in the newspapers, is herewith printed. The two pieces that completed Mr. Francis' list of original productions were the " Scheming Milliners," produced for Mrs. Oldmixon's benefit, and the " Irish Lilt," presented for the benefit of Mr. Blissett and Mrs. De Marque. The industry that Mr. Francis showed at the outset was continued for many years with great productive vigor.

The only pieces presented during the season that it seems necessary to treat separately were those of the opening night—the "Castle of Andalusia " and " Who's the Dupe? "—and the bill for the second performance—" Venice Preserved " and the " Lying Valet."

These served to introduce the new company to the patrons of the New Theatre, and for this reason the casts will be studied with peculiar interest. There were, of course, the *cognoscenti* of Philadelphia in the pit and boxes, to judge the new performers. Besides Wignell and Morris, the only familiar faces in the cast of the opening piece, the opera included all the newcomers except Mr. Fennell, Mr. and Mrs. Whitlock, Mr. and Mrs. Francis, Mr. and Mrs. Cleveland, Mr. and Mrs. Rowson, Messrs. Chalmers, Harwood and Blissett, Mr. Warrell and his two sons, Mrs. Shaw and Miss Willems. Mrs. Oldmixon had not yet arrived in the country. Of these, Messrs. Cleveland and Harwood and Mrs. Francis and Mrs. Rowson were seen in the farce the same night. The tragedy, "Venice Preserved," on the second night of the season, introduced Mr. Fennel, Mr. and Mrs. Whitlock and Messrs. Warrell and Francis; and Mrs. Shaw was brought forward the same evening as *Kitty Pry* in the "Lying Valet." These comprised all the principal members of the company, with the exception of Mr. Chalmers and Mrs. Oldmixon, the others making their first appearances as occasion served.

CASTLE OF ANDALUSIA.

Don Scipio	Mr. Finch
Don Cæsar	Mr. Darley
Don Fernando	Mr. Marshall
Don Juan	Mr. Morris
Don Alphonso	Mr. Moreton
Pedrillo	Mr. Bates
Spado	Mr. Wignell
Sanguino	Mr. Green
Phillipo	Mr. Darley, Jr
Victoria	Mrs. Warrell
Lorenza	Mrs. Marshall
Isabella	Mrs. Bates
Catalina	Miss Broadhurst

WHO'S THE DUPE?

Doiley	Mr. Morris
Sandford	Mr. Moreton
Granger	Mr. Cleveland
Gradus	Mr. Harwood
Miss Doiley	Mrs. Francis
Charlotte	Mrs. Rowson

VENICE PRESERVED.

Duke	Mr. Finch
Priuli	Mr. Whitlock
Bedamar	Mr. Marshall
Pierre	Mr. Fennell
Jaffier	Mr. Wignell
Renault	Mr. Green
Spinosa	Mr. Harwood
Elliot	Mr. Moreton
Durand	Mr. Warrell
Officer	Mr. Francis
Belvidera	Mrs. Whitlock

LYING VALET.

Sharp	Mr. Bates
Gayless	Mr. Moreton
Guttle	Mr. Warrell
Trippet	Mr. Harwood
Drunken Cook	Mr. Francis
Melissa	Mrs. Francis
Mrs. Gadabout	Mrs. Bates
Mrs. Trippet	Mrs. Rowson
Kitty Pry	Mrs. Shaw

In order to present the work of this first season in Philadelphia as compactly as possible, I have preferred to arrange the casts, except

PHILADELPHIA CASTS—FIRST SEASON.

AGREEABLE SURPRISE.

Sir Felix Friendly . . Mr. Finch
Compton . . . . . . Mr. Darley
Eugene . . . . . . Mr. Marshall
Chicane . . . . . . Mr. Warrell
John . . . . Mr. Francis
Thomas . . . . Mr. Green
Farmer Stump . . Mr. De Moulin
Cudden . . . . . . Mr. Blissett
Lingo . . . . Mr. Bates
Laura . . . . . Miss Broadhurst
Mrs. Cheshire . . . . Mrs. Shaw
Cowslip . . . . . Mrs. Marshall
Fringe . . . . . . Mrs. Rowson

AS YOU LIKE IT.

Orlando . . . . . . Mr. Moreton
Adam . . . . . . Mr. Whitlock
Banished Duke . . . Mr. Green
Duke Frederick . . Mr. Warrell
Amicus . . . . . . Mr. Marshall
Jaques . . . . . . Mr. Chalmers
Le Beau . . . . Mr. Finch
Oliver . . . . . . Mr. Harwood
Jaques De Bois . Mr. Darley, Jr
Dennis . . . . . Master Warrell
Charles . . . . . . Mr. Rowson
Touchstone . . . . . Mr. Bates
Corin . . . . . . Mr. De Moulin
Sylvius . . . . . Mr. Cleveland
William . . . . . . Mr. Francis
Rosalind . . . . Mrs. Marshall
Celia . . . . . . Mrs. Francis
Phœbe . . . . . Mrs. Cleveland
Audrey . . . . Mrs. Shaw

BATTLE OF HEXHAM.

Montague . . . . . Mr. Green
Warwick . . . . Mr. Cleveland
Somerset . . . . . . Mr. Warrell
Le Varenne . . . . Mr. Moreton
Corporal . . . . . Mr. Harwood
Drummer . . . . . Mr. Francis
Fifer . . . . Mr. Blissett
Fool . . . . . . Mr. Wignell
Barton . . . . . . Mr. Whitlock
Gondibert . . . . . Mr. Fennell
Gregory Gubbins . . . Mr. Bates
Prince Edward, Master T. Warrell
Margaret of Anjou, Mrs. Whitlock
Adeline . . . . . Mrs. Marshall

BIRTH OF HARLEQUIN.

Harlequin Skip . Mr. Milbourne
Bob Saunter . . . Mr. Cleveland
Maid . . . . . . Mrs. Rowson
Skip Harlequin . . . Mr. Francis
Pantaloon . . . . . Mr. Bellona
Clown . . . . . . Mr. Milbourne
Columbine . . . Madame Gardie

CATHARINE AND PETRUCHIO.

Petruchio . . . . Mr. Chalmers
Baptista . . . . . . Mr. Warrell
Hortensio . . . Mr. Cleveland
Grumio . . . . . . Mr. Morris
Music Master . . . Mr. Francis
Biondello . . . . Mr. Harwood
Pedro . . . . Mr. Green
Tailor . . . . . . Mr. Blissett
Catharine . . . . Mrs. Morris
Bianca . . . . Mrs. Cleveland
Curtis . . . . Mrs. Bates

CITIZEN.

Old Philpot . . . . Mr. Morris
Young Philpot . . Mr. Chalmers
Sir Jasper . . . . Mr. Warrell
Young Wilding . . . Mr. Green
Beaufort . . . . . Mr. Cleveland
Dapper . . . . . . Mr. Francis
Quilldrive . . . . Mr. Blissett
Maria . . . . . Mrs. Rowson
Corinna . . . . . Miss Rowson

COMUS.

Comus . . . . . . Mr. Fennell
First Spirit . . . . Mr. Green
Elder Brother . . . Mr. Moreton
Younger Brother . Mr. Cleveland
Lady . . . . . Mrs. Whitlock
Sabrina . . . . Miss Broadhurst
Pastoral Nymph . Mrs. Marshall
Bachante . . . . Mrs. Warrell
Euphrosyne . . . Mr. Oldmixon

CRITIC.

Dangle . . . . . . Mr. Wignell
Sneer . . . . . . Mr. Fennell
Sir Fretful Plagiary, Mr. Harwood
Sig. Pasticio . . . Mr. Marshall
Interpreter . . . . . Mr. Finch

Puff . . . . Mr. Chalmers
Mrs. Dangle . . . . Mrs. Francis
Lord Burleigh . . . . Mr. Bates
Governor . . . . . . Mr. Darley
Leicester . . . . Mr. Cleveland
Sir Walter Raleigh . . Mr. Green
Sir C. Hatton . . . Mr. Francis
Master of Horse . . Mr. Warrell
First Niece . . . Mrs. Cleveland
Second Niece . . . Miss Willems
Confidant . . . . . Mrs. Rowson
Tilburina . . . . . Mrs. Shaw
Don Whiskerandos . Mr. Moreton

CYMBELINE.

Cymbeline . . . . . Mr. Green
Cloten . . . . . . Mr. Blissett
Posthumous . . . Mr. Fennell
Arviragus . . . Mr. Harwood
Guiderius . . . Mr. Cleveland
Belarius . . . . Mr. Whitlock
Philario . . . . . Mr. Darley
Iachimo . . . . . Mr. Moreton
Caius Lucius . . . . Mr. Bates
Pisanio . . . . Mr. Marshall
Frenchman . . . . Mr. Finch
Cornelius . . . . Mr. Warrell
First Lord . . . Mr. Francis
Second Lord . . . Mr. De Moulin
Roman Captive . Mr. Darley, Jr
Queen . . . . . . Mrs. Shaw
Helena . . . . Mrs. Cleveland
Imogen . . . . Mrs. Whitlock

DESERTER.

Henry . . . . . . Mr. Marshall
Russet . . . . . . Mr. Darley
Skirmish . . . . . . Mr. Bates
Simkin . . . . . . Mr. Francis
Flint . . . . Mr. Blissett
Louisa . . . . . Mrs. Marshall
Jenny . . . . Miss Broadhurst
Margaretta . . . . Mrs. Bates

DEVIL UPON TWO STICKS.

Devil . . . . . . Mr. Wignell
Sir Thomas . . . . Mr. Finch
Invoice . . . . Mr. Cleveland
Julep . . . . . . Mr. Bates
Apoxem . . . . . Mr. Francis
Dr. Calomel . . Mr. De Moulin

those already given, in alphabetical presentment. These casts comprise all that were preserved, and show the parts of each member of

PHILADELPHIA CASTS—FIRST SEASON.

Dr. Camphire . . . Mr. Warrell
Dr. Last . . . . . . Mr. Blissett
Forceps . . . . . Mr. Darley, Jr
Secretary . . . . Mr. Harwood
Printer's Devil . Master Warrell
Mrs. Marg. Maxwell . Mrs. Shaw
Harriet . . . . Miss Broadhurst

DOUGLAS.

Lord Randolph . . . Mr. Green
Glenalvon . . . . Mr. Fennell
Old Norval . . . . Mr. Whitlock
Young Norval . . . Mr. Moreton
Lady Randolph . Mrs. Whitlock
Anna . . . . . . Mrs. Cleveland

DRAMATIST.

Lord Scratch . . . . . Mr. Bates
Neville . . . . . Mr. Cleveland
Floriville . . . . . Mr. Moreton
Willoughby . . . . . Mr. Green
Ennui . . . . Mr. Finch
Peter . . . . . . Mr. Francis
Vapid . . . . . . Mr. Chalmers
Mrs. Courtney . . . Mrs. Francis
Lady Waitford . . Mrs. Rowson
Letty . . . . . Mrs. Cleveland
Marianne . . . . Mrs. Marshall

DUENNA.

Don Jerome . . . . . Mr. Finch
Don Ferdinand . . Mr. Marshall
Antonio . . . . . . Mr. Francis
Carlos . . . . Mr. Darley, Jr
Lopez . . . . . . Mr. Blissett
Father Paul . . . . Mr. Darley
Father Frank . . . Mr. Warrell
Starved Friar . . Mr. De Moulin
Isaac Mendoza . . . . Mr. Bates
Clara . . . . . Miss Broadhurst
Louisa . . . . . . Mrs. Warrell
Flora . . . . . . Mrs. Cleveland
Margaret . . . . . . Mrs. Shaw

EVERY ONE HAS HIS FAULT.

Lord Norland . . . Mr. Whitlock
Sir Robert Ramble . Mr. Chalmers
Mr. Solus . . . . . . Mr. Morris
Mr. Harmony . . . . Mr. Bates
Capt. Irwin . . . . Mr. Fennell

Mr. Placid . . . . Mr. Moreton
Hammond . . . . . Mr. Green
Porter . . . . . . Mr. Warrell
Edward . . . . . Mrs. Marshall
Lady Eleanor . Mrs. Whitlock
Mrs. Placid . . Mrs. Rowson
Miss Spinster . . . Mrs. Bates
Miss Wooburn . . . Mrs. Morris

FAIR PENITENT.

Sciolto . . . . . Mr. Whitlock
Altamont . . . . . Mr. Green
Horatio . . . . . Mr. Fennell
Lothario . . . . Mr. Moreton
Rossano . . . . . Mr. Francis
Calista . . . . Mrs. Whitlock
Lavinia . . . . . Mrs. Francis
Lucilla . . . . . Mrs. Rowson

FARMER.

Colonel Dormant . . . Mr. Green
Valentine . . . . Mr. Marshall
Fairly . . . . . . Mr. Warrell
Flummery . . . . Mr. Blissett
Farmer Blackberry . Mr. Darley
Jemmy Jumps . . . Mr. Bates
Rundy . . . . . . Mr. Francis
Farmer Stubble . . . Mr. Morris
Louisa . . . . . Mrs. Warrell
Betty Blackberry . Mrs. Rowson
Mollie Maybush . Miss Broadhurst
Landlady . . . . . Mrs. Bates

FLITCH OF BACON.

Justice Benbow . . Mr. Warrell
Maj. Benbow . . Mr. Harwood
Captain Greville . Mr. Marshall
Captain Wilson . . . Mr. Darley
Tipple . . . . . . Mr. Francis
Eliza . . . . . Miss Broadhurst

GAMESTER.

Beverly . . . . . Mr. Fennell
Stukely . . . . . Mr. Wignell
Lewson . . . . Mr. Cleveland
Jarvis . . . . . Mr. Whitlock
Bates . . . . Mr. Green
Dawson . . . . . Mr. Moreton
Waiter . . . . Mr. De Moulin
Mrs. Beverly . . Mrs. Whitlock
Charlotte . . . Mrs. Francis
Lucy . . . . . Mrs. Cleveland

GRECIAN DAUGHTER.

Evander . . . . . Mr. Whitlock
Philotas . . . . . . Mr. Moreton
Melanthon . . . . Mr. Green
Phocion . . . . . Mr. Cleveland
Dionysius . . . . Mr. Fennell
Calippus . . . . . Mr. Warrell
Arcas . . . . . . Mr. Francis
Creek Herald . . . . Mr. Finch
Greek Officer . . Mr. Harwood
Euphrasia . . . Mrs. Whitlock
Erixene . . . . . Mrs. Cleveland

GUARDIAN.

Mr. Heartly . . . Mr. Whitlock
Sir Charles Clackit . . Mr. Morris
Young Clackit . . . . Mr. Finch
Servant . . . . Master Warrell
Lucy . . . . . . Mrs. Rowson
Harriet . . . . . Mrs. Marshall

GUSTAVUS VASA.

Christiern . . . . Mr. Marshall
Trollio . . . . . . Mr. Green
Peterson . . . . . Mr. Francis
Laertes . . . . Mr. Cleveland
Gustavus . . . . Mr. Fennell
Arvida . . . . . Mr. Wignell
Anderson . . . . . Mr. Finch
Arnoldus . . . . Mr. Harwood
Siward . . . . . Mr. Warrell
Christiana . . . Mrs. Whitlock
Augusta . . . . . . Mrs. Shaw
Marianne . . . Mrs. Cleveland

HAMLET.

Hamlet . . . . . Mr. Fennell
King . . . . Mr. Green
Ghost . . . . . Mr. Whitlock
Horatio . . . Mr. Marshall
Laertes . . . . . Mr. Moreton
Polonius . . . . Mr. Morris
Rosencranz . . . Mr. Francis
Guildenstern . . Mr. Cleveland
Player King . . Mr. De Moulin
Francisco . . . Mr. Darley, Jr
Bernardo . . . . Mr. Warrell
Marcellus . . . Mr. Harwood
Osric . . . . . . Mr. Finch
Officer . . . . . . Mr. Blissett

the company so far as they are accessible. They also present the names of the other *debutantes* of the season. These, in chronological

PHILADELPHIA CASTS—FIRST SEASON.

Gravediggers . . { Mr. Bates
{ Mr. Wignell
Queen . . . . Mrs. Shaw
Ophelia . . . . . Mrs. Marshall
Player Queen . . . Mrs. Rowson

HARLEQUIN SHIPWRECKED.

Harlequin . . . . . Mr. Francis
Genius of Liberty . . Mrs. Warrell

HARTFORD BRIDGE.

Sir Gregory Forrester . Mr. Bates
Peregrine Forrester . Mr. Moreton
Capt. Fuldair . . . Mr. Marshall
Gapt. Forrester . Mr. Cleveland
Cartridge . . . . . Mrs. Francis
Peter . . . . Mr. Blissett
Waiter . . . . Mr. Finch
Clara . . . . . . Mrs. Marshall
Susan . . . . . . Miss Willems
Barmaid . . . . . Mrs. Rowson

HIGHLAND REEL.

Laird of Col . . . . Mr. Green
Raasay . . . . . . Mr. Warrell
MacGilpin . . . . . . Mr. Finch
Sandy . . . . . . Mr. Marshall
Charley . . . . . . Mr. Francis
Shelty . . . . Mr. Bates
Croudy . . . . . Mr. Harwood
Capt. Dash . . . . Mr. Moreton
Serjt. Jack . . . . Mr. Darley
Apie . . . . Mr. Blissett
Benin . . . . . Master Warrell
Moggy . . . . . Mrs. Marshall
Jenny . . . . . . Mrs. Warrell

HOW TO GROW RICH.

Pave . . . . Mr. Chalmers
Smalltrade . . . . . Mr. Bates
Roundhead . . . . . Mr. Finch
Latitat . . . . . . Mr. Green
Hippy . . . . Mr. Francis
Warford . . . . . Mr. Moreton
Sir Chas. Dazzle . Mr. Cleveland
Plainly . . . . . Mr. De Moulin
Nab . . . . Mr. Rowson
Formal . . . . . Mr. Warrell
Lady Henrietta . Mrs. Whitlock
Rosa . . . . . Mrs. Marshall
Miss Dazzle . . . Mrs. Francis
Betty . . . . . Mrs. Cleveland

ISABELLA.

Count Baldwin . . Mr. Whitlock
Biron . . . . . . Mr. Fennell
Carlos . . . . Mr. Green
Villeroy . . . . . Mr. Wignell
Sampson . . . . . . Mr. Bates
Belford . . . . Mr. Cleveland
Pedro . . . . Mr. Green
Officer . . . . . . Mr. Warrell
Isabella . . . . Mrs. Whitlock
Nurse . . . . . . Mrs. Rowson

JEALOUS WIFE.

Oakly . . . . . . Mr. Fennell
Major Oakly . . . Mr. Whitlock
Charles . . . . . Mr. Moreton
Russet . . . . . . Mr. Wignell
Sir Harry Beagle . Mr. Chalmers
Lord Trinket . . . Mr. Finch
Captain O'Cutter . . Mr. Bates
William . . . . Mr. Darley, Jr
John . . . . . . Mr. Warrell
Tom . . . . Mr. Francis
Servant . . . . Master Warrell
Mrs. Oakly . . . Mrs. Whitlock
Lady Freelove . . . . Mrs. Shaw
Harriet . . . . . Mrs. Francis
Toilet . . . . . . Mrs. Rowson
Chambermaid . . . Miss Willems

JEANNE D'ARC.

Jeanne d'Arc . Madame Gardie
St. Denis . . . Mr. Cleveland
Dunois . . . . . Mr. Marshall
Le Tremonille . . . Mr. Bellona
Porte Guidon . . . . Mr. Darley
Chandos . . . . Mr. Moreton
Officer . . . . Mr. De Moulin
Padlock . . . . . Mr. Francis

JULIA.

Duke of Guise . . . Mr. Finch
Durazzo . . . . . . Mr. Green
Mentevole . . . . Mr. Fennell
Marcellus . Mr. Moreton
Camillo . . . . Mr. Cleveland
Officer . . . . Mr. De Moulin
Servant . . . . Master Warrell
Manon . . . . . Mr. Whitlock
Fulvia . . . . . . Mrs. Shaw

Julia . . . . . . Mrs. Whitlock
Olympia . . . . Mrs. Francis
Nerina . . . . Mrs. Cleveland

L'AMERICAIN.

Jaques Splin . . Mrs. Cleveland
Jaquot . . . . . . Mr. Finch
Loyer . . . . . . Mr. Bellona
L'Huiffier . . . . Miss Rowson
Therese . . . Madame Gardie

LIONEL AND CLARISSA.

Sir John Flowerdale, Mr. Whitlock
Colonel Oldboy . . . Mr. Bates
Jessamy . . . . . Mr. Moreton
Lionel . . . . . . Mr. Marshall
Harman . . . . . Mr. Cleveland
Jenkins . . . . . Mr. Darley
Lady Oldboy . . . . Mrs. Shaw
Clarissa . . . . . Mrs. Warrell
Diana . . . . Mrs. Oldmixon
Jenny . . . . . . Miss Willems

LOVE IN A VILLAGE.

Sir William Meadows . Mr. Morris
Justice Woodcock , . Mr. Bates
Hawthorn . . . . . Mr. Darley
Young Meadows . Mr. Marshall
Eustace . . . . . Mr. Darley, Jr
Hodge . . . . . . Mr. Francis
Deborah . . . . . . Mrs. Shaw
Lucinda . . . . Mrs. Warrell
Rosetta . . . . Mrs. Marshall
Madge . . . . Miss Broadhurst

LYAR.

Old Wilding . . . Mr. Whitlock
Young Wilding . . Mr. Chalmers
Sir James Elliot . Mr. Cleveland
Papillion . . . . . Mr. Finch
Miss Granthan . . Mrs. Francis
Miss Godfrey . . Mrs. Cleveland
Kitty . . . . . . Mrs. Rowson

MACBETH.

Macbeth . . . . . Mr. Fennell
Duncan . . . . . Mr. Green
Malcolm . . . . Mr. Cleveland
Donalbane . . . Master Warrell
Banquo . . . . . Mr. Whitlock

order, were Master Warrell, afterward Mr. Warrell, Jr., in these casts,
as the *Servant* in the " Guardian," on the 26th of February ; Miss Wil-

PHILADELPHIA CASTS—FIRST SEASON.

Macduff . . . . . . Mr. Moreton
Lenox . . . . . Mr. Harwood
Fleance . . . Master T. Warrell
Siward . . . . Mr. Warrell
Seyton . . . . Mr. Francis
Doctor . . . . . Mr. De Moulin
Messenger . . . . . Mr. Blissett
Lady Macbeth . . Mrs. Whitlock
Gentlewoman . . Mrs. Cleveland
Hecate . . . . Mr. Darley
First Witch . . . . . . Mr. Bates
Second Witch . . . . Mr. Finch
Third Witch . . . . Mr. Wignell

MAID OF THE MILL.

Lord Aimworth . . Mr. Marshall
Sir Harry Sycamore . . Mr. Bates
Mervin . . . . . Mr. Cleveland
Fairfield . . . . . Mr. Whitlock
Giles . . . . Mr. Darley
Ralph . . . . Mr. Wignell
Lady Sycamore . . . Mrs. Shaw
Theodosia . . . . Miss Willems
Patty . . . . . . Mrs. Warrell
Fanny . . . . . Mrs. Oldmixon

MERCHANT OF VENICE.

Duke . . . . Mr. Green
Antonio . . . . . Mr. Whitlock
Bassanio . . . . . Mr. Moreton
Gratiano . . . . Mr. Finch
Lorenzo . . . . . Mr. Marshall
Salerino . . . . . Mr. Cleveland
Solanio . . . . . . Mr. Harwood
Shylock . . . . . Mr. Chalmers
Tubal . . . . . . Mr. De Moulin
Launcelot . . . . . . Mr. Bates
Old Gobbo . . . . . Mr. Francis
Leonardo . . . . . Mr. Blissett
Balthazar . . . . Mr. Darley, Jr
Stephano . . . . . Mr. Warrell
Portia . . . . . . Mrs. Whitlock
Jessica . . . . . Miss Broadhurst
Nerissa . . . . . Mrs. Francis

MISS IN HER TEENS.

Captain Loveit . . . . Mr. Green
Fribble . . . . . . Mr. Marshall
Captain Flash . . . Mr. Chalmers
Puff . . . . Mr. Morris
Jasper . . . . Mr. Francis

Tag . . . . Mrs. Rowson
Miss Biddy . . . Mrs. Marshall

MODERN ANTIQUES.

Cockletop . . . . . Mr. Francis
Frank . . . . Mr. Green
Joey . . . . Mr. Bates
Napkin . . . . Mr. Blissett
Hearty . . . . . Mr. De Moulin
Thomas . . . . . Mr. Warrell
Mrs. Cockletop . . . Mrs. Shaw
Mrs. Camomile . . Mrs. Rowson
Belinda . . . . Mrs. Cleveland
Nan . . . . Mrs. Francis
Florence . . . . . Mrs Bates
Betty . . . . . . Miss. Rowson

MOURNING BRIDE.

Manuel . . . . . . Mr. Whitlock
Osmyn . . . . Mr. Fennell
Gonzales . . . . . Mr. Green
Garcia . . . . . . Mr. Wignell
Heli . . . . . . Mr. Cleveland
Perez . . . . Mr. Francis
Selim . . . . . . Mr. Harwood
Alonzo . . . . . . Mr. Warrell
Almeria . . . . . Mrs. Morris
Zara . . . . . . Mrs. Whitlock
Leonora . . . . . Mrs. Francis

NO SONG NO SUPPER.

Frederick . . . . Mr. Marshall
Crop . . . . Mr. Darley
Endless . . . . Mr. Harwood
Robin . . . . . . Mr. Bates
William . . . . Mr. Darley, Jr
Dorothy . . . . . Mrs. Shaw
Louisa . . . . Miss Broadhurst
Margaretta . . Mrs. Oldmixon
Nelly . . . . . Miss Willems

POOR SOLDIER.

Captain Fitzroy . . Mr. Darley
Father Luke . . . . Mr. Finch
Dermot . . . . Mr. Darley, Jr
Patrick . . . . . . Mr. Moreton
Darby . . . . . Mr. Wignell
Bagatelle . . . . Mr. Marshall
Boy . . . . . Master T. Warrell
Norah . . . . Miss Broadhurst
Kathleen . . . . Miss Willems

PRISONER AT LARGE.

Lord Osmond . . . Mr. Fennell
Old Dowdle . . . . . Mr. Bates
Count Fripon . . . . Mr. Finch
Jack Conner . . . Mr. Harwood
Father Frank . . . . Mr. Blissett
Frill . . . . Mr. Francis
Phelim . . . . . Master Warrell
Tough . . . . Mr. Morris
Trap . . . . . . Mr. Darley, Jr
Muns . . . . Mr. Wignell
Adelaide . . . . Mrs. Cleveland
Rachel . . . . . . Mrs. Marshall
Mary . . . . . . Mrs. Rowson
Landlady . . . . . Mrs. Bates

PRIZE.

Dr. Lenitive . . . Mr. Harwood
Mr. Heartwell . . . Mr. Moreton
Mr. Caddy . . . . . Mr. Finch
Label . . . . . . Mr. Wignell
Boy . . . . Master T. Warrell
Juba . . . . Miss Broadhurst
Mrs. Caddy . . . . Mrs. Rowson
Caroline . . . . Mrs. Oldmixon

PROVOKED HUSBAND.

Lord Townly . . . Mr. Fennell
Manly . . . . Mr. Green
Sir Francis . . . . . Mr. Morris
Count Basset . . . . Mr. Finch
Squire Richard . . . Mr. Blissett
John Moody . . . . Mr. Bates
Poundage . . . . Mr. De Moulin
Constable . . . . Mr. Warrell
James . . . . . . Master Warrell
Servant . . . . . Mr. Darley, Jr
Lady Townly . . . Mrs. Morris
Lady Grace . . . . Mrs. Francis
Lady Wronghead . . Mrs. Shaw
Jenny . . . . . Mrs. Cleveland
Trusty . . . . . . Miss Willems
Mrs. Motherly . . . . Mrs. Bates

QUALITY BINDING.

Mr. Level . . . . . Mr. Green
Colonel Modish . . Mr. Harwood
Lord Simper . . . . Mr. Moreton
Sir William Wealthy . Mr. Francis

lems as the *Chambermaid*, in the "Jealous Wife," and Mrs. Cleveland as *Miss Godfrey* in the "Lyar," on the 28th, and Master T. Warrell as

PHILADELPHIA CASTS—FIRST SEASON.

Mr. Plainwell . . . . Mr. Bates
John . . . . Mr. Blissett
William . . . . . Mr. Darley, Jr
Mrs. Level . . . . Mrs. Francis

RIVALS.
Sir Anthony Absolute . Mr. Morris
Captain Absolute . Mr. Moreton
Faulkland . . . . . Mr. Fennell
Acres . . . . Mr. Bates
Sir Lucius O'Trigger
     Mr. Whitlock
Fag . . . . . . Mr. Marshall
David . . . . Mr. Francis
Coachman . . . . . Mr. Warrell
Mrs. Malaprop . . . Mrs. Shaw
Lydia Languish . Mrs. Marshall
Julia . . . . . Mrs. Francis
Lucy . . . . . . Mrs. Rowson

ROAD TO RUIN.
Dornton . . . . . Mr. Whitlock
Harry Dornton . . . Mr. Green
Sulky . . . . Mr. Finch
Silky . . . . Mr. Bates
Goldfinch . . . . Mr. Chalmers
Milford . . . . . Mr. Cleveland
Smith . . . . Mr. Moreton
Hosier . . . . . Mr. Harwood
Sheriff's Officer . Mr. Warrell
Jacob . . . . . . Mr. Blissett
Marker . . . . . Master Warrell
Postillion . . Master T. Warrell
Mrs. Warren . . . . Mrs. Shaw
Sophia . . . . . Mrs. Marshall
Jenny . . . . . . Mrs. Francis
Mrs. Ledger . . . . Mrs. Bates

ROBIN HOOD.
Robin Hood . . . . Mr. Darley
Little John . . . . Mr. Wignell
Scarlet . . . . . Mr. Francis
Bowman . . . . . Mr. Warrell
Allan-a-Dale . . Mr. Darley, Jr
Stella . . . . . Miss Willems
Rutlekin . . . . Mr. Bates
Friar Tuck . . . Mr. Whitlock
Edwin . . . . . Mr. Marshall
Clorinda . . . . Mrs. Warrell
Annette . . . . Mrs. Marshall
Angelina . . . Miss Broadhurst

ROBINSON CRUSOE.
Robinson Crusoe . Mr. Whitlock
Pantaloon . . . . Mr. De Moulin
Pierot . . . . . Mr. Darley, Jr
Clown . . . . Mr. Blissett
Spaniard . . . . Mr. Cleveland
Captain . . . . . . Mr. Darley
Friday . . . . Mr. Bates
Columbine . . . . Miss Willems

ROMEO AND JULIET.
Romeo . . . . . . Mr. Fennell
Escalus . . . . . . Mr. Finch
Paris . . . . . . Mr. Moreton
Montagu . . . . Mr. De Moulin
Mercutio . . . . Mr. Chalmers
Benvolio . . . Mr. Cleveland
Tybalt . . . . . Mr. Harwood
Friar Laurence . . Mr. Whitlock
Friar John . . . . Mr. Warrell
Balthazar . . . . Mr. Darley, Jr
Apothecary . . . Mr. Francis
Peter . . . . . . Mr. Blissett
Juliet . . . . . Mrs. Marshall
Lady Capulet . . Mrs. Rowson
Nurse . . . . . . Mrs. Shaw

ROMP.
Watty Cockney . . Mr. Francis
Barnacle . . . . . Mr. Finch
Old Cockney . . Mr. De Moulin
Capt. Sightly . . Mr. Marshall
Priscilla Tomboy . Mrs. Marshall
Penelope . . . . Miss Willems
Mad. Le Blond . Mrs. Cleveland
Quasheba . . . . Miss Rowson

SCHOOL FOR SCANDAL.
Sir Peter Teazle . . Mr. Bates
Sir Oliver Surface . Mr. Morris
Joseph Surface . . Mr. Wignell
Charles Surface . . Mr. Chalmers
Sir Benj. Backbite . Mr. Finch
Crabtree . . . Mr. Harwood
Rowley . . . . . Mr. Warrell
Moses . . . . . . Mr. Francis
Snake . . . . . . Mr. Green
Trip . . . . . . Mr. Moreton
Lady Teazle . . . Mrs. Morris
Lady Sneerwell . . Mrs. Francis
Mrs. Candour . . . Mrs. Shaw
Maria . . . . . Mrs. Cleveland

SCHOOL FOR WIVES.
General Savage . . . . Mr. Bates
Belville . . . . . Mr. Chalmers
Torrington . . . . . Mr. Morris
Leeson . . . . . . Mr. Moreton
Captain Savage . . Mr. Cleveland
Connolly . . . . . Mr. Whitlock
Spruce . . . . . . Mr. Francis
Leech . . . . Mr. Green
Crow . . . . . . Mr. Blissett
Wolf . . . . Mr. Warrell
Miss Walsingham . . Mrs. Morris
Mrs. Belville . . . Mrs. Whitlock
Lady Rachel Mildew
     Mrs. Rowson
Mrs. Tempest . . . Mrs. Bates
Miss Leeson . . . Mrs. Francis
Maid . . . . . . Miss Willems

SELIMA AND AZOR.
Azor . . . . Mr. Marshall
Scander . . . . . Mr. Darley
Ali . . . . Mr. Bates
Fatima . . . . . Mrs. Rowson
Lesbia . . . . Miss Broadhurst
Selima . . . . . Mrs. Marshall

SHE WOULD AND SHE WOULD NOT.
Don Manuel . . . . Mr. Morris
Don Philip . . . . Mr. Fennell
Don Lewis . . . Mr. Cleveland
Octavio . . . . . . Mr. Green
Trapanti . . . . Mr. Chalmers
Soto . . . . . . Mr. Bates
Corrigidore . . . . Mr. Warrell
Diego . . . . . Mr. De Moulin
Vasquez . . . . Master Warrell
Hypolita . . . . Mrs. Marshall
Rosara . . . . . Mrs. Morris
Flora . . . . . . Mrs. Francis
Villetta . . . . . Mrs. Shaw

SON-IN-LAW.
Cranky . . . . . . Mr. Finch
Bowkit . . . . . Mr. Francis
Bourquet . . . . Mr. Moreton
Vinegar . . . . . Mr. Bates
Idle . . . . . . Mr. Harwood
Orator Mum . . . Mr. Blissett

the *Boy* in the " Poor Soldier," on the 3d of March.   Mrs. Morris

mede her first appearance in the new house on the 3d as *Lady Teazle*

PHILADELPHIA CASTS—FIRST SEASON.

Landlord . . . . . . Mr. Warrell
John . . . . . . Mr. Darley, Jr
Sig. Arionelli . . . Mr. Marshall
Cecilia . . . . . . Mrs. Warrell
Dolce . . . . . . Miss Willems

SPANISH BARBER.

Count Almaviva . . Mr. Moreton
Dr. Bartholo . . . . Mr. Green
Bazil . . . . Mr. Darley
Lazarillo . . . . . . Mr. Bates
Alcaide . . . . . Mr. Darley, Jr
Notary . . . . . . Mr. Warrell
Tallboy . . . . . . Mr. Francis
Argus . . . . Mr. Blissett
Rosina . . . . . Mrs. Oldmixon

SPOILED CHILD.

Little Pickle . . . Mrs. Marshall
Old Pickle . . . . . . Mr. Finch
Tag . . . . Mr. Francis
John . . . . Mr. Blissett
Thomas . . . . . . Mr. Darley
Miss Pickle . . . . Mrs. Rowson
Maria . . . . . . Mrs. Cleveland
Margery . . . . . . Mrs. Bates
Susan . . . . Miss Willems

ST. PATRICK'S DAY.

Lieut. O'Conner . . Mr. Whitlock
Justice Credulous . . . Mr. Bates
Dr. Rosy . . . . . Mr. Francis
Trounce . . . . . . Mr. Green
Flint . . . . Mr. Harwood
Blacksmith . . . . Mr. Moreton
Servant . . . . . Master Warrell
Bridget . . . . . Mrs. Rowson
Laura . . . . Mrs. Francis

SULTAN.

Solyman . . . . . Mr. Moreton
Osmyn . . . . . . Mr. Harwood
Elmira . . . . . . Mrs. Francis
Ismene . . . . . Miss Broadhurst
Roxalana . . . . Mrs. Oldmixon

SURRENDER OF CALAIS.

King Edward . . . Mr. Moreton
Sir Walter Many . . Mr. Warrell
Ribemont . . . . . Mr. Fennell

Le Gloire . . . . . . Mr. Bates
St. Pierre . . . . Mr. Whitlock
John de Vienne . . . Mr. Green
Old Man . . . . Mr. De Moulin
Sergeant . . . . . Mr. Wignell
O'Carrol . . . . . Mr. Marshall
Crier . . . . Mr. Blissett
First Gallowsmaker, Mr. Harwood
Second Gallowsmaker
                    Mr. Darley, Jr
Queen . . . . Mrs. Shaw
Madelon . . . . Mrs. Marshall
Julia . . . . . . Mrs. Francis

TEMPEST.

Alonzo . . . . Mr. Green
Ferdinand . . . . . Mr. Moreton
Prospero . . . . . Mr. Whitlock
Antonio . . . . . Mr. Warrell
Gonzalo . . . . . . Mr. Finch
Hippolito . . . . . Mr. Francis
Stephano . . . . . Mr. Harwood
Mustachio . . . . Mr. De Moulin
Trinculo . . . . . . Mr. Bates
Ventoso . . . . Mr. Darley, Jr
Caliban . . . . . . Mr. Darley
Miranda . . . Mrs. Cleveland
Dorinda . . . . Mrs. Marshall
Ariel . . . . . Miss Broadhurst

THREE WEEKS AFTER MARRIAGE.

Sir Charles Racket . Mr. Chalmers
Drugget . . . . . . Mr. Bates
Lovelace . . . . . Mr. Moreton
Woodley . . . . . Mr. Cleveland
Servant . . . . Mr. Darley, Jr
Lady Racket . . Mrs. Whitlock
Mrs. Drugget . . . Mrs. Rowson
Nancy . . . . . . Mrs. Francis
Dimitry . . . . . . Mrs. Shaw

TRIUMPH OF MIRTH.

Harlequin . . . . Mr. Chalmers
Mirth . . . . . Miss Broadhurst
Columbine . . . . Miss Willems

TRUE-BORN IRISHMAN.

Murrough O'Dougherty
                    Mr. Whitlock
Count Mushroom . . Mr. Wignell

Counsellor Hamilton . Mr. Green
Major Gamble . . . . Mr. Morris
John . . . . Mr. Blissett
William . . . . . Mr. Darley, Jr
James . . . . Mr. De Moulin
Mrs. Diggerty . . . Mrs. Morris
Lady Kennigad . . . Mrs. Bates
Lady Bab Frightful, Mrs. Rowson
Mrs. Gazette . . Mrs. Cleveland
Kitty Farrell . . . Miss Willems

VILLAGE LAWYER.

Scout . . . . . . Mr. Harwood
Snarl . . . . . . Mr. Francis
Sheepface . . . . Mr. Bates
Justice Mittimus . . Mr. Warrell
Charles . . . . . Mr. Cleveland
Mrs. Scout . . . . Mrs. Rowson
Kate . . . . Mrs. Bates

VIRGIN UNMASKED.

Goodwill . . . . . Mr. Warrell
Coupee . . . . . . Mr. Francis
Quaver . . . . . Mr. Marshall
Blister . . . . Mr. Bates
Thomas . . . . . . Mr. Green
Lucy . . . . . Mrs. Marshall

WATERMAN.

Mr. Bundle . . . . Mr. Francis
Tug . . . . Mr. Darley
Robin . . . . . . Mr. Bates
Mrs. Bundle . . . . Mrs. Shaw
Wilhelmina . . . Miss Broadhurst

WAYS AND MEANS.

Sir David Dunder . Mr. Harwood
Random . . . . . Mr. Moreton
Scruple . . . . Mr. Cleveland
Old Random . . . Mr. Whitlock
Carney . . . . . Mr. Blissett
Tiptoe . . . . Mr. Bates
Paul Peery . . . . Mr. Francis
Boundfee . . . . . . Mr. Finch
Bailiff . . . . . . Mr. Warrell
Lady Dunder . . . . Mrs. Shaw
Harriet . . . . . Mrs. Francis
Kitty . . . . . . Young Lady
Mrs. Peery . . . . Mrs. Rowson

in the " School for Scandal," with Bates as *Sir Peter.* Mr. Blissett
was not seen until the 12th, when he played *Counsellor Flummery* in
the " Farmer." On the 9th of April Mr. De Moulin was introduced
as *Farmer Stump* in the " Agreeable Surprise." He was probably
identical with Mr. Du Moulain, the pantomimist, who was at the
theatre in the Northern Liberties in 1792. Finally, on the 14th of
May, Mrs. Oldmixon made her first appearance in America as *Clarinda*
in " Robin Hood." Mr. Rowson, who was the prompter, was first
seen on the stage as *Charles, the Wrestler,* in " As You Like It " for
Marshall's benefit, and Miss Rowson, his adopted daughter, as *Betty*
in " Modern Antiques " for Mrs. Warrell's benefit. A young lady
made her first appearance as *Polly* in the " Woodman " for Miss Broadhurst's benefit. Mr. Bellona had speaking parts in the serious pantomime, " Jeanne d'Arc," for the benefit of Madame Gardie, and in
" L'Americain," which was played in French for the benefit of the
Clevelands. It only remains to be added that Mr. Milbourne, the
scene-painter, played *Harlequin Skip* in the dialogue to the " Birth of
Harlequin " for his own benefit.

PHILADELPHIA CASTS—FIRST SEASON.

WEST INDIAN.

Stockwell	Mr. Fennell
Belcour	Mr. Chalmers
Captain Dudley	Mr. Green
Charles Dudley	Mr. Cleveland
Maj. O'Flaherty	Mr. Whitlock
Stukely	Mr. De Moulin
Fulmer	Mr. Finch
Varland	Mr. Bates
Sailor	Mr. Blissett
Lady Rusport	Mrs. Shaw
Charlotte	Mrs. Marshall
Louisa Dudley	Miss Willems
Mrs. Fulmer	Mrs. Rowson
Lucy	Mrs. Cleveland
Housekeeper	Mrs. Bates

WIDOW OF MALABAR.

Raymond	Mr. Moreton

Albert	Mr Harwood
Chief Bramin	Mr. Fennell
Second Bramin	Mr. Warrell
Young Bramin	Mr. Cleveland
Narrain	Mr. Green
Indamora	Mrs. Whitlock
Fatima	Mrs. Cleveland

WONDER.

Don Lopez	Mr. Finch
Don Felix	Mr. Moreton
Frederick	Mr. Green
Don Pedro	Mr. Francis
Colonel Briton	Mr. Fennell
Gibby	Mr. Bates
Lissardo	Mr. Harwood
Alguazil	Mr. Warrell
Vasquez	Master Warrell
Soldier	Mr. Darley, Jr

Violante	Mrs. Whitlock
Isabella	Mrs. Francis
Flora	Mrs. Shaw
Inez	Mrs. Rowson

WOODMAN.

Sir Walter Waring	Mr. Finch
Wilford	Mr. Marshall
Capt. O'Donnell	Mr. Green
Medley	Mr. Bates
Bob	Mr. Francis
Fairlop	Mr. Darley
Filbert	Mr. Blissett
Emily	Miss Broadhurst
Dolly	Mrs. Oldmixon
Polly	Young Lady
Miss Di Clackit	Mrs. Shaw
Bridget	Mrs. Francis

Some changes in the casts during the season may be noted. Mrs. Warrell was *Clarinda* in " Robin Hood " before the arrival of Mrs. Oldmixon, and Mrs. Rowson played *Kitty Pry* in the " Lying Valet " instead of Mrs. Shaw on the 14th of April. Chalmers was the *Harlequin* in the " Triumph of Mirth " for his own benefit, " for that night only." Mrs. Marshall's appearance as *Juliet* to Fennell's *Romeo* on the 4th of June was " her first appearance in that character." The last performance of the season was for a dramatic fund, the first attempt of the kind in America. Mr. Harwood, who was something of a poet, wrote the address[1] for this occasion, which is here given as a specimen of his versification and as the first offering of this nature recited on the American stage.

As a rule, the new pieces were produced at benefits, but a number was brought forward in the regular season. Among the latter were the " Spoiled Child," given vogue in England by Mrs. Jordan, and very popular here through the piquancy of Mrs. Marshall's *Little Pickle ;* O'Keefe's " Son-in-Law," originally acted fifteen years before, but now given for the first time in the North ; the same witty writer's " Peeping Tom of Coventry," produced with success at the Haymarket

---

[1] HARWOOD'S ADDRESS.

When peace revisited this happy shore,
And war's loud clarion rent the air no more ;
When plenty from her cornucopia pour'd
Her golden produce on the festive board ;
Science reviv'd, and in her polish'd train
The muses of the drama held her reign—
Shelter'd by you, who ceaseless seek to give
Content, their happy, grateful vot'ries live,
To shelter age, to blunt misfortune's dart,
And thus to shield the wounded artist's heart,
When feebly creeps the current thro' the vein,
And the slow tot'ring step proclaims life's
        wane,

To cheer as yet the little while he stays,
And gild the vet'ran's few remaining days.
Ere yet the fires of genius faintly speak,
Or the quick hectic spreads the furrow'd
        cheek ;
Ere yet the beaming eye is languid grown,
Or dimm'd with tears for sorrows all its own—
This done, the cheering smile of former days,
The loud, resounding peal of joyous praise,
By fancy's magic rise again to view,
The faded senses all their bliss renew ;
The cordial thought is round his heart en-
        twin'd,
And his last breath in grateful pray'r resign'd.

in 1784, and "Quality Binding, or A Quarter of an Hour Before Dinner," an agreeable little piece intended to ridicule the folly of seeking the society of the great. When the benefits began, Mr. Fennell offered the younger Colman's "Surrender of Calais," anticipated by a few weeks by Mr. Henry's production of the play in New York; Mr. Morris gave an afterpiece, Prince Hoare's "Prize," first played by the Drury Lane company in 1793 for Signora Storace's benefit; Mr. Whitlock produced Jephson's tragedy, "Julia," in which Kemble's exertions had been so great as to bring on a severe illness; Mr. Marshall presented "Hartford Bridge," in which Moreton played the best part, *Peregrine Forrester*, an egotistical traveler, who talks only of himself and his adventures; Mrs. Warrell gave O'Keefe's merry trifle, "Modern Antiques," which had its first American production at the Charleston Theatre on May 6th, 1793; Mrs. Morris chose the younger Colman's "Battle of Hexham," Mrs. Whitlock playing *Queen Margaret;* Miss Broadhurst selected as a special attraction Bate Dudley's "Woodman," a comic opera in which the action takes place in Henault Forest; and Mrs. Oldmixon was first in the field in this country with one of Beaumarchais' comedies, the "Barber of Seville," adapted for the English stage by the elder Colman with the title of the "Spanish Barber."

As a whole, the season was the most brilliant that had ever been played in America.

CHAPTER IX.

THE PHILADELPHIA COMPANY, 1794-5.

HOLIDAY STREET THEATRE, BALTIMORE—WIGNELL AND REINAGLE'S FIRST
SEASON—INTERRUPTED BY YELLOW FEVER—SECOND SEASON IN
PHILADELPHIA—AMERICAN PRODUCTIONS—"THE TRIUMPHS OF
LOVE"—ESTIMATES OF SOME OF THE PERFORMERS.

FROM the outset it was part of the plans of Wignell and Reinagle
to make Baltimore a theatrical adjunct to Philadelphia. To do
this it was first necessary to build a theatre. A stock company, in the
financial sense, was organized as early as the Autumn of 1793 and the
work begun as soon as possible, so that by midsummer of the next
year the new house was completed. Better still, all the shares, which
were of the value of $100, except five, were taken before the new
theatre was finished. This theatre was built on the site of the present
house in Holiday Street, which was certainly a more convenient situation than that of the "old theatre" on Philpot's Hill. "What a superb
thing it was!—speaking now as my fancy imagined it then," wrote the
author of "Swallow Barn" many years afterward. "It had something
of the splendor of a great barn—weather-boarded, milk-white, with
many windows—and to my conception looked with a hospitable,
patronizing, tragi-comic greeting down upon the street. It never occurred to me to think of it as a piece of architecture. It was something above that—a huge, mystical Aladdin lamp, that had a magic

to repel criticism, and filled with wonderful histories." This wooden barn continued to be the "new theatre" of Baltimore until 1813, when it was replaced by the second Holiday Street Theatre.

The opening of Wignell and Reinagle's first season in Baltimore was announced for the 24th of September, 1794; but, owing to the illness of Mrs. Warrell, the initial performance was delayed until the following evening. The pieces originally chosen for the opening were "Love in a Village" and "Who's the Dupe?" Only two performances were given, when the theatre was closed at the request of the Committee of Health, because of the prevalence of yellow fever. The house was reopened on the 13th of October,

LIST OF PERFORMANCES—*Baltimore.*

1794.
Sept. 25—Every One Has His Fault
　　　　　　　　　　　　　　Mrs. Inchbald
　　　　Caledonian Frolic . . . Francis
　　　　Flitch of Bacon . . . . . . Bate
　　　26—Love in a Village . . Bickerstaff
　　　　Wrangling Lovers . . . . Lyon
Oct. 13—West Indian . . . . Cumberland
　　　　Rosina . . . . . . Mrs. Brooke
　　　17—Dramatist . . . . . . Reynolds
　　　　Sultan. 　　　　　Bickerstaff
　　　21—Venice Preserved . . . . Otway
　　　　Spoiled Child . . . . Bickerstaff
　　　24—Grecian Daughter . . . Murphy
　　　　Lying Valet . . . . . . Garrick
　　　31—Merchant of Venice . . Shakspere
　　　　Critic . . . . Sheridan

the fever having disappeared in consequence of the early October frosts. Although William Priest, a member of the band, whose "Travels in America" were published in England in 1802, noted under the date of the 14th of October that the inhabitants had returned and trade was resumed, "the late cold weather having completely destroyed the yellow fever," the season did not prove a prosperous one, and the new theatre remained open only until the close of the month.

The pieces produced during this brief Baltimore season were, without exception, reproductions from the Philadelphia repertory. The casts of two of these, "Rosina" and the "Wrangling Lovers," were not printed in the Philadelphia newspapers. A comparison of the casts in the two cities shows that there was either no change, as in the distribution of the parts in the farce of the "Sultan," or that the changes were unimportant, as will be seen from the annexed summary. Some of these changes were due to the retirement of Mr. Finch from the company, and some of the others to the absence from Baltimore of the original representatives of the roles. Among the latter were Miss Willems and Mr. Bates. In consequence of the yellow fever, the season proved colorless, being deficient both in novelty and incident. After an epidemic theatrical entertainments always fail to attract, and not even a new theatre and a remarkable company of players were able to

ROSINA.

Belville	Mr. Marshall
Captain Belville . . .	Mr. Moreton
Rustic	Mr. Rowson
First Irishman	Mr. Green
Second Irishman . . .	Mr. Blissett
Rosina	Mrs. Warrell
Dorcas	Mrs. Bates
Phœbe	Miss Broadhurst

WRANGLING LOVERS.

Don Carlos	Mr. Moreton
Don Lorenzo	Mr. Green
Lopez	Mr. Harwood
Sancho	Mr. Wignell
Leonora	Mrs. Francis
Jacintha	Mrs. Rowson

CONTRASTED CASTS—CHANGES.

PLAYS.	Phil.	Balt.	PLAYS.	Phil.	Balt.
Critic.			*Merchant of Venice.*		
Interpreter	Mr. Finch . . .	Mr. Blissett	Duke	Mr. Green . . .	Mr. Morris
Master of Horse .	Mr. Warrell . .	Mr. Darley, Jr	Gratiano	Mr. Finch . . .	Mr. Wignell
Second Niece . .	Miss Willems	Miss Rowson	Solanio	Mr. Harwood	Mr. Green
			Shylock	Mr. Chalmers	Mr. Fennell
Dramatist.			Tubal	Mr. De Moulin	Mr. Milbourne
Lord Scratch . .	Mr. Bates . . .	Mr. Wignell	Launcelot	Mr. Bates . . .	Mr. Harwood
Ennui	Mr. Finch . . .	Mr. Harwood	*Spoiled Child.*		
Lady Waitfort . .	Mrs. Rowson	Mrs. Shaw	Old Pickle	Mr. Finch . . .	Mr. Harwood
			Thomas	Mr. Darley . .	Mr. Darley, Jr
Grecian Daughter.			Susan	Miss Willems	Miss Rowson
Calippus	Mr. Warrell . .	Mr. Darley, Jr	*Venice Preserved.*		
Greek Officer . .	Mr. Finch . . .	Mr. Harwood	Duke	Mr. Finch . . .	Mr. Morris
			Bedamar	Mr. Marshall	Mr. Moreton
Lying Valet.			Elliot	Mr. Moreton .	Mr. Cleveland
Sharp	Mr. Bates . . .	Mr. Morris	*West Indian.*		
Gayless	Mr. Moreton . .	Mr. Green	Stukely	Mr. De Moulin	Mr. Moreton
Guttle	Mr. Warrell . .	Mr. Francis	Fulmer	Mr. Finch . . .	Mr. Harwood
Trippet	Mr. Harwood	Mr. Cleveland	Varland	Mr. Bates . . .	Mr. Francis
Cook	Mr. Francis . .	Mr. Blissett	Louisa Dudley . .	Miss Willems	Mrs. Cleveland
Mrs. Trippet . .	Mrs. Cleveland	Mrs. Rowson	Lucy	Mrs. Cleveland	Miss Rowson

overcome the panic caused by the plague. It is not surprising, therefore, that Wignell and Reinagle withdrew their forces and gave the company a vacation before beginning the second season in Philadelphia.

The new theatre in Chestnut Street was reopened on the 3d of December, 1794, and the performances continued without interruption, except during Passion Week, until the 4th of July following. Naturally, the list of productions was a noteworthy one. The repertory consisted of alternating tragedy and comedy, opera, farce and pantomimic ballet. The London theatres were liberally drawn upon for new English pieces. Mrs. Rowson's successful comedy of the previous season opened the way for a new comic opera from her pen, the " Volunteers," a local skit of little merit; and an ambitious Philadelphia barber, through the influence of friends, succeeded in persuading the managers to produce a local comedy called " The Triumphs of Love." Mr. Francis continued to compose new ballets and pantomimic dances; and Mr. Reinagle, as was his custom, contributed

LIST OF PRODUCTIONS.

1794.
Dec. 3—Every One Has His Fault
            Mrs. Inchbald
       Prize . . . . Hoare
     5—Highland Reel . . . . O'Keefe
       Lyar . . . . Foote
     8—Venice Preserved . . . . Otway
       Birth of Harlequin.
    10—As You Like It . . Shakspere
       Birth of Harlequin.
    12—Romeo and Juliet . . Shakspere
       Sultan . . . . Bickerstaff
    15—Lionel and Clarissa . Bickerstaff
       Ways and Means . . Colman, Jr
    17—Isabella . . . . . . Southerne
       Rosina . . . . . . Mrs. Brooke
    19—Maid of the Mill . . Bickerstaff
       Village Lawyer . . . Macready
    22—Slaves in Algiers . Mrs. Rowson
       Critic . . . . Sheridan
    24—Natural Son . . . . Cumberland
       Flitch of Bacon . . . . . . Bate
    26—George Barnwell . . . . . Lillo
       Birth of Harlequin.
    27—Lionel and Clarissa.
       Modern Antiques . . . O'Keefe
    31—Macbeth . . . . . Shakspere
       Peeping Tom of Coventry,O'Keefe
1795.
Jan. 2—Rivals . . . . Sheridan
       Harlequin Shipwrecked.
     3—Spanish Barber . . . . Colman
     5—Countess of Salisbury . Hartson
       Poor Soldier . . . . . O'Keefe

Jan. 7—Dramatist . . . . . . Reynolds
Sailor's Landlady . . . . Francis
Purse . . . . Cross
9—Hamlet . . . . Shakspere
Purse.
10—Castle of Andalusia . . O'Keefe
Lying Valet . . . . . . Garrick
12—Merchant of Venice . . Shakspere
Spoiled Child . . . . . Bickerstaff
14—School for Scandal . . Sheridan
Purse.
16—Gamester . . . . Moore
Romp . . . . Bickerstaff
17—Inkle and Yarico . . Colman, Jr
Critic . . . . Sheridan
19—Surrender of Calais . Colman, Jr
Wrangling Lovers . . . . Lyon
21—Gamester.
Volunteers . . . . Mrs. Rowson
23—Richard III . . . . . Shakspere
Deserter . . . . Dibdin
24—Clandestine Marriage
Garrick and Colman
Purse.
26—Road to Ruin . . . . . Holcroft
Volunteers.
28—Country Girl . . . . . Garrick
Comus . . . . Milton
30—Natural Son.
No Song No Supper . . . Hoare
31—Every One Has His Fault.
Robinson Crusoe . . . Sheridan
Feb. 4—Clandestine Marriage.
Robinson Crusoe.
6—Country Girl.
Rosina.
7—Cymbeline . . . . . Shakspere
Romp.
9—Highland Reel.
East Indian.
11—Jew . . . . Cumberland
Sailor's Landlady.
Purse.
13—Romeo and Juliet.
Padlock . . . . . . Bickerstaff

new overtures and accompaniments to many of the pieces. As regards the company there was little change. Mr. Finch, as already noted, had retired at the close of the first season; and Mr. Fennell, after playing with the company at Baltimore, withdrew to engage in the manufacture of salt. During the previous Winter in Philadelphia, Fennell, in order to increase his income, delivered a course of lectures on Natural Philosophy. These gave him some reputation for scientific acquirements and led to the suggestion that he should engage in salt manufacture, the suggestion, according to Fennell in his "Apology," coming from General Knox and Governor Mifflin. It proved a disastrous one for the visionary actor. When Fennell left the Philadelphia company at Baltimore in the Autumn of 1794, it was to go to Annapolis to secure a grant from the Maryland Legislature for the establishment of salt works in that State. The bill passed the Assembly, but failed in the Senate. Fennell, however, was not discouraged, and he pursued his scheme for the next two or three years, until it brought him to absolute ruin. In consequence of Fennell's retirement, the way was opened for Chalmers and Moreton, who afterward shared roles that the tragedian abandoned. Notwithstanding the loss of Fennell, the Philadelphia company at this time was beyond comparison the best and most evenly balanced that had yet been seen in America. While it had no single actor of the genius and versatility of Hodgkinson, it was claimed for Chalmers that he was in some respects the first performer on the continent and in others second only to the American Garrick. In genteel comedy he was unrivalled. Mr. Moreton, although without experience on the stage, had shown remarkable merit from the outset, and this season he made rapid

Feb. 14—Robin Hood . . . . . MacNally
Robinson Crusoe.
16—Douglas . . . . Home
Irish Lilt . . . . Francis
Ways and Means . . Colman, Jr
18—Haunted Tower . . . . . Cobb
Miller of Mansfield . . . Dodsley
20—English Merchant . . . Colman
Irish Lilt.
Three Weeks After Marriage
Murphy
21—Jew.
Flitch of Bacon.
24—Tempest . . . . Dryden
Critic.
25—Haunted Tower.
East Indian.
27—Country Girl.
Le Foret Noire.
28—Fair Penitent . . . . . . Rowe
Peeping Tom of Coventry.
Mar. 2—Lionel and Clarissa.
Le Foret Noire.
4—Isabella.,
Caledonian Frolic.
Farm House . . . . . Kemble
6— She Wou'd and She Wou'd Not
Cibber
Waterman . . . . Dibdin
7—Jew.
Prize.
9—Haunted Tower.
Farm House.
11—Every One Has His Fault.
Poor Soldier.
13—Fontainville Forest . . . Boaden
Agreeable Surprise . . . O'Keefe
14—Tempest.
Spoiled Child.
16—Fontainville Forest.
Prisoner at Large . . . O'Keefe
18—School for Wives . . . . Kelly
Irish Lilt.
Children in the Wood . . Morton
20—Busybody . . . . Mrs. Centlivre
Children in the Wood.

Mar. 21—Rivals.
  Comus.
 23—Fontainville Forest.
  Hartford Bridge . . . . Pearce
 25—Belle's Stratagem . . Mrs. Cowley
  Children in the Wood.
 27—West Indian . . . . Cumberland
  Devil to Pay . . . . . . Coffey
 28—Jew.
  Poor Vulcan . . . . . . Dibdin
 30—Orphan . . . . Otway
  Devil to Pay.
 31—Busybody.
  Deuce is in Him . . . . Colman
April 1—Love in a Village . . Bickerstaff
  Critic.
 2—Haunted Tower.
  Ways and Means.
 6—Box-Lobby Challenge,Cumberland
  Rural Revels . . . . . Francis
  Poor Vulcan.
 8—Woodman . . . . . . Dudley
  Devil to Pay.
 10—Jealous Wife . . . . . Colman
  Rural Revels.
  Lyar.
 13—Percy . . . . Miss More
  High Life Below Stairs . Townley
 15—Beaux' Stratagem . . . Farquhar
  Children in the Wood.
 17—Carmelite . . . . . Cumberland
  Two Misers . . . . . . O'Hara
 18—English Merchant.
  Two Misers.
 20—Carmelite.
  Two Misers.
 22—Tamerlane . . . . Rowe
  Tom Thumb, the Great . Fielding
 24—Inkle and Yarico . . Colman, Jr
  Tom Thumb.
 27—She Stoops to Conquer . Goldsmith
  My Grandmother . . . . Hoare
 29—Heiress . . . . Burgoyne
  Two Misers.
May 1—Jew.
  Sailor's Landlady.

strides. Mr. Finch's retirement, Mr. Moreton's promotion and Mr. Bates' indifference all contributed during the season to Mr. Harwood's opportunities. Harwood possessed gifts scarcely inferior to Moreton's, but he was slower in pressing them upon public attention, a delay that was no doubt due to his proneness to rely on the aid of Mr. Rowson, the prompter. The first part in which he made a considerable figure was *Dr. Lenitive* in the "Prize." After this his successes were numerous, and before the close of the season his popularity was established. One of the critics of the period described his articulation as either rapid like the Falls of Niagara or slow and stately like the meandering Susquehanna, according to the character he represented. These actors are thus mentioned in this place to show the effect of the changes, and to indicate that the company had already become a school of dramatic art. At the same time it must be noted that a few acquisitions were made during the season. Miss Milbourne, the daughter of the scene-painter, made her first appearance on any stage as the *Savage Princess*, afterward *Columbine* in "Harlequin Shipwrecked" on the 2d of January. Mrs. Solomon and her daughter Miss Solomon joined the company in March, the former making her first appearance as *Cowslip* in the "Agreeable Surprise," and the latter as the *Girl* in "Children in the Wood." Miss Solomon as *Tom Thumb* excited astonishment at her memory and the ease with which she went through the part. This charming little girl, it was said, was a very valuable acquisition to the new company. Later in the season a writer in the Philadelphia *Gazette* declared that her astonishing powers never shone more conspicuously than as *Juliana* in the "Prisoner." Miss Oldfield, who was among the supernumeraries

Tom Thumb.

May 4—Know Your Own Mind . Murphy
Rural Revels
Auld Robin Gray . . . . Arnold
(Mrs. Marshall's benefit.)

6—Child of Nature . . Mrs. Inchbald
Sicilian Romance . . . Siddons
(Mrs. Morris' benefit.)

8—Noble Peasant . . . . Holcroft
Apprentice . . . . . . Murphy
(Mrs. Oldmixon's benefit.)

11—Peeping Tom's Visit.
New Way to Pay Old Debts
Massinger
A Beggar on Horseback . O'Keefe
(Mr. Bates' benefit.)

13—Brothers . . . . . Cumberland
Sailor's Return . . . . . Francis
Quaker . . . . Dibdin
(Mr. Darley's benefit.)

15—Roman Father . . . . Murphy
Midnight Hour . . Mrs. Inchbald
(Mrs. Whitlock's benefit.)

18—Suspicious Husband . . Hoadley
Roman Actor . . . . Massinger
Duke and No Duke . . . . Tate
(Mr. Chalmers' benefit.)

20—Bold Stroke for a Husband
Mrs. Cowley
Scheming Milliners . . . Francis
Hob in the Well . . . . Cibber
(Mr. Moreton's benefit.)

22—Triumphs of Love . . . Murduck
Wedding Day . . Mrs. Inchbald
Tom Thumb.

25—Conscious Lovers . . . . Steele
Harlequin Hurry Scurry . Francis
Midas . . . . O'Hara
(Mr. Marshall's benefit.)

27—Duenna . . . . . . Sheridan
Little Yankee Sailor.
(Mrs. Warrell's benefit.)

29—Toy . . . . O'Keefe
Prisoner . . . . Rose
(Mr. Morris' benefit.)

June 1—Merry Wives of Windsor
                            Shakspere
        Jubilee . . . . Garrick
        (Mr. Whitlock's benefit.)
      3—Constant Couple . . . Farquhar
        Sailor's Return.
        Sicilian Romance.
          (Mr. Green's benefit.)
      5—Next-Door Neighbors
                            Mrs. Inchbald
        Prisoner.
        Mayor of Garratt . . . . Foote
        (Mr. Harwood's benefit.)
      8—Beggar's Opera . . . . . . Gay
        First Floor . . . . Cobb
        (Miss Broadhurst's benefit.)
     10—Chapter of Accidents . Miss Lee
        Linco's Travels . . . . Garrick
        Children in the Wood.
        (Mrs. Shaw's benefit.)
     12—Better Late Than Never . Andrews
        Les Armans d'Arcade . . Francis
        Le Tuteur Trompe . . . Francis
        Harlequin's Invasion . . Garrick
        (Mr. and Mrs. Francis' benefit.)
     15—Follies of a Day . . Holcroft
        Devil in the Wine Cellar . . Hill
        Florizel and Perdita . Shakspere
        (Mr. and Mrs. Cleveland's benefit.)
     17—Prisoner.
        Midnight Hour.
        Purse.
        (Miss Solomon's benefit.)
     19—Female Patriot . . Mrs. Rowson
        Travellers Preserved (Pant.).
        All the World's a Stage . Jackman
        (Mr. and Mrs. Rowson's benefit.)
     22—Rage . . . . Reynolds
        Le Tuteur Trompe.
        Irish Widow . . . . . Garrick
        (Mrs. Hervey and Miss Willems' benefit.)
     24—Every One Has His Fault.
        Sailor's Landlady.
        Tom Thumb.
        (Warrell and Sons' benefit.)
     26—Farm House.
        Irishman in London . Macready

of the previous season, was also occasionally accorded parts of some importance, as *Lucilla* in the " Fair Penitent," and *Dorinda* in the " Tempest." When the " Wedding Day " was produced as the afterpiece to the " Triumphs of Love," Mrs. Hervey, from the Haymarket Theatre, London, made her American *debut* as *Lady Contest* to Harwood's *Sir Adam.* Mrs. Hervey's second part was *Phyllis* in the " Conscious Lovers " for Mr. Marshall's benefit. None of these *debutantes,* with the exception of Miss Oldfield, became established favorites with Philadelphia playgoers.

An incident of the second season at the New Theatre, Philadelphia, was the production of an original American comedy in four acts by a Philadelphia barber named John Murduck. This production, which was called " The Triumphs of Love, or Happy Reconciliation," was important only as an early attempt at American dramatic writing. This piece was offered to the managers early in the season, who declined to produce it, but through the influence of friends of the author it was finally given a trial night while the benefits were in progress. According to the author it met with public approbation, although it must be confessed that the news-

Travellers Preserved.
(Mr. Blissett and Mrs. De Marque's benefit.)
June 29—Midnight Hour.
　　　　Love in a Camp . . . . O'Keefe
　　　　Elopement (Local Pant.).
　　　　(Mr. Milbourne's benefit.)
July　1—Rage.
　　　　Miraculous Mill . . . . Francis
　　　　Peeping Tom of Coventry.
　　　　(Mr. Wells' benefit.)
　　　3—Same bill.
　　　　(Warrell and Sons' benefit.)
　　　4—Next-Door Neighbors.
　　　　Irishman in London.
　　　　Elopement.

papers were rather lukewarm in their praise of its merits. Intoxicated with what he regarded as the success of the comedy, Murduck at once

TRIUMPHS OF LOVE.

Jacob Friendly, Sr. . . . . Mr. Morris
George Friendly, Sr. . . . . Mr. Whitlock
George Friendly, Jr. . . . . Mr. Moreton
Jacob Friendly, Jr. . . . . . . Mr. Blissett
Major Manly . . . . Mr. Green
Peevish . . . . Mr. Wignell
Trifle . . . . Mr. Marshall
Careless . . . . Mr. Francis
Beauchamp . . . . Mr. Cleveland
Patrick . . . . Mr. Harwood
Dick . . . . Mr. Mitchell
Sambo . . . . Mr. Bates
Hannah Friendly . . . . . . Mrs. Rowson
Rachel . . . . Mrs. Marshall
Mrs. Peevish . . . . Mrs. Whitlock
Jenny . . . . Mrs. Francis
Clementina . . . . Miss Willems

had it printed with an engraved frontispiece representing a scene from the play in which Moreton and Green are shown in character. Murduck was also the author of an afterpiece called " The Beau Metamorphozed, or the Generous Maid," which he wrote in full confidence that it would be produced when the comedy had its second performance early in the season of 1795–6. The managers, however, not only declined to revive the comedy, but peremptorily rejected the farce. Then the barber, like many dramatic authors of a more recent period, appealed to the public through the newspapers, alleging a temper in the managers to trample on native productions. The dramatist also complained of the excisions made in the comedy previous to its production. "At last, beyond the eleventh hour," he said, "it was shoved into the world unmercifully dissected by what the managers called necessary expungings." All this was denied on behalf of the management, and then the newspapers shut down on the controversy.

Only two pieces that were American in origin and production were presented during the season—a comic opera by Mrs. Rowson, called the "Volunteers," and a comedy, the "Little Yankee Sailor," produced for her benefit by Mrs. Warrell, with Master T. Warrell as the *Little Yankee Sailor*. Neither of these pieces attracted attention or evoked criticism. The quality of Mrs. Rowson's "Volunteers" may, perhaps, be judged by a stanza from one of the songs sung by Mr. Marshall as *Trueman*:

VOLUNTEERS.	
Trueman	Mr. Marshall
Manly	Mr. Darley
Milliken	Mr. Francis
Jerry	Mr. Bates
Grumble	Mr. Blissett
Adams	Mr. Green
Thomas	Mr. Darley, Jr
Jacob	Mr. De Moulin
Miss Aura	Mrs. Marshall
Mrs. Grumble	Mrs. Shaw
Jemima	Miss Broadhurst
Rosalind	Mrs. Rowson
Ruth	Mrs. Cleveland
Omeeah	Mrs. Oldmixon

LITTLE YANKEE SAILOR.	
Jack Worthy	Mr. Darley
Harding	Mr. Cleveland
Hatchway	Mr. Francis
Capt. Bowling	Mr. Warrell
Tangoo	Mr. Green
William	Master T. Warrell
Mary	Mrs. Warrell
Emily	Mrs. Marshall
Orra	Miss Broadhurst

> Where is the soldier will complain?
> Not one—united all agree
> To guard Columbia, follow Wayne,
> And chorus, *Vive la Liberte!*

The "Little Yankee Sailor" was probably an English nautical ballad piece localized and embellished by the introduction of Indians, men and women. These adaptations, however, were generally pantomimic in character, as in the case of the "Elopement," a local skit presented for Mr. Milbourne's benefit, and probably arranged by him.

Most of the dances, ballets and pantomimes originally produced by Mr. Francis the previous season were revived, and six new ones were added to his growing list. This season the cast of the " Sailor's Landlady" was as before, with the addition of Mr. Nugent as the *Mate*.

In " L'Amour Trove les Moyens," of which there was no cast the first season, Master Harry Warrell was now announced as making his first appearance on any stage as *Cupid*, and the cast of the " Scheming Milliners " was printed in the newspapers for the first time. The new pieces

SCHEMING MILLINERS.

Old McDonald . . Mr. Blissett
Patie . . . . . . Mr. Francis
Billy Wiffle . . . Mr. Warrell
Milliners . { Miss Milbourne
             { Mrs. De Marque

LE TUTEUR TROMPE.

Don Garcia . . . Mr. Nugent
Orsini . . . . Mr. Warrell, Jr
Alonzo . . . . . Mr. Francis
Marcella . . . Mrs. De Marque

HARLEQUIN HURRY SCURRY.

Harlequin . . . . Mr. Francis
Farmer . . . . . Mr. Rowson
Cobbler . . . . Mr. Darley, Jr
Clown . . . . . . Mr. Blissett
Barber . . Master T. Warrell
Tailor . . . Master J. Warrell

MIRACULOUS MILL.

Gaffer Thoughless . Mr. Francis
Mealey . . . . . Mr. Nugent
Bob . . . . Master J. Warrell
Goody Benson, Mrs. De Marque
Patty . . . . Miss Milbourne

were " Rural Revels," the " Sailor's Return," produced for Mr. Darley's benefit; " Harlequin Hurry Scurry," brought out for Mr. Marshall's benefit; " Les Armans d'Arcade " and " Le Tuteur Trompe, or the Guardian Outwitted," both included in the benefit bill of Mr. and Mrs. Francis; and the " Miraculous Mill," originally presented for the benefit of Mr. Wells, the box-keeper. The casts of these pieces in the advertisements show that besides Mr. Francis and Mrs. De Marque the pantomimic characters were generally accorded to Nugent, Blissett, the youthful Warrells and Miss Milbourne.

The productions of the season, comprising recent London successes and pieces that were already familiar to Philadelphia audiences, are in themselves a study. As was customary, few novelties were brought forward during the earlier part of the regular season; but the benefit successes of the previous year were accorded places in the

PHILADELPHIA CASTS—SECOND SEASON.

ALL THE WORLD'S A STAGE.

Sir Gilbert Pumpkin . Mr. Francis
Charles Stanley . . Mr. Marshall
Harry Stukely . . . . Mr. Green
William . . . Master T. Warrell
Waiter . . . . Master J. Warrell
Diggory . . . . Mr. Bates
Cymon . . . . Mr. Blissett
Wat . . . . . . Mr. Darley, Jr
Hostler . . . . . . Mr. Solomon
Miss Bridget . . . Mrs. Rowson
Kitty Sprightly . . Mrs. Marshall
Jane . . . . Mrs. Francis

AULD ROBIN GRAY.

Auld Robin Gray . . . Mr. Bates
Donald . . . . . . Mr. Francis
Fracas . . . . . . Mr. Harwood
Dorcas . . . . . Mrs. Rowson
Jenny . . . . . . Mrs. Marshall

BEAUX' STRATAGEM.

Aimwell . . . . . . Mr. Green
Archer . . . . . Mr. Chalmers
Sullen . . . . . . Mr. Whitlock
Freeman . . . . . Mr. Cleveland
Foigard . . . . . . Mr. Marshall
Gibbet . . . . . . Mr. Francis
Hounslow . . . . . Mr. Solomon
Bagshot . . . . . Mr. Darley, Jr
Boniface . . . . . . Mr. Darley
Scrub . . . . Mr. Morris
Lady Bountiful . . Mrs. Rowson
Dorinda . . . . . . Mrs. Francis
Mrs. Sullen . . . Mrs. Whitlock
Gipsy . . . . . . Miss Willems
Cherry . . . . . Mrs. Cleveland

BEGGAR ON HORSEBACK.

Old Codger . . . . . Mr. Francis
Cosey . . . . Mr. Warrell
Barney Vag . . . . Mr. Blissett
Music Master . . Mr. Darley, Jr
Corney . . . . Mr. Bates
Horace . . . . . Mr. Cleveland
Scout . . . . . . Mr. Harwood
Master Billy . . . . Mr. Darley
James . . . . . Mr. Warrell, Jr
Nancy Buttercup . Mrs. Marshall
Mrs. Mummey . . . Mrs. Shaw
Mrs. Barney Vag . Miss Rowson

BELLE'S STRATAGEM.

Doricourt . . . . Mr. Chalmers
Hardy . . . . Mr. Morris
Sir George . . . . Mr. Whitlock
Flutter . . . . . . Mr. Marshall
Saville . . . . Mr. Green
Servant . . . . . Mr. Darley, Jr
Villers . . . . . Mr. Cleveland
Courtall . . . . . . Mr Moreton
Gentleman . . . . Mr. Harwood
Gibson . . . . Mr. Warrell
Dick . . . . Mr. Blissett
Letitia Hardy . . . Mrs. Morris
Mrs. Racket . . . . Mrs. Shaw
Lady Frances . . Mrs. Cleveland
Miss Ogle . . . . Mrs. Solomon
Kitty Willis . . . . Mrs. Rowson

BETTER LATE THAN NEVER.

Saville . . . . . Mr. Moreton
Flurry . . . . . . Mr. Francis
Chouse . . . . . . Mr. Green
Grump . . . . Mr. Bates
Litigamus . . . . Mr. Harwood
Pallet . . . . . Mr. Marshall
Clerk . . . . Mr. Blissett
Richard . . . . Mr. J. Warrell
Charles . . . . Mr. Darley, Jr
Augusta . . . . Mrs. Whitlock
Mrs. Flurry . . . Mrs. Hervey
Diary . . . . . . Mrs. Francis

BOLD STROKE FOR A HUSBAND.

Don Julio . . . . Mr. Chalmers
Don Carlos . . . . Mr. Moreton
Don Vincentio . . Mr. Harwood
Don Cæsar . . . . Mr. Bates
Don Garcia . . . Mr. Cleveland
Don Vasquez . . . Mr. Francis
Don Gasper . . . Mr. Whitlock
Pedro . . . . . . Mr. Blissett
Olivia . . . . . Mrs. Marshall
Victoria . . . . Mrs. Whitlock
Laura . . . . . . Mrs. Francis
Minette . . . . . Mrs. Shaw
Marcella . . . Mrs. Cleveland
Inis . . . . . . Mrs. Solomon
Sancha . . . . . Mrs. Bates

BOX LOBBY CHALLENGE.

George Waterland . Mr. Cleveland

Capt. Waterland . . Mr. Marshall
Sir Toby Grampus . Mr. Whitlock
Squire Robert . . . Mr. Francis
Old Crotchet . . . . Mr. Green
Jack Crotchet . . . Mr. Chalmers
Fulsome . . . . . Mr. Harwood
Jones . . . . . . Mr. Warrell
Joe . . . . Mr. Blissett
Waiter . . . . . Master Warrell
Hair Dresser . . Mr. Darley, Jr
Servant . . . Master T. Warrell
Lady Jane Danvers . Mrs. Morris
Diana Grampus . . . Mrs. Shaw
Letitia Rayner . . Mrs. Marshall
Theodosia . . . . Mrs. Rowson
Lindamora . . . . Mrs. Francis

BUSYBODY.

Marplot . . . . . Mr. Chalmers
Sir George Airy . . Mr. Moreton
Charles . . . . . . Mr. Green
Sir Francis Gripe . . Mr. Morris
Sir Jealous Traffick . Mr. Francis
Whisper . . . . . . Mr. Blissett
Butler . . . . . . Mr. Warrell
Miranda . . . . . Mrs. Marshall
Isabinda . . . . . . Mrs. Francis
Patch . . . . Mrs. Shaw
Scentwell . . . . Mrs. Cleveland

CARMELITE.

Saint Valori . .   Mr. Whitlock
Lord Hilderbrand . Mr. Moreton
De Courci . . . . . . Mr. Green
Montgomeri . . . Mr. Cleveland
Gyfford . . . . . Mr. Harwood
Fitz Allan . . . . Mr. Warrell, Jr
Raymond . . . . . Mr. Warrell
Matilda . . . . . Mrs. Whitlock

CHILDREN IN THE WOOD.

Sir Rowland . . . . . Mr. Green
Lord Alford . . . Mr. Marshall
Walter . . . . . Mr. Harwood
Apathy . . . . Mr. Bates
Gabriel . . . . . . Mr. Moreton
Oliver . . . . . . ; Mr. Darley
Ruffian . . . . . Mr. De Moulin
Helen . . . . . . Mrs. Solomon
Josephine . . . . Mrs. Marshall

repertory from the outset. Thus Prince Hoare's "Prize" was the afterpiece on the opening night, and Mrs. Rowson's "Slaves in Al-

PHILADELPHIA CASTS—SECOND SEASON.

Winifred . . . . . Mrs. Rowson
Boy . . . . Master Parker
Girl . . . . Miss Solomon

CLANDESTINE MARRIAGE.

Lord Ogilby . . . Mr. Chalmers
Sir John Melville . . . Mr. Green
Sterling . . . . Mr. Morris
Lovewell . . . . . Mr. Marshall
Canton . . . . . . Mr. Harwood
Brush . . . . Mr. Moreton
Sergeant Flower . . Mr. Francis
Traverse . . . . . Mr. Cleveland
Trueman . . . . . Mr. Warrell
Servant . . . . . Mr. Darley, Jr
Mrs. Heidelberg . . . Mrs. Shaw
Miss Sterling . . . Mrs. Morris
Fanny . . . . . . Mrs. Marshall
Betty . . . . . . Mrs. Rowson
Chambermaid . . . Mrs. Francis
Trusty . . . . . . Mrs. Bates

CONSCIOUS LOVERS.

Young Bevil . . . Mr. Chalmers
Myrtle . . . . . . Mr. Cleveland
Cimberton . . . . . . Mr. Bates
Sealand . . . . . Mr. Whitlock
Sir John Bevil . . . Mr. Green
Humphrey . . . . . Mr. Warrell
Daniel . . . . . . Mr. Blissett
Tom . . . . Mr. Marshall
Indiana . . . . Mrs. Marshall
Mrs. Sealand . . . . Mrs. Shaw
Isabella . . . . . . Mrs. Rowson
Lucinda . . . . . Mrs. Cleveland
Phyllis . . . . . . Mrs. Hervey

CONSTANT COUPLE.

Sir Harry Wildair . Mrs. Marshall
Col. Standard . . . Mr. Moreton
Vizard . . . . . Mr. Cleveland
Ald. Smuggler . . . Mr. Morris
Beau Clincher . . . Mr. Green
Young Clincher . . . Mr. Bates
Tom Errand . . . . Mr. Francis
Dicky . . . . . . Mr. Blissett
Constable . . . . Mr. Darley, Jr
Angelica . . . . . Mrs. Hervey
Lady Lovewell . . . Mrs. Francis
Parly . . . . Mrs. Shaw
Errand's Wife . . . . Mrs. Bates

COUNTRY GIRL.

Moody . . . . Mr. Bates
Harcourt . . . . . Mr. Marshall
Sparkish . . . . . Mr. Moreton
Belville . . . . . Mr. Cleveland
Peggy . . . . . Mrs. Marshall
Alithea . . . . . . Mrs. Francis
Lucy . . . . Mrs. Shaw

DEVIL TO PAY.

Sir John Loverule . Mr. Marshall
Butler . . . . Mr. Francis
Cook . . . . Mr. Blissett
Footman . . . . . Mr. Solomon
Coachman . . . . Mr. Darley, Jr
Conjurer . . . . . Mr. Warrell
Jobson . . . . Mr. Bates
Lady Loverule . . . Mrs. Francis
Lucy . . . . . . Miss Willems
Lettice . . . . Mrs. Cleveland
Nell . . . . Mrs. Marshall

DUKE AND NO DUKE.

Lavino . . . . . . Mr. Moreton
Barbarino . . . . . Mr. Francis
Alberto . . . . . Mr. Warrell
Brunetto . . . . . Mr. Cleveland
Puritan . . . . . Mr. Harwood
Conjurer . . . . . Mr. Blissett
Trapolin . . . . . . Mr. Bates
Isabella . . . . Mrs. Cleveland
Prudentia . . . . Mrs. Francis
Fiametta . . . . Miss Willems
Mob Woman . . . . Mrs. Bates

EAST INDIAN.

Sir Hector Strangeways,Mr. Bates
Col. Ormsby . . . . Mr. Green
Brownlow . . . . Mr. Marshall
Orson . . . . . . Mr. Blissett
Bussora . . . . Mr. Harwood
Pillage . . . . . . Mr. Francis
James . . . . . Master Warrell
Zelide . . . . . Mrs. Marshall
Lady Di Strangeways . Mrs. Shaw
Jenny . . . . . . Miss Rowson

ENGLISH MERCHANT.

Lord Falbridge . . Mr. Moreton
Sir Wm. Douglas . Mr. Whitlock

Freeport . . . . . . Mr. Morris
Spatter . . . . . Mr. Wignell
Owen . . . . Mr. Green
La France . . . . Mr. Harwood
Officer . . . . . . Mr. Warrell
Lady Alton . . . . Mrs. Morris
Amelia . . . . . Mrs. Marshall
Mrs. Goodman . . . Mrs. Shaw
Molly . . . . . . Mrs. Francis

FARM HOUSE.

Modely . . . . . Mr. Cleveland
Freehold . . . . . Mr. Whitlock
Shacklefigure . . . Mr. Francis
Heartwell . . . . Mr. Moreton
Sir John English . . Mr. Warrell
Aura . . . . . . Mrs. Marshall
Flora . . . . . . Mrs. Francis

FEMALE PATRIOT.

Timoleon . . . . . Mr. Whitlock
Archidamus . . . . Mr. Green
Leosthenes . . . . Mr. Moreton
Hernando . . . . Mr. Francis
Diphilus . . . . . Mr. Warrell
Jailer . . . . . Mr. Darley, Jr
Graculo . . . . . Mr. Wignell
Pymbrio . . . . . Mr. Blissett
Pysander . . . . Mr. Chalmers
Cleora . . . . . Mrs. Whitlock
Olympio . . . . Mrs. Marshall
Statilla . . . . . Mrs. Rowson
Xanthia . . . . . Mrs. Francis

FONTAINVILLE FOREST.

Montault . . . . . Mr. Green
La Motte . . . . Mr. Chalmers
Louis . . . . . . Mr. Moreton
Peter . . . . . . Mr. Whitlock
Jaques . . . . . . Mr. Warrell
Nemours . . . . Mr. Cleveland
Hortensia . . . . Mrs. Shaw
Adeline . . . . Mrs. Whitlock

HARLEQUIN SHIPWRECKED.

Harlequin . . . . Mr. Francis
Leo . . . . . . Mr. Warrell, Jr
Indian Chief . . . . Mr. Nugent
Captain . . . . Mr. Cleveland
Cobbler . . . . Master Warrell

giers " was among the early productions.   Mrs. Rowson's play was
afterwards produced both in New York and Boston as a popular stock

PHILADELPHIA CASTS—SECOND SEASON.

Tailor . . . . . Mr. De Moulin
Barber . . . . Master T. Warrell
Lawyers . . . . . { Mr. Gibbon
                   { Mr. Price
Old Thoughtless . . Mr. Warrell
Tippy Bob . . . Mr. Darley, Jr
Whimsical . . . . . Mr. Green
Drowsy . . . . . . Mr. Blissett
Savage Princess . Miss Milbourne
Genius of Liberty . Mrs. Warrell

HAUNTED TOWER.

Lord William . . . Mr. Marshall
Oakland . . . . . Mr. Harwood
Edward . . . . . . Mr. Francis
Lewis . . . . Mr. Blissett
Robert . . . . . Mr. Darley, Jr
Charles . . . . . . Mr. Darley
Hugo . . . . Mr. Green
De Courcy . . . . Mr. Cleveland
Martin . . . . . . Mr. Warrell
Hubert . . . . . . Mr. Mitchell
Lady Elinor . . . . Mrs. Warrell
Adela . . . . . Mrs. Oldmixon
Cicely . . . . . Miss Broadhurst
Maud . . . . Mrs. Bates

HEIRESS.

Sir Clement Flint . Mr. Whitlock
Clifford . . . . . . Mr. Chalmers
Lord Gayville . . . Mr. Moreton
Alscrip . . . . . . Mr. Morris
Chignon . . . . . . Mr. Marshall
Mr. Blandish . . . Mr. Harwood
Prompt . . . . . . Mr. Francis
Mr. Rightly . . . Mr. Cleveland
Lady Emily . . . . Mrs. Marshall
Miss Alscrip . . . Mrs. Whitlock
Miss Alton . . . Mrs. Marshall
Mrs. Sagely . . . . Mrs. Bates
Tiffany . . . . Mrs. Cleveland
Mrs. Blandish . . . Mrs. Rowson

HIGH LIFE BELOW STAIRS.

Lovel . . . . . . Mr. Marshall
Trueman . . . . Mr. Cleveland
Sir Harry . . . . Mr. Francis
Lord Duke . . . . Mr. Harwood
Philip . . . . . . Mr. Wignell

Coachman . . . . . Mr. Warrell
Kingston . . . . Mr. Warrell, Jr
Robert . . . . . . Mr. Blissett
Tom . . . . . . Mr. Darley, Jr
Kitty . . . . . . Mr. Morris
Lady Bab . . . . Mrs. Rowson
Lady Charlotte . . Mrs. Francis
Cook . . . . Mrs. Bates
Chloe . . . . . . Miss Rowson

HOB IN THE WELL.

Trusty . . . . . . Mr. Francis
Friendly . . . . . Mr. Marshall
Hob . . . . Mr. Bates
Old Hob . . . . . Mr. Warrell
Dick . . . . . . Mr. Harwood
Roger . . . . . . Mr. Blissett
Flora . . . . . . Mrs. Warrell
Betty . . . . . . Mrs. Solomon
Hob's Mother . . . . Mrs. Bates

INKLE AND YARICO.

Inkle . . . . . Mr. Marshall
Curry . . . . . . Mr. Whitlock
Medium . . . . . . Mr. Francis
Campley . . . . . Mr. Moreton
Trudge . . . . . . Mr. Wignell
Mate . . . . Mr. Darley
Yarico . . . . . Mrs. Marshall
Narcissa . . . . Mrs. Oldmixon
Wowski . . . . Miss Broadhurst
Patty . . . . Mrs. Shaw

JEW.

Sir Stephen Bertram, Mr. Whitlock
Frederick . . . . Mr. Moreton
Charles Ratcliffe . Mr. Chalmers
Saunders . . . . . Mr. Green
Sheva . . . . . . Mr. Wignell
Jabal . . . . . . Mr. Harwood
Walter . . . . Mr. Darley, Jr
Mrs. Ratcliffe . . . . Mrs. Shaw
Eliza . . . . . . Mrs. Whitlock
Mrs. Goodison . . . . Mrs. Bates
Dorcas . . . . . . Mrs. Francis

KNOW YOUR OWN MIND.

Millamour . . . . . Mr. Moreton
Dashwood . . . . Mr. Chalmers

Malvil . . . . . . Mr. Whitlock
Bygrove . . . . Mr. Bates
Capt. Bygrove . . Mr. Cleveland
Sir John Millamour . Mr. Warrell
Sir Harry Lovewit . Mr. Harwood
Charles . . . . . . Mr. Francis
Lady Bell . . . . Mrs. Marshall
Jady Jane . . . Mrs. Cleveland
Mrs. Bromley . . . . Mrs. Shaw
Miss Neville . . . . Mrs. Francis
Mad. La Rouge . . Mrs. Rowson

LE FORET NOIRE.

Geronte . . . . Mr. Green
Lanzidan . . . . . Mr. Moreton
Adolph . . . . Master T. Warrell
Prince . . . . Mr. Francis
Lubin . . . . . . Master Warrell
Fronte . . . . Mr. Warrell
Pasquin . . . . . Mr. Darley, Jr
Le Terruer . . . . Mr. Marshall
Sans Quartier . . Mr. Cleveland
Le Fourbe . . . . . Mr. Blissett
Lucille . . . . . . Mrs. Francis
Marton . . . . . . Miss Rowson

MAYOR OF GARRATT.

Sir Jacob Jollop . . Mr. Francis
Mayor Sturgeon . Mr. Chalmers
Jerry Sneak . . . Mr Harwood
Bruin . . . . . . Mr. Green
Roger . . . . Mr. Blissett
Mrs. Sneak . . . . . Mrs. Shaw
Mrs. Bruin . . . Mrs. Cleveland

MERRY WIVES OF WINDSOR.

Sir John Falstaff . Mr. Whitlock
Fenton . . . . . . Mr. Cleveland
Justice Shallow . . Mr. Harwood
Slender . . . . . Mr. Moreton
Mr. Page . . . . . . Mr. Green
Mr. Ford . . . . Mr. Chalmers
Sir Hugh Evans . . . Mr. Bates
Dr. Caius . . . . . Mr. Marshall
Host . . . . Mr. Wignell
Bardolph . . . . Mr. Darley, Jr
Nym . . . . Mr. Warrell
Pistol . . . . . . Mr. Francis
Robin . . . . . Miss Solomon
Simple . . . . . . Mr. Blissett

piece. As before, I have arranged the casts printed for the first time during the season alphabetically, including both first productions and

PHILADELPHIA CASTS—SECOND SEASON.

Rugby . . . . . Mr. J. Warrell
Mrs. Page . . . . Mrs. Whitlock
Mrs. Ford . . . . . Mrs. Morris
Ann Page . . . . . Miss Willems
Mrs. Quickly . . . Mrs. Rowson

MIDAS.

Jupiter . . . . Mr. Warrell
Apollo . . . . . . Mr. Marshall
Momus . . . . . . Mr. Solomon
Mercury . . . . . Mr. Darley, Jr
Pan . . . . Mr. Francis
Juno . . . . Miss Willems
Midas . . ' ' . . . . Mr. Bates
Dametas . . . . . . Mr. Blissett
Sileno . . . . Mr. Darley
Mysis . . . . Mrs. Shaw
Daphne . . . . . Mrs. Oldmixon
Nysa . . . . . . Mrs. Marshall

MILLER OF MANSFIELD.

King . . . . Mr. Whitlock
Miller . . . . Mr. Morris
Richard . . . . . . Mr. Moreton
Lurewell . . . . . Mr. Cleveland
Joe . . . . Mr. Darley, Jr
Keeper . . . . Mr. Price
Peggy . . . . . . Miss Oldfield
Kate . . . . Miss Willems
Margery . . . . . . Mrs. Bates

MY GRANDMOTHER.

Sir Matthew Medley . Mr. Francis
Vapour . . . . . . Mr. Moreton
Woodley . . . . . . Mr. Darley
Gossip . . . . Mr. Bates
Souffrance . . . . Mr. Harwood
Tom . . . . Mr. Blissett
Florella . . . . . Mrs. Oldmixon
Charlotte . . Miss Broadhurst

NATURAL SON.

Sir Jeffrey Latimer . Mr. Harwood
Blushenly . . . . . Mr. Moreton
Rueful . . . . Mr. Green
Jack Hastings . . Mr. Chalmers
Major O'Flaherty . Mr. Whitlock
Dumps . . . . Mr. Bates
David . . . . Mr. Francis

Thomas . . . . . Mr. Darley, Jr
William . . . . Mr. Price
Lady Phœbe Latimer . Mrs. Shaw
Lady Paragon . . Mrs. Whitlock
Penelope . . . . Mrs. Cleveland

NEW WAY TO PAY OLD DEBTS.

Sir Giles Overreach, Mr. Chalmers
Lord Lovel . . . . Mr. Moreton
Justice Greedy . . . . Mr. Bates
Tapwell . . . . . . Mr. Wignell
Amble . . . . Mr. Blissett
Wantwell . . . . . Mr. Warrell
Welborn . . . . . Mr. Whitlock
Allworth . . . . . Mr. Cleveland
Marall . . . . . . Mr. Harwood
Order . . . . . . Mr. Warrell, Jr
Furnace . . . . . . Mr. Francis
Lady Allworth . . . Mrs. Shaw
Margaretta . . . Mrs. Marshall
Froth . . . . Mrs. Rowson

NEXT-DOOR NEIGHBORS.

Splendorville . . . Mr. Moreton
Manly . . . . Mr. Green
Blackman . . . . . . Mr. Bates
Lucre . . . . Mr. Wignell
Wilford . . . . . Mr. Whitlock
Henry . . . . . . Mr. Marshall
Bluntly . . . . . . Mr. Harwood
Shopman . . . . Mr. Darley, Jr
Lady C. Seymour . Mrs. Francis
Lady Squander . . Mrs. Rowson
Evans . . . . . Mrs. Solomon
Eleanor . . . . Mrs. Marshall

ORPHAN.

Chamont . . . . . Mr. Chalmers
Acasto . . . . . Mr. Whitlock
Castalio . . . . . Mr. Moreton
Monimia . . . . . Mrs. Whitlock

PADLOCK.

Don Diego . . . . . Mr. Darley
Leander . . . . Mr. Marshall
Mungo . . . . Mr. Bates
Leonora . . . Miss Broadhurst
Ursula . . . . . . Mrs. Shaw

PEEPING TOM OF COVENTRY.

Peeping Tom . . . . Mr. Bates
Mayor . . . . . . Mr. Harwood
Harold . . . . . Mr. Darley, Jr
Crazy . . . . Mr. Francis
Mercia . . . . . . Mr. Green
Count Lewis . . Mr. Cleveland
Maud . . . . . . Mrs. Marshall
Emma . . . . . Miss Broadhurst
Lady Godiva . . . Miss Willems
Mayoress . . . . . Mrs. Rowson

PERCY.

Percy . . . . Mr. Moreton
Douglas . . . . Mr. Green
Earl Raby . . . . Mr. Whitlock
Edric . . . . Mr. Harwood
Harcourt . . . . Mr. Warrell, Jr
Sir Herbert . . . Mr. Cleveland
Elwina . . . . . Mrs. Whitlock
Birtha . . . . . Mrs. Cleveland

POOR VULCAN.

Vulcan . . . . . . Mr. Wignell
Jupiter . . . . . . Mr. Marshall
Apollo . . . . . . Mr. Mitchell
Mars . . . . Mr. Darley
Bacchus . . . . Mr. Darley, Jr
Adonis . . . . Miss Broadhurst
Mercury . . . . . Mr. Solomon
Venus . . . . . . Mrs. Marshall
Grace . . . . . . Miss Willems

PRISONER.

Marcos . . . . . . Mr. Marshall
Bernardo . . . . . . Mr. Darley
Pasqual . . . . . Mr. Darley, Jr
Roberto . . . . . Mr. Harwood
Lewis . . . . Mr. Moreton
Narcisso . . . Young Gentleman
Clara . . . . . Miss Broadhurst
Theresa . . . . . . Mrs. Hervey
Nina . . . . . . Mrs. Marshall
Juliana . . . . . . Miss Solomon

PURSE.

Baron . . . . . . Mr. Whitlock
Theodore . . . . . Mr. Moreton

revivals. Jackman's farce, "All the World's a Stage," was the afterpiece in Mr. and Mrs. Rowson's bill, which included the "Female

PHILADELPHIA CASTS—SECOND SEASON.

Edmund . . . . Mr. Marshall
Will Steady . . . . Mr. Harwood
Page . . . . Mrs. Marshall
Sally . . . . . . Mrs. Oldmixon

RAGE.

Gingham . . . . . Mr. Wignell
Darnley . . . . . . Mr. Moreton
Sir George Gauntlet . Mr. Green
Hon. Mr. Savage . Mr. Harwood
Sir Paul Perpetual . Mr. Whitlock
Flush . . . . Mr. Francis
Ready . . . . Mr. Warrell
Waiter . . . . . Mr. Darley, Jr
Richard . . . . . . Mr. Blissett
Thomas . . . . . . Mr. Mitchell
William . . . Master T. Warrell
Groom . . . . Master J. Warrell
Lady Sarah Savage . Mrs. Hervey
Clara Sedley . . . . Miss Wells
Mrs. Darnley . . . Mrs. Marshall

RICHARD III.

Henry VI . . . . Mr. Whitlock
Prince Edward . Master Warrell
Duke of York . Master T. Warrell
Richard . . . . . Mr. Chalmers
Buckingham . . . . Mr. Wignell
Richmond . . . . . Mr. Moreton
Norfolk . . . . . . Mr. Warrell
Ratcliff . . . . . . Mr. Francis
Catesby . . . . . Mr. Cleveland
Tressel . . . . . Mr. Marshall
Oxford . . . . . . Mr. Blissett
Lieutenant . . . . Mr. Harwood
Lord Stanley . . . . Mr. Green
Lord Mayor . . . . . Mr. Bates
Tyrrell . . . . Mr. De Moulin
Queen Elizabeth . . Mrs. Morris
Lady Anne . . . . Mrs. Francis
Duchess of York . . . Mrs. Shaw

ROMAN ACTOR.

Paris . . . . Mr. Chalmers
Aretinus . . . . . Mr. Whitlock
Æsopus . . . . . . Mr. Warrell
Latinus . . . . Mr. Price

SHE STOOPS TO CONQUER.

Sir Charles Marlow . Mr. Warrell
Young Marlow . . Mr. Chalmers
Hardcastle . . . . . Mr. Morris
Hastings . . . . . Mr. Cleveland
Tony Lumpkin . . . . Mr. Bates
Diggory . . . . . . Mr. Francis
Landlord . . . . . . Mr. Darley
Jeremy . . . . Mr. Blissett
Mrs. Hardcastle . . . Mrs. Shaw
Miss Hardcastle . Mrs. Marshall
Miss Neville . . . Mrs. Francis
Maid . . . . . . Miss Willems

SICILIAN ROMANCE.

Ferrand . . . . . . Mr. Moreton
Don Lope . . . . . . Mr. Morris
Lindor . . . . . . Mr. Marshall
Martin . . . . . Mr. Harwood
Jaques . . . . . . Mr. Blissett
Sancho . . . . . . Mr. Warrell
Gerbin . . . . . . Mr. Wignell
Julia . . . . . . Miss Solomon
Alinda . . . . . Miss Broadhurst
Clara . . . . . . Mrs. Oldmixon
Adelaide . . . . . Mrs. Whitlock

SUSPICIOUS HUSBAND.

Ranger . . . . . . Mr. Chalmers
Strickland . . . . Mr. Whitlock
Frankly . . . . . . Mr. Moreton
Bellamy . . . . Mr. Cleveland
Jack Maggot . . . Mr. Harwood
Tester . . . . Mr. Bates
Milliner . . . . . Miss Willems
Buckle . . . . . . Mr. Blissett
Simon . . . . . . Mr. Warrell
Servant . . . . . Mr. Warrell, Jr
Mrs. Strickland . Mrs. Cleveland
Jacintha . . . . . Mrs. Francis
Lucetta . . . . . . Mrs. Shaw
Landlady . . . . . Mrs. Bates
Clarinda . . . . . Mrs. Marshall

TAMERLANE.

Tamerlane . . . . Mr. Whitlock
Bajazet . . . . . Mr. Chalmers
Axalla . . . . . Mr. Cleveland
Monesses . . . . . Mr. Moreton
Tanais . . . . Mr. Warrell

Omar . . . . . . Mr. Harwood
Mirvan . . . . . . Mr. Mitchell
Zama . . . . . . Mr. Darley, Jr
Hali . . . . . . Mr. Warrell, Jr
Dervise . . . . . . Mr. Morris
Arpasia . . . . . Mrs. Whitlock
Selima . . . . . . Mrs. Marshall

THREE WEEKS AFTER MARRIAGE.

Sir Charles Racket, Mr. Chalmers
Drugget . . . . . . Mr. Green
Woodley . . . . . Mr. Cleveland
Servant . . . . . Mr. Darley, Jr
Lady Racket . . Mrs. Whitlock
Mrs. Drugget . . . . Mrs. Bates
Nancy . . . . . . Miss Willems
Dimity . . . . . . Mrs. Francis

TOM THUMB, THE GREAT.

Tom Thumb . . . Miss Solomon
King Arthur . . . . . Mr. Bates
Lord Grizzle . . . Mr. Marshall
Noodle . . . . . . Mr. Francis
Doodle . . . . . Mr. Darley, Jr
Merlin . . . . Mr. Darley
Queen Dollalolla . . Mrs. Warrell
Huncamunca . . Mrs. Oldmixon
Cleora . . . . . . Miss Oldfield
Mustacha . . . . Miss Willems
Glumdalca . . . . Mrs. Rowson

TOY.

Sir Carol . . . . . Mr. Whitlock
Young Kavenagh . Mr. Moreton
Alibi . . . . Mr. Morris
Larry . . . . . . Mr. Wignell
Metheglin . . . . . Mr. Bates
Aircourt . . . . . Mr. Chalmers
Nol Pros . . . . . Mr. Warrell
Decrotan . . . . . Mr. Blissett
Footman . . . . Mr. Warrell, Jr
Boy . . . . Master T. Warrell
Lady Arable . . . . Mrs. Shaw
Lady Jane . . . . Mrs. Morris
Sophia . . . . . Mrs. Marshall
Fib . . . . Miss Willems
Katy Kavenagh . . Mrs. Rowson

Patriot," an adaptation by Mrs. Rowson from Massinger's " Bond-man," a tragedy originally acted at the Cock-pit, Drury Lane, besides a new pantomime called the " Travellers Preserved." Stephen James Arnold's " Auld Robin Gray " was given for the first time in America for Mrs. Marshall's benefit, but in spite of the excellent music con-tributed to it by the author's father it had as little success here as at the Haymarket. Mr. Bates offered for his benefit the least effective of all of O'Keefe's pieces, " A Beggar on Horseback," to which he gave the cumbrous title, " Set a Beggar on Horseback and He'll Ride to the Devil." He made some atonement, however, by presenting for the first time in the United States Philip Massinger's great comedy, " A New Way to Pay Old Debts." Originally produced at the Phœnix in Drury Lane, this great play was often revived during the following century and a half, but never with marked success until 1781, when Henderson played *Sir Giles Overreach.* That Mr. Chalmers, the original of the role in this country, was equal to its requirements is scarcely to be assumed. Mr. and Mrs. Francis for their joint benefit introduced Miles Peter Andrews' comedy, " Better Late Than Never;" but it failed to become popular. Equally unfortunate was Cumber-land's " Box-Lobby Challenge," produced immediately after the Easter holidays, but not revived. A singular revival was Tate's farce, " A Duke and No Duke," which had never been played in this country

PHILADELPHIA CASTS—SECOND SEASON.

TRAVELLERS PRESERVED.		TWO MISERS.		WEDDING DAY.	
Alberto	Mr. Moreton	Gripe	Mr. Francis	Lord Rakeland	Mr. Moreton
La Feur	Mr. Marshall	Hunks	Mr. Wignell	Sir Adam Contest	Mr. Harwood
Gerald	Mr. Warrell	Lively	Mr. Marshall	Mr. Milden	Mr. Warrell
Ramirez	Mr. Rowson	Ali	Mr. Darley	Mr. Contest	Mr. Cleveland
Old Woman	Mrs. Francis	Osman	Mr. Darley, Jr	Lady Autumn	Mr. Rowson
Rosalie	Miss Milbourne	Mustapha	Mr. Blissett	Lady Contest	Mrs. Hervey
Jacquelina	Miss Solomon	Harriet	Miss Broadhurst	Mrs. Hamford	Mrs. Shaw
		Jenny	Mrs. Oldmixon	Hannah	Mrs. Rowson

except by the Military Thespians at the Southwark Theatre in 1778. It was included in Mr. Chalmer's benefit bill, together with the "Suspicious Husband" and a condensed version of Massinger's "Roman Actor," which Chalmers called "A Defense of the Stage." The "Farm House" was a farce by John Philip Kemble, taken from Johnson's "Country Lasses" and "Fontainville Forest," a play by James Boaden, founded on Mrs. Radcliffe's "Romance of the Forest." Dunlap dramatized the story for the New York company, calling his play "Fontainville Abbey." Perhaps the most important of the pieces new to the American stage produced this season was Cumberland's "Jew." In this comedy an honest and benevolent Jew was for the first time introduced into an English play. The piece proved a great favorite with the public, both in England and America. The production of the "Merry Wives of Windsor" for Mr. Whitlock's benefit this season was the first performance of the comedy in this country. Prince Hoare's farce, "My Grandmother," acted with success at Drury Lane and long a stock piece; Mrs. Inchbald's comedy, "Next-Door Neighbors," a Haymarket success, taken from two French plays, *Le Dissipateur* and *L'Indigent;* Dibdin's burletta, "Poor Vulcan," acted at Covent Garden with applause as early as 1778; Rose's musical romance, the "Prisoner," first acted by the Drury Lane company at the Opera House in the Haymarket; Henry Siddons' opera, the "Sicilian Romance," a recent Covent Garden success, taken from the novel of the same name; and O'Keefe's "Toy," acted at Covent Garden in 1789, and said at the time to be in part the "Ward in Chancery" by Mr. Pilon, were all, excepting Dibdin's burletta, played for the first time in this country. The benefit productions among these pieces were the "Sicilian Romance," brought out by Mrs. Morris, "Next-

Door Neighbors" by Mr. Harwood, and the "Toy" and the "Prisoner" by Mr. Morris. When Morris took his benefit, a poetical admirer thus alluded to the venerable comedian and O'Keefe's new comedy in the *Aurora :*

> See, bent beneath accumulated years,
> The hoary veteran of the stage appears ;
> In spite of pain, in trembling age's spite,
> He brings a " Toy " to pleasure you to-night.
> Surviv'd the wreck of early friends he lost,
> Still on the waves of anxious being tost,
> Oh, let a ray of your mild pity shed,
> Perhaps, its last effusions on his head.

There were also some benefit pieces now played in this country for the first time of which we have no casts, including Holcroft's " Noble Peasant," in which Miss George was the original *Adela* at the Haymarket in 1784, for Mrs. Oldmixon; Cobb's " First Floor," a farce acted at Drury Lane with great success, for Miss Broadhurst; and Holcroft's " Follies of a Day," from Beaumarchais' " Marriage of Figaro," for Mr. and Mrs. Cleveland. These close the list of new productions this season.

In the long list of revivals during the season of 1794-5 there were many changes from the original casts which are chiefly interest-

CONTRASTED CASTS—CHANGES.

PLAYS.	1794.	1794-5.
Agreeable Surprise.		
Sir Felix Friendly	Mr. Finch . . .	Mr. Francis
Eugene	Mr. Marshall	Mr. Darley, Jr
John	Mr. Francis . .	Mr. Cleveland
Cowslip	Mrs. Marshall	Mrs. Solomon
Fringe	Mrs. Rowson	Miss Willems
As You Like It.		
Banished Duke .	Mr. Green . . .	Mr. Harwood
Le Beau	Mr. Finch . . .	Mr. Francis
Oliver	Mr. Harwood	Mr. Green
Corin	Mr. De Moulin	Mr. Darley
William	Mr. Francis . .	Mr. Blissett

PLAYS.	1794.	1794-5.
Birth of Harlequin.		
Pantaloon . . .	M. Bellona	Mr. Green
Maid	Mrs. Rowson	Mrs. Cleveland
Columbine . .	Madame Gardie	Mrs. De Marque
Castle of Andalusia.		
Don Scipio . .	Mr. Finch . .	Mr. Francis
Comus.		
Comus	Mr. Fennell . .	Mr. Chalmers
Critic.		
Sneer	Mr. Fennell . .	Mr. Moreton
Interpreter . . .	Mr. Finch . . .	Mr. Blissett

ing as showing the development and growth of the younger members
of the company—Moreton, Harwood and Francis—and the gradual

CONTRASTED CASTS—CHANGES.

PLAYS.	1794.	1794-5.
Lord Burleigh	Mr. Bates	Mr. Blissett
Sir W. Raleigh	Mr. Green	Mr. Francis
Sir C. Hatton	Mr. Francis	Mr. Green
Whiskerandos	Mr. Moreton	Mr. Bates

Cymbeline.

Cloten	Mr. Blissett	Mr. Wignell
Posthumous	Mr. Fennell	Mr. Chalmers
Frenchman	Mr. Finch	Mr. Warrell

Deserter.

Flint	Mr. Blissett	Mr. Green

Dramatist.

Ennui	Mr. Harwood	Mr. Marshall

Duenna.

Don Jerome	Mr. Finch	Mr. Harwood
Ferdinand	Mr. Marshall	Mr. Moreton
Antonio	Mr. Francis	Mr. Darley, Jr
Carlos	Mr. Darley, Jr	Mr. Marshall
Isaac	Mr. Bates	Mr. Wignell
Clara	Miss Broadhurst	Mrs. Warrell
Louisa	Mrs. Warrell	Miss Broadhurst

Every One Has His Fault.

Harmony	Mr. Bates	Mr. Green
Capt. Irwin	Mr. Fennell	Mr. Moreton
Hammond	Mr. Green	Mr. Cleveland
Placid	Mr. Moreton	Mr. Wignell
Mrs. Placid	Mrs. Rowson	Mrs. Shaw

Fair Penitent.

Horatio	Mr. Fennell	Mr. Chalmers
Rosario	Mr. Warrell	Mr. Francis
Lucilla	Mrs. Rowson	Miss Oldfield

Gamester.

Beverly	Mr. Fennell	Mr. Chalmers
Jarvis	Mr. Whitlock	Mr. Morris
Waiter	Mr. De Moulin	Mr. Darley, Jr

Hamlet.

Hamlet	Mr. Fennell	Mr. Chalmers
Ghost	Mr. Whitlock	Mr. Wignell
Rosencranz	Mr. Francis	Mr. Warrell, Jr
Osric	Mr. Finch	Mr. Francis
2d Gravedigger	Mr. Milbourne	Mr. Wignell

Highland Reel.

McGilpin	Mr. Finch	Mr. Harwood
Croudy	Mr. Harwood	Mr. Blissett
Apie	Mr. Blissett	Mr. T. Warrell

Isabella.

Count Baldwin	Mr. Whitlock	Mr. Green

PLAYS.	1794.	1794-5.
Biron	Mr. Fennell	Mr. Whitlock
Carlos	Mr. Green	Mr. Marshall
Villeroy	Mr. Wignell	Mr Moreton

Jealous Wife.

Oakly	Mr. Fennell	Mr. Green
Charles	Mr. Moreton	Mr. Cleveland
Lord Trinket	Mr. Finch	Mr. Marshall
Capt. O'Cutter	Mr. Bates	Mr. Harwood

Lionel and Clarissa.

Jenny	Miss Willems	Miss Broadhurst

Lyar.

Papillion	Mr. Finch	Mr. Marshall

Lying Valet.

Beau Trippet	Mr. Harwood	Mr. Cleveland
Drunken Cook	Mr. Francis	Mr. Blissett
Mrs. Trippet	Mrs. Rowson	Mrs. Cleveland

Macbeth.

Macbeth	Mr. Fennell	Mr. Chalmers
Siward	Mr. Warrell	Mr. Morris
Second Witch	Mr. Finch	Mr. Warrell

No Song No Supper.

Louisa	Miss Broadhurst	Miss Willems
Nelly	Miss Willems	Miss Broadhurst

Poor Soldier.

Capt. Fitzroy	Mr. Darley	Mr. Moreton
Father Luke	Mr. Finch	Mr. Blissett
Patrick	Mr. Moreton	Mr. Darley

Rivals.

Faulkland	Mr. Fennell	Mr. Cleveland

Road to Ruin.

Sulky	Mr. Finch	Mr. Francis

Robin Hood.

Clorinda	Mrs. Oldmixon	Mrs. Warrell
Annette	Mrs. Marshall	Mrs. Francis

Robinson Crusoe.

Robinson Crusoe	Mr. Whitlock	Mr. Bates
Friday	Mr. Bates	Mr. Francis

Romeo and Juliet.

Romeo	Mr. Fennell	Mr. Moreton
Escalus	Mr. Finch	Mr. Warrell
Paris	Mr. Moreton	Mr. Marshall
Montagu	Mr. De Moulin	Mr. Morris
Mercutio	Mr. Chalmers	Mr. Wignell

Romp.

Barnacle	Mr. Finch	Mr. Harwood

placing of Blissett in the " bits " for his excellence in which he afterward became famous. When the " Agreeable Surprise " was given
on the 13th of March, Mrs. Solomon made her first appearance with
the company as *Cowslip.* Criticism began to take form during the
season, a series of essays in the *Philadelphia Gazette* being especially
noteworthy. The first of these was devoted to Mr. Chalmers, of
whom it was said that his *Belcour* (" West Indian ") could not be ex-
celled; that his *Belville* (" School for Wives ") was equal to his *Belcour;* that the part of *Modely* (" Farm House ") fitted him as easily as
the clothes he wore, and that he did full justice to *Lord Ogilby*
(" Clandestine Marriage "). To his *Vapid* (" Dramatist ") and *Marplot*
(" Busybody ") it was objected that they were beyond nature. To
equal him as *Puff* (" Critic ") was said to be difficult—to excel him
impossible. Chalmers seldom attempted low comedy, but for his
Trappanti (" She Wou'd and She Wou'd Not ") it was claimed that he
put in the most conspicuous light all the humor, cunning and roguery

CONTRASTED CASTS—CHANGES.

Plays.	1794.	1794-5.
Old Cockney	. Mr. De Moulin..	Mr. Warrell
Penelope . . .	Miss Willems .	Miss Rowson
Quasheba . . .	Miss Rowson .	Mast. T. Warrell
School for Scandal.		
Sir Benjamin . .	Mr. Finch . . .	Mr. Marshall
Lady Sneerwell,	Mrs. Francis .	Mrs. Rowson
Maria	Mrs. Cleveland..	Mrs. Francis
School for Wives.		
Mrs. Tempest .	Mrs. Bates . .	Mrs. Solomon
She Wou'd and She Wou'd Not.		
Don Philip . . .	Mr. Fennell. . .	Mr. Cleveland
Don Lewis . . .	Mr. Cleveland .	Mr. Moreton.
Spanish Barber.		
Lazarillo . . .	Mr. Bates.. . .	Mr. Harwood
Surrender of Calais.		
Ribemont . . .	Mr. Fennell . .	Mr. Chalmers
La Gloire . . .	Mr. Bates . . .	Mr. Harwood
Gallowsmaker .	Mr. Harwood .	Mr. Blissett
Julia	Mrs. Francis . .	Mrs. Whitlock

Plays.	1794.	1794-5.
Tempest.		
Gonzalo	Mr. Finch . . .	Mr. Cleveland
Miranda	Mrs. Cleveland..	Miss Oldfield
Venice Preserved.		
Duke	Mr. Finch . . .	Mr. Morris
Pierre	Mr. Fennell . .	Mr. Chalmers
Jaffier	Mr. Wignell . .	Mr. Moreton
Elliot	Mr. Moreton .	Mr. Cleveland
West Indian.		
Stockwell . . .	Mr. Fennell . .	Mr. Morris
Stukely	Mr. De Moulin..	Mr. Moreton
Fulmer	Mr. Finch . . .	Mr. Harwood
Lucy	Mrs. Cleveland..	Mrs. Rowson
Woodman.		
Sir W. Waring .	Mr. Finch . . .	Mr. Wignell
Medley	Mr. Bates . . .	Mr. Francis
Bob	Mr. Francis . .	Mr. Darley, Jr
Polly	Young Lady . .	Miss Solomon

that Cibber bestowed upon the character.   His tragedy was inferior to
his comedy; but his *Hamlet,* it was said, was well performed, his interview with his mother being "truly great."   In the strong scenes in
tragedy he verged toward rant, his *La Motte* (" Fontainville Forest ")
being named as one of these parts; while his "thundering tones" as
Bajazet (" Tamerlane ") were pronounced exceedingly well calculated
to do justice to the tiger-like passions of the fell destroyer.   Although
Mr. Moreton was Chalmers' only real rival at this time, I find no mention of him except as *Monesses* (" Tamerlane "), the critic's favorite
phrase, "truly great," being applied to his dying scene.   Mr. Harwood,
however, was treated with more attention, the third essay in the
Gazette's series being devoted to his acting.   Greatly as his *Dr.
Lenitive* (" Prize ") was esteemed, his *Sir Fretful Plagiary* (" Critic ")
was pronounced even superior to his *Lenitive ;* his *Walter* (" Children
in the Wood ") was well performed, but inferior to Hodgkinson's; as
Sir David Dunder (" Ways and Means "), *Prattle* (" Deuce is in Him ")
and *Jabal* (" Jew ") he was received with great applause; but as the
Baron of Oakland (" Haunted Tower "), *Fulmer* (" West Indian ") and
the *Planter* (" Inkle and Yarico ") he appeared to no great advantage.
Of his interview with his *Sall* (" Purse ") it was said, however, that
even Garrick could hardly have exceeded him.   One night a sailor
and his lass were in the pit, and the jolly tar was so well pleased with
the acting that he insisted upon drinking to Harwood's health.

The only actresses belonging to the company who came under
the notice of the *Gazette's* critic at this time were Mrs. Whitlock—
claimed to be the first actress in America—and Mrs. Marshall, who
was the rival of Mrs. Hodgkinson.   These ladies were opposites in
person as they were in their parts.   Mrs. Whitlock was graceful in

carriage and animated in countenance, with a voice capable of every inflection; and except that her face and figure approached the masculine, she possessed every qualification for an actress. Mrs. Marshall, on the contrary, was *petite* and pleasing. The one had the lead in tragedy, the other in comedy. Mrs. Whitlock, it was said, displayed the unfeeling character of *Lady Macbeth* in genuine colors, and as *Mrs. Beverly* ("Gamester") she contrasted the tenderness, the sensibility and the distress of the wife with great effect. Her *Monimia* ("Orphan") was excellent. She appeared to advantage as *Lady Eleanor Irwin* ("Every One Has His Fault"), but as *Eliza Ratcliff* ("Jew") she was not so interesting. While Mrs. Whitlock was mistress of the passions and emotions, in Mrs. Marshall humor and merriment were predominant. As *Little Pickle* ("Spoiled Child") she was received with unbounded applause; as *Moggy McGilpin* ("Highland Reel") she was capital; her *Priscilla Tomboy* ("Romp") was admitted to be inferior, but her *Josephine* ("Children in the Wood") was claimed as superior to Mrs. Hodgkinson's; and her *Peggy* ("Country Girl") was pronounced nearly equal to Mrs. Jordan's. Her *Edward* ("Every One Has His Fault") was a character in which she was much admired. She could assume with equal ease, grace and propriety the forward, pouting airs of an awkward country minx; the impertinence of a rude boy, better fed than taught; the staid manners of a well-educated lady, and the softness and tenderness of a *Juliet*. She did not, however, always escape adverse comment. When "Tamerlane" was played she was severely censured for her dress as *Selima*, "which was before midleg high and displeasing alike to males and females."

CHAPTER X.

THE PHILADELPHIA COMPANY, 1795–6.

THE BALTIMORE SEASON OF 1795—OBJECTIONS OF THE COMPANY TO
ADVERSE CRITICISM—THE PHILADELPHIA SEASON OF 1795–6
—CHANGES IN THE COMPANY—THE BALTIMORE SEASON OF 1796
—WIGNELL'S FIRST COMPANY DISSOLVES.

ADVERSE criticism of the self-sufficient, dogmatic kind first met the Philadelphia company in Baltimore in the Summer and Autumn of 1795. The repertory, so far as it went, was identical with that of previous seasons in Philadelphia, nothing new being attempted except pantomimes, including "Les Deux Chasseurs," in which M. Lege, a French dancer and pantomimist, made his first appearance in America as *Cola*. Surprise was expressed that M. Lege received four guineas salary per week, the same that was paid to the favorite, Chalmers. This was a shot aimed at the management because of the retirement of Mr. Chalmers from the company after a few perform-ances at Baltimore. It may also account for much of the hostile criticism with which Mr. Moreton was received. Taking the season as a whole, however, the Baltimore public had little reason to com-plain. The engagement was a long one, extending from the 29th of July to the 3d of December; the repertory was varied, more pieces being given during that period than was customary in Philadelphia in the same length of time, and with the exception of Chalmers the company suffered no diminution of strength. Mr. Beete, whose name occurs in the bills for the first time, was probably a fair substitute for Mr. Cleveland; and the younger actresses, the Misses Willems, Oldfield and Milbourne, were ample compensation for the loss of Mrs. Cleveland. Mrs. Hervey, who failed to please the Baltimoreans at all, made her *debut* at the Holiday Street Theatre on the second night as *Louisa* in the "Irishman in London;" and Mrs. Oldmixon, who pleased them mightily, was heard there for the first time on the opening night as *Sally* in the "Purse." It may be assumed that the strictures of the Baltimore critics were of the class that has become proverbial—the severity of men new to the business.

The second Baltimore season was well under way before the onslaught began. Chalmers took his benefit on the 28th of August, and only two performances were allowed to intervene before the critical pen was called into play. The first piece chosen by the critic for his poisoned arrows was the "Rivals" when it was produced on the 2d of September. The darts were more frequently aimed at Mr. Wignell than at the others, but sooner or later nearly every member of the company felt the barb. Sometimes there was praise, but it was seldom bestowed on the Philadelphia favorites. Mr. Bates as *Bob Acres*, it was said, displayed

LIST OF PERFORMANCES—*Baltimore.*

1795.
July 29—Natural Son . . . . . Cumberland
Purse . . . . Cross
31—English Merchant . . . Colman
Irishman in London . Macready
Aug. 1—Jew . . . . Cumberland
Farmer . . . . O'Keefe
3—Every One Has His Fault
Mrs. Inchbald
Romp . . . . Bickerstaff
5—Castle of Andalusia . . O'Keefe
Farm House . . . . . Kemble
7—Next-Door Neighbors
Mrs. Inchbald
Critic . . . . Sheridan
8—Gamester . . . . . . Moore
Prize . . . . Hoare
10—Country Girl . . . . . Garrick
Flitch of Bacon . . . . . Bate
12—Maid of the Mill . . . Bickerstaff
Wrangling Lovers . . . . Lyon
14—Percy . . . . . . Miss More
Poor Soldier . . . . . O'Keefe

Aug. 15—Inkle and Yarico . . Colman, Jr
        Tom Thumb, the Great . O'Hara
    17—Countess of Salisbury . Hartson
        Prize.
    19—School for Wives . . . . Kelly
        Les Deux Chasseurs.
    21—Busybody . . . . Mrs. Centlivre
        Tom Thumb, the Great.
    22—Duenna . . . . Sheridan
        Les Deux Chasseurs.
    24—Merchant of Venice . Shakspere
        Children in the Wood . . Morton
    26—Suspicious Husband . . Hoadly
        Le Foret Noire.
    28—Road to Ruin . . . . . Holcroft
        Children in the Wood.
        (Mr. Chalmers' benefit.)
    29—Tamerlane . . . . . . Rowe
        My Grandmother . . . . Hoare
    31—Highland Reel . . . . O'Keefe
        Devil to Pay . . . . . . Coffey
Sept. 2—Rivals . . . . Sheridan
        Irish Lilt . . . . . . Francis
        Deserter . . . . . . Dibdin
    4—Isabella . . . . . . Southerne
        No Song No Supper . . . Hoare
    5—Clandestine Marriage
                 Garrick and Colman
        Sultan . . . . Bickerstaff
    7—Lionel and Clarissa . . Bickerstaff
        Le Foret Noire.
    9—Child of Nature . Mrs. Inchbald
        Sailor's Landlady . . . Francis
        Comus . . . . Milton
  11—Next-Door Neighbors.
        Peeping Tom of Coventry,O'Keefe
  14—Romeo and Juliet . . Shakspere
        Purse.
  16—Robin Hood . .   MacNally
        Les Marchandes de Mode.
  18—Jane Shore . . . . . . Rowe
        Rosina . .   . . . Mrs. Brooke
  19—Jew.
        Children in the Wood.
  21—As You Like It . . . Shakspere
        Wedding Day . . Mrs. Inchbald

a good deal of *vis comica*, and Mrs. Shaw as *Mrs. Malaprop* was " more truly in her line than since her arrival in Baltimore;" but Mr. Wignell as *Faulkland* was not suited to the character, and Mr. Moreton as *Captain Absolute* was " barely good." Mrs. Whitlock in the title-role of " Isabella " did not please the critic; and Mr. Whitlock, who played *Biron*, would have been happier as *Count Baldwin*, " poorly played by Green." Moreton " walked " through *Villeroy*. Only Miss Solomon as the *Child* gave the scribe any satisfaction. These strictures were feebly answered by " Equitas," and a few days later " Dramaticus " renewed the attack in response to " Equitas." When the " Clandestine Marriage " and the " Sultan " comprised the bill there was more tenderness shown toward the players. Mr. Marshall as *Lovewell* in the comedy, it was said, was very unhappy ; but Bates played *Lord Ogilby* with great humor; Morris as *Sterling* was chaste and laughable; Mrs. Morris as *Miss Sterling* filled the part quietly and with ease, and Mrs. Marshall as *Fanny* was tender, delicate and animated. As *Roxalana* in the farce Mrs. Oldmixon, of course, "played with her usual good fortune," and she sang "Loose were her tresses seen" with "divine melody, grace and elegance." Miss Oldfield was said to be improving. Of Mrs. Oldmixon as *Diana Oldboy* in " Lionel and Clarissa" the critic said it was scarcely necessary to say anything; Mrs. Marshall's *Clarissa* was allowed to possess a good deal of merit; Mr. Whitlock's *Sir John Flowerdale* was very happy in marking the tender solicitude of a father; Mr. Bates as *Oldboy* was excellent, and Mr. Darley sang *Jenkins'* songs with great taste, but Mr. Marshall's voice had not sufficient sweetness for *Lionel.* Wignell's *Lucre* in " Next-Door Neighbors" was "poor," and

Sept. 23—School for Scandal . . . Sheridan
Prisoner . . . . Rose
25—Percy.
Agreeable Surprise . . . O'Keefe
26—She Stoops to Conquer . Goldsmith
Quaker . . . . Dibdin
28—Orphan . . . . Otway
Spoiled Child . . . . Bickerstaff
30—Heiress . . . . Burgoyne
Padlock . . . . . . Bickerstaff
Oct. 2—Roman Father . . . Whitehead
Two Misers . . . . . . O'Hara
5—West Indian . . . . Cumberland
Two Philosophers.
My Grandmother.
7—Jealous Wife . . . . . Colman
Florizel and Perdita . Shakspere
9—Spanish Barber . . . . Colman
Prisoner.
10—Natural Son.
Romp.
12—Douglas . . . . Home
Poor Soldier.
15—Love in a Village . . Bickerstaff
Ways and Means . . Colman, Jr
16—Beaux' Stratagem . . . Farquhar
Two Misers.
21—Woodman . . . . Dudley
Who's the Dupe? . Mrs. Cowley
23—Brothers . . . . . Cumberland
Hartford Bridge . . . . Pearce
24—Gamester.
Harlequin Shipwrecked.
26—Dramatist . . . . . . Reynolds
Two Philosophers.
Quaker.
28—Grecian Daughter . . . Murphy
Prisoner at Large . . O'Keefe
29—Merry Wives of Windsor
Shakspere
Love in a Camp . . . . O'Keefe
31—Country Girl.
Sailor's Landlady.
Waterman . . . . Dibdin
Nov. 2—Toy . . . . O'Keefe
Harlequin Shipwrecked.

Nov. 4—Highland Reel.
   Modern Antiques . . . O'Keefe
  6—Fontainville Forest . . . Boaden
   All the World's a Stage . Jackman
  7—Maid of the Mill.
   Children in the Wood.
  9—Haunted Tower . . . . . Cobb
   Irishman in London.
 11—Belle's Stratagem . Mrs. Cowley
   Sicilian Romance . . . Siddons
 13—Jew.
   Harlequin Shipwrecked.
 14—Tempest . . . . Dryden
   Midnight Hour . . Mrs. Inchbald
 16—Provoked Husband . . Vanbrugh
   Jubilee . . . . Garrick
 (Mr. and Mrs. Whitlock's benefit.)
 17—George Barnwell . . . . . Lillo
   Rural Revels . . . . Francis
   Midas . . . . O'Hara
(Mrs. Oldmixon and Mr. Moreton's benefit.)
 19—How to Grow Rich . . Reynolds
   Robinson Crusoe.
  (Mr. and Mrs. Bates' benefit.)
 20—Chapter of Accidents . . Miss Lee
   Farmer.
 (Mr. Darley and Mrs. Shaw's benefit.)
 21—Wonder . . . . Mrs. Centlivre
   Miraculous Mill . . . . Francis
   Son-in-Law . . . . . . O'Keefe
 (Mr. and Mrs. Warrell's benefit.)
 23—Better Late Than Never . Andrews
   Mayor of Garratt . . . . . Foote
 (Green and Harwood's benefit.)
 24—Carmelite . . . . . Cumberland
   Les Armans d'Arcade . . Francis
   Harlequin's Invasion . . Garrick
 (Mr. and Mrs. Francis' benefit.)
 25—Romeo and Juliet.
   Tom Thumb, the Great.
 (Mrs. and Miss Solomon's benefit.)
 26—Bold Stroke for a Husband
        Mrs. Cowley
   Slaves in Algiers . Mrs. Rowson
 (Mr. and Mrs. Rowson's benefit.)

Maud in " Peeping Tom of Coventry" was a part too difficult for so young an actress as Miss Willems. The young actors, Moreton, Marshall, Harwood and Green, were unused to such harsh treatment from the newspapers, and they soon became not only angry but furious. Some of them even went so far as to threaten the critic with their vengeance. Harwood, indeed, carried their grievances before the public by making an appeal to the audience which shared in the resentment of the players. " Am I indeed in America?" he exclaimed. " Is this the country where the liberty of the press is held sacred?" This, it must be confessed, was rather illogical—it was the liberty of the press of which he was complaining. But undaunted by the threats of the players, the critic continued to distribute praise and blame according to his own sweet will. When " Romeo and Juliet" was played he found Green a good

Benvolio, but wished he could say the same for Moreton as *Romeo*. Mrs. Marshall's *Juliet* gave universal satisfaction, but Mrs. Rowson's *Nurse* was only "tolerably performed," and the younger Darley was "a miserable *Paris*," the critic doubting whether he would ever make a good actor. Other writers, however, declared that Moreton played *Romeo* with judgment; that Mrs. Rowson was a

Nov. 27—Fair Penitent . . . . . . Rowe
Le Marechal des Logis.
Midnight Hour.
(M. Lege and Mrs. Hervey's benefit.)
28—Beggar's Opera . . . . . . Gay
First Floor . . . . Cobb
(Blissett, Darley, Jr., and Mrs. De Marque's benefit.)
30—Every One Has His Fault.
Harlequin Hurry-Scurry . Francis
High Life Below Stairs . Townley
(Misses Willems, Milbourne and Oldfield's benefit.)
Dec. 1—Fontainville Forest.
Fair . . . . Francis
Purse.
2—Rage . . . . Reynolds
Harlequin Shipwrecked.
3—School for Scandal.
Poor Soldier.

very good *Nurse*, not merely tolerable; that Blissett was whimsically pleasing as *Peter;* and for Mrs. Solomon as *Lady Capulet* it was claimed as a merit that " her pleasing person and light style of dress made her appear like *Juliet* herself." With the exception of Mrs. Marshall's *Rosalind*, which was the principal support of the play, as well it might be, and Bates' *Touchstone*, which was excellent, none of the performers in "As You Like It" pleased the critic. Harwood played *Jaques* in "wretched style;" Marshall as *Amiens* was "poor and barren;" Rowson's *Charles* was "executed illy;" and Mrs. Francis as *Celia*, Mrs. Rowson as *Audrey* and Miss Oldfield as *Phœbe* were " horribly insipid." In the "Wedding Day," which was played the same night, Mrs. Hervey as *Lady Contest* was " more ridiculous than the piece." It was admitted that Mrs. Whitlock played the heroine in " Jane Shore " in a striking and beautiful manner, but Wignell's *Hastings* was " a labored piece of acting." Mrs. Warrell was said to be very pleasing as *Clarinda* in " Robin Hood," but in the title-role of

Mrs. Brooke's opera the critic declared that he "should have taken her for a landlady rather than the gentle, timid, innocent and beautiful *Rosina.*" After three weeks of this free lance the *Maryland Journal* shut down upon its critic, and we hear no more of the merits and demerits of the players through the newspapers.

The changes in the casts during the season, unimportant as they were, show us many of the inexperienced aspirants of 1793–4 in

CONTRASTED CASTS—CHANGES.

PLAYS.	Phil.	Balt.
All the World's a Stage.		
Wat	Mr. Darley, Jr .	Mr. Mitchell
Jane	Mrs. Francis .	Mrs. Solomon
As You Like It.		
Jaques	Mr. Chalmers .	Mr. Harwood
Audrey	Mrs. Shaw . .	Mrs. Rowson
Phœbe	Mrs. Cleveland .	Miss Oldfield
Belle's Stratagem.		
Doricourt . . .	Mr. Chalmers .	Mr. Moreton
Courtall	Mr. Moreton .	Mr. Harwood
Dick	Mr. Blissett . .	Mr. Mitchell
Lady Frances .	Mrs. Cleveland .	Miss Oldfield
Bold Stroke for a Husband.		
Don Garcia . .	Mr. Cleveland .	Mr. Beete
Laura	Mrs. Francis .	Mrs. Solomon
Marcella	Mrs. Cleveland .	Miss Oldfield
Luis	Mrs. Solomon .	Miss Milbourne
Carmelite.		
Montgomeri . .	Mr. Cleveland .	Mr. Harwood
Gyfford	Mr. Harwood .	Mr. Beete
Children in the Wood.		
Apathy	Mr. Bates . . .	Mr. Francis
Oliver	Mr. Darley . .	Mr. Darley, Jr
Ruffian	Mr. De Moulin .	Mr. Blissett
Boy	Master Parker .	Young Lady
Clandestine Marriage.		
Lord Ogilby . .	Mr. Chalmers .	Mr. Bates
Country Girl.		
Belville	Mr. Cleveland .	Mr. Green
Lucy	Mrs. Shaw . .	Mrs. Rowson
Critic.		
First Niece . .	Mrs. Cleveland .	Miss Milbourne
Second Niece .	Mrs. Rowson .	Miss Oldfield
Dramatist.		
Vapid	Mr. Chalmers .	Mr. Harwood
Neville	Mr. Cleveland .	Mr. Green
Willoughby . .	Mr. Green . .	Mr. Darley, Jr

PLAYS.	Phil.	Balt.
Miss Courtney .	Mrs. Francis .	Mrs. Hervey
Lady Waitford .	Mrs. Shaw . .	Mrs. Rowson
Letty	Mrs. Cleveland .	Mrs. Solomon
English Merchant.		
Mrs. Goodman .	Mrs. Shaw . .	Mrs. Solomon
Every One Has His Fault.		
Sir Robert . . .	Mr. Chalmers .	Mr. Wignell
Placid	Mr. Wignell . .	Mr. Green
Hammond . .	Mr. Cleveland .	Mr. Warrell, Jr
Miss Spinster . .	Mrs. Bates . .	Mrs. Solomon
Fair Penitent.		
Horatio	Mr. Chalmers .	Mr. Wignell
Rossano	Mr. Francis . .	Mr. Warrell
Lavinia	Mrs. Francis . .	Mrs. Hervey
Farmer.		
Louisa	Mrs. Warrell .	Mrs. Hervey
Betty	Mrs. Rowson .	Mrs. Shaw
Molly	Miss Broadhurst.	Mrs. Warrell
Flitch of Bacon.		
Justice Benbow .	Mr. Warrell . .	Mr Green
Major Benbow .	Mr. Harwood .	Mr. Bates
Fontainville Forest.		
La Motte . . .	Mr. Chalmers .	Mr. Whitlock
Peter	Mr. Whitlock .	Mr. Morris
Nemours . . .	Mr. Cleveland .	Mr. Harwood
Gamester.		
Beverly	Mr. Chalmers .	Mr. Moreton
Charlotte . . .	Mrs. Francis .	Mrs. Hervey
Lucy	Mrs. Cleveland..	Miss Oldfield
Harlequin Shipwrecked.		
Indian Chief . .	Mr. Nugent . .	Mr. Warrell, Jr
Captain	Mr. Cleveland .	Mr. Solomon
Tippy Bob . . .	Mr. Darley, Jr..	Mr. Robbins
Drowsy	Mr. Blissett .	Mr. Darley, Jr
Mme. Le Rouge		Mrs. Lege
Primrose Girl		Miss Solomon

parts that could be played only by trained actors and actresses. Mr Moreton had succeeded Chalmers as *Doricourt* in the " Belle's Stratagem," *Beverly* in the " Gamester," and *Charles Surface* in the " School for Scandal;" Mr. Harwood had been accorded Chalmers' roles of *Jaques* in " As You Like It," *Vapid* in the " Dramatist," and *Pave* in " How to Grow Rich;" and Green had for his share of the Chalmers inheritance the part of *Charles Ratcliffe* in the " Jew." To Green also

CONTRASTED CASTS—CHANGES.

PLAYS.	Phil.	Balt.	PLAYS.	Phil.	Balt.
Heiress.			*Modern Antiques.*		
Tiffany	Mrs. Cleveland.	Mrs. Hervey	Hearty	Mr. De Moulin.	Mr. Mitchell
			Nan	Mrs. Francis	Mrs. Solomon
High Life Below Stairs.			Betty	Mrs. Rowson	Miss Oldfield
Trueman . . .	Mr. Cleveland	Mr. Beete	*Peeping Tom of Coventry.*		
Lady Bab . . .	Mrs. Rowson	Miss Willems	Maud	Mrs. Marshall	Miss Willems
Cook	Mrs. Bates	Mrs. Solomon	*Percy.*		
Chloe	Miss Rowson	Miss Milbourne	Birtha	Mrs. Cleveland.	Mrs. Hervey
			Poor Soldier.		
How to Grow Rich.			Norah	Miss Broadhurst.	Miss Milbourne
Pave	Mr. Chalmers	Mr. Harwood	*Purse.*		
Roundhead . .	Mr. Finch . . .	Mr. Blissett	Baron	Mr. Whitlock	Mr. Green
Dazzle	Mr. Cleveland	Mr. Beete	Page	Mrs. Marshall	Miss Solomon
Plainly	Mr. De Moulin.	Mr. Warrell	*Rage.*		
Formal	Mr. Warrell	Mr. Solomon	Sir Paul	Mr. Whitlock	Mr. Bates
Miss Dazzle . .	Mrs. Francis	Mrs. Hervey	Lady Sarah . .	Mrs. Hervey	Mrs. Shaw
Betty	Mrs. Cleveland.	Mrs. Solomon	Clara Sedley . .	Miss Wells	Mrs. Marshall
			Mrs. Darnley .	Mrs. Marshall	Mrs. Whitlock
Jew.			*Rivals.*		
Charles Ratcliffe.	Mr. Chalmers	Mr. Green	Faulkland . . .	Mr. Cleveland	Mr. Wignell
Saunders . . .	Mr. Green . . .	Mr. Warrell	Lucy	Mrs. Rowson	Mrs. Hervey
Dorcas	Mrs. Francis	Mrs. Solomon	*Robin Hood.*		
			Annette	Mrs. Francis	Miss Milbourne
Le Teteur Trompe.			*Romeo and Juliet.*		
Don Garcia . .	Mr. Nugent	Mr. Francis	Paris	Mr. Marshall	Mr. Darley, Jr
Alonzo	Mr. Francis	Mr. Lege	Montagu . . .	Mr. Morris	Mr. Warrell
			Capulet		Mr. Morris
Lionel and Clarissa.			Benvolio . . .	Mr. Cleveland	Mr. Green
Clarissa	Mrs. Warrell	Mrs. Marshall	Balthazar . . .	Mr. Darley, Jr.	Mr. Warrell, Jr
			Lady Capulet .	Mrs. Rowson	Mrs. Solomon
Mayor of Garratt.			Nurse	Mrs. Shaw . . .	Mrs. Rowson
Major Sturgeon .	Mr. Chalmers	Mr. Green	*School for Scandal.*		
Bruin	Mr. Green . . .	Mr. Rowson	Charles Surface..	Mr. Chalmers. .	Mr. Moreton
Crispin		Mr. Darley, Jr	Careless		Mr. Darley
Mrs. Bruin . . .	Mrs. Cleveland	Mrs. Rowson	Sir Harry		Mr. Blissett
			Trip	Mr. Moreton	Mr. Warrell, Jr
Merchant of Venice.			Maria	Mr. Francis	Miss Oldfield
Solarino	Mr. Cleveland	Mr. Warrell			
Tubal	Mr. Milbourne	Mr. Harwood			
Launcelot . . .	Mr. Harwood	Mr. Bates			
Miraculous Mill.					
Mealey	Mr. Nugent	Mr. Rowson			

was allotted a number of Cleveland's parts, including *Belville* in the
" Country Girl," and *Neville* in the " Dramatist." Miss Oldfield succeeded Mrs. Cleveland as *Phœbe* in " As You Like It," *Lady Frances
Touchwood* in the " Belle's Stratagem," *Marcella* in " A Bold Stroke
for a Husband " and *Lucy* in the " Gamester." She also played *Maria*
in the " School for Scandal " instead of Mrs. Francis, and *Maud* in
" Peeping Tom of Coventry " instead of Mrs. Marshall. Miss Milbourne was also making substantial progress. She succeeded Miss
Rowson as *Harriet* in the " Wedding Day," Miss Broadhurst as *Ariel*
in the " Tempest," and Mrs. Francis as *Annette* in " Robin Hood."
As *Annette* she was complimented by the fault-finding Baltimore critic
as a promising young actress. Little Miss Solomon was also accorded
some parts not previously credited to her, as *Lord William* in the
" Countess of Salisbury " and *Cicely* in the " Quaker." The positions
held by Mrs. Hervey and Mr. Beete are also indicated in these changes.
After the play, " Fontainville Forest," on the 1st of December, a dance
by Mr. Francis, " The Fair," was given, in which Signor Joseph Doctor performed some astonishing " feats of activity." Doctor had been

CONTRASTED CASTS—CHANGES.

PLAYS.	Phil.	Balt.	PLAYS.	Phil.	Balt.
School for Wives.			Hippolito . . .	Mr. Francis . .	Mr. Warrell, Jr
Crow	Mr. Blissett . .	Mr. Solomon	Mustachio . . .	Mr. De Moulin..	Mr. Mitchell
Sicilian Romance.			Ariel	Miss Broadhurst.	Miss Milbourne
Jaques	Mr. Blissett . .	Mr. Mitchell	*Tom Thumb, the Great.*		
Alinda	Miss Broadhurst.	Mrs. Warrell	Lord Grizzle . .	Mr. Marshall	Mr. Harwood
Slaves in Algiers.			Doodle	Mr. Darley, Jr..	Mr. Blissett
Henry	Mr. Cleveland .	Mr. Beete	Huncamunca	Mrs. Oldmixon..	Mrs. Solomon
Son-in-Law.			Mustacha . . .	Miss Willems	Mrs. Bates
Cranky	Mr. Finch . . .	Mr. Warrell	*Wedding Day.*		
Landlord . . .	Mr. Warrell . .	Mr. Mitchell	Hannah . . .	Miss Rowson	Miss Milbourne
Sultan.			*Wonder.*		
Elmira	Mrs. Francis . .	Miss Oldfield	Don Lopez . .	Mr. Finch . . .	Mr. Warrell
			Col. Briton . .	Mr. Fennell . .	Mr. Whitlock
Tempest.			Alguazil	Mr. Warrell . .	Mr. Mitchell
Gonzalo	Mr. Cleveland .	Mr. Beete	Isabella	Mrs. Francis	Mrs. Warrell

with the company at Sadler's Wells from the 12th of May, 1788, to the 15th of October, 1795. He first performed the office of "clown to the tumbling," but for his last peformance " Mr. Doctor, the celebrated Spaniard," was announced to present " curious equilibres and posture work with a pyramid of glasses and the Italian serpentine on a ladder twenty feet high;" to run up a plank fifteen feet high, off which he will throw a summerset and discharge a brace of pistols at the same time, and finally to throw a summerset from the upper boxes of the theatre. Doctor was a pantomimist as well as an expert gymnast and tumbler. His appearance at Baltimore gained him an engagement the next season in Philadelphia. There were, besides, some amateur *debuts* during the season, including a young lady as *Columbine* in " Harlequin's Invasion," and a dance in the character of *Pierrot* by Mr. Bertrand at the end of the first act of the " Fair Penitent."

A number of pieces familiar to Philadelphia audiences was advertised with the casts for the first time, which are here given as part of the record. The only new piece in the list is M. Lege's pantomime, " Le Marechal des Logis." Few changes as the Baltimore casts show,

BALTIMORE CASTS OF PHILADELPHIA PRODUCTIONS.

BEGGAR'S OPERA.

Macheath . . . . . Mr. Marshall
Peachum . . . . . . Mr. Bates
Lockit . . . . Mr. Francis
Filch . . . . Mr. Blissett
Jemmy Twitcher . . . Mr. Beete
Mat . . . . Mr. Darley, Jr
Ben Budge . . . . . Mr. Green
Robin . . . . Mr. Mitchell
Nimming Ned . . Mr. Warrell, Jr
Harry . . . . Mr. Warrell
Mrs. Peachum . . . Mrs. Shaw
Polly . . . . . . Mrs. Marshall
Lucy . . . . . . Mrs. Oldmixon

CHAPTER OF ACCIDENTS.

Gov. Harcourt . . . . Mr. Green

Woodville . . . . . Mr. Moreton
Lord Glenmore . . . . Mr. Beete
Capt. Harcourt . . . Mr. Wignell
Grey . . . . Mr. Whitlock
Vane . . . . . . Mr. Francis
Jacob . . . . . . Mr. Harwood
Servant . . . . . . Mr. Mitchell
Cecilia . . . . . . Mrs. Marshall
Miss Mortimer . . . Mrs. Hervey
Warner . . . . . Mrs. Solomon
Bridget . . . . Mrs. Shaw

FIRST FLOOR.

Whimsey . . . . . Mr. Francis
Monford . . . . Mr. Beete
Young Whimsey . . Mr. Moreton
Furnish . . . . Mr. Bates

Simon . . . . Mr. Blissett
Tim Tartlet . . . Mr. Harwood
Frank . . . . . Mr. Warrell, Jr
Snap . . . . . . Mr. Darley, Jr
Landlord . . . . . . Mr. Warrell
Postboy . . . . Master Warrell
Mrs. Patty Pan . . Mrs. Rowson
Charlotte . . . . . Miss Oldfield
Nancy . . . . . . Mrs. Hervey

HARLEQUIN'S INVASION.

Harlequin . . . . . Mr. Francis
Mercury . . . . Mr. Marshall
Forge . . . . Mr. Moreton
Bounce . . . . Mr. Green
Snip . . . . Mr. Bates
Frontin . . . . . Mr. Harwood

and unimportant as they were in themselves, it is evident there was inherent weakness in the company, which sooner or later would compel its reorganization.

A fortnight after the close of the second Baltimore engagement the company began the third season in Philadelphia. It opened on the 14th of December, 1795, and closed on the 1st of July, 1796. It was not a season remarkable either for the character of its productions or the general excellence of the company. Fennell's place was still to be supplied, and Moreton was too inexperienced an actor to compensate for the loss of Chalmers. Miss Broadhurst also had left the company and joined

LIST OF PERFORMANCES—*Phil.*

1795.

Dec. 14—Carmelite . . . . . Cumberland
Romp . . . . Bickerstaff
16—Highland Reel . . . . O'Keefe
Irishman in London . Macready
18—Rage . . . . Reynolds
Les Armans d'Arcade . . Francis
Children in the Wood . . Morton
21—Child of Nature . . Mrs. Inchbald
Les Deux Chasseurs.
Midnight Hour . . Mrs. Inchbald
23—Percy . . . . Miss More
Sailor's Landlady . . . Francis
Cross Purposes . . . . O'Brien
26—George Barnwell . . . . . Lillo
Harlequin Shipwrecked.

BALTIMORE CASTS OF PHILADELPHIA PRODUCTIONS.

Abraham . . . . . . Mr. Blissett
Taffy . . . . Mr. Beete
Simon (Clown) . . . Mr. Wignell
Bog . . . . . . Mr. Darley, Jr
Padlock . . . . Mr. Warrell, Jr
Old Woman . . . . Mr. Marshall
Dolly Snip . . . . Mrs. Francis
Mrs. Snip . . . . . Mrs. Rowson
Sukey Chitterlin . . Miss Willems
Fairy . . . . Miss Solomon
Fairy Harlequin, Master Strickland
Fairy Clown . . Master Warrell

LE MARECHAL DES LOGIS.

Marechal des Logis . Mr. Moreton
Deux Voleurs { Mr. Darley, Jr
{ Mr. Blissett
Colin . . . . Mr. Lege
Colas . . . . . . Mr. Warrell
Chaffeurs . . . . . Mr. Francis

Agathe . . . . Mrs. De Marque
Margot . . . . . . Miss Solomon

MIDNIGHT HOUR.

Marquis . . . . . Mr. Marshall
General . . . . . . Mr. Harwood
Sebastian . . . . . Mr. Francis
Nicholas . . . . . . Mr. Bates
Matthias . . . . . Mr. Blissett
Ambrose . . . . . . Mr. Warrell
Julia . . . . . . Mrs. Hervey
Cicely . . . . . . Mrs. Bates
Flora . . . . . . Mrs. Whitlock

QUAKER.

Steady . . . . . Mr. Harwood
Solomon . . . . . . Mr. Bates
Lubin . . . . . Mr. Marshall
Farmer Steady . . . Mr. Warrell

Gillian . . . . . . Mrs. Marshall
Floretta . . . . . Mrs. Oldmixon
Cicely . . . . . Mrs. Solomon

ROMAN FATHER.

Tullus Hostilius . . . Mr. Green
Horatius . . . . . Mr. Whitlock
Publius . . . . . . Mr. Moreton
Valerius . . . . . Mr. Wignell
Volcinius . . . Mr. Darley, Jr
Soldier . . . . . . Mr. Warrell
First Citizen . . . . Mr. Mitchell
Second Citizen . . . Mr. Blissett
Horatia . . . . . Mrs. Whitlock
Valeria . . . . . . Mrs. Hervey

TWO PHILOSOPHERS.

Philosophers { Mr. Francis
{ Mr. Lege
Merry Girl . . Mrs. De Marque

the Old American Company in New York. Even the favorites, the Whitlocks, the Marshalls, and Bates, were no longer entirely satisfactory to the Philadelphia public, and so it was determined that Mr. Wignell should again visit England for recruits. He took his benefit and his leave of the theatre, until after his return, on the 18th of April, 1796, when he played *Roque* in the "Mountaineers." The manager's absence gave Moreton an opportunity to play at least one part before the close of the season in which Wignell was unrivalled—*Darby* in the "Poor Soldier." This was for Mrs. Warrell's benefit, when the lady absurdly appeared as *Patrick*. Subsequently, however, Mr. Chalmers returned for the remaining weeks of the season, reappearing as *Goldfinch* in the "Road to Ruin" on the 25th of May. He played *Ranger* in the "Suspicious Husband" and the title-role in "Comus" for Mr. Morris, *Mac-*

Dec. 28—Haunted Tower . . . . . Cobb
Wrangling Lovers . . . . Lyon
30—Jew . . . . Cumberland
La Boiteuse.
Tom Thumb, the Great . O'Hara
1796.
Jan. 1—Bank Note . . . . . Macready
Purse . . . . Cross
T'Other Side of the Gutter.
4—Fontainville Forest . . . Boaden
Rural Merriment . . . . Francis
High Life Below Stairs . Townley
6—Next-Door Neighbors
Mrs. Inchbald
Harlequin Shipwrecked.
8—Bank Note.
Farmer . . . . O'Keefe
11—School for Scandal . . Sheridan
Bird Catcher.
Poor Soldier . . . . . O'Keefe
13—Wheel of Fortune . Cumberland
Prize . . . . Hoare
15—Rage.
Peeping Tom of Coventry
O'Keefe
18—Douglas . . . . Home
La Boiteuse.
Deaf Lover . . . . . . Pilon
20—Rivals . . . . Sheridan
Harlequin's Invasion . . Garrick
22—Romeo and Juliet . . Shakspere
Midnight Hour.
25—Robin Hood . . . . . MacNally
Harlequin's Invasion.
27—Country Girl . . . . . Garrick
Ways and Means . . Colman, Jr
29—Wheel of Fortune.
First Floor . . . . . . Cobb
Feb. 1—Isabella . . . . . . Southerne
Devil to Pay . . . . . Coffey
3—Bank Note.
Hob in the Well . . . . Cibber
5—Married Man . . Mrs. Inchbald
La Rose et le Bouton.
Widow's Vow . . Mrs. Inchbald
8—Woodman . . . . . . Dudley

Feb. 8—All the World's a Stage . Jackman
   10—Provoked Husband . . Vanbrugh
      Warrior's Welcome Home, Francis
      Children in the Wood.
   12—Roman Father . . . Whitehead
      Spoiled Child . . . . Bickerstaff
   15—Every One Has His Fault
                     Mrs. Inchbald
      Poor Soldier.
   17—She Stoops to Conquer . Goldsmith
      Divertisement Pastoral . . Lege
      Midnight Hour.
   19—Castle of Andalusia . . O'Keefe
      As It Should Be . . . . Oulton
   20—English Merchant . . . Colman
      Tom Thumb, the Great.
   23—Zara . . . . Hill
      Agreeable Surprise . . . O'Keefe
   24—Dramatist . . . . . . Reynolds
      Padlock . . . . . . Bickerstaff
   26—Jane Shore . . . . Rowe
      Witches of the Rocks.
   29—Rage.
      Spoiled Child
Mar. 2—Gamester . . . . . . Moore
      Witches of the Rocks.
    4—Married Man.
      Prisoner . . . . Rose
    7—Merry Wives of Windsor
                     Shakspere
      Egyptian Festival . . . . . Lege
      Who's the Dupe ? . Mrs. Cowley
    9—Bold Stroke for a Husband
                     Mrs. Cowley
      Florizel and Perdita . Shakspere
   11—Orphan . . . . Otway
      Mogul Tale . . . Mrs. Inchbald
   14—Road to Ruin . . . . . Holcroft
      Lucky Escape . . . . . Francis
      Mogul Tale.
   16—Suicide . . . . Colman
      Lucky Escape.
      Deaf Lover.
   18—Inkle and Yarico . . Colman, Jr.
      Shamrock . . . . . . Francis
      Irishman in London.

beth for Mr. Green, *Richard* in
" Richard III " for Mrs. Hervey
and Miss Willems, *Mercutio* in
" Romeo and Juliet," and *Young
Wilding* in the " Lyar" for the
Warrells, father and sons; *Shylock*
for Lege and Doctor, the pantomimists ; *Sir Charles Racket* in
" Three Weeks After Marriage "
for Mrs. and Miss Solomon;
Petruchio to Mrs. Rowson's *Catharine* for the Rowsons; *Belcour*
in the " West Indian " for Mrs.
Francis, and *Zanga* in the " Revenge " for his own benefit.
When the " Children in the Wood "
was given as part of the benefit
bill of Mrs. and Miss Solomon,
Mr. Moreton made his first appearance as *Walter*, and Miss C.
Solomon appeared for the first
time on any stage as the *Boy*,
while Miss Solomon satisfied her
ambition as *Little Pickle* in the
" Spoiled Child," being introduced
in an occasional address, written
by Mrs. Rowson, of which this
was the closing couplet :

And, though at all times partial,
Forget for this one night the charming Mrs.
Marshall.

When "Harlequin Ship-
wrecked" was given for the first
time this season on the 26th of
December, the pantomime ended
with an exhibition of feats
of activity called "T'Other Side
of the Gutter," in which Signor
Doctor made his first appearance
in Philadelphia. Doctor played
in many of the pantomimes during the season, and both he and
Mrs. Doctor occasionally appeared
in small speaking parts. The
younger Darley and Miss Milbourne had a joint benefit on the
22d of June, when Chalmers
played *Vapid* and Miss Milbourne
attempted *Marianne* in the "Dramatist," while Master R. Bates made
his first appearance on the stage
as *Narcisso* in the "Prisoner."
Among the names that occasionally appeared in the bills during
the season was that of Miss Gilaspie. She made her first appearance as the *Boy* in "Children in

Mar. 21—Zara
Lucky Escape.
Deserter . . . . Dibdin
23—Duenna . . . . Sheridan
Fandango Dance . . . . Francis
Widow's Vow.
24—Tempest . . . . Dryden
Mogul Tale.
28—Earl of Essex . . . . . . Jones
Easter Gift, Francis and Milbourne
Warrior's Welcome Home.
30—George Barnwell.
Love in a Camp . . . O'Keefe
April 1—Jealous Wife . . . . . Colman
Prize.
2—Jew.
Witches of the Rocks.
4—All in the Wrong . . . Murphy
No Song No Supper . . . Hoare
6—Rage.
Shipwrecked Mariners Preserved
8—Miser . . . . Fielding
Jubilee . . . . Garrick
11—All in the Wrong.
Sicilian Romance . . . Siddons
13—Hamlet . . . . . . Shakspere
Village Lawyer . . . . . Oulton
15—Maid of the Mill . . . Bickerstaff
Le Forêt Noire.
18—Mountaineers . . . . Colman, Jr.
High Life Below Stairs.
(Mr. Wignell's benefit.)
20—Hamlet.
Robinson Crusoe . . . Sheridan
22—Rule a Wife and Have a Wife
Fletcher
Harlequin Hurry-Scurry . Francis
Two Strings to Your Bow, Jephson
(Mr. Harwood's benefit.)
25—Mountaineers.
Ways and Means.
27—Every One Has His Fault.
Irish Vagary . . . . . Francis
Romp.
(Benefit of Philadelphia Dispensary.)
29—Deserted Daughter . . Holcroft
Deserter.

May   2—Way to Keep Him . . . Murphy
        Rival Knights.
        (Mr. Moreton's benefit.)
      4—Know Your Own Mind . Murphy
        Motley Groupe . . . . Francis
        Poor Soldier.
        (Mrs. Warrell's benefit.)
      6—Deserted Daughter.
        Jubilee.
      9—Alexander the Great . . . Lee
        Deserter of Naples.
        (Mrs. Marshall's benefit.)
     11—Such Things Are . Mrs. Inchbald
        Mogul Tale.
        (Mr. Darley's benefit.)
     13—Henry II . . . . Hull
        Miraculous Mill . . . . Francis
        Love a la Mode . . . . Macklin
        (Mr. Whitlock's benefit.)
     16—Patriot.
        Barnaby Brittle . . . . Betterton
        Gil Blas . . . . Bates
        (Mr. Bates' benefit.)
     18—Count of Narbonne . . Jephson
        Lucky Escape.
        Farm House . . . . . Kemble
        (Mr. Marshall's benefit.)
     20—Speculation . . . . . Reynolds
        Miraculous Mill.
        Doctor and Apothecary . . Cobb
        (Mrs. Oldmixon's benefit.)
     23—First Love . . . . . Cumberland
        Maid of the Oaks . . . Burgoyne
        (Mrs. Whitlock's benefit.)
     25—Road to Ruin.
        Critic . . . . Sheridan
     27—Suspicious Husband . . Hoadly
        Comus . . . . Milton
        Warrior's Welcome Home.
        (Mr. Morris' benefit.)
     30—Macbeth . . . . . . Shakspere
        Harlequin's Club . . . . Francis
        Ghost . . . . . Mrs. Centlivre
        (Mr. Green's benefit.)
June 1—Busybody . . . Mrs. Centlivre
        Motley Groupe.

the Wood" on the 18th of December, 1795. She afterward played the *Fairy Columbine* in "Harlequin's Invasion," *Sally* in Francis' "Lucky Escape," and served as an extra in the processions and pageants. Together with Miss Solomon and Master Bates she was a *Pigmy* in "Harlequin Dr. Faustus," and she appeared as the *Merry Girl* in Lege's new pantomime, the "Merry Little Girl." Her last appearance on any stage was as the *Page* in the "Purse" on the 15th of June, 1796. Her brief career is only worthy of remark because the *Aurora* thought it worth while to notice her retirement. That journal spoke of her as "the little airy Gilaspie who has so often delighted the audience," and added that her connections, which were respectable, meant to transfer her budding genius to another sphere.

The changes in the casts made necessary during the season by changes in the company are at once an index to the growing strength of the younger members of the organization and of its waning importance in the eyes of the public. The most important of the vacated parts to be provided for were those of Miss Broadhurst, who was succeeded by Mrs. Marshall as *Laura* in the "Agreeable Surprise," *Leonora* in the "Padlock," *Angelina* in "Robin Hood," and *Emily* in the "Woodman;" by Miss Willems as *Catalina* in the "Castle of Andalusia," *Nelly* in "No Song No Supper," and *Phœbe* in "Rosina;" by Mrs. Hervey as *Sabrina* in "Comus" and *Cicely* in the "Haunted Tower;" by Mrs. Whitlock as *Jenny* in the "Deserter;" by Mrs. Warrell as *Louisa* in the "Duenna," *Molly Maybush* in the "Farmer," *Jessica* in the "Merchant of Venice," *Emma* in "Peeping Tom" and *Clara* in the "Prisoner;" by Miss Oldfield as *Wowski* in "Inkle and Yarico," and by Miss Milbourne as *Juba* in

June—1—Midnight Wanderers . . Pearce
   (Mrs. Shaw's benefit.)
   3—Coriolanus . . . . . Shakspere
    Harlequin Dr. Faustus . . Francis
   (Mr. and Mrs. Francis' benefit.)
   6—Richard III . . . . . Shakspere
    Barnaby Brittle.
(Mrs. Hervey and Miss Willems' benefit.)
   8—Romeo and Juliet . . . Shakspere
    Lyar . . . . Foote
   (Warrell and Sons' benefit.)
  10—Merchant of Venice . Shakspere
    Merry Little Girl . . . . . Lege
    Valiant Officer.
   (Lege and Doctor's benefit.)
  13.—Three Weeks After Marriage
              Murphy
    Children in the Wood.
  (Mrs. and Miss Solomon's benefit.)
  15—School for Soldiers . . . Henry
    Les Deux Sœurs . . . . Francis
    Purse.
(Blissett, Mrs. De Marque and Mrs. Bates'
     benefit.)
  17—Disbanded Officer . . Johnstone
    American Tar.
    Catharine and Petruchio
            Shakspere
  (Mr. and Mrs. Rowson's benefit.)
  20—Revenge . . . . Moore
    Mock Doctor . . . . . Fielding
   (Mr. Chalmers' benefit.)
  22—Dramatist.
    Prisoner.
(Mr. Darley, Jr., and Miss Milbourne's
    benefit.)
  24—West Indian . . . . Cumberland
    Crotchet Lodge . . . Hurlstone
   (Mrs. Francis' benefit.)
  27—Contrast . . . . Tyler
    Rival Knights.
   (Mr. Milbourne's benefit.)
  29—Carmelite.
    Mock Doctor.
July 1—Deserted Daughter.
    Rosina . . . . . . Mrs. Brooke
   (Mr. Wells' benefit.)

the " Prize" and *Ariel* in the " Tempest." When Miss Willems played *Phœbe* in " Rosina " on the last night of the season she was Mrs. Green,

CONTRASTED CASTS—CHANGES.

PLAYS.	1793-5.	1795-6.
Agreeable Surprise.		
John	. Mr. Cleveland	. Mr. Warrell, Jr
Stump	. Mr. De Moulin	. Mr. Solomon
Laura	. Miss Broadhurst	. Mrs. Marshall
Cowslip . . .	. Mrs. Solomon	. Miss Willems
Fringe	. Miss Willems	. Mrs. Rowson
All the World's a Stage.		
Wat	. Mr. Mitchell	. . Mr. Darley, Jr
Jane	. Mrs. Solomon	. Mrs. Francis
Bold Stroke for a Husband.		
Don Julio . . .	. Mr. Chalmers	. Mr. Green
Don Vasquez .	. Mr. Francis	. Mr. Warrell
Gasper	. Mr. Whitlock	. Mr. Francis
Busybody.		
Scentwell . . .	. Mrs. Cleveland	. Miss Oldfield
Carmelite.		
Montgomeri . .	. Mr. Harwood	. Debutante
Castle of Andalusia.		
Don Alphonso .	. Mr. Moreton .	. Mr. Darley, Jr
Philippi	. Mr. Darley, Jr	. Mr. Warrell, Jr
Catalina	. Miss Broadhurst	. Miss Willems
Catharine and Petruchio.		
Hortensio . . .	. Mr. Cleveland	. Mr. Beete
Biondello . . .	. Mr. Harwood	. Mr. Mitchell
Pedro	. Mr. Green . .	. Mr. Darley, Jr
Catharine . . .	. Mrs. Morris .	. Mrs. Rowson
Bianca	. Mrs. Cleveland	. Mrs. Hervey
Children in the Wood.		
Boy	. Master Parker	. Miss Gilaspie
Comus.		
Younger Brother.	Mr. Cleveland	. Mr. Warrell, Jr
Lady	. Mrs. Whitlock	. Mrs. Marshall
Sabrina	. Miss Broadhurst	. Mrs. Hervey
Pastoral Nymph	Mrs. Marshall	. Miss Milbourne
Critic.		
Dangle	. Mr. Wignell .	. Mr. Green
Sir Fretful . .	. Mr. Harwood	. Mr. Marshall
Pasticcio . . .	. Mr. Marshall	. Mr. Darley, Jr
Interpreter . . .	. Mr. Blissett .	. Mr. Doctor
Burleigh	. Mr. Blissett .	. Mr. Morgan
Leicester . . .	. Mr. Cleveland	. Mr. Blissett
Raleigh	. Mr. Green . .	. Mr. Beete
Deserter.		
Flint	. Mr. Green . .	. Mr. Blissett
Jenny	. Miss Broadhurst	. Mrs. Whitlock

PLAYS.	1793-5.	1795-6.
Devil to Pay.		
Footman . . .	. Mr. Solomon	. . Mr. Darley, Jr
Coachman . .	. Mr. Darley, Jr	. Mr. Morgan
Lettice	. Mrs. Cleveland	. Mrs. Solomon
Douglas.		
Glenalvon . . .	. Mr. Fennell .	. Mr. Wignell
Anna	. Mrs. Cleveland	. Mrs. Francis
Dramatist.		
Scratch	. Mr. Wignell .	. Mr. Bates
Letty	. Mrs. Solomon	. Mrs. Hervey
Duenna.		
Isaac	. Mr. Wignell .	. Mr. Bates
Porter		. Mr. Milbourne
Clara	. Mrs. Warrell	. Mrs. Oldmixon
Louisa	. Miss Broadhurst	. Mrs. Warrell
Flora	. Mrs. Cleveland	. Miss Oldfield
Lauretta		. Miss Rowson
Every One Has His Fault.		
Mrs. Placid . .	. Mrs. Rowson	. Mrs. Shaw
Farmer.		
Stubble	. Mr. Morris	. . Mr. Morgan
Betty	. Mrs. Shaw . .	. Miss Willems
Farm House.		
Modely	. Mr. Cleveland	. Mr. Marshall
Gamester.		
Beverly	. Mr. Moreton	. Mr. Whitlock
Lewson	. Mr. Cleveland	. Mr. Moreton
Dawson	. Mr. Moreton	. Mr. Beete
Hamlet.		
Hamlet	. Mr. Chalmers	. Mr. Moreton
Ghost	. Mr. Wignell .	. Mr. Whitlock
Laertes	. Mr. Moreton	. Mr. Wignell
Guildenstern . .	. Mr. Cleveland	. Mr. Beete
2d Gravedigger .	. Mr. Wignell .	. Mr. Milbourne
Harlequin Hurry-Scurry.		
Bumpkin . . .	. Mr. Blissett .	. Mr. Doctor
Harlequin Shipwrecked.		
Indian Chief . .	. Mr. Nugent .	. Mr. Warrell, Jr
Captain	. Mr. Cleveland	. Mr. Solomon
Tippy Bob . .	. Mr. Darley, Jr	. Mr. Robbins
Drowsey . . .	. Mr. Blissett .	. Mr. Darley
Harlequin's Invasion.		
Old Woman . .	. Mr. Marshall	. Mr. Darley

the wife of William Green of the company. The last time I find the
name of Miss Willems in the bill was on the 6th of June, when she

CONTRASTED CASTS—CHANGES.

PLAYS.	1793-5.	1795-6.
Haunted Tower.		
De Courci . . .	Mr. Cleveland	Mr. Moreton
Cicely	Miss Broadhurst.	Mrs. Hervey
Hob in the Well.		
Dick	Mr. Harwood	Mr. Warrell, Jr
Betty	Mrs. Solomon	Mrs. Hervey
Inkle and Yarico.		
Planter		Mr. Beete
Narcissa . . .	Mrs. Oldmixon	Miss Willems
Wowski	Miss Broadhurst.	Miss Oldfield
Isabella.		
Belford	Mr. Cleveland	Mr. Warrell
Pedro	Mr. Green . .	Mr. Beete
Officer	Mr. De Moulin	Mr. Mitchell
Jealous Wife.		
Charles	Mr. Cleveland	Mr. Moreton
Capt. O'Cutter .	Mr. Harwood	Mr. Bates
Sir Harry Beagle.	Mr. Chalmers	Mr Harwood
Paris		Mr. Blissett
Jew.		
Dorcas	Mrs. Solomon	Mrs. Rowson
Know Your Own Mind.		
Lovewit	Mr. Harwood	Mr. Francis
Malvil	Mr. Whitlock	Mr. Green
Capt. Bygrove .	Mr. Cleveland	Mr. Beete
Charles	Mr. Francis . .	Mr. Warrell, Jr
Darkwood . .	Mr. Chalmers	Mr. Marshall
Lady Jane . . .	Mrs. Cleveland	Mrs. Morris
Miss Neville . .	Mrs. Francis	Mrs. Warrell
Mad. La Rouge.	Mrs. Rowson	Miss Oldfield
Le Foret Noire.		
Adolphe	T. Warrell . .	Miss Solomon
Pasquin	Mr. Darley, Jr .	Mr. Mitchell
Sans Quartier .	Mr. Cleveland	Mr. Darley, Jr
Marton	Miss Rowson	Miss Oldfield
Lyar.		
Sir James Elliot.	Mr. Cleveland	Mr. Green
Miss Godfrey	Mrs. Cleveland	Mrs. Hervey
Macbeth.		
Malcolm	Mr. Cleveland	Mr. Warrell, Jr
Donalbane . .	Mr. Warrell, Jr.	T. Warrell
Lenox	Mr. Harwood	Mr. Marshall
Fleance	Mast.T.Warrell.	Miss Solomon
Seyton	Mr. Francis . .	Mr. Beete
Third Witch . .	Mr. Wignell . .	Mr. Francis

PLAYS.	1793-5.	1795-6.
Maid of the Mill.		
Mervin	Mr. Cleveland	Mr. Darley, Jr
Ralph	Mr. Wignell . .	Mr. Francis
Merchant of Venice.		
Shylock	Mr. Fennell . .	Mr. Chalmers
Gratiano . . .	Mr. Wignell . .	Mr. Moreton
Solanio . . .	Mr. Green . . .	Mr. Beete
Bassanio . . .	Mr. Moreton	Mr. Green
Tubal	Mr. Harwood	Mr. Morgan
Jessica	Miss Broadhurst.	Mrs. Warrell
Merry Wives of Windsor.		
Fenton	Mr. Cleveland	Mr. Warrell, Jr
Mr. Ford . .	Mr. Chalmers	Mr. Wignell
Host	Mr. Wignell . .	Mr. Darley
Bardolph . . .	Mr. Darley, Jr .	Mr. Warrell
Pistol	Mr. Francis . .	Mr. Darley, Jr
Rugby	Mr. Warrell, Jr .	Mr. Solomon
Simple	Mr. Blissett . .	Mr. Mitchell
Ann Page . . .	Miss Willems	Miss Oldfield
Midnight Hour.		
Julia	Mrs. Hervey .	Mrs. Francis
No Song No Supper.		
Louisa	Miss Willems	Miss Rowson
Nelly	Miss Broadhurst.	Miss Willems
Orphan.		
Chamont . . .	Mr. Chalmers .	Mr. Wignell
Padlock.		
Leonora	Miss Broadhurst.	Mrs. Marshall
Ursula	Mrs. Shaw . . .	Mrs. Rowson
Peeping Tom of Coventry.		
Count Lewis . .	Mr. Cleveland	Mr. Blissett
Emma	Miss Broadhurst.	Mrs. Warrell
Lady Godiva . .	Miss Willems	Miss Oldfield
Mayoress . . .	Mrs. Rowson .	Mrs. Shaw
Percy.		
Sir Hubert . . .	Mr. Cleveland	Mr. Warrell
Poor Soldier.		
Father Luke	Mr. Blissett . .	Mr. Morgan
Norah	Miss Milbourne.	Mrs. Warrell
Prisoner.		
Bernardo . . .	Mr. Darley . .	Mr. Darley, Jr
Pasqual	Mr. Darley, Jr .	Mr. Darley
Narcisso	Debutante . . .	Miss Gilaspie
Clara	Miss Broadhurst.	Mrs. Warrell
Therese	Miss Willems .	Mrs. Hervey

played *Lady Anne* in " Richard III " for her own benefit and that of
Mrs. Hervey. She was first announced as Mrs. Green on the 24th, when
she appeared as *Florella* in " Crotchet Lodge." This was the first
marriage between members of the company. An event of more than

CONTRASTED CASTS—CHANGES.

PLAYS.	1793-5.	1795-6.
Prize.		
Caddy	Mr. Finch . .	Mr. Green
Label	Mr. Wignell .	Mr. Francis
Juba	Miss Broadhurst.	Miss Milbourne
Mrs. Caddy . .	Mrs. Rowson	Mrs. Bates
Provoked Husband.		
Lord Townly .	Mr. Fennell . .	Mr. Whitlock
Basset	Mr. Finch . . .	Mr. Marshall
Poundage . . .	Mr. De Moulin .	Mr. Mitchell
Jenny	Mrs. Cleveland .	Miss Willems
Trusty	Miss Willems .	Miss Rowson
Myrtilla		Mrs. Rowson
Richard III.		
Prince Edward .	Mr. Warrell, Jr .	Mrs. Hervey
Duke of York .	T. Warrell . .	Miss Solomon
Buckingham . .	Mr. Wignell . .	Mr. Green
Catesby	Mr. Cleveland .	Mr. Darley, Jr
Lieutenant . . .	Mr. Harwood .	Mr. Warrell, Jr
Lord Stanley . .	Mr. Green . . .	Mr. Beete
Tyrrel	Mr. De Moulin .	Mr. Morgan
Lady Anne . .	Mrs. Francis . .	Miss Willems
Rivals.		
Lucy	Mrs. Rowson .	Mrs. Doctor
Road to Ruin.		
Goldfinch . . .	Mr. Chalmers .	Mr. Harwood
Milford	Mr. Cleveland .	Mr. Beete
Smith	Mr. Moreton .	Mr. Darley, Jr
Robin Hood.		
Angelina . . .	Miss Broadhurst.	Mrs. Marshall
Romeo and Juliet.		
Mercutio . . .	Mr. Chalmers .	Mr. Wignell
Escalus	Mr. Warrell .	Mr. Beete
Page		T. Warrell
Romp.		
Barnacle . . .	Mr. Harwood .	Mr. Blissett
Penelope . . .	Miss Rowson .	Miss Willems
Mad. Le Blond .	Mrs. Cleveland .	Mrs. Hervey
Rosina.		
Capt. Belville .	Mr. Moreton .	Mr. Darley, Jr
Rustic	Mr. Rowson . .	Mr. Warrell
Phœbe	Miss Broadhurst.	Mrs. Green
She Stoops to Conquer.		
Young Marlow .	Mr. Chalmers .	Mr. Moreton
Hastings . . .	Mr. Cleveland .	Mr. Green

PLAYS.	1793-5.	1795-6.
Spoiled Child.		
Maria	Mrs. Cleveland .	Mrs. Francis
Susan	Miss Rowson .	Miss Willems
Suspicious Husband.		
Bellamy . . .	Mr. Cleveland .	Mr Green
Jack Meggot . .	Mr. Harwood .	Mr. Francis
Mrs. Strickland .	Mrs. Cleveland .	Mrs. Shaw
Lucetta	Mrs. Shaw . .	Mrs. Rowson
Clarinda	Mrs. Marshall .	Mrs. Morris
Tempest.		
Prospero . . .	Mr. Whitlock .	Mr. Green
Alonzo	Mr. Green . . .	Mr. Whitlock
Three Weeks After Marriage.		
Drugget	Mr. Bates . . .	Mr. Green
Woodley . . .	Mr. Cleveland .	Mr. Beete
Dimity	Mrs. Shaw . .	Mrs. Solomon
Tom Thumb, the Great.		
Huncamunca .	Mrs. Solomon .	Miss Willems
Mustacha . . .	Mrs. Bates . .	Miss Rowson
Village Lawyer.		
Charles	Mr. Cleveland .	Mr. Darley, Jr
Mrs. Scout . .	Mrs. Rowson .	Mrs. Shaw
Ways and Means.		
Scruple	Mr. Cleveland .	Mr. Green
Lady Dunder .	Mrs. Shaw . .	Mrs. Rowson
Harriet	Mrs. Francis .	Miss Oldfield
Kitty	Debutante . . .	Miss Milbourne
West Indian.		
Stukely	Mr. Moreton .	Mr. Warrell, Jr
Fulmer	Mr. Harwood .	Mr. Green
Varland	Mr. Francis . .	Mr. Bates
Capt. Dudley .	Mr. Green . . .	Mr. Beete
Charles Dudley .	Mr. Cleveland .	Mr. Marshall
Sailor	Mr. Blissett . .	Mr. Mitchell
Louisa Dudley .	Mrs. Cleveland .	Mrs. Francis
Lucy	Miss Rowson .	Miss Oldfield
Who's the Dupe?		
Granger	Mr. Cleveland .	Mr. Green
Woodman.		
Sir Walter Waring	Mr. Wignell . .	Mr. Bates
Welford	Mr. Marshall .	Mr. Moreton
Capt. O'Donnell .	Mr. Green . . .	Mr. Mitchell
Emily	Miss Broadhurst.	Mrs. Marshall

usual importance was the first appearance of Mr. Moreton as *Hamlet* on the 13th of April. Moreton was, with the exception of Hallam, the first actor of purely American training to attempt the role that stands above all others on the English-speaking stage.

A number of casts was now given of pieces that had been made familiar to Philadelphia audiences by the Old American Com-

FIRST CASTS OF FAMILIAR PIECES.

ALEXANDER THE GREAT.

Alexander	Mr. Moreton
Hephestion . .	Mr. Warrell, Jr
Lysimachus . . .	. Mr. Marshall
Cassander	. Mr. Green
Polyperchon . .	Mr. Darley, Jr
Philip	Mr. Morgan
Clytus	Mr. Whitlock
Thessalus . . .	Mr. Warrell
Perdiccas	Mr. Beete
Eumenes	Mr. Francis
Slave	Mr. Mitchell
Roxana	Mrs. Shaw
Sysigambis . . .	Mrs. Rowson
Parisatis	Miss Willems
Statira	Mrs. Marshall

ALL IN THE WRONG.

Sir John Restless .	Mr. Whitlock
Beverly	Mr. Moreton
Sir William	Mr. Warrell
Young Belmont . . .	Mr. Green
Blandford	Mr. Francis
Robert	Mr. Beete
Brush	Mr. Blissett
Richard	Mr. Mitchell
James	Mr. Warrell, Jr
John	Mr. Darley, Jr
Lady Restless . . .	Mrs. Whitlock
Belinda	Mrs. Morris
Clarissa	Mrs. Francis
Tattle	Mrs. Rowson
Tippet	Miss Oldfield
Marmalet	Mrs. Hervey

CHILD OF NATURE.

Marquis	Mr. Whitlock
Valentia	Mr. Moreton
Mercia	Mr. Bates
Seville	Mr. Beete
Grenada	Mr. Warrell, Jr
First Peasant	Mr. Green

Second Peasant . .	Mr. Warrell
Marchioness	Mrs. Morris
Amanthis	Mrs. Marshall

CONTRAST.

Colonel Manly . . .	Mr. Green
Dimple	Mr. Marshall
Van Rough	Mr. Morris
Jessamy	Mr. Francis
Jonathan	Mr. Bates
Charlotte	Mrs. Morris
Maria	Miss Milbourne
Letitia	Mrs. Francis
Jenny	Mrs. Hervey

CROSS PURPOSES.

Grub	Mr. Morris
Consol	Mr. Francis
Frank Bevil . . .	Mr. Darley, Jr
Harry Bevil	Mr. Green
George Bevil . . .	Mr. Moreton
Chapeau	Mr. Marshall
Robin	Mr. Blissett
Mrs. Grub	Mrs. Shaw
Emily	Miss Willems
Maid	Mrs. Hervey

EARL OF ESSEX.

Essex	Mr. Wignell
Southampton . . .	Mr. Moreton
Lord Burleigh	Mr. Green
Sir Walter Raleigh .	Mr. Harwood
Lieutenant	Mr. Beete
Queen Elizabeth . .	Mrs. Morris
Lady Rutland . .	Mrs. Whitlock
Lady Nottingham . .	Mrs. Shaw

FLORIZEL AND PERDITA.

Polixenes	Mr. Green
Florizel	Mr. Moreton
Camillo	Mr. Wignell
Antigonus	Mr. Whitlock
Clown	Mr. Darley, Jr

Pedlar	Mr. Bates
Perdita	Mrs. Marshall
Mopsa	Mrs. Bates
Dorcas	Miss Milbourne

GEORGE BARNWELL.

Thorowgood . . .	Mr. Whitlock
Uncle	Mr. Wignell
George	Mr. Moreton
Trueman	Mr. Green
Blunt	Mr. Francis
Gaolor	Mr. Warrell
Maria	Mrs. Whitlock
Millwood	Mrs. Shaw
Lucy	Mrs. Francis

GHOST.

Sir Jeffrey	Mr. Warrell
Captain Constant .	Mr. Darley, Jr
Clinch	Mr. Green
Trusty	Mr. Francis
Roger	Mr. Bates
Belinda	Mrs. Hervey
Dorothy	Mrs. Shaw

IRISHMAN IN LONDON.

Captain Seymour . . .	Mr. Green
Frost	Mr. Francis
Colloney	Mr. Moreton
Murtoch Delany .	Mr. Marshall
Edward	Mr. Harwood
Cymon	Mr. Blissett
Louisa	Mrs. Hervey
Caroline	Miss Willems
Cubba	Mrs. Francis

JANE SHORE.

Gloster	Mr. Green
Hastings	Mr. Wignell
Catesby	Mr. Harwood
Ratcliffe	Mr. Warrell
Belmour	Mr. Beete
Dumont	Mr. Whitlock

pany before the New Theatre supplanted the old Southwark in the affections of playgoers, or through previous representations by Mr. Wignell's company. The only exception in the subjoined casts is " Florizel and Perdita," which was previously presented in New York

FIRST CASTS OF FAMILIAR PIECES.

Derby . . . . Mr. Francis
Alicia . . . . Mrs. Morris
Jane Shore . . . . Mrs. Whitlock

JUBILEE.
Irishman . . . . . Mr. Whitlock
Ralph . . . . Mr. Bates
First Serenade . . Mr. Marshall
Second Serenade . . Mr. Darley
Third Serenade . Mr. Darley, Jr
First Gentleman . . Mr. Moreton
Second Gentleman . . Mr. Beete
Ostler . . . . Mr. Blissett
Cook . . . . Mr. Morris
Man Singer . . . . Mr. Harwood
Trumpeter . . . . . Mr. Rowson
Goody Benson . . . . Mrs. Bates
Goody Jarvis . . . Mrs. Rowson
First Country Girl, Mrs. Oldmixon
Second Country Girl,Miss Willems
Tragic Muse . . . Mrs. Whitlock
Comic Muse . . . Mrs. Marshall

LOVE A LA MODE.
Sir Callaghan . . . Mr. Whitlock
Sir Archy . . . . . Mr. Bates
Squire Groom . . . Mr. Marshall
Beau Mordecai . . . Mr. Francis
Sir Theodore . . . . . Mr. Beete
Charlotte . . . . . Miss Willems

LOVE IN A CAMP.
Captain Patrick . . Mr. Marshall
Fehrbellin . . . . . . Mr. Green
Father Luke . . . Mr. Harwood
Olmutz . . . . . . Mr. Rowson
Quiz . . . . Mr. Blissett
Rupert . . . . . Mr. Warrell, Jr
Adjutant . . . . . Mr. Warrell
Darby . . . . Mr. Wignell
Flora . . . . . . Miss Milbourne
Mabel Flourish . Mr. Darley, Jr
Norah . . . . . . Miss Willems

MISER.
Lovegold   . . . . Mr. Bates

Frederick . . . . Mr. Marshall
Clerimont . . . . . Mr. Green
Ramilie . . . . . . Mr. Wignell
Decoy . . . . Mr. Warrell
Furnish . . . . Mr. Beete
Sparkle . . . . . Mr. Darley, Jr
Sattin . . . . . . Mr. Mitchell
List . . . . Mr. Blissett
Lawyer . . . . . . Mr. Morgan
Thomas . . . . Master Warrell
James . . . . Mr. Francis
Harriet . . . . . . Mrs. Francis
Mrs. Wisely . . . Mrs. Rowson
Mariana . . . . Mrs. Oldmixon
Wheedle . . . . Mrs. Solomon
Lappet . . . . Mrs. Morris

MOCK DOCTOR.
Sir Jasper . . . . . . Mr. Beete
Leander . . . . . Mr. Darley, Jr
Gregory . . . . Mr. Bates
Squire Robert . . Mr. Warrell, Jr
James . . . . Mr. Blissett
Harry . . . . Mr. Mitchell
Davy . . . . Mr. Morgan
Hellebore . . . . . Mr. Warrell
Dorcas . . . . . Mrs. Rowson
Charlotte . . . . Mrs. Hervey

REVENGE.
Zanga . . . . . Mr. Chalmers
Alonzo . . . . . . Mr. Moreton
Carlos . . . . Mr. Green
Alvarez . . . . . . Mr. Beete
Manuel . . . . Mr. Darley, Jr
Leonora . . . . Mrs. Whitlock
Isabella . . . . . Mrs. Hervey

SCHOOL FOR SOLDIERS.
Major Bellamy . . . Mr. Green
Bellamy . . . . . Mr. Moreton
Colonel Valentine . . Mr. Beete
Captain Valentine, Mr. Warrell, Jr

Mr. Hector . . . . . Mr. Francis
Frederick . . . . Master Warrell
Mrs. Mildmay . . . Mrs. Hervey
Clara . . . . . . Mrs. Marshall

SUCH THINGS ARE.
Sultan . . . . Mr. Green
Lord Flint . . . . . Mr. Beete
Sir Luke . . . . . . Mr. Bates
Twineall . . . . . Mr. Moreton
Hartwell . . . . . Mr. Whitlock
Elvirus . . . . . . Mr. Marshall
Meanright . . . . Mr. Darley, Jr
Zedan . . . . Mr. Darley
Messenger . . . Mr. Warrell, Jr
Lady Tremor . . . . Mrs. Shaw
Aurelia . . . . . . Mrs. Francis
Prisoner . . . . . Mrs. Whitlock

WAY TO KEEP HIM.
Lovemore . . . . Mr. Whitlock
Sir Bashful . . . . . Mr. Bates
Sir Brilliant . . . . Mr. Moreton
William . . . . . . Mr. Marshall
Sideboard . . . . . Mr. Francis
Pompey . . . . Mr. Warrell, Jr
John . . . . . . Mr. Darley, Jr
Mrs. Lovemore . . Mrs Whitlock
Widow Belmour . Mrs. Marshall
Lady Constant . . . Mrs. Francis
Muslin . . . . . . Mrs. Morris
Mignionet . . . . Mrs. Hervey
Furnish . . . . Mrs. Bates

ZARA.
Osman . . . . . . Mr. Moreton
Lusignan . . . . . Mr. Whitlock
Nerestan . . . . . Mr. Marshall
Chatillon . . . . . . Mr. Green
Orasmin . . . . Mr. Beete
Melidor . . . . . Mr. Darley, Jr
Selima . . . . . . Mrs. Hervey
Zara . . . . Mrs. Whitlock

by the Old American Company, but had been played in Philadelphia only by the Kenna troupe.

The list of pieces produced this season that were new to Philadelphia, many of which had their first production in America, was an

FIRST PRODUCTIONS—THIRD PHILADELPHIA SEASON.

AMERICAN TAR.

Will Steady	Mr. Francis
Tom Capstan . .	Mr. Warrell, Jr
Captain Trunion . . .	Mr. Beete
Midshipman . . .	Mr. Darley, Jr
Dick Hauser . . .	Mr. Rowson
Susan	Miss Rowson
Jane	Miss Milbourne

AS IT SHOULD BE.

Megrim	Mr. Moreton
Fidget	Mr. Francis
Winworth	Mr. Beete
Sparkle	Mr. Harwood
Lucy	Miss Willems
Celia	Mrs. Francis

BANK NOTE.

Sir Charles Leslie .	Mr. Moreton
Bloomfield	Mr. Wignell
Old Bloomfield . . .	Mr. Morris
Lieutenant Selby . . .	Mr. Green
Neddy Dash . . .	Mr. Harwood
Hale	Mr. Bates
Killeary	Mr. Marshall
Tim	Mr. Blissett
Young Bloomfield .	Miss Solomon
Careful	Mr. Warrell
Porter	Mr. Morgan
William	Mr. Darley, Jr
James	Mr. Warrell, Jr
Cook	Mr. Mitchell
Butler	Mr. Solomon
Lady Supple . . .	Mrs. Rowson
Mrs. Bloomfield . .	Mrs. Morris
Miss Russell . . .	Mrs. Marshall
Miss Emma Hale .	Miss Oldfield
Sally Flounce . . .	Mrs. Francis
Maid	Miss Rowson

BARNABY BRITTLE.

Barnaby Brittle . . .	Mr. Bates
Clodpole	Mr. Blissett
Jeremy	Mr. Francis

Sir Peter Pride . . .	Mr. Morgan
Livemore	Mr. Green
Jeffery	T. Warrell
Mrs. Brittle . . .	Mrs. Marshall
Lady Pride . . .	Mrs. Rowson
Damaris	Mrs. Shaw

CORIOLANUS.

Caius Marcius . . .	Mr. Moreton
Aufidius	Mr. Green
Agrippa	Mr. Bates
Cominius	Mr. Whitlock
Sicinius	Mr. Marshall
Junius Brutus . . .	Mr. Beete
Volusius	Mr. Darley, Jr
Young Marcius . .	Miss Solomon
Roman Officer .	Mr. Warrell, Jr
Volscian Officer . .	Mr. Morgan
Volumnia	Mrs. Whitlock
Virgilia	Mrs. Francis
Valeria	Mrs. Shaw
Gentlewoman . . .	Miss Rowson

COUNT OF NARBONNE.

Raymond	Mr. Whitlock
Austin	Mr. Green
Theodore	Mr. Moreton
Fabian	Mr. Beete
Hortensia	Mrs. Whitlock
Adelaide	Mrs. Marshall
Jaqueline	Miss Willems

CROCHET LODGE.

Nimble	Mr. Moreton
Truncheon	Mr. Francis
Darkly	Mr. Green
Shenkin	Mr. Blissett
De Chimic	Mr. Beete
Paddy	Mr. Morgan
Waiter	Mr. Darley, Jr
Bootcatcher	Mr. Mitchell
Hostler	Master Warrell
Sam	Mr. Solomon
Florella	Mrs. Green
Miss Crotchet . . .	Mrs. Rowson

Mrs. Truncheon . . .	Mrs. Bates
Maid	Miss Rowson
Thisbe	Mrs. Francis

DEAF LOVER.

Meadows	Mr. Green
Young Wronghead . .	Mr. Beete
Old Wronghead . .	Mr. Francis
Canteen	Mr. Harwood
Sternhold	Mr. Blissett
Groom	Mr. Bates
Cook	Mr. Morgan
William	Mr. Warrell, Jr
Joe	Mr. Mitchell
Bob	Mr. Darley, Jr
John	Mr. Warrell
Sophia	Miss Willems
Betty Blossom . . .	Mrs. Francis
Maid	Mrs. Bates

DESERTED DAUGHTER.

Mordent	Mr. Green
Chevril	Mr. Moreton
Lennox	Mr. Marshall
Item	Mr. Francis
Grime	Mr. Beete
Clement	Mr. Warrell, Jr
Donald	Mr. Bates
Joanna	Mrs. Marshall
Mrs. Sarsnet . . .	Mrs. Francis
Mrs. Enfield . . .	Mrs. Solomon
Betty	Mrs. Doctor
Lady Ann	Mrs. Whitlock

DESERTER OF NAPLES.

General	Mr. Doctor
Russet	Mr. Warrell
Henry	Mr. Marshall
Skirmish	Mr. Bates
Simkin	Mr. Francis
Jailor	Mr. Blissett
Margaret	Mrs. Rowson
Jenny	Miss Milbourne
Louisa	Mrs. Marshall

unusually long one. The first of these by alphabetical arrangement, "American Tar," was given for the benefit of the Rowsons, and, although unacknowledged, was probably one of Mrs. Rowson's adaptations. Oulton's trifle, "As It Should Be," had been previously acted

FIRST PRODUCTIONS—THIRD PHILADELPHIA SEASON.

DISBANDED OFFICER.

Colonel Holberg . .	Mr. Moreton
Paul Warmans . . .	Mr. Green
Katzenbuckle	Mr. Francis
Rouf	Mr. Beete
Count Bellair . . .	Mr. Marshall
Messenger . . .	Mr. Warrell, Jr
Boy	Master Warrell
Baroness	Mrs. Whitlock
Lisetta	Mrs. Rowson
Mrs. Marloff	Mrs. Shaw

DOCTOR AND APOTHECARY.

Thomaso	Mr. Green
Sturmwold	Mr. Bates
Carlos	Mr. Marshall
Juan	Mr. Francis
Guzman	Mr. Darley
Dr. Bilioso	Mr. Morris
Perez	Mr. Blissett
Anna	Mrs. Oldmixon
Isabella	Mrs. Marshall
Theresa	Mrs. Rowson

EASTER GIFT.

Harlequin	Mr. Francis
Pero	Mr. Doctor
Dwarf	Miss Solomon
Farmer Careful . . .	Mr. Warrell
Squire Clod	Mr. Morgan
Bootcatcher	Mr. Blissett
Statuary	Mr. Beete
Ape	Mr. Doctor
Genius of Mirth . .	Miss Willems
Columbine . . .	Miss Milbourne

FIRST LOVE.

Lord Sensitive . .	Mr. Marshall
Sir Miles Mowbray .	Mr. Whitlock
Frederick Mowbray .	Mr. Moreton
David Mowbray . . .	Mr. Bates
Wrangle	Mr. Green
Billy Bluster	Mr. Francis
Robin	Mr. Blissett
Sabina Rosny . . .	Mrs. Marshall

Lady Ruby . . .	Mrs. Whitlock
Mrs. Wrangle	Mrs. Shaw
Mrs. Kate	Mrs. Rowson
Waiting Woman .	Miss Oldfield

GIL BLAS.

Gil Blas	Mr. Bates
Young Spaniard . . .	Mr. Green
Domingo	Mr. Morgan
Domingo's Father .	Mr. Warrell
Captain	Mr. Moreton
Post-boy	Master Warrell
Gil Perot	Mr. Blissett
Pompey	Mr. Mitchell
Cook	Mr. Rowson
Spanish Lady . . .	Miss Willems
Gil Blas' Mother .	Mrs. Solomon
Harlequin . .	Mr. Warrell, Jr
Scaramouch . . .	Mr. Darley, Jr
Punch	Mr. Francis
Joany	Mrs. De Marque
Madonna	Miss Willems
Columbine . . .	Miss Milbourne

HARLEQUIN DR. FAUSTUS.

Azuria	Mrs. Francis
Faustus	Mr. Francis
Mephisto	Mr. Darley
Good Spirit	Mrs. Warrell
Evil Spirit	Mr. Darley, Jr

Dance of Furies.

Helen of Troy . .	Mrs. Marshall

Landscape and Water Mill.

Miller	Mr. Warrell
Miller's Son . . .	Mr. Darley, Jr
Clown	Mr. Blissett
Miller's Wife	Mrs. Lege
Bridesmaids .	Miss Rowson / Mrs. Doctor / Miss Gillingham
Columbine . . .	Miss Milbourne

The Magical Screen.

Scaramouch	Mr. Doctor

Cottage Changed to Inn.

Landlady	Mrs. Solomon

Street—Sedan Chair.

Chairmen	Mr. Mitchell / Mr. Morgan
Pigmies	Master Bates / Miss Solomon / Miss Gilaspie
Aerial Spirits .	Miss Solomon / Miss Gilaspie

HARLEQUIN'S CLUB.

Harlequin	Mr. Warrell, Jr
Pierrot	Mr. Doctor
Scaramouch . . .	Mr. Darley, Jr
Bumpkin	Mr. Blissett
Waiter	Master Warrell
Punch	Mr. Francis
Landlady	Mr. Rowson

HENRY II.

Henry	Mr. Moreton
Clifford	Mr. Whitlock
Prince	Mr. Warrell, Jr
Salisbury	Mr. Beete
Leicester	Mr. Warrell
Verulam	Mr. Morris
Servant	Mr. Mitchell
Abbot	Mr. Green
Queen	Mrs. Shaw
Ethelinda	Mrs. Hervey
Rosamond	Mrs. Whitlock

LA ROSE ET LE BOUTON.

Priestess	Mrs. Warrell
Colin	Mr. Francis
Agathe	Miss Milbourne

LES DEUX CHASSEURS.

Cola	Mr. Francis
Magistrate	Mr. Warrell
Guillot	Mr. Lege
Perrite	Mrs. De Marque

in New York, June 20th, 1795, for Mr. Ashton's benefit. Macready's comedy, the "Bank Note," was new in this country, having been acted at Covent Garden for the first time in 1795. It was based on Taverner's "Artful Husband," which had such success at Lincoln's Inn Fields

FIRST PRODUCTIONS—THIRD PHILADELPHIA SEASON.

LUCKY ESCAPE.

Ploughman	Mr. Francis
Jack	Mr. Warrell
Ben Block	Mr. Doctor
Bill Babler	Mr. Lege
Peggy	Mrs. De Marque
Anna	Miss Milbourne
Kate	Miss Willems
Sally	Miss Gilaspie

MAID OF THE OAKS.

Mr. Oldworth	Mr. Green
Old Grovely . . .	Mrs. Whitlock
Sir Harry	Mr. Marshall
Dupely	Mr. Moreton
Hurry	Mr. Bates
Lady Bab Lardoon,	Mrs. Whitlock
Maria	Miss Willems

MARRIED MAN.

Lord Lovmore . .	Mr. Moreton
Sir John Classick . .	Mr. Wignell
Mr. Classick . . .	Mr. Marshall
Tradewell Classick . .	Mr. Bates
Dorimant	Mr. Green
William	Mr. Blissett
Lady Classick . .	Mrs. Marshall
Emily	Mrs. Francis
Lucy	Mrs. Hervey

MERRY LITTLE GIRL.

Woodman	Mr. Lege
Pierrot	Mr. Doctor
Merry Girl	Miss Gilaspie

MIDNIGHT WANDERERS.

Marquis de Morelle . .	Mr. Bates
Julian	Mr. Marshall
Don Pedrazzo . . .	Mr. Warrell
Gasper	Mr. Francis
Dennis	Mr. Blissett
Mendicant	Mr. Beete
Guide	Mr. Morgan
Adelaide	Mrs. Warrell
Jaqueline	Mrs. Shaw

Maresa	Mrs. Oldmixon
Berilla	Miss Milbourne

MOGUL TALE.

Great Mogul . . .	Mr. Moreton
Dr. Pedant	Mr. Wignell
Omar	Mr. Green
Selim	Mr. Beete
First Guard . . .	Mr. Darley, Jr
Second Guard . . .	Mr. Mitchell
Johnny Atkins	Mr. Bates
Zaphira	Miss Oldfield
Irene	Mrs. Hervey
Sheba	Miss Willems
Fanny Atkins . .	Mrs. Marshall

MOTLEY GROUPE.

Harlequin . . .	Mr. Warrell, Jr
Pierrot	Mr. Doctor
Scaramouch . . .	Mr. Darley, Jr
Punch	Mr. Francis
Clown	Master T. Warrell

MOUNTAINEERS.

Octavian	Mr. Moreton
Virolet	Mr. Green
Kilmallock	Mr. Marshall
Roque	Mr. Wignell
Lope Tocho	Mr. Francis
Perequillo . . .	Master Warrell
Bulcazin Muley . .	Mr. Whitlock
Ganem	Mr. Beete
Pacha	Mr. Darley, Jr
Sadi	Mr. Harwood
Zorayda	Mrs. Whitlock
Floranthe	Mrs. Francis
Agnes	Mrs. Oldmixon

PATRIOT.

Albert	Mr. Green
Oscar	Mr. Moreton
Provost	Mr. Francis
Edwald . . .	Master T. Warrell
Popgun	Mr. Blissett
William Tell . . .	Mr. Whitlock

Tell's Son	Miss Solomon
Werner	Mr. Beete
Walter	Mr. Warrell
Old Man	Mr. Morgan
Court Fool	Mr. Bates

RIVAL KNIGHTS.

Duke	Mr. Doctor
Pierre	Mr. Moreton
Ferriers	Mr. Lege
Clerment	Mr. Francis
Belmonte	Mr. Green
La Gloire	Mr. Robbins
Chamont	Mr. Warrell
Du Mont	Mr. Mitchell
St. Creux	Mr. Beete
Magulonne	Mrs. Francis
Eliza	Mrs. De Marque
Sophie	Miss Willems

RULE A WIFE AND HAVE A WIFE.

Medina	Mr. Whitlock
Don Juan	Mr. Green
Sanchio	Mr. Beete
Alonzo	Mr. Darley, Jr
Cacafogo	Mr. Darley
Leon	Mr. Moreton
Copper Captain . .	Mr. Harwood
Lopez	Mr. Mitchell
Lorenzo	Mr. Warrell, Jr
Margaretta	Mrs. Shaw
Altea	Mrs. Francis
Clara	Mrs. Hervey
Estifania	Mrs. Marshall

SHIPWRECKED MARINERS PRESERVED.

Capt. Hatchway . . .	Mr. Lege
Jack Rattling . . .	Mr. Blissett
Gerald	Mr. Warrell
Ramirez	Mr. Doctor
Leonada	Mr. Francis
Rosalie	Miss Milbourne
Jaquelina	Miss Solomon

that it completely turned the author's head.   The production of
" Barnaby Brittle " was anticipated January 14th, 1795, by Charles
Powell's first company at the Boston Theatre.   Shakspere's " Corio-
lanus " had never been performed in the United States ; and Jephson's
" Count of Narbonne," founded· on Walpole's story, the " Castle of
Otranto," was also new to the American stage.   Another of Jephson's
pieces among the new productions was his farce, " Two Strings to
Your Bow," for Harwood's benefit.   It was an alteration by the
author of his farce, the " Hotel."   Hurlstone's farce, " Crotchet

FIRST PRODUCTIONS—THIRD PHILADELPHIA SEASON.

SPECULATION.

Sir Frederick Faintly,	Mr. Francis
Project	Mr. Bates
Vickery	Mr. Blissett
Ald Arable	Mr. Whitlock
Jack Arable	Mr. Marshall
Tanjore	Mr. Moreton
Promptly	Mr. Morgan
Meanwell	Mr. Beete
John	Mr. Warrell, Jr
Waiter	Mr. Mitchell
Lady Project	Mrs. Shaw
Emmeline	Mrs. Whitlock
Cecilia	Mrs. Marshall

SUICIDE.

Tobine	Mr. Moreton
Tabby	Mr. Beete
De Truby	Mr. Whitlock
Ranter	Mr. Marshall
Catchpenny	Mr. Harwood
Bounce	Mr. Darley, Jr
Squib	Mr. Blissett
Juggins	Mr. Francis
John	Mr. Warrell, Jr
Wingrave	Mr. Bates
Watchman	Mr. Warrell
Anthony	Mr. Beete
Tom Cellerman	Mr. Mitchell
Bolus	Mr. Morgan
Mrs. Grogram	Mrs. Rowson
Nancy	Mrs. Marshall
Peggy	Mrs. Hervey

TWO STRINGS TO YOUR BOW.

Don Pedro	Mr. Francis
Don Sancho	Mr. Warrell
Octavio	Mr. Beete
Ferdinand	Mr. Green
Borachio	Mr. Morgan
Lazarillo	Mr. Bates
Porter	Mr. Blissett
Donna Clara	Mrs. Francis
Leonora	Miss Willems
Maid	Mrs. Rowson

VALIANT OFFICER.

Harlequin	Mr. Francis
Pandolphe	Mr. Morgan
Watchmen	{ Mr. Bates / Mr. Blissett }
Miller	Mr. Mitchell
Valiant Officer	Mr. Darley, Jr
Maccarin	Mr. Beete
Lamp Lighter	Master Warrell
Clown	Mr. Doctor
Magician	Mr. Warrell
Columbine	Miss Milbourne
Jailer's Wife	Mrs. Lege

WHEEL OF FORTUNE.

David Daw	Mr. Francis
Tempest	Mr. Bates
Penruddock	Mr. Whitlock
Woodville	Mr. Green
Sydenham	Mr. Moreton
Weazle	Mr. Harwood
Servant	Mr. Beete
Officer	Mr. Warrell
Jenkins	Mr. Darley, Jr
James	Mr. Warrell, Jr
Richard	Mr. Morgan
Harry	Mr. Mitchell
Thomas	Master Warrell
Mrs. Woodville	Mrs. Morris
Emily Tempest	Mrs. Marshall
Dame Dunckley	Mrs. Rowson
Maid	Miss Rowson

WIDOW'S VOW.

Don Antonio	Mr. Morris
Marquis	Mr. Moreton
Carlos	Mr. Darley, Jr
Servant	Mr. Mitchell
Jerome	Mr. Bates
Countess	Mrs. Morris
Donna Isabella	Mrs. Hervey
Inis	Mrs. Rowson
Ursula	Mrs. Doctor
Flora	Mrs. Francis

WITCHES OF THE ROCK.

Harlequin	Mr. Francis
Witches	{ Mr. Darley / Mrs. Warrell }
Pantaloon	Mr. Warrell
Miser	Mr. Moreton
Lawyer	Mr. Darley, Jr
Pompey	Mr. Warrell, Jr
Drunken Valet	Mr. Milbourne
Surveyor	Mr. Beete
Pero	Mr. Doctor
Milliners	{ Miss Willems / Miss Rowson / Miss Oldfield }
Fruit Woman	Mrs. Rowson
Columbine	Miss Milbourne

Lodge," also a first production, but anticipated by a few weeks by the companies in Boston and New York, was among the successes of the previous season at Covent Garden. It was a combination of broad farce, strong caricature and whimsical situations, but it failed to become a favorite afterpiece on this side of the Atlantic. Pilon's " Deaf Lover" had its first American production in New York, March 9th, 1795. Still another Covent Garden success of the previous season was Holcroft's " Deserted Daughter," now first played in Philadelphia. The pantomimic ballet, " Deserter of Naples," also had its first American production for Mrs. Marshall's benefit. Johnstone's " Disbanded Officer, or the Baroness of Bruchsal," from the German of Lessing —a happy mixture of humor and sentiment—had been played at the Haymarket in 1786. Curiously enough, it was first produced in America February 18th, 1795, at the Church Street Theatre, Charleston. Cobb's farce, the " Doctor and Apothecary," owed its success at Drury Lane to Storace's excellent music. Mrs. Oldmixon introduced it to the American stage. M. Lege presented the first of his pantomimic dances, " Divertisement Pastoral," on the 17th of February, 1796, and his " Egyptian Festival " followed on the 7th of March. No cast of either of these productions was printed in the newspapers ; but we now have a first cast of " Les Deux Chasseurs," in which M. Lege had made his *debut* in Baltimore. Another pantomime by M. Lege was the " Merry Little Girl," which had its first production in America for the joint benefit of Lege and Doctor. The first new pantomime of the season by Francis was " Warrior's Welcome Home," which was followed by his " Lucky Escape," " Shamrock," " Fandango Dance " and " Easter Gift." We have casts of " Lucky Escape " and " Easter Gift," showing them to have been elaborate pantomimes. In the preparation of the latter Francis had the assistance of Mr. Milbourne, the scene-painter. Subsequently Francis presented " Irish Vagary," a dance; the " Motley Groupe," conventional pantomime; " Harlequin's Club " for Green's benefit, also conventional but more showy; " Harlequin Dr. Faustus," in his own behalf, the most elaborate piece of the kind he had as yet attempted, and " Les Deux Sœurs " for the benefit of Blissett, Mrs. De Marque and Mrs. Bates. In " Faustus " the changes were frequent. Besides those indicated in the cast there were a chamber scene with a trick bottle and buffet that changed to a book-case; a wood scene, with a song by Mrs. Warrell; a cavern scene with the downfall of *Faustus*, and finally the exhibition of a Temple of Glory with the descent of the Chariot of the Sun containing the two aerial spirits. Among the borrowed pieces of this class were " La Rose et le Bouton," a pantomimic ballet; " Witches of the Rock," partly by Milbourne, for the *finale* to which the artist painted a splendid view of the Falls of Niagara; " Shipwrecked Mariners Preserved," a nautical pantomime, exceedingly well cast; " Rival Knights," a serious ballet from the French; and the " Valiant Officer," brought out by Lege and Doctor for their benefit. Pantomimes were common property in those days. Even Francis borrowed the dwarf and ape scenes in " Easter Gift " from the pantomimes of " Orpheus and Eurydice " and the " Rape of Proserpine." Mr. Reinagle composed the music for the " Shamrock " and " Witches of the Rock " among others. Two of Cumberland's new comedies had their first production in Philadelphia this season—" First Love " for Mrs. Whitlock's benefit, and the " Wheel of Fortune," the latter having its first production in America. Both were Drury Lane successes of the previous season. In the former Mrs. Jordan produced a great effect as *Sabina Rosny*, thus making the part a tempting one for Mrs. Marshall; but in the latter it was not claimed that Whitlock was the rival of his brother-in-law, John Kemble, as *Penruddock*. While he was at the Royalty Theatre in 1788 Bates produced a piece of his own, partly pantomimic, " Gil Blas," which he now brought out here for his benefit. Hull's tragedy, " Henry II," was first acted in the United States for Whitlock's benefit, with Mrs. Whitlock as *Rosamond*, and the "Maid of the Oaks," for the benefit of Mrs. Whitlock, was anticipated in Boston by only a week. It is surprising that the production of Burgoyne's farce was so long delayed, but even more remarkable is the fact that John Fletcher's great comedy, " Rule a Wife and Have a Wife," was never played in this country until this season, except by the military Thespians in New York during the Revolution. Three of Mrs. Inchbald's pieces were added to the long list of her comedies already familiar to the American public—" Married Man," " Mogul Tale " and " Widow's Vow." All these had been originally acted with success at the Haymarket, but like most of her pieces they were borrowed from the French. The first American production of the younger Colman's " Mountaineers " was in Boston in 1795, where it was remarkably successful. In Philadelphia Wignell reserved it for his parting benefit this season. Mr. Bates' benefit-offering, the " Patriot," was one of the many versions of the story of William Tell which had considerable vogue in this country at that time. The only new pieces remaining to be noticed were Reynolds' " Speculation," first played at Covent Garden the previous season, and the elder Colman's comedy, the " Suicide," originally produced at the Haymarket many years before. This was, certainly, a long list of new pieces for a single season.

The third season of the Philadelphia company in Baltimore

began on the 20th of July, 1796, and lasted, with some interruptions, until the 28th of October. It had been intended to open on the 18th of July with the "Deserted Daughter," but the performance was postponed and Goldsmith's comedy substituted for Holcroft's. In Mr. Wignell's absence Mr. Moreton was the acting manager, but the company at his command was greatly enfeebled. Mr. and Mrs. Whitlock, Mr. and Mrs. Marshall, Mr. Harwood, Mr. and Mrs. Bates, Mr. Beete and Mrs. Shaw were all out of the bills. Mr. Whitlock's name appears in the advertisements as *Old Grovely* and Mrs. Whitlock's as *Lady Bab Lardoon* in "Maid of the Oaks," but this was probably a misprint. Early in the season, however, the Marshalls and Mrs. Shaw were with the company for a brief period. The substitutes were Mr. and Mrs. Chambers, Mr. Fox and Miss Sully. Mr. Chalmers, who was a great Baltimore favorite, was specially engaged. Toward the close of the season Mr. More-

LIST OF PERFORMANCES—*Baltimore.*

1796.

July	20—She Stoops to Conquer,	Goldsmith
	Mock Doctor	Fielding
	22—Deserted Daughter	Holcroft
	Barnaby Brittle	Betterton
	23—George Barnwell	Lillo
	Romp	Bickerstaff
	25—West Indian	Cumberland
	Children in the Wood	Morton
	27—Earl of Essex	Jones
	No Song No Supper	Hoare
	29—Dramatist	Reynolds
	Lucky Escape	Francis
	Catharine and Petruchio	Shakspere
	30—Provoked Husband	Vanbrugh
	Spoiled Child	Bickerstaff
Aug.	1—Busybody	Mrs. Centlivre
	Poor Soldier	O'Keefe
	3—Tempest	Dryden
	Midnight Hour	Mrs. Inchbald
	5—Rule a Wife and Have a Wife	Fletcher
	Purse	Cross
	6—Zara	Hill
	Farmer	O'Keefe
	8—Road to Ruin	Holcroft
	Rosina	Mrs. Brooke
	10—Mountaineers	Colman, Jr.
	Deaf Lover	Pilon
	12—Wild Oats	O'Keefe
	Deserter	Dibdin
	15—Carmelite	Cumberland
	Maid of the Oaks	Burgoyne
	17—Romeo and Juliet	Shakspere
	Love a la Mode	Macklin
	19—Wild Oats.	
	Mogul Tale	Mrs. Inchbald
	20—Haunted Tower	Cobb
	Widow's Vow	Mrs. Inchbald

ton made an arrangement with Mr. Fennell for twelve nights at thirty dollars a night and a benefit, Fennell making his re-entrée as *Othello* after an absence of two years from the stage, but Mr. Wignell upon his return annulled the engagement. Whether the season was a successful one there is no means of knowing, but the Baltimore Theatre had already yielded some profit to the shareholders, for simultaneously with the announcement of the opening this season, Samuel Anderson, the treasurer, informed the subscribers that a year's interest on their shares would be paid on the 10th of August. The list of performances was, as usual, made up almost wholly of previous Philadelphia successes, but the changes in the casts were so great that many of the pieces were nearly recast. Not only had the places of the absentees to be refilled, but Mr. Moreton, owing to his managerial duties, was often out of the

Aug. 22—Beaux' Stratagem . . . Farquhar
Critic . . . . Sheridan
24—Speculation . . . . . Reynolds
Lyar . . . . Foote
26—Alexander the Great . . . . Lee
Lyar.
27—Highland Reel . . . . O'Keefe
Deaf Lover.
31—Richard III . . . . . Shakspere
Prisoner . . . . Rose
Lucky Escape . . . . . Francis
(Benefit of the Warrells.)
Sept. 1—Lear . . . . Shakspere
Deserter of Naples.
(Mr. and Mrs. Marshall's benefit.)
2—Robin Hood . . . . MacNally
All the World's a Stage . Jackman
(Mr. Darley and Mrs. Oldmixon's benefit.)
3—Patriot.
Harlequin Skeleton.
(Mr. and Mrs. Bates' benefit.)
5—School for Soldiers . . . Henry
Peeping Tom of Coventry
O'Keefe
Ghost . . . . . Mrs. Centlivre
(Mr. and Mrs. Green's benefit.)
6—She Wou'd and She Wou'd Not
Cibber
Harlequin Shipwrecked.
(Mr. and Mrs. Francis' benefit.)
7—Recruiting Officer . . . Farquhar
Harlequin Hurry-Scurry . Francis
Devil to Pay . . . . . . Coffey
(Mr. Blissett and Mrs. Hervey's benefit.)
8—George Barnwell.
Spoiled Child.
(Mrs. and Miss Solomon's benefit.)
19—Bank Note . . . . . Macready
Village Lawyer . . . Macready
21—Inkle and Yarico . . Colman, Jr.
Irishman in London . Macready
23—Married Man . . Mrs. Inchbald
Rural Merriment . . . . Francis
All the World's a Stage.
26—Love in a Village . . Bickerstaff
Animal Magnetism, Mrs. Inchbald

Sept. 28—Rivals . . . . Sheridan
    Quaker . . . . Dibdin
    30—Wonder . . . . Mrs. Centlivre
    Harlequin's Invasion . . Garrick
Oct. 3—Miser . . . . Fielding
    Comus . . . . Milton
    5—Children in the Wood.
    Animal Magnetism.
    Robinson Crusoe . . . Sheridan
    7—English Merchant . . . Colman
    Modern Antiques . . . O'Keefe
    12—Othello . . . . Shakspere
    Purse.
    19—Mountaineers . . . Colman, Jr
    Ways and Means . . Colman, Jr
    28—Child of Nature . Mrs. Inchbald
    My Grandmother . . . . Hoare
    (Mr. and Mrs. Chambers' benefit.)

bill, thus making an additional vacancy. Mr. and Mrs. Chambers had been with the Old American Company at the Southwark Theatre in 1792, and had subsequently appeared in the South. Now they were, in the main, the substitutes for the Marshalls. Mr. Chambers made his first appearance at Baltimore on the 25th of July as *Walter* in "Children of the Wood," Miss Sully making her *debut* with the company the same night as the *Girl*. Mrs. Chambers was first seen as *Dorinda* in the "Tempest" on the 3d of August. Mr. Fox made

CONTRASTED CASTS—BALTIMORE CHANGES, 1796.

PLAYS.	1794-6.	Balt.
All the World's a Stage.		
Charles Stanley . Mr. Marshall	. Mr. Chambers	
Diggory . . . . Mr. Bates . .	. Mr. Blissett	
Cymon . . . . Mr. Blissett .	. Mr. Morgan	
Miss Bridget . . Mrs. Rowson	. Mrs. Doctor	
Kitty Sprightly . Mrs. Marshall	. Mrs. Chambers	
Bank Note.		
Bloomfield . . . Mr. Wignell .	. Mr. Chambers	
Lieut. Selby . . Mr. Green . .	. Mr. Fox	
Neddy Dash . . Mr. Harwood .	Mr. Francis	
Hale . . . . . Mr. Bates . .	. Mr. Blissett	
Killeary . . . . Mr. Marshall	. Mr. Green	
Tim . . . . . Mr. Blissett .	. Mr. Darley, Jr	
Young Bloomfield Miss Solomon	. Miss Sully	
Lady Supple . . Mrs. Rowson	. Mrs. Doctor	
Miss Russell . . Mrs. Marshall	. Mrs. Francis	
Sally Flounce . Mrs. Francis .	. Miss Milbourne	
Barnaby Brittle.		
Mrs. Brittle . . Mrs. Marshall	. Mrs. Francis	
Damaris . . . . Mrs. Shaw .	. Mrs. Hervey	
Busybody.		
Whisper . . . . Mr. Blissett .	. Mr. Warrell, Jr	
Patch . . . . . Mrs. Shaw .	. Mrs. Rowson	

PLAYS.	1794-6.	Balt.
Carmelite.		
Montgomeri . . Mr. Harwood .	Mr. Fox	
Gyfford . . . . Mr. Beete .	. Mr. Warrell	
Raymond . . . Mr. Warrell .	. Mr. Darley, Jr	
Catharine and Petruchio.		
Catharine . . . Mrs. Rowson	. Mrs. Francis	
Bianca . . . . Mrs. Hervey .	. Miss Rowson	
Child of Nature.		
Marquis . . . . Mr. Whitlock .	Mr. Fennell	
Murcia . . . . Mr. Bates . .	. Mr. Blissett	
Seville . . . . . Mr. Beete . .	. Mr. Warrell	
First Peasant . . Mr. Green . .	. Mr. Chambers	
Second Peasant . Mr. Warrell .	. Mr. Morgan	
Amanthis . . . Mrs. Marshall .	Mrs. Chambers	
Children in the Wood.		
Walter . . . . Mr. Harwood .	Mr. Chambers	
Gabriel . . . . Mr. Moreton .	Mr. Blissett	
Boy . . . . . Miss Gilaspie .	Miss Solomon	
Girl . . . . . Miss Solomon .	Miss Sully	
Comus.		
Comus . . . . Mr. Chalmers .	Mr. Moreton	
First Spirit . . Mr. Green . .	. Mr. Warrell	
Elder Brother . Mr. Moreton .	Mr. Fox	

his *debut* on the third night of the season in the title-role of "George Barnwell," this being his second appearance on any stage. Mr. Fox, who was then a very young man, was an engineer by profession, but he preferred the stage, for which he had some talent. It seldom happened that an aspirant obtained such an excellent line of parts as was accorded to Fox at Baltimore this season. The name of Mrs. Darley,

CONTRASTED CASTS—BALTIMORE CHANGES, 1796.

PLAYS.	1794–6.	Balt.
YoungerBrother.	Mr. Cleveland	Mr. Warrell, Jr
Lady	Mrs. Whitlock	Mrs. Oldmixon
Pastoral Nymph.	Mrs. Marshall	Miss Milbourne
Euphrosyne	Mrs. Oldmixon	Mrs. Green
Sabrina	Miss Broadhurst	Mrs. Hervey
Deaf Lover.		
Y'ng Wronghead	Mr. Beete	Mr. Darley, Jr
Canteen	Mr. Harwood	Mr. Marshall
Sternhold	Mr. Blissett	Mr. Morgan
Groom	Mr. Bates	Mr. Blissett
Bob	Mr. Darley, Jr	Mr. Solomon
Deserted Daughter.		
Grime	Mr. Beete	Mr. Warrell
Lady Ann	Mrs. Whitlock	Mrs. Shaw
Dramatist.		
Vapid	Mr. Harwood	Mr. Chalmers
Miss Courtney	Mrs. Hervey	Mrs. Francis
Earl of Essex.		
Essex	Mr. Wignell	Mr. Chalmers
Southampton	Mr. Moreton	Mr. Marshall
Raleigh	Mr. Harwood	Mr. Fox
Lieutenant	Mr. Beete	Mr. Warrell
Lady Rutland	Mrs. Whitlock	Mrs. Marshall
Nottingham	Mrs. Shaw	Mrs. Francis
English Merchant.		
Douglas	Mr. Whitlock	Mr. Green
Spatter	Mr. Wignell	Mr. Chambers
Owen	Mr. Green	Mr. Warrell
La France	Mr. Harwood	Mr. Blissett
Officer	Mr. Warrell	Mr. Morgan
Amelia	Mrs. Marshall	Mrs. Chambers
Mrs. Goodman	Mrs. Shaw	Mrs. Hervey
Farmer.		
Jemmy Jumps	Mr. Bates	Mr. Chambers
George Barnwell.		
Thoroughgood	Mr. Whitlock	Mr. Morris
Uncle	Mr. Wignell	Mr. Warrell
Barnwell	Mr. Moreton	Mr. Fox
Gaoler	Mr. Warrell	Mr. Morgan

PLAYS.	1794–6.	Balt.
Maria	Mrs. Whitlock	Mrs. Green
Millwood	Mrs. Shaw	Mrs. Francis
Lucy	Mrs. Francis	Mrs. Solomon
Harlequin's Invasion.		
Mercury	Mr. Marshall	Mr. Darley, Jr
Snip	Mr. Bates	Mr. Chambers
Frontin	Mr. Harwood	Mr. Blissett
Bog	Mr. Darley, Jr	Mr. Morgan
Simon	Mr. Wignell	Mr. Milbourne
Mrs. Snip	Mrs. Rowson	Mrs. Hervey
Fairy	Miss Solomon	Miss Sully
Fairy Harlequin.	Mast. Strickland	Mast. H. Warrell
Old Woman	Mr. Marshall	Mr. Darley
Tragic Muse	Mrs. Whitlock	Mrs. Green
Comic Muse	Mrs. Marshall	Miss Milbourne
Haunted Tower.		
Oakland	Mr. Harwood	Mr. Blissett
Lewis	Mr. Blissett	Mr. Warrell, Jr
De Courcy	Mr. Moreton	Mr. Fox
Inkle and Yarico.		
Inkle	Mr. Marshall	Mr. Chambers
Curry	Mr. Whitlock	Mr. Green
Medium	Mr. Francis	Mr. Warrell
Campley	Mr. Moreton	Mr. Darley, Jr
Trudge	Mr. Wignell	Mr. Francis
Planter	Mr. Beete	Mr. Blissett
Yarico	Mrs. Marshall	Mrs. Warrell
Narcissa	Mrs. Oldmixon	Mrs. Green
Wowski	Miss Oldfield	Mrs. Oldmixon
Patty	Mrs. Shaw	Mrs. Hervey
Irishman in London.		
Capt. Seymour	Mr. Green	Mr. Fox
Colloney	Mr. Moreton	Mr. Darley, Jr
Delaney	Mr. Marshall	Mr. Green
Edward	Mr. Harwood	Mr. Moreton
Love a la Mode.		
Sir Callaghan	Mr. Whitlock	Mr. Marshall
Squire Groom	Mr. Marshall	Mr. Chalmers
Sir Theodore	Mr. Beete	Mr. Warrell

who was probably the wife of the great *Farmer Blackberry*, occurs in the bills for the first and last time as *Cicely* in the "Quaker." The two members of the company who profited most by the changes in the casts were Mr. Blissett and Mrs. Doctor. The former obtained a number of Bates' parts among others, and the latter succeeded to some of the previous parts of Mrs. Rowson. This season Mrs. Oldmixon

CONTRASTED CASTS—BALTIMORE CHANGES, 1796.

PLAYS.	1794–6.	Balt.
Love in a Village.		
Sir William	. . Mr. Morris	. . Mr. Warrell
Meadows	. . . Mr. Marshall	. Mr. Chambers
Woodcock	. . . Mr. Bates . . .	Mr. Morris
Deborah	. . . . Mrs. Shaw . .	. Mrs. Doctor
Rosetta	. . . . Mrs. Marshall	. Mrs. Oldmixon
Madge	. . . . . Miss Broadhurst.	Mrs. Green
Lucky Escape.		
Jack	. . . . . Mr. Warrell	. . Mr. Warrell, Jr
Will Babler	. . Mr. Lege	. . . Mr. Mitchell
Peggy	. . . . . Mrs. De Marque.	Miss Rowson
Sally	. . . . . Miss Gilaspie	. Miss Solomon
Maid of the Oaks.		
Dupely	. . . . Mr. Moreton	. Mr. Chambers
Married Man.		
Sir John	. . . . Mr. Wignell .	. Mr. Chambers
Mr. Classick	. . Mr. Marshall	. Mr. Morris
Tradewell	. . . Mr. Bates . .	. Mr. Blissett
Dorimant	. . . Mr. Green . .	. Mr. Fox
William	. . . . Mr. Blissett	. Mr. Warrell, Jr
Lady Classick	. Mrs. Marshall	. Mrs. Chambers
Midnight Hour.		
General	. . . . Mr. Harwood	. Mr. Blissett
Matthias	. . . . Mr. Blissett	. . Mr. Morgan
Julia	. . . . Mrs. Francis	. Mrs. Hervey
Flora	. . . . Mrs. Whitlock	. Mrs. Francis
Miser.		
Lovegold	. . Mr. Bates . .	. Mr. Green
Frederick	. . . Mr. Marshall	. Mr. Fox
Clerimont	. . . Mr. Green . .	. Mr. Warrell, Jr
Ramillie	. . . . Mr. Wignell .	. Mr. Chambers
Furnish	. . . . Mr. Beete . .	. Mr. Morgan
Mrs. Wisely	. . Mrs. Rowson	. Mrs. Doctor
Wheedle	. . . . Mrs. Solomon	. Miss Milbourne
Mock Doctor.		
Sir Jasper	. . Mr. Beete . .	. Mr. Morgan
Gregory	. . . . Mr. Bates . .	. Mr. Morris
Davy	. . . . . Mr. Morgan .	. Mr. Solomon
Modern Antiques.		
Joey	. . . . . Mr. Bates . .	. Mr. Blissett
Napkin	. . . . Mr. Blissett	. . Mr. Warrell

PLAYS.	1794–6.	Balt.
Thomas	. . . . Mr. Warrell	. . Mr. Darley, Jr
Mrs. Cockletop	. Mrs. Shaw	. Mrs. Francis
Mrs. Camomile	. Mrs. Rowson	. Mrs. Doctor
Belinda	. . . . Mrs. Cleveland	. Miss Oldfield
Nan	. . . . . . Mrs. Solomon	. Mrs. Hervey
Flounce	. . . . Mrs. Bates	. . Mrs. Green
Betty	. . . . Miss Oldfield	. Miss Milbourne
Mountaineers.		
Virolet	. . . . Mr. Green . .	. Mr. Fox
Roque	. . . . . Mr. Wignell .	. Mr. Rowson
Bulcazin	. . . . Mr. Whitlock	. Mr. Green
Ganem	. . . Mr. Beete . .	. Mr. Warrell, Jr
Sadi	. . . . . . Mr. Harwood	. Mr. Chambers
Zorayda	. . . Mrs. Whitlock	. Mrs. Warrell
My Grandmother.		
Woodley	. . . Mr. Darley	. . Mr. Darley, Jr
Gossip	. . . . Mr. Bates . .	. Mr. Chambers
Souffrance	. . . Mr. Harwood	. Mr. Blissett
Tom	. . . . . Mr. Blissett	. . Master Warrell
Charlotte	. . . Miss Broadhurst.	Mrs. Warrell
No Song No Supper.		
Frederick	. . . Mr. Marshall	. Mr. Darley, Jr
Endless	. . . . Mr. Harwood	. Mr. Francis
Dorothy	. . . . Mrs. Shaw .	. Mrs. Rowson
Poor Soldier.		
Fitzroy	. . . . Mr. Moreton	. Mr. Darley
Patrick	. . . . Mr. Harwood	. Mr. Francis
Norah	. . . . . Miss Milbourne	. Mrs. Warrell
Provoked Husband.		
Lord Townly	. Mr. Whitlock	. Mr. Chalmers
Manly	. . . . . Mr. Green . .	. Mr. Chambers
Lady Wronghead	Mrs. Shaw	. . Mrs. Francis
Myrtilla	. . . . Mrs. Rowson	. Mrs. Hervey
Purse.		
Baron	. . . . . Mr. Green . .	. Mr. Warrell
Theodore	. . . Mr. Moreton	. Mr. Fox
Edmund	. . . . Mr. Marshall	. Mr. Darley, Jr
Steady	. . . . Mr. Harwood	. Mr. Chambers
Page	. . . . . Miss Solomon	. Miss Sully

appeared for the first time as *Mrs. Malaprop* in the "Rivals." These casts indicate the peripatetic tendencies of American players even at that early period. After leaving the South, Mr. and Mrs. Chambers and Miss Sully had been in Boston for a season, and the principal actors of Wignell's first company were to become the main support of the Boston and Charleston theatres during the rest of the century.

CONTRASTED CASTS—BALTIMORE CHANGES, 1796.

PLAYS.	1794-6.	Balt.
Quaker.		
Steady	Mr. Harwood	Mr. Chalmers
Solomon	Mr. Bates . .	Mr. Francis
Lubin	Mr. Marshall	Mr. Chambers
Gillian	Mrs. Marshall	Mrs. Doctor
Floretta		Mrs. Oldmixon
Cicily	Miss Solomon	Mrs. Darley
Rivals.		
Capt. Absolute .	Mr. Moreton	Mr. Chambers
Faulkland . . .	Mr. Wignell .	Mr. Moreton
Acres	Mr. Bates . . .	Mr. Francis
Sir Lucius . . .	Mr. Whitlock .	Mr. Green
Fag	Mr. Marshall	Mr. Warrell, Jr
David	Mr. Francis . .	Mr. Blissett
Mrs. Malaprop .	Mrs. Shaw . .	Mrs. Oldmixon
Lydia	Mrs. Marshall .	Mrs. Chambers
Lucy	Mrs. Hervey .	Mrs. Doctor
Road to Ruin.		
Dornton	Mr. Whitlock .	Mr. Green
Harry Dornton .	Mr. Green . . .	Mr. Moreton
Sulky	Mr. Francis . .	Mr. Rowson
Silky	Mr. Bates . . .	Mr. Francis
Goldfinch . . .	Mr. Harwood .	Mr. Chalmers
Milford	Mr. Beete . . .	Mr. Fox
Mrs. Warren .	Mrs. Shaw . .	Mrs. Rowson
Robinson Crusoe.		
Crusoe	Mr. Bates . . .	Mr. Chambers
Romeo and Juliet.		
Mercutio . . .	Mr. Wignell .	Mr. Chalmers
Tybalt	Mr. Harwood .	Mr. Fox
Friar Laurence .	Mr. Whitlock .	Mr. Chambers
Rule a Wife and Have a Wife.		
Medina	Mr. Whitlock .	Mr. Green
Don Juan . . .	Mr. Green . . .	Mr. Fox
Sancho	Mr. Beete . . .	Mr. Warrell, Jr
Copper Captain .	Mr. Harwood .	Mr. Chalmers
Lopez	Mr. Mitchell . .	Mr. Morgan
Lorenzo	Mr. Warrell, Jr .	Mr. Mitchell
Margaretta . .	Mrs. Shaw . .	Mrs. Rowson

PLAYS.	1794-6.	Balt.
Spoiled Child.		
Old Pickle . . .	Mr. Harwood .	Mr. Green
Maria . . .	Mrs. Francis . .	Miss Milbourne
Susan	Mrs. Green . .	Miss Rowson
Tempest.		
Alonzo . . .	Mr. Whitlock .	Mr. Green
Ferdinand . . .	Mr. Moreton . .	Mr. Fox
Prospero	Mr. Green . . .	Mr. Chambers
Gonzalo	Mr. Beete . . .	Mr. Morgan
Hippolito . . .	Mr. Warrell, Jr .	Mrs. Francis
Stephano . . .	Mr. Harwood .	Mr. Francis
Dorinda	Mrs. Marshall .	Mrs. Chambers
Village Lawyer.		
Scout	Mr. Harwood .	Mr. Green
Sheepface . . .	Mr. Bates . . .	Mr. Blissett
Mrs. Scout . . .	Mrs. Rowson .	Mrs. Francis
Kate	Mrs. Bates . .	Mrs. Doctor
West Indian.		
Capt. Dudley .	Mr. Beete . . .	Mr. Warrell
Maj. O'Flaherty .	Mr. Whitlock .	Mr. Green
Fulmer	Mr. Green . . .	Mr. Blissett
Lady Rusport .	Mrs. Shaw . .	Mrs. Rowson
Louisa Dudley .	Mrs. Francis . .	Mrs. Green
Mrs. Fulmer .	Mrs. Rowson .	Mrs. Solomon
Widow's Vow.		
Marquis	Mr. Moreton .	Mr. Fox
Wonder.		
Don Lopez . .	Mr. Finch . . .	Mr. Warrell
Frederick . . .	Mr. Green . . .	Mr. Fox
Col. Briton . .	Mr. Fennell . .	Mr. Green
Gibby	Mr. Bates . . .	Mr. Blissett
Lissardo . . .	Mr. Harwood .	Mr. Chambers
Alguazil	Mr. Warrell . .	Mr. Mitchell
Violante . . .	Mrs. Whitlock .	Mrs. Morris
Isabella	Mrs. Francis . .	Mrs. Warrell
Flora	Mrs. Shaw . .	Mrs. Francis
Inez	Mrs. Rowson .	Mrs. Hervey
Zara.		
Lusignan . . .	Mr. Whitlock .	Mr. Green
Chatillon	Mr. Green . . .	Mr. Morris
Orasmin . . .	Mr. Beete . . .	Mr. Fox
Zara	Mrs. Whitlock .	Mrs. Marshall

In some respects the Baltimore season of 1796 was distinctive. A number of the earlier pieces played by the company was revived, including the " Haunted Tower," " Love in a Village," " Modern Antiques" and the " Wonder;" and Mrs. Inchbald's " Animal Magnetism" and O'Keefe's " Wild Oats " were produced for the first time by these players. The cast of the latter, it will be observed, included Mr. Bates and Mr. and Mrs. Marshall. We now have besides the first preserved cast of " Othello" with Fennell once more in the title-role and a cast of Francis' pantomime, " Rural Merriment," originally produced in Baltimore the previous season. During the stay of the company in Baltimore Mr. Francis opened a dancing school in that city. In the meantime Mr. Wignell had returned with his reinforcements, and he carried the company back to Philadelphia to begin what proved to be the most brilliant theatrical campaign ever known in America.

ANIMAL MAGNETISM.

Marquis . . . . . Mr. Moreton
La Fleur . . . . . Mr. Green
Doctor . . . . . Mr. Francis
Picard . . . . . Mr. Warrell
Francois . . . Mr. Warrell, Jr
Jeffery . . . . . . Mr. Blissett
Constance . . . . Mrs. Green
Lisette . . . . . Mrs. Francis

WILD OATS.

Sir George Thunder . Mr. Bates
Rover . . . . . Mr. Chalmers
Harry . . . . . Mr. Marshall
John Dory . . . . Mr. Green
Banks . . . . . . Mr. Morris
Gammon . . . . Mr. Rowson
Ephraim Smooth . Mr. Blissett
Sim . . . . Mr. Francis
Twitch . . . . Mr. Darley, Jr
Lamp . . . . . . Mr. Warrell
Trap . . . . . . Mr. Mitchell
Landlord . . . . Mr. Morgan
Sailor . . . . . Mr. Solomon
Waiter . . . . Master Warrell
Midge . . . . Mr. Warrell, Jr
Lady Amaranth . Mrs. Marshall
Jane . . . . . . Mrs. Francis
Amelia . . . . Mrs. Hervey

OTHELLO.

Othello . . . . . Mr. Fennell
Cassio . . . . . Mr. Moreton
Iago . . . . Mr. Green
Roderigo . . . . Mr. Francis
Montano . . . . . . Mr. Fox
Duke . . . . . . Mr. Warrell
Brabantio . . . . . Mr. Morris
Gratiano . . . Mr. Warrell, Jr
Ludovico . . . Mr. Darley, Jr
Desdemona . . . Mrs. Morris
Emelia . . . . . Mrs. Francis

RURAL MERRIMENT.

Toby Philpot . . . Mr. Francis
Lightfoot . . . . . Mr. Doctor
Dick Chaunt . . Mr. Darley, Jr
Colin . . . . Mr. Warrell, Jr
Landlord . . . . Mr. Warrell
Phœbe . . . . Miss Milbourne

CHAPTER XI.

THE BOSTON THEATRE, 1794-5.

CHARLES POWELL'S TWO SEASONS—THE FIRST BOSTON COMPANY—PRO-
DUCTIONS—PAINE'S PROLOGUE—CASTS—THE BAKER FAMILY—THE
COMPANY REORGANIZED—SECOND SEASON—MRS. SPENCER—"THE
MEDIUM"—CHARLES POWELL'S RETIREMENT.

AFTER Joseph Harper's unsuccessful attempt to establish a
theatre in Boston, in the Summer and Autumn of 1792, the
friends of the drama were more persistent than ever in their efforts to
have the obnoxious prohibitory act of 1750 repealed. They finally
succeeded early in 1793, and on the 9th of April a meeting was
held to open subscriptions for building a house for theatrical exhibitions. The number of shares was limited to 120 at $50 per share, no
one person being allowed more than two shares. The site selected
was at the corner of Federal and Franklin Streets, where a commodi-
ous brick building 140 feet long, 61 feet wide and 40 feet in height,
was speedily erected. The new theatre was plain and substantial,
without architectural pretensions, with the exception of a colonnade in
Federal Street. One of the first acts of the trustees was to appoint
Charles Stuart Powell, who had played with Harper the previous year,
sole manager, and early in June, 1793, it was announced that he would
sail for England in a few days to engage a company for the new
theatre. Unlike Mr. Henry, Powell found no Hodgkinson at Bath

eager to engage with him, nor, like Mr. Wignell, was he able to secure a force that would have been creditable even in London. His predecessors had exhausted the immediate supply of talent eligible for the American market. The company secured for the first season at the Boston Theatre comprised Mr. and Mrs. Powell, Mr. and Mrs. Baker, Miss Baker, Mr. and Mrs. Collins, Mr. and Mrs. Jones, Messrs. Bartlett, Kenny, Nelson and Snelling Powell, a brother of the manager, Mrs. Abbot and Miss Harrison, afterward Mrs. S. Powell. These were all without reputation in the country from which they came, and such fame as they afterward acquired was confined to America.

When Mr. Powell arrived with his company he found the theatre ready for occupation, and so he proceeded to begin his campaign. The opening night was the 3d of February, 1794, with "Gustavus Vasa" and "Modern Antiques" as the initial productions. The season lasted until the 4th of July following. Probably no theatre in the United States was ever opened with so much formality and decorum. The rules and regulations adopted by the trustees were very elaborate and very strict. No infraction of them was allowed. Mr. John Hastings, the box-keeper, inadvertently let a few places in the boxes before the official announce-

LIST OF PERFORMANCES.

1794.

Feb. 3—Gustavus Vasa . . . . . Brooke
       Modern Antiques . . . O'Keefe
      7—Same bill.
     10—Belle's Stratagem . Mrs. Cowley
       Farmer . . . . O'Keefe
     12—Busybody . . . . Mrs. Centlivre
       Midnight Hour . . Mrs. Inchbald
     17—Natural Son . . . . Cumberland
       Quaker . . . . Dibdin
     19—Barbarossa . . . . . . Browne
       Quaker.
     24—Provoked Husband . . Vanbrugh
       Midnight Hour.
     26—Belle's Stratagem.
       Farmer.
     28—Child of Nature . Mrs. Inchbald
       Agreeable Surprise . . O'Keefe
March 3—Foundling . . . . . . Moore
       Bon Ton . . . . . . Garrick
      5—Which is the Man? . Mrs. Cowley
       Old Maid . . . . . . Murphy
      7—Wonder . . . . . Mrs. Centlivre
       Quaker.

ment of the opening night was made. For this he was hauled over the coals in the *Mercury*, and Mr. Powell apologized in a card, as did Hastings also. For the preservation of order both within and without the theatre a Master of Ceremonies was appointed. That this office was considered one of great dignity is apparent from the fact that Col. John S. Tyler was appointed to fill it, and so highly were Colonel Tyler's services appreciated that he was accorded the first regular benefit of the season. Not only was a master of ceremonies appointed to see that those who had taken seats should be accommodated according to contract, to direct the manner of setting down and taking up those who came to the playhouse in carriages, and to suppress " all kinds of disorder and indecorum," but the trustees reserved to themselves the power of dismissing any performer either on the stage or in the orchestra—

Mar. 10—Provoked Husband.
Rosina . . . . . . Mrs. Brooke
12—George Barnwell . . . . . Lillo
Agreeable Surprise.
14—She Stoops to Conquer . Goldsmith
Old Maid.
17—Jane Shore . . . . Rowe
Modern Antiques.
19—Natural Son.
Farmer.
21—Douglas . . . . Home
Who's the Dupe? . Mrs. Cowley
24—School for Scandal . . Sheridan
Rosina.
26—Revenge . . . . Moore
Agreeable Surprise.
31—West Indian . . . . Cumberland
Citizen . . . . Murphy
April 2—Bold Stroke for a Wife
Mrs. Centlivre
Miller of Mansfield . . Dodsley
4—George Barnwell.
Ways and Means . . Colman, Jr
8—Chapter of Accidents . Miss Lee
11—Chapter of Accidents.
Midas . . . . O'Hara
14—Love in a Village . . Bickerstaff
Miss in Her Teens . . . Garrick
16—Child of Nature.
Midas.
18—Hamlet . . . . . . Shakspere
Barnaby Brittle . . . . Betterton
21—Hamlet.
Barnaby Brittle.
23—Bold Stroke for a Wife.
Padlock . . . . . . Bickerstaff
25—Chapter of Accidents.
Midas.
28—Romeo and Juliet . . Shakspere
All in Good Humor . . . Oulton
30—School for Scandal.
Midas.
May 2—Richard III . . . . . Shakspere
All in Good Humor.
5—Twelfth Night . . . . Shakspere
Padlock.

May 7—Foundling.
　　　　Quaker.
　　9—Inkle and Yarico . . Colman, Jr
　　　　Bon Ton.
　　12—Inkle and Yarico.
　　　　Bon Ton.
　　14—Mourning Bride . . . Congreve
　　　　Lying Valet . . . . . . Garrick
　　　(For Prisoners in Algiers.)
　　16—Inkle and Yarico.
　　　　Who's the Dupe?
　　19—Child of Nature.
　　　　Agreeable Surprise.
　　(Benefit of Master of Ceremonies.)
　　21—West Indian.
　　　　Citizen.
　　　　(Mr. Collins' benefit.)
　　23—Drummer . . . . . Addison
　　　　Rosina.
　　　　(Miss Baker's benefit.)
　　26—Revenge.
　　　　Virgin Unmasked . . . Fielding
　　28—Inkle and Yarico.
　　　　Poor Soldier . . . . . O'Keefe
　　30—Wonder.
　　　　Midas.
June　2—Chapter of Accidents.
　　　　Poor Soldier.
　　　　(Mr. Kenny's benefit.)
　　4—Romeo and Juliet.
　　　　No Song No Supper . . . Hoare
　　　　(Mr. S. Powell's benefit.)
　　6—Belle's Stratagem.
　　　　Waterman . . . . . . Dibdin
　　　　(Mr. Nelson's benefit.)
　　9—Merchant of Venice . Shakspere
　　　　Son-in-Law . . . . . O'Keefe
　　　　(Mrs. Powell's benefit.)
　　11—Clandestine Marriage
　　　　　　　　Garrick and Colman
　　　　Ways and Means.
　　　　(Miss Harrison's benefit.)
　　13—Which is the Man?
　　　　Animal Magnetism, Mrs. Inchbald
　　　　(Mrs. Jones' benefit.)

a power to be exercised in the form of a request to the manager. Singularly enough, the first complaint was made against the manager himself. On the 18th of March a correspondent wrote to the *Mercury* charging Mr. Powell with improper conduct toward Mrs. Abbot, a charge that he indignantly resented in the *Centinel.* Mrs. Abbot was the leading singer —*Rosetta* in "Love in a Village," *Leonora* in the "Padlock," *Molly Maybush* in the "Farmer," and *Margaretta* in "No Song No Supper." She seems to have been too gay for a community unused to the free manners of an easy-going actress, and she left the Boston stage at the close of the first season. There was probably no occasion to discipline the gentlemen in the orchestra. On the other hand, there was difficulty in restraining them from dismissing themselves. Their situation was not an enviable one. As early as the 20th of February the musicians printed a card in the newspapers begging the thoughtless or ill-disposed not to throw apples, stones and other missiles into the orchestra. While the brutality toward the orchestra indicated by this appeal was not confined to Boston, but was equally characteristic of New York and Philadelphia, the Boston gallery audience was the only one in the country at the time that assaulted the musicians merely for the sake of assaulting them. This reprehensible conduct emanated from a class that has

June 16—Rivals . . . . Sheridan
　　　(Mr. Bartlett's benefit.)
　18—Inkle and Yarico.
　　　Son-in-Law.
　　　(Mrs. Abbot's benefit.)
　23—Grecian Daughter . . . Murphy
　　　Old Maid.
　　　(Mrs. Baker's benefit.)
　25—Natural Son.
　　　Hunt the Slipper . . . . Knapp
　　　Examination of Dr. Last . Foote
　　　(Mr. Jones' benefit.)
　27—Road to Ruin . . . . . Holcroft
　　　Irish Tailor.
　　　(Mrs. Collins' benefit.)
　30—Three Weeks After Marriage
　　　　　　　　　　　　Murphy
　　　Waterman.
　　　All the World's a Stage . Jackman
　　　(Mr. Baker's benefit.)
July 4—Lyar . . . . Foote
　　　Poor Soldier.
　　　(Mr. Powell's benefit.)

entirely passed away—a class that Mrs. John Adams was, perhaps, justified in calling the "mobility." Some of the strictures upon the management from the better part of the patrons of the Boston Theatre are equally surprising. There was a loud complaint, for instance, that an old actor who had journeyed to Boston from a far country had been refused employment in the theatre. Between newspaper suggestions and strictures, and the quarrels and jealousies in his theatrical family, the manager had a lively time from the outset.

A preliminary address was, of course, a necessary incident of the opening, and a gold medal was offered as a prize by the proprietors for a poem suited to the occasion. There was a number of competitors, and the "rejected addresses" would themselves have filled a volume of verse. The prize was adjudged to Thomas Paine, a son of

Robert Treat Paine, one of the signers of the Declaration of Independence. This Prologue[1] was recited by Mr. Powell, who at his entry was received with a cordial welcome. Mr. Paine was a very young man. He had been carefully educated according to the classical methods of the time, and his smooth but pedantic verse shows the measure of his training. He was the first American youth to set him-

[1] PROLOGUE.

When first o'er Athens learning's dawning ray
Gleamed the dim twilight of the Attic day,
To charm, improve the hours of state repose,
The deathless father of the drama rose.
No gorgeous pageantry adorned the show,
The plot was simple and the scene was low;
Without the wardrobe of the Graces dress'd,
Without the mimic blush of art caress'd,
Heroic virtue held her throne secure,
For vice was modest and ambition poor.

But soon the muse, by nobler ardors fir'd,
To loftier heights of scenic verse aspir'd;
From useful life her comic fable rose,
And curbless passions form'd the tale of woes;
For daring drama heav'n itself explor'd,
And gods descending trod the Grecian board;
Each scene expanding through the temple swell'd,
Each bosom acted what each eye beheld;
Warm to the heart each chymic fiction stole,
And purg'd, by moral alchemy, the soul.

Hence artists grac'd and heroes nerv'd the age,
The sons or pupils of a patriot stage;
Hence in this forum of the virtues fir'd,
Hence in this school of eloquence inspir'd,
With bolder crest the dauntless warrior strode;
With nobler tongue the ardent statesman glow'd;
And Athens reign'd Minerva of the globe;
First in the helmet, fairest in the robe.

In arms she triumph'd, as in letters shone,
Of taste the palace, and of war the throne.
But lo! where rising in majestic flight,
The Roman eagle sails the expanse of light!
His wings, like heaven's vast canopy, unfurl'd,
Spread the broad plumage o'er the subject world.
Behold! he soars where golden Phœbus rolls,
And, perching on his car, o'erlooks the poles.
Far, as revolves the chariot's radiant way,
He wafts his empire o'er the tide of day;
From where it rolls on yon bright sea of suns,
To where in light's remotest ebb it runs.

The globe, half ravag'd by the storm of war,
The gates of Greece admit the victor's car;
Chain'd to his wheels is captive science led,
And taste, transplanted, blooms at Tiber's head.
O'er the rude minds of empire's hardy race
The op'ning pupil beam'd of letter'd grace;
With charms so sweet the houseless drama smil'd,
That Rome adopted Athens' orphan child.
Fledg'd by her hand, the Mantuan swan aspir'd;
Aw'd by her power, e'en Pompey's self retir'd;
Sheath'd was the sword by which the world had bled,
And Janus blushing to his temple fled.
The globe's proud butcher grew humanely brave;
Earth stanch'd her wounds, and ocean hush'd his wave.

self up as a professional dramatic critic; he was the first American journalist to go to the devil, allured by the lime-light of the stage. At a later period Mr. Paine, who had his name changed from Thomas to Robert Treat Paine, Jr., by the Massachusetts Legislature because he wanted a Christian name, married Miss Baker, of the theatre, whom he neglected for other actresses. Dunlap sketched him under a thin

At length, like huge Enceladus depress'd,
Groaning with slavery's mountain on their breast,
The supine nations struggled from disgrace;
And Rome, like Etna, totter'd from her base.
Thus set the sun of intellectual light,
And, wrapt in clouds, lower'd on the Gothic night.
Dark gloom'd the storm—the rushing torrent pour'd,
And wide the deep Cimmerian deluge shower'd;
E'en learning's loftiest hills were cover'd o'er,
And seas of dulness roll'd without a shore.
Yet ere the surge Parnassus' top o'erflow'd,
The banish'd muses fled their blest abode.
Frail was their ark the heaven-topped seas to brave,
The wind their compass, and their helm the wave;
No port to cheer them, and no star to guide,
From clime to clime they rov'd the billowy tide;
At length, by storms and tempests wafted o'er,
They found an Ararat on Albion's shore.

Yet long so sterile prov'd the ravag'd age,
That scarcely seem'd to vegetate the stage;
Nature, in dotage, second childhood mourn'd,
And to her infant cradle had return'd.
But hark! her mighty rival sweeps the strings—
Sweet Avon, flow not—'tis thy Shakspere sings!

With Blanchard's* wing, in fancy's heaven he soars;
With Herschel's eye another world explores!
Taught by the tones of his melodious song,
The scenic muses tun'd their barbarous tongue;
With subtle powers the crudest soul refin'd,
And warm'd the Zembla of the frozen mind.
The world's new queen, Augusta, own'd their charms,
And clasp'd the Grecian nymphs in British arms.
Then shone the drama with imperial art,
And made a province of the human heart.
What nerve of verse can sketch th' ecstatic view
When she and Garrick sigh'd their last adieu!
Description but a shadow's shade appears,
When Siddons looks a nation into tears!

But ah! while thus unrival'd reigns the muse,
Her soul o'erflows, and grief her face bedews;
Sworn at the altar proud oppression's foe,
She weeps indignant for her Britain's woe.
Long has she cast a fondly wishful eye
On the pure climate of this western sky;
And now while Europe bleeds at every vein,
And pinion'd forests shake the crimson'd main;
While Gallia, wall'd by foes, collected stands,
And hurls her thunders from a hundred hands;
Lur'd by a clime, where—hostile arms afar—
Peace rolls luxurious in her dove-drawn car;

* A noted balloonist.

disguise as one of the characters in his theatrical novel, " The Water
Drinker." Many of his criticisms were included in a volume of his
writings in prose and verse, published after his death, Boston, 1812.
An opponent of the theatre published a prologue in the newspapers,
taking as its motto one of Mr. Paine's lines, " Apollo consecrates thy

Where freedom first awoke the human mind,
And broke th' enchantment which enslav'd
    mankind ;
Behold, Apollo seeks this liberal plain,
And brings the Thespian goddess in his train.
Oh, happy realm, to whom are richly given
The noblest bounties of indulgent heaven ;
For whom has earth her wealthiest mine be-
    stow'd,
And commerce bridg'd old ocean's broadest
    flood !
To you, a stranger guest, the drama flies,
An angel wanderer in a pilgrim's guise !
To charm the fancy and to feast the heart,
She spreads the banquet of the scenic art.
By you supported, shall her infant stage
Portray, adorn and regulate the age.
When faction rages with intemperate sway,
And gray-hair'd vices shame the face of day,
Drawn from their covert to th' indignant pit,
Be such the game to stock the park of wit ;
That park where genius all his shafts may
    draw,
Nor dread the terrors of a forest law.
But not to scenes of 'pravity confin'd,
Here polish'd life an ample field shall find ;
Reflected here, its fair perspective, view
The stage, the camera—the landscape, you.
    Ye lovely fair, whose circling beauties shine
A radiant galaxy of charms divine ;
Whose gentle hearts those tender scenes ap-
    prove,
Where pity begs, or kneels adoring love ;
Ye sons of sentiment, whose bosoms fire
The song of pathos and the epic lyre ;

Whose glowing souls with tragic grandeur
    rise,
When bleeds a hero or a nation dies ;
And ye, who thron'd on high a synod sit,
And rule the lofty atmosphere of wit ;
From whom a flash of comic lightning draws
A bursting thunder-clap of loud applause ;
If here those eyes, whose tears, with peerless
    sway
Have wept the vices of an age away ;
If here those lips, whose smiles, with magic
    art,
Have .laugh'd the foibles from the cheated
    heart ;
On mirth's gay cheek can one gay dimple
    light ;
In sorrow's breast one passion'd sigh excite :
With nobler streams the buskin's grief shall
    fall ;
With pangs sublimer throb this breathing
    wall ;
Thalia, too, more blithe, shall trip the stage,
Of care the wrinkles smooth, and thaw the
    veins of age.
    And now, thou dome, by Freedom's patrons
    rear'd,
With beauty blazon'd and by taste rever'd ;
Apollo consecrates thy walls profane,—
Hence be thou sacred to the muses' reign !
In thee three ages shall in one conspire ;
A Sophocles shall swell his chasten'd lyre ;
A Terence rise in native charms serene ;
A Sheridan display the perfect scene :
And Athens, Rome, Augusta, blush to see
Their virtues, beauty, grace, all shine—com-
    bin'd in thee.

walls profane." This was, at least, equal in literary merit to Mr. Paine's poem—it was not nearly so long as the prologue actually recited, and but for the "ifs" that implied immorality, it would have been more appropriate to the occasion—

> If, borne from far, the wit of Albion's race,
> As dissolute as gay, these walls disgrace;
> If foreign brogues and foreign manners strive
> Your speed to dictate, and the *ton* to give;
> If alien vices, here unknown before,
> Come, shameless, to pollute Columbia's shore;
> *   *   *   *   *   *   *
> O, may the lightning rend these walls profane,
> And desolation o'er the ruins reign.

The theatre as a school of vice was an assumption that at that time was generally answered by the counter-assumption that a well-regulated stage was a school of virtue. That, in fact, the playhouse was simply a place for intellectual amusement that would only reflect its environment, was a view of the subject seldom urged. But the management of the Boston Theatre certainly showed the highest respect for religion and its temples; and when the Rev. Jeremiah Belknap, D.D., chose to lecture in the church in Federal Street on a playnight the Federal Street playhouse was closed. The choice of the opening play, "Gustavus Vasa," a hundred years later would have been considered inadmissible, but in the first decade of the

GUSTAVUS VASA.

Gustavus	Mr. Baker
Trollio	Mr. Jones
Adolphus	Mr. Collins
Anderson	Mr. Nelson
Laertes	Mr. Bartlett
Christiern	Mr. Powell
Arvida	Mr. S. Powell
Sivard	Mr. Kenny
Christina	Miss Harrison
Mariana	Mrs. Jones
Augusta	Mrs. Baker
Child	Miss Cordelia Powell

(First appearance on any stage.)

MODERN ANTIQUES.

Mr. Cockletop	Mr. Jones
Frank	Mr. S. Powell
Napkin	Mr. Collins
Hearty	Mr. Nelson
Joey	Mr. Baker
Mrs. Cockletop	Miss Baker
Mrs. Camomile	Mrs. Baker
Nan	Mrs. Jones
Belinda	Mrs. Collins

Republic it was somehow considered typical of American patriotism. "Modern Antiques," the afterpiece, a merry farce by O'Keefe, first acted at Covent Garden in 1789, was a happier selection, especially as this was its first production in America. One of the Boston critics said that as *Christiern* Mr. Powell added to his previous reputation; as *Gustavus* Mr. Baker was all that could be expected; and as *Arvida* Mr. S. Powell was true to nature and made a deep and favorable impression. The ladies were received with greater warmth. Of Miss Harrison as *Christina* the critic declared it might be said, "Majestic was her form—her every action dignity and grace;" Mrs. Jones' part could not have been better filled, and Mrs. Baker's dignity of character, propriety of action and maternal tenderness at once charmed and affected. In the farce, too, the commendation was hearty. Jones as *Cockletop* appeared a genuine son of the sock; Baker as *Joey* "made the muscles of every face vibrate in unison with his own;" S. Powell displayed the genteel comedian to great advantage; and Mrs. Collins appeared to possess the *naivete* of a live actress. Miss Baker was praised for the graces of an elegant person and beauty of features, but regret was expressed that the amiable modesty of the woman proved a barrier to the fine accomplishments of the actress.

MIDNIGHT HOUR.

Marquis	Mr. S. Powell
Sebastian	Mr. Powell
Nicholas	Mr. Jones
Ambrose	Mr. Collins
Matthias	Mr. Kenny
Don Guzman . . .	Mr. Baker
Julia	Miss Baker
Cicely	Mrs. Baker
Flora	Mrs. Powell

NATURAL SON.

Sir Jeffrey Latimer .	Mr. Baker
Blushenly	Mr. Bartlett
Jack Hastings . .	Mr. S. Powell
Major O'Flaherty .	Mr. Collins
Dumps	Mr. Jones
David	Mr. Kenny
Rueful	Mr. Powell
Lady Paragon .	Miss Harrison
Penelope	Mrs. Abbott
Mrs. Phœbe Latimer,	Mrs. Baker

Among the pieces produced at the Boston Theatre this season there were six that anticipated by their first performance in Boston their American production both in Philadelphia and New York. These, taking them in the order of their presentation, were Mrs. Inchbald's "Midnight Hour," a well-contrived and pleasant entertainment from a French piece by M. Damaniant; Cumberland's " Natural Son," a comedy very lively and entertaining in the first and second acts, but in consequence of forced incidents and embarrassing situations a trial to the patience of an audience in the remaining three; " Barnaby Brittle," originally presented for Mr. Quick's benefit at Covent Garden in 1781, a farce taken from Betterton's "Amorous Widow," but based on Moliere's " George Dandin;" Oulton's "All in Good Humor," a little piece in one act, light in texture but entertaining; O'Keefe's "Son-in-Law," one of his most successful musical farces; and Mrs. Inchbald's

BARNABY BRITTLE.

Barnaby Brittle . .	Mr. Jones
Sir Peter Pride . .	Mr. Kenny
Jeremy	Mr. S. Powell
Lovemore	Mr. Bartlett
Jeffrey	Mr. Nelson
Clodpole	Mr. Baker
Mrs. Brittle . .	Miss Harrison
Lady Pride . . .	Mrs. Baker
Damaris	Mrs. Collins

SON-IN-LAW.

Old Cranky . . .	Mr. Kenny
Bowkitt	Mr. Jones
Orator Mum . . .	Mr. Powell
Vinegar	Mr. S. Powell
Idle	Mr. Baker
Bouquett : . . .	Mr. Collins
Sig. Arionelli . .	Mr. Bartlett
Cecilia	Mrs. Abbott

ALL IN GOOD HUMOR.

Chagrin	Mr. Baker
Squire Hairbrain .	Mr. S. Powell
Bellamy	Mr. Bartlett
Robin	Mr. Jones
Crop	Mr. Nelson
Mrs. Chagrin . .	Mrs. Baker
Sophia	Miss Baker
Dorothy	Mrs. Abbot

ANIMAL MAGNETISM.

Doctor	Mr. Jones
Marquis	Mr. Bartlett
Jeffrey	Mr. S. Powell
Picard	Mr. Kenny
La Fleur	Mr. Powell
Constance . . .	Miss Harrison
Lissette	Mrs. Jones

" Animal Magnetism," from the French, intended to ridicule hypnotism as then received. To these may be added the " Irish Tailor," presented for Mrs. Collins' benefit with Collins as *Roger McStrong*, Bartlett as *Captain Bounce*, and Miss Baker as *Betty*. In these casts are the names of a number of performers who were in neither of the pieces on the opening night—Mr. Bartlett, of whom one of the critics said he was new to the stage, young, extremely modest and knew his parts; Mrs. Powell, a happy acquisition, easy, natural and engaging; Mrs. Jones, modest, delicate and amiable; and Mrs. Abbot, "a siren of whose style of singing we could have formed no idea." Apparently, the siren had already begun to practise a siren's arts, for the critic added, "We trust her propriety of conduct will confirm the admiration her wonderful powers have excited."

The number of casts printed in the newspapers or otherwise accessible was unusually large. Arranged below in alphabetical order,

BOSTON THEATRE CASTS—FIRST SEASON.

AGREEABLE SURPRISE.

Sir Felix Friendly	Mr. Kenny
Compton	Mr. Collins
Eugene	Mr. Bartlett
Chicane	Mr. Nelson
Thomas	Mr. Baker
John	Mr. S. Powell
Lingo	Mr. Jones
Laura	Mrs. Abbot
Mrs. Cheshire	Mrs. Baker
Fringe	Mrs. Collins
Cowslip	Mrs. Jones

ALL THE WORLD'S A STAGE.

Charles Stanley	Mr. S. Powell
Sir Gilbert Pumpkin	Mr. Kenny
Diggory	Mr. Baker
Simon	Mr. Bartlett
Wat	Mr. Collins
Harry Stukely	Mr. Powell
Miss Bridget	Mrs. Baker
Kitty Sprightly	Miss Harrison

BARBAROSSA.

Barbarossa	Mr. Baker
Othman	Mr. Collins
Sadi	Mr. Bartlett
Aladin	Mr. Kenny
Selim	Mr. S. Powell
Zaphira	Mrs. Baker
Irene	Miss Harrison

BELLE'S STRATAGEM.

Doricourt	Mr. S. Powell
Sir Geo. Touchwood	Mr. Baker
Flutter	Mr. Powell
Saville	Mr. Bartlett
Villers	Mr. Nelson
Courtall	Mr. Collins
Hardy	Mr. Jones
Letitia Hardy	Mrs. Powell
Mrs. Racket	Mrs. Collins
Miss Ogle	Mrs. Abbot
Lady Frances	Mrs. Jones

BOLD STROKE FOR A WIFE.

Colonel Fainwell	Mr. S. Powell
Obadiah Prim	Mr. Baker
Sir Philip Modelove	Mr. Nelson
Tradelove	Mr. Collins
Freeman	Mr. Bartlett
Sackbut	Mr. Kenny
Periwinkle	Mr. Jones
Mrs. Prim	Mrs. Baker
Betty	Miss Baker
Masked Lady	Mrs. Collins
Ann Lovely	Miss Harrison

BON TON.

Sir John Trotley	Mr. Jones
Lord Minikin	Mr. S. Powell
Colonel Tivy	Mr. Collins
Jessamy	Mr. Bartlett
Mignion	Mr. Kenny
Davy	Mr. Powell
Lady Minikin	Mrs. Jones
Gymp	Mrs. Abbot
Miss Tittup	Miss Harrison

BUSYBODY.

Sir George Airy	Mr. S. Powell
Sir Francis Gripe	Mr. Jones
Sir Jealous Traffic	Mr. Nelson
Charles	Mr. Bartlett
Whisper	Mr. Collins
Butler	Mr. Kenny
Marplot	Mr. Powell
Miranda	Miss Harrison
Isabinda	Miss Baker
Scentwell	Mrs. Abbot
Patch	Mrs. Jones

CHAPTER OF ACCIDENTS.

Woodville	Mr. S. Powell
Gov. Harcourt	Mr. Baker
Lord Glenmore	Mr. Collins
Capt. Harcourt	Mr. Bartlett
Grey	Mr. Kenny
Vane	Mr. Nelson
Jacob Gawkey	Mr. Jones
Cecilia	Miss Harrison
Miss Mortimer	Miss Baker
Mrs. Warner	Mrs. Abbot
Bridget	Mrs. Powell

CHILD OF NATURE.

Marquis	Mr. Powell
Count Valentia	Mr. S. Powell
Peasant	Mr. Baker
Seville	Mr. Kenny
Granada	Mr. Bartlett
Duke Murcia	Mr. Jones
Marchioness	Mrs. Baker
Amanthis	Miss Harrison

they show the class of work performed by each member of the company during the season. There were in the company only two persons who attained distinction—Mr. S. Powell and Miss Harrison, who became his wife. Mrs. Abbot might, perhaps, have become a favorite had she not fallen under the ban—as it was, she retired at the close of the season, and her history is in her parts in these casts. Mr. Nelson joined the Old American Company in Philadelphia in the Autumn, and the Bakers also retired in consequence of a disagreement with Mr. Powell, the manager, which, like all theatrical quarrels since, was

BOSTON THEATRE CASTS—FIRST SEASON.

CITIZEN.

Young Philpot . . Mr. S. Powell
Young Wilding . . . Mr. Collins
Sir Jasper . . . . . . Mr. Kenny
Beaufort . . . . . . Mr. Bartlett
Quilldrive . . . . . Mr. Nelson
Old Philpot . . . . . Mr. Jones
Corinna . . . . . . Mrs. Abbot
Maria . . . . Mrs. Collins

CLANDESTINE MARRIAGE.

Lord Ogilby . . . . Mr. Powell
Sterling . . . . . . Mr. Kenny
Sir John Melville . . Mr. Collins
Canton . . . . Mr. Jones
Brush . . . . Mr. Baker
Sergeant Flower . . Mr. Bartlett
Lovewell . . . . . Mr. S. Powell
Miss Sterling . . . . Mrs. Powell
Mrs. Heidelberg . . Mrs. Baker
Betty . . . . Mrs. Collins
Nancy . . . . Mrs. Jones
Trusty . . . . Miss Baker
Fanny . . . . . . Miss Harrison

DOUGLAS.

Young Norval . . Mr. S. Powell
Old Norval . . . . . Mr. Jones
Officer . . . . . . Mr. Kenny
Glenalvon . . . . . . Mr. Powell
Lord Randolph . . . Mr. Collins
Lady Randolph . . Mrs. Powell
Anna . . . . Miss Baker

DRUMMER.

Tinsel . . . . . . Mr. S. Powell
Trueman . . . . . Mr. Kenny
Fantome . . . . . . Mr. Collins
Gardener . . . . . . Mr. Baker
Coachman . . . . . Mr. Nelson
Butler . . . . Mr. Bartlett
Vellum . . . . Mr. Jones
Lady Trueman . . . Miss Baker
Abagail . . . . Mrs. Baker

FARMER.

Farmer Blackberry . Mr. Collins
Capt. Valentine . . . Mr. Nelson
Col. Dormant . . Mr. S. Powell
Fairly . . . . Mr. Kenny
Rundy . . . . Mr. Bartlett
Flummery . . . . . . Mr. Baker
Jemmy Jumps . . . Mr. Jones
Betty Blackberry . . Mrs. Baker
Louisa . . . . Miss Baker
Molly Maybush . . . Mrs. Abbot

FOUNDLING.

Young Belmont . . Mr. S. Powell
Sir Charles Raymond . Mr. Baker
Sir Roger Belmont . . Mr. Jones
Colonel Raymond . . Mr. Collins
Villard . . . . Mr. Kenny
Faddle . . . . Mr. Powell
Rosetta . . . . . Miss Harrison
Fidelia . . . . Miss Baker

GEORGE BARNWELL.

George Barnwell . Mr. S. Powell

Trueman . . . . . Mr. Bartlett
Uncle . . . . Mr. Collins
Blunt . . . . Mr. Nelson
Constable . . . . . Mr. Kenny
Thoroughgood . . . . Mr. Baker
Millwood . . . . . . Mrs. Powell
Lucy . . . . . . Mrs. Collins
Maria . . . . . . Miss Harrison

GRECIAN DAUGHTER.

Evander . . . . Mr. Jones
Phocion . . . . . Mr. S. Powell
Philotas . . . . . . Mr. Bartlett
Melanthon . . . . . Mr. Collins
Calippus . . . . . . Mr. Kenny
Dionysius . . . . . . Mr. Baker
Erixene . . . . . . Miss Baker
Euphrasia . . . . . Mrs. Baker

HAMLET.

Hamlet . . . . Mr. Powell
King . . . . Mr. Collins
Polonius . . . . . . Mr. Jones
Horatio . . . . Mr. Kenny
Laertes . . . . . Mr. S. Powell
Rosencranz . . . . Mr. Bartlett
Guildenstern . . . . Mr. Nelson
Ghost . . . . Mr. Baker
Queen . . . . . . Mrs. Baker
Player Queen . . . . Mrs. Abbot
Ophelia . . . . . . Miss Baker

HUNT THE SLIPPER.

Captain Clement . . Mr. Collins
Glib . . . . Mr. Bartlett
Billy Bustle . . . . Mr. Jones

fought out in the newspapers.   Somehow, neither Mrs. Baker nor her daughter found favor with the critics, and Miss Baker's attempts at leading roles were dealt with with especial severity.   When "Hamlet" was played it was asked, " Why was not Miss Harrison or Mrs. Abbot

BOSTON THEATRE CASTS—FIRST SEASON.

INKLE AND YARICO.

Inkle . . . . Mr. Powell
Curry . . . . Mr. Baker
Campley . . . . . . Mr. Bartlett
Medium . . . . . . Mr. Kenny
Mate . . . . Mr. Collins
Trudge . . . . Mr. Jones
Yarico . . . . Mrs. Baker
Narcissa . . . . . . Miss Baker
Patty . . . . Mrs. Jones
Wowski . . . . . . Mrs. Abbot

LOVE IN A VILLAGE.

Young Meadows . . Mr. Bartlett
Woodcock . . . . . Mr. Powell
Hawthorn . . . . . Mr. Collins
Eustace . . . . . . Mr. Nelson
Sir William . . . . . Mr. Kenny
Hodge . . . . Mr. Jones
Rosetta . . . . . . Mrs. Abbot
Lucinda . . . . . . Miss Baker
Madge . . . . Mrs. Baker
Mrs. Deborah . . . Mrs. Powell

LYAR.

Young Wilding . . Mr. S. Powell
Old Wilding . . . . Mr. Powell
Sir James Elliott . . Mr. Bartlett
Papillion . . . . . . Mr. Powell
Miss Grantham . . Miss Harrison
Miss Godfrey . . . . Miss Baker
Kitty . . . . Mrs. Collins

LYING VALET.

Sharp . . . . Mr. Powell
Guttle . . . . Mr. Baker
Trippet . . . . . . Mr. Bartlett
Drunken Cook . . . Mr. Kenny
Gayless . . . . . . Mr. S. Powell
Melissa   . . . . Miss Harrison
Mrs. Gadabout . . . Mrs. Baker
Mrs. Trippet . .   . Mrs. Jones
Kitty Pry . . . . . Mrs. Powell

MIDAS.

Jupiter . . . . Mr. Nelson
Juno . . . . Miss Baker
Apollo . . . . Mr. Bartlett
Pan . . . . Mr. Collins
Midas . . . . Mr. Jones
Sileno . . . . Mr. Powell
Damætus . . . . . Mr. Kenny
Daphne . . . . . . Mrs. Powell
Mysis . . . . Mrs. Baker
Nysa . . . . Mrs. Abbot

MILLER OF MANSFIELD.

King . . . . Mr. S. Powell
Dick . . . . Mr. Kenny
Lurewell . . . . . Mr. Bartlett
Joe . . . . Mr. Nelson
Miller . . . . Mr. Jones
Madge . . . . Mrs. Baker
Peggy . . . . Miss Baker
Kate . . . . Mrs. Powell

MISS IN HER TEENS.

Captain Flash . . . . Mr. Jones
Captain Loveit . . . Mr. Collins
Puff . . . . Mr. Kenny
Fribble . . . . . Mr. Powell
Tag . . . . Mrs. Baker
Miss Biddy . . . . Mrs. Collins

MOURNING BRIDE.

King . . . . Mr. Collins
Gonzales . . . . . . Mr. Jones
Garcia . . . . . . Mr. Bartlett
Alonzo . . . . Mr. Baker
Selim . . . . Mr. Powell
Hali . . . . Mr. Kenny
Osmyn . . . . . . Mr. S. Powell
Almeria . . . . . . Mrs. Jones
Leonora . . . . . Miss Baker
Zara . . . . Miss Harrison

NO SONG NO SUPPER.

Robin . . . . Mr. Jones
Frederick . . . . . Mr. Bartlett
Endless . . . . . . Mr. Baker

William . . . . Mr. Collins
Thomas . . . . . . Mr. Kenny
Crop . . . . Mr. Nelson
Dorothy . . . . . . Mrs. Baker
Louisa . . . . Miss Baker
Nelly . . . . Mrs Collins
Margaretta . . . . Mrs. Abbot

OLD MAID.

Clerimont . . . . Mr. S. Powell
Harlow . . . . Mr. Collins
Captain Cape . . . Mr. Baker
Mrs. Harlow . . . Miss Harrison
Trifle . . . . Mrs. Abbot
Miss Harlow . . . . Mrs. Baker

PADLOCK.

Don Diego . . . . Mr. Kenny
Leander . . . . . . Mr. Nelson
Scholar . . . . . . Mr. Bartlett
Mungo . . . . Mr. Powell
Leonora . . . . . Mrs. Abbot
Ursula . . . . Mrs. Baker

POOR SOLDIER.

Patrick . . . . Mr. Nelson
Dermot . . . . . . Mr. Bartlett
Fitzroy . . . . . . Mr. Kenny
Bagatelle . . . . . Mr. Powell
Father Luke . . . . Mr. Collins
Darby . . . . Mr. Jones
Norah . . . . Mrs. Abbot
Kathleen . . . . . . Mrs. Jones

PROVOKED HUSBAND.

Lord Townly . . . . Mr. Powell
Manly . . . . . . Mr. S. Powell
Sir Francis . . . . . . Mr. Baker
Basset . . . . Mr. Collins
John Moody . . . . Mr. Kenny
James . . . . Mr. Bartlett
Squire Richard . . . . Mr. Jones
Lady Townly . . . Mrs. Powell
Lady Grace . . . Miss Harrison
Lady Wronghead . . Mrs. Baker

cast for *Ophelia* instead of Miss Baker? Why was not Mrs. Powell the *Queen* instead of Mrs. Baker?" But the Baker family did not fail to make a determined effort to establish themselves in the esteem of the Boston public. Mrs. Baker for her benefit attempted the trying

BOSTON THEATRE CASTS—FIRST SEASON.

Myrtilla . . . . . . Miss Baker
Trusty . . . . Mrs. Abbot
Miss Jenny . . . . Mrs. Collins

QUAKER.

Steady . . . . Mr. Collins
Solomon . . . . Mr. Jones
Farmer Easy . . . . Mr. Kenny
Lubin . . . . Mr. Nelson
Gillian . . . . Mrs. Abbot
Cicely . . . . Mrs. Baker
Floretta . . . . . . Mrs. Powell

REVENGE.

Don Alonzo . . . . A Gentleman
Don Carlos . . . . . Mr. Bartlett
Don Alvarez . . . . . Mr. Baker
Manuel . . . . Mr. Kenny
Zanga . . . . Mr. Powell
Leonora . . . . . Miss Harrison
Isabella . . . . . . Mrs. Baker

RICHARD III.

Richard . . . . . . Mr. Powell
Henry VI . . . . . . Mr. Jones
Prince of Wales . . A Debutante
Duke of York . . Miss C. Powell
Buckingham . . . Mr. S. Powell
Stanley . . . . . . Mr. Kenny
Lieutenant . . . . . Mr. Collins
Catesby . . . . . . Mr. Bartlett
Ratcliffe . . . . . . Mr. Nelson
Richmond . . . . . . Mr. Baker
Queen Elizabeth . . Mrs. Powell
Lady Anne . . . . Miss Harrison
Duchess of York . . Mrs. Baker

ROAD TO RUIN.

Goldfinch . . . . Mr. S. Powell
Sulky . . . . Mr. Powell
Dornton . . . . . . Mr. Kenny
Harry Dornton . . . Mr. Collins
Milford . . . . . . Mr. Bartlett
Mr. Smith . . . . . . Mr. Baker
Silky . . . . Mr. Jones
Mrs. Warren . . . . Mrs. Baker

Mrs. Ledger . . . . Mrs. Powell
Jenny . . . . Miss Baker
Sophia . . . . . . Mrs. Collins

ROMEO AND JULIET.

Romeo . . . . . . Mr. S. Powell
Mercutio . . . . . . Mr. Powell
Capulet . . . . Mr. Baker
Montagu . . . . . . Mr. Kenny
Tybalt . . . . Mr. Collins
Benvolio . . . . . . Mr. Nelson
Paris . . . . Mr. Bartlett
Friar Laurence . . . . Mr. Jones
Juliet . . . . . . Miss Harrison
Lady Capulet . . . . Mrs. Baker
Nurse . . . . Mrs. Powell

SCHOOL FOR SCANDAL.

Sir Peter Teazle . . . Mr. Jones
Sir Oliver Surface . . Mr. Baker
Joseph Surface . . . Mr. Collins
Charles Surface . . Mr. S. Powell
Crabtree . . . . . . Mr. Kenny
Sir Benjamin . . . . Mr. Bartlett
Rowley . . . . . . Mr. Powell
Careless . . . . Mr. Nelson
Mrs. Candour . . . Mrs. Powell
Maria . . . . Miss Baker
Lady Sneerwell . . . Mrs. Baker
Lady Teazle . . . Miss Harrison

SHE STOOPS TO CONQUER.

Young Marlow . . Mr. S. Powell
Hardcastle . . . . . Mr. Nelson
Hastings . . . . . . Mr. Collins
Sir Charles Marlow . Mr. Kenny
Diggory . . . . Mr. Baker
Roger . . . . Mr. Bartlett
Tony Lumpkin . . . . Mr. Jones
Mrs. Hardcastle . . Mrs. Baker
Miss Neville . . . . Miss Baker
Pimple . . . . Mrs. Abbot
Miss Hardcastle . Miss Harrison

THREE WEEKS AFTER MARRIAGE.

Sir Charles Racket . Mr. S. Powell

Woodley . . . . . . Mr. Bartlett
Drugget . . . . . . Mr. Kenny
Lady Racket . . . Miss Harrison
Mrs. Drugget . . . . Mrs. Baker
Nancy . . . . Mrs. Collins
Dimitry . . . . . . Miss Baker

VIRGIN UNMASKED.

Goodwill . . . . . . Mr. Kenny
Blister . . . . Mr. Baker
Quaver . . . . . . Mr. Bartlett
Thomas . . . . . . Mr. Nelson
Coupee . . . . Mr. Jones
Miss Lucy . . . . . Miss Baker

WATERMAN.

Tom Tug . . . . . . Mr. Jones
Bundle . . . . Mr. Collins
Robin . . . . Mr. Powell
Mrs. Bundle . . . . Mrs. Baker
Wilhelmina . . . . . Miss Baker

WAYS AND MEANS.

Sir David Dunder . . Mr. Jones
Young Random . . . Mr. Collins
Scruple . . . . . . Mr. Bartlett
Old Random . . . . Mr. Kenny
Paul Peery . . . . . Mr. Baker
Carney . . . . Mr. Nelson
Tiptoe . . . . . . Mr. S. Powell
Lady Dunder . . . . Mrs. Baker
Kitty . . . . Mrs. Collins
Harriet . . . . . Miss Harrison

WEST INDIAN.

Belcour . . . . . Mr. S. Powell
Stockwell . . . . . . Mr. Baker
Varland . . . . Mr. Jones
Captain Dudley . . Mr. Nelson
Charles Dudley . . Mr. Bartlett
Fulmer . . . . Mr. Kenny
Major O'Flaherty . . Mr. Collins
Miss Rusport . . . . Mrs. Powell
Lady Rusport . . . Mrs. Baker
Mrs. Fulmer . . . . Mrs. Abbot

part of *Euphrasia* in the "Grecian Daughter," and for his benefit on the 30th of June Mr. Baker presented a bill in which both his wife and daughter had ample opportunity to display their powers in comedy roles. He began the evening's entertainment with an original panto-mimical prologue by a gentleman of Boston—probably young Paine, who was already warmly interested in Miss Baker. Two of the pieces, Murphy's little comedy, "Three Weeks After Marriage" and Jack-man's farce, "All the World's a Stage," had often been produced else-where, but this was their first production in Boston; and the perform-ance of Dibdin's ballad opera, the "Waterman," had been anticipated in New York only within a year and in Philadelphia by only a week. As *Wilhelmina* Miss Baker had an opportunity that neither Mrs. Hodgkinson nor Miss Broadhurst disdained, but nothing availed to ex-cite interest in behalf of an actress who had dared to fascinate the son of a Signer of the Declaration of Independence. The Signer himself was implacable. Miss Eliza Baker, handsome, amiable and intelligent, was only sixteen when she came to Boston; she was married a year later, in February, 1795. In consequence young Paine was expelled from his father's house, and it was not until 1798 that there was a reconciliation. Mr. Baker afterward kept a hotel in Boston, and Mrs. Baker returned to the stage in 1796. Miss Baker's stage history ends here.

BOSTON THEATRE CASTS—FIRST SEASON.

Lucy . . . . Miss Baker	Kitty . . . . Mrs. Collins	WONDER.
Louisa Dudley . . Miss Harrison	Miss Johnstone . . . Mrs. Abbot	Don Felix . . . . Mr. S. Powell
	Sophy Pendragon . . Mrs. Jones	Colonel Briton . . . . Mr. Collins
WHICH IS THE MAN?		Don Pedro . . . . . . Mr. Jones
Lord Sparkle . . . Mr. S. Powell		Don Lopez . . . . . Mr. Nelson
Beauchamp . . . . . Mr. Collins	WHO'S THE DUPE?	Gibby . . . . Mr. Baker
Bobby Pendragon . . Mr. Jones	Gradus . . . . Mr. Jones	Frederick . . . . . Mr. Bartlett
Belville . . . . . . Mr. Bartlett	Sanford . . . . Mr. Collins	Alguazil . . . . . . Mr. Kenny
Servant . . . . Mr. Kenny	Granger . . . Mr. S. Powell	Lissardo . . . . . . Mr. Powell
Fitzherbert . . . . . Mr. Powell	Doiley . . . . . . Mr. Powell	Violante . . . . . Miss Harrison
Lady Bell Bloomer, Miss Harrison	Servant . . . . Mr. Kenny	Isabinda . . . . . . Miss Baker
Julia . . . . Miss Baker	Charlotte . . . . . . Mrs. Jones	Inis . . . . Mrs. Collins
Clarinda . . . . . . Mrs. Baker	Miss Doiley . . . Miss Harrison	Flora . . . . Mrs. Jones

The season had not been remarkably successful. Even the benefit for the American prisoners in Algiers yielded only $887.28, which was considered a very large sum. The company had not proved adequate, and it may be doubted whether even the injunction of the low comedian's benefit advertisement received a decided affirmative response—

> Then go and tell your favorite, Jones,
> That Boston his great merit owns.

After the first season ended, on the 4th of July, 1794, the Boston Theatre remained closed until the 15th of December following. In the meantime Mr. Powell made a voyage to England in search of recruits, returning with Messrs. Hipworth, Taylor, Villiers and Heeley, Mr. and Mrs. Hughes, Mrs. Hellyer, afterward Mrs. Graupner, and Miss Harrison, afterward Mrs. Dickenson. This second group of English acquisitions was like the first without previous reputation, but some of them had had considerable experience in the provincial theatres, and were not without merit. Mr. Hipworth possessed more than ordinary talent, and his conduct was exemplary, both as an actor and a man. Mr. Taylor proved more than an acceptable substitute

LIST OF PERFORMANCES.

1794.
Dec. 15—As You Like It . . . Shakspere
 Rosina . . . Mrs. Brooke
 17—Manager in Distress . . Colman
 As You Like It.
 Romp . . . . Bickerstaff
 19—Jew . . . . Cumberland
 Who's the Dupe ? . Mrs. Cowley
 24—Jew.
 Bon Ton . . . . . . Garrick
 27—Dramatist . . . . . . Reynolds
 Modern Antiques . . . O'Keefe
 29—Jew.
 Farmer . . . . O'Keefe
 31—Dramatist.
 Farmer.
1795.
Jan. 2—Jew.
 Poor Soldier . . . . . O'Keefe
 5—Such Things Are . Mrs. Inchbald
 Wrangling Lovers . . . . Lyon
 7—Such Things Are.
 Romp.
 9—George Barnwell . . . . . Lillo
 Lying Valet . . . . . . Garrick
 12—Every One Has His Fault
 Mrs. Inchbald
 Rosina.

Jan. 14—Dramatist.
    Barnaby Brittle . . . . Betterton
    17—Every One Has His Fault.
    Rosina.
    19—Every One Has His Fault.
    Deaf Lover . . . . Pilon
    21—Jew.
    Ways and Means . . Colman, Jr
    23—Inkle and Yarico . . Colman, Jr
    Midnight Hour . . Mrs. Inchbald
    26—Henry IV . . . . Shakspere
    Wrangling Lovers.
    28—West Indian . . . . Cumberland
    Miller of Mansfield . . Dodsley
    30—Wild Oats . . . . . O'Keefe
    Waterman . . . . Dibdin
Feb. 2—Every One Has His Fault.
    Mock Doctor . . . . . Fielding
    4—Wild Oats.
    All in Good Humor . . . Oulton
    6—Inkle and Yarico.
    Midnight Hour.
    9—Child of Nature . . Mrs. Inchbald
    Village Lawyer . . . Macready
    11—Rivals . . . . Sheridan
    Irishman in London . . Macready
    13—Young Quaker . . . . O'Keefe
    Village Lawyer.
    16—Jew.
    Padlock . . . . . . Bickerstaff
    18—Young Quaker.
    Irishman in London.
    20—Road to Ruin . . . . . Holcroft
    Village Lawyer.
    23—Romeo and Juliet . . Shakspere
    Seeing is Believing . . . Joddrell
    25—School for Scandal . . Sheridan
    Lying Valet.
March 2—Medium.
    4—Every One Has His Fault.
    All the World's a Stage . Jackman
    6—Beaux' Stratagem . . . Farquhar
    Poor Soldier.
    9—How to Grow Rich . . Reynolds
    Ways and Means.
    11—She Stoops to Conquer . Goldsmith
    Farmer.

for Baker, and Mrs. Hellyer eclipsed Mrs. Abbot as the leading singer of the company. During the vacation Snelling Powell married Miss Harrison, and the new Miss Harrison was her sister. The members of the original company retained were Mr. and Mrs. Powell, Mr. and Mrs. S. Powell, Mr. and Mrs. Jones, Mr. and Mrs. Collins and Messrs. Bartlett and Kenny. One or two trial nights were accorded to aspirants during the season. On the 29th of December a Mr. Clifford made his first appearance as *Captain Valentine* in the " Farmer." Notwithstanding it was said that his style of singing was that of the most approved masters, and his execution superior to any yet heard on the Boston boards, his name does not again occur in the bills. Subsequently, on the 6th of May, Mrs. Spencer, announced as from New York and the Theatre Royal, Edinburgh, made her Boston *debut* as *Juliet.* She had been coldly received in New York, but she was hailed with raptures in Boston. Young Paine, who had established the *Orrery* as his theatrical mouthpiece, declared her success a prodigy. She was mistress of the graces of the stage, he said—perfect in the letter of her author, and communicating his spirit with the most pointed elocution. Mrs. Spencer was afterward seen at the benefits as *Belvidera* in " Venice Preserved," *Mrs. Strickland* in the " Suspicious Husband," the *Queen* in " Hamlet," and *Miss Nancy* in " Neck or Nothing." She was accorded a benefit on the 5th of June, with " Percy " and the " Midnight Hour " as the bill. As a matter of course, she played *Elmira* in Miss More's tragedy. On the 15th of June a performance was given for the relief of sufferers by fire in Boston, when the receipts were $666.00. When the " Agreeable Surprise " was given as the afterpiece to the " Contrast," for Mr.

Mar. 13—Busybody . . . . Mrs. Centlivre
Deuce is in Him . . . . Colman
16—How to Grow Rich.
Deuce is in Him.
18—Romeo and Juliet.
Three Weeks After Marriage
Murphy
20—Wild Oats.
Old Maid . . . . Murphy
23—Natural Son . . . . Cumberland
Padlock.
25—Cato . . . . Addison
Miss in Her Teens . . . Garrick
27—Road to Ruin.
Prize . . . . Hoare
30—Cato.
Prize.
April 1—Inkle and Yarico.
Virgin Unmasked . . . Fielding
6—Mountaineers . . . . Colman, Jr
8—Mountaineers.
Miller of Mansfield.
13—Mountaineers.
As It Should Be . . . . Oulton
15—Mountaineers.
17—Mountaineers.
20—Mountaineers.
Deuce is in Him
22—Dramatist.
Midas . . . . O'Hara
24—Belle's Stratagem . Mrs. Cowley
Midas.
May 1—Lyar . . . . Foote
Robinson Crusoe . . . Sheridan
4—Quaker . . . . Dibdin
Robinson Crusoe.
6—Romeo and Juliet.
Quaker.
8—Prize.
Robinson Crusoe.
9—How to Grow Rich.
Ways and Means.
11—Contrast . . . . Tyler
Agreeable Surprise . . . O'Keefe
(Col. Tyler's benefit.)
13—Jew.

May 13—High Life Below Stairs . Townley
　　　　(Mr. Collins' benefit.)
　　 15—Notoriety . . . . . Reynolds
　　　　Catharine and Petruchio,Shakspere
　　　　(Mrs. S. Powell's benefit.)
　　 18—Venice Preserved . . . . Otway
　　　　(Bartlett and Heeley's benefit.)
　　 20—Notoriety.
　　　　High Life Below Stairs.
　　　　(Mr. Hipworth's benefit.)
　　 25—Orphan . . . . Otway
　　　　Mayor of Garratt . . . . . Foote
　　　　(Mr. Villiers' benefit.)
　　 27—Wild Oats.
　　　　Catharine and Petruchio.
　　　　(Mr. Kenny's benefit.)
　　 29—Richard III . . . . . Shakspere
　　　　Deuce is in Him.
　　　　(Mr. S. Powell's benefit.)
June 1—Suspicious Husband . . Hoadly
　　　　No Song No Supper . . . Hoare
　　　　(Mr. Taylor's benefit.)
　　 3—Hamlet . . . . Shakspere
　　　　Prisoner at Large . . . O'Keefe
　　　　(Mr. and Mrs. Hughes' benefit.)
　　 5—Percy . . . . Miss More
　　　　Midnight Hour.
　　　　(Mrs. Spencer's benefit.)
　　 8—Bold Stroke for a Wife
　　　　　　　　　　　Mrs. Centlivre
　　　　Neck or Nothing . . . . Garrick
　　　　(Mr. Jones' benefit.)
　　 10—Gamester . . . . . . Moore
　　　　Wedding Day . . Mrs. Inchbald
　　　　(Mrs. Collins' benefit.)
　　 12—Wonder . . . . Mrs. Centlivre
　　　　Farmer.
　　　　(Mrs. Jones and Mrs. Hellyer's benefit.)
　　 15—Mountaineers.
　　　　(For sufferers by fire.)
　　 17—Merchant of Venice . Shakspere
　　　　Prisoner at Large.
　　　　(Mr. Hipworth's benefit.)
　　 19—Inkle and Yarico.
　　　　Prize.
　　　　(S. Powell and Collins' benefit.)

Tyler's benefit, Mrs. Jones and Mrs. Hughes both laid claim to the part of *Cowslip*, both prepared to play the character, and both came on the stage at the same time, each offering her bowl of cream to *Lingo*. As Mr. Jones was playing *Lingo*, he at once settled the dispute by accepting his wife's offering. During the regular season none of the later London successes were offered, except the "Mountaineers," a great hit, and the only one brought forward at the benefits was Mrs. Inchbald's "Wedding Day," by Mrs. Collins. The season was not successful, and when it closed Mr. Powell, the manager, was bankrupt.

The pieces chosen for the opening of the second season at the Boston Theatre were Shakspere's comedy, "As You Like It," and Mrs. Brooke's comic opera, "Rosina." The comedy served for the introduction of all the new members of the company, except Mrs. Hellyer, whose *debut* was made as *Rosina* in the opera. Mr. Taylor as *Orlando* was pronounced a valuable acquisition. Mr. Paine said in the *Orrery* that he eclipsed every competitor, and it was generally admitted that he exhibited powers which placed him in the front rank of genteel comedians. Although the part of *Jaques* was said to have been feebly supported, Mr. Hipworth was accorded the distinction of having the appearance of a gentleman and being a fine vocal per-

As You Like It.

Banished Duke	Mr. Powell
Duke Frederick	Mr. Collins
Jaques	Mr. Hipworth
Amiens	Mr. Bartlett
Oliver	Mr. S. Powell
Orlando	Mr. Taylor
Adam	Mr. Hughes
Touchstone	Mr. Jones
Corin	Mr. Kenny
Silvius	Mr. Heeley
William	Mr. Villiers
Rosalind	Mrs. S. Powell
Celia	Miss Harrison
Phœbe	Mrs. Hughes
Audrey	Mrs. Powell

former. One of the critics, speaking of Mr. Hughes as *Adam,* said he never saw an old man so characteristically portrayed, but according to Mr. Paine he was above mediocrity and below excellence. A singular bit of criticism was Paine's declaration that Mr. Jones' humor as *Touchstone* was equalled only by the perfection of Mr. Villiers as *William.* Poor Heeley, on the other hand, in the little part of *Silvius* was pronounced only a speaking puppet beneath criticism, and Bartlett as *Amiens* was coupled with him. Mrs. S. Powell as *Rosalind* displayed "more than her usual excellence;" but her sister, Miss Harrison, as *Celia* had "neither face, nor voice, nor form, nor action." Mrs. Hughes had a bad cold, but she played *Phœbe* with great spirit. Mrs. Hellyer as *Rosina* in the afterpiece was said to possess a pleasing face and to sing well, but Mr. Paine could not think her equal to Mrs. Pick.

An American comedy called the "Medium, or Happy Tea-Party," was produced on the 2d of March. It was played only once

A correspondent, writing to the *Columbian Centinel* on the 11th, expressed surprise that it did not have a second performance, alleging that the imperfections of the performers had denied it a fair trial. The whole character of *Flashit*, played by Mr. Jones, this writer said, had a very forcible effect upon his mind. Boston was on the alert to ascertain the name of the author of the new comedy, but it was not divulged. Young Paine in the *Orrery* attributed the

MEDIUM.

Maitland	Mr. Kenny
Charles Maitland	Mr. S. Powell
Colonel Melfort	Mr. Hipworth
Major Bloomville	Mr. Taylor
Captain Flashit	Mr. Jones
Weston	Mr. Collins
Robert	Mr. Hughes
William	Mr. Villiers
Eliza Clairville	Mrs. S. Powell
Matronia	Mrs. Powell
Mrs. Bloomville	Mrs. Hughes
Deborah	Mrs. Hellyer
Molly	Miss Harrison
Jenny	Mrs. Collins

piece to the Rev. John Murray, the pastor of the First Universalist Church at the corner of Bennet and Hanover Streets, and the second preacher of the doctrine of universal salvation in America; but Mr. Murray denied its authorship with some asperity. The writer in the *Columbian Centinel* already cited said with peculiar suggestiveness that if the author was " this side of the State of Vermont " he " would ask him to shorten his dialogues." There is no reason to doubt that the real author of the " Medium" was Royall Tyler. Why should the " Contrast " have been revived on the 11th of May for Mr. J. S. Tyler's benefit except as a recognition of the failure to give his brother's new comedy a fair trial ? The case is one that can only be determined on circumstantial evidence, but the testimony seems to settle the question. As the first American play originally produced in Boston, the " Medium " has an interest apart from its merits, and it is to be regretted that the play was not printed and the authorship formally acknowledged.

The two pieces new to the stage in America, the younger Colman's "Mountaineers" and Mrs. Inchbald's "Wedding Day," were
destined to great popularity in every city on the continent.   Colman's
play was originally produced at the Haymarket in 1794, where it was
a great success.   It was founded on the adventures of *Cardenio Don
Fernando,* the Spanish captive, and their mistresses in "Don Quixote,"
with such additions and alterations as suggested themselves to the
author.   Mr. Taylor gained great celebrity in Boston by his perform-

CONTRASTED CASTS—CHANGES.

PLAYS.	1794.	1794–5.
Bold Stroke for a Wife.		
Sir Philip	Mr. Nelson	Mr. Taylor
Simon Pure		Mr. Kenny
Obadiah Prim	Mr. Baker	Mr. Hughes
Betty	Miss Baker	Mrs. Hellyer
Mrs. Prim	Mrs. Baker	Mrs. Jones
Bon Ton.		
Davy	Mr. Powell	Mr. Villiers
Gymp	Mrs. Abbot	Mrs. Collins
Farmer.		
Capt. Valentine	Mr. Nelson	Mr. Hipworth
Col. Dormant	Mr. S. Powell	Mr. Hughes
Betty	Mrs. Baker	Mrs. Hughes
Molly	Mrs. Abbot	Mrs. Hellyer
Louisa	Miss Baker	Miss Harrison
Hamlet.		
Ghost	Mr. Baker	Mr. Hipworth
Guildenstern	Mr. Nelson	Mr. Hughes
Player King		Mr. Heeley
Marcellus		Mr. Hughes
Gravedigger		Mr. Villiers
Queen	Mrs. Baker	Mrs. Spencer
Player Queen	Mrs. Abbot	Mrs. Collins
Ophelia	Miss Baker	Mrs. Hughes
Inkle and Yarico.		
Inkle	Mr. Powell	Mr. Hipworth
Curry	Mr. Baker	Mr. Hughes
Yarico	Mrs. Baker	Mrs. S. Powell
Narcissa	Miss Baker	Mrs. Hellyer
Wowski	Mrs. Abbot	Mrs. Hughes
Midnight Hour.		
Marquis	Mr. S. Powell	Mr. Taylor
General		Mr. Hughes
Sebastian	Mr. Powell	Mr. Hipworth
Matthias	Mr. Kenny	Mr. Villiers

PLAYS.	1794.	1794–5.
Julia	Miss Baker	Mrs. Hughes
Cicely	Mrs. Baker	Mrs. Hellyer
Flora	Mrs. Powell	Mrs. Jones
Modern Antiques.		
Hearty	Mr. Nelson	Mr. Kenny
Joey	Mr. Baker	Mr. Villiers
Thomas		Mr. Heeley
Mrs. Cockletop	Miss Baker	Mrs. S. Powell
Mrs. Camomile	Mrs. Baker	Mrs. Hughes
Flounce		Miss Harrison
Betty		Mrs. Hellyer
No Song No Supper.		
Crop	Mr. Nelson	Mr. Collins
William	Mr. Collins	Mr. Hipworth
Margaretta	Mrs. Abbot	Mrs. Hellyer
Louisa	Miss Baker	Miss Harrison
Dorothy	Mrs. Baker	Mrs. Jones
Padlock.		
Leander	Mr. Nelson	Mr. Hipworth
Leonora	Mrs. Abbot	Mrs. Hellyer
Ursula	Mrs. Baker	Mrs. Powell
Richard III.		
Richmond	Mr. Baker	Mr. Hipworth
Prince of Wales	Debutante	Boston Youth
Radcliffe	Mr. Nelson	Mr. Heeley
Lord Mayor		Mr. Hughes
Tressel		Mr. Taylor
Tyrrel		Mr. Villiers
Queen Elizabeth	Mrs. Powell	Mrs. Spencer
Duchess of York	Mrs. Baker	Mrs. Hughes
Wonder.		
Don Lopez	Mr. Nelson	Mr. Kenny
Lissardo	Mr. Powell	Mr. Hughes
Gibby	Mr. Baker	Mr. Villiers
Alguazil	Mr. Kenny	Mr. Heeley
Isabinda	Miss Baker	Mrs. Hellyer

ance of *Octavian*, but in Dunlap's estimation it was a failure. Dunlap's judgment, however, is far from conclusive. Taylor in this part wore what was a novelty at that time—a beard grown for the occcasion.

Few of the pieces presented at the Boston Theatre during the first season were revived, and in these few the changes in the casts were not important. The productions new to Boston comprised for the

BOSTON THEATRE CASTS—SECOND SEASON.

CATHARINE AND PETRUCHIO.

Petruchio	Mr. Hipworth
Baptista	Mr. Heeley
Biondello	Mr. Kenny
Tailor	Mr. Villiers
Hortensio	Mr. Bartlett
Grumio	Mr. Jones
Curtis	Mrs. Hughes
Bianca	Miss Harrison
Catharine	Mrs. S. Powell

CATO.

Cato	Mr. Hipworth
Juba	Mr. Taylor
Portius	Mr. Hughes
Marcius	Mr. S. Powell
Syphax	Mr. Powell
Sempronius	Mr. Collins
Lucius	Mr. Kenny
Decius	Mr. Jones
Marcia	Mrs. S. Powell
Lucia	Mrs. Hughes

CONTRAST.

Colonel Manly	Mr. S. Powell
Billy Dimple	Mr. Bartlett
Van Rough	Mr. Hughes
Jessamy	Mr. Hipworth
Jonathan	Mr. Villiers
Charlotte	Mrs. S. Powell
Maria	Mrs. Hughes
Letitia	Mrs. Jones
Jenny	Mr. Collins

DEUCE IS IN HIM.

Col. Tamper	Mr. S. Powell
Maj. Bedford	Mr. Hughes
Dr. Prattle	Mr. Hipworth
Emily	Mrs. S. Powell
Bell	Mrs. Collins
Florival	Mrs. Hughes

DRAMATIST.

Vapid	Mr. Hipworth
Floriville	Mr. Taylor
Scarlet	Mr. Hughes
Neville	Mr. Bartlett
Willoughby	Mr. Kenny
Peter	Mr. Villiers
Ennui	Mr. Jones
Lady Waitfort	Mrs. Powell
Miss Courtney	Mrs. Hughes
Letty	Mrs. Collins
Marianne	Mrs. S. Powell

GAMESTER.

Beverly	Mr. Hipworth
Lewson	Mr. Taylor
Stukely	Mr. Collins
Jarvis	Mr. Kenny
Dawson	Mr. Heeley
Bates	Mr. Hughes
Charlotte	Mrs. Hughes
Lucy	Miss Harrison
Mrs. Beverly	Mrs. S. Powell

HENRY IV.

King Henry	Mr. Collins
Prince of Wales	Mr. S. Powell
Prince John	Miss C. Powell
Worcester	Mr. Hughes
Northumberland	Mr. Kenny
Hotspur	Mr. Taylor
Douglas	Mr. Clifford
Westmoreland	Mr. Jones
Sir Walter Blunt	Mr. Heeley
Sir John Falstaff	Mr. Hipworth
Poins	Mr. Bartlett
Bardolph	Mr. Powell
Francis	Mr. Villiers
Lady Percy	Mrs. S. Powell
Hostess	Mrs. Powell

HIGH LIFE BELOW STAIRS.

Lovel	Mr. Hipworth
Freeman	Mr. Collins
Philip	Mr. Hughes
Lord Duke	Mr. S. Powell
Tom	Mr. Kenny
Robert	Mr. Villiers
Coachman	Mr. Heeley
Sir Harry	Mr. Powell
Kitty	Mrs. Powell
Lady Bab	Mrs. Collins
Lady Charlotte	Mrs. Hellyer
Chloe	Mrs. Hughes

JEW.

Sheva	Mr. Hipworth
Frederick	Mr. S. Powell
Charles Ratcliffe	Mr. Taylor
Sir Stephen Bertram	Mr. Kenny
Saunderson	Mr. Hughes
Jabel	Mr. Villiers
Eliza	Mrs. S. Powell
Dorcas	Mrs. Hughes
Mrs. Goodison	Mrs. Hellyer
Mrs. Ratcliffe	Mrs. Powell

MAYOR OF GARRATT.

Maj. Sturgeon	Mr. Hipworth
Sir Jacob Jollop	Mr. Kenny
Bruin	Mr. Collins
Lint	Mr. Hughes
Roger	Mr. Bartlett
Heeltap	Mr. Heeley
Jerry Sneak	Mr. Villiers
Mrs. Bruin	Mrs. Hellyer
Mrs. Sneak	Mrs. S. Powell

MERCHANT OF VENICE.

Shylock	Mr. Hipworth
Antonio	Mr. Kenny
Bassanio	Mr. Collins

most part plays that had long been familiar to New York and Philadelphia audiences. These included some of the newer comedies and
farces of Cumberland and O'Keefe, as well as earlier masterpieces of
the English drama. Upon the whole, Mr. Powell's management was
characterized by good taste and good judgment so far as the business
of the stage was concerned. Like Henry he did not look to Bath, or

BOSTON THEATRE CASTS—SECOND SEASON.

Gratiano . . . . . . Mr. Taylor
Lorenzo . . . . . . Mr. Bartlett
Duke . . . . Mr. Hughes
Tubal . . . . Mr. Villiers
Solarino . . . . . . Mr. Heeley
Launcelot . . . . . . Mr. Jones
Portia . . . . Mrs. S. Powell
Nerissa . . . . . Mrs Hughes
Jessica . . . . . . Mrs. Hellyer

NECK OR NOTHING.

Slip . . . . Mr. Jones
Stockwell . . . . Mr. Kenny
Sir Harry Harlow . Mr. Hughes
Belford . . . . . . Mr. Bartlett
Martin . . . . Mr. Taylor
Miss Nancy . . . Mrs. Spencer
Mrs. Stockwell . . Mrs. Hellyer
Jenny . . . . Mrs. Jones

ORPHAN.

Castalio . . . . . . Mr. Powell
Polydore . . . . . Mr. S. Powell
Acasto . . . . Mr. Hughes
Chaplain . . . . . . Mr. Heeley
Ernesto . . . . Mr. Kenny
Chamont . . . . . . Mr. Taylor
Monimia . . . Mrs. S. Powell
Serina . . . . Mrs. Hughes
Florella . . . . . . Mrs. Collins

PERCY.

Percy . . . . . . Mr. S. Powell
Douglas . . . . Mr. Hipworth
Sir Hubert . . . . . Mr. Jones
Edric . . . . Mr. Taylor
Harcourt . . . . . . Mr. Collins
Messenger . . . . . Mr. Bartlett
Lord Raby . . . . . Mr. Kenny
Birtha . . . . . . Mrs. Hellyer
Elwina . . . . . . Mrs. Spencer
Page . . . . Boston Youth

PRISONER AT LARGE.

Lord Edmund . . Mr. Hipworth
Old Dowdle . . . . Mr. Hughes
Frippon . . . . . . Mr. Villiers
Jack Conner . . . Mr. S. Powell
Frill . . . . Mr. Bartlett
Father Frank . . . . Mr. Kenny
Tough . . . . Mr. Heeley
Trap . . . . Mr. Collins
Muns . . . . Mr. Jones
Adelaide . . . . Mrs. S. Powell
Rachel . . . . . . Mrs. Hughes
Mary . . . . Mrs. Collins
Landlady . . . . Miss Harrison

PRIZE.

Lenitive . . . . . Mr. Hipworth
Label . . . . Mr. Villiers
Caddy . . . . Mr. Hughes
Heartwell . . . . . Mr. Kenny
Juba . . . . Mr. Heeley
Mrs. Caddy . . . . Mrs. Collins
Caroline . . . . . . Mrs. Hellyer

ROMP.

Watty Cockney . . . Mr. Jones
Barnacle . . . . . . Mr. Kenny
Old Cockney . . . . Mr. Hughes
Captain Sightly . . Mr. Hipworth
Priscilla . . . . . Mrs. Hellyer
Penelope . . . . Mrs. Hughes
Madame La Blonde . Mrs. Jones

SUSPICIOUS HUSBAND.

Ranger . . . . . . Mr. Taylor
Frankly . . . . . . Mr. Hipworth
Bellamy . . . . . . Mr. Collins
Jack Meggot . . . . Mr. Jones
Tester . . . . Mr. Villiers
Buckle . . . . Mr. Bartlett
Simon . . . . Mr. Heeley
Strickland . . . . . Mr. Kenny

Mrs. Strickland . . Mrs. Spencer
Jacintha . . . . . Mrs. Hughes
Lucetta . . . . . . Mrs. Collins
Milliner . . . . . . Mrs. Hellyer
Clarinda . . . . . Mr. S. Powell

VENICE PRESERVED.

Jaffier . . . . . . Mr. Hipworth
Pierre . . . . Mr. Kenny
Priuli . . . . Mr. Collins
Perault . . . . Mr. Powell
Bedamar . . . . . . Mr. Taylor
Elliott . . . . Mr. Heeley
Theodore . . . . . Mr. Hughes
Spinoza . . . . . . Mr. Bartlett
Belvidera . . . . . Mrs. Spencer

WEDDING DAY.

Lord Rakeland . . . Mr. Taylor
Sir Adam Contest . Mr. Hipworth
Mr. Millden . . . . Mr. Bartlett
Young Contest . . Mr. S. Powell
Lady Autumn . . . Mrs. Hellyer
Mrs. Hamford . . . Mrs. Hughes
Hannah . . . . . Miss Harrison
Lady Contest . . . . Mrs. Collins

WILD OATS.

Sir George Thunder . Mr. Jones
Rover . . . . . . Mr. Hipworth
Harry . . . . Mr. Taylor
John . . . . Mr. Kenny
Banks . . . . Mr. Hughes
Gammon . . . . . . Mr. Collins
Ephraim Smooth . . Mr. Powell
Sim . . . . Mr. Villiers
Twitch . . . . Mr. Heeley
Trap . . . . Mr. Bartlett
Landlord . . . Mr. S. Powell
Lady Amaranth . Mrs S. Powell
Jane . . . . . . Mrs. Collins
Amelia . . . . . . Mrs. Hughes

like Wignell to the leading London theatres for his people. Miss Harrison, who became Mrs. S. Powell, had played the *Marchioness* in the "Child of Nature" among other parts at Weymouth in the Summer of 1791. Mrs. Baker had been at Sadler's Wells from 1785 to 1792 as dancer, singer and actress in the pantomimes and musical pieces. Mr. Baker was at the Haymarket in 1787, but he played only small parts, such as *Borachio* in "Much Ado About Nothing." Of Messrs. Hipworth, Taylor and Villiers and Mrs. Hellyer in the reorganized company I have been able to find no English record. They do not appear, however, to have been inefficient, and it was probably to his improvident use of his resources that Mr. Powell's downfall was due. Mr. Powell retired from the management in a very discontented spirit, intending to return to London, where he

Mr. Powell's Advertisement.

Intended to be Published by Subscription.

A true and perfect account of
The Rise, Progress and Tragi-Comical Revolution of the Boston Theatre,
Interspersed with curious and whimsical anecdotes by C. S. P.,
Late Manager of said House,
With his answer to a coliquindita interrogatory (by a physical Genius),
WHAT DO YOU HERE?!!!!
A Bitter Pill to take, tho' obliged to swallow it at the time;
Likewise his true reasons for being obliged to quit it.
The Author in Court, having no Friend nor Proctor,
Was Judg'd *without Jury and Damn'd by the Doctor.*
Duo respublicæ portenta ac pæne funera
Lucius Calphurnius Piso
Join'd with Gabinius hadn't greater vice, O!!

N.B.—The Book will be neatly printed in London, where a subscription will be opened amongst P.'s friends, and Books shall be sent to Boston, early next Autumn, to those who may choose to subscribe. For very particular reasons P. wishes none to become subscribers but those who can seriously subscribe themselves his true friends. Subscriptions will be taken in at all the bookstores. *Price, One Dollar.*

April 2, 1796.

purposed publishing a pamphlet on his ejectment from the Boston Theatre. He changed his mind, however, and announced that his book would be printed in Boston.

CHAPTER XII.

HARPER IN RHODE ISLAND.

JOSEPH HARPER, after his release from arrest for giving performances in Boston in the Autumn of 1792, made his way to
Rhode Island, intending to open theatres at Providence and Newport.
There was, of course, opposition to the project, some of the writers in
the Providence *Gazette* demanding the enforcement of the prohibitory
law and denouncing the comedians for their insolence in entering the
State. The Providence Town Council, however, accorded them the
right to perform, notwithstanding the law, on condition that the proceeds of every fifth night should be paid into the city treasury. Mr.
Harper succeeded in obtaining the Court-House to be used as a
theatre, and there a number of comedies and farces was performed in
the disguise of "moral lectures" in December, 1792, and January,
1793. The subjoined advertisement from the Providence *Gazette*
shows the character of the announcements. According to Blake's
" History of the Providence Stage," the Court-House was crowded at
every performance. The season was a short one, and Mr. Harper's
company did not again appear in Providence during the next two

years, although the prohibitory law was repealed in February, 1793, and the company played two long engagements at Newport in the meanwhile. In February, 1793, Solomon and Murray undertook to give three performances in Providence, three-fourths of the proceeds of the first night being paid to the town for the use of the poor. This company was a feeble one and met with little encouragement in consequence.

On the 1st of January, 1793, while Harper was playing in the Court-House at Providence, "Venice Preserved" and the "Padlock" were announced for production at the Court-House at Newport for the benefit of the poor. The performers were either amateurs or strollers.

In the Spring of 1793 a large brick building in Newport, three stories high, was purchased by Alexander Placide and turned into a playhouse. Before the Revolution the lower part of the building was used as a market, and the upper floors for shops and offices. After the Revolution it was a printing office until it became a theatre. This was the Newport Theatre until 1842, a period of fifty years. The accompanying list of per-

PROVIDENCE ADVERTISEMENT, 1792-3.

At the Court-House
On Tuesday evening, the 1st of January, will be delivered
A MORAL LECTURE
(written by Vanbrugh), called
THE REFORMED WIFE,
After which will follow
A Pantomimical Interlude called
The *Birth, Death* and *Animation* of *Harlequin,*
To which will be added
An Entertaining Lecture called
BON TON, or *High Life Above Stairs.*
TICKETS at Half a Dollar may be had at Mr. Dixon's Stage-House, or at Wheeler's Printing Office. The doors will be opened at Five o'clock and the curtain rise at Six.

LIST OF PRODUCTIONS—*Newport.*

1793.
July   3—Gamester . . . . Moore
Bird Catcher.
Ghost . . . . . Mrs. Centlivre
10—Busybody . . . . Mrs. Centlivre
Robinson Crusoe . . . Sheridan
24—Barnaby Brittle . . . . Betterton
Two Philosophers.
All the World's a Stage . Jackman
Aug.   1—Tempest . . . . Dryden
Harlequin Skeleton.
8—She Stoops to Conquer . Goldsmith
Rosina . . . . . Mrs. Brooke

formances is far from complete, but it is sufficiently full to show the work of Harper's company. On the 10th of September Mad. Placide had a benefit, but I have not found the bill. When Mr. Moore had his benefit he delivered a eulogy on Masonry that was printed in the Newport *Mercury.* "Othello" was played during the season, when a gentleman made his first appearance as the *Moor,* and Harper as *Cassio* delivered an occasional address:

Aug. 15—Tempest.
Speaking Picture.
29—Miser . . . . Fielding
Padlock . . . . . . Bickerstaff
(Mr. Harper's benefit.)

Sept. 5—Orphan . . . . Otway
Miss in her Teens. . . . Garrick
12—Hamlet . . . . . Shakspere
Harlequin Skeleton.
(Madame Douvillier's benefit.)
19—Richard III . . . . . Shakspere
Linco's Travels . . . . Garrick
(Mr. Minchin's benefit.)
24—As It Should Be . . . . Oulton
Quality Binding . . . . . Rose
(Benefit of the Poor.)

Oct. 3—Love in a Village . . Bickerstaff
Two Philosophers.
Monody on the Chiefs.
(Mr. Moore's benefit.)
8—Prisoner at Large . . . O'Keefe
Miller of Mansfield . . Dodsley
(Last Night but One.)

Before this brilliant house behold your *Cassio* bend,
To pay a tribute to the *Moor,* his lord and friend.

Harper's plea for the *debutant,* especially in the concluding line, was scarcely poetical, but it was certainly practical and business-like:

In friendship's noble cause you're all assembled here;
What has *Othello,* then, you'll say, to fear?
Kind patrons, yes; here more from you is due—
To hear a first appearance in *Othello* through.

A sufficient number of casts has been culled from the advertisements of this first Newport season not only to show the names of Harper's Rhode Island Company, but their work and relative rank. At the head of the organization were Mr. Harper and Miss Smith, but the latter frequently yielded the supremacy to Mrs. Mechtler, who as Miss Fanny Storer had made her American *debut* at the Southwark

Theatre, Philadelphia, as early as 1767. Watts, Adams and Kenny had been with Harper in Boston in 1792. Mr. and Mrs. Moore were probably identical with the players of that name who were with Allen at Albany in 1785. Minchin was one of those actors who only appeared to disappear, but Huggins afterward became a noted barber in New York. His tonsorial advertisements in the *Evening Post*, written by Anthony Bleecker and other wits of the town among his customers, which were afterward gathered into a volume with the title of

NEWPORT CASTS—FIRST SEASON, 1793.

ALL THE WORLD'S A STAGE.

Sir Gilbert Pumpkin .	Mr. Kenny
Charles Stanley . . .	Mr. Watts
Henry Stukely . . .	Mr. Adams
Waiter	Mr. Huggins
Hostler	Mr. Minchin
Diggory	Mr. Harper
Kitty Sprightly . . .	Miss Smith
Bridget Pumpkin .	Mrs. Mechtler

AS IT SHOULD BE.

Lord Megrim	Mr. Harper
Winworth	Mr. Adams
Sparkle	Mr. Watts
Fidget	Mr. Kenny
Celia	Miss Brewer
Lucy	Miss Smith

BARNABY BRITTLE.

Barnaby Brittle . . .	Mr. Watts
Sir Peter Pride . . .	Mr. Kenny
Lovemore	Mr. Minchin
Jeremy	Mr. Adams
Clodpole	Mr. Harper
Mrs. Brittle . . .	Mrs. Mechtler
Lady Pride	Miss Brewer
Damaris	Miss Smith

BUSYBODY.

Marplot	Mr. Harper
Sir Francis	Mr. Kenny
Charles	Mr. Minchin
Sir Jealous	Mr. Adams
Whisper	Mr. Huggins
Sir George Airy . . .	Mr. Watts

Patch	Mrs. Mechtler
Isabinda	Miss Brewer
Miranda	Miss Smith

GAMESTER.

Beverly	Mr. Harper
Lewson	Mr. Kenny
Jarvis	Mr. Adams
Bates	Mr. Minchin
Dawson	Mr. Huggins
Stukely	Mr. Watts
Charlotte	Miss Smith
Lucy	Miss Brewer
Mrs. Beverly . . .	Mrs. Mechtler

GHOST.

Captain Constant . .	Mr. Adams
Sir Jeffrey	Mr. Watts
Trusty	Mr. Kenny
Clinch	Mr. Huggins
Roger	Mr. Harper
Belinda	Miss Brewer
Dolly	Miss Smith

HAMLET.

Hamlet	Mr. Harper
King	Mr. Adams
Polonius ⎫ Laertes ⎭	Mr. Watts
Horatio	Mr. Kenny
Ghost ⎫ Player King ⎭ . . .	Mr. Moore
Rosencranz	Mr. Minchin
Guildenstern	Mr. Huggins
Queen	Miss Smith

Player Queen . . .	Miss Brewer
Ophelia	Mrs. Mechtler

HARLEQUIN SKELETON.

Harlequin	Mr. Trouche
Old Man	Mr. Douvillier
Enchanter	Mr. Minchin
Lover	Mr. Huggins
Pierrot	Mr. Placide
Columbine	Mrs. Placide

LINCO'S TRAVELS.

Linco	Mr. Moore
Clodpole	Mr. Kenny
Dorcas	Mr. Huggins

MILLER OF MANSFIELD

King	Mr. Moore
Dick	Mr. Adams
Joe	Mr. Harper
Lurewell	Mr. Huggins
Miller	Mr. Watts
Margery	Mrs. Moore
Kate	Miss Brewer
Peggy	Miss Smith

MISER.

Lovegold	Mr. Adams
Ramillie	Mr. Kenny
Clerimont	Mr. Minchin
James	Mr. Moore
Furnish	Mr. Huggins
Frederick	Mr. Harper
Lappet	Mrs. Mechtler
Harriet	Miss Brewer
Marianne	Miss Smith

" Hugginiana," placed him among the literati that were then a feature of New York. Of Miss Brewer I know nothing. Mr. Prigmore put in an appearance at Newport before the close of the season, while the Old American Company was resting, his name being in the bill for the 8th of October as *Old Dowdle* in the " Prisoner at Large." Mr. Placide, apparently, was associated with Harper in the management, and together with Mrs. Placide, Mr. and Mrs. Douvillier, Mr. Trouche, Mr. Spinacuta and Mr. Mallet appeared in pantomime and ballet.

NEWPORT CASTS—FIRST SEASON, 1793.

MISS IN HER TEENS.

Captain Flash	Mr. Watts
Captain Loveit . . .	Mr. Adams
Puff	Mr. Kenny
Jasper	Mr. Minchin
Fribble	Mr. Harper
Tag	Mrs. Mechtler
Biddy	Miss Smith

ORPHAN.

Castalio	Mr. Adams
Polydore	Mr. Kenny
Acasto	Mr. Watts
Chaplain	Mr. Minchin
Ernesto	Mr. Moore
Servant	Mr. Huggins
Chamont	Mr. Harper
Serina	Miss Smith
Florella	Miss Brewer
Monimia	Mrs. Mechtler

PADLOCK.

Don Diego	Mr. Kenny
Leander	Mr. Huggins
Mungo	Mr. Harper
Ursula	Miss Smith
Leonora	Mrs. Mechtler

PRISONER AT LARGE.

Old Dowdle . . .	Mr. Prigmore
Lord Esmond	Mr. Watts
Jack Conner	Mr. Adams
Tough	Mr. Moore
Count Frippon . .	Mr. Huggins
Frill	Mr. O'Reilly

Muns	Mr. Harper
Adelaide	Mrs. Moore
Mary	Miss Brewer
Rachel	Miss Smith

QUALITY BINDING.

Mr. Lovel	Mr. Watts
Colonel Modish . .	Mr. Adams
Lord Semper	Mr. Kenny
Sir William Wealthy,	Mr. Minchin
John	Mr. Huggins
Plainwell	Mr. Harper
Mrs. Lovel	Miss Smith

RICHARD III.

Richard	Mr. Harper
Henry VI	Mr. Adams
Prince of Wales . .	Mr. Huggins
Stanley	Mr. Minchin
Catesby	Mr. Watts
Lieutenant	Mr. Kenny
Ratcliffe	Mr. O'Reilly
Halbert-bearer . . .	Mr. Trouche
Richmond	Mr. Moore
Lady Anne	Miss Smith
Duchess of York . .	Miss Brewer
Queen Elizabeth .	Mrs. Mechtler

ROSINA.

Belville	Mr. Watts
Captain Belville . . .	Mr. Kenny
Rustic	Mr. Adams
William	Mr. Harper
Rosina	Mrs Mechtler
Dorcas	Miss Smith
Phœbe	Mrs. Placide

SHE STOOPS TO CONQUER.

Hardcastle	Mr. Adams
Young Marlow	Mr. Watts
Hastings	Mr. Minchin
Sir Charles Marlow .	Mr. Kenny
Diggory	Mr. Huggins
Tony Lumpkin . . .	Mr. Harper
Mrs. Hardcastle . . .	Miss Smith
Miss Neville	Miss Brewer
Miss Hardcastle .	Mrs. Mechtler

SPEAKING PICTURE.

Cassander	Mr. Placide
Leander	Mr. Mallet
Pierrot	Mr. Douvillier
Isabella	Mrs. Placide
Columbine . . .	Mrs. Douvillier

TEMPEST.

Prospero	Mr. Adams
Hippolito	Mr. Watts
Alonzo	Mr. Minchin
Gonzalo	Mr. Huggins
Antonio	Mr. Kenny
Ferdinand	Mr. Harper
Stephano	Mr. Minchin
Ventoso	Mr. Kenny
Mustachio	Mr. Huggins
Caliban	Mr. Watts
Trinculo	Mr. Harper
Dorinda	Miss Smith
Miranda	Miss Brewer
Ariel	Mrs. Mechtler

The second Newport season began on the 1st of May, 1794, and closed on the 28th of August to allow a visit to Providence. According to Blake's "History of the Providence Stage," no performances were given in that town during the year previous to the 30th of December, 1794, and in either case the matter is not important, as an engagement there in September could only have meant a repetition of the Newport productions. In October another brief engagement was played in Newport, and then the company went to Providence for a winter season. In the meantime, Harper had almost entirely reorganized his forces. Kenny, Minchin and Huggins had retired, and the names of the Moores and Miss Brewer also disappear from the bills. The new engagements comprised Mr. Kenna, the elder, Mr. and Mrs. Solomon, Mr. Redfield, who had been with Harper in Boston, and upon occasion Fransis, Powers, Brett and Patterson. Mr. Kenna made his first appear-

LIST OF PRODUCTIONS—*Newport.*

1794.

May   1—Douglas . . . . Home
        Gallery of Portraits.
     7—Citizen . . . . Murphy
        Trick upon Trick . . . Yarrow
   15—Foundling . . . . . . Moore
        Madcap . . . . Fielding
   22—She Stoops to Conquer . Goldsmith
        Romp . . . . Bickerstaff
   29—Barbarossa . . . . . . Browne
        Thomas and Sally . . Bickerstaff
     (Benefit of Algiers Prisoners.)
June 10—Richard III . . . . . Shakspere
        Romp.
   19—Beggar's Opera . . . . . . Gay
        Ghost . . . . . . Mrs. Centlivre
   26—West Indian . . . Cumberland
        Devil to Pay . . . . . . Coffey
July   1—Countess of Salisbury . Hartson
        Quaker . . . . Dibdin
   10—Romeo and Juliet . . Shakspere
        Three Weeks After Marriage
                    Murphy
   15—Beaux' Stratagem . . Farquhar
        Romp.
   24—Bold Stroke for a Wife.
                Mrs. Centlivre
        Romp.
   31—Bold Stroke for a Wife.
        Witches.
     (Mr. Harper's benefit.)
Aug. 14—Recruiting Officer . . Farquhar
        Thomas and Sally.
     (Miss Smith's benefit.)
   28—All in the Wrong . . . Murphy
        No Song No Supper . . . Hoare
Oct. 23—Bold Stroke for a Wife.
        True-Born Irishman . . Macklin
     (Mrs. Mechtler's benefit.)
   28—Modern Antiques . . . O'Keefe
        Barataria . . . . . . Pilon
     (Mr. Harper's benefit.)

ance with the company on the opening night of the season as *Old Norval* in "Douglas." Mrs. Kenna also joined her husband and

NEWPORT CASTS—SECOND SEASON, **1794**.

ALL IN THE WRONG.

Sir John Restless . .	Mr. Harper
Beverly	Mr. Adams
Young Belmont . . .	Mr. Watts
Sir William Belmont .	Mr. Redfield
Blanford	Mr. Prigmore
Robert	Mr. Kenna
Brush	Mr. Solomon
Lady Restless	Miss Smith
Belinda	Mrs. Solomon
Tattle	Mrs Mechtler
Clarissa	Mrs. Watts

BARATARIA.

Sancho	Mr. Harper
Duke	Mr. Kenna
Don Quixote	Mr. Adams
Don Pedro	Mr. Watts
Don Alonzo	Mr. Redfield
Mary	Mrs. Harper
Teresa	Mrs. Mechtler
Duchess	Mrs. Watts
Rodriguez	Mrs. Kenna

BARBAROSSA.

Barbarossa	Mr. Kenna
Achmet	Mr. Harper
Othman	Mr. Adams
Aladin	Mr. Watts
Sadi	Mr. Redfield
Slave	Mr. Solomon
Zaphira	Mrs. Mechtler
Irene	Miss Smith
Slave	Mrs. Watts

BEAUX' STRATAGEM.

Archer	Mr. Harper
Aimwell	Mr. Patterson
Foigard	Mr. Kenna
Boniface	Mr. Adams
Sullen	Mr. Redfield
Gibbet	Mr. Watts
Freeman	Mr. Solomon
Scrub	Mr. Prigmore
Mrs. Sullen . . .	Mrs. Mechtler
Dorinda	Mrs. Solomon
Lady Bountiful . . .	Mrs. Watts

BEGGAR'S OPERA.

Macheath	Mr. Harper
Lockit	Mr. Kenna
Peachum	Mr. Adams
Mat	Mr. Watts
Filch	Mr. Solomon
Ben Budge	Mr. Redfield
Polly	Mrs. Mechtler
Lucy	Mrs. Solomon
Mrs. Peachum . . .	Miss Smith
Mrs. Slammekin . .	Mrs. Watts

BOLD STROKE FOR A WIFE.

Feignwell	Mr. Harper
Obadiah Prim	Mr. Kenna
Periwinkle	Mr. Prigmore
Sackbut	Mr. Adams
Modelove	Mr. Watts
Tradelove	Mr. Redfield
Simon Pure	Mr. Solomon
Ann Lovely . . .	Mrs. Mechtler
Mrs. Prim	Mrs Solomon
Betty	Mrs. Watts

CITIZEN.

Old Philpot	Mr. Kenna
Young Philpot . . .	Mr. Harper
Young Wilding . . .	Mr. Fransis
Beaufort	Mr. Powers
Maria	Miss Smith

COUNTESS OF SALISBURY.

Alwin	Mr. Harper
Raymond	Mr. Watts
Grey	Mr. Kenna
Morton	Mr. Adams
Leroches	Mr. Redfield
Sir Ardolf	Mr. Solomon
Ela	Miss Smith
Eleanor	Mrs. Mechtler
Lord William	Miss Brown

DEVIL TO PAY.

Sir John Loverule . .	Mr. Adams
Jobson	Mr. Harper
Conjurer	Mr. Redfield
Butler	Mr. Kenna
Coachman	Mr. Watts
Cook	Mr. Solomon
Lady Loverule . .	Mrs. Mechtler
Nell	Mrs. Solomon
Lucy	Miss Smith
Lettice	Mrs. Watts

DOUGLAS.

Old Norval	Mr. Kenny
Lord Randolph . . .	Mr. Fransis
Glenalvon	Mr. Brett
Officer	Mr. Powers
Norval	Mr. Harper
Lady Randolph . .	Miss Smith

FOUNDLING.

Sir Charles Raymond .	Mr. Kenny
Sir Roger Belmont .	Mr. Solomon
Young Belmont . . .	Mr. Fransis
Colonel Raymond .	Mr. Redfield
Faddle	Mr. Harper
Villiard	Mr. Powers
Rosetta	Mrs. Solomon
Fidelia	Miss Smith

MADCAP.

Goodwill	Mr. Redfield
Blister	Mr. Harper
Coupee	Mr. Kenna
Quaver	Mr. Solomon
Thomas	Mr. Powers
Lucy	Mrs. Solomon

MODERN ANTIQUES.

Cockletop	Mr. Adams
Frank	Mr. Watts
Joey	Mr. Harper
Napkin	Mr. Clapham
Hearty	Mr. Kenna
Thomas	Mr. Redfield
Mrs. Cockletop .	Mrs. Mechtler
Mrs. Camomile .	Mrs. Harper
Belinda	Mrs. Watts
Flounce	Mrs. Kenna

NO SONG NO SUPPER.

Robin	Mr. Harper
Crop	Mr. Prigmore
Endless	Mr. Watts
Frederick	Mr. Solomon
Thomas	Mr. Kenna
William	Mr. Adams
Margaretta . . .	Mrs. Solomon
Dorothy	Mrs. Mechtler
Louisa	Mrs. Watts
Nell	Miss Smith

the company in October.   As in the previous year, Mr. Prigmore visited Newport in the Summer of 1794, where he played low comedy
roles with Harper's company from the middle of July until the close of August.   He made his first appearance at Newport this season on the 15th of July as *Scrub* in the "Beaux' Stratagem."   After the close of the Summer season, and before the brief engagement in October, Mr. Harper and Miss Smith were married.   Besides that of Mrs. Kenna, the only new name

CONTRASTED CASTS—*Changes.*

PLAYS.	1793.	1794.
Ghost.		
Sir Jeffrey . . .	Mr. Watts . . .	Mr. Redfield
Trusty	Mr. Kenny . .	Mr. Solomon
Clinch	Mr. Huggins	Mr. Watts
Belinda	Miss Brewer . .	Mrs. Solomon
Richard III.		
Prince of Wales .	Mr. Huggins . .	Mrs. Solomon
Duke of York		Miss Brown
Stanley	Mr. Minchin . .	Mr. Kenna
Lieutenant . . .	Mr. Kenny . .	Mr. Solomon
Ratcliffe	Mr. O'Reilly . .	Mr. Redfield
Richmond . . .	Mr. Moore . . .	Mr. Adams
Duchess of York.	Miss Brewer . .	Mrs. Watts
She Stoops to Conquer.		
Hardcastle . . .	Mr. Adams . .	Mr. Kenna
Hastings	Mr. Minchin . .	Mr. Fransis
Sir Charles . . .	Mr. Kenny . .	Mr. Redfield
Diggory	Mr. Huggins	Mr. Solomon
Miss Neville . .	Miss Brewer . .	Mrs. Solomon

NEWPORT CASTS—SECOND SEASON, 1794.

QUAKER.

Steady	Mr. Kenna
Lubin	Mr. Harper
Solomon	Mr. Watts
Easy	Mr. Adams
Gillian	Mr. Solomon
Floretta	Mrs. Mechtler
Cicely	Miss Smith

RECRUITING OFFICER.

Captain Plume . . .	Mr. Harper
Captain Brazen . .	Mr. Prigmore
Sergeant Kite	Mr. Watts
Balance	Mr. Adams
Worthy	Mr. Redfield
Bullock	Mr. Kenna
Sylvia	Miss Smith
Melinda	Mrs. Mechtler
Rose	Mrs. Solomon
Lucy	Mrs. Watts

ROMEO AND JULIET.

Romeo	Mr. Harper
Mercutio	Mr. Kenna
Paris	Mr. Adams
Friar Laurence	Mr. Watts
Prince	Mr. Redfield
Capulet	Mr. Patterson
Montagu	Mr. Solomon
Juliet	Mrs. Mechtler
Nurse	Mrs. Solomon
Lady Capulet	Mrs. Watts

ROMP.

Barnacle	Mr. Watts
Old Cockney	Mr. Adams
Watty Cockney . .	Mr. Solomon
Captain Lightly . .	Mr. Redfield
Miss Le Blond . .	Mrs. Mechtler
Penelope	Mrs. Watts
Priscilla	Mrs. Solomon

THOMAS AND SALLY.

Thomas	Mr. Harper
Squire	Mr. Solomon
Sally	Mrs. Mechtler
Dorcas	Mrs. Solomon

TRICK UPON TRICK.

Mixum	Mr. Kenna
Vizard	Mr. Harper
Freeman	Mr. Fransis
Solomon Smack . .	Mr. Powers
Mrs. Mixum	Miss Smith

TRUE-BORN IRISHMAN.

O'Dogherty	Mr. Watts
Mushroom	Mr. Harper
Hamilton	Mr. Adams
Major Gamble	Mr. Kenna
John	Mr. Redfield
William	Mr. Clapham
Mrs. O'Dogherty .	Mrs. Mechtler
Kitty Farrell	Mrs. Harper
Lady Kinnegad . . .	Mrs. Watts

WEST INDIAN.

Belcour	Mr. Harper
Stockwell	Mr. Adams
Major O'Flaherty . .	Mr. Kenna
Captain Dudley . .	Mr. Redfield
Charles Dudley . . .	Mr. Watts
Fulmer	Mr. Solomon
Miss Rusport . .	Mrs. Mechtler
Louisa Dudley . . .	Miss Smith
Mrs. Fulmer . . .	Mrs. Solomon
Lady Rusport . . .	Mrs. Watts

WITCHES.

Harlequin	Mr. Prigmore
Pantaloon	Mr. Kenna
Clown	Mr. Harper
Lover	Mr. Adams
Columbine	Miss Smith

in the bills of the October season was that of Mr. Clapham, who played *Freeman* in a " Bold Stroke for a Wife" among other parts, and accompanied the company to Providence in December.

In the Autumn of 1794 a new, temporary theatre was erected in Providence, in the rear of a building known as the Old Coffee House. The season began on the 30th of December, and closed on the 13th of April following. Besides Mrs. Kenna and Mr. Clapham, the only new names in the casts were those of Copeland, Farlowe and Mc-Grath. McGrath was probably the strolling manager and actor of that name. In the early part of the season Mr. and Mrs. Watts were still with the company, but their names are not in the later

LIST OF PERFORMANCES—*Providence.*

1794.
Dec. 30—Foundling . . . . Moore
　　　　Miller of Mansfield . . . Dodsley
1795.
Feb.　9—Wonder . . . . . Mrs. Centlivre
　　　　All the World's a Stage . Jackman
　　　16—Venice Preserved . . . . Otway
　　　　Love a la Mode . . . . Macklin
March 2—Bold Stroke for a Wife
　　　　　　　　　　Mrs. Centlivre
　　　　Mayor of Garratt . . . . Foote
　　　30—Hamlet . . . . . . Shakspere
　　　　Three Weeks After Marriage
　　　　　　　　　　　　Murphy
　　　　(Mr. Kenna's benefit.)
April 13—Beggar's Opera . . . . . . Gay
　　　　Lying Valet . . . . . Garrick
　　　(Farlowe and McGrath's benefit.)

casts. Incomplete as the list of performances is, it is full enough to show the work of the season. In addition to these pieces, Mr. Blake names "Barnaby Brittle," "Provoked Wife," "Deuce is in Him" and "Beaux' Stratagem." It is likely the " Provoked Husband" was meant, the " Provoked Wife" having never been played in America.

PROVIDENCE CASTS—FIRST SEASON OF 1794-5.

BEGGAR'S OPERA.

Captain Macheath . Mr. Harper
Peachum . . . . . Mr. McGrath
Lockit . . . . Mr. Kenna
Filch . . . . Mr. Clapham
Mat . . . . Mr. Patterson
Ben Budge . . . . Mr. Copeland
Polly . . . . . . Mrs. Mechtler
Mrs. Peachum . . . Mrs. Harper
Mrs. Slammekin . . Mrs. Kenna
Diana Trapes . . . Mr. Farlowe
Lucy . . . . Mrs. Harper

FOUNDLING.

Sir Charles Raymond . Mr. Kenna
Sir Roger Belmont . Mr. Clapham
Colonel Raymond . Mr. Copeland
Young Belmont . . Mr. Harper
Faddle . . . . Mr. Watts
Rosetta . . . . . Mrs. Mechtler
Fidelia . . . . Mrs. Harper

HAMLET.

Hamlet . . . . . . Mr. Harper

In the summer of 1795 Harper found himself excluded from Newport by a rival company made up of actors and actresses from the disbanded forces of the Boston Theatre. Mr. Harper was, no doubt, content, as a new theatre was building in Providence for his occupancy and was to be opened on the 2d of September by part of the Old American Company in conjunction with his own forces. A meeting was held at McLane's Coffee House as early as the 14th of April, 1795, to raise subscriptions for a new theatre. John Brown gave a lot situated at Westminster and Mathewson Streets, where Grace Church now stands, and a sufficient sum was guaranteed in time for work on the building to begin on the 6th of August. As less than a month remained previous to the opening night, the carpenters in the town formed a "bee" and worked without pay for the purpose of completing the theatre in time. The building was 81 feet long by 50 feet in Westminster Street. Access was by three doors in front, the middle door being the entrance to the boxes, the east door to the pit, and the west door to the gallery. There were two tiers of boxes.

PROVIDENCE CASTS—FIRST SEASON OF 1794-5.

King . . . . Mr. Redfield
Ghost . . . . Mr. Kenna
Polonius . . . . . Mr. Clapham
Horatio . . . . . Mr. Patterson
Player King . . . . Mr. Farlowe
First Gravedigger . Mr. McGrath
Second Gravedigger,Mr.Copeland
Player Queen . . . Mrs. Kenna
Queen . . . . Mrs. Harper
Ophelia . . . . . Mrs. Mechtler

LOVE A LA MODE.

Sir Callaghan . . . . Mr. Kenna
Sir Archy . . . . . Mr. Clapham
Sir Theodore . . . Mr. Copeland
Beau Mordecai . . . Mr. Farlowe
Squire Groom . . . . Mr. Harper
Charlotte . . . . . Mrs. Harper

LYING VALET.

Gayless . . . . . Mr. Patterson
Sharp . . . . . . Mr. Harper
Guttle . . . . . . Mr. Kenna
Trippet . . . . . Mr. Copeland
Drunken Cook . . Mr. Clapham
Melissa . . . . . Mrs. Harper
Mrs. Gadabout . . . Mrs. Kenna
Kitty Pry . . . . Mrs. Mechtler

MILLER OF MANSFIELD.

King . . . . . . Mr. Watts
Lurewell . . . . . Mr. Copeland
Miller . . . . . . Mr. Kenna
Dick . . . . Mr. Harper
Joe . . . . Mr. Clapham
Peggy . . . . . . Mrs. Harper
Margery . . . . . Mrs. Mechtler
Kate . . . . Mr. Watts

THREE WEEKS AFTER MARRIAGE.

Sir Charles Racket . Mr. Harper
Drugget . . . . . . Mr. Kenny
Lovelace . . . . . Mr. Patterson
Woodley . . . . . Mr. Copeland
Thomas . . . . . Mr. Clapham
Lady Racket . . . Mrs. Harper
Mrs. Drugget . . Mrs. Mechtler
Dimity . . . . . . Mrs. Kenna

VENICE PRESERVED.

Jaffier . . . . . . Mr. Harper
Pierre . . . . . . Mr. Kenna
Priuli . . . . . Mr. Clapham
Renault . . . . . Mr. Redfield
Bedamar . . . . . Mr. Patterson
Elliott . . . . . Mr. Copeland
Spinosa . . . . . Mr. Farlowe
Belvidera . . . . Mrs. Harper

The proscenium was 16 feet high by 24 wide, with a motto over the arch—" Pleasure the means—the end virtue."

The opening, intended for the 2d of September, was postponed until the following evening, when a season began that lasted until the 2d of November. On the opening night Mr. Harper delivered an Occasional Address,[1] the authorship of which was attributed both to Paul Allen and Ann Maria Thayer. The opening attractions were the " Child of Nature" and " Rosina," and the season closed with

---

[1] PROVIDENCE PROLOGUE.

The eye contemplating this simple dome
Views not the art of Greece, the wealth of
    Rome ;
Nor tow'ring arch, nor roof of vast design,
Which prove the virtues of the Parian nine ;
Nor painting's touch, nor sculpture's breath-
    ing mould,
Nor life enchased in elephant and gold.
It boasts them not ; alas, it boasts alone
The wish to please—and let that wish atone.
Ye fair, who deign our efforts to repay,
Ye give it honors and ye take away.
    Here to your eyes we hold the mirror true,
Here pass your virtues in their bright review.
Nor cold reproof, nor satire's caustic smart
Can crimson virtue's cheek, or chill the heart.
Laugh then secure, or pity virtue's call—
The strokes of censure on the guilty fall.
Here view yourselves, nor fear t' applaud the
    scene,
Live o'er your lives and be what ye have
    been ;
Give to th' unbidden tear its generous flow,
Not more can pity give to fancied woe ;
Nor fear that hid beneath the mimic guise
Vice waits her victim with impatient eyes.
Here shall ye learn with purity of heart
To meet the artful in the fields of art.
The eye which beams intelligence and love

Shall learn to blend the serpent with the
    dove,
The righteous claim of bashful mirth to scan,
And well discern the coxcomb from the man.
    In ancient days when Rome could boast
    her name,
When Scipio fought and Terence wrote for
    fame,
Ere taste or genuine wit was forced to yield,
And low buffoonery had usurped the field,
The Roman stage was virtue's primal school.
There heroes learned to conquer and to rule,
And, while they wept as mimic woes were
    shown,
To feel for others' and t' endure their own.
Nor did the jest, ambiguous and obscene,
Disturb the cheek of innocence serene.
But nature's mother-wit, sublime and chaste,
Met the full voice of modesty and taste.
If such the manners of the Roman age,
Such must delight when Yankees seek the
    stage.
See a new Rome in Western forests rise,
Her manners simple and her maxims wise ;
These t' improve, to cherish fresh and fair,
Shall be our best regard, our only care.
This humble house, its office so divine,
With more than all Vitruvius' arts shall shine.
Enough for us, we rest secure the while
Of Virtue's plaudit and of Beauty's smile.

three pieces for the benefit of Mr. and Mrs. Hallam—the "Miser," "Midnight Hour" and "Robinson Crusoe." The casts show that the detachment from the Old American Company consisted of Mr. and Mrs. Hallam, Mr. Hallam, the younger, Mr. Prigmore and Mr. Woolls. Providence criticism at this time was peculiar. When "Percy" was played on the 7th of September, a writer in the *United States Chronicle* declared himself "particularly pleased with the gentleman who did the part of *Douglas*—he acted a jealous madman to the life. Old *Lord Raby* did the distressed father beyond anything I had any idea of. I could not help crying. The part of *Percy* I was much delighted with; but *Elwina*, poor girl, I shall not forget you as long as I live."

When the season closed, Harper joined the forces at the Boston Theatre, and his regular management in Rhode Island ceased.

CHILD OF NATURE.

Marquis	Mr. Harper
Valentia	Mr. Hallam
Murcia	Mr. Prigmore
Seville	Mr. Patterson
Granada	Mr. Humphreys
Peasant	Mr. Hallam
Marchioness	Mrs. Mechtler
Amanthis	Mrs. Harper

MISER.

Lovegold	Mr. Hallam
Ramillie	Mr. Hallam, Jr
Clerimont	Mr. Prigmore
Decoy	Mr. Kenna
Furnish	Mr. Tompkins
Sparkle	Mr. Woolls
Sattin	Mr. McKnight
James	Mr. Copeland
Frederick	Mr. Harper
Marianna	Mrs. Harper
Harriet	Mrs. Mechtler
Lappet	Mrs. Hallam

MIDNIGHT HOUR.

Marquis	Mr. Hallam, Jr
Sebastian	Mr. Harper
Nicholas	Mr. Hallam
Matthias	Mr. Woolls
Ambrose	Mr. Copeland
General	Mr. Prigmore
Julia	Mrs. Harper
Cicely	Mrs. Mechtler
Flora	Mrs. Hallam

ROBINSON CRUSOE.

Robinson Crusoe	Mr. Hallam
Indian Chief	Mr. Harper
Captain	Mr. Woolls
Pantaloon	Mr. Copeland
Friday	Mr. Hallam, Jr
Columbine	Mrs. Harper

CHAPTER XIII.

THE INVASION OF NEW ENGLAND.

A PART OF THE OLD AMERICAN COMPANY AT HARTFORD IN 1794—HART-
FORD CASTS—HODGKINSON LEADS THE HARTFORD DETACHMENT
IN 1795—SOME OF THE PRODUCTIONS AND CASTS—THE NEW
YORK COMPANY IN BOSTON—A BRILLIANT ENGAGEMENT.

AFTER the close of the New York season of 1793–4 and previous to the return of Hallam and Hodgkinson to the Southwark Theatre in Philadelphia for the Autumn season of 1794, a
detachment of the Old American Company ventured to invade New
England, appearing at Hartford on the 31st of July and remaining
until the 12th of September. This detachment was under the command of Mr. Martin, and the company consisted of Mr. and Mrs.
Martin, Mr. and Mrs. King, Mr. and Mrs. Ashton, Messrs. Ryan,
Bisset and Bergman, Miss Chaucer and Mrs. Wilson. Hallam and
Hodgkinson apparently had no connection with the enterprise, but
Mr. Hodgkinson was in Hartford on the 3d of September, when he
gave the rather feeble contingent the benefit of an appearance.

The list of performances and the annexed casts, though not
complete, give a satisfactory idea of the campaign with which the invasion of New England began. The plays, operas and farces were
among the most popular productions of the New York repertory,
and it is probable that the season proved reasonably remunerative.

Hartford was then a mere village, and, as it turned out in subsequent seasons, incapable of supporting an expensive organization for even a brief period. There is no hint in the advertisements of the character of the theatre, but the prices were graduated on the usual scale —three shillings and ninepence for the boxes, two shillings and thr'pence to the pit, and one shilling and sixpence to the gallery. On the opening night Mr. Ryan did not appear, and Mr. Ashton read his parts; but notwithstanding this drawback the Hartford *Gazette* said of the performance, "It pleased, and that was sufficient." An incident of the opening night was the first appearance on any stage of a young lady as *Amanthis*. She was probably Mrs. Martin. Another *debutant* was a youth of Hartford as *Edward* in "Every One

LIST OF PERFORMANCES—*Hartford.*

1794.

July 31—Child of Nature . Mrs. Inchbald
　　　　Love a la Mode . . . . Macklin
Aug. 4—West Indian . . . . . Cumberland
　　　　Prisoner at Large . . . O'Keefe
　　　7—School for Scandal . . Sheridan
　　　　Poor Soldier . . . . . O'Keefe
　　　11—Child of Nature.
　　　　No Song No Supper . . . Hoare
　　　14—Prisoner at Large.
　　　　Love a la Mode.
　　　21—Douglas . . . . Home
　　　　Ghost . . . . . . Mrs. Centlivre
　　　25—Ways and Means . . Colman, Jr.
　　　　No Song No Supper.
　　　(Mr. and Mrs. King's benefit.)
　　　28—Miser . . . . Fielding
　　　　Catharine and Petruchio, Shakspere
　　(Mr. Ryan and Miss Chaucer's benefit.)
Sept. 1—Wonder . . . . Mrs. Centlivre
　　　　Rosina . . . . . Mrs. Brooke
　　　(Bisset and Collard's benefit.)
　　　8—Every One Has His Fault
　　　　　　　　　　Mrs. Inchbald
　　　　Citizen . . . . Murphy
　　　(Mr. and Mrs. Ashton's benefit.)
　　　12—Busybody . . . . Mrs. Centlivre
　　　　Daphne and Amintor.
　　　　Death of Harlequin.
　　　(Mr. and Mrs. Martin's benefit.)

Has His Fault." The name of Mrs. Wilson was generally spelled "Willson" in the advertisements. The casts printed herewith are mainly interesting as showing the important roles assumed by the minor players of the Old American Company upon the first occasion that they organized themselves into a special company for the invasion of a quiet New England town. Martin as *Marplot, Petruchio, Young Norval, Captain*

Irwin, Charles Surface, Random, Belcour and *Don Felix;* Ashton as
Lovegold and *Sir Peter Teazle ;* King as *Lord Norland, Robin* and

HARTFORD CASTS—1794.

BUSYBODY.

Marplot	Mr. Martin
Sir George Airy	Mr. King
Sir Francis Gripe	Mr. Ashton
Charles	Mr. Bergman
Sir Jealous Traffic	Mr. Ryan
Whisper	Mr. Bisset
Miranda	Mrs. Wilson
Patch	Mrs. Martin
Scentwell	Miss Chaucer
Isabinda	Mrs. King

CATHARINE AND PETRUCHIO.

Petruchio	Mr. Martin
Baptista } Jailor }	Mr. Ryan
Hortensio	Mr. Bisset
Biondello	Mr. Bergman
Grumio	Mr. Ashton
Bianca	Mrs. King
Curtis	Mrs. Ashton
Catharine	Mrs. Wilson

CHILD OF NATURE.

Count Valentia	Mr. Martin
Alberto	Mr. Ashton
Granada	Mr. Ryan
Seville	Mr. Bisset
Marquis	Mr. King
Marchioness	Mrs. Wilson

CITIZEN.

Young Philpot	Mr. Martin
Old Philpot	Mr. Ashton
Young Wilding	Mr. King
Sir Jasper	Mr. Ryan
Beaufort	Mr. Bergman
Quilldrive	Mr. Bisset
Corinna	Miss Chaucer
Maria	Mrs. Wilson

DAPHNE AND AMINTOR.

Amintor	Mr. Bergman
First Statue	Mr. Martin
Second Statue	Mr. Ashton
Third Statue	Mr. Ryan
Mindora	Mrs. Martin
Daphne	Mrs. Wilson

DEATH OF HARLEQUIN.

Harlequin	Mr. Martin

Pantaloon	Mr. Ryan
Magician	Mr. Bisset
Clown	Mr. Ashton
Columbine	Mrs. King

DOUGLAS.

Young Norval	Mr. Martin
Lord Randolph	Mr. Ashton
Old Norval	Mr. Ryan
Officer	Mr. Bergman
Shepherd	Mr. Bisset
Glenalvon	Mr. King
Anna	Miss Chaucer
Lady Randolph	Mrs. Wilson

EVERY ONE HAS HIS FAULT.

Lord Norland	Mr. King
Harmony	Mr. Ashton
Sir Robert Ramble	Mr. Bergman
Solus	Mr. Ryan
Placid	Mr. Bisset
Capt. Irwin	Mr. Martin
Miss Wooburn	Miss Chaucer
Mrs. Placid	Mrs. King
Miss Spinster	Mrs. Ashton
Lady Elinor	Mrs. Wilson

GHOST.

Roger	Mr. Martin
Capt. Constant	Mr. Bergman
Trusty	Mr. Ryan
Sir Jeffrey	Mr. Bisset
Clinch	Mr. King
Belinda	Mrs. Martin
Dorothy	Mrs. Wilson

LOVE A LA MODE.

Sir Callaghan	Mr. King
Sir Archy	Mr. Bisset
Sir Theodore	Mr. Ryan
Beau Mordecai	Mr. Ashton
Squire Groom	Mr. Martin
Charlotte	Mrs. Wilson

MISER.

Lovegold	Mr. Ashton
Ramillie	Mr. King
Clerimont	Mr. Martin
Frederick	Mr. Bergman
Decoy	Mr. Ryan

Furnish	Mr. Bisset
Mariana	Mrs. Wilson
Harriet	Mrs. King
Mrs. Wisely	Mrs. Ashton
Wheedle	Mrs. Martin
Lappet	Miss Chaucer

NO SONG NO SUPPER.

Robin	Mr. King
Endless	Mr. Martin
Frederick	Mr. Ashton
Thomas	Mr. Ryan
William	Mr. Bisset
Crop	Mr. Bergman
Dorothy	Mrs. King
Louise	Miss Chaucer
Nelly	Mrs. Ashton
Margaretta	Mrs. Wilson

POOR SOLDIER.

Patrick	Mr. King
Capt. Fitzroy	Mr. Ashton
Dermot	Mr. Bergman
Father Luke	Mr. Ryan
Darby	Mr. Martin
Norah	Mrs. King
Kathleen	Mrs. Wilson

PRISONER AT LARGE.

Old Dowdle	Mr. Ashton
Lord Esmond	Mr. King
Jack Conner	Mr. Bergman
Frippon	Mr. Ryan
Father Frank	Mr. Bisset
Muns	Mr. Martin
Adelaide	Mrs. King
Mary	Miss Chaucer
Rachel	Mrs. Wilson

ROSINA.

Capt. Belville	Mr. Bergman
William	Mr. Martin
Rustic	Mr. Ryan
First Irishman	Mr. Ashton
Second Irishman	Mr. Bisset
Belville	Mr. King
Phœbe	Mrs. Martin
Dorcas	Mrs. Ashton
Rosina	Mrs. Wilson

Major O'Flaherty, and Bisset as *Sir Archy McSarcasm* certainly make a remarkable showing when their rank in the New York Theatre is considered.

The second season at the Hartford Theatre began August 3d, 1795, the building being probably the same that was occupied by Martin's contingent the previous year. The company comprised, besides Mr. and Mrs. Hodgkinson, a strong force from the New York Theatre as the Old American Company was previously organized. On the opening night Mr. Hodgkinson spoke a prologue, written by himself, previous to his appearance as *Vapid*. A few facts in relation to the benefits show that the season was unprofitable. Mr. Martin's first benefit failed,

LIST OF PERFORMANCES—*Hartford.*
1795.

Aug. 3—Dramatist . . . . . . Reynolds
          Rival Candidates .   . . Bate
   10—Such Things Are . Mrs. Inchbald
          Rosina . . . . . . Mrs. Brooke
   17—Belle's Stratagem . Mrs. Cowley
          Bird Catcher.
          Children in the Wood . . Morton
   24—Haunted Tower . . . . . Cobb
          Busybody . . . . Mrs. Centlivre
   31—Grecian Daughter . . . Murphy
          Triumph of Mirth.
Sept. 7—Country Girl . . . . . . Garrick
          Caledonian Frolic . . . Francis
          Poor Soldier . . . . . O'Keefe
   14—Isabella . . . . Southerne
          Le Foret Noire.
   23—Merchant of Venice . . Shakspere
          Two Philosophers.
          Agreeable Surprise . . . O'Keefe

HARTFORD CASTS—1794.

SCHOOL FOR SCANDAL.

Sir Peter Teazle . . . Mr. Ashton
Joseph Surface . . . Mr. King
Charles Surface }
Sir Benjamin   } . . Mr. Martin
Sir Oliver . . . . . . Mr. Bisset
Crabtree }
Moses   } . . . . Mr. Ryan
Rowley }
Careless } . . . . Mr. Bergman
Mrs. Candour . . . Mrs. Martin
Maria . . . . Mrs. King
Lady Sneerwell . . Mrs. Ashton
Lady Teazle . . . . Mrs. Wilson

WAYS AND MEANS.

Random . . . . . . Mr. Martin

Sample . . . . . Mr. Bergman
Sir David Dunder . . Mr. Ashton
Paul Peary . . . . . Mr. Ryan
Tiptoe . . . . Mr. King
Harriet . . . . . . Mrs. Wilson
Lady Dunder . . . Mrs. Ashton
Kitty . . . . . . Mrs. King

WEST INDIAN.

Belcour . . . . . . Mr. Martin
Stockwell . . . . Mr. Ashton
Charles Dudley . . Mr. Bergman
Capt. Dudley . . . . Mr. Bisset
Fulmer . . . . . . Mr. Ryan
Maj. O'Flaherty . . . Mr. King
Charlotte Rusport . . Mrs. Wilson

Lady Rusport . . . Mrs. Martin
Mrs. Fulmer . . . Mrs. Ashton
Louisa Dudley . . . . Mrs. King

WONDER.

Don Felix . . . . . Mr. Martin
Lissardo . . . . . Mr. Bergman
Don Pedro }
Frederick } . . . Mr. Ashton
Don Lopez . . . . Mr. Ryan
Gibby . . . . Mr. Bisset
Col. Briton . . . . . . Mr. King
Violante . . . . . . Mrs. Wilson
Flora . . . . Mrs. Martin
Inis . . . . Miss Chaucer
Isabella . . . . **Mrs. King**

that of the 5th of October being his second attempt. The benefit of Mr. and Mrs. King, Mrs. Hamilton and Mr. Lee on the 7th was also a second attempt, and the Kings made a third attempt on the last night of the season in conjunction with Mr. and Mrs. Cleveland, who had also made a previous trial. This was the first appearance of the Clevelands with the Old American Company. Hodgkinson's Address was printed, and, if not rhythmically perfect, it will be found creditable to its

Sept. 24—Deaf Lover . . . . Pilon
Sophia of Brabant.
Romp . . . . Bickerstaft
(Mad. Gardie and Miss Harding's benefit.)
28—Such Things Are.
Highland Wedding . . . Martin
Florizel and Perdita . . Shakspere
(Mr. and Mrs. Cleveland s benefit.)
30—I'll Tell You What . Mrs. Inchbald
Old Soldier.
Farmer . . . . O'Keefe
(Ashton and Durang's benefit.)
Oct. 2—Columbus . . . . . . Morton
Harlequin Gardener.
Farm House . . . . . Kemble
(Mr. King's benefit.)
5—School for Soldiers . . . Henry
Quaker . . . . Dibdin
(Mr. Martin's benefit.)
7—Midnight Hour . . Mrs. Inchbald
Highland Wedding.
American Tar . . . . . Morton
(Mr. and Mrs. King, Mrs. Hamilton and
Mr. Lee's benefit.)

HODGKINSON'S ADDRESS.

Here, while fair peace spreads her protect-
ing wing,
Science and art, secure from danger, spring;
Guarded by freedom, strengthened by the
laws,
Their progress must command the world's
applause.
While thro' all Europe horrid discord
reigns,
And the destructive sword crimsons her
plains,
Oh! be it ours to shelter the opprest;
Here let them find peace, liberty and rest,
Upheld by Washington, at whose dread name
Proud anarchy retires with fear and shame.
Among the liberal arts behold the stage
Rise, though opposed by stern, fanatic rage!
Prejudice shrinks, and, as the clouds give
way,

Reason and candor brighten up the day.
No immorality now stains our page,
No vile obscenity in this blest age.
Where mild religion takes her heav'nly reign
The stage the finest precepts must maintain.
If from this rule it swerved at any time,
It was the people's, not the stage's crime.
Let them spurn aught that's out of virtue's
rule,
The stage will ever be a virtuous school.
And tho' 'mong players some there may be
found
Whose conduct is not altogether sound,
The stage is not alone in this to blame—
Ev'ry profession will have still the same.
A virtuous sentiment from vice may come,
The libertine may praise a happy home.
Your remedy is good with such a teacher;
Imbibe the precept, but condemn the preacher.

Oct. 9—Guardian . . . . Garrick
  Sultan . . . . Bickerstaff
  Poor Vulcan.
(Mr. and Mrs. Hodgkinson's benefit.)
  14—Chapter of Accidents . Miss Lee
  Prisoner at Large . . . O'Keefe
(Mr. and Mrs. King and Mr. and Mrs.
  Cleveland's benefit.)

author. It is unnecessary to give the casts in detail, except those of the "Dramatist" and "Rival Candidates" on the opening night, and of "Such Things Are" and "Rosina," which were played a week later. These will serve to show the manner in which the Hartford contingent was constituted. The new theatre in Providence not being ready for occupancy in August, Mr. Harper visited Hartford and played the *Sultan* in Mrs. Inchbald's comedy on the 10th. These casts also show that Mr. and Mrs. Chambers were again with the company. Madame Gardie also accompanied Hodgkinson's forces. Besides his own customary parts,

DRAMATIST.

Vapid . . . Mr. Hodgkinson
Lord Scratch . . Mr. Prigmore
Neville . . . . Mr. Cleveland
Ennui . . . . Mr. King
Willoughby . . . Mr. Ashton
Peter . . . . . Mr. Durang
Floriville . . . . Mr. Martin
Louisa Courtney . Mrs. Cleveland
Lady Waitfort . Mrs. Hamilton
Letty . . . . . Mrs. Miller
Marianne . . Mrs. Hodgkinson

RIVAL CANDIDATES.

Byron . . . . . Mr. Carr
General Worry . . Mr. Ashton
Spy . . . . . . Mr. Prigmore
Sir Harry Muff . . Mr. Martin
Jenny . . . . . . Mrs. Miller
Narcissa . . Mrs. Hodgkinson

Hodgkinson played the important roles that Hallam still retained, as *Marplot* in the "Busybody," and Mr. Chambers succeeded Hallam, Jr., as *Sir George Airy*. Mrs. Cleveland was *Miranda*, instead of Mrs. Hallam. Mr. Cleveland was *De Courcey* in the "Haunted Tower," instead of the younger Hallam, while Mrs. Cleveland succeeded Mrs. Solomon as

SUCH THINGS ARE.

Mr. Howard . Mr. Hodgkinson
Sultan . . . . . Mr. Harper
Sir Luke Tremor Mr. Prigmore
Elvirus . . . . Mr. Cleveland
Lord Flint . . . Mr. Ashton
Zedan . . . . . . Mr. King
Meanright . . . . Mr. Carr
Twineall . . . . Mr. Martin
Lady Tremor . Mrs. Hamilton
Aurelia . . . . Mrs. Chambers
Female Prisoner . Mrs. Cleveland

ROSINA.

Belville . . . Mr. Hodgkinson
Captain Belville . . . Mr. Carr
Rustic . . . . . . Mr. Lee
Irishman . . . . Mr. King
Second Irishman . Mr. Durang
William . . . . Mr. Chambers
Phœbe . . . . Mrs. Chambers
Dorcas . . . . Mrs. Hamilton
Rosina . . . Mrs. Hodgkinson

Cicely, and Mrs. Chambers was the successor of Mrs. Pownall as *Lady Elinor*. These indicate the character of the changes throughout the season. It is to be regretted that no cast has been found of Morton's "Columbus," as its production at Hartford antedated the famous Philadelphia run of the piece by more than a year. A Farewell Address written by a gentleman of Hartford was spoken on the closing night of the season by Mr. Hodgkinson.

After the failure of Charles Powell as the manager of the Boston Theatre, Colonel Tyler, who had been the "master of ceremonies," assumed the management on behalf of the trustees. Colonel Tyler engaged a part of the company that had acted under Powell, including Mr. and Mrs. S. Powell, Taylor, Villiers, Kenny and Mr. and Mrs. Hughes. He also made an arrangement with Hallam and Hodgkinson for a brief engagement of the Old American Company, the two contingents that had been playing at Providence and Hartford being united for a short but brilliant season. Mr. and Mrs. Harper were also with this united company, which was still further strengthened by the engagement of Mr. Jefferson, who had been engaged by Powell, but arrived

LIST OF PERFORMANCES—*Boston*.

1795.

Nov.	2—Know Your Own Mind .	Murphy
	Caledonian Frolic . . .	Francis
	Purse	Cross
	5—Provoked Husband . .	Vanbrugh
	Rosina	Mrs. Brooke
	9—School for Scandal . . .	Sheridan
	Children in the Wood . .	Morton
	11—Jane Shore	Rowe
	Highland Reel	O'Keefe
	13—Dramatist	Reynolds
	Harlequin Restored.	
	16—Midnight Hour . .	Mrs. Inchbald
	Two Philosophers.	
	Children in the Wood.	
	18—Rivals	Sheridan
	Sultan	Bickerstaff
	20—Clandestine Marriage	
		Garrick and Colman
	Bird Catcher.	
	Spoiled Child	Bickerstaff
	23—I'll Tell You What.	Mrs. Inchbald
	Poor Jack.	
	Children in the Wood.	
	25—Rage	Reynolds
	Bird Catcher.	
	Padlock	Bickerstaff
	27—Haunted Tower	Cobb
	Love a la Mode	Macklin

Nov. 30—Haunted Tower.
　　　　Bon Ton . . . . Garrick
Dec. 2—Battle of Hexham . . Colman, Jr
　　　　Romp . . . . Bickerstaff
　　4—Deserted Daughter . . . Holcroft
　　　　Don Juan.
　　7—School for Soldiers . . . Henry
　　　　Don Juan.
　　9—Deserted Daughter.
　　　　Poor Jack.
　　　　Spoiled Child.
　　11—Country Girl . . . . . . Garrick
　　　　Harlequin Gardener.
　　　　Purse.
　　14—Robin Hood . . . . . MacNally
　　　　Bold Stroke for a Wife
　　　　　　　　　　　　Mrs. Centlivre
　　21—Macbeth . . . . . . Shakspere
　　　　Sultan.
　　23—Tempest . . . . Dryden
　　　　Le Foret Noire.
　　25—Richard III . . . . . Shakspere
　　　　Deserter . . . . Dibdin
　　28—Richard III.
　　　　Deserter.
　　　　(Mr. Deblois' benefit.)
　　30—Which is the Man ? . Mrs. Cowley
　　　　Irish Widow . . . . . . Garrick
　　　(Mr. and Mrs. Johnson's benefit.)
1796.
Jan. 1—He Would be a Soldier . . Pilon
　　　　Poor Vulcan . . . . . . Dibdin
　　(Mr. Prigmore and Mrs. Brett's benefit.)
　　4—Wheel of Fortune . Cumberland
　　　　Tammany . . . . Mrs. Hatton
　　　　(Mr. Hodgkinson's benefit.)
　　6—Alexander the Great . . . . Lee
　　　　Beggar's Opera . . . . . . Gay
　　(Hamilton and Hallam, Jr.'s, benefit.)
　　8—Inkle and Yarico . . Colman, Jr
　　　　Harlequin Shipwrecked.
　　　　Slaves Released from Algiers
　　　　　　　　　　　　Mrs. Rowson
　　(Mr. and Mrs. Cleveland's benefit.)
　　11—School for Wives . . . . . Kelly
　　　　Highland Reel.
　　　　(Mr. and Mrs. Tyler's benefit.)

after Powell's failure, and the addition of some important acquisitions from England secured by Mr. Hodgkinson. These additions were Mr. and Mrs. Johnson, Mr. and Mrs. Tyler and Mrs. Brett. Other members of the company were Mr. Hamilton, who played the testy old men of comedy, and Mrs. Pick, who was a favorite Boston singer. This remarkable organization opened the Boston Theatre on the 2d of November, 1795, and continued to give performances until the 20th of January, 1796, when the New York company withdrew to reopen the old house in John Street. No novelties were attempted, but the company was in itself a novelty, the like of which has not been seen by this generation of playgoers. The Boston contingent was in itself the nucleus of an excellent company. Harper and his wife were Boston favorites. Without the acquisitions, who were now seen in America for the first time, the New York company was far superior to either of those previously seen at the Boston Theatre, and with them it was the strongest company then on the American stage. The strength of the organization as a whole can be best understood from a glance at the casts during the stay of the Old American Company in Bos-

Jan. 13—Othello . . . . Shakspere
Man and Wife . . . . . Colman
(Mr. and Mrs. Hallam's benefit.)
15—Inconstant . . . . . . Farquhar
Les Deux Chasseurs.
Children in the Wood.
(Mad. Gardie and Miss Harding's benefit.)
18—West Indian . . . . Cumberland
Harlequin Skeleton.
No Song No Supper . . . Hoare
(King and Jefferson's benefit.)
20—Florizel and Perdita . . Shakspere
Flitch of Bacon . . . . . . Bate
Critic . . . . Sheridan
(Mrs. Hodgkinson's benefit.)

ton. Two of these, those of " Know Your Own Mind " and the " Provoked Husband," deserve to be set apart from the rest, because it was in the former, on the opening night, that Mr. Johnson as *Bygrove* and Mrs. Brett as *Mrs. Bromly* made their first appearance in America, and in the latter, on the night following, that Mr. Tyler as *Mr. Manly*,

KNOW YOUR OWN MIND.

Dashwould . Mr. Hodgkinson
Malvil . . . . Mr. Cleveland
Bygrove . . . . . Mr. Johnson
(First appearance in America.)
Sir Harry Lovewit . Mr. Martin
Captain Bygrove . Mr. Hughes
Charles . . . . . Mr. Villiers
Richard . . . . . Mr. Durang
Robert . . . . . Mr. Leonard
Millamour . . . Mr. Chambers
Miss Neville . Mrs. Cleveland
Lady Jane . . Mrs. Chambers
Mrs. Bromly . . . Mrs. Brett
(First appearance in America.)
Mad. La Rouge . Mad. Gardie
Lady Bell . . Mrs. Hodgkinson

Mrs. Tyler as *Lady Grace,* and Mrs. Johnson as *Lady Townly* made their American *debuts.* Mr. Jefferson's first appearance was reserved until the 16th of December, when he

PROVOKED HUSBAND.

Lord Townly . Mr. Hodgkinson
Sir Francis . . . Mr. Johnson
John Moody . . . Mr. Villiers
Count Basset . . . Mr. Taylor
Squire Richard . . Mr. Martin
Poundage . . . . Mr. Ashton
James . . . . . Mr. Leonard
William . . . . . Mr. Durang
Mr. Manly . . . . Mr. Tyler
(First appearance in America.)
Lady Grace . . . . Mrs. Tyler
(First appearance in America.)
Lady Wronghead . . Mrs. Brett
Miss Jenny . . Mrs. Chambers
Myrtilla . . . . . Mrs. King
Trusty . . . . Mrs. Durang
Lady Townly . . Mrs. Johnson
(First appearance in America.)

was brought forward as *La Gloire* in the "Surrender of Calais." Mr.

Jefferson was still a very young man, if, as his biographers have it, he was born in 1774. He was a son of Thomas Jefferson, an actor for many years with Garrick at Drury Lane, and afterward the manager of the theatre at Plymouth. In his father's company Joseph Jefferson received the rudiments of his theatrical education, but as soon as he reached his majority he quitted Plymouth for America. Powell had agreed to pay his passage to Boston and allow him a salary of seven-

OLD AMERICAN COMPANY CASTS—1795-6.

BATTLE OF HEXHAM.

Gondibert . . . Mr. Hodgkinson
Fool . . . . Mr. Hallam
Barton . . . . Mr. Tyler
La Varenne . . . Mr. Hallam, Jr
Montague . . . . . Mr. Harper
Warwick . . . . . Mr. Cleveland
Somerset . . . . . Mr. Taylor
Prince of Wales . . Miss Harding
Corporal . . . . . Mr. Villiers
Fifer . . . . Mr. S. Powell
Drummer . . . . . Mr. Johnson
Old Peasant . . . . Mr. Hughes
Gregory Gubbins . Mr. Prigmore
Adeline . . . . . Mrs. Cleveland
Queen Margaret . Mrs. Johnson

BIRD CATCHER.

Bird Catcher . . . . Mr. Durang
Village Maid . . . . Mad. Gardie

BOLD STROKE FOR A WIFE.

Colonel Feignwell . Mr. S. Powell
Sir Philip . . . . . . Mr. Taylor
Tradelove . . . . . Mr. Kenny
Periwinkle . . . . Mr. Prigmore
Sackbut . . . . . . Mr. Ashton
Freeman . . . . Mr. Hallam, Jr
Simon Pure . . . . . Mr. Woolls
Quaker Boy . . . . Mr. Durang
Obadiah Prim . . . Mr. Hughes
Ann Lovely . . . Mrs. S. Powell
Masked Lady . . . . Mrs. King
Mrs. Prim . . . . . . Mrs. Brett

BON TON.

Sir John Trotley . Mr. Hamilton
Colonel Tivy . . . Mr. Cleveland

Jessamy . . . . Mr. Hallam, Jr
Lord Minikin . . . Mr. S. Powell
Lady Minikin . . Mrs. Cleveland
Gymp . . . . Mrs. King
Miss Tittup . . . Mrs. S. Powell

CALEDONIAN FROLIC.

Sandy . . . . Mr. Durang
Jamie . . . . Mr. Nugent
Donald . . . . Mr. Martin
Jenny . . . . . . Mrs. Cleveland
Peggy . . . . Mad. Gardie

CLANDESTINE MARRIAGE.

Lord Ogilby . . . . Mr. Hallam
Sir John Melville . . . Mr. Tyler
Sterling . . . . . Mr. Hamilton
Canton . . . . . . Mr. Martin
Brush . . . . . . Mr. Hallam, Jr
Sergeant Flower . . . Mr. Woolls
Traverse . . . . . Mr. Durang
Trueman . . . . Mr. Tompkins
Lovewell . . . . . Mr. Harper
Miss Sterling . . . Mrs. Hallam
Mrs. Heidelberg . . . Mrs. Brett
Betty . . . . Mrs. Tyler
Chambermaid . . Mrs. Chambers
Fanny . . . . . Mrs. S. Powell

DESERTED DAUGHTER.

Cheveril . . . . Mr. Hodgkinson
Lenox . . . . Mr. Harper
Donald . . . . . Mr. Hamilton
Item . . . . Mr. Prigmore
Grime . . . . Mr. Johnson
Clement . . . . . Mr. Cleveland
Mordent · . . . . . . Mr. Tyler
Lady Ann . . . Mrs. S. Powell

Mrs. Sarsnet . Mrs. Hodgkinson
Mrs. Enfield . . . . . Mrs. Brett
Betty . . . . Mrs. King
Joanna . . . . . . Mrs. Johnson

FLITCH OF BACON.

Major Benbow . . Mr. Hamilton
Tipple . . . . . . Mr. Prigmore
Captain Wilson . . . . Mr. King
Justice Benbow . . . Mr. Ashton
Kilderkin . . . . . . Mr. Kenny
Ned . . . . Mr. Durang
Captain Greville . . . Mr. Tyler
Eliza . . . . . Mrs. Hodgkinson

IRISH WIDOW.

Whittle . . . . . . Mr. Johnson
Kecksy . . . . . Mr. Prigmore
Nephew . . . . Mr. Tyler
Bates . . . . Mr. Hughes
Sir Patrick O'Neal . . Mr. King
Thomas . . . . Mr. Hodgkinson
Widow Brady . . Mrs. Johnson

LOVE A LA MODE.

Squire Groom . Mr. Hodgkinson
Sir Callaghan . . . . Mr. King
Beau Mordecai . . Mr. Prigmore
Sir Theodore . . . . Mr. Kenny
Sir Archy . . . . . Mr. Hamilton
Charlotte . . . . . Mrs. Harper

POOR VULCAN.

Vulcan . . . . . Mr. Hodgkinson
Mars . . . . Mr. King
Adonis . . . . Mr. Tyler
Mercury . . . . . Mr. Jefferson
Apollo . . . . Mr. Durang

teen dollars per week, but Hodgkinson found him without an engagement, and employed him rather for his skill as a scene-painter than his
abilities as an actor.   By agreement, however, he was accorded a first
appearance, and he subsequently played other parts, as indicated in the
lists of full and of incomplete casts.   Dunlap describes him at this time
as of a small and light figure, well formed, with a singular physiog-
nomy, a nose perfectly Grecian, and blue eyes full of laughter.   As a

OLD AMERICAN COMPANY CASTS—1795-6.

Bacchus . . . . Mr. Lee
Jupiter . . . . . . Mr. Chambers
Grace . . . . . . Mrs. Chambers
Venus . . . . Mrs. Hodgkinson

SCHOOL FOR SCANDAL.
Sir Peter Teazle . Mr. Hamilton
Joseph Surface . . . . Mr. King
Sir Oliver . . . . . . Mr. Kenny
Crabtree . . . . . . Mr. Hughes
Sir Benjamin . . . Mr. Cleveland
Rowley . . . . . . Mr. Johnson
Moses . . . . Mr. Villiers
Trip . . . . Mr. Taylor
Snake . . . . Mr. Ashton
Charles Surface . Mr. Hodgkinson
Mrs. Candour . Mrs. Hodgkinson
Lady Sneerwell . . . Mrs. Tyler
Maria . . . . . . Mrs. Hughes
Lady Teazle . . . Mrs. Johnson

SCHOOL FOR SOLDIERS.
Major Bellamy . Mr. Hodgkinson
Captain Valentine . Mr. Cleveland
Mr. Hector . . . . Mr. Hamilton
Colonel Valentine . . Mr. Kenny
Frederick . . . . . . Mr. Woolls
Bellamy . . . . Mr. Hallam, Jr
Mrs. Mildmay . . . . Mrs. Tyler
Clara . . . . . . Mrs. S. Powell

SCHOOL FOR WIVES.
Belville . . . . Mr. Hodgkinson
Torrington . . . . . Mr. Hallam
Lewson . . . . . . Mr. Tyler
Captain Savage . Mr. Hallam, Jr
Connolly . . . . Mr. King

Spruce . . . . . Mr. Jefferson
Leech . . . . . . Mr. Johnson
Crow . . . . Mr. Kenny
Wolfe . . . . Mr. Ashton
General Savage . . Mr. Hamilton
Mrs. Walsingham . Mrs. Hallam
Lady Rachel Mildew . Mrs. Brett
Miss Lewson . . Mrs. Chambers
Mrs. Tempest . . . . Mrs. Tyler
Mrs. Belville . . . Mrs. Johnson

SLAVES RELEASED FROM ALGIERS
Ben Hassan . . . Mr. Prigmore
Muley Moloc . . . . Mr. Kenny
Mustapha . . . . . Mr. Ashton
Selim . . . . Mr. Lee
Sebastian . . . . . Mr. Villiers
Frederick . . . . Mr. Cleveland
Henry . . . . . . Mr. Harper
Constant . . . . . . Mr. Tyler
Augustus . . . . Miss Harding
Zoriana . . . . . . Mrs. Pick
Selina . . . . Mrs. King
Fetnah . . . . . Mrs. Cleveland
Rebecca . . . . . . Mrs. Tyler
Olivia . . . . . . Mrs. Johnson

SPOILED CHILD.
Little Pickle . . . Miss Harding
Tag . . . . Mr. Chambers
John . . . . Mr. Lee
Thomas . . . . . Mr. Durang
Old Pickle . . . . Mr. Prigmore
Maria . . . . . . Mrs. Chambers
Margery . . . . Mrs. Hughes
Susan . . . . . . Mrs. Durang
Miss Pickle . . . . Mrs. Brett

SULTAN.
Solyman . . . . . Mr. Cleveland
Grand Carver . . . . . Mr. Lee
Osmyn . . . . . . Mr. Johnson
Elmira . . . . . Mrs. Cleveland
Ismena . . . . Mrs. Pick
Roxalana . . . Mrs. Hodgkinson

TEMPEST.
Prospero . . . . . Mr. Hallam
Ferdinand . . . . Mr. Hallam, Jr
Anthonio . . . . . . Mr. Kenny
Alonzo . . . . . . Mr. Hamilton
Gonzalo . . . . Mr. King
Trinculo . . . . . Mr. Harper
Stephano . . . . . Mr. Hughes
Ventoso . . . . . . Mr. Ashton
Mustachio . . . . Mr. Jefferson
Caliban . . . . . . Mr. Prigmore
Sycorax . . . . . . Mr. Durang
Dorinda . . . . . . Mrs. Hallam
Miranda . . . . Mrs. King
Hyppolito . . . . Mrs. Cleveland
Ariel . . . . Miss Harding

WHEEL OF FORTUNE.
Penruddock . . Mr. Hodgkinson
Tempest . . . . . Mr. Hamilton
Woodville . . . . . Mr. Harper
Henry Woodville . Mr. Cleveland
Weazel . . . . . Mr. Johnson
Sir David Daw . . Mr. Jefferson
Jenkins . . . . . . Mr. Ashton
Servant . . . . Mr. Kenny
Sydenham . . . . . . Mr. Tyler
Mrs. Woodville . . . Mrs. Tyler
Dame Dunckly . . . Mrs. Brett
Maid . . . . Mrs. King
Emily Tempest . . Mrs. Johnson

comedian he had the power of exciting mirth by mobility of feature, and he soon obtained the first rank on the American stage in his line.

OLD AMERICAN COMPANY—INCOMPLETE CASTS.

ALEXANDER THE GREAT.

Hephestion	Mr. Tyler
Clytus	Mr. Hamilton
Roxana	Mrs. S. Powell
Statira	Mrs. Johnson

BEGGAR'S OPERA.

Macheath	Mr. Tyler
Filch	Mr. Jefferson
Lucy	Mrs. Hughes
Mrs. Peachum	Mrs. Brett

CHILDREN IN THE WOOD.

Lord Alford	Mr. Tyler
Apathy	Mr. Johnson
Winifred	Mrs. Brett
Lady Alford	Mrs. Johnson

COUNTRY GIRL.

Harcourt	Mr. Tyler
Sparkish	Mr. Chambers
Alithea	Mrs. Cleveland
Lucy	Mrs. Brett

CRITIC.

Sneer	Mr. Cleveland
Sir Fretful	Mr. Hamilton
Mrs. Dangle	Mrs. Cleveland
Whiskerandos	Mr. Prigmore
Raleigh	Mr. Johnson
Leicester	Mr. Jefferson

DESERTER.

Henry	Mr. Tyler
Russet	Mr. Johnson
Skirmish	Mr. Hamilton
Jenny	Mrs. Chambers
Margaret	Mrs. Brett

DRAMATIST.

Scratch	Mr. Hughes
Neville	Mr. Cleveland
Miss Courtney	Mrs. Cleveland
Lady Waitfort	Mrs. Brett
Marianne	Mrs. Harper

FLORIZEL AND PERDITA.

Florizel	Mr. Cleveland
Alcon	Mr. Johnson
Polixenes	Mr. Hamilton
Mopsa	Mrs. Brett
Perdita	Mrs. Johnson

HARLEQUIN GARDENER.

Pantalina	Mrs. Brett
Columbine	Mad. Gardie

HARLEQUIN SKELETON.

Harlequin	Mr. Jefferson

HAUNTED TOWER.

Lord William	Mr. Tyler
Lady Elinor	Mrs. Pick
Maud	Mrs. Brett

HE WOULD BE A SOLDIER.

Captain Crevelt	Mr. Harper
Sir Oliver Oldstock	Mr. Hamilton
Caleb	Mr. Jefferson
Amber	Mr. Johnson
Lady Oldstock	Mrs. Brett

HIGHLAND REEL.

Sandy	Mr. Chambers
Croudy	Mr. Johnson
Jenny	Mrs. Chambers

I'LL TELL YOU WHAT.

Sir George Euston	Mr. Cleveland
Sir Harry Harmless	Mr. Taylor
Lady Harriet	Mrs. S. Powell
Bloom	Mrs. Chambers
Young Lady	Mrs. Johnson

INCONSTANT.

Old Mirabel	Mr. Hamilton
Dugard	Mr. Tyler
Second Bravo	Mr. Jefferson
Oriana	Mrs. Cleveland
Bisarre	Mrs. Johnson

INKLE AND YARICO.

Inkle	Mr. Cleveland
Curry	Mr. Hughes
Wowski	Mrs. Hughes
Patty	Mrs. Chambers
Yarico	Mrs. S. Powell

JANE SHORE.

Hastings	Mr. Harper
Alicia	Mrs. Johnson
Jane Shore	Mrs. S. Powell

MACBETH.

Banquo	Mr. Harper
Malcolm	Mr. Cleveland
Sivard	Mr. Tyler
Hecate	Mr. Chambers
Lady Macbeth	Mrs. S. Powell

MIDNIGHT HOUR.

General	Mr. Hamilton
Matthias	Mr. Villiers
Marquis	Mr. Taylor
Julia	Mrs. Cleveland
Cicely	Mrs. Brett

NO SONG NO SUPPER.

Endless	Mr. Jefferson
Frederick	Mr. Tyler
Dorothy	Mrs. Pick
Nelly	Mrs. Brett

PADLOCK.

Leander	Mr. Chambers
Ursula	Mrs. Brett

RAGE.

Hon. Mr. Savage	Mr. Johnson
Sir George Gauntlet	Mr. Cleveland
Lady Sarah	Mrs. Harper
Clara Sedley	Mrs. Cleveland
Mrs. Darnley	Mrs. Johnson

RICHARD III.

Henry VI	Mr. Tyler
Queen Elizabeth	Mrs. Johnson
Lady Anne	Mrs. S. Powell

RIVALS.

Sir Anthony	Mr. Hamilton
Captain Absolute	Mr. Chambers
Bob Acres	Mr. Harper
Julia	Mrs. S. Powell
Mrs. Malaprop	Mrs. Brett
Lucy	Mrs. Tyler
Lydia Languish	Mrs. Johnson

ROBIN HOOD.

Robin Hood	Mr. Tyler
Stella	Mrs. Chambers

Mr. and Mrs. Johnson were important acquisitions to the American stage. John Johnson, who was many years his wife's senior, was a man of exemplary life and an actor of long provincial and London experience. He was engaged at the Haymarket from 1787 to 1792. In 1791 he played *Captain Greville* in the "Flitch of Bacon" at Covent Garden for Miss Brunton's benefit. His last appearance at the Haymarket that I have been able to find in a new role was in "Cross Partners," August 23d, 1792. Mrs. Johnson's English experience was entirely provincial. Her first appearance was made with Mr. Brunton's company at Norwich. When she came to America she

MR. JOHNSON'S HAYMARKET PARTS.

1787.

May 23—Much Ado About Nothing	Don Pedro
June 14—Agreeable Surprise	Sir Felix
July 6—Widow's Vow	Carlos
7—Country Attorney	Mr. Gayless
10—Romp	Capt. Sightly
23—Love in a Village	Eustace
Beggar on Horseback	Cosey
25—Henry II	Leicester
27—Merchant of Venice	Lorenzo
Mogul Tale	Selim
30—Suicide	Juggins
Aug. 1—Seeing is Believing	Capt. Nightshade
14—Intriguing Chambermaid	Valentine
21—Follies of a Day	Doubleface
29—Jane Shore	Ratcliffe
Sept. 5—Vimonda	Seton
8—Cross Purposes	George Bevil

1788.

July 24—Beaux' Stratagem	Freeman
Aug. 5—Gnome	Miser

1789.

May 20—Spanish Fryar	Alphonso

OLD AMERICAN COMPANY—INCOMPLETE CASTS.

Edwin	Mr. Chambers	Old Citizen	Mr. Johnson	Fulmer	Mr. Johnson
Angelina	Mrs. Pick	La Gloire	Mr. Jefferson	Louisa	Mrs. Johnson
Annette	Mrs. Hughes	King Edward	Mr. Harper	Lady Rusport	Mrs. Tyler
		Queen Phillippa	Mrs. Tyler	Mrs. Fulmer	Mrs. Brett
ROMP.		Julia	Mrs. Johnson	Charlotte Rusport	Mrs. S. Powell
Watty Cockney	Mr. Chambers				
Captain Sightly	Mr. Tyler	TAMMANY.		WHICH IS THE MAN ?	
ROSINA.		Columbus	Mr. Cleveland	Fitzherbert	Mr. Tyler
Belville	Mr. Tyler	Ferdinand	Mr. Tyler	Bobby Pendragon	Mr. Jefferson
Rustic	Mr. Johnson	Patanan	Mr. Chambers	Julia	Mrs. Cleveland
Phœbe	Mrs. Hughes	Rheina	Mrs. Chambers	Clarinda	Mrs. Tyler
Dorcas	Mrs. Brett			Kitty	Mrs. Brett
SURRENDER OF CALAIS.		WEST INDIAN.		Mrs. Johnson	Mrs. Durang
John de Vienne	Mr. Tyler	Varland	Mr. Jefferson	Lady Bell Bloomer	Mrs. Johnson

May 22—Polly Honeycomb . . . Ledger
    25—Miser . . . . Furnish
June 1—Hamlet . . . . Horatio
    30—Constant Couple . . . Constable

was still young, tall—almost too tall—elegant and beautiful. Mrs. Merry told Dunlap a few years later that she could scarcely recognize in the elegant Mrs. Johnson the tall, awkward girl who had made her *debut* in her father's company. Mrs. Johnson's manners were remarkably fascinating, and she was at once the most perfect example of the fine lady in comedy that had as yet been seen on the American stage, and the model in dress and demeanor for the fine ladies in private life.

Mrs. Brett was the widow of Brett, the singer of Covent Garden and the Haymarket, and the mother of Mrs. Hodgkinson and Mrs. King. Another daughter, Miss Arabella Brett, accompanied her mother to America and appeared as one of the *Apparitions* in "Macbeth," in conjunction with Miss Sully, probably a younger daughter of the tumbler and singer of Sadler's Wells, but did not make a formal *debut*. Dunlap says Mrs. Brett was a good actress and filled the line of comedy old women better than had before been seen in New York. She had been with the Bath and Bristol company while her husband was Keasebury's leading singer, and she was at the Haymarket

MRS. BRETT'S ENGLISH PARTS.
———

1786.

June	16 (Hay.)	—Separate Maintenance
		Mrs. Fustian
	17	—Quaker . . . . . Floretta
	26	—Summer Amusements
		Fidget
	30	—Widow's Vow.
July	7	—Beggar's Opera . . Lucy
	18	—Young Quaker . . . Pink
1789.		
Oct.	2 (Br.)	—Waterman . Mrs. Bundle
	17 (B.)	—As You Like It . Audrey
1790.		
Sept.	29 (Br.)	—West Indian . Mrs. Fulmer
Oct.	1	—Adventuress . . . Kitty
	29	—Castle of Andalusia
		Isabella
Nov.	4 (B.)	—Druids . . . . . Mother
	8 (Br.)	—Fashionable Lover
		Mrs. Mackintosh
	13 (B.)	—Cross Purposes . Mrs. Grub
	20	—Gentle Shepherd . Madge
	22 (Br.)	—Recruiting Officer . Lucy
	27 (B.)	—Provoked Husband, Trusty
	30	—He Wou'd be a Soldier
		Nancy

during the season of 1786. In 1789 she returned to Bath, making her first appearance at Bristol on the 2d of October after an absence of six years. The list of her Bath and Bristol parts will be found very complete, showing her work previous to her retirement in England and her coming to America. They show her to have been a trustworthy and capable actress, but it can scarcely be claimed that they established for her the rank that Dunlap accorded her. It must be remembered, however, that the comedy old woman was a line in which all the American companies were deficient up to that time.

Joseph Tyler, previous to his appearance in America, had had good provincial practice in England as actor and singer. He

Dec.	23		—No Song No Supper
			Dorothy
1791.			
Jan.	3	(Br.)	—Gentle Shepherd . Madge
Feb.	24	(B.)	—Funeral . . . Fardingale
	26		—All in the Wrong . Tippet
Mar.	14	(Br.)	—Fontainebleau . Lady Bull
	21		—Midnight Hour . . Cicely
April	11		—Ways and Means
			Lady Dunder
May	16		—Modern Antiques
			Mrs. Cockletop
	24	(B.)	—Lyar . . . . . . Kitty
	26		—Busybody . . . . Patch
	28		—Belle's Stratagem Kitty
June	4		—Highland Reel . . Moggy
	9		—Way to Keep Him, Furnish
July	6	(Br.)	—Register Office . Margery
	11		—Macbeth . . Third Witch
Oct.	3		—Wonder . . . . . . Inis
	10	(B.)	—Spoiled Child, Miss Pickle
	21	(Br.)	—George Barnwell . . Lucy
	24		—Conscious Lovers . Isabella
Dec.	22	(B.)	—Robinson Crusoe, Pantalina
1792.			
Jan.	26	(B.)	—Deaf Lover . . . . Maid
	28		—Chapter of Accidents
			Warner
April	30	(Br.)	—Road to Ruin . . . Jenny
May	19	(B.)	—Follies of a Day, Marcelina
	22		—Village Lawyer, Mrs. Scout
July	5	(Br.)	—He Wou'd be a Soldier
			Mrs. Wilkins
	6		—Lying Valet, Mrs. Gadabout
	7	(B.)	—Modern Antiques, Florence
	11	(Br.)	—Jealous Wife . . . Toilet
	23		—Duplicity . . . Mrs. Trip
	27		—Comedy of Errors, Hostess

was possessed of a manly figure, and proved an important acquisition to the Old American Company. Mrs. Tyler was without merit as an actress.

The subsequent history of these acquisitions will be found a part of the annals of the New York stage.

CHAPTER XIV.

―――

MR. SOLLEE'S CHARLESTON COMPANY, 1794–6.

BOSTON PLAYERS ENGAGED FOR CHARLESTON—THEY APPEAR AT NEW-
PORT—CITY THEATRE, CHARLESTON—SOLLEE'S SEASON, 1795–6
—THE COMPANY AND THE PLAYS—THE MISSES WRIGHTEN—MRS.
POWNALL'S DEATH AND ITS CAUSE—HER PARTS.

WHEN the Boston Theatre Company disbanded in the Summer
of 1795, Mr. Sollee, the proprietor of the City or Church
Street Theatre at Charleston, engaged a number of the Boston players
for his approaching Charleston season, including Mr. and Mrs. Jones,
Mr. and Mrs. Collins, Messrs. Hipworth, Bartlett and Heely and Mrs.
Hellyer. Besides these he had secured Mrs. Pownall and her two
daughters, the Misses Wrighten; Mr. and Mrs. Turnbull, who had just
arrived from London; Mr. and Mrs. Miller, of the Old American
Company; and Mr. Patterson, a dancer. All these arrived at Charleston early in November. Mr. Watts, who was also engaged, had pre-
ceded them by a few days, and it was announced that Mr. and Mrs.
King, also of the Old American Company, would join Mr. Sollee's
forces at a later period. M. Audin, a French scene-painter, had also
been secured; and Mr. Graupner, who subsequently gave his name to
Mrs. Hellyer, was the leader of the orchestra. Mr. Turnbull aspired
to be a poet and dramatist, filling the Charleston papers with his
effusions and presenting a piece of his own for his benefit. Mr. Patter-

(280)

son died on the 11th of July, 1796, at the age of thirty-two. "As a dancer," one of the Charleston papers said, "he was equal, perhaps, to any in America, possessed commendable talents as a musical performer, and he was a man of an affectionate, honest mind." After leaving the Old American Company, Mrs. Pownall went to Boston, where she gave a concert on the 5th of October, 1795, at which she was assisted by her daughters, the Misses Wrighten, who had joined her after the death of their father, James Wrighten, in 1793. Miss M. A. Wrighten played the "Battle of Prague" on the pianoforte, and Miss C. Wrighten joined in trios with her mother and sister. Felix Pownall, a child only four years old, sang "Little Felix is my name," his first attempt at singing in public.

At this time there were two theatres in Charleston—the Charleston Theatre, built by Bignall and West in 1792, and the City or Church Street Theatre, which is generally identified with Harmony Hall, built for Godwin in 1786. In the Summer of 1794 the latter was occupied by the Placide troupe. It was then called the French Theatre. The performances were confined to pantomime, dancing and tumbling. It would be useless to give a complete list of the performances, but the names of a few of the pieces are printed herewith to indicate the character of the productions. One of these was a local skit representing a Revolutionary episode in Charleston history. In the "Deserter" Placide was *Montariel*, and Madame Placide *Jeannette ;* Douvillier

PARTIAL LIST OF PLACIDE'S PIECES.

1794.

June 12—Deserter.
   Two Game Keepers.
   18—Jeannette.
   Attack on Fort Moultrie.
July 21—Fusileer.
   Le Devin Deritage.
   Indian Heroine.
   (Mad. Placide's benefit.)
Aug. 9—Statue Lover.
   Genevieve of Brabant.
   (Mr. Placide's benefit.)

Alexis, and Madame Douvillier *Louisa;* Val the *Old Lover*, and
Madame Val *Alexis' Aunt;* Francisquy *Bertan;* Darville *Jean Lois*,
and Spinacuta and Latte the *Soldiers*. These were the strolling pantomimists of the period, who appeared at intervals in all the leading
cities from Boston to Charleston.

It was not until near the close of 1794 that the name City
Theatre was given to Harmony Hall. The stage was then occupied
by a company of which Mr. Edgar was the head, and it is not improbable that Mr. Sollee was the manager. The company had
played at Savannah during the Summer, where " Tancred and
Sigismunda" and the " Romp " were produced on the 25th of
September for Edgar's benefit. The Charleston repertory, like the
two pieces played at Savannah,

LIST OF PERFORMANCES.

1795.
Jan. 3—Earl of Essex . . . . . . Jones
     10—Zara . . . . Hill
        Polly Honeycomb . . . Colman
     13—All in Good Humor . . . Oulton
        Provoked Husband . . Vanbrugh
        Farm House . . . . . Kemble
     31—Baroness of Bruchsal . Johnstone
        Virgin Unmasked . . . Fielding
Feb. 14—Louis XVI . . . . . Preston
        Farm House.
     18—Baroness of Bruchsal.
        Tristram Shandy . . . MacNally
     21—Oroonoko . . . . . . Southerne
        (Mr. Edgar's benefit.)

was singularly incongruous. Mr. Edgar's tragedy parts, as in " Zara "
and " Oroonoko," and some of the musical pieces and farces, as
" Polly Honeycomb " and the " Virgin Unmasked," had already fallen
into desuetude. The " Baroness of Bruchsal " had been played at the
Haymarket in 1786 with the title of the " Disbanded Officer." It was
taken from the German of Lessing, of whom the prologue to Mr.
Johnstone's version declared :

> His play's as much applauded at Vienna,
> As here the " School for Scandal " or " Duenna."

When the " Baroness of Bruchsal " was acted for the last time, on the 18th of February, MacNally's bagatelle from Sterne's " Tristram Shandy " had its first production in America. It had not been well executed by the adapter, and, although it was kindly received in London, it had been condemned in Dublin. The only American production of the season was William Preston's tragedy, " Louis XVI." This play was printed in Philadelphia in 1794, and afterward acted in Boston in 1797 by Charles Powell's company at the Haymarket. The piece was played more than once in Charleston, the performance of the 14th of February being advertised as the last night of its production.

CHARLESTON CASTS—CITY THEATRE, 1795.

ALL IN GOOD HUMOR.

Bellamy	Mr. Edgar
Chagrin	Mr. Lewis
Cross	Mr. Bernard
Robin	Mr. Francis
Hairbrain	Mr. Henderson
Servant	Master C. Sully
Dorothy	Mrs. Edgar
Mrs. Chagrin	Mrs. Davids

BARONESS OF BRUCHSAL.

Colonel Holtberg	Mr. Edgar
Rouf	Mr. Henderson
Skatzenbuckle	Mr. Lewis
Bellair	Mr. Bernard
Messenger	Mr. Thompson
Paul Wermans	Mr. Francis
Lisetta	Mrs. Henderson

DEUCE IS IN HIM.

Colonel Tamper	Mr. Edgar
Major Belford	Mr. Henderson
Dr. Prattle	Mr. Francis
Emily	Mad. Spinacuta
Mad. Florival	Mrs. Henderson
Bell	Mrs. Edgar

DOUGLAS.

Young Norval	Mr. Edgar
Glenalvon	Mr. Lewis
Lord Randolph	Mr. Francis
Old Norval	Mr. Henderson
Anna	Mrs. Henderson
Lady Randolph	Mrs. Edgar

EARL OF ESSEX.

Rutland	Mad. Spinacuta

FARM HOUSE.

Modely	Mr. Edgar
Heartwell	Mr. Francis
Shacklefigure	Mr. Lewis
Sir John English	Mr. Bernard
Freehold	Mr. Henderson
Flora	Mrs. Edgar
Aura	Mrs. Henderson

LOUIS XVI.

Marat } Citizen } Louis }	Mr. Edgar
Robespierre } Cleri }	Mr. Henderson
Orleans } Lemoignon } Petron }	Mr. Lewis
Gustin	Mr. Brown
Dauphin	Master Davids
Queen	Mrs. Edgar
Princess Elizabeth,	Mrs. Henderson
Princess Royal	Mad. Spinacuta

OROONOKO.

Oroonoko	Mr. Edgar
Governor	Mr. Henderson
Blanford	Mr. Francis
Aboan } Captain Driver }	Mr. Lewis
Planter	Mr. Thompson

Widow Racket	Mrs. Edgar
Lucy Waldron	Mad. Spinacuta
Imoinda	Mrs. Henderson

POLLY HONEYCOMB.

Honeycomb	Mr. Lewis
Ledger	Mr. Henderson
Scribble	Mr. Edgar
Nurse	Mrs. Edgar
Polly	Mrs. Henderson

PROVOKED HUSBAND.

Lord Townly	Mr. Edgar
Manly	Mr. Henderson
Lady Grace	Mrs. Henderson
Lady Townly	Mrs. Edgar

TRISTRAM SHANDY.

Mr. Shandy	Mr. Francis
Uncle Toby	Mr. Lewis
Obadiah	Mr. Henderson
Dr. Slop	Mr. Francis
Corporal Trim	Mr. Edgar
Susannah	Mrs. Edgar
Widow Wadman	Mrs. Henderson

ZARA.

Osman } Lusignan }	Mr. Edgar
Chatillon	Mr. Lewis
Nerestan	Mr. Henderson
Orasmin	Mr. Francis
Melidor	Mr. Carey
Selima	Mrs. Henderson
Zara	Mrs. Edgar

Before the departure of the Boston contingent of Sollee's company, in the Autumn of 1795, it is not improbable that the players engaged for Charleston joined with other members of Powell's disbanded organization in giving a season at Newport. No casts were printed in the newspapers, but the "Mountaineers" was announced to be played "as performed at the Boston Theatre thirty-six consecutive nights," and on the last night of the season,

LIST OF PERFORMANCES—*Newport.*

1795.
July 22—Inkle and Yarico .   Colman, Jr
          Village Lawyer . . . Macready
Aug. 19—School for Scandal . . Sheridan
          Seeing is Believing . . Joddrell
      26—Such Things Are . Mrs. Inchbald
          Mayor of Garratt . . . . Foote
Sept. 2—Road to Ruin . . . . . Holcroft
          Miller of Mansfield . . Dodsley
      30—Mountaineers . . .   Colman, Jr
          Miss in Her Teens . . . Garrick
Oct.   6—George Barnwell . . . . . Lillo
          Village Lawyer.
          (Benefit of the poor.)

the 6th of October, Mr. Hipworth was underlined for a comic song. These two facts seem to establish the identity of the Newport players of 1795 with the company engaged for Charleston.

Mr. Sollee's season with the company that he transferred from Boston to Charleston began on the 10th of November, 1795, and lasted until the 3d of May, 1796. The company was then disbanded, some of the actors joining West's forces for the rest of the season at the Charleston Theatre. The list of performances comprised the popular pieces of the time in the Northern cities, the only original productions being an interlude written by Mr. Turnbull, with the title of the "Recruit," and pre-

LIST OF PERFORMANCES.

1795.
Nov. 10—Every One Has His Fault
                          Mrs. Inchbald
          Double Disguise . . Mrs. Hook
      12—Dramatist . . . . . . Reynolds
          Poor Soldier . . . . . O'Keefe
      14—Such Things Are . Mrs. Inchbald
          Romp . . . . Bickerstaff
      17—Every One Has His Fault.
          Romp.
      19—Jealous Wife . . . . . . Colman
          Barnaby Brittle . . . . Betterton
      21—Love in a Village . . Bickerstaff
          Miss in Her Teens . . . Garrick
      24—Jew . . . . Cumberland
          Romp.

sented for his benefit, and a benefit offering by Mr. Audin, Jr., one of the scene-painters, called " The Apotheosis of Franklin," a spectacular pantomime in two acts and five scenes. The entire cast of " Every One Has His Fault," on the opening night, was new to Charleston ; but only Miss Caroline Wrighten, the daughter and pupil of Mrs. Pownall, who played *Miss Wooburn*, made her first appearance on any stage. Mrs. Miller was seen the same evening as *Miss Dorothy Evergreen* in the afterpiece. Mrs. Collins appeared on the 12th of November as *Marianne* in the " Dramatist." Miss Mary Wrighten's first appearance on any stage was on the 14th as *Priscilla Tomboy* in the " Romp." Mr. Fawcett, from the New York Theatre, appeared on the 19th as *Charles Oakly* in the " Jealous Wife." Mr. Chalmers, from the Philadelphia Company, was secured for a brief engagement, and made his entry as *Ranger* in the

Nov. 26—She Stoops to Conquer . Goldsmith
Midnight Hour . . Mrs. Inchbald
28—Highland Reel . . . . O'Keefe
Bon Ton . . . . Garrick
Dec. 9—School for Scandal . . Sheridan
Farmer . . . . O'Keefe
11—Heigho for a Husband . Waldron
Midnight Hour.

1796.
Jan. 1—Robin Hood . . . . . MacNally
Miller of Mansfield . . Dodsley
4—Heigho for a Husband.
Purse . . . . Cross
7—Suspicious Husband . . Hoadly
Quaker . . . . Dibdin
9—Beaux' Stratagem . . . Farquhar
Village Lawyer . . . Macready
Feb. 1—West Indian . . . . Cumberland
Lyar . . . . Foote
3—Douglas . . . . Home
Farmer.
10—Busybody . . . . Mrs. Centlivre
Peeping Tom of Coventry,O'Keefe
12—Romeo and Juliet . . Shakspere
Agreeable Surprise . O'Keefe
(Mrs. Jones' benefit.)
15—Mountaineers . . . . Colman, Jr
Barnaby Brittle.
16—Young Quaker . . . . O'Keefe
Rosina . . . . . . Mrs. Brooke
(Mrs. Pownall's benefit.)
17—Hamlet . . . . Shakspere
Agreeable Surprise.
18—Mountaineers.
Modern Antiques . . . O'Keefe
19—Dramatist.
No Song No Supper . . . Hoare
22—Richard III . . . . . Shakspere
Purse.
(Mr. Chalmers' benefit.)
24—Merchant of Venice . . Shakspere
Midnight Hour.
26—Robin Hood.
Catharine and Petruchio,Shakspere
27—Mountaineers.
Catharine and Petruchio.

Feb. 29—Suspicious Husband.
   Ways and Means . . Colman, Jr
March 4—Fair Penitent . . . . . . Rowe
   Quaker.
  9—Robin Hood.
   Love a la Mode . . . . Macklin
  10—Notoriety . . . . . Reynolds
   Poor Soldier.
  12—Orphan . . . . Otway
   Recruit . . . . Turnbull
   Deuce is in Him . . . . Colman
   (Mr. Turnbull's benefit.)
  15—Mountaineers.
   High Life Below Stairs . Townley
   (Mrs. Hellyer's benefit.)
  17—Macbeth . . . . . . Shakspere
   Children in the Wood . . Morton
   (Mr. Jones' benefit.)
  19—Lyar.
   Children in the Wood.
  23—Duenna . . . . Sheridan
   Love a la Mode.
  31—Natural Son . . . . Cumberland
   Comus . . . . Milton
   (Mr. Bartlett's benefit.)
April 2—Road to Ruin . . . . . Holcroft
   Two Strings to Your Bow, Jephson
   (Miss C. Wrighten's benefit.)
  5—Bold Stroke for a Husband
       Mrs. Cowley
   True-Born Irishman . . Macklin
   (Mrs. Henderson's benefit.)
  7—Recruiting Officer . . . Farquhar
   Irish Tailor.
   Miss in Her Teens.
   (Mr. Collins' benefit.)
  9—Critic . . . . Sheridan
   Children in the Wood.
   Apprentice . . . . . . Murphy
   (Mr. Fawcett's benefit.)
  12—West Indian.
   Midas . . . . O'Hara
(Mr. and Mrs. Turnbull's benefit.)
  14—She Stoops to Conquer.
   Brave Irishman . . T. Sheridan
   (Mr. Patterson's benefit.)
  16—Richard III.
   Apotheosis of Franklin Audin, Jr
   (Mr. Audin, Jr.'s, benefit.)

"Suspicious Husband" on the 7th of January, 1796. Mr. and Mrs. Henderson, who had played at the City Theatre the previous season, were also added to the company. When Miss C. Wrighten took her benefit, on the 2d of April, Mr. Pownall played *Harry Dornton* in the "Road to Ruin" "for that night only," and Mr. Bergman volunteered for *Ferdinand* in "Two Strings to Your Bow." Mr. Chalmers intended to present Boaden's "Fontainville Forest," and subsequently substituted the "Gamester," but owing to the fact that Mrs. Pownall was delivered of a daughter the morning previous, the "Dramatist" was played. When the season closed some of the performers remained in Charleston, but many of them returned to Boston. Among the features of Mr. Sollee's advertisements was an announcement that no person of color would be admitted to the theatre, by regulation of the Common Council.

The two new productions, Turnbull's interlude, the " Recruit," and the younger Audin's pantomime, "Apotheosis of Franklin," deserve a few lines of description. Mr. Turnbull's little piece was only a military skit, in which the author, in the title-role, was a Scotch cobbler turned into a comedy recruit; but the pantomime of the younger Audin was, perhaps, the most ambitious attempt

April 19—Dramatist.
    Critic.
    (Mr. Chalmers' benefit.)
   22—Romp.
    Rosina.
    Apotheosis of Franklin.
    (Mr. Audin's benefit.)
   23—Son-inLaw . . . . . . O'Keefe
    Midas.
    Chrononhotonthologos . . Carey
    (Watts and Heely's benefit.)
   26—Chapter of Accidents . Miss Lee
    Doctor and Apothecary . . Cobb
    (Mr. Bergman's benefit.)
   30—Manager in Distress . . Colman
    My Grandmother . . . . Hoare
    Gentle Shepherd . . . . Ramsay
    (Mr. Henderson's benefit.)
May 3—Manager in Distress.
    Inkle and Yarico . . Colman, Jr
    Doctor and Apothecary.

yet made in this country in the way of scenic production. The advertisements declared that nothing like it was ever before performed

RECRUIT.

Sampson . . . . Mr. Turnbull
Sergeant . . . . . Mr. Bartlett
Drummer . . . Mr. Henderson
Nell . . . . . Mrs. Turnbull
Polly . . . . . . Mrs. Hellyer

on this continent for the honor and dignity of Americans and to the

glorious energies and virtues of Franklin. The first scene represented the sculptor Houdon at work on the tomb of Franklin. The tomb itself, in marked contrast with the modest slab that covers the grave of Ben-

APOTHEOSIS OF FRANKLIN.

Franklin . . . . Mr. Turnbull
Voltaire . . . . . Mr. Bartlett
Shakspere . . . . . Mr. Heely
Newton . . . . . Mr. Parsons
Houdon . . . . . Mr. Collins
Diard . . . . Mr. Watts
Countryman . . . . Mr. Jones
Envy . . . . Mr. Henderson
Philosophy . Miss M. Wrighten
Charon . . . . . Mr. Fawcett
Goddess of Fame . Mast. Johnson
Clio . . . . Miss C. Wrighten
Euterpe . . . . Mrs. Graupner

jamin and Deborah Franklin, at Fifth and Arch Sts. in Philadelphia, was adorned with two beautiful statues, one representing the United States holding the American eagle in one hand, and in the other a shield and buckler inscribed, *Unitale populoque Americano;* the other the Goddess

of Prudence holding a tablet inscribed, *Prudentia deresit eam.*   The
second act was in three scenes.   The first scene represented a gloomy

PARTIAL CASTS—CITY THEATRE, 1795-6.

AGREEABLE SURPRISE.

Sir Felix . . . . . Mr. Turnbull
Chicane . . . . . . Mr. Watts
Farmer Stump . . . . Mr. Heely
Laura . . . . Mrs. Hellyer

APPRENTICE.

Dick . . . . Mr. Fawcett
Wingate . . . . Mr. Watts
Gargle . . . . Mr. Heely
Scotchman . . . . Mr. Turnbull
Irishman . . . . . Mr. Collins
Simon . . . . Mr. Jones
Charlotte . . . Miss M. Wrighten

BARNABY BRITTLE.

Sir Peter Pride . . . Mr. Collins
Clodpole . . . . . Mr. Turnbull
Lady Pride . . . . Mrs. Miller
Mrs. Brittle . . . . Mrs. Jones

BOLD STROKE FOR A HUSBAND.

Don Julio . . . . Mr. Chalmers
Don Carlos . . . . . Mr. Collins
Don Cæsar . . . . Mr. Turnbull
Don Vincentio . . . . Mr. Jones
Don Garcia . . . . Mr. Bartlett
Gaspar . . . . . Mr. Henderson
Vasquez . . . . Mr. Heely
Pedro . . . . Mr. Watts
Olivia . . . . . Mrs. Henderson
Victoria . . . Miss M. Wrighten
Laura . . . . Miss C. Wrighten
Marcella . . . . . Mrs. Hellyer
Minette . . . . . . Mrs. Collins
Sancha . . . . . Mrs. Turnbull

BUSYBODY.

Marplot . . . . . Mr. Chalmers
Sir Jealous . . . . Mr. Turnbull
Whisper . . . . . Mr. Fawcett
Miranda . . . . . . Mrs. Jones
Isabinda . . . Miss M. Wrighten
Scentwell . . . . . Mrs. Hellyer
Patch . . . . . . Mrs. Collins

CATHARINE AND PETRUCHIO.

Petruchio . . . . Mr. Chalmers
Bianca . . . . . . Mrs. Hellyer
Curtis . . . . . . Mrs. Turnbull

CHILDREN IN THE WOOD.

Walter . . . . Mr. Jones
Sir Rowland . . . Mr. Turnbull
Apathy . . . . . Mr. Henderson
Gabriel . . . . . Mr. Fawcett
Oliver . . . . Mr. Watts
Lord Alford . . . . Mr. Collins
Josephine . . Miss M. Wrighten
Winifred . . . . . Mrs. Turnbull
Lady Alford . Miss C. Wrighten

COMUS.

Comus . . . . . Mr. Chalmers
Attendant Spirit . . Mr. Fawcett
Elder Brother . . . Mr. Turnbull
Pastoral Nymph . . Mrs. Hellyer
Bacchant . . Miss M. Wrighten
Lady . . . . Miss C. Wrighten

CRITIC.

Puff . . . . . . Mr. Chalmers
Plagiary }
Leicester } . . . Mr. Turnbull
Sneer . . . . . . Mr. Fawcett
Dangle . . . . . . Mr. Bartlett
Hatton . . . . . . Mr. Watts
Don Whiskerandos . . Mr. Jones
Mrs. Dangle . . . Mrs. Turnbull
Tilburina . . . . . Mrs. Jones

DEUCE IS IN HIM.

Col. Tamper . . . Mr. Chalmers
Maj. Belford . . . . Mr. Collins
Dr. Prattle . . . . Mr. Jones
Florival . . . Miss M. Wrighten
Emily . . . . Miss C. Wrighten

DOUBLE DISGUISE.

Lord Hartwell . . Mr. Hipworth
Sir Richard . . . . Mr. Turnbull
Tinsel . . . . . . Mr. Jones
Sam . . . . Mr. Miller
Emily . . . . Miss C. Wrighten
Dorothy . . . . . Mrs. Miller
Rose . . . . . . Mrs. Pownall

DRAMATIST.

Vapid . . . . . Mr. Chalmers
Scratch . . . . . Mr. Turnbull

Neville . . . . . . Mr. Bartlett
Ennui . . . . Mr. Collins
Floriville . . . . . . Mr. Jones
Louisa . . . . . . Mrs. Jones
Lady Waitfort . . . Mrs. Miller
Letty . . . . . . Mrs. Hellyer
Marianne . . . . Mrs. Collins

EVERY ONE HAS HIS FAULT.

Lord Norland . . . Mr. Turnbull
Sir Robert . . . . Mr. Hipworth
Solus . . . . Mr. Jones
Harmony . . . . . Mr. Collins
Placid . . . . . . Mr. Bartlett
Irwin . . . . . Mr. Patterson
Hammond . . . . . Mr. Heely
Porter . . . . Mr. Miller
Edward . . . . Mrs. Hellyer
Lady Eleanor . . . Mrs. Jones
Mrs. Placid . . . Mrs. Pownall
Miss Spinster . . Mrs. Turnbull
Miss Wooburn, Miss C. Wrighten

FAIR PENITENT.

Horatio . . . . Mr. Chalmers
Sciolto . . . . . Mr. Turnbull
Altamont . . . . Mr. Fawcett
Rossano . . . . . Mr. Bartlett
Lothario . . . . . Mr. Collins
Calista . . . Mrs. Henderson
Lucilla . . . . . Mrs. Hellyer
Lavinia . . . Miss C. Wrighten

GENTLE SHEPHERD.

Patie . . . . Miss M. Wrighten
Roger . . . . . . Mr. Collins
Sir William . . . . Mr. Watts
Bauldy . . . . . Mr. Turnbull
Gland . . . . Mr. Henderson
Peggy . . . . Miss C. Wrighten
Jenny . . . . Mrs. Henderson
Mause . . . . . Mrs. Turnbull
Madge . . . . . . Mrs. Jones

HAMLET.

Hamlet . . . . . Mr. Chalmers
Horatio . . . . . Mr. Turnbull
Laertes . . . . . Mr. Fawcett
Ghost . . . . Mr. Watts

cavern, through which were seen the river Styx and the banks of the Stygian lake. Charon was in his boat, ready to convey Franklin to

PARTIAL CASTS—CITY THEATRE, 1795-6.

Gravedigger . . . Mr. Henderson
Ophelia . . . . Miss C. Wrighten
Player Queen . . Mrs. Turnbull

HEIGHO FOR A HUSBAND.

Fairlove . . . . . . Mr. Collins
Rackrent . . . . . Mr. Turnbull
Squire Edward . . Mr. Fawcett
Timothy . . . . . . Mr. Jones
Player . . . . Mr. Heely
William . . . . Mr. Miller
Charlotte . . . Miss C. Wrighten
Maria . . . . . . Mrs. Collins
Mrs. Millclack . . . Mrs. Miller
Chambermaid . . . Mrs. Hellyer

HIGH LIFE BELOW STAIRS.

Lovel . . . . . Mr. Henderson
Sir Harry . . . . Mr. Bartlett
Philip . . . . . . Mr. Turnbull
Tom . . . . Mr. Watts
Lord Duke . . . . . . Mr. Jones
Lady Charlotte . Mrs. Henderson
Kitty . . . . . . Mrs. Hellyer
Chloe . . . . . Master Johnson

INKLE AND YARICO.

Inkle . . . . . . Mr. Fawcett
Medium . . . . Mr. Henderson
Curry . . . . Mr. Watts
Campley . . . . . . Mr. Collins
Yarico . . . . Miss C. Wrighten
Wowski . . . Miss M. Wrighten

IRISH TAILOR.

Betty . . . . . Mrs. Graupner

JEALOUS WIFE.

Major Oakly . . . Mr. Turnbull
Sir Harry Beagle . . . Mr. Jones
Lord Trinket . . . Mr. Bartlett
Captain O'Cutter . . Mr. Collins
Charles Oakly . . . Mr. Fawcett
Lady Freelove . . . Mrs. Miller
Harriet . . . . Miss C. Wrighten
Toilet . . . . . . Mrs. Hellyer

JEW.

Sir Stephen . . . . Mr. Turnbull
Charles Ratcliffe . . Mr. Collins

Frederick . . . . . Mr. Fawcett
Saunders . . . . . . Mr. Bartlett
Jabel . . . . Mr. Jones
Eliza . . . . Mrs. Jones
Mrs. Ratcliffe . . Mrs. Turnbull
Dorcas . . . . Mrs. Miller

LOVE A LA MODE.

Sir Archy . . . . . Mr. Turnbull
Sir Callaghan . . . . Mr. Collins
Mordecai . . . . . Mr. Bartlett
Sir Theodore . . . . Mr. Heely
Squire Groom . . . Mr. Chalmers
Charlotte . . . . . Mrs. Hellyer

LOVE IN A VILLAGE.

Woodcock . . . . Mr. Turnbull
Sir William . . . . Mr. Heely
Eustace . . . . . Mr. Bartlett
Footman . . . . . . Mr. Watts
Lucinda . . . Miss C. Wrighten
Madge . . . . . Mrs. Hellyer
Deborah . . . . . Mrs. Miller

LYAR.

Young Wilding . . Mr. Chalmers
Old Wilding . . . Mr. Turnbull
Papillion . . . . . . Mr. Jones
Miss Godfrey . . . Mrs. Hellyer
Miss Grantham . Miss C. Wrighten

MACBETH.

Macbeth . . . . . Mr. Chalmers
Macduff . . . . . . Mr. Collins
Banquo . . . . . Mr. Fawcett
Duncan . . . . . Mr. Turnbull
Malcolm . . . . . . Mr. Bartlett
Fleance . . . . . Mrs. Hellyer
Singing Witch . Miss C. Wrighten
Hecate . . . Miss M. Wrighten
Lady Macbeth . . . Mrs. Jones

MERCHANT OF VENICE.

Shylock . . . . . Mr. Chalmers
Antonio . . . . . . Mr. Turnbull
Duke . . . . Mr. Watts
Gratiano . . . . . Mr. Fawcett
Gobbo . . . . . Mr. Henderson
Portia . . . . . Mrs. Henderson
Nerissa . . · Miss M. Wrighten

MIDAS.

Jupiter . . . . . . Mr. Fawcett
Juno . . . . . Miss M. Wrighten
Sileno . . . . . Mr. Henderson
Damætas . . . . . Mr. Turnbull
Daphne . . . . Miss C. Wrighten
Mysis . . . . . . Mrs. Turnbull
Nysa . . . . . . Mrs. Graupner

MIDNIGHT HOUR.

General . . . . . . Mr. Turnbull
Marquis . . . . . . Mr. Fawcett
Matthias . . . . . . Mr. Watts
Cicely . . . . . Mrs. Turnbull
Julia . . . . Miss M. Wrighten

MISS IN HER TEENS.

Puff . . . . Mr. Turnbull
Jasper . . . . Mr. Watts
Tag . . . . Mrs. Jones

MODERN ANTIQUES.

Cockletop . . . . . Mr. Turnbull
Joey . . . . Mr. Watts
Frank . . . . . Mr. Henderson
Mrs. Cockletop . Miss M. Wrighten
Mrs. Camomile . . . Mrs. Miller
Flounce . . . . . Mrs. Hellyer
Betty . . . . . Mrs. Turnbull

MOUNTAINEERS.

Octavian . . . . . Mr. Chalmers
Virolet . . . . . . Mr. Fawcett
Roque . . . . Mr. Watts
Muley . . . . . Mr. Turnbull
Lope Toche . . Mr. Henderson
Zorayda . . . Miss C. Wrighten
Floranthe . . Miss M. Wrighten
Agnes . . . . . . Mrs. Hellyer

MY GRANDMOTHER.

Sir Matthew Medley, Mr. Turnbull
Vapour . . . . . . Mr. Fawcett
Woodley . . . . . Mr. Collins
Gossip . . . . . . Mr. Jones
Souffrance . . . . . Mr. Watts
Florella . . . Miss M. Wrighten
Charlotte . . . Miss C. Wrighten

the Elysian Fields. When Elysium was revealed, the Goddess of Fame descended and proclaimed the virtues of Franklin, who was then conducted by Philosophy to the abodes of Peace, where Diogenes, the Cynic, introduced him to all the wise and learned men who inhabit the abodes of eternal rest. The last scene represented the Temple of Memory adorned with the statues and busts of all the deceased philosophers, poets and patriots who had gone before Franklin to the

PARTIAL CASTS—CITY THEATRE, 1795-6.

NATURAL SON.

Jack Hastings . .	Mr. Chalmers
Sir Jeffrey Latimer .	Mr. Turnbull
Rueful	Mr. Fawcett
David	Mr. Watts
Mrs. Phœbe Latimer	Mrs. Henderson
Penelope	Mrs. Hellyer
Lady Paragon	Mrs. Jones

NO SONG NO SUPPER.

Endless	Mr. Watts
Thomas	Mr. Heely
Crop	Mr. Turnbull
Louisa	Miss C. Wrighten
Nelly	Mrs. Miller
Margaretta . .	Miss M. Wrighten

NOTORIETY.

Nominal	Mr. Chalmers
Colonel Hubbub . . .	Mr. Jones
Sir Andrew Acid .	Mr. Turnbull
Clairville	Mr. Fawcett
Lord Jargon	Mr. Bartlett
Saunter	Mr. Heely
James	Mr. Henderson
Blunder O'Whack .	Mr. Collins
Honoria . . .	Miss C. Wrighten
Lady Acid	Mrs. Hellyer
Sophia Strangeways .	Mrs. Collins

ORPHAN.

Chamont	Mr. Chalmers
Polydore	Mr. Collins
Castalio	Mr. Fawcett
Page	Mrs. Hellyer
Ernesto	Mr. Bartlett
Acasto	Mr. Turnbull

Monimia . . .	Miss C. Wrighten
Serina	Miss M. Wrighten

PEEPING TOM OF COVENTRY.

Peeping Tom	Mr. Jones
Mayor	Mr. Turnbull
Harold	Mr. Collins
Count Lewis	Mr. Bartlett
Crazy	Mr. Henderson
Earl Mercia	Mr. Heely
Lady Godiva . . .	Mrs. Hellyer
Mayoress	Mrs. Miller
Emma	Miss C. Wrighten

POOR SOLDIER.

Fitzroy	Mr. Collins
Father Luke . . .	Mr. Turnbull
Bagatelle	Mr. Miller
Norah	Mrs. Hellyer

PURSE.

Will Steady	Mr. Jones
General	Mr. Turnbull
Theodore	Mr. Fawcett
Edmund	Mr. Bartlett
Page	Master Johnson
James	Mr. Heely

QUAKER.

Easy	Mr. Watts
Cicely	Mrs. Miller
Gillian	Mrs. Hellyer

RECRUITING OFFICER.

Capt. Plume . . .	Mr. Chalmers
Capt. Brazen	Mr. Jones
Balance	Mr. Turnbull
Worthy	Mr. Bartlett

Bullock	Mr. Henderson
Constable	Mr. Fawcett
Sergeant Kite	Mr. Collins
Sylvia	Miss M. Wrighten
Melinda	Mrs. Graupner
Rose	Mrs. Henderson

RICHARD III.

Richard	Mr. Chalmers
Richmond	Mr. Collins
King Henry . . .	Mr. Turnbull
Buckingham	Mr. Fawcett
Prince of Wales,	Miss M. Wrighten
Duke of York . . .	Mrs. Hellyer
Stanley	Mr. Watts
Oxford	Mr. Miller
Lord Mayor . .	Mr. Henderson
Duchess	Mrs. Turnbull
Lady Anne . .	Miss C. Wrighten

ROAD TO RUIN.

Goldfinch	Mr. Chalmers
Dornton	Mr. Turnbull
Sulky	Mr. Henderson
Harry Dornton . .	Mr. Pownall
Widow Warren . .	Mrs. Hellyer
Jenny . . .	Miss M. Wrighten
Sophia	Miss C. Wrighten
Mrs. Ledger . . .	Mrs. Turnbull

ROBIN HOOD.

Robin Hood . . .	Mr. Chalmers
Little John . . .	Mr. Turnbull
Scarlet	Mr. Fawcett
Allen-a-Dale	Mr. Bartlett
Ruttekin	Mr. Jones
Fitzherbert	Mr. Collins
Edwin	Mr. Bergman
Stella	Miss C. Wrighten

Elysium beyond. As the curtain fell, Franklin's statue was placed on a vacant pedestal facing that of Sir Isaac Newton. As an early attempt at the spectacular, this outline is interesting. Between the production of the " Recruit," on the 12th of March, and the " Apotheosis of Franklin," on the 16th of April, Mrs. Hellyer, the *Polly* of the former, became Mrs. Graupner, the *Euterpe* of the other.

As was customary at that time, nearly all the casts were printed

PARTIAL CASTS—CITY THEATRE, 1795-6.

Annette . . . Miss M. Wrighten
Angelina . . . . . Mrs. Hellyer

ROMEO AND JULIET.

Romeo . . . . . . Mr. Chalmers
Friar Laurence . . Mr. Turnbull
Paris . . . . Mr. Fawcett
Benvolio . . . . . . Mr. Bartlett
Capulet . . . . Mr. Watts
Montagu . . . . . . Mr. Heely
Apothecary . . . . . Mr. Jones
Peter . . . . . . Mr. Henderson
Juliet . . . . Mrs. Jones
Lady Capulet . . Mrs. Turnbull
Nurse . . . . Mrs. Miller

ROMP.

Barnacle . . . . . Mr. Turnbull
Old Cockney . . . . . Mr. Heely
Dick . . . . Mr. Miller
Penelope . . . . . . Mrs. Collins
Priscilla . . . Miss M. Wrighten

ROSINA.

Belville . . . . Mr. Collins
Capt. Belville . . . Mr. Bartlett
William . . . . Mr. Jones
Dorcas . . . . Mrs. Miller
Rosina . . . . . . Mrs. Hellyer

SHE STOOPS TO CONQUER.

Hardcastle . . . . Mr. Turnbull
Diggory . . . . . . Mr. Watts
Jeremy . . . . Mr. Miller
Miss Hardcastle Miss M. Wrighten
Miss Neville . Miss C. Wrighten
Mrs. Hardcastle . . Mrs. Miller

SON-IN-LAW.

Old Cranky . . . . . Mr. Watts
Idle . . . . Mr. Henderson
Vinegar . . . . Mr. Heely
Orator Mum . . . . Mr. Parsons
Cecilia . . . . . . Mrs. Hellyer
Dolce . . . . . . Mrs. Turnbull

SUCH THINGS ARE.

Twineall . . . . . . Mr. Jones
Sultan . . . . Mr. Collins
Sir Luke Tremor . Mr. Turnbull
Zedan . . . . Mr. Heely
Elvirus . . . . Mr. Bartlett
Aurelia . . . . Miss C. Wrighten
Female Prisoner . . . Mrs. Jones

SUSPICIOUS HUSBAND.

Ranger . . . . . . Mr. Chalmers
Strickland . . . . Mr. Turnbull
Frankly . . . . . Mr. Fawcett
Tester . . . . Mr. Watts
Clarinda . . . . . . Mrs. Jones
Jacintha . . . Miss M. Wrighten
Landlady . . . . Mrs. Turnbull

TRUE-BORN IRISHMAN.

Delany . . . . Mr. Collins
Mushroom . . . . . Mr. Bartlett
Counsellor . . . . . Mr. Fawcett
Maj. Gamble . . . Mr. Turnbull
John . . . . Mr. Watts
Lady Kinnegad . . Mrs. Hellyer
Lady Bab . . . . Mrs. Turnbull
Mrs. Gazette . Miss C. Wrighten
Kitty Farrell . . Mrs. Henderson

TWO STRINGS TO YOUR BOW.

Don Pedro . . . . . Mr. Watts
Don Sancho . . . . Mr. Heely
Octavio . . . . . . Mr. Bartlett
Ferdinand . . . . . .M. Bergman
Borachio . . . . . Mr. Turnbull
Lazarillo . . . . Mr. Jones
Donna Clara . Miss M. Wrighten
Leonora . . . Miss C. Wrighten
Maid . . . . . . Mrs. Turnbull

WEST INDIAN.

Belcour . . . . . Mr. Chalmers
Stockwell . . . . . Mr. Turnbull
Charles Dudley . . Mr. Fawcett
Fulmer . . . . Mr. Watts
Louisa Dudley, Miss C. Wrighten
Lady Rusport . . . . Mrs. Miller
Charlotte . . . . . . Mrs. Jones
Mrs. Fulmer . . . Mrs. Turnbull
Lucy . . . . Mrs. Collins

YOUNG QUAKER.

Young Sadboy . . Mr. Chalmers
Chronicle . . . . . Mr. Turnbull
Capt. Ambush . . . Mr. Fawcett
Spatterdash . . . . Mr. Collins
Shadrach . . . . . . Mr. Miller
Old Sadboy . . . . . Mr. Watts
Lounge . . . . Mr. Heely
Goliah . . . . . Master Johnson
Clod . . . . Mr. Jones
Dinah Primrose,Miss C.Wrighten
Judith . . . . . Mrs. Hellyer
Araminta . . . Miss M. Wrighten
Mrs. Millefleur . . Mrs. Turnbull
Lady Rouncival . . . Mrs. Miller

in the newspapers; but, as a rule, they were devoid of interest, and no attempt has been made to preserve them, except so far as they illustrate dramatic development in the South. The Boston contingent was in Charleston only what it had been in Boston—Jones, Collins, Bartlett and Heely, Mrs. Jones and Mrs. Collins having many of the parts they had previously played. Their new parts of importance are noted. Mrs. Hellyer, or Mrs. Graupner as she was called before the season closed, is treated in the same way. The parts of Mr. Hipworth, Mr. Patterson and Mrs. Pownall in these pieces are reserved for a *résumé* of their work, as they died during the Summer of 1796. The most interesting feature of these casts is the prominence that was given to the Wrighten twin sisters, Miss C. Wrighten being apparently the better actress and Miss M. Wrighten the better singer. Another feature was the fact that the Boston contingent, outside of Jones in low comedy and Collins in Irishmen, was subordinate to the New York and Philadelphia actors. Mr. Hipworth, who had been engaged for the lead in high comedy, was soon supplanted by Mr. Chalmers, but Mrs. Jones was accorded two great Shaksperean parts, *Juliet* and *Lady Macbeth.* There were some attempts at dramatic criticism in the Charleston papers early in the season. Mrs. Pownall as *Rosetta* in "Love in a Village" was pronounced perfection, her songs being given "in a style far superior to anything ever heard in this city before." It was said of Miss C. Wrighten that as *Lucinda* she was animated and improves fast. Mr. Hipworth was less fortunate, his *Young Meadows* being declared "at war with propriety." When Miss M. Wrighten made her *debut* as *Priscilla Tomboy* in the "Romp," she, too, was unkindly treated by one of the critics. On her second appearance in the part, another critic said her improvement was rapid and visible, and that her efforts to please were crowned with deserved applause. "Where was, then," he asked, "the would-be critic, who with feeble and malignant pen attempted to write this young lady down on her first night?" Mr. Jones as *Watty* was described as admirable. In the "Jew" Mr. Fawcett was accorded much discriminating praise as *Frederick*. In the scene with *Mrs. Ratcliffe, Eliza* and *Charles*, his acting was described as tender, animated and correct. His person, voice and action, it was said, were manly, and his walk graceful. The critic thought his *forte* was tragedy and sentimental comedy. Others in the cast were described in a word. Mr. Collins as *Charles* was excellent, Mr. Turnbull as *Sir Stephen* very well, Mrs. Jones as *Eliza* charming, Mrs. Turnbull as *Mrs. Ratcliffe* good, and Mrs. Miller as *Dorcas* at home. Mr. Hipworth, who seems to have been entirely out of place in Sollee's company, seceded early in February, 1796, and joined West's forces at the Charleston Theatre on the 15th, the opening night, playing *Jaffier* in "Venice Preserved" to the *Pierre* of Mr. J. West. After the close of Mr. Sollee's season at the City Theatre, Mr. Godwin, whose name has frequently occurred in this history, made his reappearance in Charleston after an absence of ten years as *Lovegold* in "Miser," for the "benefit of the sufferers by the late fire." An occasional address descriptive

LIST OF PERFORMANCES—*Godwin.*

1796.
June 28—Miser . . . . Fielding
       Old Soldier.
      (For Sufferers by the late Fire.)
    30—Miller of Mansfield . . Dodsley
       Farmer . . . . O'Keefe
       Laborers' Return.
July   2—Farmer.
       American Heroine.
     4—Poor Soldier . . . . . O'Keefe
       Apotheosis of Franklin . Audin, Jr
     9—Duenna . . . . Sheridan
       French Vauxhall Gardens.
    12—Inkle and Yarico . . Colman, Jr
       French Vauxhall Gardens.

of the fire was spoken by Mrs. Pownall, who played *Lappet* with her daughter, Miss M. Wrighten, as *Harriet.* Mr. J. West was

Frederick, and Mrs. J. West *Marianne*. The rest of the cast comprised Nelson as *Ramilie*, Collins as *Clerimont*, Sully as *Decoy*, Master Duport as *Sattin*, J. Jones as *James*, and Mrs. Miller as *Wheedle*. The pantomime was given by the Placide troupe. Godwin's parts at this time were the *Miller* in the "Miller of Mansfield," *Father Luke* in the "Poor Soldier," and *Don Jerome* in the "Duenna." He also personated *Old Charon* in young Audin's pantomime, in which Mr. Placide was seen as *Franklin*. This brief season in Charleston closed Mr. Godwin's career as a strolling player.

The appearances of Mrs. Pownall and her two daughters in these performances led to unexpected results. This great actress had been a singularly obliging performer as a member of the Old American Company. She not only played the old ladies of comedy whenever she was asked to do so, but she yielded many of the singing roles in which her supremacy was established. This obliging disposition led her to support Godwin's ill-considered undertaking, and besides *Lappet* in the "Miser" she appeared during the engagement as *Betty Blackberry* in the "Farmer," and *Clara* in the "Duenna." She also placed the services of her daughters at Godwin's disposal, Miss M.

MRS. POWNALL'S AMERICAN PARTS.

All in the Wrong	Lady Restless
Animal Magnetism	Lisette
Beaux' Stratagem	Cherry
Beggar's Opera	Lucy
Bold Stroke for a Husband	Minette
Chapter of Accidents	Bridget
Child of Nature	Marchioness
Country Girl	Lucy
Demolition of the Bastile	Matilda
Deserter	Jenny
Duenna	Louisa
English Merchant	Molly
Every One Has His Fault	Mrs. Placid
Farmer	Betty Blackberry
Gentle Shepherd	Peggy
Haunted Tower	Lady Elinor
Heigho for a Husband	Dorothy
Heiress	Miss Alten
Jealous Wife	Mrs. Oakly
Know Your Own Mind	Mad. Larouge
Liberty Restored	Paulina
Lionel and Clarissa	Clarissa
Love in a Camp	Norah
Love in a Village	Madge
Love's Frailties	Nannette
Maid of the Mill	Patty

Wrighten being *Molly Maybush* in the "Farmer" as well as *Wowski* in "Inkle and Yarico" with Miss C. Wrighten as *Yarico.* Miss C. Wrighten was also *Louisa* both in the "Farmer" and the "Duenna." Caroline Wrighten was thus brought into contact with Alexander Placide, the strolling pantomimist and tumbler from Sadler's Wells, who appeared as *Bagatelle* in the "Poor Soldier" and as *Lucas* in the "Bird Catcher" and in other pantomimes. Subsequently Mrs. Pownall and her daughters appeared at the Charleston Theatre in an opera called the "Caravan of Cairo," for the benefit of M. Douvillier, a French pantomimist, and at a musical festival given on the 16th of June, in which Mrs. Pownall sang the soprano solos in the "Stabat Mater," and the Misses Wrighten were in the chorus. On the 1st of August, 1796, Mrs. Pownall was advertised to sing at Williams' Long Room on the 4th for the

Midas . . . . Daphne
Midnight Hour . . . . Flora
Needs Must . . . . Marianne
No Song No Supper . . . . . . Dorothy
Padlock . . . . Leonora
Poor Soldier . . . . { Norah / Kathleen
Prize . . . . Caroline
Rival Candidates . . . . Jenny
Road to Ruin . . . . . . Widow Warren
Robin Hood . . . . { Angelina / Clarinda
Rosina . . . . Phœbe
School for Greybeards . . . . . . Rachel
Such Things Are . . . . . . Lady Tremor
Sultan . . . . Ismene
Three Weeks After Marriage . . . Dimitry
Waterman . . , ... Mrs. Bundle
Wedding Ring . . . . Lisetta
Which is the Man ? . . . . Kitty
Wild Oats . . . . Jane
World in a Village . . . . . Mrs. Alebut
Young Quaker . . . . Pink

City Theatre, Charleston.

Agreeable Surprise . . . . . Cowslip
Catharine and Petruchio . . . . Catharine
Comus . . . . Euphrosyne
Double Disguise . . . . Rose
Every One Has His Fault . . . Mrs. Placid
Hamlet . . . . Queen
Heigho for a Husband . . . . . Dorothy
Jealous Wife . . . . Mrs. Oakly
Love in a Village . . . . Rosetta
Midnight Hour . . . . Flora
No Song No Supper . . . . . . Dorothy
Peeping Tom of Coventry . . . . . Maud
Poor Soldier . . . . Kathleen
Purse . . . . Sally
Quaker . . . . Floretta
Richard III . . . . . . Queen Elizabeth
Robin Hood . . . . Clarinda
Rosina . . . . , . Phœbe
Such Things Are . . . . . . Lady Tremor
Suspicious Husband . . . . Mrs. Strickland
True-born Irishman . . . . . Mrs. Diggory
Young Quaker . . . . Pink

last time in America, but on the morning of the concert she printed a card in the newspapers, in which she said "that from an unforeseen and unnatural change which has taken place in her family she is rendered totally incapable of appearing this evening; she, therefore, declines giving the entertainment at Williams' and requests those persons who have bought tickets to return them to her at Mr. Rogers' in Broad Street and receive their money." The unforeseen and unnatural event in Mrs. Pownall's family was the elopement of her daughter, Caroline Wrighten, with Alexander Placide. As Mrs. Placide this young woman became a distinguished actress on the Southern stage, and she was the mother of the celebrated Placide family of actors. Up to this time, however, there had been a Madame Placide who played *Rosetta* in the "Bird Catcher" to Placide's *Lucas* as late as the opening night of Godwin's brief season, and appeared in most of the pantomimes. The name of this Mrs. Placide is found in conjunction with that of Mr. Placide during his whole previous career. The effect of the elopement upon Mrs. Pownall was completely to prostrate her, the shock proving so severe that she died on the 11th of August, only eight days afterward, it was said, of a broken heart. Although this distinguished actress had made her London *debut* under the name of Mrs. Wrighten as early as 1770, she was, according to the obituary notices in the Charleston papers, only in her fortieth year at the time of her death.

CHAPTER XV.

THE BOSTON THEATRE, 1796.

MR. AND MRS. WILLIAMSON—COLONEL TYLER'S MANAGEMENT—THE PRO-
DUCTIONS AND CASTS—" TRAVELLER RETURNED "—A CONTRO-
VERSY OVER THE AMERICAN COMEDY—THE SEASON A FAILURE
—A WORD ABOUT THE RETIRING PLAYERS.

SOME time before the Old American Company took its departure
from Boston two distinguished English players arrived under
engagement for the Boston Theatre. These were John Brown Williamson, for many years a favorite actor at the Haymarket, London, and
his wife, better known in theatrical history as Miss Fontenelle, the
original *Molly McGilpin* in the " Highland Reel." Williamson might
have had a brilliant and prosperous career in America had it not been
for his unfortunate habit of undervaluing everything American and of
promoting dissensions in which he was in no way concerned. His
manners were as offensive as his language was impertinent. " We remember," Dunlap wrote, " hearing Williamson, with all the swelling
port of *My Lord Duke*, tell Hodgkinson that Tyler, the Yankee manager, had run away, and then thank heaven he was not a regular-bred
manager." In the quarrels between Hodgkinson and Hallam, Williamson stimulated Hodgkinson in his hostility to his partner for no other
reason than that Hodgkinson was by training an English actor. The
result of this narrow and meddlesome spirit was that while William-

son became the manager of the Boston Theatre, after his first season, he failed in the management through a want of co-operation and support from the stockholders.

Mr. Williamson, who was the son of a London saddler but was announced as from Edinburgh, made his first appearance at the Haymarket, London, June 6th, 1783, as *Hamlet.* He was not seen again until the 12th of August, when he appeared in the humble part of *Don Frederick* in O'Keefe's "Birthday." On the 19th he played *Charles Powys* in the "Lawyer," after which I do not find his name in the Haymarket bills until July 19th, 1785, when he was *Captain Ambush* in the "Young Quaker." This was not a very auspicious beginning, it must be confessed; but in 1786 he was able to assert his rank as the principal tragedian in a theatre "where tragedy was not the order of the day, and a kind of stiff, handsome 'walking gentleman' of comedy." This criticism, coming from Dunlap, who thoroughly disliked him, not without reason, must be taken with some grains

MR. WILLIAMSON'S HAYMARKET PARTS.

1783.
June   6—Hamlet . . . . Hamlet
Aug. 12—Birthday . . . . Don Frederick
19—Lawyer . . . . . Charles Powys
1785.
July 19—Young Quaker . . Capt. Ambush
1786.
July   8—Mogul Tale . . . . . . Mogul
11—I'll Tell You What
Sir George Euston
13—Conscious Lovers . . . . . Bevil
Aug. 12—Siege of Curzola . . . Frederick
28—Peep Behind the Curtain . Mervin
1787.
May. 25—Much Ado about Nothing, Claudio
June 14—English Merchant, Lord Falbridge
18—Separate Maintenance
Lord Newberry
July 27—Merchant of Venice . . Shylock
Aug. 28—Sir John Cockle at Court . King
29—Jane Shore . . . . . . Gloster
1788.
July 10—Ways and Means . . . . Scruple
24—Beaux' Stratagem . . . Aimwell
1789.
May 18—English Merchant
Sir William Douglas
21—Quality Binding . . . . . Lovel
Spanish Friar . . . . . Lorenzo
25—Miser . . . . Frederick
Half an Hour After Supper
Bentley
June 1—Hamlet . . . . Ghost
July 15—Married Man . . . . Dorimont
30—Constant Couple . Col. Standard

of allowance. This view of his acting was supported, however, by an English critic as late in his London career as 1791, who said of Williamson's *King* in the " Battle of Hexham " that he " was upright and as little royal as ever." Between his first ap-

1790.
June 15—Battle of Hexham . La Varenne
    18—Ways and Means . . . Random
July 12—Spanish Barber . . . . Almaviva
Aug. 11—Child of Nature . . . . Marquis
1791.
June 30—Henry V . . . . . King Henry
July 22—Two to One . . Young Townly
    26—She Wou'd and She Wou'd Not
                                    Octavio
    30—Surrender of Calais, King Edward
1792.
Aug. 23—Cross Partners . George Cleveland

pearance at the Haymarket in 1783 and his return near the close of the season of 1785 Williamson had a trial at Bath, where he made his first appearance as *Hamlet* on October 9th, 1783, and appeared on the 23d as *Bellair* in " More Ways Than One." Mr. Benson took his place at the Haymarket in 1793.

Miss Fontenelle, now Mrs. Williamson, had sprung into favor on the London boards at a single bound. Before her first appearance at Covent Garden, November 6th, 1788, as *Moggy McGilpin* in the original production of the " High- land Reel," it was announced that she had never trod a stage, and in the prologue to the comedy she was alluded to as " Priscilla Tom- boy of Cheapside." On the oc- casion of her *debut* she dis- tinguished herself by a greater flow of animal spirits than any heroine ever exhibited before. " She appears to have a good

MISS FONTENELLE'S ENGLISH PARTS.

Covent Garden.
1788.
Nov. 6—Highland Reel . Moggy McGilpin
1789.
Feb. 3—Toy . . . . Sophia
Mar. 3—Beggar's Opera . . . Macheath
April 24—Cries of London and Dublin
                            Mlle. D'Epingle
May 2—Sultan . . . . Roxalana
    Romp . . . . Priscilla Tomboy
Haymarket.
1790.
June 17—Follies of a Day . . . . . Page
    22—Merchant of Venice . . Nerissa
    28—Inkle and Yarico . . . Wowski
    29—Gretna Green . . . Miss Plumb
July 16—New Spain . . . . Flora
    28—Farm House . . . . . Aura
Aug. 25—Who's the Dupe ? . . . . Charlotte

Sept. 4—Basket Maker . . . Parisian Girl
    15—Battle of Hexham . . . Adeline
1791.
June 23—Young Quaker . . . . Araminta
July 22—Two to One . . . . . . Tippet
    26—She Wou'd and She Wou'd Not
                         Flora
Aug. 13—Irishman in Spain.
    16—Northern Inn.
    19—Beggar's Opera . . . . . Filch
1792.
June 15—Young Quaker . . . . . . Pink
    27—Village Lawyer . . . . . Kate
July 9—I'll Tell You What . . . Bloom
Aug. 23—Cross Partners . . . Mrs. Mutter
Sept. 6—Family Compact.
1793.
June 12—Deaf Lover . . . . Maid
    25—Commissary . . . . . . Jenny
Aug. 27—Agreeable Surprise . . . Fringe

countenance and expressive features," said one of her critics, "but her action was so extremely nimble that a painter's eye could scarce catch a feature." When she played her second part at Covent Garden, *Sophia* in the " Toy," it was admitted that she showed glimpses of exquisite comedy; but these, it was said, were "succeeded by such ungraceful and girlish fooleries as prejudice any man of taste against her and attract only the unthinking." Her *Captain Macheath* in the " Beggar's Opera " was declared to be " without musical talents that could compensate for the impropriety." Miss Fontenelle was introduced to Mr. Harris by Mr. Woodfall, the editor of the *Morning Chronicle*. Although her engagement at Covent Garden was for three years, she retired after her first season. Early in 1790 it was announced that she had been engaged for the Haymarket, and she made her first appearance there on the 17th of June as the *Page* in " Follies of a Day." The only allusion that I have found to her acting during the season was the remark that she supported the character of a Parisian girl in the " Basket Maker " with great spirit. On the 12th of January, 1793, Miss Fontenelle appeared as *Moggy* in the " Highland Reel " at Edinburgh, where Williamson was engaged; but she returned to the Haymarket for the Summer. Her last appearance there was on the 14th of September, 1793, as *Kate* in the " Village Lawyer."

Five days after the retirement of the Old American Company the regular season at the Boston Theatre began, under the direction of Col. John S. Tyler, with "Othello" and the "Spoiled Child" as the opening pieces. Mr. Williamson made his first appearance in America as the *Moor*, and Mrs. Williamson effected her American *debut* the same night as *Little Pickle* in the afterpiece. Mr. Paine said in the *Orrery* that Williamson's elocution was marked by singular propriety, but that the tragedian lacked flexibility of countenance. There was, however, no half-hearted praise of Mrs. Williamson. Her *Little Pickle* was declared to be the most astonishing and brilliant display of theatrical genius ever exhibited in America. Besides those of the two principals there were no new names in the casts of the opening pieces. The other *debutants* in their order were Miss Green as *Miss Neville* in "She Stoops to Conquer," and Mr. Clarke as *Gregory* in the "Mock Doctor," on the 3d of

LIST OF PRODUCTIONS.

1796.

Jan. 25—Othello . . . . . . Shakspere
Spoiled Child . . . . Bickerstaff
27—Every One Has His Fault
Mrs. Inchbald
Romp . . . . Bickerstaff

Feb. 2—Mountaineers . Colman, Jr
Old Maid . . . . Murphy
3—She Stoops to Conquer, Goldsmith
Mock Doctor . . . . . Fielding
5—Mountaineers.
Old Maid.
8—Gamester . . . . . . Moore
Spoiled Child.
10—Foundling . . . . . . Moore
Virgin Unmasked . . . Fielding
12—Love in a Village . . Bickerstaff
Deuce is in Him . . . . Colman
15—Jew . . . . Cumberland
Crotchet Lodge . . . Hurlstone
17—George Barnwell . . . . . Lillo
Lying Valet . . . . . . Garrick
19—Mountaineers.
True-Born Irishman . . Macklin
22—Every One Has His Fault.
Wrangling Lovers . . . . Lyon
Monody to the Chiefs.
24—Love in a Village.
High Life Below Stairs . Townley
27—Brothers (Shipwreck),Cumberland
Prize . . . . Hoare
29—Mountaineers.
Devil to Pay . . . . . . Coffey

March 2—Child of Nature . Mrs. Inchbald
True-Born Irishman.
4—Wild Oats . . . . . . O'Keefe
All the World's a Stage . Jackman
7—Mountaineers.
Miller of Mansfield . . Dodsley
9—Traveller Returned.
Prize.

Mar. 11—Traveller Returned.
Romp.
14—Jew.
Oscar and Malvina.
16—Brothers.
Oscar and Malvina.
18—First Love . . . . . Cumberland
Oscar and Malvina.
21—Child of Nature.
Oscar and Malvina.
23—Bank Note . . . . . Macready
Quaker . . . . Dibdin
24—Crotchet Lodge.
Oscar and Malvina.
28—Spoiled Child.
Romp.
Oscar and Malvina.
(Mrs. Williamson's benefit.)
30—Romeo and Juliet . . Shakspere
Midas . . . . O'Hara
(Mr. S. Powell's benefit.)

April 1—Recess.
Peep Behind the Curtain . Garrick
Orpheus.
(Mrs. Harper's benefit.)
4—Seduction . . . . . . Holcroft
Prisoner at Large . . . O'Keefe
(Mrs. Ashton's benefit.)
6—Bank Note.
Cymon and Sylvia . . . Garrick
(Mrs. Pick's benefit.)
8—Conscious Lovers . . . . Steele
Farmer.
(Mrs. Chambers' benefit.)
11—Bold Stroke for a Husband
Mrs. Cowley
Love in a Camp . . . . O'Keefe
(Mr. J. Hughes' benefit.)
13—Spoiled Child.
Hob in the Well . . . . Cibber
Witches.
(Mr. Harper's benefit.)
15—Mysteries of the Castle . Andrews
Rosina . . . . . . Mrs. Brooke
(Mrs. Arnold's benefit.)

February, and Mrs. Arnold as *Rosetta* in " Love in a Village " on the 12th. Miss Green was from London, but Mr. Clarke was an American. He was underlined as making " his first appearance in the United States." Mrs. Arnold was from Covent Garden, where she was in the chorus. She was advertised among the vocalists in the " Woodman " in 1789, in " Blue Beard " in 1791, and in " Zelma " in 1792; but I have not found her credited with a speaking character. In Boston, however, she played a number of very ambitious parts for a brief period. She was prominent in comedy, farce, opera and panto-mime, ranking with Mrs. S. Powell in fine comedy ladies, and above Mrs. Williamson, whom she suc-ceeded as *Agnes* in the " Moun-taineers " on the 19th of February, except in romps and the sprightly heroines of musical comedy. Ten days later Mrs. Williamson again played *Agnes*, and Mrs. Arnold

Zorayda, previously Mrs. S. Powell's part. The company comprised, besides those already mentioned, Mr. and Mrs. Harper, who had temporarily abandoned the Providence and Newport theatres; Mr. and Mrs. Chambers and Mr. Hamilton from West's company; Mr. Ashton from the Old American Company; Mr. and Mrs. S. Powell, Mr. and Mrs. Hughes, and Messrs. Taylor, Kenny and Villiers, retained from the previous season; and Mrs. Baker, of Charles Powell's first company, who now returned to the stage. Other additions were Miss Sully, of the celebrated Sully family of actors and artists; Mrs. Pick, who had returned from the South; Mr. Maginnis, who had been giving monologue entertainments in Boston; and Mr. Ratcliffe, one of the Rhode Island

April 18—Better Late Than Never . Andrews
　　　　Oscar and Malvina.
　　　（Mrs. S. Powell's benefit.）
　　20—Sicilian Romance . . . Siddons
　　　　Half an Hour After Supper.
　　　　Village Lawyer . . . Macready
　　　（Mr. Villiers' benefit.）
　　25—Fashionable Lover . Cumberland
　　　　No Song No Supper . . . Hoare
　　　（Mr. Hamilton's benefit.）
　　27—Lear . . . . Shakspere
　　　　Devil to Pay.
　　　（Mr. Chambers' benefit.）
　　29—Sicilian Romance.
　　　　Spoiled Child.
　　　（Mr. Tyler's benefit.）
May　2—First Love.
　　　　Mogul Tale . . . Mrs. Inchbald
　　　（Mrs. Baker's benefit.）
　　4—World in a Village . . O'Keefe
　　　　Old Soldier.
　　　（Mr. Ashton's benefit.）
　　6—Every One Has His Fault.
　　　　Love of Fame.
　　　　Farm House . . . . . Kemble
　　　（Mrs. Hughes' benefit.）
　　9—Jealous Wife . . . . . Colman
　　　　Lying Valet.
　　　　Agreeable Surprise . . O'Keefe
　　　（Mr. Kenny's benefit.）
　　11—Bold Stroke for a Husband.
　　　　Children in the Wood . . Morton
（Miss Sully and Mr. Campbell's benefit.）
　　13—Traveller Returned.
　　　　Who's the Dupe? . Mrs. Cowley
（For Widows and Orphans of Boston.）
　　16—Highland Reel . . . . O'Keefe
　　　　Maid of the Oaks . . Burgoyne
　　　（Mr. Williamson's benefit.）

company. In "Mysteries of the Castle" Miss Arnold, afterward Mrs. Poe, sang "The Market Lass" between the second and third acts, her first appearance in public. Mr. Harper was the acting manager.

The season yielded only one American production, the " Traveller Returned," ostensibly written by a lady, although Paine in the *Orrery*, as in the case of the "Medium," attributed the authorship to the Rev. John Murray, and was not contradicted. This comedy was

TRAVELLER RETURNED.

Mr. Rambleton . . . . Mr. Harper
Mr. Stanhope . . . . Mr. Kenny
Alberto Stanhope . . . . . Mr. Chambers
Mr. Vansittart . . . . Mr. Hughes
Patrick O'Neal . . . . . . Mr. Hamilton
Obadiah . . . . Mr. Villiers
Officer . . . . Mr. Clarke
Major Camden . . . . . . Mr. S. Powell
Mrs. Montague . . . . Mrs. Arnold
Emily Lovegrove . . . . . . Mrs. Hughes
Mrs. Vansittart . . . . Mrs. Harper
Bridget . . . . Mrs. Chambers
Harriet Montague . . . . Mrs. Williamson

played twice in succession, being brought forward for the first time on the 9th of March, and it was finally presented a third time for the benefit of the widows and orphans of Boston on the 13th of May. Intense feeling was excited in behalf of the play and its author in consequence of Mr. Paine's criticism of the comedy in the *Orrery*. To the ears of a less sensitive age the critique has not a sound of violent fury, and it might well have passed unchallenged, but the author's friends were determined the play should not be immured " in despot cell." Foremost among her champions was the Rev. Mr.

[1] PAINE'S CRITICISM.—(From the *Orrery*.) —On Wednesday and Thursday evening was performed a new comedy entitled the "Traveller Returned." As an American production it met with a very favorable reception. The author, we think, possesses a dramatic talent which is capable of improvement. But experience is necessary to theatrical effect; and in producing it art is equally as essential as genius. The tedium of uninteresting solemnity constitutes the principal defect in the "Traveller Returned." That it has many good scenes cannot be denied, and the second act is undisputably the best in the piece. But the author seems not to be aware that novelty of incident, picturesque situation and brilliancy of dialogue are cardinal requisites in a genteel comedy. We hope the public have not condemned him for substituting broad humor for wit, and dulness for pathos. Long and frequent soliloquies are in comedy highly unnatural; and in the social interviews of polished life pedantry should never intrude. In the construction of his fable the author admits episode, but does not support it; for the principal characters of the underplot are introduced in some of his scenes although not a syllable " is set down for them." To the successful representation of the piece the almost unparalleled exertions of the performers contributed. They seemed inspired by a spirit of emulation which entitled them to the best thanks of the author and the universal applause of the public.

Murray, a fact that explains Paine's imputation of the authorship to that "reverend scribbler and Parson Flummery." To the criticism Mr. Paine appended a long recital of the fable. A wealthy American, Mr. Montague, had long lived abroad, unknown to his family, having separated from his wife on account of her fashionable dissipations. His son he committed to the care of his friend, *Mr. Camden*, with injunctions not to divulge to the boy the secret of his birth, and his daughter *Harriet* grew to womanhood in charge of her mother, who had abandoned the fashionable world, and, confining herself to her library, become a literary recluse. The play began with the return of Mr. Montague during the Revolution, who found his son gallantly serving as a major in the American army. By his intrepidity *Major Camden* had recently saved the life of *Mrs. Montague*, who, to reward her deliverer, made every exertion to bestow her daughter's hand upon him. Fortunately, her heart was prepossessed by *Alberto Stanhope ;* and *Major Camden*, finding his addresses coldly received by *Harriet*, was attracted by the engaging modesty of *Miss Emily Lovegrove*, who was living in the same house with her aunt, *Mrs. Montague*. Mr. Montague upon his return had assumed the name of *Rambleton* and, with his servant, *Patrick O'Neal*, taken up his abode at a tavern kept by *Mr. Vansittart*, a Dutch settler.— Through *Patrick*, *Mrs. Vansittart* learned that *Rambleton* was possessed of great wealth in English guineas and crowns, and wishing

APOLOGY FOR THE AUTHOR.

(Spoken by Mrs. S. Powell.)

Ambitious of that fame which you can give,
And seeking in your fair award to live,
Full freighted with apologies I bend,
Solicitous our author to defend.
Who would not tolerate a female pen ?
Women, perhaps, were born a match for men :
But natal rights by education crampt,
The sex's inequality is stampt.
Yet sure in this celebrious age design'd,
To crown the struggles of the opening mind,
To equal efforts you will point the way,
Nor e'en the emulative wish betray.
The Author of to-night has aim'd to please

Her budding hopes let no fell mildew seize.
'Twere pitiful to blast that early growth,
Which may, perchance, produce maturer
　　worth;
If she hath err'd her heart is not to blame—
'Tis laudable to seek an honest fame;
Lur'd by the soothing voice of dulcet praise,
Which oft hath beam'd conspicuous in her
　　lays,
She mark'd that candor which, embosom'd
　　here,
Assumes no aspect stern or brow severe;
And fondly thought beneath so mild a sun,
Some ripening fruit by culture might be won,
Nor dream'd of sable pall, or passing bell,
Or screech-owl rancor hooting her death
　　knell,
Unconscious of offense no speeches rose,
Or open graves her steps to interpose.
But ah! alas! the pick-axe was prepar'd,
And with the play her bright'ning views in-
　　terr'd!
Her comedy, by critic hands inhum'd,
Beyond resuscitation was presum'd!
And since in despot cell it was immur'd,
Ah me! what sorrows hath her heart endur'd.
With Orphean lyre 'tis you can charm it
　　thence,
And all the vigor of new life dispense;
For Pagan bard ne'er issued sweeter strains,
Than in the gift of echoing fame remains.
Her confidence in you she hath exprest,
And your full patronage devoutly blest.
Forth from her lips those fervid thanks which
　　flow,
With warmth meridian in her bosom glow.
And gratitude triumphant in her breast,
A coward host of fears hath dispossess'd,
And, reassur'd, she will her course pursue,
With ample chart provided thus by you.
Charybdian gulfs and Scyllian rocks in vain
Molest the voyagers whom you sustain.

to do a "jonteel thing" for herself and country she induced her husband to cause a charge of Toryism to be made against her lodger, alleging that he was a British spy. *Mr. Rambleton* was arrested and taken before the Committee of Public Safety, while *Vansittart* and his wife, having plied *Patrick* with liquor, secured the treasure. In order to procure cash for traveling expenses, *Vansittart* disposed of a miniature portrait of *Mrs. Montague,* which *Rambleton* had always carried; but the jeweler, recognizing it as one he had set for Mr. Montague many years before, sent it to *Mrs. Montague,* at the same time informing her of the innkeeper's suspicious conduct. Through *Major Camden* the thieves were pursued and the property recovered, *Mr. Rambleton* released, and a happy *denouement* effected, with everybody reconciled or

married. When the criticism and synopsis appeared, "Fair Play" at once rushed into print to defend the comedy, alleging that "the author of that piece aimed at furnishing it with humor from characters that should not possess uncommon talents of any description, much less that wit which is confessedly rare." The introduction of soliloquies was justified by *Sir Peter Teazle's* in the "School for Scandal" and those in the "Jew." The author also responded, wanting to know which of the characters were without a syllable set down for them. The critic was called invidious, envious and mercenary. But even more silly than the foolish answers to Paine's strictures was the "Apology," spoken by Mrs. S. Powell when the piece was played the third and last time. To all this Paine finally answered: *Nil de mortuis nisi bonum*—"Damn not a play which has gone to that bourne from which no Traveller Returns."

The productions of the season comprised many pieces new to Boston and a few now first made known to the American stage.

FIRST BOSTON PRODUCTIONS—CASTS.

BANK NOTE.
Sir Charles Leslie . Mr. Chambers
Mr. Bloomfield . . . Mr. Harper
Father . . . . Mr. Kenny
Lieut. Selby . . . Mr. S. Powell
Ned Dash . . . . . Mr. Taylor
Mr. Hale . . . . . Mr. Hughes
Tim . . . . Mr. Villiers
Careful . . . . Mr. Ashton
Young Bloomfield . . Miss Sully
Servant . . . . . Mr. Maginnis
Porter . . . . Mr. Clarke
Killeary . . . . Mr. Williamson
Lady Supple . . . . Mrs. Baker
Mrs. Bloomfield . . Mrs. Arnold
Miss Emma Hale . Mrs. Chambers
Sally Flounce . . . Mrs. Hughes
Miss Russell . . Mrs. Williamson

BETTER LATE THAN NEVER.
Saville . . . . Mr. Harper
Flurry . . . . Mr. Kenny
Grump . . . . Mr. Hamilton
Litigamus . . . . Mr. Chambers
Sir Charles Chouse Mr. S. Powell

Pallet . . . . Mr. Hughes
Lawyer's Clerk . . Mr. Maginnis
Augusta . . . . . Mrs. S. Powell
Mrs. Flurry . . . . Mrs. Hughes
Diary . . . . . . Mrs. Chambers

BOLD STROKE FOR A HUSBAND.
Don Julio . . . . Mr. Chambers
Don Carlos . . . . . Mr. Harper
Don Cæsar . . . . Mr. Hamilton
Don Vincentio . . Mr. S. Powell
Don Garcia . . . . . Mr. Kenny
Vasquez . . . . Mr. Clarke
Pedro . . . . . . Mr. Maginnis
Sancho . . . . . . Mr. Ratcliffe
Gasper . . . . Mr. Hughes
Olivia . . . . . . Mrs. S. Powell
Victoria . . . . . . Mrs. Hughes
Laura . . . . Miss Green
Marcella . . . . Mrs. Pick
Inis . . . . Mrs. Ashton
Minette . . . . . Mrs. Chambers

BROTHERS.
Sir Benjamin Dove Mr. Hamilton

Belfield . . . . . Mr. Chambers
Old Belfield . . . . . Mr. Ashton
Patterson . . . . . . Mr. Kenny
Francis . . . . Mr. S. Powell
Goodwin . . . . . . Mr. Hughes
Philip . . . . Mr. Villiers
Skiff . . . . Mr. Clarke
Jonathan . . . . . Mr. Maginnis
Captain Ironsides . . Mr. Harper
Lady Dove . . . . . Mrs. Baker
Sophia . . . . . . Mrs. Harper
Lucy Waters . . . . Miss Green
Fanny Goodwin . . Mrs. Hughes
Kitty . . . . Mrs. Ashton
Violetta . . . . . . Mrs. Arnold

CONSCIOUS LOVERS.
Young Bevil . . . . Mr. Harper
Cimberton . . . . . Mr. Hughes
Sealand . . . . Mr. Hamilton
Myrtle . . . . . . Mr. Ashton
Sir John Bevil . . . Mr. Kenny
Humphrey . . . . Mr. Maginnis
Daniel . . . . Mr. Villiers
Tom . . . . Mr. S. Powell

Those new to America comprised the "Crotchet Lodge," produced later in the season in New York and Philadelphia; "Half an Hour

FIRST BOSTON PRODUCTIONS—CASTS.

Indiana . . . . . Mrs. S. Powell
Lucinda . . . . . Mrs. Chambers
Mrs. Sealand . . . . Mrs. Baker
Isabella . . . . . . Mrs. Ashton
Phyllis . . . . Mrs. Williamson

CROTCHET LODGE.

Timothy Truncheon . Mr. Harper
Shinkin ap Lloyd . . Mr. Kenny
Paddy . . . . . . Mr. Hamilton
Dr. Chimic . . . . . Mr. Clarke
Waiter . . . . Mr. Ashton
Boots . . . . Mr. Maginnis
Nimble . . . . . Mr. S. Powell
Miss Crotchet . . . . Mrs. Baker
Florella . . . . . . Mrs. Harper
Landlady . . . . . Mrs. Hughes
Maid . . . . Mrs. Ashton
Thisbe . . . . . Mrs. Chambers

CYMON AND SYLVIA.

Cymon . . . . . . Mr. Chambers
Merlin . . . . . . Mr. S. Powell
Denis . . . . Mr. Hughes
Damon . . . . Mr. Kenny
Dorilas . . . . . . Mr. Maginnis
Linco . . . . Mr. Harper
Urganda . . . . . Mrs. Arnold
Fatima . . . . . Mrs. Chambers
Shepherdesses . { Mrs. Hughes / Miss Green
Dorcas . . . . Mrs. Baker
Sylvia . . . . Mrs. Pick

FASHIONABLE LOVER.

Lord Aberville . . . Mr. Harper
Aubrey . . . . . Mr. Williamson
Mortimer . . . . . Mr. Kenny
Tyrrell . . . . . . Mr. Chambers
Dr. Druid . . . . . Mr. Hughes
Napthali . . . . . . Mr. Villiers
Bridgmore . . . . . Mr. Ashton
Jarvis . . . . . . Mr. Maginnis
La Jeunesse . . . . . Mr. Clarke
Colin Macleod . . Mr. Hamilton
Augusta Aubrey . Mrs. S. Powell
Mrs. Bridgmore . . . Mrs. Baker
Mrs. Macintosh . . Mrs. Ashton
Jenny . . . . Mrs. Pick
Lucinda . . . . . Mrs. Arnold

FIRST LOVE.

Lord Sensitive . . Mr. S. Powell
Sir Miles Mowbray . Mr. Hamilton
Fred'k Mowbray Mr. Williamson
David Mowbray . . Mr. Harper
Mr. Wrangle . . . . Mr. Ashton
Billy Bustler . . . . Mr. Villiers
Robin . . . . . . Mr. Maginnis
Lady Ruby . . . . Mrs. Arnold
Mrs. Wrangle . . . Mrs. Hughes
Mrs. Kate . . . . . Mrs. Baker
Waiting Woman . . . Miss Green
Sabina Rosny . Mrs. Williamson

HALF AN HOUR AFTER SUPPER.

Mr. Sturdy . . . . Mr. Hamilton
Bentley . . . . Mr. Ashton
Berry . . . . Mr. Kenny
Frank . . . . Mr. Hughes
Miss Tabitha . . . . Mrs. Baker
Miss Sukey . . . . Mrs. Arnold
Miss Elizabeth . . . Miss Green
Nanny . . . . . . Mrs. Hughes

HOB IN THE WELL.

Testy . . . . Mr. Kenny
Friendly . . . . . Mr. Chambers
Old Hob . . . . . Mr. Hamilton
Dick . . . . Mr. S. Powell
Roger . . . . . . Mr. Maginnis
Hob . . . . Mr. Harper
Flora . . . . . . Mrs. Arnold
Hob's Mother . . . . Mrs. Baker
Betty . . . . Mrs. Harper

JEALOUS WIFE.

Oakly . . . . Mr. Harper
Major Oakly . . Mr. Hamilton
Rupert . . . . Mr. Hughes
Charles Oakly . . . Mr. Ashton
Lord Trinket . . . . Mr. Taylor
Captain O'Cutter . . Mr. Kenny
Tom . . . . Mr. Clarke
John . . . . Mr. Ratcliffe
Lady Freelove . . . Mrs. Arnold
Harriet . . . . . . Mrs. Harper
Toilet . . . . . . Miss Green
Mrs. Oakly . . . Mrs. S. Powell

LEAR.

Lear . . . . Mr. Chambers
Kent . . . . Mr. Hamilton
Gloster . . . . . . Mr. Kenny
Bastard . . . . . . Mr. Ashton
Usher . . . . Mr. S. Powell
Albany . . . . . . Mr. Taylor
Burgundy . . . . . Mr. Hughes
Cornwall . . . . . Mr. Sweeney
Physician . . . . . Mr. Villiers
Officer . . . . Mr. Clarke
Gentleman . . . . Mr. Ratcliffe
Edgar . . . . Mr. Harper
Goneril . . . . . Mrs. Harper
Regan . . . . . . Mrs. Hughes
Arante . . . . . . Mrs. Ashton
Cordelia . . . . Mrs. S. Powell

LOVE IN A CAMP.

Captain Patrick . Mr. Chambers
Quid . . . . Mr. Villiers
Father Luke . . . Mr. Hamilton
Fehrbellin . . . . Mr. S. Powell
Olmutz . . . . Mr. Hughes
Rupert . . . . Mr. Kenny
Darby . . . . Mr. Harper
Mabel Flourish . . Mr. Maginnis
Norah . . . . Mrs. Pick
Flora . . . . . Mrs. Williamson

MAID OF THE OAKS.

Old Groveby . . . . Mr. Hughes
Dupely . . . . . Mr. Chambers
Oldworth . . . . . . Mr. Kenny
Sir Harry Groveby . Mr. Ashton
Robin . . . . Mr. Ratcliffe
Hurry . . . . Mr. Villiers
Maria . . . . . . Mrs. Chambers
Lady Bab . . . Mrs. Williamson

MOGUL TALE.

Mogul . . . . Mr. Kenny
Omar . . . . . . Mr. Hamilton
Eunuch . . . . Mr. Ashton
Johnny Atkins . . . Mr. Villiers
Dr. Gass . . . . . Mr. Hughes
Fatima . . . . . . Mrs. Hughes
Fanny Atkins . . . . Mrs. Baker

After Supper," an interlude from the Haymarket, intended to expose
the dangers in the sentimental trash of the circulating libraries ; Cum-

FIRST BOSTON PRODUCTIONS—CASTS.

MYSTERIES OF THE CASTLE.

Hilario . . . . Mr. Harper
Tractioso . . . . . Mr. Hamilton
Count Montini . . . Mr. Taylor
Montauban . . . Mr. Chambers
Cloddy . . . . Mr. Villiers
Valoury . . . . . Mr. S. Powell
Bernardo . . . . . . Mr. Ashton
Centinel . . . . Mr. Clarke
Sergeant . . . . . Mr. Maginnis
Captain . . . . . . Mr. Ratcliffe
Carlos . . . . . Mr. Williamson
Julia . . . . . . Mrs. S. Powell
Constantia . . . . . Mrs. Arnold
Annette . . . . Mrs. Williamson

Bards . . . . { Mr. Harper
Mr. Chambers
Mr. Villiers
Mrs. Arnold
Mrs. Chambers
Mrs. Pick

ORPHEUS.

Orpheus . . . . . Mr. Chambers
Old Shepherd . . . Mr. Hamilton
Rhodope . . . . . . Mrs. Arnold

OSCAR AND MALVINA.

Fingal . . . . . . Mr. Hamilton
Oscar . . . . . . Mr. S. Powell
Mervin . . . . Mr. Harper
Draco . . . . Mr. Taylor
Dumoth . . . . . . Mr. Ashton
Carrol . . . . . Mr. Williamson
Farmer . . . . . . Mr. Hughes
Farmer's Wife . . . . Mrs. Baker
Pedlar . . . . . Mr. Chambers
Page . . . . Miss Sully
Shepherd . . . . Mrs. Pick
Shepherdess . . . Mrs. Chambers
Malvina . . . . Mrs. Williamson

OTHELLO.

Othello . . . . . Mr. Williamson
Iago . . . . Mr. Harper
Roderigo . . . . . Mr. Taylor
Brabantio . . . . . Mr. Hamilton
Duke . . . . Mr. Hughes
Ludovico . . . . . . Mr. Ashton

Montano . . . . . Mr. Kenny
Gratiano . . . . . Mr. Villiers
Emilia . . . . . . Mrs. Hughes
Desdemona . . . Mrs. S. Powell

PEEP BEHIND THE CURTAIN.

Glib . . . . Mr. Harper
Sir Toby Fuz . . . Mr. Hughes
Sir Macron Virtu . Mr. S. Powell
Patent . . . . Mr. Kenny
Hopkins . . . . Mr. Maginnis
Saunders . . . . . Mr. Clarke
Wilson . . . . . . Mr. Ashton
Mervyn . . . . . . Mr. Ratcliffe
Lady Fuz . . . . . . Mrs. Baker
Miss Fuz . . . . Mrs. Harper

RECESS.

Don Carlos . . . Mr. Williamson
Don Guzman . . . Mr. Hamilton
Don Ferdinand . . Mr. Chambers
Don Pedro . . . . Mr. S. Powell
Lazarillo . . . . . Mr. Villiers
Octavio . . . . Mr. Ashton
Officer . . . . Mr. Kenny
Alguazil . . . . . Mr. Maginnis
Lopez . . . . Mr. Ratcliffe
Muskato . . . . . . Mr. Harper
Donna Aurora . . Mrs. S. Powell
Donna Marcella . . Mrs. Harper
Leonorda . . . . Mrs. Chambers
Beatrice . . . . Mrs. Williamson

SEDUCTION.

Lord Morden . . Mr. Chambers
Gabriel . . . . . . Mr. S. Powell
General Burland . . . Mr. Ashton
Lapelle . . . . Mr. Kenny
Bailiff . . . . Mr. Clarke
Constable . . . . . Mr. Maginnis
Servant . . . . . . Mr. Ratcliffe
Sir Fred'k Fashion . Mr. Harper
Mrs. Modely . . . . Mrs. Arnold
Harriet . . . . . . Mrs. Harper
Emily . . . . . . Mrs. Chambers
Mrs. Pinup . . . . Mrs. Ashton
Lady Morden . . Mrs. S. Powell

SICILIAN ROMANCE.

Ferrand . . . . . Mr. S. Powell
Lindor . . . . . . Mr. Chambers
Martin . . . . Mr. Harper
Don Lope . . . . . Mr. Hughes
Prior . . . . Mr. Ashton
Sancho . . . . . . Mr. Ratcliffe
Vincent . . . . . . Mr. Maginnis
Jacques . . . . Mr. Clarke
Gerbin . . . . Mr. Villiers
Marchioness . . . Mrs. S. Powell
Alinda . . . . Mrs. Arnold
Clara . . . . . . Mrs. Chambers
Julia . . . . . . A Boston Lady

WITCHES.

Harlequin . . . . . . Mr. Clarke
Pantaloon . . . . . Mr. Hughes
Clown . . . . . . Mr. Maginnis
Lamplighter . . . Mr. Chambers
Lover . . . . Mr. Taylor
First Witch . . . . . . Mrs. Pick
Second Witch . . Mrs. Chambers
Third Witch . . . Mr. Hamilton
Fourth Witch . . . . Miss Green
Hecate . . . . Mr. Harper
Genius . . . . Mrs. Arnold
Pantalina . . . . . . Mrs. Baker
Nurse . . . . Mrs. Ashton
Fairy . . . . Miss Sully
Columbine . . . . Mrs. Harper

WORLD IN A VILLAGE.

Dr. Grigsby . . . Mr. Chambers
Sir Harry Check . Mr. Harper
Charles Willows . . . Mr. Taylor
William Bellevue . Mr. S. Powell
Jollyboy . . . . . . Mr. Kenny
Capt. Mullinahack . Mr. Hamilton
Albert . . . . Mr. Ashton
Willows . . . . . . Mr. Villiers
Capt. Van Sluesin . . Mr. Clarke
Hedgeworth . . . . Mr. Ratcliffe
Briers . . . . Mr. Sweeney
Edward Bellevue . . . Miss Sully
Mrs. Bellevue . . . Mrs. Arnold
Mrs. Allbut . . . . . Mrs. Baker
Maria . . . . . Mrs. Chambers
Margery . . . . . Mrs. Hughes
Louisa . . . . . Mrs. S. Powell

berland's "First Love," also produced in New York and Philadelphia later in the season, but called "Little Pickle" in the Boston bills; Burgoyne's "Maid of the Oaks," which anticipated the Philadelphia production by a week; "Mysteries of the Castle," a gallery piece originally acted at Covent Garden; and "A Peep Behind the Curtain," one of Garrick's most successful farces, into the second act of which was introduced the burletta of "Orpheus," of which Barthelomon was the composer.   I have given full casts of all these, including the pieces long familiar in other cities, but only now brought forward for the first

THIRD BOSTON SEASON—INCOMPLETE CASTS.

AGREEABLE SURPRISE.

Compton	Mr. Chambers
Eugene	Mr. Harper
Chicane	Mr. Hughes
Lingo	Mr. Villiers
Laura	Mrs. Pick
Cowslip	Mrs. Williamson

ALL THE WORLD'S A STAGE.

Charles Stanley	Mr. Taylor
Harry Stukely	Mr. Ashton
Diggory	Mr. Villiers
Kitty Sprightly	Mrs. Hughes

CHILD OF NATURE.

Marquis	Mr. Williamson
Murcia	Mr. Hamilton
Marchioness	Mrs. Arnold
Amanthis	Mrs. Williamson

CHILDREN IN THE WOOD.

Walter	Mr. Chambers
Apathy	Mr. Villiers
Lord Alford	Mr. Harper
Lady Alford	Mrs. Arnold
Josephine	Mrs. Williamson

DEUCE IS IN HIM.

Dr. Prattle	Mr. Harper
Bell	Miss Green
Florival	Mrs. Hughes

DEVIL TO PAY.

Sir John Loverule,	Mr. Chambers
Jobson	Mr. Harper
Nell	Mrs. Chambers

EVERY ONE HAS HIS FAULT.

Sir Robert Ramble,	Mr. Chambers
Lord Norland	Mr. Kenny
Edward	Miss Sully
Placid	Mr. Hamilton
Irwin	Mr. S. Powell
Lady Eleanor	Mrs. S. Powell
Mrs. Placid	Mrs. Harper
Miss Wooburn	Mrs. Hughes

FARMER.

Farmer Blackberry,	Mr. Hamilton
Capt. Valentine	Mr. Harper
Molly Maybush	Mrs. Pick
Betty Blackberry,	Mrs. Chambers

FARM HOUSE.

Freehold	Mr. Hamilton
Shacklefigure	Mr. Hughes
Modely	Mr. Chambers
Flora	Mrs. Pick
Aura	Mrs. Williamson

FOUNDLING.

Sir Chas. Raymond,	Mr. Hamilton
Young Belmont	Mr. Chambers
Faddle	Mr. S. Powell
Fidelia	Mrs. Harper

GAMESTER.

Beverly	Mr. Williamson
Stukely	Mr. Harper

GEORGE BARNWELL.

Millwood	Mrs. S. Powell

HIGHLAND REEL.

Shelty	Mr. Harper
Sandy	Mr. Chambers
Charley	Mr. Villiers
McGilpin	Mr. Hughes
Jenny	Mrs. Pick
Moggy	Mrs. Williamson

HIGH LIFE BELOW STAIRS.

Lovel	Mr. Harper
Kitty	Mrs. Harper
Lady Charlotte	Mrs. Hughes
Lady Bab	Miss Green

JEW.

Sheva	Mr. Williamson
Eliza Ratcliffe	Mrs. Arnold
Mrs. Ratcliffe	Mrs. Harper

LOVE IN A VILLAGE.

Young Meadows	Mr. Chambers
Woodcock	Mr. Hamilton
Hodge	Mr. Villiers
Hawthorn	Mr. Harper
Rosetta	Mrs. Arnold

LYING VALET.

Sharp	Mr. Harper
Kitty Pry	Mrs. Chambers

MIDAS.

Midas	Mr. Hamilton
Sileno	Mr. Harper

time in Boston. The rest of the casts, those of the productions already known to Boston theatre-goers, will be found sufficiently complete to cover the parts played during the season by the important acquisitions—Mr. and Mrs. Williamson, Mr. and Mrs. Chambers, Mr. Hamilton, Mrs. Pick and Mrs. Arnold—together with the important roles accorded to the old members of the company. The season was not remarkable for incident. When the benefit of Mr. Villiers, "our favorite son of Momus," was announced, it was said that he had intended producing a piece of his own on that occasion, but "the present

THIRD BOSTON SEASON—INCOMPLETE CASTS.

Jupiter . . . . . . Mr. Hughes
Apollo . . . . . . Mr. Chambers
Momus . . . . Mr. Villiers
Juno . . . . . . Mrs. Chambers
Minerva . . . . . . Mrs. Harper
Venus . . . . Miss Green
Daphne . . . . . . Mrs. Arnold
Nysa . . . . Mrs. Pick

MOCK DOCTOR.
Gregory . . . . Mr. Clarke
Charlotte . . . . . Mrs. Harper

MOUNTAINEERS.
Kilmallock . . . . Mr. Hamilton
Zorayda . . . . . Mrs. Arnold
Agnes . . . . . Mrs. Williamson

NO SONG NO SUPPER.
Crop . . . . . . Mr. Hamilton
Endless . . . . . . Mr. Taylor
Robin . . . . Mr. Harper
Dorothy . . . . Mrs. Pick
Margaretta . . Mrs. Williamson

OLD SOLDIER.
Lucas . . . . . . Mr. Chambers
Flora . . . . Mrs. Pick
Colette . . . . . . Mrs. Arnold

POOR SOLDIER.
Patrick . . . . . . Mrs. Pick
Darby . . . . Mr. Harper
Bagatelle . . . . Mr. Hamilton

Norah . . . . . Mrs. Chambers
Kathleen . . . . Mrs. Williamson

PRISONER AT LARGE.
Trap . . . . Mr. Sweeney
Muns . . . . Mr. Harper
Adelaide . . . . Mrs. Chambers
Mary . . . . Mrs. Pick
Rachel . . . . Mrs. Williamson

PRIZE.
Lenitive . . . . Mr. Chambers
Caroline . . . . . . Mrs. Arnold

ROMEO AND JULIET.
Romeo . . . . Mr. Harper
Mercutio . . . . . Mr. S. Powell

ROMP.
Watty Cockney . Mr. Chambers
Miss La Blond . . . Miss Green
Priscilla . . . Mrs. Williamson

ROSINA.
Belville . . . . . Mr. Chambers
Rustic . . . . . . Mr. Hamilton
William . . . . . Mr. Williamson
Rosina . . . . . Mrs. Arnold

SHE STOOPS TO CONQUER.
Young Marlow . Mr. Williamson
Tony Lumpkin . . . Mr. Harper
Miss Neville . . . . Miss Green
Mrs. Hardcastle . . Mrs. Harper

SPOILED CHILD.
Little Pickle . . Mrs. Williamson
Tag . . . . Mr. Chambers

TRUE-BORN IRISHMAN.
O'Dogherty . . . Mr. Hamilton
Mushroom . . . . . Mr. Harper
Mrs. Diggerty . . . Mrs. Harper
Lady Kinnegad . . Mrs. Hughes
Lady Bab Frightful . Mrs. Baker

VILLAGE LAWYER.
Scout . . . . Mr. Taylor
Snarl . . . . Mr. Hughes
Sheepface . . . . . Mr. Villiers
Mrs. Scout . . . . Mrs. Baker
Kitty . . . . Mrs. Pick

VIRGIN UNMASKED.
Coupee . . . . . . Mr. Taylor
Quaver . . . . . Mr. Chambers
Lucy . . . . Mrs. Williamson

WILD OATS.
Sir George Thunder, Mr. Hamilton
Rover . . . . Mr. Harper
John Dory . . . . . Mr. Kenny
Ephraim Smooth . Mr. Chambers
Lady Amarath . . . Mrs. Harper

WRANGLING LOVERS.
Don Carlos . . . . Mr. S. Powell
Leonora . . . . . Mrs. Harper

state of the company precludes its exhibition." Mr. Williamson wrote a prologue for Villiers' benefit and one also to introduce the young lady who played *Julia* in the "Sicilian Romance" on the 20th of April, the *debutante* being a protege of Mrs. Williamson. The only actor who gave offense during the season was Mr. Taylor. On

WILLIAMSON'S PROLOGUE.

———

(Spoken by Mrs. Williamson.)

Bless me! What, here again? Well, this
   is clever;
Our lucky barque makes frequent trips, and
   never
Returns to port unfreighted with your favor.
Our little Jabal sees with pride to-night
How well you're stow'd—I think you're
   pretty tight!
So kindly pack'd together, I dare say
Not one ill natur'd thought can here fetch
   way;
Though candor, taste and judgment who have
   come
As cabin passengers have always room.
   Small tho' our barque, 'tis yet well built
   and sound;
No fears that she will ever run aground!
The owners, too—too spirited to shrink,—
Will never see their gallant vessel sink;
If, with a pilot's care, in the command,
Our captain steers her with an artist's hand.
That hope's our venture; boldly we em-
   bark it;
Nor wish to seek or find a better market.
   To-night one novel article's on board—
A sample merely—drawn from nature's hoard.
A native young adventurer comes forth;
The growth is genuine—you must rate its
   worth.
The tender plant puts forth its trembling
   leaves,
E'en shrinking from the favor it receives;

New to the art, a stranger to its laws,
I come, a suppliant in my sex's cause!
Come, do now be good-humor'd—'tis by half
More pain to you, I'm sure, to frown than
   laugh.
I found that secret out as, in your eyes,
I've marked the beams of genuine pleasure
   rise!
   To our young friend within shall I impart
This clue—this master key to gain the heart?
To nature true your judgment can't be fickle,
You'll raise, perhaps, another *Little Pickle;*
Grateful as in the first and all your own,
Nurs'd, rear'd and tutor'd by your smiles
   alone.
Candor and critic taste have kindly view'd
The first expansion of the opening bud;
And thro' the o'erwhelming blush—the stifled
   power,
Augur'd the future harvest's ripen'd store.
Merit is ever modest—to be led,
Like your own Independence, from its shade,
Requires a fostering art, a guardian arm,
To shield the growth from each insidious
   harm.
So worth expands, and so your freedom grew;
And such your glorious Leader prov'd to you.
With watchful care, with patient toil, he
   rear'd
The healthful plant; and as he watch'd, he
   cheer'd
The rapid growth, till nations saw it rise,
A solid column, tow'ring to the skies!
   Oh! be to merit, opening to your view,
What nature was to man—and Washington
   to you.

the 23d of March he inserted an apology, under the advertisements of the day, regretting that his conduct on the previous Friday evening had been construed into an intention to insult the audience, and asking forgiveness on the ground that it was an accidental error. When the theatre closed with Mr. Williamson's benefit, Mr. Harper in a graceful speech took leave of the public as acting manager, and Mr. Williamson announced his appointment to the management.

The retiring members of the company were Mr. and Mrs. S. Powell, who joined Charles S. Powell's forces at the new Boston Haymarket; Mr. and Mrs. Chambers, who together with Miss Sully became the theatrical features of Rickett's Circus; Mr. and Mrs. Hughes, Mr. Taylor, Mr. Maginnis, Mrs. Pick and Mrs. Arnold, besides Mr. and Mrs. Harper. A summer campaign in Rhode Island intervened under Mr. Harper's management, the company being the same as at the Boston Theatre, with the exception of Mr. and Mrs. Williamson and Mrs. Arnold. Mr. Williamson was busy organizing his forces for the next season, and visited New York and Philadelphia to secure players. Mrs. Arnold gave concerts at Portsmouth, N. H., and other New England towns during the summer, assisted by her daughter, Miss Arnold. As Miss Arnold after this year was in charge of Mr. and Mrs. Tubbs, the inference is a natural one that the grandmother of Edgar Allan Poe became the wife of Tubbs, a strolling player.

CHAPTER XVI.

NEW HAY AT THE OLD MARKET.

RETURN OF THE OLD AMERICAN COMPANY TO NEW YORK—INTRODUC-
TION OF THE NEW PLAYERS—PRODUCTIONS OF THE SEASON—
"THE ARCHERS"—DUNLAP ENTERS THE MANAGEMENT—MANA-
GERIAL QUARRELS—MRS. HALLAM'S RETIREMENT—"MOHAWKS."

AFTER the return of the Old American Company from Boston to New York little time was lost in beginning the season. All the recent acquisitions who had been introduced to the American public at the Boston Theatre were now brought forward in New York, and the season was the most brilliant that had ever been known in the old theatre in John Street. The pieces chosen for the opening night were the "Provoked Husband" and the "Spoiled Child." In the former Johnson as *Sir Francis Wronghead*, Jefferson as *Squire Richard*, Tyler as *Manly*, Mrs. Tyler as *Lady Grace*, Mrs. Brett as *Lady Wronghead*, and Mrs. Johnson as *Lady Townly* made their first appearance in New York. Jefferson also played *Tag* and Mrs. Brett *Miss Pickle* in the afterpiece. On the second night Miss Broadhurst appeared for the first time on the New York stage as *Yarico*, and Miss Arabella Brett made her first appearance on any stage as *Narcissa* in "Inkle and Yarico." Miss Arabella Brett, who had accompanied her mother to America, was, according to Dunlap, a child in years, but a woman in appearance. She was devoid of personal beauty, but possessed a powerful voice, and achieved marked success as a singer. Apart from the introduction of these important players to the New York audience, the only noteworthy *debut* was that of John Hogg, who made his first appearance on the 30th of March as *Virolet* in the "Mountaineers." Mr. Hogg's *debut*, apparently, was unsatisfactory, for he was not seen again during the season. He was a good-looking young man, diffident and easily disconcerted. His forte was comic old men. In serious parts he often forgot his lines and sometimes was unable to proceed. Mr. Hogg had married Ann Storer, who had been the first Mrs. Henry, and who subsequently shared his distinction on the New York stage. After the first night this season the younger Hallam played *Virolet* in the "Mountaineers." Mr. and Mrs. Cleveland made their New York entrance in "Mahomet" on the 13th of February. The produc-

LIST OF PERFORMANCES.

1796.

Feb. 10—Provoked Husband . . Vanbrugh
Spoiled Child . . . . Bickerstaff
12—Inkle and Yarico . . Colman, Jr
Guardian . . . . Garrick
13—Mahomet . . . . Miller
15—Surrender of Calais . Colman, Jr
Midnight Hour . . Mrs. Inchbald
17—Earl of Essex . . . . . . Jones
Rosina . . . . . . Mrs. Brooke
19—I'll Tell You What . Mrs. Inchbald
Children in the Wood . . Morton
22—School for Soldiers . . . Henry
Two Philosophers.
Purse . . . . Cross
24—Deserted Daughter . . . Holcroft
Padlock . . . . . . Bickerstaff
26—Robin Hood . . . . . MacNally
Irish Widow . . . . . . Garrick
27—Bold Stroke for a Husband
Mrs. Cowley
Don Juan.
29—Carmelite . . . . . Cumberland
Sultan . . . . . . Bickerstaff
March 2—Deserted Daughter.
Highland Reel . . . . O'Keefe
4—Wheel of Fortune . Cumberland
Spoiled Child.
5—Inconstant . . . . . . Farquhar
Bird Catcher.
Harlequin Gardener.
7—Wheel of Fortune.
Flitch of Bacon . . . . . Bate
9—Deserted Daughter.
Agreeable Surprise . . . O'Keefe
11—Young Quaker . . . . O'Keefe
No Song No Supper . . . Hoare
14—School for Scandal . . Sheridan
Quaker . . . . Dibdin
16—Deserted Daughter.
Poor Vulcan . . . . . . Dibdin

Mar. 18—Know Your Own Mind . Murphy
Cooper.
No Song No Supper.
21—Jew . . . . Cumberland
Children in the Wood.
23—Clandestine Marriage
Garrick and Colman
Midnight Hour.
26—Jane Shore . . . . . . Rowe
Whims of Galatea.
28—Haunted Tower . . . . . Cobb
Lyar . . . . Foote
30—Mountaineers . . . . Colman, Jr
Irish Widow.
April 1—Belle's Stratagem . . Mrs. Cowley
Florizel and Perdita . . Shakspere
4—Mountaineers.
Romp . . . . Bickerstaff
6—Alexander the Great . . . . Lee
Whims of Galatea.
Rosina.
8—Mountaineers.
Bon Ton . . . . Garrick
9—Mountaineers.
Le Foret Noire.
11—Maid of the Mill . . Bickerstaff
Tempest . . . . . . Dryden
13—Deserted Daughter.
Milliners.
Purse.
15—Mountaineers.
Busybody . . . . Mrs. Centlivre
18—Archers . . . . Dunlap
Edgar and Emmeline
Hawkesworth
20—Macbeth . . . . . . Shakspere
Deserter . . . . Dibdin
21—Children in the Wood.
Two Hunters.
Enraged Musicians . Francisquy
(Mrs. Val's benefit.)
22—Archers.
Critic . . . . Sheridan
25—Romeo and Juliet . . Shakspere
Three Weeks After Marriage
Murphy
(Mrs. Hallam's benefit.)

tions of the season show little in the way of novelty, the only piece of American origin, aside from two or three pantomimes, being Dunlap's " Archers." What, however, was in itself a novelty was an agreement with Hallam and Hodgkinson by which Dunlap became an associate manager of the Old American Company. The suggestion came from Hodgkinson, Dunlap being allured by the temptation of having the sole control of the pieces produced, including the power to bring forward his own. Hodgkinson's suggestion was made on the 19th of March, while Dunlap's opera was in preparation. Hallam's concurrence was obtained in April. Immediately after the production of the "Archers," Dunlap met the two managers for the purpose of signing the Articles of Agreement. At this meeting Hallam began to raise difficulties, claiming that, Hodgkinson and Dunlap being a majority, he would be bound by their acts. To this it was answered that, his property being equal to that of the other two, his voice in all matters relating to the property would be equal to both his colleagues. Still Hallam declined to sign, but finally, on the 1st of May, he unbosomed his grievances to Dunlap. These, of course, consisted mainly in Hodgkinson's usurpation of power and of parts, Hallam being deprived of his authority in the theatre and of the roles that still gave him consequence with the public, while Mrs. Hallam was not only aggrieved and misrepresented, but the parts in which she was most acceptable were given to others. Hodgkinson, on the other hand, ridiculed Hallam's wish to keep the parts, but finally, through Dunlap's mediation, the characters that Hodgkinson claimed and Hallam refused to yield were reduced to four—*Orestes, Ranger, Hamlet* and *Benedick.* Why *Orestes* and *Ranger* should have

April 27—Roman Father . . . Whitehead
    Sicilian Romance . . . Siddons
    (Mrs. Cleveland's benefit.)
  29—As You Like It . . . Shakspere
    Poor Soldier . . . . . O'Keefe
    (Mr. King's benefit.)
May 3—Every One Has His Fault
               Mrs. Inchbald
    American Heroine.
    (Mad. Gardie's benefit.)
  4—School for Greybeards
               Mrs. Cowley
    Prisoner . . . . Rose
    (Miss Broadhurst's benefit.)
  6—Speculation . . . . . Reynolds
    (Mrs. Hodgkinson's benefit.)
  9—Werter and Charlotte . Reynolds
    Slaves in Algiers . Mrs. Rowson
  11—Mountaineers.
    Crotchet Lodge . . . Hurlstone
    (Mr. Woolls' benefit.)
  13—Masked Apparition . . . . Cross
    Highland Reel.
    Man and Wife . . . . . Colman
    (Mr. Hallam, Jr.'s, benefit.)
  18—Tancred and Sigismunda, Thomson
    Old Man Grown Young
               Francisquy
    Two Misers . . . . . . O'Hara
    (Mr. Tyler's benefit.)
  20—First Love . . . . . Cumberland
    Auld Robin Gray . . . . Arnold
    Thomas and Sally . . Bickerstaff
    (Mrs. Johnson's benefit.)
  23—Speculation.
    Adopted Child . . . . . . Birch
    (Mr. Jefferson's benefit.)
  25—Earl of Warwick . . . Franklin
    Poor Soldier.
    (Mrs. Melmoth's benefit.)
  30—Much Ado About Nothing
               Shakspere
    My Grandmother . . . . Hoare
    (Mr. Hodgkinson's benefit.)
June 3—Child of Nature . Mrs. Inchbald
    Son-in-Law . . . . . O'Keefe
    (Mr. and Mrs. Tyler's benefit.)

June 6—Road to Ruin . . . . . Holcroft
        Adopted Child.
        (Mr. Faulkner's benefit.)
        8—Love Makes a Man . . . Cibber
        Independence of America.
        (Mr. Cleveland's benefit.)
        11—Hamlet . . . . Shakspere
        Prisoner at Large . . . O'Keefe
        (Mr. King's benefit.)
        13—Better Late Than Never . Andrews
        Farmer . . . . O'Keefe
        (Mr. Johnson's benefit.)
        15—Lear . . . . Shakspere
        Robinson Crusoe . . . Sheridan
        (Mr. Francisquy's benefit.)
        17—He Would Be a Soldier . . Pilon
        Two Philosophers.
        Children in the Wood.
        (Mr. Hallam's benefit.)
        20—Wild Oats . . . . . . O'Keefe
        Love in a Camp . . . . O'Keefe
        (Durang and Lee's benefit.)
        22—As You Like It.
        Adopted Child.
    (Gill, Vincent, Handasy, Munto and Master
        Stockwell's benefit.)
        25—Inkle and Yarico.
        Catharine and Petruchio, Shakspere
    (Miss Brett and Miss Harding's benefit.)

been in dispute it is difficult to understand, as neither the " Distressed Mother " nor " Suspicious Husband " was a necessary part of the repertoire. This, in fact, reduced the parts in dispute to two, which were divided between the disputants, Hodgkinson bringing out " Much Ado About Nothing " for his benefit on the 30th of May, and Hallam appearing as *Hamlet* for King's benefit on the 11th of June. While the dispute was in progress Hodgkinson swore he would have the parts or not play, notwithstanding he had just bound himself to the new purchaser of a part of the property, while Hallam expressed as much surprise at Hodgkinson's demand as if his associate had claimed his tables and chairs.

When the season opened on the 10th of February Mr. Hodgkinson delivered an introductory [1] address written by William Miln, a

---

[1] OPENING ADDRESS.

The wandering traveler, compell'd to roam,
Is not more pleas'd to reach his native home
Than we our patrons thus again to meet,
Whom here with joy and gratitude we greet;
So long an absence with regret we mourn,
Respect alone prevented our return;

While dire calamity oppress'd the town,
And death wore terror's most distressing frown;
We view'd its sorrows stung with poignant grief,
Pitied, alas! but could not send relief.
Enough!—o'er such a scene we draw a veil,
Reflection shudders at the horrid tale.
See rosy health, array'd in smiles, appears,

friend of Hodgkinson. " It was commonplace in the serious and silly in the attempted comic parts," Dunlap says of it, and there is no occasion to challenge his judgment.

Dunlap's opera, " The Archers," produced on the 18th of April, was the only ambitious attempt at a native production during the season. The music was by Carr and, according to Dunlap, " was

Blooms on each cheek and dissipates our fears,
Bids mirth and cheerfulness resume their sway,
And ev'ry muse her ev'ry charm display.
We joyfully obey—for you again
We tune the lyre and wake the swelling strain.
Your favor to deserve we long have tried—
That we have gain'd it is our greatest pride.
Friends we have met in ev'ry port, 'tis true,
But our sheet anchor rests secure with you.
Of our desire to please behold the fruits—
From distant lands we bring you new recruits,
Whose various merits will conspicuous shine,
Warm'd by the influence of your smile benign.
With you sit plenty, riches, mirth and pleasure—
Your kind applause is true theatric treasure;
With your assistance soon we'll cut a dash
In our new house—we only want more cash.
Poetic merit, too, your smiles can raise.
And fan the spark of genius to a blaze;
While giddy fashion's nursery of satire
Shall find the comic muse in richest matter;
Folly and fashion are theatric game,
And we at manners, not at men, take aim.
We claim a right to hunt pit, box and lobby,
Where Uncle Toby-like each rides his hobby;
Hence will we ferret witlings, beaux and fops,
Who, though no conjurors, perhaps are crops.
And you, ye belles, I vow you must not frown
Should we attack cap, petticoat and gown—
In days of yore hips were not so disgraced;
Six yards of hoop encircl'd beauty's waist.

Stiff stays, tight-lac'd, like sugar loaf inverted,
Show'd that the body was not quite deserted.
Two ladies then, of consequence, when drest,
Requir'd twelve yards, at least, to walk abreast;
Could Miss' grandmama rise from her grave,
'Twere droll to see how Miss and she'd behave;
" Why Nancy, child, Lord bless me, where's your body?
Mercy upon us—what a hoddy-doddy ! "
" La, grandmama, don't be in such a passion,
To look like nobody is all the fashion."
" The girl's stark mad—why, Nancy, where's your waist ? "
" Up here, grandma—to wear it high's the taste."
" If it grows higher, child, as you grow older,
In half a year 'twill be above the shoulder."
" No fear of that, grandma, for you will see
It falls next year an inch below the knee;
I dearly love extremes—oh ! what a treat
'Twould be to wear one's waist about one's feet."
Pardon the bold digression, oh ! ye fair:
Nature has form'd you with peculiar care;
Wisdom and wit with beauty have combin'd
To grace your person and adorn your mind;
And though the whims of fashion, for a day,
May loveliness in folly's garb display,
The charm soon breaks—detraction rails in vain—
Beauty triumphant is itself again.

pleasing and well got up." Hodgkinson and Mrs. Melmoth, according to the same authority, were forcible, and the comic parts told well with Hallam and Mrs. Hodgkinson, " although *Conrad* ought to have been given to Jefferson." The last suggestion was probably a late after-thought with Dunlap. The author, in his later character of historian, says the piece was received with applause, repeatedly played and immediately printed.

ARCHERS.

William Tell	Mr. Hodgkinson
Walter Furst	Mr. Johnson
Arnold Melchthal	Mr. Tyler
Werner Staffach	Mr. Hallam, Jr
Gestler	Mr. Cleveland
Burgomaster	Mr. Prigmore
Lieutenant . . . . . . , . .	Mr. Jefferson
Leopold	Mr. King
Conrad	Mr. Hallam
Portia	Mr. Melmoth
Rhodolpha	Miss Broadhurst
Cicely	Mrs. Hodgkinson

It was played twice and printed. The music, unfortunately, is lost. For this loss the book is no compensation.

During the season a part of the Boston repertory was played in New York with casts modified by the exigencies of the company.

CONTRASTED CASTS—NEW YORK AND BOSTON.

Alexander the Great.

	New York.	Boston.
Thessalus . . .	Mr. Woolls	. . Mr. Ashton
Perdiccas . . .	Mr. Durang	. . Mr. Kenny
Eumenes . . .	Mr. Munto	. . Mr. Woolls
Clytus	Mr. Hallam	. . Mr. Hamilton
Roxana	Mrs. Melmoth	. Mrs. S. Powell

Bon Ton.

Sir John Trotley.	Mr. Prigmore	. Mr. Hamilton
Lord Minikin	. Mr. Cleveland	. Mr. S. Powell
Colonel Tivy .	. Mr. King .	. . Mr. Cleveland
Davy	Mr. Jefferson	. Mr. Villiers
Gymp	Mrs. Munto	. . Mrs. King
Miss Tittup . .	Mrs. Johnson	. Mrs. S. Powell

Children in the Wood.

Gabriel	Mr. Jefferson	. Mr. Martin
Lady Alford . .	Mrs. Melmoth	. Mrs. Johnson

Clandestine Marriage.

Sterling	Mr. Johnson .	. Mr. Hamilton
Canton . . .	Mr. Roberts .	. Mr. Martin
Trueman . . .	Mr. Munto	. . Mr. Tompkins
Traverse . . .	Mr. Tompkins	. Mr. Durang
Lovewell . . .	Mr. Hodgkinson.	Mr. Harper
Fanny	Mrs. Johnson	. Mrs. S. Powell

Critic.

	New York.	Boston.
Sir Fretful . . .	Mr. Prigmore	. Mr. Hamilton
Hatton	Mr. McKenzie	..Mr. Ashton
Whiskerandos	. Mr. Hallam, Jr..	Mr. Prigmore

Deserted Daughter.

Lenox	Mr. King . . .	Mr. Harper
Grime	Mr. Jefferson	. Mr. Johnson
Donald	Mr. Johnson	. Mr. Hamilton
Lady Ann . . .	Mrs. Melmoth	. Mrs. S. Powell

Don Juan.

Scaramouch . .	Mr. Jefferson	. Mr. Prigmore

Flitch of Bacon.

Tipple	Mr. Jefferson	. Mr. Prigmore
Benbow	Mr. Johnson	. Mr. Ashton
Maj. Benbow .	Mr. Prigmore	. Mr. Hamilton
Kilderkin . . .	Mr. Woolls	. . Mr. Kenny
Eliza	Miss Broadhurst.	Mrs. Hodgkinson

Florizel and Perdita.

Polixenes . . .	Mr. King . . .	Mr. Hamilton
Camillo	Mr. Munto	. . Mr. Kenny
Mopsa	Mrs. Munto	. . Mrs. Brett
Dorcas	Mrs. Brett . . .	Mrs. King

These changes are interesting in showing the progress of the recent acquisitions, especially Mrs. Johnson and Mr. Jefferson. Among the

CONTRASTED CASTS—NEW YORK AND BOSTON.

Harlequin Gardener.

	New York.	Boston.
Pantaloon	Mr. Johnson	Mr. Ashton
Lover	Mr. Hallam, Jr.	Mr. Leonard
Clown	Mr. Jefferson	Mr. Prigmore

Haunted Tower.

Charles	Mr. Munto	Mr. Chambers
Hugo	Mr. De Moulin	Mr. Ashton
De Courcy	Mr. Hallam, Jr.	Mr. Cleveland
Martin	Mr. Lee	Mr. Villiers
Edward	Mr. Jefferson	Mr. Hodgkinson
Lady Elinor	Miss Broadhurst.	Mrs. Pick
Cicely	Mrs. Brett	Mrs. Chambers

Highland Reel.

Sandy	Mr. Tyler	Mr. Chambers
Charley	Mr. Jefferson	Mr. Martin
Coll	Mr. Munto	Mr. Ashton
Raasay	Mr. Roberts	Mr. Kenny
Jenny	Miss Broadhurst.	Mrs. Chambers

I'll Tell You What.

Charles Euston	Mr. Hallam, Jr.	Mr. Martin
Sir H'y Harmless	Mr. Jefferson	Mr. Taylor
Lady Harriet	Mrs. Tyler	Mrs. S. Powell
Bloom	Mrs. Cleveland	Mrs. Chambers

Inconstant.

Old Mirabel	Mr. Prigmore	Mr. Hamilton
Lamorce	Mrs. Munto	Mrs. King

Inkle and Yarico.

Inkle	Mr. Tyler	Mr. Cleveland
Curry	Mr. King	Mr. Hughes
Medium	Mr. Johnson	Mr. Kenny
Campley	Mr. Munto	Mr. Hallam, Jr
Wowski	Mrs. Hodgkinson	Mrs. Hughes
Narcissa	Miss Brett	Mrs. Hodgkinson
Patty	Mrs. Brett	Mrs. Chambers
Yarico	Miss Broadhurst.	Mrs. S. Powell

Irish Widow.

Nephew	Mr. Cleveland	Mr. Tyler
Thomas	Mr. Woolls	Mr. Hodgkinson
Bates	Mr. Roberts	Mr. Hughes
Blackboy	Mr. McKnight	

Jane Shore.

Hastings	Mr. Hodgkinson.	Mr. Tyler
Belmour	Mr. Tyler	Mr. Hallam, Jr
Ratcliff	Mr. Woolls	Mr. Hughes
Catesby	Mr. Cleveland	Mr. Ashton
Derby	Mr. Johnson	
Alicia	Mrs. Melmoth	Mrs. Johnson
Jane Shore	Mrs. Johnson	Mrs. S. Powell

Know Your Own Mind.

	New York.	Boston.
Sir H'y Lovewit	Mr. Tyler	Mr. Martin
Capt. Bygrove	Mr. Munto	Mr. Hughes
Millamour	Mr. Hallam, Jr	Mr. Chambers
Charles	Mr. Jefferson	Mr. Villiers
Lady Jane	Miss Broadhurst.	Mrs. Chambers

Le Foret Noire.

Le Terreur	Mr. Francisquy	Mr. Hodgkinson
Lauridan	Mr. Jefferson	Mr. King
Geronte	Mr. Val	Mr. Hallam
Confidante	Mrs. Munto	Mrs. Hughes

Macbeth.

Banquo	Mr. Tyler	Mr. Harper
Duncan	Mr. Johnson	Mr. Kenny
Seyton	Mr. Munto	Mr. Ashton
Second Witch	Mr. Jefferson	Mr. Johnson
Third Witch	Mrs. Brett	Mrs. Hamilton
Lady Macbeth	Mrs. Melmoth	Mrs. S. Powell

Midnight Hour.

General	Mr. Prigmore	Mr. Hamilton
Nicholas	Mr. Hallam	Mr. Prigmore
Sebastian	Mr. Jefferson	Mr. Martin
Matthias	Mr. Johnson	Mr. Villiers
Marquis	Mr. Tyler	Mr. Taylor

No Song No Supper.

Dorothy	Miss Broadhurst.	Mrs. Pick
Louisa	Mrs. Munto	Mrs. King

Padlock.

Don Diego	Mr. Woolls	Mr. Kenny
Leander	Mr. Tyler	Mr. Chambers

Poor Vulcan.

Adonis	Mr. Jefferson	Mr. Tyler
Mercury	Mr. Munto	Mr. Jefferson
Jupiter	Mr. Tyler	Mr. Chambers
Grace	Mrs. Hodgkinson	Mrs. Chambers
Venus	Miss Broadhurst.	Mrs. Hodgkinson

Provoked Husband.

Lord Townly	Mr. Hallam	Mr. Hodgkinson
Moody	Mr. Prigmore	Mr. Villiers
Basset	Mr. Hallam, Jr	Mr. Taylor
Squire Richard	Mr. Jefferson	Mr. Martin
Miss Jenny	Mrs. Hallam	Mrs. Chambers
Myrtilla	Mrs. Munto	Mrs. King

Purse.

Edward	Mr. Tyler	Mr. Chambers
Thomas	Mr. Jefferson	Mr. Villiers

productions in this list were two comedies that had not been played in New York—Holcroft's "Deserted Daughter" and Cumberland's "Wheel of Fortune." The former was produced by the Old American Company in both cities before its production in Philadelphia, but the "Wheel of Fortune" was played by the Philadelphia company the evening previous to its production in Boston. Another piece in the list not previously given was Dibdin's burletta, "Poor Vulcan," played in Philadelphia during the season 1794–5.

Besides those already mentioned a long list of pieces was presented for the first time in New York, some of which had their initial performance in America. These comprised the "Adopted Child," a musical drama by Samuel Birch that had been acted with success at Drury Lane; the "Masked Apparition," of which there is no cast, probably identical with Cross' musical romance, the "Apparition," originally produced at the Haymarket; the "Milliners," probably the

CONTRASTED CASTS—NEW YORK AND BOSTON.

Robin Hood.

	New York.	Boston.
Robin Hood . .	Mr. King . . .	Mr. Tyler
Allan-a-Dale . .	Mr. Munto . .	Mr. Cleveland
Fitzherbert . .	Mr. Johnson .	Mr. Ashton
Edwin	Mr. Tyler . . .	Mr. Chambers
Annette	Mrs. Brett . . .	Mrs. Hughes
Angelina . . .	Miss Broadhurst.	Mrs. Pick

Romp.

Watty Cockney .	Mr. Jefferson .	Mr. Jefferson
Old Cockney . .	Mr. Johnson . .	Mr. Ashton
Miss Le Blond .	Mrs. Tyler . . .	Mrs. Chambers
Penelope . . .	Mrs. Munto . .	Mrs. King

Rosina.

Capt. Belville .	Mr. Munto . .	Mr. King
Irishman . . .	Mr. King . . .	Mr. Kenny
Will	Mr. Durang . .	Mr. Jefferson
Phœbe	Mrs. Hodgkinson	Mrs. Hughes
Rosina	Miss Broadhurst.	Mrs. Hodgkinson

School for Scandal.

Sir Peter Teazle .	Mr. Hallam . .	Mr. Hamilton
Sir Oliver . . .	Mr. Johnson . .	Mr. Kenny
Crabtree	Mr. Prigmore .	Mr. Hughes

	New York.	Boston.
Rowley	Mr. Woolls . .	Mr. Johnson
Snake	Mr. Munto . .	Mr. Ashton
Trip	Mr. Durang . .	Mr. Taylor
Moses	Mr. Jefferson .	Mr. Villiers
Mrs. Candour .	Mrs. Brett . . .	Mrs. Hodgkinson
Maria	Mrs. Cleveland .	Mrs. Hughes
Lady Teazle . .	Mrs. Hallam . .	Mrs. Johnson

School for Soldiers.

Col. Valentine .	Mr. Prigmore .	Mr. Kenny
Hector	Mr. Johnson . .	Mr. Hamilton
Clara Mildmay .	Mrs. Cleveland .	Mrs. S. Powell

Spoiled Child.

Tag	Mr. Jefferson .	Mr. Chambers
Maria	Mrs. Munto . .	Mrs. Chambers

Sultan.

Ismene	Miss Broadhurst.	Mrs. Pick

Wheel of Fortune.

Tempest	Mr. Prigmore .	Mr. Hamilton
Woodville . . .	Mr. King . . .	Mr. Harper
Jenkins	Mr. Munto . .	Mr. Ashton
Maid	Mrs. Munto . .	Mrs. King

two-act burletta of T. Harpley acted at Liverpool in 1790; "Speculation," a satire by Reynolds, aimed at the swindling projects then so

FIRST NEW YORK PRODUCTIONS—CASTS.

ADOPTED CHILD.

Boy	Miss Harding
Sir Bertrand	Mr. Cleveland
La Sage	Mr. Tyler
Record	Mr. Johnson
Spruce	Mr. Hallam, Jr
Flint	Mr. Munto
Michael	Mr. Jefferson
Clara	Miss Broadhurst
Lucy	Miss Brett
Sarsnette	Mrs. Munto
Nell	Mrs. Cleveland

AULD ROBIN GRAY.

Jamie	Mr. Francisquy
Donald	Mr. Durang
Auld Robin	Mr. Johnson
Goody Toothless	Mrs. Brett
Jenny	Mad. Gardie

BETTER LATE THAN NEVER.

Saville	Mr. Hodgkinson
Flurry	Mr. Prigmore
Sir Charles	Mr. Tyler
Pallet	Mr. Cleveland
Grump	Mr. Johnson
Clerk	Mr. Durang
Litigamus	Mr. Jefferson
Diary	Mrs. Hodgkinson
Mrs. Flurry	Mrs. Hallam
Augusta	Mrs. Johnson

CROTCHET LODGE.

Truncheon	Mr. Hallam
Nimble	Mr. Jefferson
Dr. Chronic	Mr. Johnson
Paddy	Mr. King
Darnly	Mr. Cleveland
Waiter	Mr. Durang
Bootcatcher	Mr. Lee
Simpkin	Mr. Prigmore
Florella	Miss Broadhurst
Miss Crotchet	Mrs. Brett
Landlady	Mrs. Tyler
Maid	Mrs. Munto
Thisbe	Mrs. Cleveland

ENRAGED MUSICIANS.

Woodcutters	{ Mr. Durang
	Mr. Lee

Lucas	Mr. Dubois
Colas	Mr. Francisquy
Innkeeper	Mr. Lee
Colette	Mad. Val
Lucille	Miss Brett
Shepherdess	Mrs. Durang
Finette	Mad. Gardie

FIRST LOVE.

Fred'k Mowbray	Mr. Hodgkinson
David Mowbray	Mr. Jefferson
Sir Miles Mowbray	Mr. Johnson
Billy Bustler	Mr. Prigmore
Wrangle	Mr. Cleveland
Robin	Mr. Durang
Lord Sensitive	Mr. Tyler
Sabina Rosny	Mrs. Cleveland
Mrs. Wrangle	Mrs. Tyler
Mrs. Kate	Mrs. Brett
Waiting Woman	Mrs. Munto
Lady Ruby	Mrs. Johnson

INDEPENDENCE OF AMERICA.

America	Mad. Gardie
Britannia	Mrs. Cleveland
Goddess of Liberty	Mrs. Hallam
Senator	Mr. Cleveland
British Officers	{ Mr. Munto
	Mr. Lee
The General	Mr. Tyler
Officer	Mr. Jefferson
Citizen	{ Mr. Durang
	Mr. Woolls
Boston Messenger	Mr. Lee
President	Mr. Hallam, Jr
Old Woman	Mr. Francisquy

MILLINERS.

Abbe	Mr. Francisquy
Husband	Mr. Val
Officers	{ Mr. Jefferson
	Mr. Hallam, Jr
	Mr. Prigmore
	Mr. Durang
Hairdresser	Mr. Tompkins
Music Master	Mr. Munto
Old Servant	Mr. Lee
Simpleton	Mr. Dubois
Wife	Mad. Val
Nannette	Mrs. Brett
Sylvia	Mrs. Cleveland

Fanny	Mrs. Munto
Rachel	Mrs. Tompkins
Emma	Mad. Gardie

MY GRANDMOTHER.

Vapour	Mr. Hodgkinson
Sir Matthew	Mr. Johnson
Woodly	Mr. Tyler
Souffrance	Mr. Cleveland
Tom	Mr. Munto
Dicky Gossip	Mr. Jefferson
Charlotte	Miss Broadhurst
Florella	Mrs. Hodgkinson

OLD MAN GROWN YOUNG.

Old Man	Mr. Francisquy
Colas	Mr. Durang
Cupid	Master Stockwell
Finette	Mrs. Cleveland
Laurette	Mad. Gardie

PRISONER.

Marcus	Mr. Hodgkinson
Pasqual	Mr. King
Robert	Mr. Jefferson
Lewis	Mr. Johnson
Narcisso	Master Stockwell
Bernardo	Mr. Tyler
Clara	Miss Broadhurst
Nina	Miss Brett
Juliana	Miss Harding
Theresa	Mrs. Munto

SPECULATION.

Tanjore	Mr. Hodgkinson
Ald. Arable	Mr. Prigmore
Jack Arable	Mr. Jefferson
Capt. Arable	Mr. Tyler
Sir Frederick	Mr. Cleveland
Vickery	Mr. Durang
Promptly	Mr. Munto
Meanwell	Mr. Lee
Project	Mr. Johnson
Lady Project	Mrs. Melmoth
Cecilia	Mrs. Hallam
Emmeline	Mrs. Johnson

TANCRED AND SIGISMUNDA.

Tancred	Mr. Hodgkinson
Sifredi	Mr. Cleveland

common in London; "Werter and Charlotte," a tragedy based on Goethe's novel which Reynold's wrote when he was a boy at Westminster School; and the two pantomimes, "Old Men Grown Young" and "Whims of Galatea," which owed their production to Mr. Francisquy. All the other first productions in New York this season were anticipated by other companies elsewhere—"Hurlstone's farce, "Crotchet Lodge," and Cumberland's "First Love" at the Boston Theatre, since the retirement of the Old American Company; the two pantomimes, "Enraged Musicians" and "Independence of America," at Richmond the previous season; Thomson's tragedy, "Tancred and Sigismunda," by Mr. and Mrs. Edgar at Savannah in 1794; and the rest by the Philadelphia company. The American pantomime, "Independence of America," which had probably been elaborated in New York, began with an allegorical prologue, included a pastoral dance, and ended with the Declaration of Independence. Madame Gardie must have made a charming figure as *America*, and Mr. Tyler in his "make-up" as the *General*, it was said, greatly resembled Washington. Mr. Francisquy, to whom the production of the panto-

FIRST NEW YORK PRODUCTIONS—CASTS.

Rodolpho	Mr. King
Officer	Mr. Munto
Osmond	Mr. Tyler
Laura	Mrs. Tyler
Sigismunda	Mrs. Johnson

WERTER AND CHARLOTTE.

Werter	Mr. Hodgkinson
Sebastian	Mr. Cleveland
Lenthup	Mr. Johnson
Albert	Mr. Hallam
Laura	Mrs. Munto
Charlotte	Mrs. Johnson

WHIMS OF GALATEA.

Damon	Mr. Francisquy
Dorilas	Mr. Jefferson
Alexis	Mr. Durang
Strephon	Mr. Munto
Palemon	Mr. Leonard
Dametas	Mr. McKnight
Cupid	Master Stockwell
Sylvia	Mrs. Cleveland
Phyllis	Miss Brett
Louisa	Mrs. Munto
Pastora	Mrs. Tompkins
Phillida	Mrs. Durang
Galatea	Mad. Gardie

MOUNTAINEERS.

Octavian	Mr. Hodgkinson
Bulcazin Muley	Mr. Tyler
Sadi	Mr. Jefferson
Virolet	Mr. Hallam, Jr
Kilmallock	Mr. King
Ganem	Mr. Cleveland
Muleteers	Mr. Prigmore / Mr. Woolls / Mr. Munto / Mr. Lee
Goatherds	Mr. Roberts / Mr. De Moulin
Goatherd's Son	Mr. Durang
Perequillo	Mr. Leonard
Lope Tocho	Mr. Hallam
Agnes	Mrs. Hodgkinson
Floranthe	Mrs. Cleveland
Zorayda	Mrs. Johnson

mimes this season was due, had brought his troupe of French performers from Richmond to New York. He began by giving special
performances in the theatre on the 3d and 12th of March by agreement with the managers of the Old American Company.

Among the pieces produced during the season there were
three in this list of which no casts had been preserved, or preserved
only in part. In the latter class were the " Belle's Stratagem " and

NEW CASTS OF FAMILIAR PIECES.

As You Like It.

Orlando . . . . . Mr. Cleveland
Oliver . . . . . . Mr. Prigmore
Duke . . . . . Mr. Hallam, Jr
Banished Duke . . . . Mr. King
Jaques . . . . . Mr. Hodgkinson
Amiens . . . . Mr. Tyler
Adam . . . . Mr. Johnson
Le Beau . . . . . Mr. Jefferson
Sylvius . . . . Mr. Munto
Jaques de Bois . . Mr. McKenzie
Charles . . . . Mr. Lee
Touchstone . . . . Mr. Hallam
Audrey . . . . Mrs. Brett
Phœbe . . . . Mrs. Munto
Celia . . . . . . Miss Broadhurst
Rosalind . . . . Mrs. Johnson

Belle's Stratagem.

Doricourt . . . Mr. Hodgkinson
Flutter . . . . . Mr. Hallam, Jr
Sir George Touchwood . Mr. King
Courtall . . . . . . Mr. Hallam
Saville . . . . . Mr. Cleveland
Dick . . . . Mr. Durang
Pilgrim . . . . . . Mr. Munto
Villers . . . . Mr. Woolls
Mr. Hardy . . . . Mr. Prigmore
Widow Racket . . Mrs. Melmoth
Lady Frances . . . Mrs. Hallam
Miss Ogle . . . Mrs. Cleveland
Kitty Willis . . . . Mrs. Munto
Letitia Hardy . Mrs. Hodgkinson

Guardian.

Heartly . . . . . . Mr. Hallam
Sir Charles Clackit . Mr. Prigmore
Young Clackit . . . Mr. Jefferson
Lucy . . . . Mrs. Brett
Harriet . . . . . . Mrs. Hallam

Hamlet.

Hamlet . . . . . Mr. Hallam
King . . . . . . Mr. Cleveland
Horatio . . . . . . Mr. Tyler
Laertes . . . . . Mr. Hallam, Jr
Polonius . . . . . Mr. Johnson
Rosencranz . . . . Mr. Woolls
Guildenstern . . . . Mr. Munto
Osric . . . . . . Mr. Jefferson
Bernardo . . . . . . Mr. Lee
Francisco . . . . Mr. McKenzie
Gravediggers . { Mr. Prigmore
                { Mr. Roberts
Ghost . . . . Mr. King
Queen . . . . . Mrs. Melmoth
Player Queen . . . Mrs. Brett
Ophelia . . . . Mrs. Hodgkinson

Love Makes a Man.

Carlos . . . . . Mr. Hodgkinson
Clodio . . . . . . Mr. Cleveland
Governor . . . . . . Mr. Tyler
Sanche . . . . . Mr. Jefferson
Antonio . . . . Mr. King
Charico . . . . . . Mr. Johnson
Don Duart . . Mr. Hallam, Jr
Don Lewis . . . . Mr. Prigmore
Louisa . . . . . Mrs. Cleveland
Elvira . . . . . . Mrs. Tyler
Angelina . . . . . Mrs. Johnson

Lyar.

Young Wilding . Mr. Hodgkinson
Old Wilding . . . . Mr. Johnson
Sir James Elliott . Mr. Cleveland
Papillion . . . . . Mr. Jefferson
Miss Godfrey . . Mrs. Cleveland
Kitty . . . . Mrs. Brett
Miss Grantham . . Mrs. Hallam

Much Ado About Nothing.

Benedick . . . Mr. Hodgkinson
Leonato . . . . . . Mr. Tyler
Claudio . . . . . Mr. Cleveland
Prince . . . . . Mr. Johnson
Don John . . . . Mr. Hallam, Jr
Anthonio . . . . . . Mr. King
Verges . . . . . . Mr. Jefferson
Dogberry . . . . . Mr. Prigmore
Hero . . . . . . Mrs. Cleveland
Margaret . . . . . . Mrs. Brett
Beatrice . . . . . Mrs. Johnson

Thomas and Sally.

Thomas . . . . Mr. Hodgkinson
Squire . . . . Mr. Tyler
Dorcas . . . . . . Mrs. Brett
Sally . . . . . Miss Broadhurst

Two Misers.

Gripe . . . . . . Mr. Hallam
Hunks . . . . . Mr. Johnson
Osman . . . . . Mr. Jefferson
Ali . . . . Mr. Prigmore
Mustapha . . . . . . Mr. King
Selim . . . . Mr. Munto
Lively . . . . Mr. Tyler
Jenny . . . . Miss Brett
Harriett . . . . Miss Broadhurst

Two Philosophers.

Philosophers . . { Mr. Jefferson
                  { Mr. Durang
Drummer . . . . . . Mr. Munto
Fifer . . . . . Mr. McKnight
Sergeant . . . . Mr. Lee
Merry Girl . . . . Mad. Gardie

the " Lyar ; " the others were " Hamlet " and the pantomime, " Two Philosophers." That the remaining productions in the list of familiar pieces had not been revived since the reorganization of the Old American Company in 1792 is surprising, but such is the fact. The New Yorkers had seen only Mrs. Kenna as *Rosalind ;* and " Much Ado About Nothing," although played by the Old American Company in Philadelphia with Hallam as *Benedick* and Mrs. Morris as *Beatrice*, had not previously been produced in New York. Even now Hodgkinson only presented the comedy for his benefit for the sake of appearing as *Benedick*, to Hallam's discomfiture.

The casts in which the players can be placed in juxtaposition with the previous representatives of the roles in the principal pieces

CONTRASTED CASTS—CHANGES.

PLAYS.	1792-5.	1796.
Bold Stroke for a Husband.		
Don Carlos	. Mr. King . .	. Mr. Cleveland
Don Garcia	. . Mr. Hammond	.Mr. Munto
Gasper	. . . . Mr. Richards	. Mr. Johnson
Don Vincentio	. Mr. Martin . .	. Mr. Jefferson
Victoria	. Mrs. Wilson . .	. Mrs. Cleveland
Minette	. Mrs. Pownall	. Mrs. Hodgkinson
Laura	. Mrs. Kenna .	. Mrs. Tyler
Marcella	. Mrs. Hamilton	. Mrs. Munto
Inis		. Mrs. Brett
Carmelite.		
Montgomeri . .	Mr. Martin . .	. Mr. Cleveland
Gyfford	. Mr. Ashton . .	. Mr. Johnson
Fitz-Allan . . .	. Mr. Kenna . .	. Mr. Munto
Hildebrand . .	. Mr. Richards	. Mr. Tyler
Child of Nature.		
Granada	. Mr. Martin . .	. Mr. Munto
Seville	. Mr. Ryan . . .	. Mr. McKenzie
Marchioness . .	. Mrs. Pownall	. Mrs. Hallam
Edgar and Emmeline.		
Florimund . . .	. Mr. Martin . .	. Mr. Jefferson
Emmeline . . .	. Mrs. Marriott	. Mrs. Cleveland
Farmer.		
Valentine . . .	. Mr. West . . .	. Mr. Tyler
Rundy	. Mr. Martin . .	. Mr. Jefferson
Fairly	. Mr. Heard . .	. Mr. Johnson
Col. Dormant	. Mr. Ashton . .	. Mr. Munto

PLAYS.	1792-5.	1796.
Jemmy Jumps	Mr. Prigmore	. Mr. Hodgkinson
Betty	. Mrs. Pownall	. Miss Broadhurst
Louisa	. Mrs. Kenna .	. Mrs. Johnson
Landlady . . .	. Mrs. Rankin .	. Mrs. Munto
Jew.		
Charles Ratcliffe	.Mr. Martin . .	. Mr. Cleveland
Fred'k Bertram	.Mr. Fawcett . .	. Mr. Hallam, Jr
Sir Stephen . .	. Mr. Richards	. Mr. Tyler
Mrs. Ratcliffe .	. Mrs. Hamilton	. Mrs. Tyler
Dorcas	. Mrs. Miller . .	. Mrs. Brett
Mrs. Goodison	. Miss Chaucer	. Mrs. Durang
Eliza	. Mrs. Hallam .	. Mrs. Johnson
Maid of the Mill.		
Aimworth . . .	. Mr. Hodgkinson	.Mr. Tyler
Mervyn	. Mr. West . . .	. Mr. Munto
Fairfield	. Mr. Ashton .	. Mr. Johnson
Fanny	. Mrs. Kenna . .	. Mrs. Hodgkinson
Theodosia . .	Mrs. Hallam . .	. Mrs. Munto
Lady Sycamore	.Mrs. Hamilton	. Mrs. Brett
Patty	. Mrs. Pownall	. Miss Broadhurst
Quaker.		
Steady	. Mr. King . . .	. Mr. Tyler
Lubin	. Mr. Nelson . .	. Mr. Prigmore
Farmer Easy .	. Mr. Ashton . .	. Mr. Roberts
Floretta	. Mrs. Solomon	. Miss Broadhurst
Cicely	. Mrs. Miller . .	. Mrs. Brett

always serve to show the character, value and importance of the changes in the company. Most of these pieces had not been revived since early in the epoch, hence the frequent recurrence of the names of Messrs. Hammond, Heard, Richards, Ryan and West, and of Mrs. Kenna, Mrs. Pownall and Mrs. Marriott. Mrs. Hamilton had ceased to be a member of the company, and Mrs. King and Mr. Martin were out of the bills this season. Mr. and Mrs. Munto had returned to New York after a year's absence in the South. It is unnecessary to analyze the relations of the new players to the old, as the order of succession can be seen in a glance at the contrasted casts.

This is a fitting place to recite the relations of Mrs. Hallam to the theatre, and especially toward Mr. and Mrs. Hodgkinson, up to the close of this season. The recital is from a pamphlet that Hodgkinson caused to be printed in 1797. When the story was originally published it was as unnecessary as it was cruel, because all causes for its recital had disappeared with Mrs. Hallam's final withdrawal from the stage, its publication being due to malice because Hodgkinson was hissed after

CONTRASTED CASTS—CHANGES.

PLAYS.	1792-5.	1796.
Road to Ruin.		
Dornton	Mr. Henry	. . Mr. Johnson
Milford	Mr. Martin	. . Mr. Cleveland
Smith	Mr. Ashton	. . Mr. Munto
Jacob	Mr. Ryan .	. . Mr. Lee
Hosier		. Mr. Tyler
Mrs. Ledger . .	Mrs. Kenna	. . Mrs. Munto
Jenny	Mrs. Hamilton	. Mrs. Cleveland
Widow Warren .	Mrs. Pownall	. Mrs. Brett
School for Greybeards.		
Don Octavio . .	Mr. Martin . .	Mr. Cleveland
Peter	Mr. Ashton . .	Mr. Roberts
Pedrillo		. Mr. Lee
Jaques		. Mr. Munto
Antonia	Mrs.Hodgkinson	Miss Broadhurst
Rachel	Mrs. Pownall	. Mrs. Brett
Viola	Mrs. Marriott	. Mrs. Cleveland

PLAYS.	1792-5.	1796.
Clara	Mrs. King . .	. Mrs. Tyler
Carlotta	Mrs. Miller	. . Miss Harding
Wild Oats.		
Smooth	Mr. Henry	. . Mr. Jefferson
Harry Thunder .	Mr. West .	. . Mr. Cleveland
Banks	Mr. Heard .	. . Mr. Johnson
Gammon . . .	Mr. Hammond	. Mr. Lee
Jane	Mrs. Pownall	. Mrs.Hodgkinson
Amelia	Mrs. Kenna .	. Mrs. Tyler
Lady Amaranth.	Mrs. Henry .	. Mrs. Johnson
Young Quaker.		
Capt. Ambush .	Mr. Martin . .	Mr. Hallam, Jr
Shadrach . . .	Mr. Hammond	. Mr. Jefferson
Goliah	Miss Hatton .	. Miss Harding
Pink	Mrs. Pownall	. Mrs. Cleveland
Lady Rounceval.	Mrs. Miller .	. Mrs. Brett
Mrs. Millefleur .	Mrs. Hamilton	. Mrs. Tyler
Judith	Mrs. King . .	. Mrs. Munto

the Hallam riot.   Dunlap may have been ignorant of Mrs. Hallam's persistent intemperance, but Hodgkinson, if his own story is true, knew all about it long before he enticed the ambitious dramatist to buy a share in the business.   According to his pamphlet, Mrs. Hallam, as early as October 20th, 1794, while playing *Lady Racket* in Philadelphia, was "in too degraded a state to be seen."   When she observed, Hodgkinson adds, that some of the ladies noticed her condition, she assailed them with bad language.   Again, on the 27th of October, in a violent fit of intemperance, she quarrelled with Ashton, and, when Hodgkinson interfered, she called him rascal, scoundrel, swindler and other pet names, and, while he was playing in "Don Juan," the afterpiece, baited him with "every mock and ridicule that could be."   The next day Mrs. Hallam apologized to Hodgkinson, pretending to have no knowledge of the events of the previous evening, and the two managers dined together at Oeller's, where a reconciliation was effected, Hallam saying, "I know that girl so well I'm sure she never will forgive herself, or drink anything but water as long as she lives."   Notwithstanding Hallam's assurances, she was intoxicated again while playing *Lady Fancourt* in "Love's Frailties" on the 14th of November, was incapacitated from playing *Miss Walsingham* in the "School for Wives" on the 20th of December, and was even worse as *Marianne* in the "Dramatist" on the 29th.   The first of these three scenes occurred in Philadelphia, and the last two in New York.   On the 5th of January, 1795, Hodgkinson accidentally cut Hallam's hand in the fight with *Douglas* in "Percy," whereupon Mrs. Hallam went into a violent rage, exclaiming, "That damn'd butcher has cut Mr. Hallam."   The next day Hodgkinson wrote to Hallam : "Sir, we are a city talk ; and it would certainly be better to endeavor that Mrs. Hallam should be kept at home than suffered to expose us and herself when she is unfit to be seen." No immediate action was taken; but on the 10th the actress, as *Lady Euston* in " I'll Tell You What," was in a "state of partial intoxication;" on the 28th, as the *Marchioness* in the "Child of Nature," she was again intoxicated, and on the 5th of February, as *Eliza Ratcliffe* in the " Jew," she was " an exhibition too disgustful to remember and too disgraceful to the stage to be dwelt upon." On the last occasion there was a cry in the audience—" She must insult us no more "—and Hallam finally consented to his wife's temporary sequestration. She was, however, restored to the stage as *Lady Teazle* on the 25th of March; but on the 30th, as *Cordelia*, she was not perfectly herself; and on the 10th of April, when she appeared as *Louise* in " World in a Village," " several people, in disgust, left the theatre." On the 11th of May Mrs. Hallam played *Miss Neville* in " Know Your Own Mind," dressing in the same room with Mrs. Hodgkinson. During the progress of the piece she insulted Mrs. Hodgkinson in very energetic language. " Damn the play," she exclaimed, " damn the person who got it up, and damn the person for whom it was got up!" Hodgkinson then threatened to offer his share in the property to the highest bidder; but again, on the 18th, Mrs. Hallam made an exhibition of herself in " Which is the Man?" for Woolls' benefit. Hallam then agreed to withdraw her at the close of the season, and authorized Hodgkinson to write to England to procure an actress in her place. The engagement of Mrs. Johnson was the outcome. Mrs. Hallam, however, played with the Providence contingent in the Autumn of 1795, and when the " Clandestine Marriage" was produced at the Boston Theatre, Mr. Hallam insisted that his wife should play *Miss Sterling*, notwithstanding his agreement with Hodgkinson in regard to her retirement. Hodgkinson yielded, and Mrs. Johnson agreed to allow Mrs. Hallam all the parts she had previously played, but demanded the elegant characters in comedy in the new pieces, in accordance with her contract. All this knowledge Hodgkinson possessed before he invited Dunlap into the partnership, and yet he not only used Mrs. Hallam's failings as an excuse for breaking his covenants with Dunlap, but engaged himself to Wignell almost before the ink of his first contract with Dunlap was dry. The Wignell agreement, however, was cancelled almost immediately.

There was some rather free criticism of the plays and players during the season, which originated with a band of critics who called themselves the Mohawks. Farquhar's " Inconstant," which had been revived by Hodgkinson, was condemned by these theatrical reformers. Cumberland's " Wheel of Fortune " did not meet their approbation, although Hodgkinson as *Penruddock*, Jefferson's *Daw* and Mrs. Johnson's *Emily Tempest* were praised. King as *Woodville* and Cleveland as *Harry* were censured. The only difference between Prigmore's acting as *Tempest* and his acting generally was that between a hat cocked up and a cocked-up hat. Hodgkinson was justly rebuked for casting a man named Lee for *Widow Cheshire* in the " Agreeable Surprise "— " a heavy, vulgar, stupid fellow, with no requisite for the stage, except a bass voice and some knowledge of music." Jefferson fell under the lash as *Endless* in " No Song No Supper," but the Mohawks praised Prigmore's *Crop*. Miss Broadhurst was always a favorite with these savages. Mr. and Mrs. Hallam as *Sir Peter* and *Lady Teazle* were reminded that the critics could not forget Mr. and Mrs. Henry in these parts; that they could not but remember that such things were, and were most precious. " Poor Vulcan " was pronounced " insipid, tasteless and unentertaining." They wanted to know why *Miss Neville* in "Know Your Own Mind," played by Mrs. Cleveland, was not given to Mrs. Hallam or Mrs. Johnson; and they asked, "Where was Mr. Hallam when the part of *Captain Bygrove* was cast upon Mr. Munto, who, whenever he appears in uniform, reminds us of a servant in livery?" The managers were blamed for putting "a poor, deformed idiot," Roberts, in the fine part of *Canton* in the "Clandestine Marriage." Sometimes there was generous praise, however, Mrs. Melmoth's *Alicia,* for instance, being said to have been full of fiery passion, and Mrs. Johnson's *Jane Shore* of tender pathos. One critic charged King with neglecting to commit the words as *Lenox* in the "Deserted Daughter" and of his part in the "Agreeable Surprise" on the 9th of March, and suggested that he ought to be displaced. King replied in a letter in the *Gazette*, in which he denied the charge and called the critic a liar and an assassin. On the 23d "A Citizen" wrote to the *Gazette*, saying of the *Diary* critics: "I understand there are three whose cleverness abuses merit! A pretty coalition when three cannot write common sense! Yet these are the reptiles who judge for the city of New York and descant on the merits of performers; these are the snakes which sting people in the dark who endeavor to get their bread by indefatigable study; these are the caterpillars who would nip merit in the bud." It will be observed there was strong and coarse language on both sides.

When the season closed Mr. Prigmore, Mr. and Mrs. Cleveland, Mr. and Mrs. King, Miss Broadhurst and Madame Gardie retired from the company. Mrs. King had been ill during almost the whole season.

CHAPTER XVII.

THE BOSTON THEATRE, 1796–7.

MR. WILLIAMSON'S SEASON — THE PRODUCTIONS — MRS. WHITLOCK — MR.
JONES—MR. BATES—WILLIAM CHARLES WHITE—HIS "ORLANDO"—
"AMERICANS IN ENGLAND"—NEW ENGLISH PIECES—WORK OF
THE COMPANY—RETIREMENT OF THE ROWSONS—THEIR PARTS.

POLITICAL feeling ran very high in the theatres during the last
decade of the last century, the English actors, as a rule, becoming intense Republicans. Mr. Williamson, apparently, was an exception, for which, however, he had other motives than mere partisan
sentiment. "We have the opinion hollow as to the merits of the
company and the patronage of the 'better sort,'" he wrote to Hodgkinson; "but the rage for novelty in Boston and prevailing Jacobin
spirit in the lower ranks are our strongest opponents." To a great extent the Boston Theatre depended for its patronage on the Federalist
element, while the new Boston Haymarket was avowedly built to cater
for the Republicans. As a matter of course the divided patronage
consequent upon such narrow views, leading to the creation of two
theatres in a city that could not more than support one, brought about
the failure of both. "Two theatres cannot be supported," Williamson said in his letter; "an additional public could not be created with
an additional theatre." The old theatre naturally strove to retain as
much of the "Jacobin" element as possible, and the consequent efforts

(332)

to avoid offense to the partisans of France were sometimes very amusing. The production of the " Poor Soldier " was a case in point. The character of *Bagatelle* had become very offensive to American Frenchmen, and it was therefore cut out of the opera by Williamson's direction, *Domingo*, a negro valet, being substituted. Such makeshifts, however, could not appease a public seeking a patriotic drama, with "Bunker Hill " and all the glare of Charlestown on fire at the other house.

Williamson's season, which opened on the 19th of September, began with a great flourish of trumpets. Besides the members of the Boston Theatre company whom he retained, he engaged a number of the principal performers from the Philadelphia company, including Mrs. Whitlock and Mr. Bates for limited engagements, and Mr. Chalmers, Mr. and Mrs. Marshall, the Rowsons and the Solomons. To these he added Jones for a limited engagement, and Fawcett, who, like Jones, had been with Sollee at Charleston. Chalmers made his first appearance in Boston on the opening night as *Vapid* in the " Dramatist," and Jones reappeared the same night as *Jemmy Jumps* in the " Farmer." Another name in the opening bill was that of Mr. Downie, who made his

LIST OF PRODUCTIONS.

1796.

Sept.	19—Dramatist . . . . . . Reynolds	
	Farmer . . . . O'Keefe	
	21—School for Scandal . . Sheridan	
	Lyar . . . . Foote	
	23—West Indian . . . . . Cumberland	
	Spoiled Child . . . . Bickerstaff	
	26—Much Ado About Nothing	
	Shakspere	
	Modern Antiques . . . O'Keefe	
	28—Romeo and Juliet . . Shakspere	
	30—Know Your Own Mind . . Kelly	
	Rosina . . . . . Mrs. Brooke	
Oct.	3—Isabella . . . . . . Southerne	
	Lyar.	
	5—Provoked Husband . . Vanbrugh	
	Maid of the Oaks . . Burgoyne	
	6—Percy . . . . Miss More	
	Purse . . . . Cross	
	10—Isabella.	
	Oscar and Malvina.	
	12—Venice Preserved . . . . Otway	
	14—Way to Keep Him . . . Murphy	
	Rosina.	
	17—Cymbeline . . . . . Shakspere	
	Romp . . . . Bickerstaff	
	19—Jealous Wife . . . . . Colman	
	Purse.	
	21—Fontainville Forest . . . Boaden	
	Farmer.	

Oct. 24—Way to Keep Him.
    Irishman in London . Macready
   26—Jealous Wife.
    Love a la Mode . . . . Macklin
   28—Fair Penitent . . . . . . Rowe
    Virgin Unmasked . . . Fielding
   31—Roman Father   Whitehead
    Highland Reel . . . . O'Keefe
    (Mrs. Whitlock's benefit.)

Nov. 2—Mountaineers . . . Colman, Jr
    Purse.
   4—Inkle and Yarico . . Colman, Jr
    First Floor . . . . Cobb
    (Mr. Jones' benefit.)
   7—Love in a Village . . Bickerstaff
    Lying Valet . . . . . . Garrick
   9—As You Like It . . . Shakspere
    My Grandmother . . . . Hoare
  11—Suspicious Husband . . Hoadly
    Tom Thumb, the Great . O'Hara
  14—Lionel and Clarissa . Bickerstaff
    Sultan . . . . Bickerstaff
  16—As You Like It.
    Tom Thumb.
  18—Miser . . . . Fielding
    Catharine and Petruchio
               Shakspere
  21—Hamlet . . . . . Shakspere
    Spoiled Child.
  23—George Barnwell . . . . . Lillo
    Peeping Tom of Coventry,O'Keefe
  25—Speculation . . . . . Reynolds
    Virgin Unmasked.
  28—Hamlet.
    Poor Soldier   . . . . O'Keefe
  30—Belle's Stratagem . Mrs. Cowley
    Tom Thumb.

Dec. 2—Inkle and Yarico.
    Harlequin's Invasion . . Garrick
   5—Patriot.
    Harlequin Skeleton.
    Beggar on Horsback . . O'Keefe
    (Mr. Bates' benefit.)
   7—Chances . . . . . . Garrick
    Harlequin's Invasion.
   9—Busybody . . . . Mrs. Centlivre

debut as *Neville* in the comedy. For his first appearance in Boston Mr. Rowson was given the part of *Farmer Blackberry* in the "Farmer," to which he must have been grotesquely unequal, and Mrs. and Miss Rowson were respectively *Betty Blackberry* and *Molly Maybush*. Mr. Fawcett was first seen as *Sir James Elliott* in the "Lyar" on the second night, and Mr. Beete also modestly appeared as *Joseph's Servant* in the "School for Scandal." Although Mr. Marshall afterward played *Ennui* in the "Dramatist" and *Valentine* in the "Farmer," his Boston *debut* was made as *Mercutio* on the 28th, Mrs. Marshall making her first appearance in Boston as *Juliet*. Mrs. Solomon as *Lady Jane* and Madame Gardie as *Mad. La Rouge* in "Know Your Own Mind" were seen for the first time on the 30th. On the 3d of October Mrs. Whitlock made her Boston *debut* in the title-role of "Isabella." Her engagement was not merely a special one, being limited to twelve nights; it was the first star engagement in America. According to the newspapers of the time she was paid $450 and given a benefit. Mr. Whitlock made his only appearance in Boston as *Horatius* to his wife's *Horatia* in the "Roman Father" for her benefit. Mrs. Whitlock's parts[1] comprised those only in which she had been most popular in Philadelphia. Two days after Mrs. Whitlock's benefit Mr. Jones' engagement also closed, a benefit following. Jones, who appeared nearly every night, sometimes twice, played a round of his favorite characters in Boston, together with two or three new parts. This brief engagement was

[1] MRS. WHITLOCK'S PARTS.

Cymbeline . . . . Imogen
Fair Penitent . . . . Calista
Fontainville Forest . . . . Adeline
Isabella . . . . Isabella
Maid of the Oaks . . . Lady Bab Lardoon
Percy . . . . Elwina
Provoked Husband . . . . . Lady Townly
Roman Father . . . . Horatia
Venice Preserved . . . . Belvidera
Way to Keep Him . . . . Mrs. Lovemore

Dec. 9—Agreeable Surprise . . O'Keefe
  12—Henry IV . . . . . Shakspere
    Death of Captain Cook.
    (Mr. Chalmer's benefit.)
  14—Douglas . . . . Home
    Harlequin's Invasion.
  16—Mountaineers.
    My Grandmother.
  19—Douglas.
    Death of Captain Cook.
  21—Oroonoko . . . . . Southerne
    Sultan.
  23—Richard III . . . . . Shakspere
    Rosina.
  26—Way to Get Married . . Morton
    Three Weeks After Marriage
                              Murphy
  27—Suspicious Husband.
    Critic . . . . Sheridan
  28—Way to Get Married.
    Harlequin's Invasion.
1797.
Jan. 2—Tancred and Sigismunda, Thomson
    Poor Soldier.
  4—Lionel and Clarissa.
    Critic.
  6—Next-Door Neighbors
                      Mrs. Inchbald
    Children in the Wood . . Morton
  9—Rivals . . . . Sheridan
    Death of Captain Cook.
  11—Castle of Andalusia . . O'Keefe
    Children in the Wood.
  13—Tancred and Sigismunda.
    Rosina.
  16—Way to Get Married.
    Wedding Day . . Mrs. Inchbald
  18—She Wou'd and She Woul'd Not
                              Cibber
    All the World's a Stage . Jackman
  20—Way to Get Married.
    Oscar and Malvina.
  23—Next-Door Neighbors.
    Richard Cœur de Lion . Burgoyne
  25—Three Weeks After Marriage.
    Richard Cœur de Lion.

Jan. 27—Count of Narbonne . . . Jephson
          Highland Reel.
Feb. 1—Mountaineers.
          Agreeable Surprise.
      3—Merchant of Venice . . Shakspere
          Wedding Day.
      6—Romeo and Juliet.
          Two Hunters and the Milkmaid.
      8—Spanish Barber . . Beaumarchais
          Two Hunters.
          Critic.
    13—Merry Wives of Windsor
                     Shakspere
          American Heroine.
    15—Dramatist.
          Richard Cœur de Lion.
    17—Jew . . . . Cumberland
          American Heroine.
    20—Spanish Barber.
          My Grandmother.
    22—Man of Ten Thousand . Holcroft
          Birthday . . . . Lege
    24—Young Quaker . . . . O'Keefe
          Birthday.
          Wedding Day.
    27—Preservation . . . . Williamson
          Two Philosophers.
          Romp.
Mar. 1—Preservation.
      3—Preservation.
          Spanish Barber.
      6—Maid of the Mill . . . Bickerstaff
          Cripples (Pant.).
          Spoiled Child.
      8—Maid of the Mill.
          American Heroine.
    10—Orlando . . . . White
          La Boiteuse.
          Peeping Tom of Coventry.
    13—Orlando.
          Highland Reel.
          (Author's benefit.)
    15—Preservation.
          La Boiteuse.
          Midnight Hour . . Mrs. Inchbald
          (Author's benefit.)

previous to his departure for Charleston, where he had become the manager of the City or Church Street Theatre.[1] A somewhat unusual "first appearance in America" was that of William Priest, a member of the band, who had previously been with the Philadelphia orchestra. Priest played *Sciolto* in the "Fair Penitent" on the 28th of October, but was not seen again. Mr. Bates, the Philadelphia comedian, succeeded Jones in the low comedy roles, making his first appearance in Boston as *Woodcock* in " Love in a Village "

[1] MR. JONES' PARTS.

Cymbeline	Cloten
Farmer	Jemmy Jumps
First Floor	Tim Tartlet
Highland Reel	Shelty
Inkle and Yarico	Trudge
Lyar	Papillion
Modern Antiques	Cockletop
Mountaineers	Sadi
Much Ado About Nothing	Dogberry
Oscar and Malvina	Pedlar
Purse	Will Steady
Romeo and Juliet	Friar Laurence
Romp	Watty Cockney
Rosina	William
School for Scandal	Sir Peter Teazle
Spoiled Child	Tag
Virgin Unmasked	Coupee
West Indian	Varland

on the 7th of November. Bates' engagement was also a limited one, his parts,[1] like Mrs. Whitlock's, being mostly those in which he had been most popular. *Sir John Falstaff*, for Chalmers' benefit, he now played for the first time. Mr. Williamson reserved his first appearance this season until the 14th of November, when he played *Sir John Flowerdale* in "Lionel and Clarissa." Mrs. Hogg, who was known as Miss Storer, and for a brief period as Mrs. Henry, on the colonial stage, made her Boston *debut* as *Lappet*

[1] MR. BATES' PARTS.

Agreeable Surprise	Lingo
As You Like It	Touchstone
Beggar on Horseback	Corney
Hamlet	First Gravedigger
Harlequin's Invasion	{ Snip, Old Woman
Henry IV	Sir John Falstaff
Lionel and Clarissa	Colonel Oldboy
Love in a Village	Woodcock
Lying Valet	Sharp
Miser	Lovegold
Mountaineers	Sadi
My Grandmother	Dicky Gossip
Peeping Tom of Coventry	Tom
Poor Soldier	Darby
Speculation	Project
Tom Thumb, the Great	King Arthur

Mar. 17—St. Patrick's Day . . . Sheridan
Le Foret Noire.
　(Mr. Tyler's benefit.)
20—Roman Actor . . . . . Massinger
Critic.
Prisoner . . . . Rose
　(Mr. Chalmer's benefit.)
22—Day in Turkey . . Mrs. Cowley
Miraculous Mill . . . . Francis
Old Maid . . . . . . Murphy
Lethe . . . . . . Garrick
　(Mr. T. Paine's benefit.)
24—Merchant of Venice.
Two Hunters.
My Grandmother.
　(Ticket night.)
27—Country Girl . . . . . Garrick
Bird Catcher.
Midas . . . . O'Hara
　(Mrs. Marshall's benefit.)
29—Lock and Key . . . . . Hoare
Prisoner.
Oscar and Malvina.
　(Mrs. Williamson's benefit.)
31—Life's Vagaries . . . . O'Keefe
Devil Upon Two Sticks (Pant.).
Selima and Azor . . . . Collier
　(Mr. Cleveland's benefit.)
April 3—Follies of a Day . . . Holcroft
Iron Mask.
　(Mr. Marshall's benefit.)
5—Deserted Daughter . . . Holcroft
Triumph of Washington.
Island of Calypso.
　(Mad. Gardie's benefit.)
7—Mountaineers.
Spoiled Child.
　(Mr. White's benefit.)
10—Little Yankee Sailor.
Lock and Key.
Triumph of Washington.
Prisoner.
(Mrs. and the Misses Solomon's benefit.)
12—Americans in England
　　　　　　　Mrs. Rowson
Shipwrecked Mariners Preserved.

April 12—Poor Soldier.
   (Mr. and Mrs. Rowson's benefit.)
      17—Heigho for a Husband . Waldron
         La Petite Espiegle.
         Day in Boston.
         (Mr. Villiers' benefit.)
      19—Americans in England.
      21—Americans in England.
         Shipwrecked Mariners Preserved.
         Lock and Key.
      26—Americans in England.
         Shipwrecked Mariners Preserved.
         Spanish Barber.
            (Author's benefit.)
      28—Hamlet.
         Purse.
May   1—Mahomet . . . . Miller
         Magic Cauldron.
         No Song No Supper . . . Hoare
         (Mrs. Cleveland's benefit.)
       3—Slaves in Algiers . . Mrs. Rowson
         Midnight Hour.
   (Mr. Downie and Miss Rowson's benefit.)
       5—Way to Get Married.
         Children in the Wood.
   (M. Leaumont, Miss Green and Miss
         Solomon's benefit.)
       8—As You Like It.
         Mock Doctor . . . . . Fielding
         (Coles and Clarke's benefit.)
      10—Follies of a Day.
         Pygmalion.
         Paul and Virginia.
         (Dubois and Renaud's benefit.)
      12—Every One Has His Fault
                        Mrs. Inchbald
         Miraculous Mill
         Prisoner.
      15—Wonder . . . . . Mrs. Centlivre
         Agreeable Surprise.
         (Mrs. Graupner's benefit.)
      17—Jane Shore.
         Spoiled Child.
   (Mr. and Mrs. Marshall's benefit.)
      22—Wild Oats . . . . . . O'Keefe
         Agreeable Surprise.
            (Mr. Villiers' benefit.)

in the " Miser " on the 18th,
playing *Catharine* in " Catharine
and Petruchio" the same night.
Two nights later Mr. Hogg made
his first appearance as *Tag* in the
" Spoiled Child." Both Mr. and
Mrs. Hogg had been with West's
Company at Norfolk in the Summer of 1796. An interesting first
appearance this season was that of
a young Bostonian, the son of a
merchant, who abandoned the
counting-room for the stage—
William Charles White.[1] Young
White, who was only in his twen-
tieth year, made his first appearance on any stage on December
14th as *Young Norval* in " Douglas." His career as an actor lasted
not quite four months, during

[1] Mr. White's Parts.

Count of Narbonne	Theodore
Douglas	Young Norval
Man of Ten Thousand . . .	Lord Laroon
Merry Wives of Windsor	Fenton
Mountaineers	Octavian
Next-Door Neighbors	Henry
Orlando	Orlando
Preservation	Randall
Romeo and Juliet	Romeo
Tancred and Sigismunda	Tancred

which he attempted both *Romeo* and *Tancred*, and, on the 7th of of April, 1797, took a formal leave of the stage with a benefit, playing *Octavian* and delivering a valedictory address.   Miss Solomon, who had been a popular little actress in Philadelphia, was seen in Boston this season, among other parts in her favorite role of the hero in " Tom Thumb," and as *Lucianus* to the *Duchess* of Miss Hogg and the *Ganzalo* of Master Gower in the mock play in " Hamlet."   Miss C. Solomon made her first appearance on the stage of the Boston Theatre on the 6th of January,

May 24—Town Before You . Mrs. Cowley
Taste of the Times (Local Pant.).
(Paine and Campbell's benefit.)
29—Town Before You.
Taste of the Times.
(Mr. Campbell's benefit.)
31—Mountaineers.
Taste of the Times.
June 2—Such Things Are . Mrs. Inchbald
Agreeable Surprise.
(Mr. Kenny's benefit.)
5—Dramatist.
Ways and Oddities.
Melocosmiotis.
(Mr. Chalmers' benefit.)
7—Rivals.
No Song No Supper.
(Mr. Williamson's benefit.)
16—Midnight Hour.
Son-in-Law . . . . . . O'Keefe
All in Good Humor . . . Oulton
(Dickenson and Prompter's benefit.)
19—Wheel of Fortune . . Cumberland
Ghost . . . . . . Mrs. Centlivre
(Mrs. Bayles' benefit.)
22—Romeo and Juliet.
Poor Soldier.
(Mr. Deblois' benefit.)

1797, as the *Boy* in " Children in the Wood."   Miss M. Solomon was in the cast of " Every One Has His Fault," on May 12th, as *Edward*, a part that indicates that Miss M. Solomon was in fact Miss Solomon. Mrs. Graupner, formerly Mrs. Hellyer, reappeared in Boston on the 23d as *Lauretta* in " Richard Cœur de Lion," after an absence of two years.   On the 27th Mr. Coles was noted as making his second appearance on any stage as *Austin* in the " Count of Narbonne," and on the 6th of February Mr. Lege, the pantomimist, made his first appearance in Boston as *Guillot* in the " Two Hunters."   There were no other first appearances during the season, except those of one or two nameless amateurs.

Native productions were, as a matter of course, a feature of the season. Among these, the most important, historically considered, were "Orlando," a tragedy by young White, and "Americans in England," by Mrs. Rowson.

ORLANDO.

Orlando	Mr. White
Lysander	Mr. Downie
Danfred	Mr. Kenny
Somerville	Mr. Coles
Albert	Mr. Cleveland
Lucretia . . .	Miss Green
Boy	Miss C. Solomon
Cecilia . . .	Mrs. Marshall

AMERICANS IN ENGLAND.

Courtland	Mr. Kenny
Folio	Mr. Hamilton
Snap	Mr. Rowson
Waiter	Mr. McKenzie
Capt. Ormsby . .	Mr. Downie
Jack Acorn	Mr. Hogg
Thomas	Mr. Coles
Bailiff's Man . . .	Mr. Clarke
Rhymer	Mr. Marshall
Mrs. Ormsby . .	Mrs. Rowson
Arabella	Mrs. Hogg
Betty	Miss Rowson
Melissa	Mrs. Cleveland

Americans.

Ezekiel Plainly,	Mr. Williamson
Horace Winship .	Mr. Cleveland
Jemima Winship .	Mrs. Rowson

"Orlando" was a very immature work, but it had the regulation productions—two performances and an "author's night." After leaving the stage, Mr. White studied law, and opened an office for the practice of his profession at Providence, R. I., in 1800, but he returned to the stage for another brief period the same year. He was at one time editor of the *National Ægis*, and was the author of a number of plays, besides his tragedy of "Orlando," including "The Clergyman's Daughter," "The Country Cousin" and "The Poor Lodger." He also compiled a "Compendium and Digest of the Laws of Massachusetts" (1809–10), in three volumes, of which it was said it was "made up of here a little Blackstone and there a little White." Mrs. Rowson's "Americans in England"

PRESERVATION.

Characters from Lillo.

Old Wilmot . .	Mr. Williamson
Randall	Mr. White
Young Wilmot .	Mr. Chalmers
Mrs. Wilmot . . .	Mrs. Hogg
Maria	Miss Green
Charlotte	Mrs. Marshall

Original Characters.

Arnold	Mr. Cleveland
Malign	Mr. Kenny
Flint	Mr. Rowson
Sailor	Mr. McKenzie
Boy	Mrs. Williamson

DAY IN BOSTON.

Old Hominy . .	Mr. Hamilton
Spry	Mr. McKenzie
Capt. Wayne . . .	Mr. Downie
Kiddy Crispin . .	Mr. Villiers
Miss Tabitha . .	Mrs. Rowson
Nabby	Miss Rowson
Peggy	Mrs. Collins

made no distinct impression in Boston at the time of its production. She subsequently disposed of the right to act the play to Hodgkinson in consideration of a benefit, saying she had lost money by it when originally produced. It was printed, but became one of the scarcest plays of American origin. Mr. Williamson's "Preservation" was composed in part of Lillo's "Fatal Curiosity," played at the Haymarket as early as 1736. In the original, which was in three acts, *Young Wilmot* was murdered by his father, at the instigation of his mother, while he slept, for a casket of jewels, his parents not knowing his identity. The other characters in Lillo's play were *Young Wilmot's* sister *Maria*, her husband *Randall*, and his affianced *Charlotte*. In an alteration, by Henry Mackenzie, produced at Covent Garden in 1784, the *Boy* was introduced. The characters introduced by Mr. Williamson were probably no embellishment to the tragedy. Mr. Villiers' play for his benefit, "A Day in Boston," had, perhaps, no originality, except in name and the names of the characters. To these pieces were added three new pantomimes—the "Birthday," by Lege; "Taste of the Times, or Laugh! Laugh! Laugh!" probably by Paine, as it was given for the joint benefit of Mr. Paine, the dramatist, and Mr. Campbell, the prompter of the theatre, with Mr. Baker, Paine's father-in-law, as the *Clown;* and the "Triumph of Washington" for Madame Gardie's benefit. It is a curious fact that the American patriotic and historical drama at this time took the form of pantomime. Madame Gardie's piece was probably adapted from the production called "Independence of America," first presented by the Francisquy troupe in Richmond in 1795, and afterward in New York. In the Boston cast, Mr. Cleveland was *General Washington*, Madame Gardie *America*, and Mrs. Cleveland the *Goddess of Liberty*, with Lege and Dubois as Indians instead of British officers, and Renaud as an *Old Soldier* instead of the *Senator* of the earlier piece. The Boston pantomime, " Taste of the Times," made an attempt at scenic realism, views being presented of Mount Vernon, the new Boston State House, Beacon Hill and the Monument. It is not recorded who painted the scenery.

PHILADELPHIA PLAYERS IN BOSTON—CONTRASTED CASTS.

PLAYS.	Boston.	Phil.	PLAYS.	Boston.	Phil.
Castle of Andalusia.			*My Grandmother.*		
Pedrillo	Mr. Marshall	Mr. Bates	Vapour	Mr. Marshall	Mr. Moreton
Cæsar	Mr. Rowson .	Mr. Darley	Woodley	Mr. Rowson .	Mr. Darley
Catalina	Mrs. Rowson	Miss Broadhurst	Souffrance . . .	Mr. Cleveland	Mr. Harwood
Victoria	Mrs. Marshall	Mrs. Warrell	Charlotte . . .	Miss Rowson	Miss Broadhurst
Count of Narbonne.			Florella	Mrs. Marshall	Mrs. Oldmixon
Adelaide	Mrs. Marshall	Mrs. Marshall	*Next-Door Neighbors.*		
Jaqueline . . .	Mrs. Rowson	Miss Willems	Splendorville . .	Mr. Cleveland	Mr. Moreton
Cymbeline.			Shopman . . .	Mr. Rowson .	Mr. Darley, Jr
Posthumous . .	Mr. Chalmers	Mr. Fennell	LadyC. Seymour	Mrs. Cleveland	Mrs. Francis
Iachimo	Mr. Cleveland	Mr. Moreton	Evans . . .	Mrs. Rowson	Mrs. Solomon
Frenchman . .	Mr. Beete . .	Mr. Finch	*Peeping Tom of Coventry.*		
Pisanio	Mr. Marshall	Mr. Marshall	Emma	Miss Rowson	Miss Broadhurst
Helena	Miss Rowson	Mrs. Cleveland	*Prisoner.*		
First Floor.			Marcos	Mr. Marshall	Mr. Marshall
Young Whimsey.	Mr. Cleveland	Mr. Moreton	Pasqual	Mr. Rowson .	Mr. Darley, Jr
Monford	Mr. Beete . .	Mr. Beete	Lewis	Mr. Cleveland	Mr. Moreton
Charlotte . . .	Mrs. Cleveland	Miss Oldfield	Juliana	Miss Solomon	Miss Solomon
Nancy	Miss Rowson	Mrs. Hervey	Clara	Mrs. Cleveland	Miss Broadhurst
Mrs. Patty Pan.	Mrs. Rowson	Mrs. Rowson	Theresa	Mrs. Solomon	Mrs. Hervey
Fontainville Forest.			*Selima and Azor.*		
Montault . . .	Mr. Cleveland	Mr. Green	Azor	Mr. Marshall	Mr. Marshall
Lamotte	Mr. Chalmers	Mr. Chalmers	Scander	Mr. Rowson .	Mr. Darley
Nemours . . .	Mr. Beete . .	Mr. Cleveland	Ali	Mr. Cleveland	Mr. Bates
Harlequin's Invasion.			Fatima	Mrs. Rowson	Mrs. Rowson
Harlequin . . .	Mr. Chalmers	Mr. Francis	Lesbia	Mrs. Solomon	Miss Broadhurst
Mercury . . .	Mr. Marshall	Mr. Marshall	Selima	Mrs. Marshall	Mrs. Marshall
Mrs. Snip . . .	Mrs. Rowson	Mrs. Rowson	*She Wou'd and She Wou'd Not.*		
Lionel and Clarissa.			Trapanti	Mr. Chalmers	Mr. Chalmers
Lionel	Mr. Marshall	Mr. Marshall	Don Philip . .	Mr. Marshall	Mr. Fennell
Jenkins	Mr. Rowson .	Mr. Darley	Octavio	Mr. Cleveland	Mr. Green
Harman	Mr. Cleveland	Mr. Cleveland	Diego	Mr. Rowson .	Mr. De Moulin
Clarissa	Mrs. Marshall	Mrs. Warrell	Flora	Mrs. Cleveland	Mrs. Francis
Diana	Miss Rowson	Mrs. Oldmixon	Rosara	Mrs. Rowson	Mrs. Morris
Little Yankee Sailor.			Hypolita . . .	Mrs. Marshall	Mrs. Marshall
William	Miss Solomon	Mast. T. Warrell	*Shipwrecked Mariners Preserved.*		
Merry Wives of Windsor.			Capt. Hatchway.	Mr. Lege . . .	Mr. Lege
Ford	Mr. Chalmers	Mr. Chalmers	Jacquelina . . .	Miss Solomon	Miss Solomon
Dr. Caius . . .	Mr. Marshall	Mr. Marshall	*Speculation.*		
Pistol	Mr. Cleveland	Mr. Francis	Tanjore	Mr. Chalmers	Mr. Moreton
Bardolph . . .	Mr. Rowson .	Mr. Darley, Jr	Jack Arable . .	Mr. Marshall	Mr. Marshall
Robin	Miss Solomon	Miss Solomon	Lady Project .	Mrs. Rowson	Mrs. Shaw
Mrs. Page . . .	Mrs. Cleveland	Mrs. Whitlock	Cecilia	Mrs. Cleveland	Mrs. Marshall
Mrs. Ford . . .	Mrs. Marshall	Mrs. Morris			
Mrs. Quickly . .	Mrs. Rowson	Mrs. Rowson			

The productions new to Boston comprised many pieces in which the acquisitions to the company had previously appeared in Philadelphia, now either retaining their former roles or succeeding to others of more importance. The Rowsons, it is apparent, were held in higher esteem in Boston than elsewhere, even Mr. Rowson being accorded parts of some importance. The Clevelands made some progress, but Mr. Marshall remained where he began, and Mrs. Marshall, in consequence of the rivalry of Mrs. Williamson, receded a

NEW BOSTON PRODUCTIONS—SUPPLEMENTARY CASTS.

CASTLE OF ANDALUSIA.

Don Scipio . . . . Mr. Hamilton
Don Juan . . . . . Mr. Kenny
Don Alphonso . . . Mr. Downie
Spado . . . . Mr. Villiers
Sanguino . . . . . . Mr. Hogg
Phillipo . . . . Mrs. Williamson
Lorenza . . . . . . Mad. Gardie
Isabella . . . . Mrs. Hogg

COUNT OF NARBONNE.

Count . . . . . . Mr. Chalmers
Theodore . . . . . . Mr. White
Fabian . . . . Mr. Kenny
Austin . . . . Mr. Coles
Countess . . . . . . Mrs. Hogg

CYMBELINE.

Cymbeline . . . . . Mr. Kenny
Belarius . . . . . Mr. Hamilton
Arviragus . . . . . Mr. Downie
Queen . . . . Mrs. Baker

FIRST FLOOR.

Old Whimsey . . Mr. Hamilton
Landlord . . . . . . Mr. Kenny
Simon . . . . . . Mr. McKenzie
Furnish . . . . . . Mr. Ashton
Snap . . . . Mr. Clarke

FONTAINVILLE FOREST.

Louis . . . . Mr. Downie
Peter . . . . Mr. Kenny
Jaques . . . . Mr. Fawcett
Laval . . . . . . Mr. Radcliffe
Hortensia . . . . . . Mrs. Baker

HARLEQUIN'S INVASION.

Bog . . . . Mr. Collins
Capt. Bounce . . . Mr. Fawcett
Abraham . . . . . Mr. Villiers
Forge . . . . . . Mr. Hamilton
Taffy . . . . Mr. Hogg
Dolly Snip . . . . . Mrs. Collins

LIONEL AND CLARISSA.

Sir John . . . . Mr. Williamson
Jenny . . . . . Mrs. Williamson
Lady Mary . . . . . Mrs. Baker

MERRY WIVES OF WINDSOR.

Sir John Falstaff . Mr. Williamson
Shallow . . . . Mr. Kenny
Slender . . . . Mr. Villiers
Sir Hugh Evans . Mr. Hamilton
Mr. Page . . . . . . Mr. Hogg
Host . . . . Mr. Downie
Nym . . . . Mr. Clarke
Rugby . . . . . Mr. McKenzie
Simple . . . . . . Miss Green
Ann Page . . . . . Mrs. Collins

MY GRANDMOTHER.

Sir Matthew . . . Mr. Hamilton

NEXT-DOOR NEIGHBORS.

Blackman . . . . Mr. Hamilton
Bluntly . . . . . . Mr. Villiers
Manly . . . . Mr. Collins
Wilford . . . . . . Mr. Kenny
Lucre . . . . Mr. Downie
Lord Hazard . . . . Mr. Hogg
Henry . . . . Mr. White
Lady Bridget . . . . Miss Green
Eleanor . . . . Mrs. Williamson

PEEPING TOM OF COVENTRY.

Mayor . . . . . . Mr. Hamilton
Harold . . . . . . Mr. Downie
Count Lewis . . . Mr. McKenzie
Goodwin . . . . . . Mr. Kenny
Crazy . . . . Mr. Villiers
Lady Godiva . . . . Miss Green
Mayoress . . . . . . Mrs. Baker
Maud . . . . . Mrs. Williamson

PRISONER.

Bernardo . . . . . Mr. Downie
Roberts . . . . . . Mr. Villiers
Nina . . . . . Mrs. Williamson

SHE WOU'D AND SHE WOU'D NOT

Soto . . . . Mr. Villiers
Don Louis . . . . . . Mr. Hogg
Corrigidore . . . . . Mr. Downie
Host . . . . Mr. Kenny
Don Manuel . . . Mr. Hamilton
Villetta . . . . . . Mrs. Collins

SHIPWRECKED MARINERS PRESERVED.

Jack Rattling . . . . Mr. Hogg
Gerald . . . . Mr. Kenny
Ramirez . . . . . . Mr. Dubois
Rosalie . . . . . . Mad. Gardie

SPECULATION.

Ald. Arable . . . . Mr. Hamilton
Capt. Arable . . . Mr. Cleveland
Sir Frederick Faintly, Mr. Fawcett
Vickery . . . . . Mr. McKenzie
Emmeline . . . Mrs. Williamson

point as regarded the hoydens, advancing, however, in high comedy. The annexed summary will show the relative position of the Philadelphia players in the two theatres, the parts of the other members of the company in these pieces being added in a separate list. I have preserved full casts of only such of the new Boston productions as were not previously played in Philadelphia. The first of these, by alphabetical arrangement, was "A Day in Turkey," one of Mrs. Cowley's least successful pieces, produced for the benefit of Mr. T. Paine, the literary adjunct of the theatre. Mrs. Pownall had previously included it in one of her benefit bills with the title of " Liberty Restored."

FIRST BOSTON PRODUCTIONS—COMPLETE CASTS.

A DAY IN TURKEY.

Ibrahim	Mr. Cleveland
Orloff	Mr. White
Mustapha	Mr. Downie
Muley	Mr. Rowson
Azim	Mr. Hamilton
Old Man	Mr. Kenny
Son	Mr. McKenzie
Ismael	Mr. Clarke
A la Greque	Mr. Marshall
Alexina	Mrs. Cleveland
Lauretta	Mrs. Collins
Fatima	Mrs. Solomon
Paulina	Mrs. Williamson

FOLLIES OF A DAY.

Almaviva	Mr. Cleveland
Don Guzman	Mr. Kenny
Dr. Bartholo	Mr. Hamilton
Antonio	Mr. Villiers
Doublefee	Mr. Downie
Bazil	Mr. Hogg
Bounce	Mr. Rowson
Figaro	Mr. Marshall
Page	Mrs. Williamson
Countess	Mrs. Cleveland
Marcellina	Mrs. Rowson
Agnes	Mrs. Collins
Susan	Mrs. Marshall

HEIGHO FOR A HUSBAND.

Gen. Fairlove	Mr. Kenny
Rackrent	Mr. Hamilton

Squire Edward	Mr. Cleveland
Frank	Mr. Downie
Player	Mr. Hogg
William	Mr. Clarke
Timothy	Mr. Villiers
Charlotte	Mrs. Cleveland
Maria	Mrs. Collins
Millclack	Mrs. Hogg
Maid	Miss Green
Dorothy	Mrs. Williamson

IRON MASK.

Mask	Mr. Marshall
Caroline	Mrs. Marshall

ISLAND OF CALYPSO.

Telemachus	Mr. Lege
Cupid	Miss Solomon
Eucledus	Mrs. Cleveland
Minerva	Mad. Lege
Calypso	Mad. Gardie

LA PETITE ESPIEGLE.

Blaise	Mr. Lege
Bazily	Mr. Dubois
La Petite Espiegle	Miss Solomon

LIFE'S VAGARIES.

Lord Arthur	Mr. Cleveland
Sir Hans	Mr. Kenny
Dickens	Mr. Hogg
Robin	Mr. McKenzie
Coachman	Mr. Rowson

George Burgis	Mr. Villiers
Lord Torrendil	Mr. Downie
L'Œillet	Mr. Clarke
Robinson	Mr. Coles
Timolin	Mr. Marshall
Augusta	Mrs. Cleveland
Lady Torrendil	Mrs. Rowson
Miss Clare	Miss Green
Landlady	Mrs. Collins
Fanny	Mrs. Williamson

LOCK AND KEY.

Capt. Cheerly	Mr. Marshall
Brummagem	Mr. Hamilton
Vane	Mr. Downie
Ralph	Mr. Villiers
Fanny	Mrs. Solomon
Selina	Miss Green
Dolly	Miss Rowson
Laura	Mrs. Marshall

MAN OF TEN THOUSAND.

Torrington	Mr. Chalmers
Major Rampart	Mr. Cleveland
Lord Laroon	Mr. White
Sir Pertinax Pitiful	Mr Hogg
Hudson	Mr. Rowson
Thomas	Mr. McKenzie
Herbert	Mr. Villiers
Curfew	Mr. Hamilton
Consol	Mr. Kenny
Robert	Mr. Downie
Clerk	Mr. Clarke

Another of Mrs. Cowley's pieces, "Town Before You," originally acted at Covent Garden, was played for the first time in this country for Paine and Campbell's benefit. The remaining productions that were new, not only to Boston, but had not been brought forward previous to this season, either in New York or Philadelphia, were O'Keefe's "Life's Vagaries," Hoare's "Lock and Key," Holcroft's "Man of Ten Thousand," Burgoyne's "Richard Cœur de Lion" and Morton's "Way to Get Married." O'Keefe's comedy had been acted with success at Covent Garden, and, like most of his pieces, it was at once characteristic of his irregularities and of his genius. Prince Hoare's opera was also a Covent Garden success. It long continued a stock piece, both in England and in this country. Holcroft's new comedy failed at Drury Lane for political reasons, being acted only seven nights, but in

FIRST BOSTON PRODUCTIONS—COMPLETE CASTS.

Hairbrain . . . . . Mr. Marshall
Lady Taunton . . . . Mrs. Hogg
Girl . . . . Miss Green
Annabel . . . . Mrs. Cleveland
Olivia . . . . . . Mrs. Marshall

MUCH ADO ABOUT NOTHING.

Benedick . . . . . Mr. Chalmers
Claudio . . . . . Mr. Cleveland
Leonato . . . . . . Mr. Kenny
Prince . . . . Mr. Downie
Don John . . . . . Mr. Fawcett
Balthazar . . . . . Mr. Rowson
Conrade . . . . Mr. Radcliffe
Borachio . . . . Mr. McKenzie
Dogberry . . . . . . Mr. Jones
Verges . . . . . . Mr. Villiers
Sexton . . . . Mr. Beete
Friar . . . . Mr. Clarke
Anthonio . . . . . . Mr. Ashton
Hero . . . . . . Mrs. Cleveland
Margaret . . . . . Mrs. Rowson
Ursula . . . . . . Miss Green
Beatrice . . . . Mrs. Williamson

OROONOKO.

Oroonoko . . . . Mr. Cleveland
Blandford . . . . . Mr. Downie

Lieutenant-Governor . Mr. Hogg
Stanmore . . . . . . Mr. Kenny
Jack Stanmore . . Mr. McKenzie
Holman . . . . . . Mr. Fawcett
Capt. Driver . . . Mr. Hamilton
Aboan . . . . . Mr. Williamson
Imoinda . . . . . Mrs. Marshall

RICHARD CŒUR DE LION.

Richard . . . . . . Mr. Marshall
Blondel . . . . . Mr. Cleveland
Sir Owen . . . . . . Mr. Rowson
Florestan . . . . . Mr. Downie
Seneschal . . . . . . Mr. Hogg
Guillot . . . . Mr. Villiers
Old Matthew . . . . Mr. Kenny
William . . . . . Mr. McKenzie
Pilgrim . . . . . . Mr. Clarke
Antonio . . . . Mrs. Williamson
Lauretta . . . . Mrs. Graupner
Julie . . . . Mrs. Solomon
Dorcas . . . . . Mrs. Rowson
Collette . . . . . . Miss Green
Matilda . . . . . Mrs. Marshall

TANCRED AND SIGISMUNDA.

Tancred . . . . . . Mr. White

Earl Osmond . . . Mr. Marshall
Pharoa . . . . . . Mr. Downie
Rhodolpho . . . . . Mr. Hogg
Siffredi . . . . . Mr. Cleveland
Laura . . . . . . Mrs. Solomon
Sigismunda . . . . Mrs. Marshall

TOWN BEFORE YOU.

Tippy . . . . . . Mr. Chalmers

WAY TO GET MARRIED.

Tangent . . . . . Mr. Chalmers
Dashall . . . . . . Mr. Marshall
Toby Allspice . . . Mr. Hamilton
Caustic . . . . Mr. Kenny
McQueery . . . . . Mr. Collins
Landlord . . . . . Mr. Rowson
Surgeon . . . . . . Mr. Hogg
Shopman . . . . . . Mr. Clarke
Ned . . . . Mr. Fawcett
Postillion . . . . . Miss Solomon
Jeffrey . . . . . . Mr. Villiers
Capt. Faulkner . Mr. Williamson
Clementina . . . Mrs. Cleveland
Lady Sorrel . . . . Mrs. Hogg
Fanny . . . . . . Miss Green
Julia Faulkner . Mrs. Williamson

this country its politics gave it popularity.   The opera " Richard Cœur de Lion " was an almost literal transcript from Sedaine's drama of that name, first acted in Paris in 1784.   Two versions were brought out in London two years later—one at Drury Lane by General Burgoyne, and one at Covent Garden by Leonard MacNally.   The former was the more successful, and was the version played in Boston.   Morton's new comedy, " The Way to Get Married," was a great success on both sides of the Atlantic.   It was a Covent Garden production, and was what would now be called a comedy-drama, humor and pathos being blended with great skill and effect.   Charles Powell brought out two of these pieces at his new theatre, anticipating the production of Holcroft's comedy at the Boston Theatre by more than a week.   Besides these, Mrs. Marshall produced for her benefit a little piece called the " Iron Mask, or Destruction of the Bastile ; " Madame Gardie brought out a new ballet, the " Island of Calypso ; " the two French pantomimists, Dubois and Renaud, offered " Pygmalion " and " Paul and Virginia," both French pieces ; and finally a skit called " Ways and Oddities " was produced the same night, with the Covent Garden interlude " Melocosmiotis."   In the interlude Mr. Chalmers had the assistance of Mr. Williamson, the Covent Garden singer, at the Boston Haymarket, who gave " The Tobacco-Box " and " The Hobbies."

The full casts of the new pieces show the *personnel* and relative rank of the company ; but the strength of Mr. Williamson's com-

TWO BOSTON COMPANIES—CONTRASTED CASTS.

PLAYS.	Col. Tyler's Co.	Williamson's Co.	PLAYS.	Col. Tyler's Co.	Williamson's Co.
Agreeable Surprise.			Cudden	Mr. Radcliffe	. Mr. Clarke
Compton . . .	. Mr. Chambers	. Mr. Collins	Stump	. Mr. Clarke	. . Mr. Solomon
Eugene	. Mr. Harper	. . Mr. Downie	Lingo	. Mr. Villiers	. . Mr. Bates
Chicane . . .	. Mr. Hughes	. . Mr. Rowson	Laura	. Mrs. Pick	. . . Mrs. Marshall
John	. Mr. S. Powell	. Mr. McKenzie	*All the World's a Stage.*		
Thomas . . .	Mr. Ashton	. Mr. Hogg	Harry Stukely	. Mr. Ashton	. . Mr. Cleveland

pany, as compared with that of the previous season, is best illustrated
by the changes in the casts of the pieces played by both. A glance
at these shows that Cleveland and Marshall shared Snelling Powell,
Harper and Chambers' better parts, but Chalmers succeeded to the
best. Downie, Fawcett, Hamilton, Hogg and Rowson took their
minor roles, besides those of Taylor and Hughes. An exception was
Octavian, in which Taylor had acquired a prescriptive right, which

TWO BOSTON COMPANIES—CONTRASTED CASTS.

PLAYS.	Col. Tyler's Co.	Williamson's Co.
Charles Stanley	Mr. Taylor	Mr. Downie
Cymon	Mr. Clarke	Mr. Rowson
Kitty Sprightly	Mrs. Hughes	Mrs. Collins
Miss Bridget	Mrs. Baker	Mrs. Rowson
Children in the Wood.		
Walter	Mr. Chambers	Mr. Marshall
Sir Rowland	Mr. Ashton	Mr. Kenny
Gabriel	Mr. Hughes	Mr. McKenzie
Oliver	Mr. Kenny	Mr. Rowson
Lord Alford	Mr. Harper	Mr. Cleveland
Girl	Miss Sully	Miss Solomon
Lady Alford	Mrs. Arnold	Mrs. Hogg
Winifred	Mrs. Baker	Mrs. Rowson
Every One Has His Fault.		
Sir Robert	Mr. Chambers	Mr. Chalmers
Harmony	Mr. Ashton	Mr. Cleveland
Solus	Mr. Hughes	Mr. Hamilton
Placid	Mr. Hamilton	Mr. Hogg
Edward	Miss Sully	Miss Solomon
Hammond	Mr. Maginnis	Mr. Downie
Irwin	Mr. S. Powell	Mr. Marshall
Miss Wooburn	Mrs. Hughes	Mrs. Graupner
Mrs. Placid	Mrs. Harper	Mrs. Rowson
Miss Spinster	Mrs. Baker	Mrs. Cleveland
Farmer.		
Jemmy Jumps	Mr. Chambers	Mr. Jones
Blackberry	Mr. Hamilton	Mr. Rowson
Col. Dormant	Mr. Ashton	Mr. Kenny
Fairly	Mr. Kenny	Mr. Ashton
Flummery	Mr. Maginnis	Mr. Hamilton
Capt. Valentine	Mr. Harper	Mr. Marshall
Molly Maybush	Mrs. Pick	Miss Rowson
Landlady	Mrs. Ashton	Mrs. Baker
Betty	Mrs. Chambers	Mrs. Rowson
George Barnwell.		
George Barnwell	Mr. S. Powell	Mr. Cleveland
Blunt	Mr. Hughes	Mr. McKenzie
Trueman	Mr. Taylor	Mr. Hogg

PLAYS.	Col. Tyler's Co.	Williamson's Co.
Maria	Mrs. Harper	Mrs. Cleveland
Lucy	Mrs. Hughes	Mrs. Solomon
Millwood	Mrs. S. Powell	Mrs. Hogg
Highland Reel.		
Shelty	Mr. Harper	Mr. Jones
McGilpin	Mr. Hughes	Mr. Hamilton
Sergt. Jack	Mr. Kenny	Mr. Rowson
Capt. Dash	Mr. Taylor	Mr. Fawcett
Sandy	Mr. Chambers	Mr. Marshall
Jenny	Mrs. Pick	Miss Rowson
Jew.		
Frederick	Mr. S. Powell	Mr. Downie
Charles Ratcliffe	Mr. Taylor	Mr. Cleveland
Saunders	Mr. Hughes	Mr. Rowson
Mrs. Ratcliffe	Mrs. Harper	Mrs. Hogg
Mrs. Goodison	Mrs. Ashton	Mrs. Solomon
Dorcas	Mrs. Hughes	Mrs. Rowson
Eliza	Mrs. Arnold	Mrs. Marshall
Love in a Village.		
Young Meadows	Mr. Chambers	Mr. Marshall
Woodcock	Mr. Hamilton	Mr. Bates
Hawthorn	Mr. Harper	Mr. Rowson
Eustace	Mr. Ashton	Mr. Downie
Madge	Mrs. Pick	Mrs. Williamson
Lucinda	Miss Green	Mrs. Solomon
Rosetta	Mrs. Arnold	Mrs. Marshall
Lying Valet.		
Sharp	Mr. Harper	Mr. Bates
Trippet	Mr. Ashton	Mr. Downie
Cook	Mr. Villiers	Mr. Clarke
Gayless	Mr. S. Powell	Mr. Fawcett
Melissa	Mrs. Hughes	Mrs. Cleveland
Mrs. Gadabout	Miss Green	Miss Rowson
Mrs. Trippet	Mrs. Ashton	Mrs. Solomon
Kitty Pry	Mrs. Chambers	Mrs. Rowson
Maid of the Oaks.		
Dupely	Mr. Chambers	Mr. Downie

went to Chalmers. Instead of Mrs. S. Powell, Mrs. Harper, Mrs. Arnold, Mrs. Pick and Mrs. Hughes, we have Mrs. Marshall, Mrs. Cleveland, Mrs. and Miss Rowson and Mrs. Collins. Mrs. Williamson retained such of her previous roles as pleased her, taking whatever else commended itself to the ambition of the manager's wife. To these summaries I have added a number of incomplete casts, comprising only pieces long familiar to the American theatre-going public, al-

TWO BOSTON COMPANIES—CONTRASTED CASTS.

PLAYS.	Col. Tyler's Co.	Williamson's Co.
Old Groveby	Mr. Hughes	Mr. Hamilton
Maria	Mrs. Chambers	Miss Rowson
Midas.		
Jupiter	Mr. Hughes	Mr. Clarke
Apollo	Mr. Chambers	Mr. Marshall
Pan	Mr. Maginnis	Mr. Kenny
Sileno	Mr. Harper	Mr. Rowson
Damætas	Mr. Kenny	Mr. Downie
Juno	Mrs. Chambers	Miss Rowson
Minerva	Mrs. Harper	Miss Green
Venus	Miss Green	Mrs. Collins
Daphne	Mrs. Arnold	Mrs. Solomon
Mysis	Mrs. Baker	Mrs. Rowson
Nysa	Mrs. Pick	Mrs. Marshall
Mountaineers.		
Octavian	Mr. Taylor	Mr. Chalmers
Bulcazin	Mr. Kenny	Mr. Cleveland
Kilmallock	Mr. Hamilton	Mr. Marshall
Virolet	Mr. Ashton	Mr. Downie
Roque	Mr. Hughes	Mr. Rowson
Old Goatherd	Mr. S. Powell	Mr. Kenny
Ganem	Mr. Hutchins	Mr. Beete
Sadi	Mr. Chambers	Mr. Marshall
Zorayda	Mrs. S. Powell	Mrs. Marshall
Floranthe	Mrs. Hughes	Mrs. Cleveland
Oscar and Malvina.		
Oscar	Mr. S. Powell	Mr. Chalmers
Marvin	Mr. Harper	Mr. Cleveland
Draco	Mr. Taylor	Mr. Fawcett
Carrol	Mr. Williamson	Mr. Marshall
Pedlar	Mr. Chambers	Mr. Jones
Page	Miss Sully	Miss Solomon
Shepherdess	Mrs. Chambers	Mrs. Solomon
Malvina	Mrs. Williamson	Mad. Gardie
Poor Soldier.		
Patrick	Mrs. Pick	Mrs. Williamson
Darby	Mr. Harper	Mr. Bates
Capt. Fitzroy	Mr. S. Powell	Mr. Downie

PLAYS.	Col. Tyler's Co.	Williamson's Co.
Dermot	Mr. Chambers	Mr. Collins
Father Luke	Mr. Kenny	Mr. Hamilton
Norah	Mrs. Chambers	Miss Rowson
Kathleen	Mrs. Williamson	Mrs. Solomon
Romeo and Juliet.		
Romeo	Mr. Harper	Mr. Chalmers
Mercutio	Mr. S. Powell	Mr. Marshall
Paris	Mr. Ashton	Mr. Downie
Benvolio	Mr. Hughes	Mr. Ashton
Montagu	Mr. Maginnis	Mr. Rowson
Tybalt	Mr. Taylor	Mr. Fawcett
Friar Laurence	Mr. Hamilton	Mr. Jones
Apothecary	Mr. Clarke	Mr. Hamilton
Lady Capulet		Mrs. Rowson
Juliet	Mrs. S. Powell	Mrs. Marshall
Romp.		
Watty Cockney	Mr. Chambers	Mr. Jones
Capt. Sightly	Mr. Kenny	Mr. Downie
Barnacle	Mr. Hughes	Mr. Hamilton
Penelope	Mrs. Hughes	Miss Rowson
Rosina.		
Belville	Mr. Chambers	Mr. Marshall
Capt. Belville	Mr. Ashton	Mr. Downie
Rustic	Mr. Hamilton	Mr. Rowson
William	Mr. Williamson	Mr. Jones
Phœbe	Miss Green	Miss Solomon
Rosina	Mrs. Arnold	Mrs. Marshall
Spoiled Child.		
Tag	Mr. Chambers	Mr. Hogg
Old Pickle	Mr. Hughes	Mr. Hamilton
Margery	Mrs. Hughes	Mrs. Rowson
Susan	Mrs. Ashton	Miss Rowson
Virgin Unmasked.		
Coupee	Mr. Taylor	Mr. Jones
Blister	Mr. Hughes	Mr. Hamilton
Thomas	Mr. Ashton	Mr. Beete
Quaver	Mr. Chambers	Mr. Marshall

though not all of them had been seen in Boston before this season. In these and in the new productions also Mr. Villiers retained his rank

INCOMPLETE CASTS OF FAMILIAR PIECES.

As You Like It.

Adam	Mr. Hamilton
Oliver	Mr. Fawcett
Sylvius	Mr. Downie
Celia	Mrs. Cleveland
Audrey	Mrs. Rowson
Rosalind	Mrs. Marshall

Busybody.

Sir George Airy . .	Mr. Marshall
Whisper	Mr. Downie
Sir Francis	Mr. Hamilton
Isabinda	Mrs. Cleveland
Scentwell	Miss Rowson
Patch	Mrs. Rowson
Marinda	Mrs. Marshall

Catharine and Petruchio.

Grumio	Mr. Hamilton
Hortensio	Mr. Downie
Bianca	Miss Green
Catharine	Mrs. Hogg

Country Girl.

Moody	Mr. Kenny
Sparkish	Mr. Marshall
Harcourt	Mr. Williamson
Peggy	Mrs. Marshall

Critic.

Sir Fretful	Mr. Hamilton
Dangle	Mr. Downie
Sneer	Mr. Cleveland
Mrs. Dangle . . .	Mrs. Rowson
Raleigh	Mr. Fawcett
Leicester	Mr. Rowson
Beefeater	Mr. Hogg
Whiskerandos . . .	Mr. Marshall
Tilburina	Mrs. Hogg

Douglas.

Lord Randolph . . .	Mr. Kenny
Glenalvon	Mr. Cleveland
Old Norval . .	Mr. Williamson
Lady Randolph . . .	Mrs. Hogg

Dramatist.

Scratch	Mr. Hamilton
Lady Waitfort . . .	Mrs. Hogg

Louisa Courtney .	Mrs. Cleveland
Letty	Miss Green
Marianne . . .	Mrs. Williamson

Fair Penitent.

Altamont	Mr. Downie
Rossano	Mr. Beete
Lavinia	Mrs. Cleveland
Lucilla	Mrs. Solomon

Hamlet.

Polonius	Mr. Hamilton
Laertes	Mr. Cleveland
Horatio	Mr. Fawcett
Guildenstern . . .	Mr. Downie
Francisco	Mr. Rowson
Ghost	Mr. Williamson
Queen	Mrs. Hogg
Player Queen . . .	Miss Rowson
Ophelia	Mrs. Williamson

Henry IV.

Prince of Wales .	Mr. Cleveland
King	Mr. Collins
Poins	Mr. Downie
Westmoreland . .	Mr. Hamilton
Worcester	Mr. Hogg
Northumberland . . .	Mr. Kenny
Prince John . . .	Miss Solomon
Sir Walter Blunt . .	Mr. Fawcett
Hostess	Mrs. Baker
Lady Percy . . .	Mrs. Cleveland

Inkle and Yarico.

Inkle	Mr. Marshall
Curry	Mr. Hamilton
Mate	Mr. Rowson
Campley	Mr. Downie
Yarico	Mrs. Marshall
Narcissa	Miss Rowson
Patty	Mrs. Rowson
Wowski	Mrs. Williamson

Irishman in London.

Delany	Mr. Marshall
Callooney	Mr. Cleveland
Capt. Seymour . . .	Mr. Downie
Mr. Frost	Mr. Hamilton
Louisa	Mrs. Cleveland

Carline	Mrs. Solomon
Cubba	Mrs. Rowson

Isabella.

Carlos	Mr. Fawcett
Sampson	Mr. Hamilton
Belford	Mr. Beete

Jane Shore.

Hastings	Mr. Chalmers
Belmour	Mr. Downie
Dumont	Mr. Marshall
Alicia	Mrs. Cleveland
Jane Shore	Mrs. Marshall

Know Your Own Mind.

Millamour	Mr. Chalmers
Dashwould	Mr. Marshall
Sir Harry	Mr. Downie
Old Bygrove . . .	Mr. Hamilton
Capt. Bygrove . . .	Mr. Fawcett
Miss Neville . . .	Mrs. Cleveland
Lady Bell . .	Mrs. Marshall

Le Foret Noire.

Le Terreur	Mr. Lege
Geronte	Mr. Hamilton

Lyar.

Young Wilding .	Mr. Chalmers
Sir James Elliott . .	Mr. Fawcett
Miss Grantham .	Mrs. Cleveland
Miss Godfrey	Miss Green
Kitty	Mrs. Rowson

Midnight Hour.

Ambrose	Mr. Downie
Matthias	Mr. Rowson
Cicely	Mrs. Rowson
Flora	Mrs. Williamson

Miser.

Clerimont	Mr. Downie
Decoy	Mr. Rowson
Harriet	Miss Green
Lappet	Mrs. Hogg

Modern Antiques.

Joey	Mr. Villiers

as the principal low comedian, except when displaced by Jones or Bates, and Kenny played nearly all his former parts and many new ones. When Kenny took his benefit it was announced that the receipts would

INCOMPLETE CASTS OF FAMILIAR PIECES.

Coachman . . . . . Mr. Rowson
Mrs. Cockletop . Mrs. Cleveland
Nan . . . . Mrs. Rowson
Flounce . . . . Miss Green

OLD MAID.

Clerimont . . . . . . Mr. Hogg
Trifle . . . . Miss Rowson

PERCY.

Percy . . . . . Mr. Cleveland
Douglas . . . . . Mr. Chalmers
Raby . . . . . Mr. Hamilton
Sir Hubert . . . . Mr. Fawcett
Harcourt . . . . . . Mr. Downie
Birtha . . . . . Mrs. Cleveland

PROVOKED HUSBAND.

Lord Townly . . . Mr. Chalmers
Sir Francis . . . . Mr. Hamilton
Manly . . . . . . Mr. Cleveland
Basset . . . . Mr. Downie
Squire Richard . . . Mr. Villiers
Poundage . . . . . . Mr. Beete
Lady Grace . . . Mrs. Cleveland
Lady Wronghead . . Mrs. Baker

PURSE.

Edmund . . . . . Mr. Marshall
Page . . . . Miss Solomon
Sally . . . . Mrs. Solomon

RICHARD III.

Richard . . . . . Mr. Chalmers
Richmond . . . . Mr. Cleveland
Henry VI. . . . . . Mr. Collins
Buckingham . . . . Mr. Fawcett
Catesby . . . . . . Mr. Rowson
Lady Anne . . Mrs. Cleveland
Duchess of York . Mrs. Rowson
Queen Elizabeth . . . Mrs. Hogg

SCHOOL FOR SCANDAL.

Charles Surface . . Mr. Chalmers
Joseph Surface . . Mr. Cleveland
Crabtree . . . . . Mr. Hamilton
Rowley . . . . . . Mr. Rowson

SLAVES IN ALGIERS.

Constant . . . . Mr. Williamson
Mustapha . . . . . Mr. Hogg
Ben Hassan . . . . Mr. Rowson
Zoriana . . . . . Miss Rowson
Selima . . . . . Miss Green
Frederick . . . . . Mr. Downie
Henry . . . . . Mr. Cleveland
Olivia . . . . . . Mrs. Rowson
Rebecca . . . . . Mrs. Hogg

ST. PATRICK'S DAY

Lieutenant . . . . Mr. Marshall
Credulous . . . . . Mr. Kenny
Trounce . . . . . Mr. Rowson
Flint . . . . . . Mr. Hogg
Dr. Rosy . . . . Mr. Hamilton
Bridget . . . . Mrs. Rowson
Laurilla . . . . . Mrs. Collins

SULTAN.

Grand Carver . . Mr. Rowson
Osmyn . . . . . . Mr. Villiers
Ismene . . . . . Miss Rowson
Roxalana . . . Mrs. Marshall

SUSPICIOUS HUSBAND.

Jack Meggot . . . . Mr. Downie
Mrs. Strickland . . Mrs. Solomon
Clarinda . . . . Mrs. Marshall

THREE WEEKS AFTER MARRIAGE.

Sir Charles Racket, Mr. Chalmers
Woodley . . . . . Mr. Downie
Lovelace . . . . . . Mr. Hogg
Drugget . . . . . Mr. Hamilton
Mrs. Drugget . . . Mrs. Rowson
Dimitry . . . . Mrs. Solomon
Lady Racket . . Mrs. Marshall

TOM THUMB.

Ghost . . . . . . Mr. Rowson
Huncamunca . . . Mrs. Solomon
Cleonora . . . . . Miss Green
Dollalolla . . . Mrs. Williamson

TWO HUNTERS.

Guillot . . . . M. Lege
Colas . . . . M. Dubois
Perrette . . . . . Mad. Gardie

VENICE PRESERVED.

Jaffier . . . . . . Mr. Chalmers
Pierre . . . . . Mr. Cleveland
Priuli . . . . Mr. Kenny
Bedamar . . . . . Mr. Downie
Elliott . . . . . . Mr. Beete
Spinosa . . . . . Mr. Rowson

WAY TO KEEP HIM.

Lovemore . . . . . Mr. Chalmers
Sir Brilliant . . . Mr. Cleveland
Sir Bashful . . . . Mr. Hamilton
William . . . . . Mr. Downie
Sideboard . . . . . Mr. Beete
Widow Belmour . Mrs. Marshall
Lady Constant Mrs. Cleveland
Muslin . . . . . Miss Rowson
Mignon . . . . Mrs. Collins

WEDDING DAY.

Rakeland . . . . Mr. Cleveland
Millden . . . . . . Mr. Kenny
Mr. Contest . . . . Mr. Downie
Sir Adam Contest . Mr. Hamilton
Mrs. Hamford . . . . Mrs. Hogg
Lady Autumn . . . Mrs. Rowson
Hannah . . . . . Miss Rowson
Lady Contest . Mrs. Williamson

WEST INDIAN.

Belcour . . . . . Mr. Chalmers
Capt. Dudley . . . Mr. Fawcett
Stukely . . . . . Mr. Downie
Fulmer . . . . . . Mr. Rowson
Maj. O'Flaherty . Mr. Hamilton
Lady Rusport . . . Mrs. Baker
Mrs. Fulmer . . . . Mrs. Rowson
Lucy . . . . Miss Green
Charlotte . . . Mrs. Williamson

all go to Mrs. Kenny and her children, and S. Powell postponed his benefit at the Haymarket to befriend his former associate. Mr. Baker made his first appearance in three years as *Captain Cape* in the "Old Maid" for Mr. T. Paine's benefit. Mrs. Marshall chose the "Country Girl" as a benefit piece, that she might play *Peggy*. Mr. Clarke also asserted himself on his benefit night by appearing as *Gregory* in the "Mock Doctor," when Mr. Coles was seen as *Orlando* in "As You Like It." Jones, who had returned from Charleston, played *Bob Acres* in the "Rivals" for Williamson's last benefit. The season had been disastrous, the expenditures exceeding the receipts, in consequence of the competition of the rival house.

When Williamson's season closed, the company was scattered, but none finally retired from the stage, except the Rowson family, after a brief summer engagement with Harper at Newport. During the three years that the Rowsons were with the Philadelphia company, Mrs. Rowson's list of parts was a long one, but she played nothing above the rank of mere respect-

MRS. ROWSON'S PARTS.
Phil. Co.

Agreeable Surprise. . . Fringe
Alexander the Great, Sysagambis
All in the Wrong . . . . Tattle
All the World's a Stage
             Miss Bridget
As You Like It . . . . Audrey
Auld Robin Gray . . . Dorcas
Bank Note . . . Lady Supple
Barnaby Brittle . . Lady Pride
Beaux' Stratagem
            Lady Bountiful
Belle's Stratagem . Kitty Willis
Birth of Harlequin . . . Maid
Box Lobby Challenge, Theodosia
Busybody . . . . Patch
Catharine and Petruchio
            Catharine
Children in the Wood
            Winifred
Citizen . . . . Maria
Clandestine Marriage . . Betty
Conscious Lovers . . . Isabella

MR. ROWSON'S PARTS.
Phil. Co.

American Tar . . Dick Hauser
As You Like It . . . . Charles
Gil Blas . . . . Cook
Harlequin Hurry Scurry, Farmer
Harlequin's Club . . Landlady
How to Grow Rich . . . Nab
Jubilee . . . . . . Trumpeter
Love in a Camp . . . Olmutz
Miraculous Mill . . . Mealey
Mountaineers . . . . . Roque
Rosina . . . . Rustic
Travellers Preserved . Ramirez
Wild Oats . . . . . Gammon

MISS ROWSON'S PARTS.

American Tar . . . . . Susan
Bank Note . . . . . . Maid
Beggar on Horseback
            Mrs. Barney Vag

Country Girl . . . . . . Lucy
Critic . . . . Confidante
Crotchet Lodge . Mrs. Crotchet
Deserter of Naples . . Margaret
Disbanded Officer . . Lisetta
Doctor and Apothecary, Theresa
Dramatist . . . Lady Waitfort
Every One Has His Fault
     Mrs. Placid
Fair Penitent . . . . . Lucilla
Farmer . . . Betty Blackberry
Female Patriot . . . . Statilla
First Love . . . . . Mrs. Kate
Guardian . . . . Lucy
Hamlet . . . . Player Queen
Hartford Bridge . . . Barmaid
Heiress . . . . Mrs. Blandish
High Life Below Stairs
     Lady Bab
Isabella . . . . Nurse
Jealous Wife . . . . . Toilet
Jew . . . . Dorcas
Jubilee . . . . . Goody Jarvis
Know Your Own Mind
     Mad. La Rouge
Lyar . . . . Kitty
Lying Valet . . . Mrs. Trippet
Mayor of Garratt . Mrs. Bruin
Merry Wives of Windsor
     Mrs. Quickly
Miser . . . . . . Mrs. Wisely
Miss in Her Teens . . . . Tag
Mock Doctor . . . . . Dorcas
Modern Antiques
     Mrs. Camomile
New Way to Pay Old Debts
     Froth
Next-Door Neighbors
     Lady Squander
No Song No Supper . Dorothy
Padlock . . . . Ursula
Peeping Tom of Coventry
     Mayoress
Prisoner at Large . . . . Mary
Prize . . . . . Mrs. Caddy
Provoked Husband . . Myrtilla

Catharine and Petruchio, Bianca
Citizen . . . . Corinna
Coriolanus . . . Gentlewoman
Critic . . . . . Second Niece
Crotchet Lodge . . . . . Maid
Duenna . . . . Lauretta
East Indian . . . . . . Jenny
Harlequin Dr. Faustus
     Bridesmaid
High Life Below Stairs . Chloe
L'Americain . . . . L'Huiffier
Le Foret Noire . . . . Marton
Lucky Escape . . . . . Peggy
Modern Antiques . . . . Betty
No Song No Supper . . Louisa
Romp . . . . . { Quasheba
      { Penelope
Spoiled Child . . . . . Susan
Tom Thumb . . . . Mustacha
West Indian . . . . . . Lucy
Wheel of Fortune . . . . Maid
Witches of the Rock . Milliner

ability. At the Boston Theatre she repeated many of her Philadelphia roles, but, on the whole, enjoyed greater importance as an actress. Mr. and Miss Rowson, on the other hand, obtained a higher rank than they had previously been accorded. Rowson's position as prompter kept him off the stage, and it was only during the last season of Wignell's first company in Baltimore, when it was greatly enfeebled, that he secured his two best parts—*Roque* in the " Mountaineers," and *Gammon* in " Wild Oats." These he made the measure of his standing in Boston. Miss Rowson's Boston success was warranted by her growth in years and experience. Charlotte Rowson was still almost a child when she came to Philadephia. She was born in London in 1779, and married William J. Johnston, a bookkeeper in the office of Claypoole's *Advertiser*, before she was eighteen. David Claypoole Johnston, the eminent caricaturist, often called the American Cruikshank, was her son. Mrs. Johnston died in July, 1855. Mrs. Rowson's last part at the Boston Theatre was *Miss Pickle* in the "Spoiled Child," on the 17th of May, 1797. After her retirement she opened a young ladies' school in Boston, which she conducted with great success for many years, numbering among her pupils the daughters of some of the principal families of Beacon Hill, by whom she was held in great esteem. She died in 1824, but her school was continued for a number of years after her death.

The fortunes of the other members of Mr. Williamson's disbanded company will be developed as a subsequent part of this history. Some of them obtained engagements at Charleston, where Mr. Sollee has previously carried so many Boston players, thus crowding out those who had gone before. The latter found a refuge in other Southern towns or made their way back to the Northern cities, even Alexandria becoming in 1798 an important theatrical town.

Rivals . . . . Lucy
Road to Ruin . . Mrs. Warren
Romeo and Juliet { LadyCapulet / Nurse
Rule a Wife and Have a Wife
                Margaretta
School for Scandal
            Lady Sneerwell
School for Wives, Lady Rachel
Selima and Azor . . . Fatima
Slaves in Algiers . . . . Olivia
Spoiled Child . . . Miss Pickle
St. Patrick's Day . . . Bridget
Suicide . . . . Mrs. Grogram
Suspicious Husband . . Lucetta
Three Weeks After Marriage
            Mrs. Drugget
Tom Thumb . . . Glumdalca
Toy . . . . . Katy Kavenagh
Triumphs of Love
          Hannah Friendly
True-Born Irishman . Lady Bab
Two Strings to Your Bow, Maid
Village Lawyer . . . Mrs. Scout
Volunteers . . . . . Rosalind
Ways and Means { Mrs. Peery / Lady Dunder
Wedding Day . . . . Hannah
West Indian . { Mrs. Fulmer / Lady Rusport
Wheel of Fortune
          Dame Dunckley
Who's the Dupe? . . Charlotte
Widow's Vow . . . . . . Inis
Witches of the Rock
           Fruit Woman
Wonder . . . . Inez
Wrangling Lovers . . Jacintha

CHAPTER XVIII.

THE BOSTON HAYMARKET, 1796–7.

BUILDING THE NEW HOUSE—POWELL'S RECRUITS—MR. AND MRS. BAR-
RETT—THE SIMPSONS—WILLIAMSON, THE SINGER—MR. DICKENSON
—THE PRODUCTIONS—" BUNKER HILL "—" WEST POINT PRE-
SERVED"—THE CASTS—A DISASTROUS SEASON.

O N the 11th of April, 1796, Charles S. Powell advertised proposals for building a new theatre in Boston. The capital was
placed at £3,400—two hundred shares of stock at $60 per share—
making $12,000 in American money. Powell was to have a lease of
the new house, to which he gave the name of the Haymarket, for
fourteen years at an annual rental of $1,200. Such was the eagerness
with which the shares were taken that on the 18th of May an advertisement was printed for bids for the contract for furnishing stone for
the new building. Each share of stock carried with it free admission
to the theatre during the season, and the desire to become stockholders
was so great that some Boston mechanics even undertook to give their
labor in payment for their shares. So rapidly was the work pushed
forward that before the close of the year the house was ready for occupancy. The new theatre was situated near the corner of Tremont
and Boylston Streets, and was an immense wooden pile, overtopping
every building in the vicinity. It had three tiers of boxes, together
with a pit and gallery. While the theatre was building, Mr. Powell

went to England to engage a company, again going into the English provinces for his recruits. The only London engagement that he effected was that of Mr. Williamson, a singer of some repute at Covent Garden. The English provincial players were Mr. and Mrs. Barrett, Mr. and Mrs. Simpson, and the three Misses Westray, daughters of Mrs. Simpson by a former marriage.

Mr. Powell had left behind him the nucleus of a very fair company for the time—Mr. and Mrs. S. Powell, Mr. and Mrs. Hughes, Mr. Taylor and Mrs. Pick from the Boston Theatre, together with such other players and aspirants for theatrical fame as were available. The new theatre was opened on the 26th of December, 1796, the "Belle's Stratagem" and "Mirza and Lindor" comprising the bill. Mr. S. Powell appeared as *Doricourt*, Mr. Charles Powell was once more seen in his old part of *Flutter*, and Mr. Taylor, from the Boston Theatre, played *Courtall*. Mrs. S. Powell was the *Letitia Hardy*, Mrs. Hughes *Lady Touchwood*, Miss Harrison, the sister of Mrs. S. Powell, *Miss Ogle*, and Mrs. Pick *Kitty Willis*. Mr. Marriott, who had been with the Old American Company and

LIST OF PERFORMANCES.

1796.
Dec. 26—Belle's Stratagem . Mrs. Cowley
Mirza and Lindor.
28—Suspicious Husband . . Hoadly
Cooper.
1797.
Jan. 2—She Stoops to Conquer, Goldsmith
Waterman . . . . Dibdin
4—Beaux' Stratagem . . . Farquhar
Padlock . . . . . . Bickerstaff
6—Variety . . . . Griffith
Mirza and Lindor.
9—Jew . . . . Cumberland
Rosina . . . . . Mrs. Brooke
11—Upholsterer . . . . . . Murphy
Padlock.
13—Variety.
New French Deserter.
16—Alexander the Great . . . . Lee
New French Deserter.
18—Way to Get Married . . Morton
Deserter . . . . . . Dibdin
20—Alexander the Great.
Quaker . . . . Dibdin
23—Way to Get Married.
Waterman.
25—Battle of Hexham . . Colman, Jr
Animal Magnetism, Mrs. Inchbald
27—Merchant of Venice . Shakspere
New French Deserter.

Jan. 30—Mountaineers . . . . Colman, Jr
　　　Milliners.
　　　Miller of Mansfield . . Dodsley
Feb.　1—Battle of Hexham.
　　　Milliners.
　　　Quaker.
　　　3—Richard III . . . . . Shakspere
　　　Inkle and Yarico . . Colman, Jr
　　　6—Merchant of Venice.
　　　Siege of Quebec (Pant.)
　　　Two Hunters and the Milkmaid.
　　　8—Inkle and Yarico.
　　　Siege of Quebec.
　　　Two Hunters.
　　10—Road to Ruin . . . . Holcroft
　　　Animal Magnetism.
　　13—Man of Ten Thousand . Holcroft
　　　Wood Cutters.
　　　Agreeable Surprise . . O'Keefe
　　15—Mountaineers.
　　　Wood Cutters.
　　　Retaliation . . . . . MacNally
　　20—Battle of Bunker Hill . . . Burk
　　　Padlock.
　　22—Bunker Hill.
　　　Poor Jack.
　　　Prize . . . . Hoare
　　24—Bunker Hill.
　　　Deuce is in Him . . . . Colman
　　　(Author's Night.)
　　27—Bunker Hill.
　　　Poor Jack.
March　1—Bunker Hill
　　　Bon Ton . . . . . . Garrick
　　　3—Bunker Hill.
　　　Midnight Hour　. Mrs. Inchbald
　　　(Author's Second Night.)
　　　6—Bunker Hill.
　　　Double Disguise . . Mrs. Hook
　　　8—Double Disguise.
　　　Deuce is in Him.
　　　Robinson Crusoe . . . Sheridan
　　10—Alexander the Great.
　　　Robinson Crusoe.
　　13—Child of Nature . Mrs. Inchbald
　　　Chrononhotonthologos . . Carey

afterward with the Virginia company, made his first appearance in Boston as *Sir George Touchwood.* There was now a second Mrs. Marriott, who was among the attendants of *Mirza* in " Mirza and Lindor." The name of Mr. Cunnington, who was *Gibson* in the comedy and the *Valet* in the ballet, was new, as was also that of Mr. Dickenson, who made " his first appearance on any stage " as *Saville.* Dickenson, whose real name was Dickson, was born in London in 1774, but went to Philadelphia at the age of twenty-one, where he was engaged by Mr. Powell during a visit of the Haymarket manager to the Quaker City. He married Miss Harrison and achieved success in Boston both as actor and manager. The important *debuts* of the opening comedy were those of Mr. Simpson as *Hardy* and Mrs. Simpson as *Mrs. Racket.* Mrs. Simpson was underlined as from the Theatre Royal, Bath ; but the Mrs.

Simpson who succeeded to the roles of Mrs. Siddons in 1782 and was the Bath heroine for a number of years was not this Mrs. Simpson. In the pantomime, besides Mr. Cunnington, were Mrs. Pick, Mr. and Mrs. Val, Mr. and Mrs. Lege and Mr. Francisquy. Mrs. Simpson's daughter, Miss Westray, who became Mrs. William B. Wood, made her American *debut* on the 28th as *Jacintha* in the "Suspicious Husband." The same night Mr. Barrett made his first appearance in the United States as *Ranger*. There were three Barretts on the English and Irish stage—Barrett, of the Haymarket, who played subordinate parts there for many years; "Jew" Barrett, best known in Dublin and so called because he loaned money to the actors at high interest; and Barrett, of Norwich. The last was Giles Leonard Barrett, now the leading player of the new Boston Haymarket. The first mention of him in a London paper

Mar. 15—Adopted Child . . . . . Birch
Deserter.
17—George Barnwell . . . . . Lillo
New French Deserter.
20—Every One Has His Fault
Mrs. Inchbald
Ghost . . . . . Mrs. Centlivre
27—Columbus . . . . . . Morton
Adopted Child.
29—Columbus.
Ghost.
Garden of Love.
31—Columbus.
Garden of Love.
Double Disguise.
April 3—Columbus.
Adopted Child.
5—Columbus.
Whims of Galatea . . Francisquy
7—Bunker Hill.
Prize.
10—Love in a Village . . Bickerstaff
Garden of Love.
17—West Point Preserved . . Brown
Agreeable Surprise.
19—West Point Preserved.
Prize.
21—West Point Preserved.
Padlock.
24—West Point Preserved.
Irish Widow . . . . . Garrick
(For the Sisters of the Author.)
26—West Point Preserved.
Harlequin Doctor.
28—Inkle and Yarico.
Lying Valet . . . . . . Garrick
May 3—He Would be a Soldier . . Pilon
Milliners.
Irishman in London . Macready
8—Rule a Wife and Have a Wife
Fletcher
Quality Binding . . . . . Rose
(Mr. Williamson's benefit.)
10—Bunker Hill.
Wrangling Lovers . . . . Lyon
Indian War Feast . . . . Burk
(Author's Night.)

May 15—Zorinski . . . . . . Morton
    Sportsman Outwitted.
    Romance of an Hour . . Kelly
    (Mr. Simpson's benefit.)
   17—Rule a Wife and Have a Wife.
    Clemency of Charlemagne.
    (Madame Val's benefit.)
   19 —Love Makes a Man . . . Cibber
    Clemency of Charlemagne.
    (Mrs. S. Powell's benefit.)
   22—Rage . . . . Reynolds
    Don Juan.
    (Mr. Francisquy's benefit.)
   24—Death of Louis XVI . . Preston
    Poor Jack.
    Son-in-Law . . . . . O'Keefe
    (Mr. Fawcett's benefit.)
   26—Three and the Deuce . . Hoare
    Destruction of the Bastile.
    Don Juan.
    (Mr. Barrett's benefit.)
   29—Werter . . . . . . Reynolds
    Mountaineers.
    Absent Man . . . . Bickerstaff
    (Mr. Taylor's benefit.)
   31—School for Scandal . . Sheridan
    Son-in-Law.
    (Brother Barrett's benefit.)
June 5—Zorinski.
    Adopted Child.
(Mrs. Simpson and Miss Westray's benefit.)
    7—Duplicity . . . . . . Holcroft
    Divorce . . . . Jackman
  (Mr. and Mrs. Hughes' benefit.)
   12—Child of Nature.
    Medea and Jason.
    All in Good Humor . . . Oulton
    (Mr. S. Powell's benefit.)
   14—Death of Louis XVI.
    Zorinski.
  (Fawcett and Taylor's benefit.)

was in July, 1785, when it was said that the Brunton, our Mrs. Merry, before her *entree* on the Covent Garden boards, would keep Stabich Fair in the most noble booth of Mr. Barrett. A letter from Norwich dated February 4th, 1788, speaks of Barrett as manager of the Norwich Theatre, and says he had engaged Palmer and Bannister and wanted Mrs. Siddons. In 1790 Barrett was engaged at the Royal Circus, where he made his first appearance on the 16th of April. In 1791 he appeared as *Ranger* at Derby, and afterward played at Nottingham and Margate the same year. " Charity here triumphs over taste," said a letter from Norwich, dated March 14th, 1792, " for Mrs. Barrett's benefit at the theatre overflowed, although her husband performed two principal characters." There is no reason to suppose that this sarcasm was aimed at Barrett as an actor. It is, perhaps, explained by the fact that Barrett married the daughter of a Norwich alderman, whom he had abandoned for Mrs. Belfield, an actress. Although Mrs. Barrett was originally announced in Boston as from Covent Garden and the Haymarket, I have not been able to find her name in the bills as Mrs. Belfield, Mrs. Rivers, or her real name, Mrs. Barrett; but she was an actress of experience in the English provinces, as is apparent from the fact that her American *debut* was announced to be made as *Mrs. Beverly* in the " Gamester" on the 2d of January, 1797. For some reason " She Stoops to Conquer" and the " Waterman " were substituted for the " Gamester " and the "Upholsterer," and in consequence she actually appeared in Boston for the first time two days later as *Mrs. Sullen* in the " Beaux' Stratagem." The change of bill had the effect of hastening the American *debut* of Mr. Williamson, the singer, who made his first appearance as *Tom Tug.* David Williamson was a singer of repute at Covent Garden, where he was first heard February 26th, 1791, as *Bob*, the miller, in the " Woodman." One of the critics said of him on this occasion that he had a sound, clear voice, and had only to learn a more skilful management of it to become an acquisition to the stage. He also appeared during his first season at Covent Garden as *Maleager* in " Alexander the Little," and the *Rustic* in " Rosina." Another first appearance in Boston that was deferred in consequence of the change of bill was that of Mrs. Allen, which was announced for *Termagant* in the " Upholsterer." Mrs. Allen had played in New York and Albany in 1785–6. She made her Boston *debut* on the 6th of January as *Lady Fallal* in " Variety." Miss Broadhurst, from the Philadelphia and New York theatres, was also engaged and made her first appearance in Boston on the 4th as *Leonora* in the " Padlock." There were no further introductions until the 25th, when Miss Eleanor Westray made her first appearance as the *Prince of Wales* in the " Battle of Hexham." She afterward became Mrs. Darley, the wife of the actor recorded in this volume as Darley, Jr.   When the " Road to Ruin " was given on the 10th of February, Mr. Fawcett, who had been with the company at the Boston Theatre, played *Sulky*, and Miss Gowen, who previously appeared as *Joan* in the " New French Deserter," had the little part of *Sophia*.   The other names that occur in the bills during the season, apart from the performers in the pantomimes, were Wilson, Sprague and Clough, who made themselves useful in minor roles.

Although the company was not to be compared with that at the Boston Theatre, the season was made a memorable one by the successful production of two dramas on Revolutionary themes.   The first of these was the " Battle of Bunker Hill," by John Burk, an Irishman, who had arrived in Boston early in 1796. A report was circulated soon after his arrival that a reward for his arrest had been offered by the

BUNKER HILL.

General Warren	Mr. Barrett
Colonel Prescott	Mr. S. Powell
Colonel Putnam	Mr. Hughes
Governor Gage	Mr. Marriott
Lord Percy	Mr. Williamson
General Howe	Mr. Dickenson
Colonel Harman	Mr. Fawcett
American Grenadier	Mr. Wilson
Colonel Abercrombie	Mr. Taylor
Elvira	Mrs. Barrett
Anna	Mrs. Hughes
Principal Mourner	Miss Broadhurst

British government, but the *Columbian Centinel* denied this, saying he had fled not from prosecution, but from persecution.   " He is a gentleman of talents and modesty," the *Centinel* added, " and his principles of government are rational and republican."   This " deplorable " play, as Dunlap calls it, was first produced on the 20th of February, 1797, and enjoyed the unprecedented run of nine nights during the season to crowded houses.   There is no difference of opinion as to the houses.   " They have brought out a new play," Williamson wrote in his letter to Hodgkinson, " called ' Bunker's Hill,' a tragedy, the most execrable of the Grub Street kind; but from its locality in title, the burning of Charlestown and peppering of the British, which are superadded to the tragedy in pantomime, to the utter disgrace of Boston theatricals, has brought full houses." The praise of the *Centinel* was as unstinted as Williamson's condemnation was sweeping and severe. "'Bunker Hill' is not less unrivalled as a play," said that journal, "than it has been unequalled in the history of military glory." The play was offered to Hodgkinson for production in a let-

BURK'S LETTER TO HODGKINSON.

Dear Sir,

From a wish that you should be possessed of my play as early as possible, I have preferred sending on the original copy rather than wait to have a fair one transcribed— where it was incomplete I have written and made it good, interspersing such remarks as, from seeing the effect in representation, appeared to me serviceable in getting it up. It was played seven nights successively, and on the last night was received with the same enthusiasm as on the first—it revived old scenes, and united all parts of the house. Mr. Powell intends it for a stock play, and it will be represented on all festivals—such as 4th July, 19th June, &c. It will be played here in a few nights again, immediately after Columbus. The lines marked by inverted commas are those spoken. The hill is raised gradually by boards extended from the stage to a bench. Three men should walk abreast in it, and the side where the English march up, should for the most part be turned towards the wings; on our hill there was room for eighteen or twenty men, and they were concealed by a board painted mud colour, and having two cannon painted on it—which board was three feet and a half high. The English marched in two divisions from one extremity of the stage, where they ranged, after coming from the wings, when they

come to the foot of the hill. The Americans fire—the English fire—six or seven of your men should be taught to fall—the fire should be frequent for some minutes. The English retire to the front of the stage—second line of English advance from the wing near the hill—firing commences — they are again beaten back—windows on the stage should be open to let out the smoak. All the English make the attack and mount the hill. After a brisk fire, the Americans leave works and meet them. Here is room for effect, if the scuffle be nicely managed. Sometimes the English falling back, sometimes the Americans—two or three Englishmen rolling down the hill. A square piece about nine feet high and five wide, having some houses and a meeting-house painted on fire, with flame and smoak issuing from it, should be raised two feet distance from the horizon scene at the back of your stage, the windows and doors cut out for transparencies—in a word, it should have the appearance of a town on fire. We had painted smoak suspended —it is raised at the each wing, and is intended to represent Charlestown, and is on a line with the hill, and where it is lowest. The fire should be played skilfully (this puts one in mind of Bottom playing Moonshine) behind this burning town, and the smoak to evaporate. When the curtain rises in the fifth, the appearance of the whole is

ter that Dunlap printed as " too great a curiosity " to be suppressed;
but Hodgkinson returned it, partly through the terms demanded by the
author, and finally refused it altogether, in consequence of Dunlap's

good—Charlestown on fire, the breastwork of wood, the Americans appearing over the works and the muzzles of their guns, the English and the American music, the attack of the hill, the falling of the English troops, Warren's half-descending the hill and animating the Americans, the smoak and confusion, all together produce an effect scarce credible. We had a scene of State-street—if you had one it would not be amiss—we used it instead of the scene of Boston Neck —it appears to me you need not be particular, but the hill and Charlestown on fire. We had English uniforms for men and officers. You can procure the coats of some company at New-York, which dresses in red. Small cannon should be fired during the battle, which continued with us for twelve or fifteen minutes. I am thus prolix that you may find the less difficulty in getting it up—it is not expensive, and will always be a valuable stock piece. I should not wonder if every person in New-York, and some miles around it, should go to see it represented. There will no doubt be some who will call in question your prudence in getting up this piece, as being not in favour of England. Those are blockheads, and know not the public opinion in America. Boston is as much divided as New York—party was forgotten in the representation of it. Others there are who will endeavour to prejudice you against its merit; of them I shall say nothing. You have the play and can judge for yourself—my reason for mentioning the latter description of men is, that a man from Boston, who pretends to criticise without knowing how to *spell*, has been industrious in depreciating the value of my piece in Boston, and I conceived it not improbable that he would act in the same manner in New-York. When he found it

had succeeded, he ascribed its success alone to its locality. This man took a letter to you from Mr. Barrett. I send you the prologue and elegy.

After consulting Mr. Barrett, who was delicate in advising, lest he should be thought partial to one interest or the other, I have concluded to charge you one hundred guineas for the copy, seventy of which I request you will send to Mr. Barrett immediately on receipt of the piece, the remaining thirty on the fourth night of representation. Mr. Barrett thinks it will run ten nights in succession at New-York. I think not of printing it for one year, when I do I shall dedicate it to the President. Mr. Bates has sent on to me for a copy. I am in treaty with Mr. Wignell. The terms shall not be lower than with you. I shall send you on from time to time such pantomimes and entertainments as I shall arrange, on reasonable terms. I have three at present, which I shall send on when you please, as cheap as you can get a pirated copy of a farce. My new tragedy, entitled Joan of Arc, or the Maid of Orleans, is ready for representation. Excuse this wretched scrawl, it has been written too hastily.

JOHN BURK.

We had our hill on the left side of the stage—the painting of Charlestown on fire should not be seen till the fifth act. If there is anything you would wish to be informed on further, by directing a line to me, you shall receive the speediest answer. As I look on this only as the *basis* of a future negotiation, I shall not be averse to abate something of my demand, if you think it high, though I am tolerably certain you will clear four thousand dollars in its run only.

opposition, to whom its scenic effects were an abomination, as is clearly indicated by his sneer—"how to play a tragedy." The scenery, by the way, was by Audin, and the dirge in the transformation was sung by Miss Broadhurst as the principal mourner, assisted by Mrs. Pick, Miss Elizabeth Westray—who became successively Mrs. Villiers and Mrs. Twaits—Miss Gowen, Miss Westray and Miss Eleanor Westray as mourners. Burk made $2,000 by the production in Boston. The play was printed, but the dedication was to Aaron Burr, not to the President, as the author intended. As a play it has little literary or dramatic merit.

Two months after the production of "Bunker Hill" another American play, "West Point Preserved," was brought out at the Boston Haymarket. This piece was written by an American, "the late William Brown, well known to amateurs of science and poesy." As Mr. Brown did not live to see the production of his drama, the proceeds of the "author's night" were given to his sisters. Dunlap does not mention this production at all, notwithstanding it was played six nights in succession and antedated his "André" by a year. Only the prologue, which was spoken by Mr. Barrett, was printed.

WEST POINT PRESERVED.

Washington	Mr. Barrett
La Fayette	Mr. Taylor
Arnold	Mr. Powell
Greene	Mr. S. Powell
Knox	Mr. Fawcett
Hamilton	Mr. Hughes
Robertson	Mr. Dickenson
Humphreys	Mr. Clough
Volunteer	Mr. Simpson
Messenger	Mr. Sprague
Major André	Mr. Williamson
Mrs. Arnold	Mrs. Simpson
Louisa	Miss Gowen
Honoria	Mrs. S. Powell

PROLOGUE.

When first indignant of the wrongs they bore,
Your valiant sires explor'd this distant shore,
Thro' pathless oceans undismayed they pass'd,
And found fair Freedom in the boundless waste.
From meagre famine, and the savage foe,
Their hardy souls experienced many a woe;
Till thro' the devious wilds they forc'd their way,

Mr. Powell displayed as much vigor in bringing out new English pieces and pieces new to Boston as he showed tact in the production of American dramas, but his selections did not always approve his judgment.   His first new piece, Richard Griffith's "Variety," is an

And op'd the darkling forest to the day.
   Here each new sun their growing power
      beheld,
To the wild wood succeeds the fertile field;
Before the hamlet and the town remove
The thorny thicket and the gloomy grove;
From distant climes adventurous barques resort,
And various nations crowd each rising port.
   But still, the arts of polished life unknown,
Each formal visage wore a gloomy frown;
In bigot bonds th' imprisoned thought confined,
Stern superstition held the captive mind.
Few pleasures were allowed to soften toil,
'Twas sin to laugh, and hardly safe to smile.
The buskined muse they never could endure,
Perhaps too rigid, and perhaps too poor.
   But when fair science spread her radiant
      light,
Dark superstition sought her native night.
Then, first each breast immortal Shakspere
      fired;
All read the scenes—to view all they desired.
Hence into being rose Columbia's stage,
The cherished offspring of a liberal age.
    And now since commerce to the genial
      gale
Spreads o'er each watery world her wealthy
      sail,
On canvas pinions circles every zone,
To make the treasures of a world your own,
These splendid seats your attic taste has
      rais'd,
Are nobly patronized, as justly prais'd;
Here youth and age their leisure hours employ,

On scenes of useful woe or harmless joy.
   Born on Columbia's shore, a bard, this
      night,
Plumes his young wing, and tempts a daring
      flight;
With native notes presumes to please the ear,
And force from patriot eyes the tender tear.
Deep in your minds the well-known tale's
      engraved,—
A hero sacrificed—a traitor saved.
From disappointed justice Arnold flies,
And oh! hard fate! the noble André dies,
Though pleas'd that heaven preserved th'
      important post,
The prized palladium of Columbia's coast,
Not sternest veterans e'er the tale relate,
But pour a pitying tear on André's fate.
   Be yours this night to rear, with fost'ring
      hand,
The rare production of your native land;
With just applause the toils of genius crown,
The scene, the fable and the bard your own,
Thus warm'd in approbation's ripening ray,
Shall future bards their scenic power display,—
Your venial faults, your glorious deeds rehearse,
With comic wit or tragic charm of verse.
Columbian Shaksperes shall adorn the age—
Columbian Garricks grace Columbia's stage.
Then shall the full resounding trump of fame,
To earth's remotest bounds your praise proclaim;
On distant shores your envied sons declare
The first in genius, freedom, arts and war—
Till e'en proud Europe deign to learn from
      you,
And the Old World be lessoned by the New.

illustration. It was without plot or characterization, and had failed at Drury Lane fifteen years before. The second of his new pieces, Morton's comedy, the " Way to Get Married," had been produced at the Boston Theatre on the night that the Haymarket opened. The cast was not printed with the advertisements. Powell's production of Holcroft's " Man of Ten Thousand " anticipated its first performance by Williamson's company by a week. Then came MacNally's farce,

NEW BOSTON PRODUCTIONS—CASTS.

ABSENT MAN.

Dr. Gruel . . . . . Mr. Hughes
Welldon . . . . Mr. Dickenson
Capt. Slang . . . . Mr. Fawcett
Coxcomb . . . . . . Mr. Clough
Frank . . . . Mr. Simpson
Robin . . . . . . Mr. S. Powell
Shatterbrain . . . . Mr. Taylor
Mrs. Junkett . . . Mrs. Simpson
Miss Frolic . . . . Mrs. Hughes
Landlady . . . . . . Mrs. Allen
Flavia . . . . . . Miss Westray

COLUMBUS.

Harry Herbert . . . Mr. Barrett
Alonzo . . . . . . Mr. S. Powell
Dr. Dolores . . . . Mr. Simpson
Bribon . . . . Mr. Hughes
Roldan . . . . Mr. Marriott
Valverdo . . . . . . Mr. Wilson
Moscovo . . . . Mr. Cunnington
Columbus . . . . . Mr. Taylor
Orozimbo . . . . Mr. Williamson
Solasco . . . . . . Mr. Fawcett
Catulpo . . . . . Mr. Dickenson
Cuto . . . . Mr. Sprague
Nelti . . . . . Miss E. Westray
Cora . . . . Mrs. Barrett

DUPLICITY.

Mr. Osborn . . . . Mr. Barrett
Old Vandervelt . . . Mr. Hughes
Sir Hornet Armstrong, Mr. Kenny
Squire Turnbull . . Mr. Simpson
Timid . . . . . . Mr. S. Powell
Scrip . . . . Mr. Taylor
Sir Harry Portland
        Mr. Williamson

Miss Barbara . . . Mrs. Hughes
Melissa . . . . . Miss Westray
Mrs. Trip . . . . . . Mrs. Allen
Clara Forrester . . Mrs. Barrett

LOUIS XVI.

Louis . . . . Mr. Barrett
Orleans . . . . . . Mr. Simpson
Peasant . . . . . Mr. Dickenson
Sauterre . . . . . Mr. Hughes
Marat . . . . Mr. Fawcett
Robespierre . . . . Mr. Taylor
Pelitier . . . . . Mr. S. Powell
Cleri . . . . Mr. Clough
Dauphin . . . . . Miss Westray
Princess Royal . Mrs. S. Powell
Princess Elizabeth, Mrs. Simpson
Queen . . . . . . Mrs. Barrett

MAN OF TEN THOUSAND.

Torrington . . . . Mr. S. Powell
Hairbrain . . . . . . Mr. Powell
Sir Pertinax Pitiful . Mr. Fawcett
Lord Laroon . . . . Mr. Taylor
Maj. Rampart . . . Mr. Marriott
Consol . . . . Mr. Hughes
Curfue . . . . . Mr. Dickenson
Hudson . . . . . . Mr. Wilson
Herbert . . . . . . Mr. Simpson
Lady Taunton . . . Mrs. Hughes
Annabel . . . . . Miss Westray
Girl . . . . Mrs. Marriott
Olivia . . . . . Mrs. S. Powell

ROMANCE OF AN HOUR.

Sir Hector . . . . . Mr. Hughes
Col. Ormsby . . . . Mr. Fawcett
Brownlow . . . . Mr. Dickenson

Orson . . . . . . Mr. S. Powell
Pillage . . . . Mr. Clough
Bussora . . . . . . Mr. Simpson
Lady Di . . . . . Mrs. Simpson
Jenny . . . . Miss Gowen
Zeliday . . . . . Miss Westray

THREE AND THE DEUCE.

Three Singles . . . Mr. Barrett
Taffline . . . . . . Mrs. Barrett

VARIETY.

Com. Broadside . . Mr. Marriott
Capt. Seafort . . Mr. Williamson
Sir Tim. Valerian . . Mr. Hughes
Lord Frankly . . . . Mr. Taylor
Major Seafort . . . . Mr. Powell
Charles Steady . . Mr. Dickenson
Sir Fred'k Fallal . . Mr. Wilson
Mr. Mosely . . Mr. S. Powell
Harriet Temple . Mrs. S. Powell
Lady Fallal . . . . . Mrs. Allen
Lady Frankly . . Mrs. Hughes
Mrs. Buckle . . . . . Mrs. Pick
Lady Courtney . . Mrs. Simpson

ZORINSKI.

Zorinski . . . . . . Mr. Barrett
Cassimer . . . . . . Mr. Taylor
Witski . . . . . . Mr. Simpson
O'Carrah . . . . . Mr. Fawcett
Radzano . . . . . Mr. S. Powell
Amalekite . . . . . Mr. Hughes
Rodansko . . . . Mr. Dickenson
Nacho . . . . Mr. Clough
Zarus . . . . . Mr. Williamson
Winifred . . . . . . Mrs. Barrett
Rachel . . . . Miss E. Westray
Rosalia . . . . . Mrs. S. Powell

"Retaliation," originally acted at Covent Garden in 1782. It was played in Boston only once, and there is no cast of it. The success of the season among the English pieces was Morton's "Columbus," which was played five nights in succession, rivalling the two American dramas in popularity. It may be that the piece called "Columbus" which Hodgkinson produced at Hartford in 1795 was "Tammany" under another name. In that case, this was the first production north of the Delaware. This so-called historical play was originally acted at Covent Garden in 1792 with great success. The episode of *Cora* and *Alonzo*, which was very pleasing, was taken from Marmontel's "Incas." Mr. Morton scarcely succeeded in the introduction of the manners and customs of the native Peruvians and Mexicans into his play, but the characters of *Harry Herbert, Dr. Dolores* and *Bribon* greatly contributed to the success of the piece. Another of Morton's plays, "Zorinski,"

PANTOMIMES AND BALLETS—CASTS.

CLEMENCY OF CHARLEMAGNE.

Charlemagne	Mr. Val
Rowland	Mr. Spinacuta
Renault	Mr. Francisquy
Alard	Mr. Fawcett
Guichard	Mr. Sevens
Richard	Mr. Dickenson
Clara	Mad. Val

COOPER.

Martin	Mr. Val
Cosin	Mr. Francisquy
Father Cap	Mr. Dubois
Bailiff	Mr. Sevens
Miller	Mr. Amean
Fanchette	Mad. Val

GARDEN OF LOVE.

Tircio	Mr. Francisquy
Palemont	Mr. Bowen
Alexis	Mr. Sevens
Cupid	Master Shaffer
Collette	Miss Gowen

Finette	Mad. Sevens
Estelle	Mad. Val

MIRZA AND LINDOR.

Mondor	Mr. Val
Commander	Mr. Lege
Valet	Mr. Cunnington
Mrs. Mondor	Mrs. Pick
Mondor's Friend	Mr. Francisquy
Mirza	Mad. Val
Negro Woman	Mad. Lege

NEW FRENCH DESERTER.

Alexis	Mr. Francisquy
Jean Louis	Mr. Powell
Bertrand	Mr. Lege
Montariel	Mr. Dubois
General	Mr. Taylor
Mayor	Mr. S. Powell
Aid	Mr. Marriott
Louisa	Mad. Val
Joan	Miss Gowen
Martin	Mad. Lege
Mad. de Clairville	Mrs. Pick

SPORTSMAN OUTWITTED.

Damon	Mr. Francisquy
Squire	Mr. Val
Phœbe	Mad. Val

WHIMS OF GALATEA.

Paris	Mr. Francisquy
Dorilas	Mr. Borier
Alexis	Mr. Sevens
Strephon	Mr. Dickenson
Palemon	Mr. Val
Dametus	Mr. Sprague
Cupid	Master Shaffer
Sylvia	Mrs. Pick
Laura	Mad. Sevens
Phyllis	Miss Gowen
Pastora	Miss Harrison
Phillida	Young Lady
Galatea	Mad. Val

WOOD CUTTERS.

William	Master Shaffer
Joseph	Master Gowen

was also produced, this one certainly for the first time in America. It was founded on the then recent abduction of the King of Poland, Stanislaus being introduced under the name of *Casimer*. It was originally acted at the little theatre in the Haymarket in 1795. "Zorinski" was produced for Mr. Simpson's benefit, whose bill also included Hugh Kelly's "Romance of an Hour." The production of Preston's "Louis XVI" was due to Mr. Fawcett, who had it "altered by a citizen of Boston." For his first benefit Mr. Barrett brought out Prince Hoare's comic drama, the "Three and the Deuce." It was then a recent Haymarket success, and turned upon the close resemblance of three brothers. The remaining pieces new to Boston were Holcroft's "Duplicity" and Jackman's "Divorce."

This season was remarkable for the number of pantomimes and ballets that was produced, beginning with "Mirza and Lindor" on the opening night. Nearly all these pieces were of French origin, the noteworthy exceptions being the "Siege of Quebec," acted at Covent Garden as early as 1760, but of which there is no Boston cast, and the "Indian War Feast," by Burk, produced on his last benefit night, but also without the cast. A feature was made of the appearance of a Boston boy, only 8 years old, as *Thomas* in the "Wood Cutters."

The casts of the more important of the familiar pieces are given as the best means of showing the strength of the company and the

HAYMARKET CASTS OF FAMILIAR PIECES.

AGREEABLE SURPRISE.

Sir Felix	Mr. Hughes
Compton	Mr. Williamson
Eugene	Mr. Dickenson
Chicane	Mr. Marriott
John	Mr. S. Powell
Lingo	Mr. Simpson
Laura	Miss Broadhurst
Mrs. Cheshire	Mrs. Allen
Fringe	Miss Westray
Cowslip	Mrs. Pick

ALEXANDER THE GREAT.

Alexander	Mr. Barrett
Hephestion	Mr. Williamson
Lysimachus	Mr. Hughes
Cassander	Mr. Taylor
Polyperchon	Mr. S. Powell
Perdiccas	Mr. Dickenson
Clytus	Mr. Marriott
Thessalus	Mr. Wilson
Eumenes	Mr. Smith
Statira	Mrs. S. Powell
Sysigambis	Mrs. Allen
Parisatis	Mrs. Hughes
Roxana	Mrs. Barrett

initial work of actors and actresses, whose names are a part of the history of the American theatre. Mr. Barrett, it will be observed, had

HAYMARKET CASTS OF FAMILIAR PIECES.

ANIMAL MAGNETISM.

Doctor . . . . . . Mr. Simpson
La Fleur . . . . . . Mr. Powell
De Lancy . . . Mr. Williamson
Jeffrey . . . . . . Mr. S. Powell
Constance . . . . Miss Westray
Lisette . . . . Mrs. Pick

BATTLE OF HEXHAM.

Gondibert . . . . . Mr. Barrett
Prince of Wales, Miss E. Westray
La Varenne . . . . . Mr. Taylor
Fool . . . . Mr. S. Powell
Barton . . . . . . Mr. Marriott
Drummer . . . . Mr. Dickenson
Fifer . . . . Mr. Wilson
Robber . . . . . Mr. Williamson
Corporal . . . . . . Mr. Hughes
Gregory . . . . . . Mr. Simpson
Adeline . . . . . Mrs. S. Powell
Queen . . . . . . Mrs. Simpson

BEAUX' STRATAGEM.

Archer . . . . Mr. Barrett
Aimwell . . . . . . Mr. Taylor
Boniface . . . . . . Mr. Hughes
Gibbet . . . . . Mr. Williamson
Freeman . . . . . . Mr. Wilson
Foigard . . . . . . Mr. Marriott
Scrub . . . . Mr. Simpson
Sullen . . . . . . Mr. Dickenson
Lady Bountiful . . . Mrs. Powell
Dorinda . . . . . Mrs. Hughes
Cherry . . . . . . Miss Westray
Gipsey . . . . . . Miss Harrison
Mrs. Sullen . . . . Mrs. Barrett

DEUCE IS IN HIM.

Col. Tamper . . . Mr. S. Powell
Maj. Belford . . . . Mr. Fawcett
Dr. Prattle . . . . . Mr. Powell
Mad. Florival . . . Mrs. Hughes
Bell . . . . Miss Westray
Emily . . . . . . Mrs. Simpson

EVERY ONE HAS HIS FAULT.

Norland . . . . . . Mr. Marriott
Sir Robert . . . Mr. Williamson
Solus . . . . . . Mr. Hughes

Harmony . . . . . Mr. Fawcett
Placid . . . . . . Mr. Simpson
Hammond . . . . . Mr. Wilson
Porter . . . . . . Mr. Dickenson
Edward . . . . . . Miss Gowen
Irwin . . . . . . Mr. S. Powell
Miss Wooburn . . Mrs. Hughes
Mrs. Placid . . . Mrs. Simpson
Miss Spinster . . . . Mrs. Powell
Lady Eleanor . . Mrs. S. Powell

GEORGE BARNWELL.

Barnwell . . . . Mr. S. Powell
Thorowgood . . . . Mr. Marriott
Uncle . . . . . . Mr. Fawcett
Blunt . . . . Mr. Hughes
Trueman . . . . . . Mr. Taylor
Maria . . . . . . Mrs. Hughes
Lucy . . . . Mrs. Allen
Millwood . . . . Mrs. S. Powell

GHOST.

Sir Jeffrey . . . . . Mr. Fawcett
Capt. Constant . . . Mr. Taylor
Trusty . . . . . . Mr. Hughes
Clinch . . . . . . Mr. S. Powell
Roger . . . . Mr. Powell
Belinda . . . . . Miss Westray
Dolly . . . . Mrs. Hughes

HE WOULD BE A SOLDIER.

Col. Talbot . . . . Mr. Fawcett
Sir Oliver Oldstock . Mr. Hughes
Capt. Crevelt . . . . Mr. Taylor
Count Pierpont . . . Mr. Powell
Mandeville . . . Mr. Dickenson
Amber . . . . . . Mr. S. Powell
Johnson . . . . Mr. Williamson
Wilkins . . . . . . Mr. Clough
Caleb . . . . Mr. Simpson
Lady Oldstock . . . . Mrs. Allen
Harriet . . . . . . Miss Westray
Mrs. Wilkins . . . Mrs. Simpson
Betty . . . . Miss Gowen
Nancy . . . . . . Miss Harrison
Charlotte . . . . Mrs. S. Powell

IRISH WIDOW.

Sir Patrick O'Neal . Mr. Barrett

Kecksey . . . . . . Mr. Powell
Bates . . . . Mr. Fawcett
Thomas . . . . . . Mr. Simpson
Nephew . . . . . Mr. Dickenson
Footman . . . . . . Mr. Clough
Whittle . . . . . . Mr. Hughes
Mrs. Brady . . . . Mrs. Barrett

IRISHMAN IN LONDON.

Mr. Frost . . . . . Mr. Hughes
Colloony . . . . . Mr. Fawcett
Edward . . . . Mr. Williamson
Capt. Seymour . . Mr. Dickenson
Cymon . . . . . Mr. S. Powell
Delany . . . . . . Mr. Simpson
Caroline . . . . . Mrs. Hughes
Harriett . . . . . Miss Westray
Cubba . . . . . . Mrs. Simpson

LOVE MAKES A MAN.

Don Lewis . . . . . Mr. Barrett
Don Antonio . . . Mr. Simpson
Don Charino . . . Mr. Hughes
Carlos . . . . Mr. Fawcett
Don Duart . . . . . Mr. Taylor
Sancho . . . . . Mr. Williamson
Don Manuel . . . Mr. Dickenson
Governor . . . . . . Mr. Clough
Don Dismallo . . Mr. S. Powell
Louisa . . . . Mrs. Barrett
Elvira . . . . . . Miss Westray
Honoria . . . . . Miss Harrison
Angelina . . . . Mrs. S. Powell

MERCHANT OF VENICE.

Shylock . . . . . . Mr. Barrett
Bassanio . . . . Mr. Williamson
Gratiano . . . . . . Mr. Taylor
Launcelot . . . . . Mr. Simpson
Old Gobbo . . . . . Mr. Hughes
Solanio . . . . . . Mr. Wilson
Lorenzo . . . . . Mr. Dickenson
Leonardo . . . . . . Mr. Smith
Antonio . . . . . . Mr. Marriott
Jessica . . . . Miss Broadhurst
Nerissa . . . . . . Mrs. Hughes
Portia . . . . Mrs. Barrett

MOUNTAINEERS.

Octavian . . . . . . Mr. Taylor

the lead in high comedy, and occasionally appeared in what was called, in the stilted language of the time, the tragic walk. Among his parts

HAYMARKET CASTS OF FAMILIAR PIECES.

Bulcazin . . . . Mr. Williamson
Virolet . . . . . . Mr. S. Powell
Kilmallock . . . . Mr. Fawcett
Roque . . . . Mr. Hughes
Sadi . . . . Mr. Simpson
Floranthe . . . . . Mrs. Hughes
Zorayda . . . . . Mrs. S. Powell
Agnes . . . . . Miss E. Westray

PADLOCK.

Diego . . . . Mr. Simpson
Leander . . . . Mr. Williamson
Mungo . . . . Mr. Powell
Ursula . . . . . . Mrs. Powell
Leonora . . . . Miss Broadhurst

QUAKER.

Steady . . . . . . Mr. Simpson
Solomon . . . . . Mr. Powell
Easy . . . . . . Mr. Dickenson
Lubin . . . . . Mr. Williamson
Floretta . . . . . . Mrs. Hughes
Cecilia . . . . Mrs. Powell
Gillian . . . . . Miss Broadhurst

QUALITY BINDING.

Mr. Lovel . . . . . Mr. Fawcett
Col. Modish . . . . Mr. Taylor
Lord Simper . . . Mr. S. Powell
Sir William Wealthy, Mr. Simpson
John . . . . . . Mr. Dickenson
William . . . . . . Mr. Clough
Plainwell . . . . . . Mr. Barrett
Mrs. Lovel . . . . Mrs. Hughes

RAGE.

Gingham . . . . . . Mr. Barrett
Darnly . . . . . Mr. S. Powell
Sir George Gauntlet, Mr. Fawcett
Hon. Mr. Savage . Mr. Simpson
Sir Paul Perpetual . Mr. Hughes
Flash . . . . Mr. Dickenson
Sig. Cygnet . . . Mr. Francisquy
Lady Sarah . . . . Mrs. Barrett
Clara Sedley . . . Miss Westray
Mrs. Darnly . . Mrs. S. Powell

ROAD TO RUIN.

Harry Dornton . . . Mr. Taylor

Old Dornton . . . Mr. Marriott
Silky . . . . Mr. Hughes
Sulky . . . . Mr. Fawcett
Milford . . . . . Mr. Dickenson
Mr. Smith . . . . . Mr. Wilson
Officer . . . . Mr. Smith
Goldfinch . . . . Mr. S. Powell
Widow Warren . . . Mrs. Allen
Jenny . . . . Mrs. Hughes
Mrs. Ledger . . . Mrs. Marriott
Sophia . . . . . . Miss Gowen

RULE A WIFE AND HAVE A WIFE.

Duke . . . . Mr. Taylor
Copper Captain . . . Mr. Barrett
Don Juan . . . . . Mr. Fawcett
Cacafojo . . . . . Mr. Hughes
Sancho . . . . Mr. Clough
Alonzo . . . . . Mr. Dickenson
Old Woman . . . Mr. Simpson
Maid . . . . . . Mr. S. Powell
Leon . . . . . . Mr. Williamson
Margaretta . . . Mrs. S. Powell
Altea . . . . . . Mrs. Simpson
Clara . . . . . . Miss Westray
Lady . . . . . . Miss Harrison
Estifania . . . . . . Mrs. Barrett

SCHOOL FOR SCANDAL.

Sir Peter Teazle . . Mr. Simpson
Sir Oliver . . . . Mr. Fawcett
Charles Surface . . . Mr. Barrett
Joseph Surface . Mr. Williamson
Crabtree ⎫ . . . . Mr. Hughes
Moses ⎭
Sir Benjamin . . . Mr. S. Powell
Rowley . . . . . Mr. Dickenson
Snake . . . . Mr. Clough
Mrs. Candour . . Mrs. Simpson
Lady Sneerwell . . Mrs. Hughes
Maria . . . . . . Miss Westray
Lady Teazle . . . . Mrs. Barrett

SHE STOOPS TO CONQUER.

Young Marlow . . Mr. S. Powell
Hardcastle . . . . . Mr. Hughes
Hastings . . . . . . Mr. Taylor
Sir Charles Marlow, Mr. Marriott
Diggory . . . . . Mr. Dickenson

Tony Lumpkin . . . Mr. Simpson
Mrs. Hardcastle . Mrs. Simpson
Miss Hardcastle . Mrs. S. Powell
Miss Neville . . . Mrs. Hughes
Pimple . . . . . . Mrs. Marriott

SUSPICIOUS HUSBAND.

Ranger . . . . . . Mr. Barrett
Strickland . . . . . Mr. Marriott
Frankly . . . . . . Mr. Taylor
Bellamy . . . . . Mr. Dickenson
Jack Meggot . . . Mr. Powell
Buck . . . . . Young American
Tester . . . . . . Mr. Simpson
Servant . . . . Mr. Cunnington
Mrs. Strickland . . Mrs. Simpson
Clarinda . . . . . Mrs. S. Powell
Jacintha . . . . . Miss Westray
Lucette . . . . Mrs. Pick
Landlady . . . . . Mrs. Marriott
Milliner . . . . . Miss Harrison

UPHOLSTERER.

Quidnunc . . . . . Mr. Hughes
Razor . . . . . . Mr. Simpson
Pamphlet . . . . . Mr. Powell
Buck . . . . Mr. Wilson
Belman . . . . . . Mr. Taylor
Rovewell . . . . . Mr. Marriott
Feeble . . . . . . Mr. Dickenson
Harriet . . . . . . Miss Westray
Termagant . . . . . Mrs. Allen

WATERMAN.

Tom Tug . . . . Mr. Williamson
Bundle . . . . . . Mr. Hughes
Robin . . . . Mr. Simpson
Mrs. Bundle . . . . Mrs. Powell
Wilhelmina . . . . . Mrs. Pick

WERTER.

Werter . . . . . . Mr. Barrett
Sebastian . . . . Mr. Fawcett
Lathrop . . . . . Mr. Dickenson
Albert . . . . Mr. Williamson
Laura . . . . . . Miss Harrison
Charlotte . . . . Mrs. S. Powell

not included in these casts were *Sheva* in the " Jew," *Don Juan* in the pantomime of that name, *Henry Dubois* in the " Destruction of the Bastile," and *Signor Arionelli* in the " Son-in-Law" for his last benefit. On that occasion Mrs. S. Powell delivered a poetic address on the immortal Washington. Miss Broadhurst was, of course, *Rosina* in Mrs. Brooke's opera, and *Wowski* in " Inkle and Yarico," with Mrs. S. Powell as *Yarico*. When " Columbus " was repeated on the 3d of April, Mr. Powell played *Harry Herbert*, and Mrs. S. Powell was *Cora*. Madame Spinacuta made her only appearance during the season as *Donna Anna* in " Don Juan " for Mr. Francisquy's benefit. Mrs. Barrett played the heroines to the detriment of Mrs. S. Powell, and Miss Westray made her mark in walking ladies. But the success of the company as a whole was not great; and Mr. Powell, according to Mr. Williamson of the Boston Theatre, was not always able to pay salaries. The result was that he gave up his lease at the close of the season, and the company was scattered. Mr. Barrett played *Tangent* and Mrs. Barrett *Julia Faulkner* in the " Way to Get Married " at Newport on the 22d of November, 1797, in which they were assisted by Mr. Hallam as *Dashall*, Mr. Simpson as *Toby Allspice*, Mrs. Simpson as *Lady Sorrel*, Miss Westray as *Clementina*, and Miss Eliza Westray as *Fanny*. Miss Westray played *Cowslip*, Miss Eleanor Westray *Laura*, and Miss Eliza Westray *Fringe* in the " Agreeable Surprise " the same night. The Boston Haymarket having passed into the control of Mr. Hodgkinson, who gave a Summer and Autumn season, the Simpsons and the Misses Westray appeared with the New York company, as did also Mr. and Mrs. S. Powell, Mr. Fawcett and Mrs. Pick. The house was afterward used as a Summer theatre until it was finally abandoned.

CHAPTER XIX.

A RHODE ISLAND INTERLUDE.

HARPER AGAIN AT PROVIDENCE AND NEWPORT—THE PROVIDENCE
SEASON—BOSTON PLAYERS THE PERFORMERS—MRS. ALLEN—
HARPER'S SECOND COMPANY—A QUEER ASSORTMENT—MR. AND
MRS. TUBBS—MISS ARNOLD'S FIRST APPEARANCE.

AFTER Mr. Harper relinquished the acting management of the Boston Theatre he returned to Rhode Island and gave brief seasons at Providence and Newport in the Summer of 1796. The Providence engagement began on the 6th of June and lasted far into September, the brief Newport season, which was for five nights only, being confined to the last week in August and the first week in September. Previous to Harper's return and for a few nights after his departure the Newport Theatre was occupied by the Francisquy troupe of pantomimists, who presented harlequinades at intervals from the 7th of July to the 7th of September. The company included, besides its ordinary complement of Frenchmen, Mr. and Mrs. Durang, Mr. Roberts, Mr. Tompkins, Mr. Hallam, from Virginia, and Madame Gardie. On the last night of the season, for Mr. Durang's benefit, these bold players attempted the " Beaux' Stratagem " and " Poor Soldier," Durang playing *Archer*, and Mrs. Durang *Cherry* and *Kathleen*. While this feeble force was entertaining the Newport amusement lovers, Harper gave performances three times a week at Providence with a part of the company that had been at the Boston Theatre under his stage direction.

On his opening night in Providence Mr. Harper spoke an Occasional Address, and produced as the play of the evening Mrs. Cowley's comedy, " A Bold Stroke for a Husband." The afterpiece was not named in the advertisement in the Providence *Gazette*. A complete list of the performances is of course unattainable, but this is not so much to be regretted, as the plays and the players and consequently the casts were in the main repetitions of the previous season at the Boston Theatre. Singing between the pieces, by Miss Sully and Mrs. Pick, was often a feature. The only new name that occurred in the bills during the season was that of Mrs. Allen, who appeared as the *Widow Warren* in the " Road to Ruin " for Mr. Taylor's benefit. She was announced as from the theatres of New York, Philadelphia and Quebec. Mrs. Allen also played *Patty* in " Inkle and Yarico " at Newport. I give casts of six pieces not included in those of the Boston repertory, four of which were played at Providence and two at Newport. In a few

LIST OF PERFORMANCES—*Providence.*

1796.

June 6—Bold Stroke for a Husband
                          Mrs. Cowley
     13—Jew . . . . Cumberland
         Village Lawyer . . . Macready
     20—Better Late Than Never, Andrews
         Who's the Dupe ? . Mrs. Cowley
     27—Farm House . . . . . Kemble
         Two Philosophers.
         Farmer . . . . O'Keefe
July 4—Richard III . . . . . Shakspere
         Monody to the Chiefs.
     11—Mountaineers . . . . Colman, Jr
         Wrangling Lovers . . . Lyon
     18—Belle's Stratagem . Mrs. Cowley
         Ghost . . . . . Mrs. Centlivre
Aug. 8—Road to Ruin . . . . Holcroft
         Son-in-Law . . . . O'Keefe
         (Mr. Taylor's benefit.)
     11—Rivals . . . . Sheridan
         Catharine and Petruchio
                          Shakspere
         (Mrs. S. Powell's benefit.)
Sept. 10—Midnight Hour . Mrs. Inchbald
         Oscar and Malvina.

Newport.

Aug. 24—Grecian Daughter . . . Murphy
         Spoiled Child . . . . Bickerstaff
     31—Such Things Are . Mrs. Inchbald
         Inkle and Yarico . . Colman, Jr

of the casts there were changes in consequence of the absence of the Williamsons, Mrs. Arnold and Mrs. Baker. Among these Mrs. Hughes played *Aura* in the " Farm House " instead of Mrs. Williamson ; Mr. Harper succeeded Mr. Williamson as *Sheva* in the " Jew," and Mrs. S. Powell was *Eliza* instead of Mrs. Arnold ; Taylor was *Mervin*, Kenny *Draco*, Harper *Carrol*, and Mrs. Harper *Malvina* in " Oscar and Malvina " instead respectively of Harper, Taylor, Williamson and Mrs. Williamson ; Mrs. Harper was *Little Pickle* in the " Spoiled Child," and Hamilton was *Snarl*, Hughes *Sheepface*, and Mrs. Ashton *Mrs. Scout* in the " Village Lawyer " instead respectively of Taylor, Villiers and Mrs. Baker. When the season closed, the Boston players returned, but Mr. and Mrs. Harper, however, remained in Rhode Island.

It was not until the Spring of 1797 that Mr. Harper felt himself strong enough to begin giving regular performances in the two Rhode

PROVIDENCE AND NEWPORT CASTS—1796.

Providence.

MIDNIGHT HOUR.

General . . . . . . Mr. Hughes
Marquis . . . . . Mr. S. Powell
Nicholas . . . . . . Mr. Ashton
Ambrose . . . . . . Mr. Clarke
Matthias . . . . . . Mr. Kenny
Sebastian . . . . . Mr. Taylor
Julia . . . . Mrs. Hughes
Cicely . . . . Mrs. Ashton
Flora . . . . Mrs. Pick

ROAD TO RUIN.

Mr. Dornton . . . . Mr. Kenny
Goldfinch . . . . . Mr. S. Powell
Sulky . . . . Mr. Harper
Milford . . . . Mr. Ashton
Silky . . . . Mr. Hughes
Mr. Smith . . . . Mr. Ratcliffe
Jacob . . . . Mr. Clarke
Harry Dornton . . . Mr. Taylor
Mrs. Warren . . . . Mrs. Allen
(Her first appearance.)
Jenny . . . . . . Mrs. Hughes

Providence.

Mrs. Ledger . . . . Mrs. Ashton
Milliner . . . . . Miss Harrison
Sophia . . . . . Mrs. S. Powell

SON-IN-LAW.

Cranky . . . . Mr. Kenny
Vinegar . . . . . . Mr. Hughes
Bouquet . . . . . . Mr. Harper
Orator Mum . . . Mr. S. Powell
Idle . . . . Mr. Ashton
Bowket . . . . . Mr. Taylor
Sig. Arionelli . . . . . Mrs. Pick
Dolce . . . . . . Miss Harrison
Cecilia . . . . . . Mrs. Hughes

WHO'S THE DUPE?

Old Doiley . . . . Mr. Hughes
Granger . . . . . Mr. S. Powell
Sandford . . . . . . Mr. Kenny
Servant . . . . . . Mr. Ratcliffe
Gradus . . . . . Miss Harrison
Charlotte . . . . Mrs. Chambers

Newport.

GRECIAN DAUGHTER.

Evander . . . . . . Mr. Harper
Dionysius . . . . . . Mr. Kenny
Melanthon . . . . . Mr. Ashton
Philotus . . . . . Mr. Ratcliffe
Arcus . . . . Mr. Taylor
Calippus . . . . . . Mr. Clarke
Perdiccas . . . . . Mr. Durang
Phocian . . . . . Mr. S. Powell
Eurixene . . . . . Miss Harrison
Euphrasia . . . . Mrs. S. Powell

SUCH THINGS ARE.

Mr. Howard . . . . Mr. Harper
Sir Luke Tremor . . Mr. Hughes
Sultan . . . . Mr. Ashton
Elvirus . . . . . Mr. S. Powell
Lord Flint . . . . . Mr. Kenny
Twineall . . . . . . Mr. Taylor
Arabella . . . . Mrs. S. Powell
Aurelia . . . . . Miss Harrison
Lady Tremor . . . Mrs. Hughes

Island capitals. He began at Newport, the performance of the 12th of April being announced as the last night but one, but between the 5th and 12th the "Mountaineers" was played, with Harper as *Octavian*. On the 24th of April the company was at Providence, where "Love in a Village" and the "Lying Valet" were produced, the cast of the opera in the two cities being identical. The stay in Providence was short, as Harper was again performing in Newport on the 2d of May. In order to show the rather remarkable force with which he was working, I give casts of four of the pieces—

LIST OF PERFORMANCES—*Newport.*

1797.

Mar. 28—Deuce is in Him . . . . Colman
        Devil to Pay . . . . . . Coffey
April 5—Love in a Village . . Bickerstaff
        Trick Upon Trick . . . Yarrow
   12—Rosina . . . . . . Mrs. Brooke
        Ghost . . . . . . Mrs. Centlivre
        Spoiled Child . . . . Bickerstaff
        (Mrs. Tubbs' benefit.)
May 2—West Indian . . . . Cumberland
        Ghost.

LOVE IN A VILLAGE.

Justice Woodcock . Mr. Kenna
Sir William Meadows . Mr. King
Young Meadows . Mr. Harper
Eustace . . . . . Mr. Peters
Hodge . . . . . . Mr. Tubbs
Hawthorn . . . . . Mr. Rose
Rosetta . . . . . Mrs. Tubbs
Madge . . . . . Mrs. Harper
Deborah . . . . . Mrs. Kenna
Lucinda . . . . . Mrs. Peters

LYING VALET.

Sharp . . . . . . Mr. Harper
Guttle . . . . . . Mr. Kenna
Trippet . . . . . . Mr. Peters
Cook . . . . . . Mr. Tubbs
Gayless . . . . . . Mr. King
Melissa . . . . . Mrs. Harper
Mrs. Gadabout . . Mrs. Kenna
Mrs. Trippet . . . Mrs. Peters
Kitty Pry . . . . Mrs. Tubbs

"Love in a Village," the same in both theatres; the "Lying Valet," as played in Providence; and the "West Indian" and the "Ghost" produced on the 2d of May. Mrs. Tubbs had her benefit on the 12th of April, when she appeared as *Rosina*, while Miss Arnold, a

WEST INDIAN.

Belcour . . . . . Mr. Harper
Stockwell . . . . . Mr. King
Capt. Dudley . . . Mr. Rose
Charles Dudley . . Mr. Callen
Fulmer . . . . . . Mr. Peters
Maj. O'Flaherty . . Mr. Kenna
Charlotte Rusport . Mrs. Harper
Lady Rusport . Mrs. Kenna
Louisa Dudley . . Mrs. Peters

GHOST.

Sir Jeffrey Constant . Mr. King
Capt. Constant . . . Mr. Rose
Trusty . . . . . . Mr. Kenna
Clinch . . . . . . Mr. Peters
Roger . . . . . . Mr. Harper
Belinda . . . . . Mrs. Peters
Dolly . . . . . . Mrs. Harper

young girl of ten years, was announced for *Little Pickle*, with songs. This, however, was not the young actress' first appearance in a speaking part, as on the 5th she was in the bill for *Solomon Smack* in "Trick upon Trick." She had probably been acting in a mild way even before this season, as the *Eastern Herald*, speaking of an entertainment given by the Tubbses at Portland, Me., early in the previous December, alluded to "the beautiful Miss Arnold, whose powers as an actress command admiration." If, therefore, the Newport announcement fails to fix the date of Miss Arnold's formal *debut* as an actress, the line in which our *Little Pickle* was called "a young miss of ten years" may be accepted as establishing the year of the birth of the future Mrs. Poe as 1787. Although the Tubbs family accompanied Harper to Providence, there was evidently a rupture before the return to Newport, as the same night that the company played the "West Indian" and the "Ghost" at the theatre, Mr. and Mrs. Tubbs, assisted by Miss Arnold, gave a reading and concert that they called "Oddities after the Manner of Dibdin" at Mrs. Penrose's Hall in Church Street. Tubbs accompanied Mrs. Tubbs and Miss Arnold on the piano and made himself generally useful. The secession of the Tubbses brought Harper's second attempt at management with his own company in Rhode Island to an end.

After the dissolution of Harper's ill-assorted force "the celebrated Mr. Maginnis, from London," gave entertainments at the theatre, beginning on the 6th of June and lasting until the 28th, the last night but one, when the bill was the "Country Girl" and the "Poor Soldier." The company comprised Mr. and Mrs. Harper, Mr. and Mrs. Marshall, Mr., Mrs. and Miss Rowson and Messrs. Kenny, Downie, J. Jones and McKenzie.

CHAPTER XX.

HALLAM, HODGKINSON AND DUNLAP.

AT HARTFORD, 1796—JOHN D. MILLER—THE NEW YORK SEASON OF
1796-7—MRS. SEYMOUR—THE HALLAM RIOT—HALLAM GOES TO
JAIL—" MYSTERIOUS MONK "—" EDWIN AND ANGELINA "—" BOUR-
VILLE CASTLE "—" COMET "—" MAN OF FORTITUDE."

WITH the beginning of Hodgkinson's second season in Hartford, on the 11th of July, 1796, Dunlap's attempt at management as one of the firm of Hallam, Hodgkinson and Dunlap began in
earnest. As early as the 4th of July the new manager was at Hartford with the company in anticipation of the opening. He remained
in Connecticut until the 19th, by which time he had already advanced
between four and five hundred dollars toward the expenses, it being
apparent from the receipts on the opening night that Hartford could
not afford such an organization. It had been the intention to go to
Philadelphia to reopen the old Southwark Theatre, but as neither Hallam nor Hodgkinson offered to assist in the expenses necessary to remove the company and repair the theatre, the plan, which was apparently Dunlap's, was given up. The result was that the Hartford season
was prolonged until the 13th of September.

The opening pieces were the " Provoked Husband " and the
" Purse." The list of productions comprised nothing that was new,
and was without incident except the *debut* of John D. Miller as

Clement in the "Deserted Daughter." Miller was born in New York in 1771, being the son of Philip Miller, a well-to-do German baker. According to Dunlap he was a good-looking young man, but without education or talent. Miller subsequently became a grocer in conjunction with his brother, an orator in Tammany Hall, and an alderman. On the night of his *debut*, Jefferson as *Item*, the attorney, whose clerk *Clement* was, seized Miller in a frenzy of feigned passion and shook him so violently that the young baker's blood boiled, and he threw off the comedian with a vigor that was not feigned. Near the close of the season Hodgkinson wrote to Dunlap a letter in which there are some curious references to the players of the period—

LIST OF PRODUCTIONS.

1796.

July 11—Provoked Husband . . Vanbrugh
    Purse . . . . Cross
Aug. 1—Jew . . . . Cumberland
    Poor Soldier . . . . . O'Keefe
    3—Road to Ruin . . . . . Holcroft
    Adopted Child . . . . . Birch
    5—School for Scandal . . Sheridan
    My Grandmother . . . . Hoare
    22—School for Soldiers . . . Henry
    Catharine and Petruchio, Shakspere
    24—Americans in Algiers
                            Mrs. Rowson
    Harlequin's Restoration.
    26—George Barnwell . . . . . Lillo
    Highland Reel . . . . O'Keefe
    29—Inkle and Yarico . . Colman, Jr.
    Lyar . . . . Foote
    (Mr. and Mrs. Tyler's benefit.)
    31—Speculation . . . . . Reynolds
    Adopted Child.
    (Mr. Jefferson and Mrs. Brett's benefit.)
Sept. 2—Midnight Hour . . Mrs. Inchbald
    Prisoner . . . . Rose
    (Misses Brett and Harding's benefit.)
    13—Wonder . . . . . Mrs. Centlivre
    Shelty's Travels . . . . Dunlap
    Waterman . . . . . . Dibdin
    (Mr. Hodgkinson's benefit.)

Crosby, who was the Richards of previous seasons; Mr. and Mrs. Collins, returned from Charleston, where they had been members of Sollee's company; and Mr. and Mrs. Hughes, who had lately retired from the Boston Theatre. There is a tradition that afterward Crosby and Collins, whose real name was Phipps, quarrelled in Boston, and were preparing to fight a duel when the authorities interfered and imprisoned both, their release being conditioned upon their leaving the State. The misunderstanding with Tyler to which Hodgkinson alludes was smoothed over, Crosby rejoined the company the next season in New York, and Collins, " from England," was engaged while the season was in progress. The allusion to Mr. Hallam at Newport might convey the impression that he was performing there with part of the company. Such, however, was not the case, the Newport Theatre at the time

HODGKINSON TO DUNLAP.—*Dear Sir:* I received your favor. The terms of the Collins's are 28 *dollars pr. week*, she finding her own wardrobe, which I think cheap. Crosby is wanted principally for the Irishman, and as that line is to be supplied by Collins, there is not occasion for him. Hughes is a favorite actor in Boston in the old Comic Character, *a line we want.*

His wife is a decent, sprightly actress. I beg you to use your own discretion in all these things. You cannot estimate Mr. Tyler's loss beyond what I should, as a man of ability, but I never did nor never shall *prize* the services of any man who can forfeit the good opinion I labored to entertain of him, in so open a manner as he has done. I think the late misunderstanding a premeditated plan and carried even to the pitch of insult, that the Play and Farce I had fixed on and publickly given out I meant to take for my Benefit, he took and *would have*, or take *none*, even after he had thrown and I won his Right ☞ I am opposed to every principle of unfair monopoly as man can be, but at the same time confess, I believe it the *first* instance where a Manager had not the power of withdrawing any piece he choose for himself in his own property, and I hope while I am concerned will be the *last*.

Add to which, the entire music of the Opera *was by right* my own private property, 'tho I had *given* it sometime ago to the House, a circumstance that he was perfectly apprised of, and that had not given it out for

a stock night, because I meant to take it. I suppose on Mr. Tyler's arrival in New York, you will hear his expectations from himself: I will neither *make terms with him* nor *offer him any;* only this—I was upwards of TWO YEARS in the Company on 16⅓ dollars weekly, and I don't yet see that he earns or deserves *more*, nor so *much* as I did. This I will allow; I think he ought to have as much as any male member of the Company.

I remitted to Mr. Hallam, at Newport, last Monday, 70 dollars, requesting him to Husband it for the necessities of the Company with economy, and if not sufficient I would send him more. I also sent to Nicolai Jr., 20 dollars to Boston, that he might be enabled to join the Company on its commencement in New York. My Balance in hand at *present* is 700 dollars, so you see I have enough for every purpose. The Rent is 316. Friday night was unfortunate from *very bad weather* when we expected the *greatest* House there had been, had the day prov'd *favorable.*

☞ Monday, *Inckle and Yarico* and *Lyar*—Mr. and Mrs. Tyler 239 dollars 12½ cents; charges 190 dollars.

Wednesday, *Speculation* and *Adopted Child*, Jefferson and Mrs. Brett, 220 dollars 25 cents; charges 190 dollars.

Friday, *Midnight Hour* and *Prisoner:* Miss Brett and Miss Harding, 130 dollars. I close *next Friday.*

Your Friend Sincerely, JNO. HODGKINSON.

being occupied by the French troupe of pantomimists in which Francisquy, Val, Dubois, Durang and Madame Gardie were the principal performers. In addition to the stock pantomimes, then very popular, a number of serious pieces, comedy and opera, were made to do pantomimic duty. Curiously enough, there was a Mr. Hallam with this company, but it is impossible to imagine the New York manager acting *Sam Shroud* in "Jack in Distress," *Harlequin* in "Harlequin Rambler," the *Hairdresser* in "Milliners," and a *Sportsman* in the "Bird Catcher," or, with pantomimic performers, of *Sandy* in "Auld Robin Gray," *Darby* in the "Poor Soldier," and *Aimwell* in the "Beaux' Stratagem." The pantomimic Hallam was probably identical with the Mr. Hallam who was with Bignall and West's company at Richmond in 1792.

Almost immediately after the return of the Old American Company from Hartford to New York the theatre was reopened, the season lasting from the 26th of September, 1796, to the 16th of June, 1797. An opening address, written by Mr. Miln, was spoken by Mr. Hodgkinson. The productions were strictly within the line

HARTFORD, 1796—SPECIMEN CASTS.

CATHARINE AND PETRUCHIO.

Petruchio	Mr. Hodgkinson
Baptista	Mr. Johnson
Hortensio	Mr. Cleveland
Tailor	Mr. Leonard
Music Master	Mr. Woolls
Biondello	Mr. Munto
Pedro	Mr. Lee
Grumio	Mr. Jefferson
Bianca	Mrs. Munto
Curtis	Mrs. Brett
Catharine	Mrs. Johnson

POOR SOLDIER.

Patrick	Mr. Tyler
Capt Fitzroy	Mr. Munto
Dermot	Mr. Hodgkinson
Father Luke	Mr. Johnson
Bagatelle	Mr. Cleveland
Boy	Master Stockwell
Darby	Mr. Jefferson
Norah	Miss Brett
Kathleen	Mrs. Hodgkinson

WATERMAN.

Tom Tug	Mr. Tyler
Bundle	Mr. Johnson
Mr. Wick	Mr. Leonard
Robin	Mr. Jefferson
Mrs. Bundle	Mrs. Brett

Wilhelmina	Mrs. Hodgkinson

WONDER.

Don Felix	Mr. Hodgkinson
Col. Briton	Mr. Tyler
Don Lopez	Mr. Johnson
Don Pedro	Mr. Munto
Gibby	Mr. Cleveland
Frederick	Mr. Miller
Alguazil	Mr. Woolls
Vasquez	Mr. Leonard
Lissardo	Mr Jefferson
Flora	Mrs. Brett
Isabella	Mrs. Tyler
Inis	Mrs. Munto
Violante	Mrs. Johnson

that had been established by previous usage—stock pieces, with occasional performances of recent English successes. This rule was varied, however, by the amateur management of the new partner, who brought out two of his own pieces and the pieces of two of his cronies during the season. There were some additions to the performers—Miller returned to New York with the company; Martin, as well as Crosby, resumed his old place, and Mrs. Seymour was an acquisition of some importance. She was an illiterate woman, but a great beauty. She made her *debut* as *Narcissa* in "Inkle and Yarico" on the 14th of October. Mrs. Seymour was the substitute for Miss Broadhurst. There was a Mr. Seymour, but as an actor he was of no consequence. Another member of the company this season in small parts was Mr. McGrath, probably Christopher Charles McGrath, comedian. Mr. Collins, who had been with Williamson's company in Boston at the beginning of the

LIST OF PERFORMANCES—*New York.*

1796.

Sept. 26—Wonder . . . . . Mrs. Centlivre
      Poor Soldier . . . . . O'Keefe
    28—Carmelite . . . . . Cumberland
      Romp . . . . Bickerstaff
Oct. 1—Jew . . . . Cumberland
      Lyar . . . . Foote
    3—Road to Ruin . . . . . Holcroft
      Spoiled Child . . . . Bickerstaff
    5—Jane Shore . . . . Rowe
      Old Maid . . . . Murphy
    7—Battle of Hexham . . Colman, Jr
      Three Weeks After Marriage
                          Murphy
    10—School for Soldiers . . . Henry
      Waterman . . . . . . Dibdin
    12—Deserted Daughter . . . Holcroft
      Adopted Child . . . . . Birch
    14—Inkle and Yarico . . Colman, Jr
      Old Maid.
    17—Mountaineers . . . . Colman, Jr
      Rosina . . . . . . Mrs. Brooke
    20—First Love . . . . . Cumberland
      Farmer . . . . O'Keefe
    22—Country Girl . . . . . Garrick
      Purse . . . . Cross
    26—Romeo and Juliet . . Shakspere
      Sultan . . . . Bickerstaff
    28—Child of Nature . Mrs. Inchbald
      Children in the Wood . . Morton
    31—Mysterious Monk . . . Dunlap
      Midnight Hour . . Mrs. Inchbald
Nov. 2—Which is the Man ? . Mrs. Cowley
      No Song No Supper . . . Hoare
    4—School for Scandal . . Sheridan
      Agreeable Surprise . . O'Keefe
    7—Mysterious Monk.
      Catharine and Petruchio
                        Shakspere.
    9—Such Things Are . Mrs. Inchbald
      Waterman.

season, made his first appearance as *Kilmallock* in the "Mountaineers" on the 30th of January, 1797. The season was not without incident, but the disorders that attended it reflected little credit either upon the audience or the management. The introduction of liquor into the house during the performance led to a riot on the 2d of November. Two sea captains becoming intoxicated in one of the stage boxes demanded "Yankee Doodle" during the overture to the farce. The audience hissed them, whereupon they threw missiles at the orchestra. A riot was the consequence, the disturbers being dragged from their box, and one turned into the street, the other carried into a dressing-room. Subsequently they attacked the doors of the theatre, aided by a number of sailors, but were finally arrested by the city watch. The managers then made it a rule not to allow the introduction of liquor

Nov. 11—Surrender of Calais . Colman, Jr
Romp.
14—Belle's Stratagem . Mrs. Cowley
Quaker . . . . Dibdin
16—Earl of Essex . . . . . . Jones
Padlock . . . . . Bickerstaff
18—Young Quaker . . . . O'Keefe
My Grandmother . . . . Hoare
21—Wheel of Fortune . . Cumberland
My Grandmother.
23—Othello . . . . . . Shakspere
Rosina.
28—Speculation . . . . . Reynolds
Children in the Wood.
30—Mountaineers.
Midnight Hour.
Dec. 2—She Stoops to Conquer, Goldsmith
Prize . . . . Hoare
5—Provoked Husband . . Vanbrugh
Poor Soldier.
7—Deserted Daughter.
Deserter . . . . . . Dibdin
10—Road to Ruin . . . . . Holcroft
Adopted Child.
12—Romeo and Juliet.
Spoiled Child.
14—As You Like It . . . Shakspere
Farmer.
16—Macbeth . . . . . . Shakspere
Modern Antiques . . . O'Keefe
19—Edwin and Angelina . . . Smith
Florizel and Perdita . Shakspere
21—Haunted Tower . . . . . Cobb
Two Strings to Your Bow
Jephson
23—Much Ado About Nothing
Shakspere
My Grandmother.
26—Clandestine Marriage
Garrick and Colman
Don Juan.
28—Isabella . . . . . . Southerne
Two Strings to Your Bow.
30—Siege of Belgrade . . . . Cobb
Modern Antiques.
31—George Barnwell . . . . . Lillo
Deserter.

1797.

Jan.   2—Much Ado About Nothing.
            Sultan.
        4—Siege of Belgrade.
            Two Strings to Your Bow.
        6—Man of Ten Thousand . Holcroft
            Prize.
        9—Alexander the Great . . . . Lee
            Tell Truth and Shame the Devil
                                      Dunlap
        11—Siege of Belgrade.
            Old Maid.
        13—Man of Ten Thousand.
            Highland Reel . . . . O'Keefe
        16—Bourville Castle . . . . . Linn
            Modern Antiques.
        18—Siege of Belgrade.
            Tell Truth and Shame the Devil.
        20—Bourville Castle.
            All the World's a Stage, Jackman
        23—Man of Ten Thousand.
            No Song No Supper.
        25—Bourville Castle.
            Two Strings to Your Bow.
        27—Siege of Belgrade.
            All the World's a Stage.
        30—Mountaineers.
            Romp.
Feb.   1—Comet . . . . Miln
            Spoiled Child.
        3—Every One Has His Fault
                                  Mrs. Inchbald
            Agreeable Surprise.
        6—Comet.
            Adopted Child.
        8—Comet.
            All the World's a Stage.
        10—Gamester .   .   .   .   . Moore
            Waterman.
        13—Man of Ten Thousand.
            Critic . . . . Sheridan
        15—Comet.
            Rosina.
        17—Siege of Belgrade.
            Poor Soldier.
        20—School for Arrogance . . Holcroft
            Children in the Wood.

into the house until the conclusion of the first piece, and respectfully hoped gentlemen would not call for any. A more serious riot occurred on the 29th of March following because of Mrs. Hallam's enforced retirement. Hallam made strenuous efforts to secure his wife's return to the stage, but failing he gave it out that she should play for his benefit. To prevent this, Hodgkinson relieved Dunlap of his duties as the acting manager and announced a code of rules for the ensuing benefits that would enable him to exclude Mrs. Hallam. Hallam refused to assent to these regulations and had them torn down. But even before Hallam took this step there were indications that he and his friends were resolved upon strong measures for Mrs. Hallam's restoration. On the evening after the new regulations were posted in the green-room, Hodgkinson was met by an audible hiss when as *Puff* in the "Critic" he mentioned himself, as was usual. Hodgkinson resented this by adding to *Puff's* speech: "To be sure, he was goosed, but that's of little consequence ; it is not the first time this season that some envious scoundrel has insulted him," and then went on with the part. The trouble between the two actor-managers came to a public·issue on the evening of the 29th. When Hodgkinson, who was to play *Colin McLeod* in the "Fashionable Lover," came on the stage, he was greeted with hisses and cries of "Off, off." He was astounded. At this moment Mrs. Hallam entered from the right. She was dressed in black silk, her powdered hair being parted on the top of her head and combed down on each side of her face. She looked, Dunlap says, beauty in distress. The plaudit that greeted her entrance was the first notice Hodgkinson had of her purpose. She held a paper in her hand and courtesied most profoundly. "Out with the

Feb. 23—Speculation.
Don Juan.
25—Dramatist . . . . Reynolds
Prisoner at Large . . . O'Keefe
27—School for Arrogance.
Double Disguise . . Mrs. Hook
March 1—Comet.
Harlequin's Restoration.
3—Chapter of Accidents . Miss Lee
Double Disguise.
6—Siege of Belgrade.
Two Strings to Your Bow.
8—Wheel of Fortune.
Lock and Key . . . . . Hoare
10—As You Like It.
Lock and Key.
13—Surrender of Calais.
New York Balloon . . . Wignell
15—Deserted Daughter.
New York Balloon.
17—Carmelite.
Lock and Key.
20—Comet.
Double Disguise.
22—Werter and Charlotte . Reynolds
Purse.
Harlequin's Restoration.
24—Child of Nature.
Critic.
25—Young Quaker.
Lock and Key.
27—Siege of Belgrade.
Lyar . . . . Foote
29—Fashionable Lover . Cumberland
Quaker.
31—Macbeth.
Adopted Child.
April 3—Wonder.
Children in the Wood.
5—Such Things Are.
Adopted Child.
7—Way to Get Married . . Morton
Modern Antiques.
17—Next-Door Neighbors
Mrs. Inchbald
Romp.

April 17—Highland Reel.
   (Mrs. Hodgkinson's benefit.)
    19—Way to Get Married.
     Poor Soldier.
     (Mrs. Tyler's benefit.)
    21—Suspicious Husband . . Hoadly
     Alonzo and Imogene.
     (Mr. Martin's benefit.)
    24—Cymbeline . . . . . Shakspere
     Lock and Key.
     (Mrs. Johnson's benefit.)
    26—School for Wives . . . . Kelly
     All in Good Humor . . . Oulton
     Ariadne Abandoned by Theseus.
     (Mrs. Melmoth's benefit.)
    28—Life's Vagaries . . . . O'Keefe
     Double Disguise.
     (Mr. Jefferson's benefit.)
May 1—Way to Get Married.
     Padlock.
     3—Midnight Wanderers . . Pearce
     Next-Door Neighbors.
     All the World's a Stage.
     (Mrs. Seymour's benefit.)
     5—Lear . . . . Shakspere
     Quality Binding . . . . . Rose
     Mirror . . . . Miln
     Half an Hour After Supper.
     (Mr. Johnson's benefit.)
     8—Way to Get Married.
     Lock and Key.
     (Mr. Woolls' benefit.)
    10—Fortune's Fool . . . . Reynolds
     Selima and Azor . . . . Collier
    (Mr. Hodgkinson's benefit.)
    12—Richard III . . . . . Shakspere
     Deserter.
  (Roberts and Seymour's benefit.)
    15—Fontainebleau . . . . O'Keefe
     Three Weeks After Marriage.
     (Mr. Tyler's benefit.)
    17—Siege of Belgrade.
     Doldrum . . . . O'Keefe
  (Mrs. Brett and Mrs. King's benefit.)
    19—No One's Enemy but His Own
            Murphy

rascal," was the cry that came from the pit, but this was superseded by another cry, " Hear Mrs. Hallam." Just then Mr. Hallam, dressed in black, was seen stalking down the stage. He bowed, and addressing the audience asked permission for Mrs. Hallam to read the paper she held in her hand. There being no objection, Mrs. Hallam read her statement, asserting that she had never willingly insulted the public, and claiming that she was wrongfully excluded from her profession. She then retired, leaving Hallam and Hodgkinson on the stage. Both addressed the audience, Hodgkinson, in spite of the hisses that greeted him, succeeding in saying that Mrs. Hallam's withdrawal was the basis of the existing copartnership. This Hallam denied, whereupon Hodgkinson appealed to Philip Ten Eyck, as the bearer of the proposition from Hallam, and Mr. Ten Eyck, who was present, confirmed

Hodgkinson's statement. Hallam's friends, however, were not satisfied, and their anger was raised to a very high pitch when Hodgkinson alluded to the disturbance as a riot. "You are guilty of a riot," exclaimed John Cozine, a leading member of the New York bar, speaking from a box near the stage, "and liable for the consequent damage that may ensue. If Mr. Hallam is aggrieved he has his remedy in a court of justice. You are rioters; you will know to-morrow that the grand jury is sitting."

"It is very hard that the public is not to be indulged with a favorite actress," some one said.

"You are not the public, sir," Hodgkinson aptly said. He

May 19—Deaf Lover . . . . . . Pilon
No Song No Supper.
(Mr. Miller's benefit.)
22—Mountaineers.
Tom Thumb, the Great . O'Hara
(Misses Brett and Harding's benefit.)
24—Hamlet . . . . . . Shakspere
Old Thomas Day.
High Life Below Stairs . Townley
(Mr. Lee's benefit.)
26—Chapter of Accidents.
Tom Thumb.
(Mr. Crosby's benefit.)
29—Love Makes a Man . . . Cibber
First Floor . . . . Cobb
(Mr. Faulkner's benefit.)
31—School for Scandal . . Sheridan
Pannel . . . . Kemble
(Mr. Hallam, Jr.'s, benefit.)
June 5—Spanish Barber . . . . Colman
Rural Merriment . . . . Francis
Two Strings to Your Bow.
(Mr. Martin's benefit.)
7—Man of Fortitude . . Hodgkinson
Quality Binding.
Mogul Tale . . . Mrs. Inchbald
(Mr. Johnson's benefit.)
12—Toy . . . . O'Keefe
Lock and Key.
(Mr. Hallam's benefit.)
16—Inkle and Yarico.
(Crosby, Woolls, Faulkner and Mrs. Collins' benefit.)

was asked whether he would permit Mrs. Hallam to play, and answered, "Never while I have anything to do with the theatre." At last Hallam withdrew in despair, desiring that the play might proceed, and the performance went on to the close without further interruption. On the next play night, however, Hodgkinson was hissed so persistently that he finally retired and did not appear again during the season except for the benefit of Seymour and Roberts, when he played *Richard* in

"Richard III." On the day following Hodgkinson's withdrawal he brought suit against Hallam for breach of covenant. The process was served on the 17th of April, all that was required of Hallam being to indorse his appearance on the writ. This Hallam refused to do and announced his intention to go to jail, which he insisted upon doing. He soon tired of being a martyr, however, and went home. Hodgkinson, in his malice, proceeded to put the woman's faults upon record forever; and then, within a few weeks, in order to secure a share in the lease of the new theatre, known in history as the Park, he agreed to engage both Mr. and Mrs. Hallam as members of the company. The actress returned to the stage on the occasion of the younger Hallam's benefit, playing *Lady Teazle* in the "School for Scandal," and *Beatrice* in Kemble's farce, the "Pannel," which then had its first New York production. As a matter of course, she delivered an Occasional Address,[1] which was written for her by Mr.

---

[1] MRS. HALLAM'S ADDRESS.

These flattering plaudits can not fail to raise
A wish to merit such transcendent praise;
It can but be a wish, for ah! my heart
Knows merit could not claim a thousandth part;
But like the lavish hand of heaven, you
Give largely e'en though nothing should be due.
O'ercome with joy, my anxious, throbbing heart,
Disdaining all the little tricks of art,
Conceals those feelings in a grateful breast
Which may be felt but can not be express'd.
Time has now swept ten rolling years away*
Since flattering plaudits graced my first essay;

* This would make her *debut* as late as 1787.

Young, giddy, rash, ambitious and untaught,
You still caress'd, excusing many a fault;
With friendly hand safe led me through the way,
Where lurking error watches to betray.
And shall I such advantages forego
With my consent? I frankly answer, " No."
I may through inadvertency have stray'd;
But who by folly never was betray'd?
If e'er my judgment play'd the foolish part,
I acted not in concert with my heart.
I boldly can defy the world to say,
From my first entrée to the present day,
Whate'er my errors, numerous or few,
I never wanted gratitude to you.
On your indulgence still I rest my cause;
Will you support me with your kind applause?
You verify the truth of Pope's fine line—
" To err is human; to forgive, divine."

Miln. Although sneered at by Dunlap as an " extraordinary performance," it had at least one merit—it was short. Mrs. Hallam was also announced to appear for Mr. Munto's benefit on the 3d of June, but I have been able to find no record of the performance.

Dunlap's influence upon the productions of the season can only be described as grotesque. Vanity and friendship were his only motives in bringing forward the feeble pieces that he put in rehearsal when the season began. His own play, the " Mysterious Monk," produced on the 31st of October, and afterward printed with the title of " Ribbemont, or the Feudal Baron," was Dunlap's third tragedy. It was played only twice, its failure being due to a want of skill in the management of the plot and the insufficiency of the characters and incidents. The afterpiece, " Tell Truth and Shame the Devil," was not played until the 9th of January, and was scarcely more fortunate than the tragedy; but it had the distinction of being produced at Covent Garden May 18th, 1799. It was based on a French piece in one act called " Jerome Pointu," and was also printed. In the " Biographia Dramatica " it is said to be " by no means an unentertaining piece." Dr. Elihu Hubbard Smith, the author of " Edwin and Angelina, or the Bandit," was a young

MYSTERIOUS MONK.

Ribbemont . .	Mr. Hodgkinson
Manuel	Mr. Tyler
Theodore	Mr. Martin
Jacques	Mr. Johnson
Francis	Mr. Munto
Countess	Mrs. Melmoth

TELL TRUTH AND SHAME THE DEVIL.

Semblance . . .	Mr. Johnson
Whitely	Mr. Tyler
Tom Holton . .	Mr. Jefferson
Susan . . .	Mrs. Hodgkinson

EDWIN AND ANGELINA.

Edwin	Mr. Tyler
Ethelbert	Mr. Martin
Walter	Mr. Crosby
Edred	Mr. Munto
Hugo	Mr. Miller
Sifred	Mr. Hodgkinson
Angelina . .	Mrs. Hodgkinson

BOURVILLE CASTLE.

Chas. Bourville,	Mr. Hodgkinson
Guthrum	Mr. Crosby
Bernard	Mr. Johnson
James	Mr. Jefferson
William	Mr. McGrath
Strabo	Mr. Munto
Alfred	Mr. Tyler
Marcia	Mrs. Tyler

New York physician who fell a victim to the yellow fever in 1798. The piece was an opera, so called, the music by Pelisier. It had no dramatic merit, and was played only once, but was printed for the author. The last of the pieces by the three cronies was "Bourville Castle," by John Blair Linn. This piece was more successful than any of the others, but Dunlap only mentions its production. The author, who afterward became the pastor of a Presbyterian church in Philadelphia, was a law student in the office of Alexander Hamilton.

Two pieces were produced during the season that have curious histories—one a comedy by William Miln called the "Comet;" the other a drama with the title of the "Man of Fortitude," the authorship of which was assigned to Hodgkinson, but

COMET.		MAN OF FORTITUDE.	
Plotwell . . .	Mr. Hodgkinson	Sir Bertrand .	Mr. Hodgkinson
Belmont	Mr. Tyler	Carlos	Mr. Jefferson
Stitch	Mr. Lee	Peasant	Mr. Johnson
John	Mr. Leonard	Spectre	Mr. Tyler
Testy	Mr. Johnson	Captive	Mrs. Johnson
Jenny . . .	Mrs. Hodgkinson		
Lady Candour .	Mrs. Seymour		
Emily	Mrs. Johnson		

which Dunlap claimed was in fact a piece of his own that he had called the "Knight's Adventure." Miln's piece had previously been produced in London for Bannister's benefit as a farce, but it was now re-written and enlarged into a comedy in five acts. Subsequently it was again reduced to a farce in two acts, of which there is an American edition published as late as 1817. Dunlap's piece was in blank verse, which Hodgkinson partly turned into prose, adding the comic character and the lady. It was printed with Hodgkinson's name on the title-page.

The number of new English pieces produced in New York for the first time during the season was not as great as usual, owing, no doubt, to the slovenly way in which the benefits were conducted because of the managerial quarrels. The pieces that had casts with the advertisements are noticed in the order of their production. Jephson's farce, "Two Strings to Your Bow," had been played by the Philadelphia company, so that the first production of the season new to the American stage was Cobb's "Siege of Belgrade," a comic opera originally acted at Drury Lane. It was presented in New York with new scenery painted by Jefferson. After these came Holcroft's two comedies, "Man of Ten Thousand" on the 6th of January, and "School for Arrogance" on the 20th of February. It is likely the

FIRST NEW YORK PRODUCTIONS—1796-7.

FIRST FLOOR.

Whimsey	Mr. Johnson
Young Whimsey . .	Mr. Martin
Monford	Mr. Munto
Furnish	Mr. Crosby
Simon	Mr. Miller
Landlord	Mr. Collins
Frank	Mr. Seymour
Snap	Mr. Lee
Postboy	Mr. Leonard
Tartlet	Mr. Jefferson
Charlotte	Mrs. Seymour
Nancy	Mrs. Collins
Mrs. Patty Pan . . .	Mrs. Brett

FONTAINEBLEAU.

Lackland	Mr. Hallam
Henry	Mr. Tyler
Sir John Bull . . .	Mr. Johnson
Sir Shinkin	Mr. Jefferson
Lapoche	Mr. Martin
Col. Epaulette .	Mr. Hallam, Jr
Lord Winlove	Mr. Munto
Waiters . . . . {	Mr. Miller / Mr. Leonard
Robin	Mr. Lee
Postboy	Mr. McKnight
Jockey	Mr. Seymour
French Innkeeper . .	Mr. Roberts
Miss Bull	Mrs. Johnson
Mrs. Casey . . .	Mrs. Melmoth
Nannette	Mrs. Collins
Lady Bull	Mrs. Brett
Celia · ·	Mrs. Seymour
Rosa	Mrs. Hodgkinson

FORTUNE'S FOOL.

Capt. Hazard	Mr. Martin
Sir B. Blackletter .	Mr. Johnson
Sir Charles . . .	Mr. Hallam, Jr
Orville	Mr. Munto
Tom Seymour . . .	Mr. Jefferson
Mrs. Seymour . .	Mrs. Melmoth
Miss Uncore	Mrs. Brett
Lady Danvers . .	Mrs. Johnson

HARLEQUIN'S RESTORATION.

Harlequin	Mr. Martin
Pantaloon	Mr. Johnson
Magician	Mr. Crosby
Gladiator	Mr. Tyler
Lover	Mr. Munto
Swiss Servant . . .	Mr. Leonard
Landlord	Mr. Lee
Clown	Mr. Jefferson
Mirth	Miss Brett
Pantalina	Mrs. Brett
Columbine	Mrs. Seymour

LOCK AND KEY.

Ralph	Mr. Hodgkinson
Cheerly	Mr. Tyler
Vain	Mr. Martin
Pages . . . . {	Miss Harding / Mast. Stockwell
William	Mr. McGrath
Thomas	Mr. Munto
Peter	Mr. Lee
Brummagem	Mr. Johnson
Laura	Mrs. Seymour
Dolly	Mrs. Munto

Selima	Mrs. King
Fanny	Mrs. Hodgkinson

MAN OF TEN THOUSAND.

Torrington . . .	Mr. Hodgkinson
Herbert	Mr. Jefferson
Curfew	Mr. Johnson
Consol	Mr. Tyler
Major Rampart . . .	Mr. Crosby
Lord Laroon	Mr. Martin
Hudson	Mr. Hallam, Jr
Sir Pertinax Pitiful .	Mr. Munto
Robert	Mr. Seymour
Thomas	Mr. McGrath
Hairbrain	Mr. Hallam
Lady Taunton	Mrs. Tyler
Annabel	Mrs. Seymour
Girl	Mrs. Munto
Olivia	Mrs. Johnson

MIDNIGHT WANDERERS.

Marquis de Morelle .	Mr. Johnson
Julian	Mr. Tyler
Don Pedrazzo . . .	Mr. Crosby
Dennis	Mr. Martin
Guide	Mr. Lee
Gasper	Mr. Jefferson
Adelais	Mrs. Seymour
Jaquelin	Miss Brett
Bercilla	Mrs. Munto
Maresa	Mrs. Hodgkinson

MOGUL TALE.

Johnny Atkins .	Mr. Hodgkinson
Mogul	Mr. Tyler

pantomime, " Harlequin's Restoration," previously presented at Hartford, was an old one with a new variation in the name.   Prince Hoare's " Lock and Key," of which the first production in New York had been anticipated by the Philadelphia company, although devoid of literary merit, was successful in both cities as it had been at Covent Garden.   The " New York Balloon," which the advertisements said had been localized by Mr. Wignell from " A Mogul Tale," was produced in Philadelphia simply as Mrs. Inchbald's farce, so far as the announcements show.   The production of Morton's play, the " Way

FIRST NEW YORK PRODUCTIONS—1796-7.

Doctor . . . . . . Mr. Johnson
Fanny . . . . Mrs. Hodgkinson

NEW YORK BALLOON.

Johnny Atkins . Mr. Hodgkinson
Dr. Phlogiston . . . Mr. Johnson
Omar . . . . Mr. Martin
Mustapha . . . . . . Mr. Munto
Selim . . . . Mr. Miller
Great Mogul . . . . . Mr. Tyler
Zaphira . . . . . Mrs. Seymour
Sheba . . . . Miss Brett
Irene . . . . Mrs. Munto
Fanny . . . . Mrs. Hodgkinson

NEXT-DOOR NEIGHBORS.

Splendorville . . Mr. Hallam, Jr
Manly . . . . Mr. Tyler
Blackman . . . . . Mr. Johnson
Lucre . . . . Mr. Munto
Lord Hazard . . . . . Mr. Miller
Wilford . . . . Mr. Crosby
Henry . . . . Mr. Martin
Bluntly . . . . . . Mr. Jefferson
Lady Caroline . . Mrs. Seymour
Lady Bridget . . . . Mrs. Tyler
Evans . . . . Mrs. Brett
Eleanor . . . . . . Mrs. Johnson

OLD THOMAS DAY.

Gammer Gurton . . Mr. Johnson
Dame Turton . . . . . Mr. Lee
Goody Burton . . . Mr. Jefferson

QUALITY BINDING.

Mr. Level . . . . . Mr. Tyler
Lord Simper . . Mr. Hallam, Jr
Colonel Modish . . . Mr. Munto
Sir William Wealthy . Mr. Collins
John . . . . Mr. Johnson
Plainwell . . . . . Mr. Jefferson
William . . . . . . Mr. Seymour
Mrs. Level . . . . Mrs. Melmoth

SCHOOL FOR ARROGANCE.

Count Villiers . Mr. Hodgkinson
Sir Paul Peckham . Mr. Johnson
Sir Samuel Sheepy . Mr. Jefferson
McDermot . . . . . Mr. Crosby
Dorimont . . . . . . Mr. Tyler
Edmond . . . . Mr. Hallam, Jr
Picard . . . . Mr. Martin
Lady Peckham . . Mrs. Melmoth
Lucy . . . . . . Mrs. Johnson
Lydia . . . . . Mrs. Seymour

SIEGE OF BELGRADE.

Col. Cohenburg . Mr. Hodgkinson
Leopold . . . . . . Mr. Jefferson
Peter . . . . Mr. Munto
Useph . . . . Mr. Johnson
Ismael . . . . . . Mr. Seymour
Anselm . . . . . . Mr. McGrath
Michael . . . . . . Mr. Miller
Seraskin . . . . . . Mr. Tyler
Lilla . . . . Mrs. Seymour
Ghitta . . . . Miss Brett
Fatima . . . . Mrs. Munto
Catharine . . . Mrs. Hodgkinson

TWO STRINGS TO YOUR BOW.

Don Pedro . . . . Mr. Johnson
Don Sancho . . . . Mr. Crosby
Ferdinand . . . . . . Mr. Tyler
Octavio . . . . Mr. Martin
Borachio . . . . . . Mr. Munto
Drunken Porter . . . . Mr. Lee
Waiter . . . . Mr. Miller
Lazarillo . . . . Mr. Hodgkinson
Leonora . . . . . Mrs. Seymour
Maid . . . . Mrs. Munto
Donna Clara . . . Mrs. Johnson

WAY TO GET MARRIED.

Tangent . . . . . . Mr. Martin
Toby Allspice . . . Mr. Jefferson
Caustic . . . . . . Mr. Johnson
Dashall . . . . . Mr. Hallam, Jr
McQueery . . . . . Mr. Crosby
Landlord }
Jailer   } . . . . Mr. Munto
Shopman . . . . . Mr. Seymour
Sheriff's Servant }
Undertaker   } . . Mr. Lee
Ned . . . . Mr. Miller
Postillion . . . . Mr. McKnight
Caustic's Servant . . Mr. Leonard
Bailiff . . . . Mr. Roberts
Solicitor . . . . . . Mr. Woolls
Captain Faulkner . . Mr. Tyler
Clementina . . . . Mrs. Seymour
Lady Sorrel . . . . Mrs. Brett
Fanny . . . . Mrs. Munto
Julia Faulkner . . Mrs. Johnson

to Get Married," was delayed until late into the regular season, although it was the comedy success of the year both in Boston and Philadelphia. For the benefits there were some new pieces, including Mrs. Inchbald's "Next-Door Neighbors," for Mrs. Hodgkinson, for the first time in New York;" "Alonzo and Imogene," a Sadler's Well's production, for Mr. Martin;" O'Keefe's "Life's Vagaries," for Mr. Jefferson; the comic opera, "Midnight Wanderers," which had had some vogue at Covent Garden, though not equal to "Hartford Bridge" by the same author, for Mrs. Seymour, for the first time in America; O'Keefe's "Fontainebleau," a satire on the English habit of traveling in France previous to the Revolution, for Mr. Tyler; the same author's "Doldrum," a farce based on the idea of a man sleeping from 1796 to 1803, and his surprise at the changes around him, thus anticipating Rip Van Winkle, for Mrs. Brett and Mrs. King; Murphy's "No One's Enemy but His Own," never played in this country except by the British Military Thespians in Philadelphia in 1778, for Mr. Miller; the Haymarket interlude, "Half an Hour After Supper," for Mr. Johnson; "Fortune's Fool," Reynolds' latest Covent Garden success, for Mr. Hodgkinson, for the first time in America; "Ariadne Abandoned by Theseus," the music by Pelisier, for Mrs. Melmoth; the catch, "Old Thomas Day," for Mr. Lee; John Philip Kemble's "Pannel," a lively and pleasant farce taken from Bickerstaff's "'Tis Well 'Tis No Worse," with Mrs. Hallam as *Beatrice*, for the younger Hallam; Cobb's "First Floor," for Mr. Faulkner, the box-keeper; and the "Mogul Tale," for Mr. Johnson's second benefit.

The familiar pieces were recast to a considerable extent because of the acquisitions of the previous season, the return of Martin and Crosby, and the engagement of Mr. and Mrs. Seymour, Mr. Collins,

Mr. Miller and Mr. McGrath. Among these are a few complete casts of pieces which either had not been played since 1792 or of which no

RECASTS OF FAMILIAR PIECES—1796-7.

ALEXANDER THE GREAT.

Clytus	Mr. Hallam
Cassander	Mr. Crosby
Hephestion	Mr. Martin
Thessalus	Mr. Miller
Eumenes	Mr. McGrath
Perdiccas	Mr. Seymour
Sysigambis	Mrs. Tyler
Parisatis	Mrs. Seymour

ALL THE WORLD'S A STAGE.

Sir Gilbert Pumpkin .	Mr. Crosby
Charles Stanley . . .	Mr. Martin
Harry Stukely .	Mr. Hallam, Jr
Cymon	Mr. Johnson
Wat	Mr. Lee
Hostler	Mr. Miller
Diggery	Mr. Jefferson
Miss Bridget	Mrs. Brett
Kitty Sprightly . .	Mrs. Seymour

BATTLE OF HEXHAM.

Barton	Mr. Johnson
Somerset	Mr. Miller
Gregory Gubbins .	Mr. Jefferson
Adeline	Mrs. Johnson
Queen Margaret .	Mrs. Melmoth

CHAPTER OF ACCIDENTS.

Lord Glenmore . . .	Mr. Collins
Grey	Mr. Tyler
Vane	Mr. Munto
Governor Harcourt .	Mr. Johnson
Bridget	Mrs. Hodgkinson
Miss Mortimer . .	Mrs. Seymour
Mrs. Warner	Mrs. Brett
Cecilia	Mrs. Johnson

COUNTRY GIRL.

Sparkish	Mr. Martin
Alithea	Mrs. Tyler

CRITIC.

Sir Fretful	Mr. Jefferson
Sneer	Mr. Collins
Dangle	Mr. Martin
Mrs. Dangle	Mrs. Tyler
Leicester	Mr. Miller
Hatton	Mr. McGrath

Burleigh	Mr. Seymour
Whiskerandos . .	Mr. Hallam, Jr

DESERTER.

Simpkin	Mr. Jefferson
Jenny	Mrs. Seymour

DON JUAN.

Don Juan	Mr. Johnson
Don Ferdinand	Mr. Tyler
Pedro	Mr. Martin
Scaramouch	Mr. Jefferson
Confidante	Mrs. Brett
Donna Anna . . .	Mrs. Johnson

DOUBLE DISGUISE.

Tinsel	Mr. Jefferson
Evergreen	Mr. Crosby
Sam	Mr. Munto
Heartwell	Mr. Tyler
Rose	Mrs. Hodgkinson
Miss Dorothy	Mrs. Brett
Emily	Mrs. Seymour

DRAMATIST.

Lord Scratch . . .	Mr. Johnson
Neville	Mr. Martin
Ennui	Mr. Jefferson
Willoughby	Mr. Munto
Peter	Mr. McGrath
Louisa	Mrs. Johnson

EARL OF ESSEX.

Lord Burleigh	Mr. Crosby
Raleigh	Mr. Munto
Lieutenant	Mr. Miller
Southampton	Mr. Tyler
Lady Rutland . . .	Mrs. Johnson
Lady Nottingham . .	Mrs. Tyler
Queen Elizabeth .	Mrs. Melmoth

FASHIONABLE LOVER.

Mortimer	Mr. Hallam
Aubrey	Mr. Tyler
Tyrrel	Mr. Munto
Abberville . .	Mr. Hallam, Jr
Bridgemore	Mr. Johnson
Dr. Druid	Mr. Crosby
La Jeanesse	Mr. Roberts

Jarvis	Mr. Woolls
Colin MacLeod .	Mr. Hodgkinson
Miss Bridgemore . .	Mrs. Tyler
Mrs. Bridgemore . .	Mrs. Brett
Mrs. MacIntosh . .	Mrs. Munto
Maid	Mrs. King
Augusta Aubrey .	Mrs. Johnson

GAMESTER.

Lewson	Mr. Tyler
Jarvis	Mr. Crosby
Stukely	Mr. Collins

GRECIAN DAUGHTER.

Dionyslus . . .	Mr. Hodgkinson
Evander	Mr. Hallam
Philotas	Mr. Martin
Phocian	Mr. Tyler
Melanthon	Mr. Crosby

HIGHLAND REEL.

Sandy	Mr. Munto
Charley	Mr. Jefferson
Sergt. Jack	Mr. Tyler
Capt. Dash . .	Mr. Hallam, Jr
McGilpin	Mr. Johnson
Jenny	Miss Brett

HIGH LIFE BELOW STAIRS.

Lovel	Mr. Hallam
Lord Duke	Mr. Jefferson
Sir Harry	Mr. Martin
Freeman	Mr. Munto
Philip	Mr. Hallam, Jr
Tom	Mr. Woolls
Coachman	Mr. Lee
Kingston	Mr. McKnight
Kitty	Mrs. Collins
Lady Charlotte . . .	Mrs. Tyler
Lady Bab	Mrs. Seymour

MACBETH.

Banquo	Mr. Tyler
Malcolm	Mr. Martin
Duncan	Mr. Crosby
Lenox	Mr. Hallam, Jr

MODERN ANTIQUES.

Cockletop	Mr. Johnson

previous casts had been preserved, including "All the World's a Stage," "Double Disguise," "Earl of Essex," "Fashionable Lover,"

RECASTS OF FAMILIAR PIECES—1796-7.

Napkin . . . . . . Mr. Crosby	Queen Elizabeth . Mrs. Melmoth	Drugget . . . . . . Mr. Johnson
Thomas . . . . Mr. Lee	Lady Anne . . . . Mrs. Tyler	Mrs. Drugget . . . . Mrs. Brett
Joey . . . . Mr. Jefferson		Dimitry . . . . Mrs. Tyler
Mrs. Cockletop . . . Mrs. Brett		Miss Nancy . . . . . Miss Brett
Mrs. Camomile . . . Mrs. Tyler	**ROMEO AND JULIET.**	Lady Racket . . . Mrs. Johnson
Flounce . . . . . Miss Harding	Romeo . . . . Mr. Hodgkinson	
Nan . . . . Mrs. Munto	Mercutio . . . . . . Mr. Hallam	**TOM THUMB THE GREAT.**
Belinda . . . . . Mrs. Seymour	Friar Laurence . . . . Mr. Tyler	Tom Thumb . . Mast. Stockwell
	Capulet . . . . . . Mr. Crosby	Grizzle . . . . . . Mr. Jefferson
OLD MAID.	Montagu . . . . . . Mr. Munto	Noodle . . . . . . Mr. Martin
Capt. Cape . . Mr. Hodgkinson	Prince . . . . Mr. Hallam, Jr	Doodle . . . . Mr. Munto
Harlow . . . . . Mr. Hallam, Jr	Benvolio . . . . Mr. Miller	Merlin . . . . Mr. Collins
Footman . . . . . Mr. Leonard	Paris . . . . Mr. McGrath	Ghost . . . . Mr. Lee
Clerimont . . . . . . Mr. Tyler	Tybalt . . . . Mr. Martin	Arthur . . . . . . Mr. Johnson
Mrs. Harlow . . . . Mrs. Tyler	Peter . . . . Mr. Jefferson	Dollalolla . . . . Mrs. Seymour
Trifle . . . . . . Miss Harding	Apothecary . . . . Mr. Johnson	Huncamunca . . . . . Miss Brett
Miss Harlow . . . . Mrs. Brett	Lady Capulet . . . . Mrs. Tyler	Cleora . . . . Mrs. Munto
	Nurse . . . . Mrs. Brett	Mustachio . . . . . . Mrs. King
PRISONER AT LARGE.	Juliet . . . . Mrs. Johnson	Glumdalca . . . . . Mr. Crosby
Old Dowdle . . . . . Mr. Crosby		
Lord Esmond . . . . Mr. Collins	**SELIMA AND AZOR.**	**WHEEL OF FORTUNE.**
Frippon . . . . Mr. Martin	Azor . . . . Mr. Tyler	Tempest . . . . . . Mr. Johnson
Jack Conner . . . Mr. Hallam, Jr	Scandar . . . . . . Mr. Collins	Woodville . . . . . . Mr. Munto
Frill . . . . Mr. McGrath	Ali . . . . . . Mr. Jefferson	Harry . . . . Mr. Martin
Father Frank . . . . Mr. Woolls	Fatima . . . . . Mrs. Seymour	Weazel . . . . Mr. Crosby
Tough . . . . . . Mr. Munto	Lesbia . . . . Miss Brett	Jenkins . . . . Mr. Miller
Landlord . . . . . Mr. Roberts	Fairy . . . . . . Miss Harding	Maid . . . . Mrs. Munto
Philemon . . . . . . Mr. Miller	Selima . . . Mrs. Hodgkinson	
Trap . . . . Mr. Lee		**WHICH IS THE MAN?**
Muns . . . . Mr. Jefferson	**SUCH THINGS ARE.**	Sparkle . . . . Mr. Hallam, Jr
Adelaide . . . . . Mrs. Seymour	Twineall . . . . . . Mr. Martin	Fitzherbert . . . . . Mr. Johnson
Mary . . . . Mrs. Munto	Sultan . . . . . Mr. Hallam, Jr	Belville . . . . Mr. Tyler
Landlady . . . . . . Mrs. Brett	Sir Luke Tremor . . Mr. Johnson	Tom . . . . Mr. Leonard
Rachel . . . . Mrs. Hodgkinson	Elvirus . . . . Mr. Miller	Harry . . . . Mr. Miller
	Lord Flint . . . . Mr. Munto	Julia . . . . . . Mrs. Seymour
PRIZE.	Zedan . . . . Mr. Tyler	Kitty . . . . Mrs. Munto
Caddy . . . . . . Mr. Crosby	Meanright . . . . Mr. Jefferson	Mrs. Johnson . . . . Mrs. Brett
Juba . . . . . . Mrs. Seymour	Lady Tremor . . . Mrs. Brett	Tiffany . . . . . Miss Harding
Mrs. Caddy . . . . Mrs. Brett	Aurelia . . . . . . Mrs. Munto	
Caroline . . . Mrs. Hodgkinson	Arabella . . . . Mrs. Johnson	**WONDER.**
		Don Felix . . . Mr. Hallam, Jr
RICHARD III.	**SURRENDER OF CALAIS.**	Colonel Briton . . . . Mr. Tyler
Buckingham . . . Mr. Collins	Ribbemont . . . . Mr. Martin	Don Lopez . . . Mr. Johnson
Tressel . . . . . . Mr. Martin	John de Vienne . . . Mr. Crosby	Don Pedro . . . . Mr. Munto
Catesby . . . . . . Mr. Munto	O'Carrol . . . . . . Mr. Tyler	Gibby . . . . Mr. Martin
Stanley . . . . . . Mr. Crosby	King Edward . . Mr. Hallam, Jr	Frederick . . . . . Mr. Miller
Oxford . . . . . Mr. Seymour	John D'Aire . . Mr. Seymour	Lissardo . . . . . Mr. Jefferson
Duke of York . Mast. Stockwell	Harcourt . . . . . Mr. Miller	Isabella . . . . . Mrs. Tyler
Lord Mayor . . . Mr. Johnson		Flora . . . . . . Mrs. Brett
Duchess of York . . . Mrs. Brett	**THREE WEEKS AFTER MARRIAGE.**	Inis . . . . Mrs. Munto
	Woodley . . . . . . Mr. Miller	Violante . . . . Mrs. Johnson

"Grecian Daughter," "High Life Below Stairs," "Old Maid," "Prisoner at Large," "Romeo and Juliet," "Selima and Azor," and "Tom Thumb, the Great." Of some of the others there were Boston casts of which only the characters are here given in which there were changes. These casts are important in showing the working strength of the Old American Company during the last full season at the old theatre in John Street.

There were many changes in the pieces that had been played during the previous season and were now repeated, important parts finding new and in some cases inferior representatives, in consequence

CONTRASTED CASTS—CHANGES.

PLAYS.	1796.	1796-7.
Adopted Child.		
Sir Bertrand . .	Mr. Cleveland .	Mr. Crosby
Flint	Mr. Munto . .	Mr. Lee
Clara	Miss Broadhurst.	Mrs. Hodgkinson
Nell	Mrs. Cleveland .	Mrs. Brett
As You Like It.		
Orlando	Mr. Cleveland .	Mr. Martin
Oliver	Mr. Prigmore .	Mr. Munto
Duke	Mr. King . . .	Mr. Tyler
Amiens	Mr. Tyler . . .	Mr. McGrath
Sylvius . .	Mr. Munto . .	Mr. Miller
Celia	Miss Broadhurst.	Mrs. Tyler
Belle's Stratagem.		
Flutter	Mr. Hallam, Jr	Mr. Hallam
Sir George . . .	Mr. King . . .	Mr. Tyler
Courtall	Mr. Hallam . .	Mr. Hallam, Jr
Saville . .	Mr. Cleveland .	Mr. Martin
Dick	Mr. Durang . .	Mr. Leonard
Hardy	Mr. Prigmore .	Mr. Johnson
Lady Frances	Mrs. Hallam .	Mrs. Tyler
Miss Ogle . . .	Mrs. Cleveland .	Mrs. Seymour
Kitty Willis . .	Mrs. Munto . .	Mrs. Brett
Carmelite.		
Montgomeri . .	Mr. Cleveland .	Mr. Martin
De Courcy . .	Mr. King . . .	Mr. Hailam, Jr
Raymond . . .	Mr. Durang . .	Mr. Miller
Child of Nature.		
Marquis	Mr. King . .	Mr. Hodgkinson
Valentia	Mr. Hodgkinson	Mr. Martin
Mercia	Mr. Prigmore .	Mr. Johnson
Marchioness . .	Mrs. Hallam . .	Mrs. Johnson

PLAYS.	1796.	1796-7.
Children in the Wood.		
Sir Rowland . .	Mr. Cleveland .	Mr. Crosby
Deserted Daughter.		
Chevaril	Mr. Hodgkinson	Mr. Martin
Item	Mr. Prigmore .	Mr. Jefferson
Grime	Mr. Jefferson .	Mr. Munto
Lenox	Mr. King . . .	Mr. Hallam, Jr
Clement	Mr. Cleveland .	Mr. Miller
Betty	Mrs. King . . .	Mrs. Munto
Farmer.		
Blackberry . .	Mr. King . . .	Mr. Seymour
Flummery		Mr. Martin
Betty	Miss Broadhurst	Mrs. Hodgkinson
Louisa	Mrs. Johnson .	Mrs. Munto
Landlady . . .	Mrs. Munto . .	Mrs. Brett
Molly	Mrs. Hodgkinson	Mrs. Seymour
First Love.		
Billy Bustler . .	Mr. Prigmore .	Mr. Munto
Wrangler . . .	Mr. Cleveland .	Mr. Martin
Robin	Mr. Durang . .	Mr. Miller
Sabina Rosny .	Mrs. Cleveland .	Mrs. Hodgkinson
Hamlet.		
King	Mr. Cleveland .	Mr. Munto
Horatio	Mr. Tyler . . .	Mr. Martin
Guildenstern . .	Mr. Munto . .	Mr. Miller
Bernardo . . .	Mr. Lee . . .	Mr. Seymour
Gravedigger . .	Mr. Prigmore .	Mr. Lee
Ghost	Mr. King . . .	Mr. Tyler
Haunted Tower.		
Oakland	Mr. King . . .	Mr. Johnson
Robert	Mr. Prigmore .	Mr. Munto

of the sequestration of Mrs. Hallam, the withdrawal of Mr. Hodgkinson after the Hallam riot, and the retirement from the company of Mr.

CONTRASTED CASTS—CHANGES.

PLAYS.	1796.	1796–7.	PLAYS.	1796.	1796–7.
Lewis	Mr. Johnson	Mr. Martin	Smith	Mr. Munto	Mr. Miller
Charles	Mr. Munto	Mr. McGrath	Sophy	Mrs. Hallam	Mrs. Hodgkinson
Hugo	Mr. De Moulin	Mr. Crosby	Mrs. Ledger	Mrs. Munto	Mrs. Tyler
Servant	Mr. Tompkins	Mr. Leonard	*Romp.*		
Lady Elinor	Miss Broadhurst	Mrs. Seymour	Old Cockney	Mr. Johnson	Mr. Munto
Inkle and Yarico.			Barnacle	Mr. King	Mr. Johnson
Curry	Mr. King	Mr. Hallam	Miss Le Blond	Mrs. Tyler	Mrs. Munto
Narcissa	Miss Brett	Mrs. Seymour	Penelope	Mrs. Munto	Miss Brett
Patty	Mrs. Brett	Miss Harding	*Rosina.*		
Yarico	Miss Broadhurst	Mrs. Johnson	Irishman	Mr. King	Mr. Crosby
Lyar.			Rosina	Miss Broadhurst	Mrs. Seymour
Old Wilding	Mr. Johnson	Mr. Crosby	*School for Scandal.*		
Elliott	Mr. Cleveland	Mr. Munto	Joseph Surface	Mr. King	Mr. Tyler
Papillion	Mr. Jefferson	Mr. Martin	Sir Oliver	Mr. Johnson	Mr. Crosby
Miss Godfrey	Mrs. Cleveland	Mrs. Munto	Crabtree	Mr. Prigmore	Mr. Johnson
Miss Grantham	Mrs. Hallam	Mrs. Tyler	Sir Benjamin	Mr. Cleveland	Mr. Martin
Mountaineers.			Careless		Mr. Seymour
Kilmallock	Mr. King	Mr. Crosby	Trip	Mr. Durang	Mr. Miller
Ganem	Mr. Cleveland	Mr. Miller	Maria	Mrs. Cleveland	Mrs. Seymour
First Muleteer	Mr. Prigmore	Mr. Martin	Lady Teazle	Mrs. Hallam	Mrs. Johnson
Second Muleteer	Mr. Woolls	Mr. McGrath	*Speculation.*		
Floranthe	Mrs. Cleveland	Mrs. Johnson	Ald. Arable	Mr. Prigmore	Mr. Crosby
Zorayda	Mrs. Johnson	Mrs. Tyler	Sir Frederick	Mr. Cleveland	Mr. Munto
Much Ado About Nothing.			Vickery	Mr. Durang	Mr. Leonard
Claudio	Mr. Cleveland	Mr. Martin	Promptly	Mr. Munto	Mr. Miller
Antonio	Mr. King	Mr. Crosby	Cecilia	Mrs. Hallam	Mrs. Seymour
Dogberry	Mr. Prigmore	Mr. Hallam	*Spoiled Child.*		
Hero	Mrs. Cleveland	Mrs. Seymour	Old Pickle	Mr. Prigmore	Mr. Johnson
My Grandmother.			Maria	Mrs. Munto	Miss Brett
Souffrance	Mr. Cleveland	Mr. Martin	Susan	Mrs. Durang	Mrs. Munto
Charlotte	Miss Broadhurst	Miss Brett	*Sultan.*		
No Song No Supper.			Solyman	Mr. Cleveland	Mr. Martin
Frederick	Mr. Tyler	Mr. Munto	Ismene	Miss Broadhurst	Mrs. Seymour
Thomas	Mr. Durang	Mr. Leonard	*Werter and Charlotte.*		
Crop	Mr. Prigmore	Mr. Tyler	Sebastian	Mr. Cleveland	Mr. Martin
Dorothy	Miss Broadhurst	Mrs. Seymour	Lenthorp	Mr. Johnson	Mr. Crosby
Purse.			Albert	Mr. Hallam	Mr. Tyler
Baron	Mr. King	Mr. Johnson	Laura	Mrs. Tyler	Mrs. Munto
Theodore	Mr. Cleveland	Mr. Hallam, Jr	*Wheel of Fortune.*		
Quaker.			Woodville	Mr. King	Mr. Munto
Lubin	Mr. Prigmore	Mr. Hodgkinson	Harry	Mr. Cleveland	Mr. Martin
Solomon		Mr. Jefferson	*Young Quaker.*		
Easy	Mr. Roberts	Mr. Munto	Chronicle	Mr. Prigmore	Mr. Johnson
Floretta	Miss Broadhurst	Miss Brett	Capt. Ambush	Mr. Hallam, Jr	Mr. Tyler
Road to Ruin.			Twig	Mr. Durang	Mr. Miller
Dornton	Mr. Johnson	Mr. Crosby	Goliah	Miss Harding	Mast. Stockwell
Sulky	Mr. King	Mr. Jefferson	Spatterdash	Mr. King	Mr. Martin
Milford	Mr. Cleveland	Mr. Martin	Pink	Mrs. Cleveland	Mrs. Seymour
			Dinah	Mrs. Hallam	Mrs. Johnson

Prigmore, Mr. King, Mr. and Mrs. Cleveland and Miss Broadhurst. These changes in the casts are a better index to the changes in the company than can be obtained in any other way.

Some of the minor incidents of the season are worth noting. For Mr. Johnson's benefit Mr. Miln wrote a monologue, called the "Mirror," which was spoken by Mrs. Johnson. It was repeated on Mr. Miller's night. Miller also spoke an address, for which there was no apparent reason. As was Mr. Hodgkinson's custom at his benefits, he gave the "Dissertation on Hobby Horses," with "for this night only, Mr. Hodgkinson's Hobby." Hodgkinson's hobby, it may be assumed, related to the managerial troubles in the theatre. Mrs. Hallam's address, when she made her reappearance for the younger Hallam's benefit, was merely exculpatory; but the young man's championship of his step-mother recalls the effective lines in the introductory address spoken by Hodgkinson when Hallam, Jr., made his *debut* in New York in 1793:

> Poor Lewis Hallam, anxious for his son,
> With tragic phiz, thus makes his piteous moan—
> "Oh! Hodg., my friend, the fatal time draws near
> That gives the keenest throes—paternal fear ;
> O'er the same ground where many years his father
> Did, with applause, theatric laurels gather,
> My boy, unpractised in the mimic art,
> A candidate for favor now must start."
>   *   *   *   *   *
> I at his fears endeavored, sirs, to laugh,
> But all in vain, for here in his behalf
> He swore I trespassed friendship's sacred laws,
> If I refused to plead their mutual cause.

When the season closed, Hodgkinson carried the company to Hartford for a brief season of ten nights, and then to the Boston Hay-market, the negotiations for the control of the new theatre, then build-ing in New York, being completed before his departure.

EPILOGUE.

THE abrupt and in some respects inconclusive close of this volume brings with it a regret that I am unable to put a bushel of plums into a peck measure. Before me lies the MS. of chapters telling the story of Bignall and West's company in the South, 1792–7; of the second company of Boston players at Charleston, 1796–7; of the English career of Wignell's recruits for the Philadelphia Theatre— Mrs. Merry, Mr. Cooper, Mr. Warren, Mr. and Mrs. L'Estrange, and Mr. and Mrs. Byrne—and of the first season of the second Philadelphia company. To have included all this would have compelled incompleteness in other respects, thus defeating the main purpose of my self-imposed task. So far as I may be able to tell the "History of the American Theatre," I wish to do it with absolute fulness, so that those who use my volumes will not find it necessary to search out the widely scattered and almost inaccessible sources of information from which I have drawn my material. In my next volume I shall resume the narrative where it is interrupted by the limitations incident to a work of this kind.

END OF THE VOLUME.

INDEX.